A BRIEF HISTORY OF WESTERN CIVILIZATION

FOURTH EDITION

A BRIEF HISTORY OF WESTERN CIVILIZATION
THE UNFINISHED LEGACY

VOLUME I: TO 1715

MARK KISHLANSKY
Harvard University

PATRICK GEARY
University of California, Los Angeles

PATRICIA O'BRIEN
University of California, Riverside

PEARSON
Longman

New York   San Francisco   Boston
London   Toronto   Sydney   Tokyo   Singapore   Madrid
Mexico City   Munich   Paris   Cape Town   Hong Kong   Montreal

Vice President and Publisher: Priscilla McGeehon
Acquisitions Editor: Erika Gutierrez
Development Manager: Lisa Pinto
Development Editor: Nancy Crochiere
Executive Marketing Manager: Sue Westmoreland
Supplements Editor: Kristi Olson
Media Editor: Patrick McCarthy
Production Manager: Donna DeBenedictis
Project Coordination, Text Design, and Electronic Page Makeup: Elm Street Publishing Services, Inc.
Cover Design Manager: Wendy Ann Fredericks
Cover Designer: Joel Zimmerman
Cover Image: Detail from *Children's Games*, by Pieter Bruegel the Elder, 1560, Flemish. Kunsthistoriches Museum, Vienna, Austria/Superstock.
Photo Researcher: Photosearch, Inc.
Manufacturing Buyer: Lucy Hebard
Printer and Binder: Quebecor World Dubuque
Cover Printer: Coral Graphic Services, Inc.

Library of Congress Cataloging-in-Publication Data
Kishlansky, Mark A.
    A brief history of Western civilization: the unfinished legacy / Mark Kishlansky, Patrick Geary, Patricia O'Brien.—4th ed.
        p. cm.
    Includes bibliographical references and index.
    ISBN 0-321-19675-9 (complete ed.)—ISBN 0-321-19676-7 (v. 1)—ISBN 0-321-19677-5 (v. 2)
    1. Civilization, Western—History. I. Geary, Patrick J., 1948– II. O'Brien, Patricia, 1945– III. Title.

CB245.C545 2005
909' .09821—dc22   2003022063

Please visit our website at http://www.ablongman.com/kishlansky

ISBN 0-321-19675-9 (Complete Edition)
ISBN 0-321-19676-7 (Volume I)
ISBN 0-321-19677-5 (Volume II)

1 2 3 4 5 6 7 8 9 10—QWD—07 06 05 04

BRIEF CONTENTS

DETAILED CONTENTS

CHAPTER 4

EARLY ROME AND THE ROMAN REPUBLIC, 800–146 B.C.E.   68

CHAPTER 5

IMPERIAL ROME, 146 B.C.E.–192 C.E.   86

CHAPTER 6

THE TRANSFORMATION OF THE CLASSICAL WORLD   110

CHAPTER 14

EUROPE AT WAR, 1555–1648   280

CHAPTER 15

THE EXPERIENCES OF LIFE IN EARLY MODERN EUROPE, 1500–1650   298

CHAPTER 16

THE ROYAL STATE IN THE SEVENTEENTH CENTURY   318

MAPS AND GEOGRAPHICAL TOURS

CHRONOLOGIES, GENEALOGIES, AND FIGURES

DOCUMENTS

PREFACE

When we set out to write *Civilization in the West,* we tried to write, first of all, a book that students would *want* to read. Throughout many years of planning, writing, revising, rewriting, and numerous meetings together, this was our constant overriding concern. Would the text work across the variety of Western civilization courses, with the different levels and formats that make up this fundamental course? We also solicited the reactions of scores of reviewers to this single question: "Would students *want* to read these chapters?" Whenever we received a resounding "No!" we began again—not just rewriting, but rethinking how to present material that might be complex in argument or detail or that might simply seem too remote to engage the contemporary student. Though all three of us were putting in long hours in front of word processors, we quickly learned that we were engaged in a teaching rather than a writing exercise. And though the work was demanding, it was not unrewarding. We enjoyed writing this book, and we wanted students to enjoy reading it. We have been gratified to learn that our book successfully accomplished our objectives. It stimulated student interest and motivated students to want to learn about European history. *Civilization in the West* was successful beyond our expectations.

The text has been so well received, in fact, that we decided to publish this alternative, brief version: *A Brief History of Western Civilization: The Unfinished Legacy.* In an era of rapidly changing educational materials, alternative formats and models should be available. We believe that students and general readers alike will enjoy a conveniently sized book that offers them a coherent, well-told story. In this edition of the brief text, we have increased the size of many of the full-color maps and photographs so that they are easier to see and use. We have also added 10 new excerpts from primary source documents to give students a feel for the concreteness of the past, and we have replaced several of the chapter-opening "Visual Record" narratives.

APPROACH

The approach used in *A Brief History of Western Civilization: The Unfinished Legacy,* Fourth Edition, upholds and confirms a number of decisions made early in the writing of *Civilization in the West.* First, this brief, alternative version is, like the full-length text, a mainstream text in which most energies have been placed in developing a solid, readable narrative of Western civilization that integrates coverage of women and minorities into the discussion. We highlight personalities while identifying trends. We spotlight social history, both in sections of chapters and in separate chapters, while maintaining a firm grip on political developments.

Neither *A Brief History of Western Civilization: The Unfinished Legacy* nor *Civilization in the West* is meant to be an encyclopedia of Western civilization. Information is not included in a chapter unless it fits within the themes of that chapter. In both the full-length and brief versions of this text, we are committed to integrating the history of ordinary men and women into our narrative. We believe that isolated sections placed at the end of chapters that deal with the experiences of women or minority groups in a particular era profoundly distort historical experience. We call this technique "ca-boosing," and whenever we found ourselves segregating women or families or the masses, we stepped back and asked how we might recast our treatment of historical events to account for a diversity of actors. How did ordinary men, women, and children affect the course of world historical events? How did world historical events affect the fabric of daily life for men, women, and children from all walks of life? We tried to rethink critical historical problems of civilization as gendered phenomena.

C H A P T E R

21

INDUSTRIAL EUROPE

- THE VISUAL RECORD: An Iron Forge
- THE TRADITIONAL ECONOMY
- THE INDUSTRIAL REVOLUTION IN BRITAIN
- THE INDUSTRIALIZATION OF THE CONTINENT

THE VISUAL RECORD

AN IRON FORGE

THE KEY TO INDUSTRIALIZATION was the replacement of muscle with machine. This demanded ingenuity on the part of inventors, capital on the part of investors, and adaptability on the part of workers.

that almost resembles a nativity scene except that the birth being celebrated is the machine forging of iron, the miracle product of the age.

Joseph Wright of Derby was born and bred in the English Midlands where the Industrial Revolution first began. He was fascinated by the scientific developments of his age and specialized in paintings that were technically accurate. *An Iron Forge* was one of a number of industrial scenes that Wright painted in the 1770s when advances in technology were changing the face of rural

had previously been associated with smithing. Indeed, of the three workmen in the picture, only one is actually laboring and he is simply holding the tongs which keeps the iron in place. It is the machine that labors—the drum turning, the cam lifting, the hammer falling—and the people who benefit—proud parents, healthy and happy children. All are the product, the artist seems to be saying, of the new industrialization.

LOOKING AHEAD

As this chapter will discuss, industrialization began in Great Britain around forges like the one portrayed by Joseph Wright. It was the result of changes in agricultural practices that allowed for a larger population to be supported by fewer farmers. It was powered first by coal and its use in the production of iron and then by steam wh

We take the same approach to the coverage of central and eastern Europe that we did to women and minorities. Even before the epochal events of the late 1980s and early 1990s that returned this region to the forefront of international attention, we realized that many textbooks treated the Slavic world as marginal to the history of Western civilization. Therefore, we worked to integrate more of the history of eastern Europe into our text than is found in most others and to do so in a way that presented these regions, their cultures, and their institutions as integral rather than peripheral to Western civilization.

FEATURES

In *A Brief History of Western Civilization: The Unfinished Legacy*, we wanted to reuse the features that had the most immediate and positive impact on our readers and fulfill our goal of involving students in learning. Therefore, this edition features the following:

The Visual Record: Pictorial Chapter Openers

In these pictorial chapter openers, an illustration—a painting, a photograph, an artifact, or an edifice—appears at the beginning of each chapter, accompanied by text through which we explore the picture, guiding students across a canvas or helping them to see in an artifact or a piece of architecture details that are not immediately apparent. It is the direct combination of text and image that allows us to achieve this effect, to "unfold" both an illustration and a theme. All of the opening images have been chosen to illustrate a dominant theme within the chapter, and the dramatic and lingering impression they make helps to reinforce that theme. A new section at the end of each essay called *Looking Ahead* provides a brief overview of chapter coverage and further strengthens the connection between the subject of the opener and the major topics and themes of the chapter.

Geographical Tours of Europe

A Brief History of Western Civilization: The Unfinished Legacy continues the image-based approach to the presentation of geography used in *Civilization in the West*. When teachers of Western civilization courses are surveyed, no single area of need is cited more often than geographical knowledge. Many American students have no mental image of Europe, no familiarity with those geophysical features that are a fundamental

Christian Institutions. As the number of Christians increased in the face of persecution, the organization and teaching of this new faith began to evolve. A hierarchy developed within the various communities that Paul and the other apostles established. The leader of each community was the bishop, an office derived from the priestly leader of the Jewish synagogue, who was responsible for both charity and the Torah. Assisted by *presbyters* (priests), deacons, and deaconesses, bishops assumed growing responsibilities as expectations for the second coming receded. These respon-

damental role in the transformation of the Roman world would not become clear until the third and fourth centuries.

GEOGRAPHICAL TOUR
A Tour of the Empire

Each town in the sprawling empire, from York in the north of Britain to Dura Europus on the Euphrates, was a center

▼ **Map A. The Roman Empire at the Time of Hadrian.** Hadrian's empire was a well-ordered world of provinces governed by a vast bureaucracy and held together by a common culture and the power of the imperial army.

DISCOVERING WESTERN CIVILIZATION ONLINE

You can obtain more information about Europe and the world between 1870 and 1914 at the websites listed below. See also the companion website that accompanies this text: www.ablongman.com/kishlansky, which contains an online study guide and additional resources.

The European Balance of Power, 1870–1914
www.lordham.edu/halsall/mod/modsbook38.html
This site is part of a larger site on World War I primary and secondary sources, but it contains a section on the developments among the great powers from the 1870s to 1914.

The New Imperialism
www.lordham.edu/halsall/mod/modsbook34.html
A comprehensive site of links arranged by continent to primary source materials and bibliographies on imperialism.

The European Search for Territory and Markets
www.hum.port.ac.uk/slas/francophone/bibliographies.htm
A collection of bibliographies on the partition of Africa and the impact of colonization in Africa.
www.geocities.com/Vienna/5048/TREATY01.html
This site is devoted to the treaties that gave foreign governments access to political and commercial power in China.
www.chinaexhibit.org
A virtual museum exhibit of photographs taken in 1903 of the Chinese countryside after the Boxer Rebellion.

A WOMAN REPORTER BEHIND THE LINES OF THE WAR IN CHECHNYA

Anne Nivat was the Moscow correspondent for the French daily newspaper Liberation in October 2000 when she interviewed the rebel president of Chechnya. Fluent in Russian and holding a doctorate in political science, Nivat traveled to southern Russia disguised as a Chechen woman to cover the war from the Chechen side. Her newspaper reports led to antiwar protests in Paris.

FOCUS QUESTIONS

What indications does the Chechen rebel leader give that he sees guerrilla warfare within Chechnya as the best means of defeating Russia? What are his motives for opposition to the presence of Russian troops in Chechnya?

I FINALLY FIND MASKHADOV. He is wearing a military uniform with a pistol in his belt and appears to be in perfect health. Seated on a comfortable sofa in a "safe house," he seems relaxed and eager to share his thoughts on the situation in Chechnya. Outside, Russian armored vehicles pass through the autumn mist. Since he left Grozny the previous winter, the rebel president hasn't spent more than two consecutive days in any one spot. He usually communicates with his men and with the outside world by means of audiotapes. Few journalists take the

our territory—that is, while they remain inactive—their forces grow weaker, while ours get stronger. Our men are everywhere. The Russians know it, and yet they never mount an offensive. Their army is demoralized." . . .

Maskhadov is silent for a moment. He lets out a deep sigh. The Chechens, he admits, are tired of this war. "I recognize that the situation is difficult for the civilian population, which has become the target of the Russian army. I also regret that thousands of my countrymen have had to leave for Ingushetia or elsewhere. But each time I send out my representatives, they come back with the same message: 'Continue the fight. We're with you.' We can't afford to lose face, and the population knows it as well as I do. One way or another, the Russians will be forced to come to the negotiating table. I am constantly reminding Putin that he will be better off negotiating with me, as long as I am alive. It will be worse without me. And the Russians will leave in the end. Last time they led us to believe that they would never leave and then they disappeared. The worse thing would be if they stayed and we had to defend the

---

part of the geopolitical realities of Western history. Maps, carefully planned and skillfully executed, are an important component of our text.

To complement the standard map program of the text, we have added a special geographical feature, the "Geographical Tour of Europe." Six times throughout the book, we pause in the narrative to take a tour of Europe. Sometimes we follow an emperor as he tours his realm; sometimes we examine the impact of a peace treaty; sometimes we follow the travels of a merchant. Whatever the thematic occasion, our intention is to guide students around the changing contours of the geography of Western history. In order to do this effectively, we include several small, detailed maps to complement the overview map that appears at the beginning of each tour section. Using small maps allows us to integrate maps directly into the relevant text so that they are easy to locate and immediately available as the students follow the "tour." In addition, in this fourth edition, we have added specific in-text references to direct students to the corresponding map at key points in the narrative. The number of maps throughout the text, the specially designed tour-of-Europe geographical feature, and the ancillary program of map transparencies and workbook exercises combine to provide the strongest possible program for teaching historical geography.

Discovering Western Civilization Online

Discovering Western Civilization Online encourages students to explore the study of Western civilization beyond the confines of a textbook. These end-of-chapter website resources link students to enriching documents, images, and cultural sites. They have been thoroughly updated for this fourth edition.

Primary Sources

A Brief History of Western Civilization: The Unfinished Legacy contains selections from primary sources in order to stimulate students' interest in history by allowing them to hear the past speak in its own voice. The extracts relate directly to discussion within the chapter, thus providing students with a fuller understanding of a significant thinker or event. Each selection is accompanied by an explanatory head-note that identifies the author and work and provides the necessary historical context. New to this edition are Focus Questions following the headnote; these questions guide students' reading and spark critical thinking about the document.

CHANGES IN THE NEW EDITION

In the fourth edition of *A Brief History of Western Civilization: The Unfinished Legacy*, we have made several changes to the book's coverage.

Chapter Content

- The text now opens with a two-page introductory essay: *The Idea of Western Civilization*.
- Chapter 9: The High Middle Ages, 900–1300 includes more on the status of women in medieval society.
- In Chapter 10: The Later Middle Ages, 1300–1500, there is more extensive treatment of the multiethnic world of medieval Spain.
- Parts of Chapter 20: The French Revolution and the Napoleonic Era, 1789–1815 were reorganized to present more clearly the factors leading to the crisis of the Old Regime and the early stages of the revolution.
- Chapter 30: The West Faces the New Century, 1989 to the Present has been updated through the War in Iraq and also includes expanded coverage of the European Union, the women's movement, and terrorism in the early twenty-first century.

New Pictorial Essays

Several new *The Visual Record* pictorial essays were added to the fourth edition as well.

- Chapter 1: The First Civilizations opens with a pictorial essay on the discovery of the ancient iceman Ötzi.
- Chapter 5: Imperial Rome, 146 B.C.E.–192 C.E. examines the Augustan Altar of Peace.
- Chapter 18: The Balance of Power in Eighteenth-Century Europe explores the rise of militarism through an examination of military portraiture.
- Chapter 21: Industrial Europe considers imagery of technology in the early industrial period.
- Chapter 28: Global Conflagration: Hot and Cold War opens with Hitler's entry into Austria in 1938.
- Chapter 29: Postwar Recovery and the New Europe to 1989 illustrates the devastation of postwar Europe in Warsaw, 1946.

We believe that each of these new pictorial essays will help students in understanding the dominant themes of their respective chapters.

New Primary Source Documents

To freshen the fourth edition, new primary source documents replace the previous documents in many chapters.

- Chapter 4 has a document from Greek historian Polybius describing the siege of New Carthage.
- Chapter 9 includes the appeal from Pope Urban II that launched the First Crusade.
- Chapter 10 includes a new document on religious intolerance in medieval Spain.
- Chapter 15 includes an excerpt from a document explaining how to root out witches.
- Chapter 17 has a first-hand account of encountering pirates while at sea.

- Chapter 19 includes an excerpt on love and marriage from an eighteenth-century periodical.
- Chapter 23 contains a document from a member of the Paris Commune.
- Chapter 24 includes an account of the abuse endured by a British suffragette.
- Chapter 28 has the text of FDR's request for a declaration of war against Japan.
- Chapter 30 contains a reporter's insight on the war in Chechnya.

Expanded Heading Structure

Finally, to make the book more accessible to students, additional headings have been incorporated to allow easier comprehension and mastery of a chapter's main ideas. These headings break the text into smaller segments, aiding students in identifying and retaining key information.

* * *

There are many new features in our text and much that is out of the ordinary. But there are important traditional aspects of the narrative itself that also deserve mention. *A Brief History of Western Civilization: The Unfinished Legacy* is a mainstream text in which most of our energies have been placed in developing a solid, readable narrative of Western civilization that integrates coverage of women and minorities into the discussion. We have highlighted personalities while identifying trends. We have spotlighted social history, both in sections of chapters and in separate chapters, while maintaining a firm grip on political developments. We hope that there are many things in this book that teachers of Western civilization will find valuable. But we also hope that there are things here with which you will disagree, themes that you can develop better, arguments and ideas that will stimulate you. A textbook is only one part of a course, and it is always less important than a teacher. What we hope is that by having done our job successfully, we will have made the teacher's job easier and the student's job more enjoyable.

ACKNOWLEDGMENTS

We want to thank the many conscientious historians who gave generously of their time and knowledge to review our manuscript. We would like to thank the reviewers of the first three editions as well as those of the current edition. Their valuable critiques and suggestions have contributed greatly to the final product. We are grateful to the following:

Daniel F. Callahan, *University of Delaware;* Gary P. Cox, *Gordon College;* Peter L. de Rosa, *Bridgewater State College;* Frank Lee Earley, *Arapahoe Community College;* Patrick Foley, *Tarrant County College;* Charlotte M. Gradie, *Sacred Heart University;* Richard Grossman, *Northeastern Illinois University;* Gary L. Johnson, *University of Southern Maine;* Oscar Lansen, *University of North Carolina at Charlotte;* Michael R. Lynn, *Agnes Scott College;* John M. McCulloh, *Kansas State University;* Martha G. Newman, *University of Texas at Austin;* Lisa Pace-Hardy, *Jefferson Davis Community College;* Marlette Rebhorn, *Austin Community College;* Steven G. Reinhardt, *University of Texas at Arlington;* Robert Rockwell, *Mt. San Jacinto College;* Maryloy Ruud, *University of West Florida;* Jose M. Sanchez, *St. Louis University;* Erwin Sicher, *Southwestern Adventist College;* and John E. Weakland, *Ball State University.*

Our special thanks go to our colleagues at Marquette University for their longstanding support, valuable comments, and assistance on this edition with the design of the book: Lance Grahn, Lezlie Knox, Timothy G. McMahon, and Alan P. Singer.

We also acknowledge the assistance of the many reviewers of *Civilization in the West* whose comments have been invaluable in the development of *A Brief History of Western Civilization: The Unfinished Legacy:*

Achilles Aavraamides, *Iowa State University*; Meredith L. Adams, *Southwest Missouri State University*; Arthur H. Auten, *University of Hartford*; Suzanne Balch-Lindsay, *Eastern New Mexico University*; Sharon Bannister, *University of Findlay*; John W. Barker, *University of Wisconsin*; Patrick Bass, *Mount Union College*; William H. Beik, *Northern Illinois University*; Patrice Berger, *University of Nebraska*; Lenard R. Berlanstein, *University of Virginia*; Raymond Birn, *University of Oregon*; Donna Bohanan, *Auburn University*; Werner Braatz, *University of Wisconsin, Oshkosh*; Thomas A. Brady, Jr., *University of Oregon*; Anthony M. Brescia, *Nassau Community College*; Elaine G. Breslaw, *Morgan State University*; Ronald S. Brockway, *Regis University*; April Brooks, *South Dakota State University*; Daniel Patrick Brown, *Moorpark College*; Ronald A. Brown, *Charles County Community College*; Blaine T. Browne, *Broward Community College*; Kathleen S. Carter, *High Point University*; Robert Carver, *University of Missouri, Rolla*; Edward J. Champlin, *Princeton University*; Stephanie Evans Christelow, *Western Washington University*; Sister Dorita Clifford, BVM, *University of San Francisco*; Gary B. Cohen, *University of Oklahoma*; Jan M. Copes, *Cleveland State University*; John J. Contreni, *Purdue University*; Tim Crain, *University of Wisconsin, Stout*; Norman Delaney, *Del Mar College*; Samuel E. Dicks, *Emporia State University*; Frederick Dumin, *Washington State University*; Laird Easton, *California State University, Chico*; Dianne E. Farrell, *Moorhead State University*; Margot C. Finn, *Emory University*; Allan W. Fletcher, *Boise State University*; Luci Fortunato De Lisle, *Bridgewater State College*; Elizabeth L. Furdell, *University of North Florida*; Thomas W. Gallant, *University of Florida*; Frank Garosi, *California State University, Sacramento*; Lorne E. Glaim, *Pacific Union College*; Joseph J. Godson, *Hudson Valley Community College*; Sue Helder Goliber, *Mount St. Mary's College*; Manuel G. Gonzales, *Diablo Valley College*; Louis Haas, *Duquesne University*; Eric Haines, *Bellevue Community College*; Paul Halliday, *University of Virginia*; Margaretta S. Handke, *Mankato State University*; David A. Harnett, *University of San Francisco*; Paul B. Harvey, Jr., *Pennsylvania State University*; Neil Heyman, *San Diego State University*; Daniel W. Hollis, *Jacksonville State University*; Kenneth G. Holum, *University of Maryland*; Patricia Howe, *University of St. Thomas*; David Hudson, *California State University, Fresno*; Charles Ingrao, *Purdue University*; George F. Jewsbury, *Oklahoma State University*; Donald G. Jones, *University of Central Arkansas*; William R. Jones, *University of New Hampshire*; Richard W. Kaeuper, *University of Rochester*; David Kaiser, *Carnegie-Mellon University*; Jeff Kaufmann, *Muscatine Community College*; Carolyn Kay, *Trent University*; William R. Keylor, *Boston University*; Joseph Kicklighter, *Auburn University*; Charles L. Killinger, III, *Valencia Community College*; Alan M. Kirshner, *Ohlone College*; Charlene Kiser, *Milligan College*; Alexandra Korros, *Xavier University*; Cynthia Kosso, *Northern Arizona University*; Lara Kriegel, *Florida International University*; Lisa M. Lane, *Mira Costa College*; David C. Large, *Montana State University*; Catherine Lawrence, *Messiah College*; Bryan LeBeau, *Creighton University*; Robert B. Luehrs, *Fort Hays State University*; Donna J. Maier, *University of Northern Iowa*; Margaret Malamud, *New Mexico State University*; Roberta T. Manning, *Boston College*; Lyle McAlister, *University of Florida*; Therese M. McBride, *College of the Holy Cross*; David K. McQuilkin, *Bridgewater College*; Victor V. Minasian, *College of Marin*; David B. Mock, *Tallahassee Community College*; Robert Moeller, *University of California, Irvine*; R. Scott Moore, *University of Dayton*; Ann E. Moyer, *University of Pennsylvania*; Pierce C. Mullen, *Montana State University*; John A. Nichols, *Slippery Rock University*; Thomas F. X. Noble, *University of Virginia*; J. Ronald Oakley, *Davidson County Community College*; Bruce K. O'Brien, *Mary Washington College*; Dennis H. O'Brien, *West Virginia University*; Maura O'Connor, *University of Cincinnati*; Richard A. Oehling, *Assumption College*; James H. Overfield, *University of Vermont*; Catherine Patterson, *University of Houston*; Sue Patrick, *University of Wisconsin, Barron County*; Peter C. Piccillo, *Rhode Island College*; Peter O'M. Pierson, *Santa Clara University*; Theophilus Prousis, *University of North Florida*; Marlette Rebhorn, *Austin Community College*; Jack B. Ridley, *University of Missouri, Rolla*; Constance M. Rousseau, *Providence College*; Thomas J. Runyan, *Cleveland State University*; John P. Ryan, *Kansas City Community College*; Geraldine Ryder, *Ocean County College*; Joanne Schneider, *Rhode Island College*; Steven Schroeder, *Indiana University of Pennsylvania*; Steven C. Seyer, *Lehigh County Community*

College; Lixin Shao, *University of Minnesota, Duluth;* George H. Shriver, *Georgia Southern University;* Ellen J. Skinner, *Pace University;* Bonnie Smith, *University of Rochester;* Patrick Smith, *Broward Community College;* James Smither, *Grand Valley State University;* Sherill Spaar, *East Central University;* Charles R. Sullivan, *University of Dallas;* Peter N. Stearns, *Carnegie-Mellon University;* Saulius Suziedelis, *Millersville University;* Darryl B. Sycher, *Columbus State Community College;* Roger Tate, *Somerset Community College;* Janet A. Thompson, *Tallahassee Community College;* Anne-Marie Thornton, *Bilkent University;* Donna L. Van Raaphorst, *Cuyahoga Community College;* James Vanstone, *John Abbot College;* Steven Vincent, *North Carolina State University;* Richard A. Voeltz, *Cameron University;* Faith Wallis, *McGill University;* Sydney Watts, *University of Richmond;* Eric Weissman, *Golden West College;* Christine White, *Pennsylvania State University;* William Harry Zee, *Gloucester County College.*

Each author also received invaluable assistance and encouragement from many colleagues, friends, and family members over the years of research, reflection, writing, and revising that went into the making of this text:

Mark Kishlansky thanks Ann Adams, Robert Bartlett, Ray Birn, David Buisseret, Ted Cook, Frank Conaway, Constantine Fasolt, James Hankins, Katherine Haskins, Richard Hellie, Matthew Kishlansky, Donna Marder, Mary Beth Rose, Victor Stater, Jeanne Thiel, and the staffs of the Joseph Regenstein Library, the Newberry Library, and the Widener and Lamont Libraries at Harvard.

Patrick Geary wishes to thank Mary, Catherine, and Anne Geary for their patience, support, and encouragement; he also thanks Anne Picard, Dale Schofield, Hans Hummer, and Richard Mowrer for their able assistance throughout the project.

Patricia O'Brien thanks Elizabeth Sagias for her encouragement and enthusiasm throughout the project and Robert Moeller for his keen eye for organization and his suggestions for writing a gendered history.

MARK KISHLANSKY
PATRICK GEARY
PATRICIA O'BRIEN

SUPPLEMENTS

FOR QUALIFIED COLLEGE ADOPTERS

Instructor's Resource Manual

Prepared by David B. Mock of Tallahasee Community College, this thorough Instructor's Manual includes an introductory essay on teaching Western civilization and a bibliographic essay on the use of primary sources for class discussion and analytical thinking. Each chapter contains a chapter summary, key terms, list of important geographic locations, discussion questions, and an annotated list of films (not supplied by Longman) that may be used to enrich the course.

Test Bank

Prepared by Chris Howell of Red Rocks Community College, this supplement contains more than 1,200 multiple-choice, true/false, and essay questions. Multiple-choice and true/false questions are referenced by topic and text page number.

TestGen-EQ Computerized Testing System

This flexible, easy-to-master computerized test bank on a dual-platform CD includes all of the items in the printed test bank and allows instructors to select specific questions, edit existing questions, and add their own items to create exams. Tests can be printed in several different fonts and formats and can include figures, such as graphs and tables.

Companion Website (*www.ablongman.com/kishlansky*)

Instructors can take advantage of the Companion Website that supports this text. The instructor section includes teaching links and downloadable maps, tables, and graphs from the text for use in PowerPoint™.

Supplements Central™ (*http://suppscentral.ablongman.com*)

A helpful website where instructors can download supplements including: Instructor's Manuals, Test Banks, TestGens, Power Point™ presentations, as well as CourseCompass®, WebCT, and BlackBoard materials. Instructors will need to request a password from their sales representative to gain access.

Text-Specific Transparency Set

A set of full-color transparency map acetates drawn from *Civilization in the West,* Fifth Edition.

History Video Program

A list of over 100 videos from which qualified college adopters can choose. Restrictions apply.

History Digital Media Archive CD-ROM

This CD-ROM contains electronic images and interactive and static maps, along with media elements such as video. It is fully customizable and ready for classroom presentation. All images and maps are available in PowerPoint™ as well.

CourseCompass (*http://www.ablongman.com/techsolutions*)

Focus on teaching the course, not the technology! CourseCompass combines the strength of Longman content with state-of-the-art technology that simplifies online course management for you. This easy-to-use and customizable program enables you to tailor the content and functionality to meet your individual needs. You can create an online presence—for ANY course you teach—in under an hour. This course contains several dozen primary sources, Western civilization maps from Longman textbooks, and the map exercises from both *Mapping Western Civilization* and *Western Civilization Map Workbook*, all of which you can customize for your own class and text.

BlackBoard (*http://www.ablongman.com/techsolutions*)

Longman's rich Western civilization content is available in BlackBoard's course management system. The BlackBoard format enables you to quickly and easily customize any course to meet your specific needs. This downloadable course contains several dozen primary sources, Western civilization maps from Longman textbooks, and the map exercises from both *Mapping Western Civilization* and *Western Civilization Map Workbook*, all of which you can customize for your own class and text.

WebCT (*http://www.ablongman.com/techsolutions*)

WebCT offers a host of online course management tools. Longman will provide qualified college adopters with a wealth of material to customize their own WebCT course. Available content includes several dozen primary sources, Western civilization maps from Longman textbooks, and the map exercises from both *Mapping Western Civilization* and *Western Civilization Map Workbook*, all of which you can customize for your own class and text. Contact your sales representative for more information.

Discovering Western Civilization Through Maps and Views

Created by Gerald Danzer, University of Illinois at Chicago, and David Buisseret, this unique set of 140 full-color acetates contains an introduction to teaching history through maps and a detailed commentary on each transparency. The collection includes cartographic and pictorial maps, views and photos, urban plans, building diagrams, and works of art. Available to qualified college adopters.

FOR STUDENTS

Study Guide

Revised by Paul Brasil of Mountain Community College, this *Study Guide* is available in two volumes. Each chapter includes a summary; a timeline activity; map and geography questions; key terms, people, and events; and identification, multiple-choice, and critical-thinking questions.

Companion Website (*www.ablongman.com/kishlansky*)

Providing a wealth of resources for students using *Civilization in the West*, this Companion Website contains chapter summaries, interactive practice test questions, and web links for every chapter in the text.

Research Navigator and Research Navigator Guide

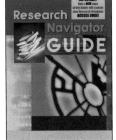

Research Navigator is a comprehensive website comprising three exclusive databases of credible and reliable source material for research and for student assignments: EBSCO's ContentSelect Academic Journal Database, the New York Times Search by Subject Archive, and "Best of the Web" Link Library. The site also includes an extensive help section. The Research Navigator Guide provides your students with access to the Research Navigator website and includes reference material and hints about conducting online research. **Free to qualified college adopters when packaged with the text.**

Multimedia Edition CD-ROM for *Civilization in the West*

This unique CD-ROM takes students beyond the printed page, offering them a complete multimedia learning experience. It contains the full annotatable textbook on CD-ROM, with contextually placed media—audio, video, interactive maps, photos, and figures—that link students to additional content directly related to key concepts in the text. The CD also contains the *Study Guide*, map workbooks, a primary source reader, and more than a dozen supplementary books, most often assigned in Western civilization courses, including Plato, *The Republic*, and Machiavelli, *The Prince*. **Free to qualified college adopters when packaged with the text.**

Mapping Western Civilization: **Student Activities**

Created by Gerald Danzer, University of Illinois at Chicago, this FREE map workbook for students is designed as an accompaniment to *Discovering Western Civilization Through Maps and Views*. It features exercises designed to teach students to interpret and analyze cartographic materials such as historical documents. **Free to qualified college adopters when packaged with the text.**

Western Civilization Map Workbook

The map exercises in these two volumes by Glee Wilson test and reinforce basic geography literacy while building critical-thinking skills. **Free to qualified college adopters when packaged with the text.**

Full-Color Longman Western Civilization Timeline

Noting key events and trends in political and diplomatic, social and economic, and cultural and technological history, this fold-out illustrated timeline provides a thorough and accessible chronological reference guide for Western civilization. **Free to qualified college adopters when packaged with the text.**

Longman Atlas of Western Civilization

This 52-page atlas features carefully selected historical maps that provide comprehensive coverage for the major historical periods. Each map has been designed to be colorful, easy-to-read, and informative, without sacrificing detailed accuracy. This atlas makes history—and geography—more comprehensible.

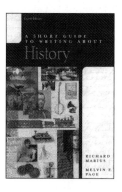

A Short Guide to Writing About History, **Fourth Edition**

Written by Richard Marius, late of Harvard University, and Melvin E. Page, Eastern Tennessee State University, this engaging and practical text helps students get beyond merely compiling dates and facts; it teaches them how to incorporate their own ideas into their papers and to tell a story about history that interests them and their peers. Covering both brief essays and the documented resource paper, the text explores the writing and researching processes, identifies different modes of historical writing, including argument, and concludes with guidelines for improving style.

Longman World History—Primary Sources and Case Studies *(http://longmanworldhistory.com)*

The core of this website is its large database of thought-provoking primary sources, case studies, maps, and images—all carefully chosen and edited by scholars and teachers of world history. The content and organization of the site encourage students to analyze the themes, issues, and complexities of world history in a meaningful, exciting, and informative way. Offered at a significant discount to *A Brief History of Western Civilization: The Unfinished Legacy* users, professors can visit the site for a free three-day trial.

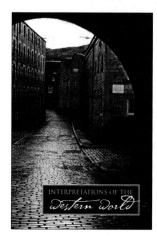

Interpretations of the Western World

General Editor Mark Kishlansky has prepared a customizable database of secondary source readings in Western civilization. Selections are grouped topically so that instructors can assign readings that illustrate different points of view about a given historical debate (e.g., How democratic was Athens? Did the Industrial Revolution improve the standard of living?). Interpretations of the Western World can be packaged at a discount with *A Brief History of Western Civilization: The Unfinished Legacy*, Fourth Edition.

PENGUIN-LONGMAN PARTNERSHIP

The partnership between Penguin Books and Longman Publishers offers your students a discount on the titles below when instructors bundle them with any Longman survey. Visit www.ablongman.com/penguin for more information.

Available Titles

Peter Abelard, *The Letters of Abelard and Heloise*
Dante Alighieri, *Divine Comedy: Inferno*
Dante Alighieri, *The Portable Dante*
Anonymous, *The Song of Roland*

Anonymous, *The Epic of Gilgamesh*
Anonymous, *Vinland Sagas*
Aristophanes, *The Knights, Peace, The Birds, Assemblywomen, Wealth*
Louis Auchincloss, *Woodrow Wilson* (Penguin Lives Series)
Jane Austen, *Emma*

Jane Austen, *Pride and Prejudice*
Jane Austen, *Persuasion*
Jane Austen, *Sense and Sensibility*
Edward Bellamy, *Looking Backward*
Richard Bowring, *Diary of Lady Murasaki*
Charlotte Brontë, *Jane Eyre*
Charlotte Brontë, *Villette*
Emily Brontë, *Wuthering Heights*
Benvenuto Cellini, *The Autobiography of Benvenuto Cellini*
Geoffrey Chaucer, *The Canterbury Tales*
Marcus Tullius Cicero, *Cicero: Selected Political Speeches*
Miguel de Cervantes, *The Adventures of Don Quixote*
Bartolome de las Casas, *A Short Account of the Destruction of the West Indies*
René Descartes, *Discourse on Method and The Meditations*
Charles Dickens, *Hard Times*
Charles Dickens, *Great Expectations*
John Dos Passos, *Three Soldiers*
Einhard, *Two Lives of Charlemagne*
Olaudah Equiano, *The Interesting Narrative and Other Writings*
Jeffrey Gantz (tr.), *Early Irish Myths and Sagas*
Peter Gay, *Mozart* (Penguin Lives Series)
William Golding, *Lord of the Flies*
Kenneth Grahame, *The Wind in the Willows*
Grimm & Grimm, *Grimms' Fairy Tales*
Thomas Hardy, *Jude the Obscure*
Herodotus, *The Histories*
Thomas Hobbes, *Leviathan*
Homer, *The Iliad*
Homer, *Odyssey: Revised Prose Translation*
Homer, *Odyssey Deluxe*
The Koran
Lemisch, *B. Franklin*
Primo Levi, *If Not Now, When?*
Machiavelli, *The Prince*
Karl Marx, *The Communist Manifesto*
John Stuart Mill, *On Liberty*
Jean-Baptiste Molière, *Tartuffe and Other Plays*
Charles-Louis Montesquieu, *Persian Letters*
Sir Thomas More, *Utopia and Other Essential Writings*
Sherwin Nuland, *Leonardo DaVinci*
George Orwell, *1984*
George Orwell, *Animal Farm*

Plato, *Great Dialogues of Plato*
Plato, *The Republic*
Plato, *The Last Days of Socrates*
Marco Polo, *The Travels*
Procopius, *The Secret History*
Jean-Jacques Rousseau, *The Social Contract*
Sallust, *The Jugurthine Wars, The Conspiracy of Cataline*
William Shakespeare, *Hamlet*
William Shakespeare, *Macbeth*
William Shakespeare, *The Merchant of Venice* (Pelican Series)
William Shakespeare, *The Merchant of Venice* (Signet Classics)
William Shakespeare, *Othello*
William Shakespeare, *The Taming of the Shrew*
William Shakespeare, *Twelfth Night*
William Shakespeare, *King Lear*
William Shakespeare, *Four Great Comedies: The Taming of the Shrew, A Midsummer's Night Dream, Twelfth Night, The Tempest*
William Shakespeare, *Four Great Tragedies: Hamlet, Macbeth, King Lear, Othello*
William Shakespeare, *Four Histories: Richard II, Henry IV: Part I, Henry IV: Part II, Henry V*
William Shakespeare, *The Tempest*
Mary Shelley, *Frankenstein*
Aleksandr Solzhenitsyn, *One Day in the Life of Ivan Denisovich*
Sophocles, *The Three Theban Plays*
St. Augustine, *The Confessions of St. Augustine*
Robert Louis Stevenson, *The Strange Case of Dr. Jekyll and Mr. Hyde*
Suetonius, *The Twelve Caesars*
Jonathan Swift, *Gulliver's Travels*
Tacitus, *The Histories*
Voltaire, *Candide, Zadig and Selected Stories*
Goethe, *Faust, Part 1*
Goethe, *Faust, Part 2*
Edith Wharton, *Ethan Frome*
M. Willet, *The Signet World Atlas*
Gary Wills, *Saint Augustine* (Penguin Lives Series)
Virginia Woolf, *Jacob's Room*

ABOUT THE AUTHORS

MARK KISHLANSKY   Mark Kishlansky is Frank B. Baird, Jr. Professor of English and European History and has served as the Associate Dean of the Faculty at Harvard University. He was educated at the State University of New York at Stony Brook where he first studied history and at Brown University where he received his Ph.D. in 1977. For 16 years, he taught at the University of Chicago and was a member of the staff that taught Western Civilization. Currently, he lectures on the History of Western Civilization at Harvard. Professor Kishlansky is a specialist on seventeenth-century English political history and has written, among other works, *A Monarchy Transformed, The Rise of the New Model Army* and *Parliamentary Selection: Social and Political Choice in Early Modern England.* From 1984 to 1991 he was editor of the *Journal of British Studies* and is presently the general editor of the *History Compass,* the first on-line history journal. He is also the general editor for Pearson Custom Publishing's source and interpretations databases, which provide custom book supplements for Western Civilization courses.

PATRICK GEARY   Holding a Ph.D. in Medieval Studies from Yale University, Patrick Geary has broad experience in interdisciplinary approaches to European history and civilization. He has served as the director of the Medieval Institute at the University of Notre Dame as well as director for the Center for Medieval and Renaissance Studies at UCLA where he is currently Professor of History. He has also held positions at the University of Florida and Princeton University and has taught at the École des Hautes Études en Sciences Sociales in Paris and the University of Vienna. His many publications include *Readings in Medieval History; Before France and Germany: The Creation and Transformation of the Merovingian World; Phantoms of Remembrance: Memory and Oblivion at the End of the First Millennium;* and *The Myth of Nations: The Medieval Origins of Europe.*

PATRICIA O'BRIEN   Between 1995 and 1999, Patricia O'Brien worked to foster collaborative interdisciplinary research in the humanities as director of the University of California Humanities Research Institute. Since 1999, she has held the position of Dean of the College of Humanities, Arts, and Social Sciences at the University of California, Riverside. She has held appointments at the University of California, Irvine, Yale University, and at the École des Hautes Études en Sciences Sociales in Paris. Professor O'Brien is a specialist in modern French cultural and social history and has published widely on the history of crime, punishment, cultural theory, urban history, and gender issues. Representative publications include *The Promise of Punishment: Prisons in Nineteenth-Century France;* "The Kleptomania Diagnosis: Bourgeois Women and Theft in Late Nineteenth-Century France" in *Expanding the Past: A Reader in Social History;* and "Michel Foucault's History of Culture" in *The New Cultural History,* edited by Lynn Hunt. Professor O'Brien's commitment to this textbook grew out of her own teaching experiences in large, introductory Western civilization courses. She has benefited from the contributions of her students and fellow instructors in her approach to the study of Western civilization in the modern period.

A BRIEF HISTORY OF WESTERN CIVILIZATION

INTRODUCTION

THE IDEA OF WESTERN CIVILIZATION

THE WEST IS AN IDEA. It is not visible from space. An astronaut viewing the blue-and-white terrestrial sphere can make out the forms of Africa, bounded by the Atlantic, the Indian Ocean, the Red Sea, and the Mediterranean. Australia, the Americas, and even Antarctica are distinct patches of blue-green in the darker waters that surround them. But nothing comparable separates Asia from Europe, East from West. Viewed from 100 miles up, the West itself is invisible. Although astronauts can see the great Eurasian landmass curving around the Northern Hemisphere, the Ural Mountains—the theoretical boundary between East and West—appear faint from space. Certainly they are less impressive than the towering Himalayas, the Alps, or even the Caucasus. People, not geology, determined that the Urals should be the arbitrary boundary between Europe and Asia.

Even this determination took centuries. Originally, Europe was a name that referred only to central Greece. Gradually, Greeks extended it to include the whole Greek mainland and then the landmass to the north. Later, Roman explorers and soldiers carried Europe north and west to its modern boundaries. Asia too grew with time. Initially, Asia was only that small portion of what is today Turkey inland from the Aegean Sea. Gradually, as Greek explorers came to know of lands farther east, north, and south, they expanded their understanding of Asia to include everything east of the Don River to the north and of the Red Sea to the south.

Western civilization is as much an idea as the West itself. Under the right conditions, astronauts can see the Great Wall of China snaking its way from the edge of the Himalayas to the Yellow Sea. No comparable physical legacy of the West is so massive that its details can be discerned from space. Nor are Western achievements rooted forever in one corner of the world. What we call Western civilization belongs to no particular place. Its location has changed since the origins of civilization, that is, the cultural and social traditions characteristic of the *civitas*, or city. "Western" cities appeared first outside the "West," in the Tigris and Euphrates river basins in present-day Iraq and Iran, a region that we today call the Middle East. These areas have never lost their urban traditions, but in time, other cities in North Africa, Greece, and Italy adapted and expanded this heritage.

Until the sixteenth century C.E., the western end of the Eurasian landmass was the crucible in which disparate cultural and intellectual traditions of the Near East, the Mediterranean, and northern and western Europe were smelted into a new and powerful alloy. Then "the West" expanded by establishing colonies overseas and by giving rise to the "settler societies" of the Americas, Australia and New Zealand, and South Africa.

Western technology for harnessing nature, Western forms of economic and political organization, Western styles of art and music are—for good or ill—dominant influences in world civilization. Japan is a leading power in the Western traditions of capitalist commerce and technology. China, the most populous country in the world, adheres to Marxist socialist principles—a European political tradition. Millions of people in Africa, Asia, and the Americas follow the religions of Islam and Christianity, both of which developed from Judaism in the cradle of Western civilization.

Many of today's most pressing problems are also part of the legacy of the Western tradition. The remnants of European colonialism have left deep hostilities throughout the world. The integration of developing nations into the world economy keeps much of humanity in a seemingly hopeless cycle of poverty as the wealth of poor countries goes to pay interest on loans from Europe and America. Hatred of Western civilization is a central, ideological tenet that inspired the attacks on symbols of American economic and military strength on September 11, 2001, and that fuels anti-Western terrorism around the world. The West itself faces a crisis. Impoverished citizens of former colonies flock to Europe and North America seeking a better life but often finding poverty, hostility, and racism instead. Finally, the advances of Western civilization endanger our very existence. Technology pollutes the world's air, water, and soil, and nuclear weapons threaten the destruction of all civilization. Yet these are the same advances that allow us to lengthen life expectancy, harness the forces of nature, and conquer disease. It is the same technology that allows us to view our world from outer space.

How did we get here? In this book we attempt to answer that question. The history of Western civilization is not simply the triumphal story of progress, the creation of a better world. Even in areas in which we can see development, such as technology, communications, and social complexity, change is not always for the better. However, it would be equally inaccurate to view Western civilization as a progressive decline from a mythical golden age of the human race. The roughly 300 generations since the origins of civilization have bequeathed a rich and contradictory legacy to the present. Inherited political and social institutions, cultural forms, and religious and philosophical traditions form the framework within which the future must be created. The past does not determine the future, but it is the raw material from which the future will be made. To use this legacy properly, we must first understand it, not because the past is the key to the future, but because understanding yesterday frees us to create tomorrow.

1

THE FIRST CIVILIZATIONS

- THE VISUAL RECORD: Ötzi's Last Meal
- BEFORE CIVILIZATION
- MESOPOTAMIA: BETWEEN THE TWO RIVERS
- THE GIFT OF THE NILE
- BETWEEN TWO WORLDS
- NINEVEH AND BABYLON
- THE NEW BABYLONIAN EMPIRE

T H E   V I S U A L   R E C O R D

ÖTZI'S LAST MEAL

THE IDEA THAT WE CAN VISIT WITH AN ANCESTOR from three hundred generations past seems incredible. And yet a discovery in the Italian Alps a decade ago has brought us face to face with Ötzi (so-named for the valley where he was found), an ordinary man who faced a cruel death more than five thousand years ago. Ötzi's perfectly preserved body, clothing, tools, and weapons allow us to know how people lived and died in Western Europe before it was Europe—before indeed it was the West.

Ötzi was small by modern European standards: he stood at just 5 feet 4 inches. Around 40 years old, he was already suffering from arthritis, and his several tattoos were likely a kind of therapy. He probably lived in a village below the mountain whose inhabitants survived from hunting, simple agriculture, and goat herding.

One spring day around 3000 B.C.E., Ötzi enjoyed what would be his last meal of meat, some vegetables, and flat bread made of einkorn wheat. He dressed warmly but simply in a leather breechcloth with a calfskin belt covered by a leather upper garment of goatskin sewn together with animal sinews. Below, he wore leather leggings and sturdy shoes made of bearskin soles and deerhide tops, lined with soft grasslike socks. On his head was a warm bearskin cap.

Ötzi carried an ax with a blade of almost pure copper and a flint knife in a fiber scabbard. He secured his leather backpack on a pack-frame made of a long hazel rod bent into a U-shape and reinforced with two narrow wooden slats. Among other things it held birch bark containers, one filled with materials to start a fire, which he could ignite with a flint he carried in his pouch. He also equipped himself with a multi-purpose mat made from long stalks of Alpine grass and a simple first-aid kit consisting of inner bark from the birch tree—a substance with antibiotic and styptic properties.

For so small a man, Ötzi carried an imposing weapon: a yew-wood bow almost six feet long and a quiver of arrows. He must have been working on the weapon shortly before he died; the bow and most of the arrows were unfinished.

For ten years after the discovery of Otzi's body, scholars and scientists studied his remains and speculated on why and how he died. Was he caught by a sudden storm or did he perhaps injure himself and die of exposure? And what was he doing so high in the mountains—six hours from the valley where he had his last meal, without adequate food or water? Finally, another X-ray of his frozen corpse revealed a clue: the shadow of a stone point lodged in his back.

Apparently, Ötzi left the lower villages that fateful spring day frightened and in a great hurry. Alone at an altitude of over 10,000 feet, desperately trying to finish his bow and arrows, he was fleeing for his life, but his luck ran out. Ötzi was shot in the back with an arrow. It pierced his shoulder between his shoulder blade and ribs, paralyzing his arm and causing extensive bleeding. Exhausted, he lay down in a shallow cleft in the snowy rocks. In a matter of hours he was dead, and the snows of centuries quietly buried him.

What does Ötzi's life and death tell us about the story of Western civilization? Although during his lifetime radically new urban societies and cultures were appearing just east of the Mediterranean, Ötzi still belonged to the Stone Age. None of his clothing was woven, although such basic technology was common in western Asia. The only metal was his ax head of soft copper, not the much harder bronze favored in the eastern Mediterranean. And yet, something vital connected Ötzi's world and that distant cradle of civilization: his last meal. Einkorn is not native to western Europe but originated in the region of the Tigris and Euphrates. From there, both the grain itself and the technology of its cultivation spread slowly, ultimately reaching Ötzi's Alpine village. Other components of civilization would follow: weaving, metal working urbanization, writing, and ways to kill men and women like Ötzi with greater efficiency.

LOOKING AHEAD

This first chapter begins before Ötzi with the origins of humankind and chronicles the great discoveries that led to the first urban-based civilizations of Mesopotamia and Egypt. It examines as well the seminomadic herding societies that lived on their margins and developed the first great monotheistic religious tradition.

BEFORE CIVILIZATION

The human race was already ancient by the time civilization first appeared around 3,500 years before the Common Era, the period following the traditional date of the birth of Jesus. (Such dates are abbreviated B.C. for "before Christ" or B.C.E. for "Before the Common Era"; A.D., the abbreviation of the Latin for "in the year of the Lord," is used to refer to dates after the birth of Jesus. Today, scholars use simply C.E. to mean the Common Era. To indicate an approximate date for an event that cannot be dated precisely, the abbreviation *ca.*, or *circa*, "approximately," is used.) The first humanlike creatures whose remains have been discovered date from as long as five million years ago. One of the best-known finds, nicknamed "Lucy" by the scientist who discovered her skeleton in 1974, stood only about four feet tall and lived on the edge of a lake in what is now Ethiopia. Lucy and her band did not have brains that were as well developed as those of modern humans. They did, however, use simple tools such as sticks, bone clubs, and chipped rocks. Although small and relatively weak compared with other animals, Lucy's species of creatures—neither fully apes nor human—survived for over four million years.

Varieties of the modern species of humans, *Homo sapiens* ("thinking human"), appeared well over 100,000 years ago and spread across the Eurasian landmass and Africa. The earliest *Homo sapiens* in Europe, the *Neanderthal*, differed little from us today. They were roughly the same size and had the same cranial capacity as we. They spread throughout much of Africa, Europe, and Asia during the last great ice age. To survive in the harsh tundra landscape, they developed a cultural system that enabled them to modify their environment. Customs such as the burial of their dead with food offerings indicate that Neanderthals may have developed a belief in an afterlife. Although a bit shorter and heavier than most people today, they were clearly our close cousins. Nevertheless, DNA studies suggest that Neanderthals are not directly related to modern humans. Their subspecies appears to have been a dead end.

No one knows why or how the Neanderthals were replaced by our subspecies, *Homo sapiens sapiens* ("thinking thinking human"), around 40,000 years ago. Whatever the reason and whatever the process—extinction, evolution, or extermination—this last arrival on the human scene was universally successful. All humans today—whether blond, blue-eyed Scandinavians, Australian aborigines, Africans, Japanese, or Amerindians—belong to this same subspecies. Differences in skin color, type of hair, and build are minor variations on the same theme. The identification of races, while selectively based on some of these physical variations, is, like civilization itself, a fact not of biology but of culture.

Early *Homo sapiens sapiens* lived in small kin groups of 20 or 30, following game and seeking shelter in tents, lean-tos, and caves. People of the Paleolithic era or Old Stone Age (ca. 600,000–10,000 B.C.E.) worked together for hunting and defense and apparently formed emotional bonds that were based on more than sex or economic necessity. The skeleton of a man found a few years ago in Iraq, for example, suggests that although he was born with only one arm and was crippled further by arthritis, the rest of his community supported him and he lived to adulthood. Clearly, his value to his society lay in something more than his ability to make a material contribution to its collective life.

The Dominance of Culture

During the upper or late Paleolithic era (ca. 35,000–10,000 B.C.E.), *culture*, meaning everything about humans that is not inherited biologically, was increasingly determinant in human life. Paleolithic people were not on an endless and all-consuming quest to provide for the necessities of life. They spent less time on such things than we do today. Therefore they were able to find time to develop speech, religion, and artistic expression. Wall paintings, small clay and stone figurines of female figures (which may reflect concerns about fertility), and finely decorated stone and bone tools indicate not just artistic ability but also abstract and symbolic thought.

The end of the glacial era marked the beginning of the Mesolithic, or Middle Stone Age (ca. 10,000–8000 B.C.E.). This period occurred at different times in different places as the climate grew milder, vast expanses of glaciers melted, and sea levels rose. Mesolithic peoples began the gradual domestication of plants and animals and sometimes formed settled communities. They developed the bow and arrow and pottery, and they made use of small flints (microliths) and fishhooks.

Paintings: A Cultural Record. An amazing continuous record of the civilizing of the West is found in the arid wastes of Africa's Sahara Desert. At the end of the last ice age, around 10,000 B.C.E., much of North Africa enjoyed a mild, damp climate and supported a diverse population of

C H R O N O L O G Y	
BEFORE CIVILIZATION	
ca. 100,000 B.C.E.	*Homo sapiens*
ca. 40,000 B.C.E.	*Homo sapiens sapiens*
ca. 35,000–10,000 B.C.E.	Late Paleolithic era (Old Stone Age)
ca. 8000–6500 B.C.E.	Neolithic era (New Stone Age)
ca. 3500 B.C.E.	Civilization begins

animals and humans. At Tassili-n-Ajjer in modern Algeria, succeeding generations of inhabitants left over 4,000 paintings on cliff and cave walls that date from about 6000 B.C.E. until the time of Jesus. Like a pictorial time line, these paintings show the gradual transformations of human culture.

The earliest cave paintings were produced by people who, like the inhabitants of Europe and the Near East, lived by hunting game and gathering edible plants, nuts, and fruit. Through this long period, humans perfected the making of stone tools; learned to work bone, antler, and ivory into weapons and utensils; and organized an increasingly complex society.

Sedentarization. Sometime around 5000 B.C.E., the artists at Tassili-n-Ajjer began to include in their paintings images of domesticated cattle and harnesslike equipment. Such depictions give evidence of the arrival in North Africa of two of the most profound transformations in human history: sedentarization, that is, the adoption of a fixed dwelling place, and the agricultural revolution. These fundamental changes in human culture began independently around the world and continued for roughly 5,000 years. They appeared first around 10,000 B.C.E. in the Near East, then elsewhere in Asia around 8000 B.C.E. By 5000 B.C.E. the domestication of plants and animals was under way in Africa and what is today Mexico.

Around 10,000 B.C.E., many hunter-gatherers living along the coastal plains of what is today Syria and Israel and in the valleys and the hill country near the Zagros Mountains between modern Iran and Iraq began to develop specialized strategies that led, by accident, to a transformation in human culture. Rather than constantly traveling in search of food, people living near the Mediterranean coast stayed put and exploited the various seasonal sources of food, fish, wild grains, fruits, and game. In communities such as Jericho, people built and rebuilt their mud brick and stone huts over generations rather than moving on as their ancestors had. Such a sedentary existence was easier on the very young and the very old, and consequently infant mortality dropped and life expectancy rose. In the Zagros region, sedentary communities focused on single, abundant sources of food at specific seasons, such as wild sheep and goats in the mountains during summer and pigs and cattle in the lower elevations in winter. These people also harvested the wild forms of wheat and barley that grew in upland valleys.

Social Organization, Agriculture, and Religion

No one really knows why settlement led to agriculture. As population growth put pressure on the local food supply,

▶ In this cave painting in northern Africa, animal magic evokes help from the spirit world in ensuring the prosperity of the cattle herd. A similar ceremony is still performed by members of the Fulani tribes in the Sahel, on the southern fringe of the Sahara.

gathering activities demanded more formal coordination and organization and led to the development of political leadership. This leadership and the perception of safety in numbers may have prevented the traditional breaking away to form other similar communities in the next valley, as had happened when population growth pressured earlier groups. In any case, people no longer simply looked for favored species of plants and animals where they occurred naturally. Now they introduced these species into other locations and favored them at the expense of plant and animal species that were not deemed useful. Agriculture had begun.

Control of Nature.   The ability to domesticate goats, sheep, pigs, and cattle and to cultivate barley, wheat, and vegetables changed human communities from passive harvesters of nature to active partners with it. These peoples of the Neolithic, or New Stone Age (ca. 8000–6500 B.C.E.), organized sizable villages. Jericho, which had been settled before the agricultural revolution, grew into a fortified town complete with ditch, stone walls, and towers and sheltered perhaps 2,000 inhabitants. Çatal Hüyük in southern Turkey may have been even larger.

The really revolutionary aspect of agriculture was not simply that it ensured settled communities a food supply. The true innovation was that agriculture was portable. For the first time, rather than looking for a place that provided them with the necessities of life, humans could carry with them what they needed to make a site inhabitable. This portability also meant the rapid spread of agriculture throughout the region.

Religion.   Agricultural societies brought changes in the form and organization of formal religious cults. Elaborate sanctuary rooms decorated with frescoes, bulls' horns, and sculptures of heads of bulls and bears indicate that structured religious rites were important to the inhabitants of Çatal Hüyük. At Jericho, human skulls covered with clay, presumably in an attempt to make them look as they had in life, suggest that these early settlers practiced ancestor worship. In these larger communities the bonds of kinship that had united small hunter-gatherer bands were being supplemented by religious organization, which helped to control and regulate social behavior. The nature of this religion is a matter of speculation. Images of a female deity, interpreted as a guardian of animals, suggest the religious importance of women and fertility.

Around 1500 B.C.E., a new theme was depicted on the cliff walls at Tassili-n-Ajjer: men herding horses and driving horse-drawn chariots. These drawings indicate that the use of horses and chariots, which had developed over 1,500 years before in Mesopotamia, had now reached the people of North Africa. Chariots symbolized

a new, dynamic, and expansive phase in Western culture. Constructed of wood and bronze and used for transport and especially for aggressive warfare, they are symbolic of the culture of early river civilizations, the first civilizations in western Eurasia.

MESOPOTAMIA: BETWEEN THE TWO RIVERS

Need drove the inhabitants of Mesopotamia—a name that means "between the rivers"—to create a civilization; nature itself offered little for human comfort or prosperity. The upland regions of the north receive most of the rainfall, but the soil is thin and poor. In the south the soil is fertile, but rainfall is almost nonexistent. There the twin rivers provide life-giving water but also bring destructive floods that normally arrive at harvest time. Therefore, agriculture is impossible without irrigation. But irrigation systems, if not properly maintained, deposit harsh alkaline chemicals on the soil, gradually reducing its fertility. In addition, Mesopotamia's only natural resource is clay. It has no metals, no workable stone, no valuable minerals of use to ancient people. These very obstacles pressed the people to cooperative, innovative, and organized measures for survival. Survival in the region required planning and the mobilization of labor, which was possible only through centralization.

Until around 3500 B.C.E., the inhabitants of the lower Tigris and Euphrates lived in scattered villages and small towns. Then the population of the region, which was known as Sumer, began to increase rapidly. Small settlements became increasingly common; then towns such as Eridu and Uruk in what is now Iraq began to grow rapidly. These towns developed in part because of the need to concentrate and organize population in order to carry on the extensive irrigation systems necessary to support Mesopotamian agriculture. These towns soon spread their control out to the surrounding cultivated areas, incorporating the smaller towns and villages of the region. They also fortified themselves against the hostile intentions of their neighbors.

Nomadic peoples inhabited the arid steppes of Mesopotamia, constantly trading with and occasionally threatening settled villages and towns. Their menace was as ever-present in Near Eastern history as drought and flood. But nomads were a minor threat compared with the dangers posed by settled neighbors. As population growth increased pressure on the region's food supply, cities supplemented their resources by raiding their more prosperous neighbors. Victims sought protection within the ramparts of the settlements that had grown up around religious centers. As a result, the populations of the towns rose along with their towering temples, largely at the expense of the countryside. Between about 3500 and 3000 B.C.E., the population of Uruk quadrupled, from 10,000 to

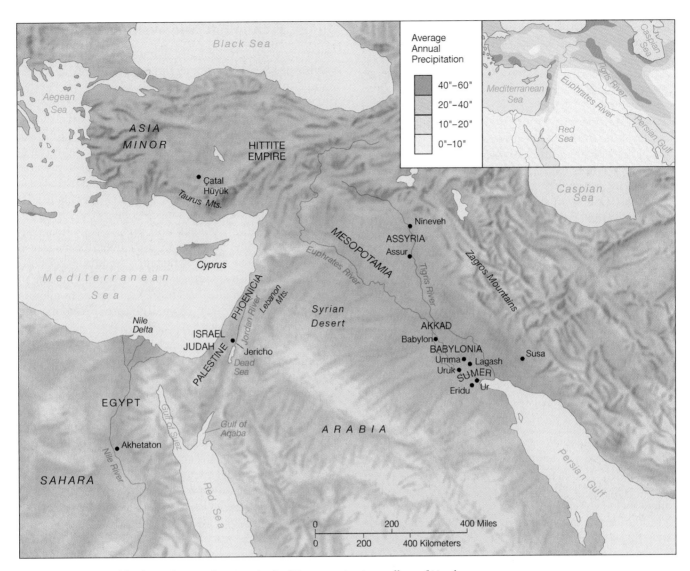

▲ The Ancient World. The earliest civilizations in the West arose in river valleys of Northern
Africa and Western Asia where life depended on control of water.

40,000. Other Mesopotamian cities, notably Umma, Eridu, Lagash, and Ur, developed along the same general lines as they concentrated water supplies within their districts with artificial canals and dikes. At the same time, the number of smaller towns and villages in the vicinity decreased rapidly. The city had become the dominant force in the organization of economy and society, and the growth of the Sumerian cities established a precedent that would continue throughout history.

The Ramparts of Uruk

Cities did more than simply concentrate population. Within the walls of the city, men and women developed new technologies and new social and political structures. They created cultural traditions such as writing and literature. The pride of the first city dwellers is captured in a passage from the *Epic of Gilgamesh*, the earliest known great heroic poem, which was composed sometime before 2000 B.C.E. In the poem, the hero Gilgamesh boasts of the mighty walls he had built to encircle his city, Uruk:

> *Go up and walk on the ramparts of Uruk*
> *Inspect the base terrace, examine the brickwork:*
> *Is not its brickwork of burnt brick?*
> *Did not the Seven Sages lay its foundations?*

Gilgamesh was justifiably proud of his city. In his day (ca. 2700 B.C.E.) these walls were marvels of military engineering; even now their ruins remain a tribute to his age. Archaeologists have uncovered the remains of the ramparts of Uruk, which stretched over five miles and were protected by some 900 semicircular towers. These massive protective walls enclosed about two square miles of houses, palaces, workshops, and temples. Uruk may with reason be called the first true city in the history of Western civilization.

Urban Life.   Within Uruk's walls the peculiar circumstances of urban life changed the traditional social structure of Mesopotamia. In Neolithic times, social and economic differences within society had been minimal. Urban immigration increased the power, wealth, and status of two groups. In the first group were the religious authorities who were responsible for the temples. The second consisted of the emerging military and administrative elites, such as Gilgamesh, who were responsible for the construction and protection of the cities. These two groups probably encouraged much of the migration to the cities.

Whether they lived inside the city or on the farmland it controlled, Mesopotamians formed a highly stratified society that shared unequally in the benefits of civilization. Slaves, who did most of the unskilled labor within the city, were the primary victims of civilization. Most were prisoners of war, but some were people forced by debt to sell themselves or their children. Most of the remaining rural people were peasants who were little more than slaves. Better off were soldiers, merchants, and workers and artisans who served the temple or palace. At the next level were landowning free persons. Above all of these were the priests responsible for temple services and the rulers. Rulers included the *ensi*, or city ruler, and the *lugal*, or king, the earthly representative of the gods. Kings were powerful and feared.

Women's Status.   Urban life also redefined the role and status of women, who in the Neolithic period had enjoyed roughly the same roles and status as men. In cities, women tended to exercise private authority over children and servants within the household, while men controlled the household and dealt in the wider world. This change in roles resulted in part from the economic basis of the first civilization. Southern Mesopotamia has no sources of metal or stone. To acquire these precious commodities, trade networks were extended into Syria, the Arabian Peninsula, and even India. The primary commodities that Mesopotamians produced for trade were textiles, and these were produced largely by women captured in wars with neighboring city-states. Some historians suggest that the disproportionate numbers of low-status women in Mesopotamian cities affected the status of women in general. Although women could own property and even appear as heads of households, by roughly 1500 B.C.E. the pattern of patriarchal households predominated. Throughout Western history, while individual women might at times exercise great power, they did so largely in the private sphere.

Tools: Technology and Writing

Changes in society brought changes in technology. The need to feed, clothe, protect, and govern growing urban populations led to major technological and conceptual discoveries. Canals and systems of dikes partially harnessed water supplies. Farmers began to work their fields with improved plows and to haul their produce to town, first on sleds and ultimately on carts. These land-transport devices, along with sailing ships, made it possible not only to produce greater agricultural surplus but also to move this surplus to distant markets. Artisans used a refined potter's wheel to produce ceramic vessels of great beauty. Government officials and private individuals began to use cylinder seals, small stone cylinders engraved with a pattern, to mark ownership. Metalworkers fashioned gold and silver into valuable items of adornment and prestige. They also began to cast bronze, an alloy of copper and tin, which came into use for tools and weapons about 3000 B.C.E.

Pictograms.   Perhaps the greatest invention of early cities was writing. As early as 7000 B.C.E., small clay or stone tokens with distinctive shapes or markings were being used to keep track of animals, goods, and fruits in inventories and bartering. By 3500 B.C.E., government and temple administrators were using simplified drawings—today termed *pictograms*—that were derived from these tokens to assist them in keeping records of their transactions. Scribes used sharp reeds to impress the pictograms on clay tablets. Thousands of these tablets have survived in the ruins of Mesopotamian cities.

Cuneiform.   The first tablets were written in Sumerian, a language related to no other known tongue. Each pictogram represented a single sound, which corresponded to a single object or idea. In time, these pictograms developed into a true system of writing called *cuneiform* (from the Latin *cuneus*, "wedge") after the wedge shape of the characters. Finally, scribes took a radical step. Rather than simply using pictograms to indicate single objects, they began to use cuneiform characters to represent concepts. For example, the pictogram for "foot" could also mean "to stand." Ultimately, pictograms came to represent sounds divorced from any particular meaning.

The implications of the development of cuneiform writing were revolutionary. Since symbols were liberated from meaning, they could be used to record any language. Over the next thousand years, scribes used these same symbols to write not only in Sumerian but also in the other languages of Mesopotamia, such as Akkadian, Babylonian, and Persian. Writing soon allowed those who had mastered it to achieve greater centralization and control of government, to communicate over enormous distances, to preserve and transmit information, and to express religious and cultural beliefs. Writing reinforced memory, consolidating and expanding the achievements of the first civilization and transmitting them to the future. Writing was power, and for much of subsequent history a small minority of merchants and elites and the scribes in their employ wielded this power. In Mesopotamia, this power served to increase the strength of the king, the servant of the gods.

Gods and Mortals in Mesopotamia

Uruk had begun as a village like any other. Its rise to importance resulted from its significance as a religious site. A world of many cities, Mesopotamia was also a world of many gods, and Mesopotamian cities bore the imprint of the cult of their gods.

Mesopotamian Divinities.   The gods were like the people who worshipped them. They lived in a replica of human society, and each god had a particular responsibility. Every object and element from the sky to the brick or the plow had its own active god. The gods had the physical appearance and personalities of humans as well as human virtues and vices. Greater gods such as Nanna and Ufu were the protectors of Ur and Sippar. Others, such as Inanna, or Ishtar, the goddess of love, fertility, and wars, and her husband Dumuzi, were worshiped throughout Mesopotamia. Finally, at the top of the pantheon were the gods of the sky, the air, and the rivers.

Temples and Rituals.   Mesopotamians believed that the role of mortals was to serve the gods and to feed them through sacrifice. Towns had first developed around the gods' temples for this purpose. By around 2500 B.C.E., although military lords and kings had gained political power at the expense of the temple priests, the temples still controlled a major portion of economic resources. They owned vast estates where peasants cultivated crops and tended flocks to support the priests, scribes, artisans, laborers, farmers, teamsters, smiths, and weavers who operated these complex religious centers. A ziggurat, or tiered tower, dedicated to the god stood near many temples.

Although Mesopotamians looked to hundreds of personal divinities for assistance, they did not attempt to establish personal relationships with their great gods. However, since they assumed that the gods lived in a structured world that operated rationally, they believed that mortals could deal with the gods and enlist their aid by following the right rituals. Rites centered on the veneration of idols. The most important care was feeding. At the temple of Uruk the gods were offered two meals a day, each consisting of two courses served in regal quantity and style.

Through the proper rituals a person could buy the god's protection and favor. Still, mortal life was harsh, and the gods offered little solace in coping with the great issues of human existence. This attitude is powerfully presented in the *Epic of Gilgamesh*, which, while not an accurate picture of Mesopotamian religion, does convey much of the values of this civilization. In this popular legend, Gilgamesh, king of Uruk, civilizes the wild man Enkidu, who was sent by the gods to temper the king's harshness. Gilgamesh and Enkidu become friends and undertake a series of adventures. However, even their great feats cannot overcome death. Enkidu displeases the gods and dies. Gilgamesh then sets out to find the magic plant of eternal life with which to return his friend from the somber underworld. On his journey he meets Ut-napishtim, the Mesopotamian Noah, who recounts the story of the Great Flood and tells Gilgamesh where to find the plant. Gilgamesh follows Ut-napishtim's advice and is successful but loses the plant on his journey home. The message is that only the gods are immortal, and the human afterlife is at best a shadowy and mournful existence.

Sargon and Mesopotamian Expansion

The temple was one center of the city; the palace was the other. As representative of the city's god, the king was the ruler and highest judge. He was responsible for the construction and maintenance of religious buildings and the complex system of canals that maintained the precarious balance between swamp and arid steppe. Finally, he commanded the army, defending his community against its neighbors and leading his forces against rival cities.

Competition and War.   The cultural and economic developments of early Mesopotamia occurred within the context of almost constant warfare. From around 3000 B.C.E. until 2300 B.C.E. the rulers of Ur, Lagash, Uruk, and Umma fought among themselves for control of Sumer, their name for the southern region of Mesopotamia. The population was a mixture of Sumerians and Semites, peoples who spoke Semitic languages related to modern Arabic or Hebrew, all jealously protective of their cities and gods and eager to extend their domination over their weaker neighbors.

The Akkadian Empire.   The extraordinary developments in this small corner of the Middle East might have remained isolated phenomena were it not for Sargon (ca. 2334–2279 B.C.E.), king of Akkad and the most important figure in Mesopotamian history. During his long reign of 55 years, Sargon built on the conquests and confederacies of the past to unite, transform, and expand Mesopotamian civilization. Born in obscurity, he was worshipped as a

The Standard of Ur, made of shells, lapis lazuli, and limestone, was found at Ur. In the top panel, known as *War,* soldiers and horse-drawn chariots return victorious from battle. In the lower panel *Peace,* the king celebrates the victory, captives are paraded before him, and the conquered people bring him tribute.

god after his death. In his youth he was the cupbearer to the king of Kish, another Sumerian city. Later, Sargon overthrew his master and conquered Uruk, Ur, Lagash, and Umma. This made him lord of Sumer. Such glory had satisfied his predecessors, but not Sargon. Instead, he extended his military operations east across the Tigris, west along the Euphrates, and north into modern Syria, thus creating the first great multiethnic empire state in the West.

The Akkadian state—so named by contemporary historians for Sargon's capital at Akkad—consisted of a vast and heterogeneous collection of city-states and territories. Sargon attempted to rule it by transforming the traditions of royal government. Rather than eradicating the traditions of conquered cities, he allowed them to maintain their own institutions but replaced many of their autonomous ruling aristocracies with his own functionaries. At the same time, however, he tried to win the loyalty of the ancient cities of Sumer by naming his daughter high priestess of the moon-god Nanna at Ur. He was thus the first in a long tradition of Near Eastern rulers who sought to unite his disparate conquests into a true state.

Sargon did more than just conquer cities. Although a Semite, he spread the achievements of Sumerian civilization throughout his vast state. Akkadian scribes used cuneiform to write the Semitic Akkadian language. So important did Sargon's successors deem his accomplishments that they ordered him to be worshiped as a god.

The Akkadian state proved as ephemeral as Sargon's accomplishments were lasting. All Mesopotamian states tended to undergo a cycle of rising rapidly under a gifted military commander and then beginning to crumble under the internal stresses of dynastic disputes and regional assertions of autonomy. Thus weakened, they could then be conquered by other expanding states. First Ur, under its Sumerian king and first law codifier, Shulgi (2094–2047 B.C.E.), and then Amoritic Babylonia, under its great ruler, Hammurabi (1792–1750 B.C.E.), assumed dominance in the land between the rivers. From about 2000 B.C.E. on, the political and economic centers of Mesopotamia were in Babylonia and in Assyria, the region to the north at the foot of the Zagros Mountains.

Hammurabi and the Old Babylonian Empire

In the tradition of Sargon, Hammurabi expanded his state through arms and diplomacy. He expanded his power

THE CODE OF HAMMURABI

The society revealed in the Code of Hammurabi was a complex world of landed aristocrats, merchants, and simple workers and shopkeepers. Its economy functioned on a complex system of credit relationships binding the various members of the society together, as seen in the following selections.

FOCUS QUESTIONS

What occupations were pursued in the Old Babylonian Empire?

How did gender and social status affect legal penalties?

IF A MERCHANT LENT GRAIN AT INTEREST, he shall receive sixty *qu* of grain per *jur* as interest [equal 20 percent rate of interest]. If he lent money at interest, he shall receive one-sixth shekel six *se* (i.e., one-fifth shekel) per shekel of silver as interest.

If a seignior who incurred a debt does not have the money to pay it back, but has the grain, the merchant shall take grain for his money with its interest in accordance with the ratio fixed by the king.

If a seignior gave money to another seignior for a partnership, they shall divide equally in the presence of god the profit or loss which was incurred.

If a woman wine seller, instead of receiving grain for the price of a drink, has received money by the large weight and so has made the value of the drink less than the value of the grain, they shall prove it against that wine seller and throw her into the water.

If an obligation came due against a seignior and he sold the services of his wife, his son, or his daughter, or he has been bound over to service, they shall work in the house of their purchaser or obligee for three years, with their freedom reestablished in the fourth year.

If an obligation came due against a seignior and he has accordingly sold [the services of] his female slave who bore him children, the owner of the female slave may repay the money which the merchant paid out and thus redeem his female slave.

---

south as far as Uruk and north to Assyria. In the tradition of Shulgi, he promulgated an important body of law, known as the Code of Hammurabi. In the words of its prologue, this code sought

> To cause justice to prevail in the country
> To destroy the wicked and the evil,
> That the strong may not oppress the weak.

Law and Society. As the favored agent of the gods, the king had responsibility for regulating all aspects of Babylonian life, including dowries and contracts, agricultural prices and wages, and commerce and money lending. Hammurabi's code addresses professional behavior of physicians, veterinarians, architects, and boat builders. It offers a view of many aspects of Babylonian life, though always from the perspective of the royal law. The code lists offenses and prescribes penalties, which vary according to the social status of the victim and the perpetrator. Hammurabi's code thus creates a picture of a prosperous society composed of three legally defined social strata: a well-to-do elite, the mass of the population, and slaves. Each group had its own rights and obligations in proportion to its status. Even slaves enjoyed some legal rights and protection, could marry free persons, and might eventually obtain freedom.

Much of the code sought to protect women and children from arbitrary and unfair treatment. Husbands ruled their households but did not have unlimited authority over their wives. Women could initiate their own court cases, practice various trades, and even hold public positions. Upon marriage, husbands gave their fathers-in-law a payment in silver or in furnishings. The wife's father gave her a dowry over which she had full control. Some elite women personally controlled great wealth.

The Code of Hammurabi was less a royal attempt to restructure Babylonian society than an effort to reorganize, consolidate, and preserve previous laws in order to maintain the established social and economic order. What innovation it did show was in the extent of such punitive measures as death or mutilation. Penalties in earlier codes had been primarily compensation in silver or valuables.

Mathematics. Law was not the only area in which the Old Babylonian kingdom began an important tradition. To handle the economics of business and government administration, Babylonians developed the most sophisticated mathematical system known before the fifteenth century C.E. Babylonian mathematics was based on a numerical system from 1 to 60. (Today we still divide hours and minutes into 60 units.) Babylonian mathematicians devised multiplication tables and tables of reciprocals.

They also devised tables of squares and square roots, cubes and cube roots, and other calculations needed for computing such important figures as compound interest. Although Babylonian mathematicians were not interested primarily in theoretical problems and were seldom given to abstraction, their technical proficiency indicates the advanced level of sophistication with which Hammurabi's contemporaries could tackle the problems of living in a complex society.

For all its achievements, Hammurabi's state was no more successful than those of his predecessors at defending itself against internal conflicts or external enemies. Despite his efforts, the traditional organization that he inherited from his Sumerian and Akkadian predecessors could not ensure orderly administration of a far-flung collection of cities. Hammurabi's son lost over half of his father's kingdom to internal revolts. Weakened by internal dissension, the kingdom fell to a new and potent force in Western history: the Hittites.

The Hittite Empire. The Hittite state emerged in Anatolia in the shadow of Mesopotamian civilization. The Hittite court reflected Mesopotamian influence in its art and religion and in its adaptation and use of cuneiform script. Unlike the Sumerians, the Semitic nomads, the Akkadians, and the Babylonians, the Hittites were an Indo-European people. Their language was part of the linguistic family that includes most modern European languages as well as Persian, Greek, Latin, and Sanskrit. From their capital of Hattushash (modern Bogazköy in Turkey), they established a centralized state based on agriculture and trade in the metals mined from the ore-rich mountains of Anatolia and exported to Mesopotamia. The Hittites were among the earliest people to succeed in smelting iron.

Perfecting the light horse-drawn war chariot, the Hittites expanded into northern Mesopotamia and along the Syrian coast. They were able to destroy the Babylonian state around 1600 B.C.E. The Hittite Empire was the chief

C H R O N O L O G Y	
BETWEEN THE TWO RIVERS	
ca. 3500 B.C.E.	Pictograms appear
ca. 3000–2316 B.C.E.	War for control of Sumer
ca. 2700 B.C.E.	Gilgamesh
ca. 2334–2279 B.C.E.	Sargon
1792–1750 B.C.E.	Hammurabi
ca. 1600 B.C.E.	Hittites destroy Old Babylonian state
ca. 1286 B.C.E.	Battle of Kadesh

political and cultural force in western Asia from about 1400 to 1200 B.C.E. Its gradual expansion south along the coast was checked at the battle of Kadesh about 1286 B.C.E., when Hittite forces encountered the army of an even greater and more ancient power: the Egypt of Ramses II.

THE GIFT OF THE NILE

Like that of the Tigris and Euphrates valleys, the rich soil of the Nile Valley can support a dense population. There, however, the similarities end. Unlike the Mesopotamian floodplain, the Nile floodplain required little effort to make the land productive. Each year, the river flooded at exactly the right time to irrigate crops and to deposit a layer of rich, fertile silt. The Nile flows from south to north, emptying into the Mediterranean Sea. South of the last cataracts (rapids or falls), the fertile upriver region called Upper Egypt is about eight miles wide and is flanked by high desert plateaus. Down river, in Lower Egypt near the Mediterranean, the Nile spreads across a lush marshy delta more than one hundred miles wide. Egypt knew only two environments: the fertile Nile Valley and the vast wastes of the Sahara Desert surrounding it. This inhospitable and largely uninhabitable region limited Egypt's contact with outside influences. Thus while trade, communication, and violent conquest characterized Mesopotamian civilization, Egypt knew self-sufficiency, an inward focus in culture and society, and stability. In its art, political structure, society, and religion, the Egyptian universe was static. Nothing was ever expected to change.

The earliest sedentary communities in the Nile Valley appeared on the western margin of the Nile Delta around 4000 B.C.E. In villages such as Merimda, which had a population of over 10,000, huts constructed of poles and adobe bricks huddled together near *wadis,* fertile riverbeds that were dry except during the rainy season. Farther south, in Upper Egypt, similar communities developed somewhat later but achieved an earlier political unity and a higher level of culture. By around 3200 B.C.E., Upper Egypt was in contact with Mesopotamia and had apparently borrowed something of that region's artistic and architectural traditions. During the same period, Upper Egypt developed a pictographic script.

These cultural achievements coincided with the political centralization of Upper Egypt under a series of kings. Probably around 3150 B.C.E., King Narmer or one of his predecessors in Upper Egypt expanded control over the fragmented south, uniting Upper and Lower Egypt and establishing a capital at Memphis on the border between these two regions. For over 2,500 years, the Nile Valley, from the first cataract to the Mediterranean, enjoyed the most stable civilization the Western world has ever known.

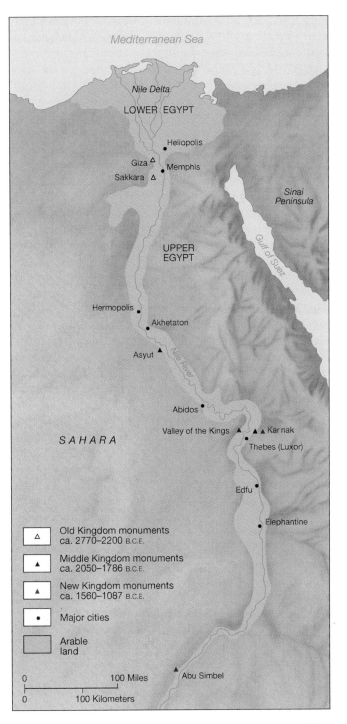

▲ Ancient Egypt. The thin strip of rich land bordering the Nile saw the development of an extraordinary civilization that endured for more than 2,000 years.

Tending the Cattle of God

Historians divide the vast sweep of Egyptian history into 31 dynasties, regrouped in turn into four periods of political centralization: pre- and early dynastic Egypt

(ca. 3150–2770 B.C.E.), the Old Kingdom (ca. 2770–2200 B.C.E.), the Middle Kingdom (ca. 2050–1786 B.C.E.), and the New Kingdom (ca. 1560–1087 B.C.E.). The time gaps between kingdoms were periods of disruption and political confusion termed intermediate periods. While minor changes in social, political, and cultural life certainly occurred during these centuries, the changes were less significant than the astonishing stability and continuity of the civilization that developed along the banks of the Nile.

God Kings. Divine kingship was the cornerstone of Egyptian life. Initially, the king was the incarnation of Horus, a sky and falcon god. Later, the king was identified with the sun-god Ra (subsequently known as Amen-Re, the great god), as well as with Osiris, the god of the dead. As divine incarnation, the king was obliged above all to care for his people. It was he who ensured the annual flooding of the Nile, which brought water to the parched land. His commands preserved *maat*, the ideal state of the universe and society, a condition of harmony and justice. In the poetry of the Old Kingdom, the king was the divine herdsman; the people were the cattle of god:

> *Well tended are men, the cattle of god.*
> *He made heaven and earth according to their desire*
> *and repelled the demon of the waters . . .*
> *He made for them rulers (even) in the egg,*
> *a supporter to support the back of the disabled.*

Unlike the rulers in Mesopotamia, the kings of the Old Kingdom were not warriors but divine administrators. Protected by the Sahara, Egypt had few external enemies and no standing army. A vast bureaucracy of literate court officials and provincial administrators assisted the god-king. They wielded wide authority as religious leaders, judicial officers, and, when necessary, military leaders. A host of subordinate overseers, scribes, metalworkers, stonemasons, artisans, and tax collectors rounded out the royal administration. At the local level, governors administered provinces called *nomes*, the basic units of Egyptian local government.

Gender and Bureaucracy. Women of ancient Egypt were more independent and involved in public life than those of Mesopotamia. Egyptian women owned property, conducted their own business, entered legal contracts, and brought lawsuits. They shared in the economic and professional life of the country at every level except one: women were apparently excluded from formal education. The professional bureaucracy was open only to those who could read and write. As a result, the primary route to public power was closed to women, and the bureaucratic machinery remained firmly in the hands of men.

The role of this bureaucracy was to administer estates, collect taxes, and channel revenues and labor toward vast public works projects, which focused on the king. The king lived in the royal city of Memphis in the splendor of a *Per-ao,* or "Great House," from which comes the word *pharaoh,* the Hebrew term for the Egyptian king.

The Pyramids.   During the Old and Middle Kingdoms, great pyramid temple-tomb complexes more imposing than the Great House were built for the kings. Within the temples, priests and servants performed rituals to serve the dead kings just as they had served the kings when they were alive. Even death did not disrupt the continuity that was so vital to Egyptian civilization. The cults of dead kings reinforced the monarchy, since veneration of past rulers meant veneration of the reigning king's ancestors.

Building and equipping the pyramids focused and transformed Egypt's material and human resources. Artisans had to be trained, engineering and transportation problems had to be solved, quarrying and stone-working techniques had to be perfected, and laborers had to be recruited. In the Old Kingdom, whose population has been estimated at perhaps 1.5 million, more than 70,000 workers at a time were employed in building these great temple-tombs. No smaller work force could have built such a massive structure as the Great Pyramid of Khufu (ca. 2600 B.C.E.), which stood 481 feet high and contained almost 6 million tons of stone. In comparison, the great Ziggurat of Ur, built around 2000 B.C.E., rose only some 120 feet above the Mesopotamian plain. The pyramids were constructed by peasants working when the Nile was in flood and they could not till the soil. Although actual construction was seasonal, the work was unending. No sooner was one complex completed than the next was begun.

Feeding the masses of laborers absorbed most of the country's agricultural surplus. Equipping the temples and pyramids provided a constant demand for the highest-quality luxury goods, since royal tombs and temples were furnished as luxuriously as palaces. Thus the construction and maintenance of these vast complexes focused the organization and production of Egypt's economy and government.

Democratization of the Afterlife

In the Old Kingdom, future life was available through the king. The graves of thousands of his attendants and servants surrounded his temple. All the wealth, labor, and expertise of the kingdom thus flowed into these temples, reinforcing the position of the king. Like the tip of a pyramid, the king was the summit, supported by all of society.

Decline of Royal Power.   Gradually, however, the absolute power of the king declined. The increasing demands for consumption by the court and the cults forced agricultural expansion into areas where returns were poor, thus decreasing the flow of wealth. As bureaucrats increased their efforts to supply the voracious needs of living and dead kings and their attendants, they neglected the maintenance of the economic system that supplied these needs. The royal government was not protecting society; the "cattle of god" were not being well tended. Finally, tax-exempt religious foundations, established to ensure the perpetual cult of the dead, received donations of vast amounts of property, and their power came to rival the king's. This removed an ever greater amount of the country's wealth from the control of the king and his agents. Thus the wealth and power of the Egyptian kings declined at roughly the time that Sargon was expanding his Akkadian state in Mesopotamia. By around 2200 B.C.E., Egyptian royal authority collapsed entirely, leaving political and religious power in the hands of provincial governors.

The Middle Kingdom.   After almost 200 years of fragmentation, the governors of Thebes in Upper Egypt reestablished centralized royal traditions, but with a difference. Kings continued to build vast temples, but they did not resume the tremendous investments in pyramid complexes on the scale of the Old Kingdom. The bureaucracy was opened to all men, even sons of peasants, who could master the complex pictographic writing. Private temple-tombs proliferated and with them new pious foundations. These promised eternal care by which anyone with sufficient wealth could enjoy a comfortable afterlife.

The memory of the Old Kingdom's shortcomings introduced a new ethical perspective that was expressed in the literature written by the elite. For the first time, the elite voiced the concern that justice might not always be served and that the innocent might suffer at the hands of royal agents. In a popular tale from around 1900 B.C.E., Sinuhe, an official of Amenemhet I (d. 1962 B.C.E.), flees Egypt after the death of his king. He fears that through false reports of his actions he will incur the wrath of Amenemhet's son. Though he returns in his old age and is received honorably, the moral is clear: The state system at times failed in its responsibility to safeguard *maat.*

The Hykos.   The greater access to power and privilege in the Middle Kingdom benefited foreigners as well as Egyptians. Assimilated Semites rose to important administrative positions. By around 1600 B.C.E., when the Hittite armies were destroying the state of Hammurabi's successors, large bands of Semites had settled in the eastern Delta, setting the stage for the first foreign conquest of Egypt. A series of kings referred to by Egyptian sources as "rulers of foreign lands," or Hyksos, overran the country and ruled the Nile Valley as far south as Memphis. These foreigners adopted the traditions of Egyptian kingship and continued the tradition of divine rule.

The Hyksos kings introduced their military technology and organization into Egypt. In particular, they brought with them the light horse-drawn war chariot. This mobile fighting platform—manned by warriors armed with bows, bronze swords of a type previously unknown in Egypt, and lances—transformed Egyptian military tactics. These innovations remained even after the Hyksos were expelled by Ahmose I (1552–1527 B.C.E.), the Theban founder of the Eighteenth Dynasty, with whose reign the New Kingdom began.

The Egyptian Empire

Ahmose did not stop with the liberation of Egypt. He forged an empire. He and his successors used their new-found military might to extend the frontiers of Egypt south up the Nile beyond the fourth cataract and well into Nubia. To the east they absorbed the caravan routes to the Red Sea, from which they were able to send ships to Punt (probably modern Somalia), the source of the myrrh and frankincense that were needed for funeral and religious rituals. Most important was the Egyptian expansion into Canaan. Here Egyptian chariots crushed their foes as kings pressed on as far as the Euphrates. Thutmose I (1506–1494 B.C.E.) proclaimed, "I have made the boundaries of Egypt as far as that which the sun encircles."

Thutmose's immediate successors were his children, Thutmose II (1494–1490 B.C.E.) and Hatshepsut (1490–1468 B.C.E.), who married her brother. After the death of Thutmose II, Hatshepsut ruled both as regent for her stepson Thutmose III (1490–1436 B.C.E.) and as co-ruler. She was by all accounts a capable ruler, preserving stability and even personally leading the army on several occasions to protect the empire.

In spite of the efforts of Hatshepsut and her successors, the Egyptian empire was never as grand as its kings proclaimed. Many of the northern expeditions were raids rather than conquests. Still, the expanded political frontiers meant increased trade and unprecedented interaction with the rest of the ancient world. The cargo excavated from the wreck of a ship that sank off the coast of what is now Turkey around 1350 B.C.E. vividly portrays the breadth of international exchange in the New Kingdom. The lost ship carried a cargo of exotic merchandise from around the Mediterranean world. As private merchants were virtually unknown in the Egyptian empire, the voyage was likely a royal venture or perhaps carried gifts and tributes to the god-king.

Religious and Royal Consolidation Under Akhenaten

Religion was both the heart of royal power and its only limiting force. Although the king was the embodiment of

▲ This painted limestone head of Hatshepsut was originally from a statue. She is shown wearing the crown of Egypt and the stylized beard that symbolized royalty and was often seen on the statues and death masks of pharaohs.

the religious tradition he was also bound by that tradition as it was interpreted by an ancient and powerful system of priesthoods, pious foundations, and cults. The intimate relationship between royal absolutism and religious cult culminated in the reign of Amenhotep IV (1364–1347 B.C.E.), the most controversial and enigmatic ruler of the New Kingdom, who challenged the very basis of royal religious control. In a calculated break with over a thousand years of Egyptian religious custom, Amenhotep attempted to abolish the cult of Amen-Re along with all of the other traditional gods, their priesthoods, and their festivals. In their place he promoted a new divinity, the sun-disk god Aten. Amenhotep moved his capital from Thebes to a new temple city, Akhetaton, near modern Tel al-'Amarna, and changed his own name to Akhenaten ("It pleases Aten").

Akhenaten has been called the first monotheist, a reformer who sought to revitalize a religion that had decayed into superstition and magic. Yet his monotheism was not complete. The god Aten shared divine status with Akhenaten himself. Akhenaten attacked other cults, especially that of Amen-Re, to consolidate royal power and to replace the old priesthoods with his own family members and supporters.

A New Aesthetic.   In attempting to reestablish royal divinity, Akhenaten temporarily transformed the aesthetics of Egyptian court life. Traditional archaic language gave way to the everyday speech of the fourteenth century B.C.E. Wall paintings and statues showed people in the clothing that they actually wore rather than in stylized parade dress. This new naturalism rendered the king at once more human and more divine. It differentiated him from the long line of preceding kings, emphasizing his uniqueness and his royal power.

The strength of royal power was so great that during his reign, Akhenaten could command acceptance of his radical break with Egyptian tradition. However, his ambitious plan did not long survive his death. His innovations annoyed the Egyptian elite, while his abolition of established festivals alienated the masses. His son-in-law, Tutankhamen (1347–1337 B.C.E.), the son of Akhenaten's predecessor, was a child when he became king upon Akhenaten's death. Under the influence of his court advisers, probably inherited from his father's reign, he restored the ancient religious traditions and abandoned the new capital of Akhetaton for his father's palace at Thebes.

The Hittites.   Return to the old ways meant return to the old problems. Powerful pious foundations controlled fully 10 percent of the population. Dynastic continuity ended after Tutankhamen, and a new military dynasty seized the throne. These internal problems provided an opportunity for the growing Hittite state in Asia Minor to expand south at the expense of Egypt. Ramses II (1289–1224 B.C.E.) checked the Hittite expansion at the battle of Kadesh, but the battle was actually a draw. Eventually, Ramses and the Hittite king Hattusilis III signed a peace treaty whose terms included nonaggression and mutual defense. The agreement marked the failure of both states to unify the Fertile Crescent, the region stretching from the Persian Gulf northwest through Mesopotamia and down the Mediterranean coast to Egypt.

The mutual standoff at Kadesh did not long precede the disintegration of both Egypt and the Hittite state. Within a century, states large and small along the Mediterranean coast from Anatolia to the Delta and from the Aegean Sea in the west to the Zagros Mountains in the east collapsed or were destroyed in what seems to have been a general crisis of the civilized world. The various raiders, sometimes erroneously called the "Sea Peoples," who struck Egypt, Syria, the Hittite state, and elsewhere, were not the primary cause of the crisis. It was rather internal political, economic, and social strains within both Egypt and the Hittite state that provided the opportunity for various groups—including Anatolians, Greeks, Israelites, and others—to raid the ancient centers of civilization. In the ensuing confusion, the small Semitic kingdoms of Syria and Canaan developed a precarious independence in the shadow of the great powers.

BETWEEN TWO WORLDS

City-based civilization was an endangered species throughout antiquity. Just beyond the well-tilled fields of Mesopotamia and the fertile delta of the Nile lay the world of the Semitic tribes of seminomadic shepherds and traders. Of course, not all Semites were nonurban. Many had formed part of the heterogeneous population of the Sumerian world. Sargon's Semitic Akkadians and Hammurabi's Amorites created great Mesopotamian nation-states, adopting the ancient Sumerian cultural traditions. Along the coast of Canaan, other Semitic groups established towns and joined in the trade between Egypt and the north. But the majority of Semitic peoples continued to live a life that was radically different from that of the people of the floodplain civilizations. From these, one small group, the Hebrews, emerged to establish a religious and cultural tradition that was unique in antiquity.

C H R O N O L O G Y	
THE GIFT OF THE NILE	
ca. 3150–2770 B.C.E.	Predynastic and early dynastic Egypt
ca. 2770–2200 B.C.E.	Old Kingdom
ca. 2600 B.C.E.	Pyramid of Khufu
ca. 2050–1786 B.C.E.	Middle Kingdom
ca. 1560–1087 B.C.E.	New Kingdom
1552–1527 B.C.E.	Ahmose I
1506–1494 B.C.E.	Thutmose I
1494–1490 B.C.E.	Thutmose II
1490–1468 B.C.E.	Hatshepsut
1364–1347 B.C.E.	Amenhotep IV (Akhenaten)
1347–1337 B.C.E.	Tutankhamen
1289–1224 B.C.E.	Ramses II

The Hebrew Alternative

Sometime after 2000 B.C.E., small Semitic bands under the leadership of patriarchal chieftains spread into what is today Syria, Lebanon, Israel, and Palestine. These bands crisscrossed the Fertile Crescent, searching for pasture for their flocks. Occasionally, they participated in the trade uniting Mesopotamia and the towns of the Mediterranean coast. For the most part, however, they pitched their tents on the outskirts of towns only briefly, moving on when their sheep and goats had exhausted the supply of pasturage. Semitic Aramaeans and Chaldeans brought with them not only their flocks and families, but Mesopotamian culture as well.

Mesopotamian Origins.   Hebrew history records such Mesopotamian traditions as the story of the flood (Genesis, chapters 6–10), legal traditions strongly reminiscent of those of Hammurabi, and the worship of the gods on high places. Stories such as that of the Tower of Babel (Genesis, chapter 11) and the garden of Eden (Genesis, chapters 2–4) likewise have a Mesopotamian flavor, but with a difference. For these wandering shepherds, urban culture was a curse. In the Hebrew Bible (the Christian Old Testament) the first city was built by Cain, the first murderer. The Tower of Babel, probably a ziggurat, was a symbol not of human achievement but of human pride.

At least some of these wandering Aramaeans, among them the biblical patriarch Abraham, rejected the gods of Mesopotamia. Religion among these nomadic groups focused on the specific divinity of the clan. In the case of Abraham, this was the god El. Abraham and his successors were not monotheists. They did not deny the existence of other gods. They simply believed that they had a personal pact with their own god.

In its social organization and cultural traditions, Abraham's clan was no different from its neighbors. These independent clans were ruled by a senior male (hence the Greek term *patriarch*—"rule by the father"). Women, whether wives, concubines, or slaves, were treated as distinctly inferior, virtually as property.

Egypt and Exodus.   Some of Abraham's descendants must have joined the steady migration from Canaan into Egypt that took place during the Middle Kingdom and the Hyksos period. Although they were initially well treated, after the expulsion of the Hyksos in the sixteenth century B.C.E., many of the Semitic settlers in Egypt were reduced to slavery. Around the thirteenth century B.C.E., a small band of Semitic slaves numbering fewer than 1,000 left Egypt for Sinai and Canaan under the leadership of Moses. The memory of this departure, known as the Exodus, became the formative experience of the descendants of those who had taken part and those who later joined them. Moses, a Semite who carried an Egyptian name and who, according to tradition, had been raised in the royal court, was the founder of the Israelite people.

During the years that they spent wandering in the desert and then slowly conquering Canaan, the Israelites forged a new identity and a new faith. From the Midianites of the Sinai Peninsula, they adopted the god Yahweh as their own. Although composed of various Semitic and even Egyptian groups, the Israelites adopted the oral traditions of the clan of Abraham and identified his god, El, with Yahweh. They interpreted their extraordinary escape from Egypt as evidence of a covenant with this god, a treaty similar to those concluded between the Hittite kings and their dependents. Yahweh was to be the Israelites' exclusive god; they were to make no alliances with any others. They were to preserve peace among themselves, and they were obligated to serve Yahweh with arms. This covenant was embodied in the law of Moses, a series of terse absolute commands ("Thou shall not . . .") that were quite unlike the conditional laws of Hammurabi ("if . . ., then . . ."). Inspired by their new identity and their new religion, the Israelites swept into Canaan. Taking advantage of the vacuum of power left by the Hittite-Egyptian standoff following the battle of Kadesh, they destroyed or captured the cities of the region. In some cases the local population welcomed the Israelites and their religion. In other places the indigenous people were slaughtered down to the last man, woman, and child.

A King Like All the Nations

During its first centuries, Israel was a loosely organized confederation of tribes whose only focal point was the religious shrine at Shiloh. This shrine, in contrast with the temples of other ancient peoples, housed no idols, only a chest, known as the Ark of the Covenant, which contained the law of Moses and mementos of the Exodus. In times of danger, temporary leaders would lead united tribal armies. The power of these leaders, who were called judges in the Hebrew Bible, rested solely on their personal leadership qualities. This charisma indicated that the spirit of Yahweh was with the leader. Yahweh alone was the ruler of the people.

By the eleventh century B.C.E., this disorganized political tradition placed the Israelites at a disadvantage in fighting their neighbors. The Philistines, who dominated the Canaanite seacoast and had expanded inland, posed the greatest threat. By 1050 B.C.E., the Philistines had defeated the Israelites, captured the Ark of the Covenant, and occupied most of their territory. Many Israelites clamored for "a king like all the nations" to lead them to victory. To consolidate their forces, the Israelite religious leaders reluctantly established a kingdom. Its first king was Saul, and its second was David.

David (ca. 1000–962 B.C.E.) and his son and successor, Solomon (ca. 961–922 B.C.E.), brought the kingdom of

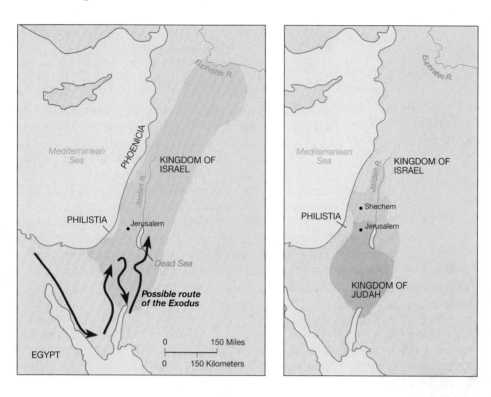

The Kingdoms of Israel and Judah. From its greatest extent under Solomon, the Kingdom of Israel split into rival northern and southern kingdoms and then progressively lost ground against Assyria and Babylon.

Israel to its peak of power, prestige, and territorial expansion. David defeated and expelled the Philistines, subdued Israel's other enemies, and created a united state that included all of Canaan from the desert to the sea. He established Jerusalem as the political and religious capital. Solomon went still further, building a magnificent temple complex to house the Ark of the Covenant and to serve as Israel's national shrine. David and Solomon restructured Israel from a tribal to a monarchical society. The old tribal structure remained only as a religious tradition. Solomon centralized land divisions, raised taxes, and increased military service to strengthen the monarchy.

The cost of this transformation was high. The kingdom under David and especially under Solomon grew more tyrannical as it grew more powerful. Solomon behaved like any other king of his time. He contracted marriage alliances with neighboring princes and allowed his wives to practice their own cults. He demanded extraordinary taxes and services from his people to pay for his lavish building projects. When he was unable to pay his Phoenician creditors for supplies and workers, he deported Israelites to work as slaves in Phoenician mines.

Exile

Not surprisingly, the united kingdom did not survive Solomon's death. The northern region broke off to become the Kingdom of Israel with its capital in Shechem. The south, the Kingdom of Judah, continued the tradition of David from his capital of Jerusalem. These small, weak kingdoms did not long maintain their independence. Beginning in the ninth century B.C.E., a new Mesopotamian power, the Assyrians, began a campaign of conquest and unprecedented brutality throughout the Near East. The Hebrew kingdoms were among their many victims. In 722 B.C.E., the Assyrians destroyed the Kingdom of Israel and deported thousands of its people to upper Mesopotamia. In 586 B.C.E., the Kingdom of Judah was conquered by Assyria's destroyers, the New Babylonian empire under King Nebuchadnezzar II (604–562 B.C.E.). The temple of Solomon was destroyed, Jerusalem was burned, and Judah's elite were deported to Babylon.

The Babylonian captivity ended some 50 years later when the Persians, who had conquered Babylonia, allowed the people of Judah to return to their homeland. Those who returned did so with a new understanding of themselves and their covenant with Yahweh, who was now seen as not just one god among many but as the one universal God. This new understanding was central to the development of Judaism.

The fundamental figures in this transformation were Ezra and Nehemiah (fifth and fourth centuries B.C.E.), who were particularly concerned with keeping Judaism uncontaminated by other religious and cultural influences. They condemned those who had remained in Judaea and who had intermarried with foreigners during the exile. Only the exiles who had remained faithful to Yahweh and who had avoided foreign marriages could be the true interpreters of the Torah. This ideal of separatism and national purity came to characterize the Jewish religion in the post-exilic period.

▶ In this gypsum bas-relief panel, Israelite refugees are seen sadly departing their home city of Lachish after its subjugation by the Assyrians in 701 B.C.E. The sculpture was commissioned by the tyrant Sennacherib to commemorate his victory.

Among its leaders were the Pharisees, a group of zealous adherents to the Torah, who produced a body of oral law termed the Mishnah, or second law, by which the law of Moses was to be interpreted and safeguarded. In subsequent centuries this oral law, along with its interpretation, developed into the Talmud, which did not assume its final form until almost a thousand years after the Babylonian exile. Pharisees believed in resurrection and in spirits such as angels and devils. They also believed that a messiah, or savior, would arise as a new David to reestablish Israel's political independence. Among the priestly elite, the hope for a Davidic messiah was seen as more universal: a priestly messiah would arise and bring about the kingdom of glory. Some Jews actively sought political liberation from the Persians and their successors. Others were more intent on preserving ritual and social purity until the coming of the messiah. Still others, such as the Essenes, withdrew into isolated communities to await the fulfillment of the prophecies.

NINEVEH AND BABYLON

The Assyrian state that destroyed Israel accomplished what no other power had ever achieved. It tied together the floodplain civilizations of Mesopotamia and Egypt. But the Assyrian state was not just larger than the nation-states that had preceded it; it differed in nature as well as in size. The nation-states of Akkadia, Babylonia, the Hittites, and even the Egyptian empire were essentially diverse collections of city-states. Each preserved its own institutions and cultural traditions while diverting its economic resources to the capital. The Assyrian empire was an integrated state in which conquered regions were reorganized and remade along the model of the central government. By the middle of the seventh century B.C.E., the Assyrian empire stretched from the headwaters of the Tigris and Euphrates rivers to the Persian Gulf, along the coast from Syria to beyond the Delta, and up the Nile to Thebes.

The Assyrian Empire

The Assyrian plain north of Babylonia had long been the site of a small Mesopotamian state threatened by seminomads and great powers such as the Babylonians and later the Hittites. When King Assur-dan II mounted the throne in 934 B.C.E., his country was, as he himself later said, exhausted. Gradually, he and his successors began to strengthen the state against its enemies and to allow its population to rebuild its agricultural and commercial base. The Assyrian army, forged by constant warfare into a formidable military machine, began to extend the frontiers of the kingdom both toward the Mediterranean and down the twin rivers toward the Persian Gulf. However, like its predecessors, within a century this empire seemed destined for collapse.

Rapid growth and unprecedented wealth had created a new class of noble warriors who were resented and mistrusted by the petty nobility of the old heartland of the Assyrian kingdom. The old nobility demanded a greater share in the imperial wealth and a more direct role in the administration of the empire. When the emperors ignored their demands, they began a long and bitter revolt that lasted from 827 B.C.E. until 750 B.C.E. This internal crisis put Assyria at the mercy of its external enemies, who seemed on the verge of destroying the Assyrian state. Instead, the revolt paved the way for the ascension of Tiglath-pileser III (746–727 B.C.E.), the greatest empire builder of Mesopotamia since Sargon. Tiglath-pileser and his successors transformed the structure of the Assyrian state and expanded its empire. In the sense that the Assyrians not only conquered but created an administrative system by which to rule, theirs was the first true empire, and as such, it served as a model for Persia, Macedonia, and Rome.

From his palace at Nineveh, Tiglath-pileser combined all of the traditional elements of Mesopotamian statecraft with a new religious ideology and social system to create the framework for a lasting multiethnic imperial system. The heart of Tiglath-pileser's program was the most modern army the world had ever seen. In place of traditional armies of peasants and slaves supplied by great aristocrats, he raised professional armies from the conquered lands of the empire and placed them under the command of Assyrian generals. The Assyrian army was also the first to make massive use of iron weapons, which were superior to the bronze swords and shields of their enemies. Assyrian forces were well balanced, including not only infantry, cavalry, and chariots, but also engineering units for constructing the siege equipment that was needed to capture towns. Warfare had become a science.

In addition to the professional army, Tiglath-pileser created the most developed military-religious ideology of any ancient people. Kings had long been agents of the gods, but Ashur, the god of the Assyrians, had but one command: Enlarge the empire! Thus warfare was the mission and duty of all, a sacred command paralleled through the centuries in the cries of "God wills it" of the Christian crusaders and "God is great" of Muslims.

Tiglath-pileser restructured his empire, both at home in Assyria and abroad, so that revolts of the sort that had nearly destroyed it would be less likely. Within Assyria he increased the number of administrative districts, thus decreasing the strength of each. This reduced the likelihood of successful rebellions launched by dissatisfied governors. Outside Assyria proper, the king liquidated traditional leaders whenever possible and appointed Assyrian governors or at least assigned loyal overseers to protect his interests. To shatter regional identities, which could lead to separatist movements, Tiglath-pileser deported and resettled conquered peoples on a massive scale. He transported the Hebrews to Babylon, sent 30,000 Syrians to the Zagros Mountains, and moved 18,000 Aramaeans from the Tigris to Syria.

Finally, in the tradition of his Assyrian predecessors, Tiglath-pileser and his successors maintained control of conquered peoples through a policy of unprecedented cruelty and brutality. One ruler, for example, boasted of once having flayed an enemy's chiefs and used their skins to cover a great pillar that he erected at their city gate and on which he impaled his victims.

The New Babylonian Empire

Ironically, while the imperial military and administrative system created by the Assyrians became in time the blueprint for future empires, its very ferocity led to its downfall. The hatred inspired by such brutality led to the destruction of the Assyrian empire at the hands of a coalition of its subjects. In what is today Iran, Indo-European tribes coalesced around the Median dynasty. Egypt shook off its Assyrian lords under the leadership of the pharaoh Psamtik I (664–610 B.C.E.). In Babylon, which had always proven difficult for the Assyrians to control, a new Aramaean dynasty began to oppose Assyrian rule. In 612 B.C.E., the Medes and Babylonians joined forces to attack and destroy Nineveh. Once more, the pattern begun by Sargon, of imperial expansion, consolidation, decay, and destruction, was repeated.

However, the lessons that the Assyrians taught the world were not forgotten by the Babylonians, who modeled their imperial system on that of their predecessors. Administration of the New Babylonian empire, which extended roughly over the length of the Tigris and extended west into Syria and Canaan, owed much to Assyrian tradition. The Code of Hammurabi once more formed the fundamental basis for justice. Babylonian kings restored and enriched temples to the Babylonian gods, and temple lands, administered by priests appointed by the king, played an important role in Babylonian economy and culture. Babylonian priests, using the mathematical methods developed during the Old Kingdom, made important advances in mathematical astronomy.

Under King Nebuchadnezzar II, the city of Babylon reached its zenith, covering some 500 acres and containing a population of over 100,000, more than twice the population of Uruk at its height. The city walls, later counted among the seven wonders of the world by the Greeks, were so wide that two chariots could ride abreast on them. Yet this magnificent fortification was never tested. In 539 B.C.E., a Persian army under King Cyrus II (ca. 585–ca. 529 B.C.E.), who had ousted the Median dynasty in 550 B.C.E., slipped into the city through the Euphrates riverbed at low water and took the city by surprise.

Conclusion

THE LEGACY OF THE FIRST 3,000 YEARS OF CIVILIZATION is more than a tradition of imperial conquest, exploitation, and cruelty. It goes beyond a mere catalog of discoveries, inventions, and achievements, impressive as they are. The legacy includes the basic structure of Western civilization. The floodplain civilizations and their neighbors provided the first solutions to problems of social and political organization and complex government. They built what we now recognize to have been the first cities, city-states, nation-states, and finally multinational empires. They attacked the problems of uneven distribution of natural resources through irrigation, long-distance trade, and communication. Their religious traditions, from polytheism to monotheism, provided patterns for subsequent Western religious traditions. Mesopotamian astronomy and mathematics and Egyptian engineering and building were fundamental for future civilizations. The immediate successors of these civilizations, however, would be to the west of the great river valleys, in the mountainous peninsulas and scattered islands of southern Europe.

QUESTIONS FOR REVIEW

1. What cultural developments allowed people to secure food, organize society, and overcome hostile environments before the rise of the first cities?
2. How did urbanization, the invention of writing, and political centralization first develop in the resource-poor area between the Tigris and Euphrates rivers?
3. How did the differing geographic conditions of Mesopotamia and Egypt shape the development of civilization in each?
4. What was the Hebrew people's covenant with Yahweh, and how did this help make a society quite different from the societies around it?
5. What political, religious, and military innovations made the Assyrian Empire more vast and powerful than any previously seen?

DISCOVERING WESTERN CIVILIZATION ONLINE

You can obtain more information about the first civilizations at the websites listed below. See also the companion website that accompanies this text: www.ablongman.com/kishlansky, which contains an online study guide and additional resources.

General Websites

history.evansville.net/referenc.html#West
This section of Nancy V. Mautz's "Creative Impulse: The Artist's View of World History and Western Civilization" provides a directory of Western Civilization websites and pages for further exploration.

Before Civilization

www.versiontech.com/origins/
Educational information on prehistory of humanity.

history.evansville.net/prehist.html
Prehistoric links.

rupestre.net/ralinks/index.html
Online database of links to prehistoric rock art throughout the world.

catal.arch.cam.ac.uk/catal/catal.html
A site devoted to Çatal Hüyük, one of the earliest settlements to have developed into a sedentary agricultural community.

Mesopotamia

www-oi.uchicago.edu/OI/DEPT/RA/ABZU/ABZU.HTML
A major site for all aspects of Ancient Mesopotamia and Egypt maintained by the Oriental Institute of The University of Chicago.

www.taisei.co.jp/cg_e/ancient_world/ur/aur.html
The city of Ur reproduced with computer graphics.

Egypt

history.Evansville.net/egypt.html
Award-winning site for Egyptian history.

touregypt.net/kings.htm
A site that provides information on all of the pharaohs.

www.oi.uchicago.edu/OI/DEPT/COMP/GIZ/MODEL/Giza_Model.html
A site devoted to Giza with a computer model of its pyramids and other monuments.

Israel

An excellent course site devoted to the ancient Hebrews.

Nineveh and Babylon

A 3-D animated fly-through of The Palace of Ashurnasirpal II.

A tour of Babylon in the year 580 B.C.E.

SUGGESTIONS FOR FURTHER READING

General Reading

Cambridge Ancient History, Vol. 1, Part 1 (Cambridge, England: Cambridge University Press, 1990). Contains essays on every aspect of ancient civilizations.

Gerda Lerner, *The Creation of Patriarchy* (New York: Oxford University Press, 1986). A study of gender and politics in antiquity by a leading feminist historian.

Barbara S. Lesko, ed. *Women's Earliest Records from Ancient Egypt and Western Asia: Proceedings of the Conference on Women in the Ancient Near East* (Atlanta: Scholar's Press, 1989). Important collection of essays on all aspects of women in ancient societies.

Donald B. Redford, *Egypt, Canaan, and Israel in Ancient Times* (Princeton: Princeton University Press, 1992). A synthesis of the interrelations among three great Near Eastern civilizations.

Before Civilization

Barry Cunliffe, *Prehistoric Europe: An Illustrated History* (Oxford: Oxford University Press, 1997). An engaging introduction to early Europe.

Brian M. Fagan, *People of the Earth: An Introduction to World Prehistory,* 7th ed. (New York: HarperCollins, 1992). Excellent introduction to the prehistory of Europe and Asia.

Mesopotamia: Between the Two Rivers

Jean Bottero, *Everyday Life in Ancient Mesopotamia* (Baltimore: Johns Hopkins University Press, 2001). Social history of Mespotamia by a leading expert.

Susan Pollock, *Ancient Mesopotamia: The Eden that Never Was* (Cambridge: Cambridge University Press, 1999). An original introduction to the earliest phase of Mesopotamian history.

The Gift of the Nile

Cyril Aldred, *The Egyptians,* 3rd Rev. ed. (New York: Thames & Hudson, 1998). Readable general history of ancient Egypt focusing on culture.

Erik Hornung, *History of Ancient Egypt: An Introduction* (Ithaca, N.Y.: Cornell University Press, 1999). A brief survey of Egypt by a great European scholar.

Ian Shaw, ed. *The Oxford History of Ancient Egypt* (Oxford: Oxford University Press, 2000). Comprehensive collaborative survey of ancient Egypt.

Between Two Worlds

John Curtis, *Ancient Persia* (Cambridge, Mass. Harvard University Press, 1990). Brief overview of ancient Iran.

Roland De Vaux, *Ancient Israel: Its Life and Institutions* (Grand Rapids, Mich.: Wm. B. Eerdmans Publishing Co., 1997). A classic account of religious and social life in ancient Israel.

Henry Jackson Flanders, Robert Wilson Crapps, and David Anthony Smith, *People of the Covenant: An Introduction to the Hebrew Bible,* 4th ed. (New York: Oxford University Press, 1996). A balanced introduction to Hebrew and Jewish history that draws on both Jewish and Christian scholarship.

A. T. Olmstead, *History of Assyria* (Chicago: University of Chicago Press, 1975). The fundamental survey of the Assyrian empire.

CHAPTER 2

EARLY GREECE, 2500–500 B.C.E.

- THE VISUAL RECORD: Hecuba and Achilles
- GREECE IN THE BRONZE AGE TO 700 B.C.E.
- ARCHAIC GREECE, 700–500 B.C.E.

- A TALE OF THREE CITIES
- THE COMING OF PERSIA AND THE END OF THE ARCHAIC AGE

HECUBA AND ACHILLES

THE WRATH OF THE GREAT WARRIOR ACHILLES is the subject of Homer's *Iliad,* the first and greatest epic poem of the Mediterranean West, written shortly after 750 B.C.E. Angered by a perceived slight to his honor, Achilles sulks in his tent while the other Achaeans, or Greeks, fight a desperate and losing battle against their enemies, the defenders of the city of Troy. Only after his friend Patroclus is slain by the Trojan Prince Hector does Achilles return to the battle to avenge his fallen comrade and propel the Achaeans to victory. Near the end of the epic, after he has slain Hector in hand-to-hand combat, Achilles ties his foe's body to the back of his chariot and drags it three times around Patroclus's tomb to appease his friend's spirit. The gods are horrified at this demeaning treatment of the body of one who had always been faithful in his sacrifices. Zeus, the chief god, sends his messenger Iris to Hector's mourning parents, his father, Priam, king of Troy, and his mother, Hecuba. Iris urges them to ransom their son's body from Achilles. Moved by the message, Priam goes to Achilles' tent to plead for Hector's body. Achilles, moved by pity and grief for his own father and for Patroclus, grants the old king his request, and Priam returns in sorrow to Troy bearing the body of his son for burial.

The first portions of this episode are brilliantly rendered on the side of the sixth century B.C.E. *hydria,* or water pitcher, shown here. At the center, Achilles leaps into his chariot. The naked body of Hector stretches below him, and the chariot rushes around the tumulus, or burial mound, of Achilles' friend, represented by the white hill to the right. Above it, the small winged spirit of Patroclus watches. But even as Achilles carries out his deed of vengeance, Iris, the winged messenger of Zeus, rushes to Hector's parents, who are shown under a columned portico, which represents Troy. Typically, the artist has taken some liberty with the story. It is not the grieving father the artist has chosen to feature but rather Hecuba, Hector's disconsolate mother. In a vivid manner, totally alien to previous artistic traditions, the Greek artist, like the Greek poet, has captured the essentials of human tragedy.

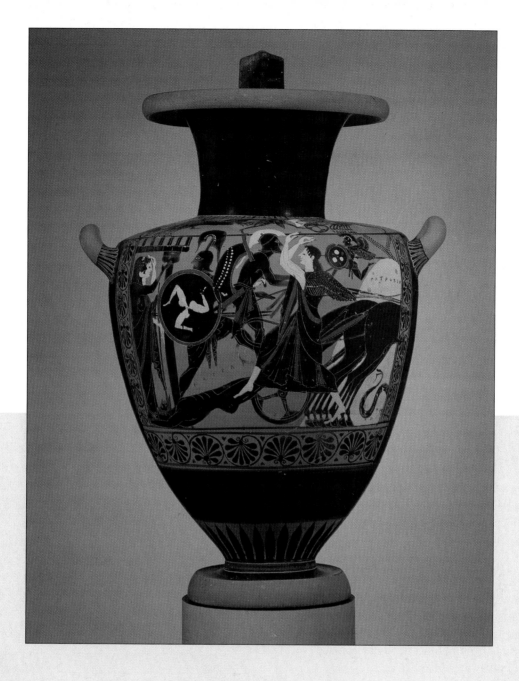

For all its violent action, the *Iliad* is concerned less with what people do than with how they face the great challenges of life and death. Hector had died well and, in so doing, won immortal fame from his enemies, the Greeks. Achilles eventually acted well and, in his encounter with Priam, faced the universal elements of human destiny: life, love, suffering, endurance, death. Such sentiments, expressed by Homer, became an enduring heritage of Greek civilization and, through it, the civilization of the West.

LOOKING AHEAD

In this chapter, we will explore the first Greek-speaking societies in the Eastern Mediterranean, their collapse, and then the emergence of a new and powerful form of civilization created in the cities of Archaic Greece.

27

GREECE IN THE BRONZE AGE TO 700 B.C.E.

Early in the *Iliad*, Homer pauses to list the captains and ships of the besieging forces. The roll call of heroes and their homelands is more than a literary device. It is the distant echo of a vanished world, the world of "the goodly citadel of Athens, wealthy Corinth, Knossos and Gortys of the great walls, and the established fortress of Mycenae." The poet lived in an age of illiterate warrior herdsmen, of impoverished, scattered, and sparsely populated villages. Still, in the depths of this "Dark Age," roughly from 1200 to 700 B.C.E., the distant memory of a time of rich palaces, teeming cities, and powerful kings lived on. Homer and his contemporaries could not know that these confused memories stemmed from the last great Bronze Age (ca. 3500–1200 B.C.E.) civilization of the Mediterranean. Still less could they have imagined that they were preparing the foundations of a far greater and lasting civilization, that of classical Greece.

Unlike the rich floodplains of Mesopotamia and Egypt, Greece is a stark world of mountains and sea. The rugged terrain of Greece, only 10 percent of which is flat, and the scores of islands that dot the Aegean and Ionian seas favor the development of small, self-contained agricultural societies. The Greek climate is uncertain, constantly threatening Greek farmers with failure. Rainfall varies enormously from year to year, and arid summers alternate with cool, wet winters. Wheat, barley, and beans were the staples of Greek life. Greek farmers struggled to produce the Mediterranean triad of grains, olives, and wine, which first began to dominate agriculture around 3000 B.C.E. Constant fluctuations in climate and weather from region to region helped to break down the geographical isolation by forcing insular communities to build contacts with a wider world in order to survive.

Islands of Peace

To Homer, the Greeks were all Achaeans, whether they came from the Greek mainland, the islands in the Aegean Sea, or the coast of Asia Minor. Since the late nineteenth century, archaeologists have discerned three fairly distinct late Bronze Age cultures—the Cycladic, the Minoan, and the Mycenaean—that flourished in the Mediterranean before the end of the twelfth century B.C.E.

The Cyclades. The first culture appeared on the Cyclades, the rugged islands strewn across the bottom of the Aegean from the Greek mainland to the coast of Asia Minor. As early as 2500 B.C.E., artisans in small settlements on the islands of Naxos and Melos developed a high level of metallurgical and artistic skill. Cycladic society was not concentrated into towns, nor, apparently, was it particularly warlike. Many of the largest Cycladic settlements were unfortified. Cycladic religion, to judge from fragments of large clay statues of female figures found in a temple on the island of Ceos, focused on female deities, perhaps fertility goddesses.

This early Bronze Age society slowly faded, but not before influencing its neighbors, especially Crete, the large Mediterranean island to the south. There, beginning around 2500 B.C.E., a sophisticated centralized civilization developed that was termed Minoan after the legendary King Minos of Crete.

Minoan Crete. Knowledge of Minoan civilization burst on the modern world suddenly in 1899. In that year, the English archaeologist Sir Arthur Evans made the first of a series of extraordinary archaeological discoveries at Knossos, the legendary palace of Minos. Crete's location between the civilizations of the Fertile Crescent, Egypt, and the barbarian worlds of the north and west made the island a natural point of exchange and amalgamation of cultures. Still, during the golden age of Crete, roughly between 2000 and 1550 B.C.E., the island developed its unique traditions.

Great palace complexes were constructed at Knossos, Phaistos, Hagia Triada, and elsewhere on the island. They appear as a maze of storerooms, workrooms, and living quarters clustered around a central square. Larger public rooms may have existed at an upper level, but all traces of them have disappeared. Palace bureaucrats, using a unique form of syllabic writing known as Linear A, controlled agricultural production and distribution as well as the work of skilled artisans in their surrounding areas.

C H R O N O L O G Y	
GREECE IN THE BRONZE AGE	
ca. 2500 B.C.E.	Beginning of Minoan civilization in Crete
ca. 2000–1500 B.C.E.	Golden Age of Crete
ca. 1600 B.C.E.	Beginning of Mycenaean civilization in Greece
ca. 1450 B.C.E.	Cretan cities, except Knossos, destroyed
ca. 1375 B.C.E.	Knossos destroyed
ca. 1200–700 B.C.E.	Greek Dark Age
ca. 1200 B.C.E.	Mycenaean sites in Greece destroyed; Knossos destroyed again
ca. 1100–1000 B.C.E.	Writing disappears from Greece

▲ Greece in the Bronze Age. Three distinctive civilizations—Cycladic, Minoan, and Mycenaean—developed around the Aegean Sea in the third and second millennia B.C.E.

Cretan Society and Religion. Like other ancient civilizations, Minoan Crete was strongly stratified. The vast peasantry paid a heavy tribute in olive oil and other produce. Tribute or taxes flowed to local and regional palaces and ultimately to Knossos, which stood at the pinnacle of a four-tiered network uniting the island. To some extent, the palace elites redistributed this wealth back down the system through their patterns of consumption.

Though the system may have been exploitive, it was not militaristic. None of the palaces or towns of Crete was fortified. Nor was the cult of the ruler particularly emphasized. Monumental architecture and sculpture designed to exalt the ruler and to overwhelm the commoner are entirely absent from Crete. A key to this unique social tone may be Cretan religion and, with it, the unusually high status of women. Although male gods received veneration, Cretans particularly worshipped female deities. Chief among the female deities was the mother goddess, who was the source of good and evil. However, one must be careful not to paint too idyllic an image of Cretan religion. Children's bones found in excavations of the palace of Knossos show traces of butchering and the removal of slices of flesh.

Although Minoan society was not clearly matriarchal, it nevertheless differed considerably from the floodplain civilizations of the Near East and the societies that were developing on the mainland. At least until the fourteenth century B.C.E., both men and women seem to have played important roles in religious and public life and together built a structured society without the need for vast armies or warrior kings.

Around 1450 B.C.E., a wave of destruction engulfed all of the Cretan cities except Knossos, which was finally

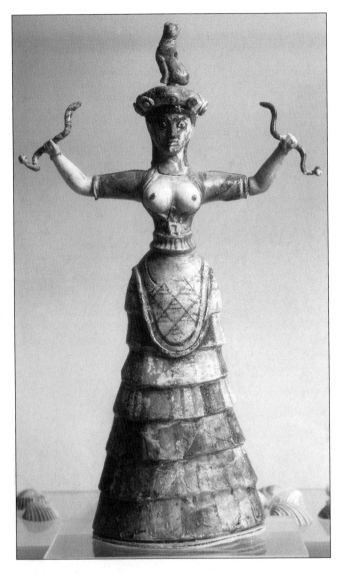

▲ Female divinity from Knossos, ca. 1600 B.C.E. Snakes, symbols of the underworld, are balanced by the bird of prey on the head of this divinity.

Mainland of War

The contrast between the vulnerable islands and the violent Greek mainland was particularly marked. Around 1600 B.C.E., a new and powerful warrior civilization arose on the Peloponnesus at Mycenae. The only remains of the first phase of this civilization are 30 graves found at the bottom of deep shafts arranged in two circles. The swords, axes, and armor that fill the graves emphasize the warrior lives of their occupants. By 1500 B.C.E., mainland Greeks were using huge *tholoi*, or beehive-shaped tombs, for royal burials. Over 50 such tombs have been found on the Greek mainland, as have the remains of over 500 villages and great palaces at Mycenae, Tiryns, Athens, Thebes, Gla, and Pylos. This entire civilization, which encompassed not only the mainland but also parts of the coast of Asia Minor, is called Mycenaean, although there is no evidence that the city of Mycenae actually ruled all of Greece.

The Mycenaeans quickly adopted artisanal and architectural techniques from neighboring cultures, especially from the Hittites and from Crete, and incorporated these techniques into a distinctive tradition of their own. Unlike the open Cretan palaces and towns, Mycenaean palaces were strongly walled fortresses. From these palaces, Mycenaean kings and their staffs controlled the collection of taxes and tribute as well as the production of bronze and woolen cloth and governed maritime trade. Palace administrators adopted the Linear A script of Crete, transforming it to write their own language, a Greek dialect, in a writing known as Linear B, which appears to have been used almost exclusively for record keeping in palaces.

The Dark Age

Mycenaean domination did not last for long. Around 1200 B.C.E., many of the mainland and island fortresses and cities were sacked and totally destroyed. In some areas, such as Pylos, the population fell to roughly 10 percent of what it had been previously. Centralized government, literacy, urban life—civilization itself—disappeared from Greece for over 400 years. Why and how this happened are one of the great mysteries of world history.

In later centuries, the Greeks believed that after the Trojan War, new peoples, especially the Dorians, had migrated into Greece, destroying Mycenae and most of the other Achaean cities. More recently, some historians have argued that catastrophic climatic changes, volcanic eruptions, or some other natural disaster wrecked the cities and brought famine and tremendous social unrest in its wake. Neither theory is accurate. No single invasion or natural disaster destroyed Mycenaean Greece. It self-destructed. Its disintegration was part of the widespread crisis affecting the eastern Mediterranean in the twelfth century B.C.E. The pyramid of Mycenaean lordship, built by small military elites commanding maritime commercial networks,

annihilated around 1375 B.C.E. The causes of this catastrophe continue to inspire historical debate. Some argue that a natural disaster such as an earthquake or the eruption of a powerful volcano on Thera was responsible for the destruction. More likely, given the martial traditions of the continent and their total absence on Crete, the destruction was the work of mainland Greeks taking control of Knossos and other Minoan centers. Around this same time, true warrior graves equipped with weapons and armor begin to appear on Crete and at Knossos for the first time. Following this violent conquest, only Knossos and Phaistos were rebuilt, presumably by Greek lords who had eliminated the other political centers on the island. Knossos was ravaged again around 1200 B.C.E.

▲ A golden funeral mask (ca. 1500 B.C.E.) found in the royal tombs of Mycenae. The mask was once thought to be the likeness of Agamemnon, the king of Mycenae in the Homeric epics.

was always threatened with collapse. Overpopulation, the fragility of the agrarian base, the risks of overspecialization in cash crops such as grain in Messenia and sheep raising in Crete, and rivalry among states—all made Mycenaean culture vulnerable. The disintegration of the Hittite empire and the near-collapse of the Egyptian empire disrupted Mediterranean commerce, exacerbating hostilities among Greek states.

As internal warfare raged, the delicate structures of elite lordship disappeared in the mutual sackings and destructions of the palace fortresses. The Dark Age poet Hesiod (ca. 800 B.C.E.), although writing about his own time, probably got it about right:

> Father will have no common bond with son
> Neither will guest with host, nor friend with friend
> The brother-love of past days will be gone . . .
> Men will destroy the towns of other men.

With the collapse of the administrative and political system on which Mycenaean civilization was built, the tiny elite that had ruled it vanished as well. From roughly 1200 until 800 B.C.E., the Aegean world entered what is generally termed the Dark Age, a confused period about which little is known, during which Greece returned to a more primitive level of culture and society.

A New Material Culture.   In the wake of the Mycenaean collapse, bands of northerners moved slowly into the

Peloponnesus while other Greeks migrated out from the mainland to the islands and the coast of Asia Minor. As these tribal groups merged with the indigenous populations, they gave certain regions distinctive dialectic and cultural characteristics. Thus, the Dorians settled in much of the Peloponnesus, Crete, and southwest Asia Minor. Ionians made Attica, Euboea, and the Aegean islands their home; a mixed group called Aeolians began to migrate to central and northwest Asia Minor. As a result, from the eleventh century B.C.E., both shores of the Aegean became part of a Greek-speaking world. Still later, Greeks established colonies in what is today southern Ukraine, Italy, North Africa, Spain, and France. Throughout its history, Greece was less a geographical than a cultural designation.

Everywhere in this world, between roughly 1100 and 1000 B.C.E., architecture and urban traditions declined, and writing disappeared along with the elites for whose exclusive benefit these achievements had served. The Greece of this Dark Age was much poorer, more rural, and more simply organized. It was also a society of ironworkers. Iron began to replace bronze as the most common metal for ornaments, tools, and weapons. At first this was a simple necessity. The collapse of long-distance trade deprived Greeks of access to tin and copper, the essential ingredients of bronze. Gradually, however, the quality of iron tools and weapons began to improve as smiths learned to work hot iron into a primitive steel.

What little is known of this period must be gleaned from archaeology and from Homer's two great epic poems that were written down around 750 B.C.E., near the end of the Dark Age. The archaeological record is bleak. Pictorial representation of humans and animals almost disappears. Luxury goods and most imports are gone from tombs. Pottery made at the beginning of the Dark Age shows little innovation, crudely imitating forms of Mycenaean production.

Gradually, beginning in the eleventh century B.C.E., things began to change a bit. New geometric forms of decoration began to appear on pottery. New types of iron pins, weapons, and decorations appeared that owed little or nothing to the Mycenaean tradition. Cultural changes accompanied these material changes. Around the middle of the eleventh century B.C.E., Greeks in some locations stopped burying their dead and began to practice cremation. Whatever the meaning of these changes, they signaled something new on the shores of the Aegean.

The Evidence of Homer.   The two epic poems—the *Iliad* and the *Odyssey*—hint at this something new. The *Iliad* is the older poem, dating probably to the second half of the eighth century B.C.E. The *Odyssey* dates from perhaps 50 years later. Traditionally ascribed to Homer, these epics were actually the work of oral bards or performers who composed as they chanted. Although the Homeric poems explicitly harken back to the Mycenaean age, much of the description of life, society, and culture actually reflects Dark

HECTOR AND ANDROMACHE

The Trojan hero Hector is almost as central to the Iliad *of Homer as is Achilles. Unlike the latter, Hector is a dutiful, reliable support to his city and to Andromache, who is not only his wife but his closest and dearest companion. The description of their last meeting is one of the great expressions of the heroic ethos and of the bonds of man and woman in that culture.*

FOCUS QUESTIONS

How would you describe the relationship between Hector and Andromache? What is the ideal future that Hector wishes for his son?

AT LAST HIS OWN GENEROUS WIFE CAME RUNNING TO MEET HIM, Andromache, the daughter of high-hearted Eëation . . . . She came to him there, and beside her went an attendant carrying the boy in the fold of her bosom, a little child, only a baby, Hector's son, the admired, beautiful as a star shining . . . . Andromache, stood close beside him, letting her tears fall, and clung to his hand and called him by name and spoke to him: "Dearest, your own great strength will be your death, and you have no pity on your little son, nor on me, ill-starred, who soon
  must be your widow" . . . .
Then tall Hector of the shining helm answered her: "All these things are in my mind also, lady; yet I would feel deep shame before the Trojans, and the Trojan women with trailing garments, if like a coward I were to shrink aside from fighting . . . . But it is not so much the pain to come of the Trojans that troubles me . . . as the thought of you, when some bronze-armored Achaian leads you off, taking away your day of liberty in tears; and in Argos you must work at the loom of another" . . .
Then taking up his dear son he tossed him about in his arms and kissed him, and lifted his voice in prayer to Zeus and the
  other immortals:
"Zeus, and you other immortals, grant that this boy, who is my son, may be as I am, pre-eminent among the Trojans, great in strength, as I am, and rule strongly over Ilion;
And someday let them say of him: 'He is better by far than his
  father,'
as he comes from the fighting; and let him kill his enemy and bring home the blooded spoils, and delight the heart of his
  mother."

From the *Iliad* of Homer, Book VI.

Age conditions. Thus Homer's heroes were petty kings, chieftains, and nobles, whose positions rested on their wealth, measured in land and flocks, on personal prowess, on networks of kin and allies, and on military followings. The Homeric hero Odysseus is typical of these Dark Age chieftains. In the *Iliad* and the *Odyssey* he is king of Ithaca, a small island on the west coast of Greece. He retained command of his men only as long as he could lead them to victory in the raids against their neighbors. Odysseus describes his departure for home after the fall of Troy with pride:

> The wind that bore me from Ilios brought me . . . to Ismarus, whereupon I sacked their city and slew the people. And from the city we took their wives and much goods, and divided them among us, that none through me might go lacking his proper share.

When present, the king was judge, gift giver, lawgiver, and commander. Absent, no legal or governmental institutions preserved his authority. Instead, the nobility, lesser warriors who were constantly at odds with the king, sought to take his place. In the *Odyssey*, only their mutual rivalry saves Odysseus's wife, Penelope, from being forced to marry one of these haughty aristocrats who were eager to replace the king. Odysseus's son Telemachus summoned the assembly of the people to listen to his complaints against the noble suitors of his mother. Thus the people were not entirely excluded from public life; but this does not mean that they were particularly effective. The assembly listened to both sides and did nothing. Still, a time was coming when changes in society would give hitherto unimagined power to the silent farmers and herdsmen of the Dark Age.

From the Bronze Age civilizations, speakers of Greek had inherited distant memories of an original, highly organized urban civilization grafted onto the rural, aristocratic warrior society of the Dark Ages. Most important, this common dimly recollected past gave all Greek-speaking inhabitants of the Mediterranean world common myths, values, and identity.

ARCHAIC GREECE, 700–500 B.C.E.

Between roughly 800 and 500 B.C.E., extraordinary changes took place in the Greek world. The descendants of the farmers and herdsmen of Homer's Dark Age brought about a revolution in political organization, artistic traditions, intellectual values, and social structures. In a burst of creativity forged in conflict and competition, they invented politics, abstract thought, and the individual. Greeks of the Archaic Age (ca. 700–500 B.C.E.) set the agenda for the rest of Western history.

The first sign of radical change in Greece was a major increase in population in the eighth century B.C.E. In Attica, for example, between 780 and 720 B.C.E., the population increased perhaps sevenfold, possibly because of a shift from herding to agriculture. The consequences were enormous. First, population increase meant more villages and towns, greater communication among them, and thus the more rapid circulation of ideas and skills. Second, the rising population placed impossible demands on the agricultural system of much of Greece. Third, it led to greater division of labor and, with an increasingly diverse population, to fundamental changes in political systems. The old structure of loosely organized tribes and chieftains became inadequate to deal with the more complex nature of the new society.

The multiplicity of political and social forms developing in the Archaic Age set the framework within which the first flowering of Greek culture developed. Economic and political transformations laid the basis for intellectual advance by creating a broad class with the prosperity to enjoy sufficient leisure for thought and creative activity. Finally, maritime relations brought people and ideas from around the Greek world together, cross-fertilizing artists and intellectuals in a way never before seen in the West.

Ethnos and Polis

In general, two forms of political organization developed in response to the population explosion of the eighth century B.C.E. On the mainland and in much of the western Peloponnesus, people continued to live in large territorial units called *ethne* (sing. *ethnos*). In each ethnos, people lived in villages and small towns scattered across a wide region. Common customs and a common religion focusing on a central religious sanctuary united them. The ethnos was governed by an elite, or oligarchy (meaning "rule by the few"), made up of major landowners who met from time to time in one or another town within the region. This form of government, which had its roots in the Dark Ages, continued to exist throughout the classical period.

A much more innovative form of political organization, which developed on the shores of the Aegean and on the

▼ Greek Cities and Colonies of the Archaic Age. Greek civilization was never limited geographically but thrived in trading and agricultural colonies ringing the Mediterranean and Black Seas.

islands, was the *polis* (pl. *poleis*), or city-state. Initially, *polis* meant simply "citadel." Villages clustered around these fortifications, which were both protective structures and cult centers for specific deities. These high, fortified sites—*acropolis* means "high citadel"—were sacred to specific gods: in Athens and Sparta, to Athena; in Argos and Samos, to Hera; at Corinth and Thermon, to Apollo. In addition to protection, the polis offered a marketplace, or *agora,* where farmers and artisans could trade and conduct business. The rapid population growth of the eighth century B.C.E. led to the fusion of these villages and the formation of real towns. Each town was independent, each was ruled by a monarchy or an oligarchy, and each controlled the surrounding region, the inhabitants of which were on an equal footing with the townspeople. At times of political or military crisis, the rulers might summon an assembly of the free males of the community to the agora to participate in or to witness the decision-making process. In the following centuries these city-states became the center for that most dramatic Greek experiment in government: democracy.

Technology of Writing and Warfare

The general model of the polis may have been borrowed from the eastern Mediterranean Phoenicians, the merchant society that was responsible for much of the contact Greeks of the eighth century B.C.E. had with the surrounding world. The Phoenicians were certainly the source of an equally important innovation that appeared in Greece at the same time: the reintroduction of writing. Sometime in the eighth century B.C.E., Greeks adopted the Phoenician writing system. But unlike the abandoned Mycenaean script, the purpose of the new writing system was not primarily central administrative record keeping. From the start, this writing system was intended for private, personal use and was available to virtually anyone. The Greeks radically transformed the Phoenician system, making its Semitic characters stand for arbitrary sounds and adding vowel notation in order to record poetry. Soon this writing system was used to indicate ownership of objects, to record religious and secular vows, and even to entertain.

Within the polis, political power was not the monopoly of the aristocracy. The gradual expansion of the politically active population resulted largely from the demands of warfare. In the Dark Age, warfare had been dominated by heavily armed, mounted aristocrats who engaged their equals in single combat. In the Archaic Age, such individual combat between aristocratic warriors gave way to battles that were decided by the use of well-disciplined ranks of infantrymen called *phalange* (sing. *phalanx*). Although few Greeks could afford costly weapons, armor, and horses, between 25 and 40 percent of the landowners

could provide the shields, lances, and bronze armor needed by the infantrymen, or *hoplites.*

The democratization of war led gradually to the democratization of political life. Those who brought victory in the phalanx were unwilling to accept total domination by the aristocracy in the agora. The rapid growth of the urban population, the increasing impoverishment of the rural peasantry, and the rise of a new class of wealthy merchant commoners were all challenges that traditional forms of government failed to meet. Everywhere, traditional aristocratic rule was being undermined, and cities searched for ways to resolve this social conflict. No one solution emerged, and one of the outstanding achievements of archaic Greece was the almost limitless variety of political forms elaborated in its city-states.

Colonists and Tyrants

Colonization and tyranny were two intertwined results of the political and social turmoil of the seventh century B.C.E. Population growth, changes in economy, and opposition to aristocratic power led Greeks to seek change externally through emigration and internally through political restructuring.

Late in the eleventh century B.C.E., Greeks had begun to migrate to new homes on the islands and along the coast of Asia Minor, in search of commercial advantages or a better life. By the eighth century B.C.E., Greeks had pushed east as far as Al Mina in northern Syria and Tarsus in eastern Asia Minor.

Beginning around 750 B.C.E., a new form of colonization began in the western Mediterranean. The impetus for this expansion was not primarily trade, but rather the need to reduce population pressure at home. The first noteworthy colony, Cumae, near Naples, was founded by emigrants from Euboea. Soon other cities sent colonists to southern Italy and Sicily. Around 700 B.C.E., similar colonies appeared in the northeast in Thrace, on the shores of the Black Sea, and as far as the mouth of the Don River. The colonists were not always volunteers. At Thera, for example, young men were chosen by lot to colonize Cyrene. The penalty for refusing to participate was death and confiscation of property. Usually, colonists were only single males, the most volatile portion of the community. Colonies were thus a safety valve to release the pressures of population growth and political friction. Although colonies remained attached culturally to their mother cities, they were politically independent. The men who settled them were warriors as well as farmers or traders and carved out their new cities at the expense of the local population.

Colonization relieved some of the population pressure on Greek communities, but it did not solve the problem of political conflict. As opposition to entrenched aristocracies grew, first in Argos, then at Corinth, Sicyon, Elis, Mytilene, and elsewhere, new leaders opposed to aristocratic rule seized power. These rulers were known as *tyrants,* a term that originally meant the same as king. In the course of the later sixth century B.C.E., "tyrant" came to designate those who had achieved supreme power without benefit of official position. Often, this rise to power came through popularity with hoplite armies. However, the term tyrant did not carry the negative connotation associated with it today. Early tyrants were generally welcomed by their fellow citizens and played a crucial role in the destruction of aristocratic government and the creation of civic traditions.

Tyrants weakened the power of entrenched aristocratic groups, promoted the prosperity of their supporters by protecting farmers and encouraging trade, undertook public works projects, founded colonies, and entered into marriage alliances with rulers of other cities, which provided some external peace. Although they stood outside the traditional organs of government, tyrants were frequently content to govern through them, leaving magistracies and offices intact but ensuring that through elections these offices were filled with the tyrant's supporters. Thus at Corinth, Mytilene, Athens, and elsewhere, tyrants preserved and even strengthened constitutional structures as a hedge against the return to power of aristocratic factions.

The great weakness of tyrannies was that they depended for their success on the individual qualities of the ruler. Tyrants tended to pass their powers on to their sons, and as tyrannies became hereditary, cities came to resent incompetent or excessively cruel successors. As popular tyranny gave way to harsh and arbitrary rule, opposition brought on civil war and the deposition or abdication of the tyrant. Gradually, "tyranny" acquired the meaning it bears today, and new forms of government emerged. Still, in spite of the bitter memory Greek tyranny left in people's minds, in many cities tyrants had for a time solved the crisis of political order and had cleared the way for broader participation in public life than had ever before been known.

Gender and Power

Military, political, and cultural life in the city-states became more democratic, but this democratization did not extend to women. Greek attitudes toward gender roles and sexuality were rigid. Except in a few cities and in certain religious cults, women played no public role in the life of the community. They remained firmly under male control throughout their lives, passing from the authority of their fathers to that of their husbands. For the most part, friendship existed only between members of the same sex, and this friendship was often intensely sexual. Bisexuality was the norm in Greek society, although neither Greek homosexuality nor heterosexuality was the same as in modern society. Rather, they coexisted and formed parts of a sexuality of domination by those considered superior in age, rank, or sex over others. Mature men took young boys as

▶ A Corinthian vase showing hoplites marching into battle.

their lovers, helped to educate them, and inspired them by word and deed to grow into ideal warriors and citizens. We know less about such practices among women, but teachers such as Sappho of Lesbos (ca. 610–ca. 580 B.C.E.), who was also a wife and mother, formed similar bonds with their pupils, even while preparing them for marriage.

Those women who were in public life were mostly slaves, frequently prostitutes. These ranged from impoverished streetwalkers to *hetairai,* educated, sophisticated courtesans who entertained men at *symposia* (sing. *symposion*), or male banquets, which were the centers of cultural and social life. Many female slaves were acquired by collecting and raising female infants who had been abandoned. Greek society did not condemn or even question abandonment of infants, prostitution, or sexual exploitation of women and slave boys. These practices formed part of the complex and varied social systems of the developing city-states.

Gods and Mortals

Greeks and their gods enjoyed an ambivalent, almost irreverent relationship. On the one hand, Greeks made regular offerings to the gods, pleaded with them for help, and gave them thanks for assistance. On the other, the gods were thoroughly human, sharing in an exaggerated manner not only human strengths and virtues but also weaknesses and vices.

Greeks offered sacrifices to the gods on altars, which were raised everywhere—in homes, in fields, in sacred groves. No group had the sort of monopoly on the cult of the gods that Mesopotamian and Egyptian priests enjoyed. Unlike the temples of other societies, Greek temples were houses of the gods, not centers of ritual. The so-called Doric temple, which housed a statue of the god, consisted of an oblong or rectangular room covered by a pitched roof and circled by columns. These temples reflected the wealth and patriotism of the city. They stood as monuments to the human community rather than to the divine.

On special occasions, festivals were celebrated at sanctuaries, honoring the gods of the city with processions, athletic contests, and feasts. Some of these celebrations drew participants from all of the Greek world. The two greatest pan-Hellenic (meaning "all Greek," from *Hellas,* the Greek word for Greece) sanctuaries were Olympia and Delphi. Because both were remote from centers of political power, they were insulated from interstate rivalry and provided neutral ground on which hostile neighbors could meet in peace.

Beginning in 776 B.C.E., every four years, wars and conflicts were temporarily suspended while athletes from the whole Greek world met at Olympia to participate in contests in contests in honor of Zeus. The competitions were sometimes violent. Wrestling in particular could be deadly, since matches continued until one participant signaled that he had had enough. Many wrestlers chose death rather than defeat. Olympic victors were treated as national heroes.

Delphi, the site of the shrine of Apollo, god of music, archery, medicine, and prophecy, was the second pan-Hellenic cult center. Like Olympia, Delphi drew athletes from the whole Greek world to its athletic contests. However, Delphi's real fame lay in its oracle, or spokeswoman, for the god Apollo. From the eighth century B.C.E., before undertaking any important decision such as establishing a colony, beginning a war, or even contracting a marriage, individuals and representatives of distant cities traveled to Delphi to ask Apollo's advice or to seek purification from the guilt attached to shedding others' blood and reconciliation with their fellow citizens. For a stiff fee, visitors were allowed to address questions to the god through a female medium. She entered a trance state and uttered a reply, which lay priests at the shrine then put into verse form and transmitted to the petitioner. The ambiguity of the Delphic replies was legendary.

Though gods were petitioned, placated, and pampered, they were not privileged or protected. Unlike the awe-inspiring gods of the Mesopotamians and Egyptians, the traditional Greek gods, inherited from the Dark Age, were represented in ways that showed them as all too human, vicious, and frequently ridiculous. Zeus was infamous for his frequent rapes of boys and girls. His lust was matched only by the fury of his jealous wife, Hera. According to one story, a visitor to Athens asked why its citizens so often use the phrase "By Zeus!" The answer came back: "Because so many of us are." The Greek gods were immortal, superhuman in strength, and able to interfere in human affairs. But in all things they reflected the values and weaknesses of the Greek mortals, who could bargain with them, placate them, and even trick them.

Religious cults were not under the exclusive control of any priesthood or political group. Therefore there were no official versions of stories of gods and goddesses. This is evident both from Greek poetry, which often presents contradictory stories of the gods, and from pottery, which bears pictorial versions of myths that differ greatly from written ones. No one group or sacred site enjoyed a monopoly on access to the gods. Like literacy and government, the gods belonged to all.

Myth and Reason

The glue holding together the individual and frequently hostile Greek poleis and the ethne scattered throughout the Mediterranean was their common stock of myths. Stories of gods and heroes, told and retold, were fashioned into *mythoi* (myths, literally, "formulated speech"), which explained and described the world both as it was and as it should be. Myths were told about every city, shrine, river, mountain, and island. Myths explained the origins of cities, festivals, the world itself. What is the place of humans in the cosmos? They stand between beasts and gods because Prometheus tricked Zeus and gave men fire with which they cook their food and offer the bones and fat of sacrificial animals to the gods. Why is there evil and misfortune? Because in revenge for Prometheus's trickery, Zeus offered humans Pandora (the name means "all gifts"), the first woman, whose beauty hid her evil nature. By accepting this gift, humans brought evil and misfortune on themselves. Such stories were more than simply fanciful explanations of how things came to be. Myths sanctioned and supported the authority of social, political, and religious traditions and provided a means of reasoning about the world.

Art and the Individual

Archaic Greeks borrowed from everywhere and transformed all that they borrowed. Just as they adopted and adapted the Phoenician alphabet and Mesopotamian science, they took Near Eastern and Egyptian painting and sculpture and made them their own. During the Dark Age, the Mycenaean traditions of art had entirely disappeared. Pottery showed only geometric decorations; sculpture was unknown. Gradually, from the ninth century B.C.E., stylized human and animal figures, lions, griffins, and other strange beasts began to appear within the tightly composed geometric patterns. By the eighth century B.C.E., such exotic subjects had given way to the Greek passion for human images taken from their own myths and legends. The preferred technique was the so-called black figure style, which developed first at Corinth. Subjects were painted in black silhouette on red clay, and then details were cut with a sharp point so that the background could show through.

As the popularity of these mythic and heroic scenes increased, so too did the artists' technical competence. Greek artists competed with one another to overcome technical problems of perspective and foreshortening. From the sixth century B.C.E., many of the finest examples were signed. Such masterpieces celebrated not only the heroes of the past but also the artist as individual and as the interpreter of culture no less original than the poet.

Greek sculpture underwent a similar dramatic development. The earliest and most common subject of archaic sculpture was the standing male nude, or *kouros* figure, which was in wide demand as a grave monument, dedication to a god, or even cult statue of male deity. In Egypt, seventh century B.C.E. Greeks had seen colossal statues and had learned to work stone. They brought these techniques home, improved on them by using iron tools (the Egyptians knew only bronze ones), and began to create their own human images. The rigidly formulaic position of the kouros—standing, arms by the sides, looking straight ahead, left foot extended—followed Egyptian tradition and left little room for originality. Thus sculptors sought to give their statues originality and individuality, not as representations of individuals, but as the creations of the individual sculptor. To this end, they experimented with increasingly natural molding of limbs and body and began signing their works. Thus, as in vase painting, Greek sculpture reflected the importance of the individual, not in its subject matter, but in its creator. The female counterparts of the kouros figures, called *korai*, followed similarly rigid traditions to which sculptors added female attributes.

The real challenges in sculpture came in the portrayal of narrative in decorations on monuments, primarily temples. Unlike kouroi, which were usually private commissions intended to adorn the tombs of aristocrats, these public buildings were constructed as expressions of civic pride and were accessible to everyone. Here the creativity and dynamism of Greek cities could be paralleled in stone. Figures such as the Calf-Bearer (ca. 590 B.C.E.) from the Athenian acropolis are daring in the complexity of composition and the delicacy of execution. (See photo on p. 38.) These are statues that tell stories. In the Calf-Bearer, a master farmer carries a calf to be sacrificed to Athena. The two gentle heads and the cross formed by the farmer's hands and the calf's legs are individual traits without precedent in ancient art. Although formally intended for religious purposes, these figures serve not only the gods and the aristocratic elite, but the whole community.

C H R O N O L O G Y	
ARCHAIC GREECE	
ca. 780–720 B.C.E.	Population increase in Greece
776 B.C.E.	First Olympic Games held
ca. 750–700 B.C.E.	Greeks develop writing system based on Phoenician model; Greeks begin colonizing western Mediterranean
ca. 700–500 B.C.E.	Archaic Age of Greece
ca. 700 B.C.E.	First stone temples appear in Greece
ca. 650 B.C.E.	Cypselus breaks rule of Bacchiads in Corinth; rules city as tyrant
594 B.C.E.	Solon elected chief archon of Athens; institutes social and political reforms
586 B.C.E.	Death of Periander ends tyrants' rule in Corinth
499 B.C.E.	Ionian cities revolt

A TALE OF THREE CITIES

The political, social, and cultural transformations that occurred in the Archaic Age took different forms across the Greek world. No community or city-state was typical of Greece. The best way to understand the diversity of Archaic Greece is to examine three very different cities that

▲ The Calf-Bearer was commissioned for the temple of Athena, which was destroyed by the Persians in 480 B.C.E. when they captured Athens and burned the Acropolis.

by the end of the sixth century B.C.E. had become leading centers of Greek civilization. Corinth, Sparta, and Athens present something of the spectrum of political, cultural, and social models of the Hellenic world. Corinth, like many cities, developed into a commercial center in which the assembly of citizens was dominated by an oligarchy. Sparta developed into a state in which citizenship was radically egalitarian but restricted to a small military elite. In Athens, the Archaic Age saw the foundations of an equally radical democracy.

Wealthy Corinth

Corinth owed its prosperity to its privileged site, dominating both a rich coastal plain and the narrow isthmus connecting the Peloponnesus to the mainland. In the eighth century B.C.E., as Greeks turned their attention to the west, Corinthians led the way. Corinthian pottery appeared throughout western Greece and southern Italy. Corinthian trade led to colonization, and settlers from Corinth founded Syracuse and other cities in Sicily and Italy, which served as markets for Corinthian products. Even more important to Corinthian prosperity was its role in the transport of other cities' products from east to west. By carrying goods across the isthmus and loading them onto other ships, merchants could avoid the long, dangerous passage around the Peloponnesus.

Social Tensions. The precise details of early Corinthian government are uncertain. Still, it appears that in Corinth, as in many other cities, a tyranny replaced a ruling clan, and in time this tyranny ended with an oligarchic government. Until the middle of the seventh century B.C.E., Corinth and its wealth were ruled in typical Dark Age fashion by an aristocratic clan known as the Bacchiads. Corinth began its rise under this aristocratic rule, and individual Bacchiads led colonizing expeditions to Italy and Sicily. However, the increasing pressures of population growth, rapidly expanding wealth, and dramatic changes in the economy produced social tensions that the traditional aristocratic rulers were unable to handle. As in cities throughout the Greek world, these tensions led to the creation of a new order.

The early history of Corinth is obscure, but apparently around 650 B.C.E. a revolution led by a dissident Bacchiad named Cypselus (ca. 657–627 B.C.E.) and supported by non-Bacchiad aristocrats and other Corinthians broke the Bacchiads' grip on the city. The revolution led to the establishment of Cypselus as tyrant. Cypselus and his son Periander (ca. 627–586 B.C.E.) seem to have been generally popular with most Corinthians.

Corinth Under Its Tyrants. In Corinth, as in many other cities, the tyrants restructured taxes, relying primarily on customs duties, which were less of a burden on the peasantry. Around 600 B.C.E., Periander began construction of a causeway across the isthmus on which ships could be hauled from the Aegean to the western Mediterranean. This causeway eventually became a major source of Corinth's wealth. Periander attacked conspicuous consumption on the part of the aristocracy. He introduced laws against idleness and put thousands of Corinthians to work in extensive building programs. He erected temples and sent colonists to Italy. Under his leadership, the Corinthian fleet developed into the most powerful naval force in the Adriatic and Aegean Seas. Under its tyrants, Corinth led the Greek world in the production of black figure pottery, which spread throughout the Mediterranean.

The tyrants also laid the foundation for broader political participation. Cypselus divided the population into eight tribes, based not on traditional ethnic divisions, but on arbitrary groupings by region. All of Corinth was divided into three large regions. The population of each region was distributed among each of the eight tribes. This assignment prevented the emergence of political factions based on regional disputes. Ten representatives from each tribe formed a council of 80 men. Under the tyrants this council was largely advisory and provided a connection between the autocratic rulers and the citizens.

In Corinth, as elsewhere, the strength or weakness of tyranny rested on the abilities and personality of individual tyrants. Cypselus had been a beloved liberator. His son Periander, in spite of his accomplishments, was remembered for his cruelty and violence. Shortly after Periander's death in 586 B.C.E., a revolt killed his successor, and tyranny in Corinth ended.

Oligarchy. The new government continued the tribal and council system established by Cypselus. From the sixth century B.C.E. until its conquest by Macedonia in 338 B.C.E., Corinth was ruled by an oligarchy. Although an assembly of the *demos,* or adult males, met occasionally, actual government was in the hands of eight deliberators, or *probouloi,* and nine other men from each tribe who together formed the council of eighty. The oligarchs who made up the council avoided the kind of exclusive and arbitrary tendencies that had destroyed both the Bacchiads and the tyrants. They were remarkably successful in maintaining popular support among the citizens and provided a reliable and effective government.

Thus Corinth flourished, a city that was more open to commerce and wealth than most, moderate in its political institutions and eager for stability. As one fourth century B.C.E. poet wrote:

> [There] lawfulness dwells, and her sister,
> Safe foundation of cities,
> Justice, and Peace, who was bred with her;
> They dispense wealth to men.

Martial Sparta

At the beginning of the eighth century B.C.E., the Peloponnesus around Sparta and Laconia faced circumstances similar to those of Corinth and other Greek communities. Population growth, increasing disparity between rich and poor, and an expanding economy created powerful tensions. However, while Corinthian society developed into a complex mix of aristocrats, merchants, artisans, and peasants ruled by an oligarchy, the Spartan solution was a rigid two-tiered social structure. By the end of the Archaic Age, a small, homogeneous class of warriors called *homoioi*

("those alike"), or equals, ruled a vast population of state serfs, or *helots.* The two classes lived in mutual fear and mistrust. Spartans controlled the helots through terror and ritual murder. The helots in turn were "an enemy constantly waiting for the disasters of the Spartans." Yet, throughout antiquity the Spartans were the Greeks who were most praised for their courage, simplicity of life, and service to the state.

Messenia. War was the center of Spartan life, and war lay at the origin of the Spartans' extraordinary social and political organization. In the eighth century B.C.E., the Spartans conquered the fertile region of Messenia and compelled the vanquished Messenians to turn over one-half of their harvests. The spoils were not divided equally but went to increase the wealth of the aristocracy, thus creating resentment among the less privileged. Early in the seventh century B.C.E., the Spartans attempted a similar campaign to take the plain of Thyreatis from the city of Argos. This time they were not so fortunate; they were defeated, and resentment of the ordinary warriors toward their aristocratic leaders flared into open conflict. The Messenians seized on this time as a moment to revolt, and for a time, Sparta was forced to fight at home and abroad for its very existence. In many cities, such crises gave rise to tyrants. In Sparta, the crisis led to radical political and social reforms that transformed the polis into a unique military system.

Reforms of Lycurgus. The Spartans attributed these reforms to the legendary lawgiver Lycurgus (seventh century B.C.E.). Whether or not Lycurgus ever existed and was responsible for all of the reforms, they saved the city and ended its internal tensions at the expense of abandoning the mainstream of Greek development. Traditionally, Greeks had placed personal honor above communal concerns. During the crisis of the second Messenian war, Spartans of all social ranks were urged to look not to individual interest but to *eunomia,* good order and obedience to the laws, which alone could unite Spartans and bring victory. United, the Spartans crushed the Messenians. In return for obedience, poor citizens received equality before the law and benefited from a land distribution that relieved their poverty. Conquered land, especially that in Messenia, was divided and distributed to Spartan warriors. However, the Spartan warriors were not expected to work the land themselves. Instead, the state reduced the defeated Messenians to the status of helots and assigned them to individual Spartans. While this system did not erase all economic inequalities among the Spartans (aristocrats continued to hold more land than others), it did decrease some of the disparity. It also provided a minimum source of wealth for all Spartan citizens and allowed them to devote themselves to full-time military service.

This land reform was coupled with a political reform that incorporated elements of monarchy, oligarchy, and democracy. The state was governed by two hereditary kings, probably representing different groups that had formed the Spartan polis earlier, and a council of elders, the *gerousia.* In peacetime, the authority of the two royal families was limited to familial and religious affairs. In war, they commanded the army and held the power of life and death.

In theory at least, the central institution of Spartan government was the gerousia, which was composed of 30 men at least 60 years of age and included the two kings. The gerousia directed all political activity, especially foreign affairs, and served as high court. Members were elected for life by the assembly, or *apella,* which was composed of all equals over the age of 30 and approved decisions of the gerousia. However, this approval, made by acclamation, could easily be manipulated, as could the course of debate within the gerousia itself. Wealth, cunning, and patronage were more important than its formal structures in the direction of the Spartan state.

Actual administration was in the hands of five magistrates, termed *ephors,* whose powers were extremely broad. They presided over joint sessions of the gerousia and apella. They held supreme authority over the kings during wartime, acted as judges for noncitizens, and controlled the *krypteia,* or secret police. The krypteia were a band of youths who practiced state terrorism as part of their rite of passage to the status of equal. On the orders of the ephors, the krypteia assassinated, intrigued, arrested powerful people, and terrorized helots. Service in this corps was considered a necessary part of a youth's education.

Social Control.   The key to the success of Sparta's political reform was an even more radical social reform that placed everyone under the direct supervision and service of the state from birth until death. Although admiring aristocratic visitors often exaggerated their accounts of Spartan life, the main outlines are clear enough. Eunomia was the sole guiding principle, and service to the state came before family, social class, and every other duty or occupation.

Spartan equals were made, not born. True, only a man born of free Spartan parents could hope to become an equal, but birth alone was no guarantee of admission to this select body, or even of the right to live. Public officials examined infants and decided whether they were sufficiently strong to be allowed to live or should be exposed on a hillside to die. From birth until age seven, a boy lived with his mother; he then entered the state education system, or *agoge,* living in barracks with his contemporaries and enduring 13 years of rigorous military training. At age 12, training with swords and spears became more intense, as did the rigors of the lifestyle. Boys were given only a single cloak to wear and slept on thin rush mats. They were encouraged to supplement their meager diet by stealing food, although if they were caught, they were severely whipped, not for the theft but for the failure. All of this they were expected to endure in silence.

Much of the actual education of the youths was entrusted to older, accomplished warriors, who selected boys as their homosexual lovers. Such relationships were the norm throughout Greece but were more important in Sparta. The lover served as tutor and role model, and in time the two became a fighting team. At age 20, Spartan youths were enrolled in the krypteia. Each was sent out into the countryside with nothing but a cloak and a knife, forbidden to return until he had killed a helot.

If a youth survived the rigors of his training until age 30, he could at last be incorporated into the rank of equals, provided that he could pass the last obstacle. He had to be able to furnish a sufficient amount of food from his own lands for the communal dining group to which he would be assigned. This food might come from inherited property or, if he had proved himself an outstanding warrior, from the state. Those who passed this final qualification became full members of the assembly, but they continued to live with the other warriors. Men could marry at age 20, but family life in the usual sense was nonexistent. A man could not live with his wife until age 30 because he was bound to the barracks.

Although their training was not as rigorous as that of males, Spartan women were given an education and allowed a sphere of activity unknown elsewhere in Greece. Girls, like boys, were trained in athletic competition and, like boys, competed naked in wrestling, footraces, and spear throwing. This training was based not on a belief in the equality of the sexes but simply on the desire to improve the physical stamina and childbearing abilities of Spartan women. Women were able to own land and to participate widely in business and agricultural affairs; since men were entirely involved in military pursuits, women were expected to look after economic and household affairs. When a foreign woman commented that Spartan women were the only women who could rule men, a Spartan woman replied, "With good reason, for we are the only women who bring forth men."

Few Lacedaemonians (as Spartans were also called) ever became equals. Not only were there far more helots than Spartans, but many inhabitants of the region, termed *perioikoi,* or peripherals, although they were free citizens of their local communities, were not allowed into the agoge. Others were unable to endure the harsh life, and still others lacked the property qualifications to supply their share of the communal meals. For all the trappings of egalitarianism, equality in Sparta was the privilege of a tiny minority.

The total dedication to military life was reinforced by a deliberate rejection of other activities. From the time of the second Messenian war, Sparta withdrew from the mainstream of Greek civilization. Equals could not engage in crafts, trade, or any other forms of economic activity. Because Sparta banned silver and gold coinage, it could not participate in the growing commercial network of the Greek world. Although a group of free citizens of subject towns could engage in such activities, the role of Sparta in the economic, architectural, and cultural life of Greece was negligible after the seventh century B.C.E. Militarily, Sparta cast a long shadow across the Peloponnesus and beyond, but the number of equals was always too small to allow Sparta both to create a vast empire and to maintain control over the helots at home. Instead, Sparta created a network of alliances and nonaggression pacts with oligarchic neighbors. In time this network came to be known as the Peloponnesian League.

Democratic Athens

Athens did not enjoy the advantages of a strategic site such as that of Corinth, nor was it surrounded by rich plains like Sparta. However, the "goodly citadel of Athens" was one of the few Mycenaean cities to have escaped destruction at the start of the Dark Age. Gradually, Athens united the whole surrounding region of Attica into a single polis, by far the largest in the Greek world. Well into the seventh century B.C.E., Athens followed the general pattern of the polis seen in Corinth and Sparta. Like other Dark Age communities, Athens was ruled by aristocratic clans, particularly the Alcmaeonids. Only the members of these clans could participate in the *areopagus*, or council, which they entered after serving a year as one of the nine *archons*, or magistrates, elected yearly. Until the seventh century B.C.E., Athens escaped the social pressures brought on by population growth and economic prosperity that led to civil strife, colonialism, and tyranny elsewhere. This was due largely to its relative abundance of arable land and its commercial prosperity based on the export of grain.

Social Tensions.   By the late seventh century B.C.E., however, Athens began to suffer from the same class conflict that had shaken other cities. Sometime around 630 B.C.E.,

an aristocrat named Cylon attempted to seize power as tyrant. His attempt failed, but when he was murdered by one of the Alcmaeonids, popular revulsion drove the Alcmaeonids from the city. A decade of strife ensued as aristocratic clans, wealthy merchants, and farmers fought for control of the city. Violence between groups and families threatened to tear the community apart.

Reforms of Solon.   In 621 B.C.E., the Athenians granted a judge, Draco, extraordinary powers to revise and systematize traditional laws concerning vengeance and homicide. His restructuring of procedures for limiting vengeance and preventing bloodshed were harsh enough to add the term "Draconian" to Western legal vocabulary. When asked why death was the most common penalty he imposed, Draco explained that minor offenses merited death and he knew of no more severe penalty for major ones. Still, these measures did nothing to solve the central problems of political control. Finally, in 594 B.C.E., an Athenian merchant who was respected by both aristocrats and commoners was elected chief archon and charged with reforming the city's government. Solon (ca. 630–ca. 560 B.C.E.) based his reform on the ideal of eunomia, as had the Spartans, but he followed a very different path to secure good order.

In Sparta, Lycurgus had begun with a radical redistribution of land. In Athens, Solon began with the less extreme measure of eliminating debt bondage. Athenians who had been forced into slavery or into sharecropping because of their debts were restored to freedom. A law forbade mortgaging free men and women as security for debts. Athenians might be poor, but they would be free.

▶ An Athenian silver coin called a *tetradrachm*, dating from the fifth century B.C.E. The owl is the symbol of the goddess Athena.

This free peasantry formed the basis of Athenian society throughout its history.

Solon also reorganized the rest of the social hierarchy and broke the aristocracy's exclusive control of the areopagus by dividing the society into four classes based on wealth rather than birth and opening the archonship to the top two classes. He further weakened the areopagus by establishing a council of 400 members drawn from all four classes, to which citizens could appeal decisions of the magistrates.

Solon's efforts to resolve Athens's social tensions did not entirely succeed. His laws were more humane than those of Draco, but Solon himself did not consider his new constitution perfect, only practical. Asked whether he had given the Athenians the best laws that he could give them, he answered, "The best that they could receive." Resistance from the still powerful aristocracy prompted some Athenians to urge Solon to assume the powers of a tyrant to force through his reforms. He refused, but after his death, Peisistratus (d. 527 B.C.E.), an aristocrat who was strongly supported by the peasants against his own class, hired a mercenary force to seize control of the city. After two abortive attempts, Peisistratus ruled as tyrant from 545 B.C.E. until his death.

Athenian Tyranny. Peisistratus and later his son Hippias (d. 490 B.C.E.), who succeeded him until 510 B.C.E., ruled through Solon's constitution but took care to ensure that the archons who were elected each year were their agents. Thus they strengthened the constitution even while they further weakened the aristocracy.

Peisistratus and Hippias drew their support from the *demos*, or people at large, rather than from an aristocratic faction. They claimed divine justification for their rule and made a great show of devotion to the Athenian gods. Peisistratus promoted annual festivals and, in so doing, began the great tradition of Athenian literature. At the festival of Athena, professional reciters of *rhapsoidiai* (epic poetry) recited large portions of the *Iliad* and the *Odyssey*. During a festival in honor of Dionysus, actors performed the first tragedies and comedies. The tyrants also directed a series of popular nationalistic public works programs that beautified the city, increased national pride, and provided work for the poor. They rebuilt the temple of Athena on the acropolis, for which the statue of the Calf-Bearer was commissioned. These internal measures were accompanied by support for commerce and export, particularly of grain. Soon, Athens was challenging Corinth as the leading commercial power and was trading in grain as far away as the Black Sea.

Peisistratus was firm. His son Hippias was harsh. Still, even Hippias enjoyed the support of the majority of the citizens of both popular and aristocratic factions. Only after the assassination of his younger brother did Hippias become sufficiently oppressive to drive his opponents into exile. Some of these exiles obtained the assistance of Sparta and returned to overthrow Hippias in 510 B.C.E. Hippias's defeat ended the tyrants' rule in Athens and won for Sparta an undeserved reputation as the opponent of all tyranny.

Athenian Democracy. Following the expulsion of Hippias, some aristocrats attempted to return to the "good old days" of aristocratic rule. However, Athenians had been accustomed to Solon's constitution for more than 80 years and were unwilling to give it up. Moreover, the tyrants had created a fierce sense of nationalistic pride among all ranks of Athenians, and few were willing to turn over government to the hands of only a few. When the aristocrats made their bid to recover power, their primary opponent, Cleisthenes (ca. 570–ca. 507 B.C.E.), a descendant of the Alcmaeonids, made the demos his faction and pushed through a final constitutional reform that became the basis for Athenian democracy.

The essence of Cleisthenes' reform lay in his reorganization of the major political units by which members of the council were selected. Previously, each citizen had belonged to one of four tribes, which were further broken down into 12 brotherhoods, or *phratries*, which were administrative and religious units. In a manner similar to that of Cypselus in Corinth, Cleisthenes reshuffled these phratries into 30 territorial units comprising urban, inland, or coastal regions. These 30 units in turn were grouped into 10 tribes, each consisting of one unit from each of the urban, inland, and coastal regions. The tribes elected the members of the council, military commanders, jurors, and magistrates. As in Corinth, this reorganization destroyed the traditional kin-based social and political pattern and integrated people of differing social, economic, and regional backgrounds. Aristocrats, merchants, and poor farmers had to work together to find common ground for political action, both regionally and nationally. With this new integrated democracy and its strong sense of nationalism, Athens emerged from the Archaic Age as the leading city of the Hellenic world.

THE COMING OF PERSIA AND THE END OF THE ARCHAIC AGE

By the end of the sixth century B.C.E., the products of Greek experimentation were evident throughout the Mediterranean. Greek city-states had resolved the crises of class conflict. Greek merchants and artisans had found ways to flourish despite poor soil and uncertain climate. Greek philosophers, poets, and artists had begun to celebrate the human form and the human spirit. Still, these achievements were the product of small, independent, and relatively weak communities on the fringe of the civilized world.

In the second half of the sixth century B.C.E., all this changed. The Persian empire, under its dynamic king Cyrus II, began a process of conquest and expansion west into Asia Minor, absorbing the kingdom of Lydia and conquering

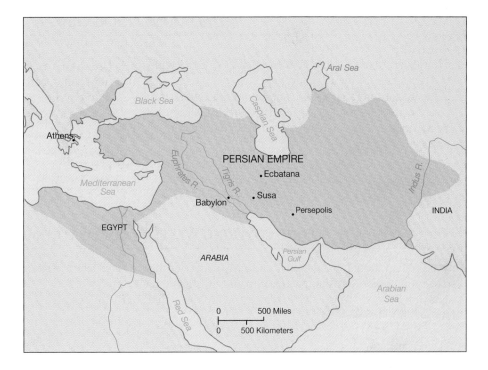

▶ The Persian Empire, ca. 500 B.C.E. Even larger than the Assyrians and Babylonians, the Persian Empire stretched from India to Europe and incorporated all of the civilized world except for Greece.

Ionia on the coast of Asia Minor. The Persians placed tyrants loyal to Cyrus to rule over these Greek communities, and for a few decades these centers of Greek culture and thought accepted foreign control. In 499 B.C.E., the passion for democracy, which had swept much of mainland Greece, reached Ionia. Cities such as Miletus, Ephesus, Chios, and Samos revolted, expelled their Persian-appointed tyrants, established democracies, and sent ambassadors to the mainland to seek assistance. Eretria and Athens, two mainland cities with Ionian roots, responded, sending ships and men to aid the Ionian rebels. Athenian interests were more than simple solidarity with their Ionian cousins. Athens depended on grain from the Black Sea region and believed its direct interests to lie with the area. The success of the revolt was short lived. The puny Greek cities were dealing with the largest empire the West had yet known. By 500 B.C.E., the Persian empire included Asia Minor, Mesopotamia, Palestine, and Egypt, uniting all peoples from the Caucasus to the Sudan.

The giant Persian empire responded slowly, but with force, to the Greek revolt. King Darius I (522–486 B.C.E.) gathered a vast international force from throughout his empire and set about recapturing the rebellious cities. The war lasted five years and ended in a Persian victory. By 494 B.C.E., the Persians had retaken the cities of the coast and nearby islands. In the cities that were deemed most responsible for the revolt, the population was herded together, the boys were castrated and made into royal eunuchs, the girls were sent to Darius's court, the remainder of the population was sold into slavery, and the towns were burned to the ground. Once the rebels had been disposed of, Darius set out to punish their supporters on the mainland, Eretria and Athens. With the

same meticulous planning and deliberate pace, the Persian king turned his vast armies toward the Greek mainland.

Conclusion

CIVILIZATION DEVELOPED MUCH LATER in the Mediterranean world than it had in the floodplains of the Near East. The earliest Bronze Age societies of Greece and the neighboring islands, while influenced by contact with the great civilizations of Mesopotamia and Egypt, developed distinctive societies and cultures that were tied closely to the sea around them. Still, they too were caught up in the general cataclysm of the twelfth century B.C.E. Out of the ruins emerged a society that was much less centralized, wealthy, or powerful but possessed an extraordinary dynamism.

The Archaic Age was an age of experimentation. Propelled by demographic and political pressures and inspired by the legends of vanished heroes, Greeks began in the eighth century B.C.E. to recast traditions and techniques acquired from their ancient neighbors into new forms. The multiplicity of independent communities, their relative isolation, and their differing traditions created a wide spectrum of political forms, social structures, and cultural values. Yet from Sicily to Asia Minor, Greeks felt themselves united by a common language, a common cultural heritage, and a common commitment to individual freedom within the community, whether that freedom was protected within a monarchy, a tyranny, an oligarchy, or a democracy. That commitment to freedom, fostered in the hoplite ranks, protected in the assembly, and increasingly expressed in poetry and sculpture, hung in the balance as Darius and the Persians marched westward.

QUESTIONS FOR REVIEW

1. What social and geographic factors shaped Greek culture in the age of the *Iliad* and the *Odyssey*?
2. What social forces spurred colonization, and what impact did colonization have on Archaic Greek civilization?
3. What do the gods, myths, and art of the Greek people reveal about their lives?

4. How did the Corinthian, Spartan, and Athenian cultures differ, and why did these city-states evolve in such different directions?

DISCOVERING WESTERN CIVILIZATION ONLINE

You can obtain more information about early Greece at the websites listed below. See also the companion website that accompanies this text: www.ablongman.com/kishlansky, which contains an online study guide and additional resources.

General Websites

www.perseus.tufts.edu/
A digital library dedicated to all aspects of ancient Greek civilization.

history.evansville.net/greece.html
Links to Greek history and civilization.

www.perseus.tufts.edu/cgi-bin/ptext?doc=1999.04.0009
This page of The Perseus Digital Project includes an extremely detailed outline of Greek history up to the death of Alexander with wonderful links to other sources.

Greece in the Bronze Age

www.dilos.com/region/crete/kn_01.html
A site devoted to the city of Knossos.

Archaic Greece

www.museum.upenn.edu/Greek_World/Index.html
A comprehensive site dedicated to ancient Greece from the University of Pennsylvania Museum.

w3.arizona.edu/~ws/ws200/fall97/grp3/grp3.htm
A site devoted to elite women in Greece and their education.

www.pantheon.org/mythica.html
A site devoted to mythology with excellent resources on Greek myth.

A Tale of Three Cities

www.Indiana.edu/~kglowack/athens/
A site dedicated to ancient Athens including architecture and sources.

www.geocities.com/Athens/Aegean/7849
A site dedicated to Sparta.

www.agn.gr/hellas/map.htm
A Greek government site with an interactive map of Greek locations including historical and modern information.

The Coming of Persia

www.livius.org/persia.html
Links to articles on many aspects of ancient Persian history.

SUGGESTIONS FOR FURTHER READING

General Reading

S. B. Pomeroy, et al., *Ancient Greece: A Political, Social, and Cultural History* (Oxford: Oxford University Press, 1998). An important introduction to Greek society and culture.

Greece in the Bronze Age to 700 B.C.E.

M. I. Finley, *Early Greece: The Bronze and Archaic Ages*, 2nd ed. (New York: W. W. Norton, 1982). A very readable overview by a leading Greek historian.

Susan Langdon, ed. *New Light on a Dark Age: Exploring the Culture of Geometric Greece* (Columbus, Mo: University of Missouri Press, 1997). Current essays on every aspect of society and culture in Dark Age Greece.

N. K. Sandars, *The Sea Peoples* (New York: Thames & Hudson, 1985). A survey of the controversy over the crisis of the twelfth century B.C.E.

William Taylour, *The Mycenaeans* (London: Thames & Hudson, 1990). General overview of Mycenaean civilization and daily life based on archaeology.

Archaic Greece, 700–500 B.C.E.

A. Andrewes, *The Greek Tyrants* (Atlantic Highlands, N. J.: Humanities Press International, 1956). A standard survey of Greek tyranny.

John Boardman, *The Greeks Overseas* (New York: Thames & Hudson, 1982). A description of varieties of Greek involvement abroad and their effects on Greece.

John Boardman, *Greek Sculpture: Archaic Period* (New York: Thames & Hudson, 1985). A well-illustrated survey of early Greek sculpture.

Walter Burkert, *Structure and History in Greek Mythology and Ritual* (Berkeley: University of California Press, 1980). Relates myth and religion to society and history.

W. G. Forrest, *The Emergence of Greek Democracy* (New York: McGraw-Hill, 1966). Covers the politics of the Archaic period.

S. B. Pomeroy, *Families in Classical and Hellenistic Greece: Representation and Realities* (Oxford: Oxford University Press, 1999). A history of the family in Greece by a leading feminist historian.

Anthony Snodgrass, *Archaic Greece: The Age of Experiment* (Totowa, N.J.: Biblio Distribution Center, 1980). An excellent survey of the creative achievements of the Archaic period.

Christopher Tadgell, *Hellenic Classicism: The Ordering of Form in the Ancient Greek World.* (New York: Whitney Library of Design, 1998). A survey of Greek art and architecture to the construction of Athens' Acropolis.

A Tale of Three Cities

Paul Cartledge, *Sparta and Lakonia: A Regional History 1300–362 B.C.* (New York: Routledge, Chapman & Hall, 1978). The best survey of Spartan history.

J. R. Salmon, *Wealthy Corinth: A History of the City to 338 B.C.* (New York: Oxford University Press, 1984). A comprehensive history of early Corinth.

David Whitehead, *The Demes of Attica (ca. 508–250 B.C.)* (Princeton, N.J.: Princeton University Press, 1986). An excellent study of Athenian politics and society.

3

CLASSICAL AND HELLENISTIC GREECE, 500–100 B.C.E.

- THE VISUAL RECORD: Alexander at Issus
- WAR AND POLITICS IN THE FIFTH CENTURY B.C.E.
- ATHENIAN CULTURE IN THE HELLENIC AGE

- FROM CITY-STATES TO MACEDONIAN EMPIRE, 404–323 B.C.E.
- THE HELLENISTIC WORLD

ALEXANDER AT ISSUS

THE CENTURIES OF GREEK GLORY OPENED AND CLOSED with war with Persia. The invasion of the Greek mainland by Darius I in 490 B.C.E. pitted the greatest empire the West had ever known against a few small, mutually suspicious states. His failure created among the Greeks a new belief in the superiority of the Greek world over the barbarian and of free men over Eastern despots. Darius III (336–330 B.C.E.) suffered a far more devastating defeat than his ancestor at the hands of Alexander the Great (336–323 B.C.E.) and a combined Greek army 157 years later. Darius I had lost his pride. Darius III lost his empire and, shortly afterward, his life.

Alexander had announced his expedition as a campaign to punish the Persians for their invasion of Greece over a century and a half earlier. Greeks rightly viewed Alexander's victory at Issus in 333 B.C.E. as the beginning of the end for the Persians, and it was long celebrated by Greek poets and artists. The most famous of these was Philoxenus of Eretria, whose paintings marked the high point of Greek pictorial art. His masterpiece, like all other Greek paintings executed on wood, is long vanished. In the first century B.C.E., however, a wealthy Roman commissioned a mosaic copy of the painting for his villa at Pompeii in southern Italy. The mosaic, measuring some 16 feet by 8 feet and containing 1.5 million stones, each the size of a grain of rice, is itself a masterpiece. It is also a faithful copy of Philoxenus's painting, which a Roman critic had characterized as "surpassed by none."

In muted tones of red, brown, black, and yellow, Philoxenus captures this most dramatic moment of the battle. Alexander, with reckless disregard for his own safety, has routed the Persians' left flank, cutting Darius's Greek mercenaries to pieces, scattering his Persian guard, and forcing Darius to flee for his life. The artist's use of bold foreshortening renders the rear of the horse in the center almost three dimensional as it runs in blind fury toward Darius's chariot. Although the entire scene is wildly chaotic, each man and each mount is portrayed as an individual, with his own expression of emotion and his own part to play in the violent action.

The young Alexander exudes the reckless courage and violence for which he was so famous. Yet he is not the center of the composition. That place of honor goes to Darius, whose kindly, tortured face looks back as his horses pull his chariot to safety. His hand stretches out in helpless sympathy toward the young Persian who has thrown himself between his king and Alexander, taking through his chest the spear that the Greek king had intended for the Persian ruler.

The artist has not depicted a simple juxtaposition of civilization against barbarity. Greeks fought on both sides at Issus, just as they had in the Persian wars of the fifth century B.C.E. Nor did Alexander's warriors despise their Persian enemies. Philoxenus's depictions of Darius and Alexander reflect the complexity of the situation. A similar degree of complexity characterized the entire panorama of classical Greek history.

LOOKING AHEAD

The victories over the Persian forces of Darius and his successors brought an unprecedented period of political and cultural freedom and creativity, but also a deadly rivalry between Athens and Sparta, the leaders of the victorious Greeks. Only a generation after Athenian and Spartan troops had faced the Persians, they fought each other in a long and futile war. This left the Greek world exhausted and easy prey for the ambitious Macedonian dynasty, which nevertheless spread Greek culture through the Eastern Mediterranean and western Asia.

WAR AND POLITICS IN THE FIFTH CENTURY B.C.E.

The vast Persian army moving west in 490 B.C.E. threatened the fruits of three centuries of Greek political, social, and cultural experimentation. The shared ideal of freedom within community and the common bond of language and culture seemed no basis on which to build an effective resistance to the great Persian Empire. Moreover, Darius I was not marching against the Greeks as such. Few Greek states other than Athens had supported the Ionians against their Persian conquerors. Many Greeks saw the Persians as potential allies or even rulers who were preferable to their more powerful Greek neighbors and to rivals within their own states. Separated by political traditions, intercity rivalries, and cultural differences, the Greeks did not feel any sense of national or ethnic unity. Particular interest, rather than patriotism or love of freedom, determined which cities opposed the Persian march. In the end, only Eretria, a badly divided Athens, and the small town of Plataea were prepared to refuse the Persian king's demand for gifts of earth and water, the traditional symbols of submission.

The Persian Wars

Initially, the Persian campaign followed the pattern established in Ionia. In the autumn of 490 B.C.E., Darius quickly destroyed the city of Eretria and carried off its population in captivity. The victorious Persian forces, numbering perhaps 20,000 infantrymen and mounted archers, then landed at the Bay of Marathon. Even with around 600 Plataeans, the total Athenian force was no more than half that of its enemies, but the Greeks were better armed and commanded the hills facing the Marathon plain on which the Persian troops had massed. The Athenians also benefited from the leadership of Miltiades (ca. 544–489 B.C.E.), an experienced soldier who had served Darius and who knew the Persian's strengths and weaknesses. For over a week, the two armies faced each other in a battle of nerves. Growing dissension in the Athenian ranks finally led the Greek generals to make a desperate and unexpected move. Abandoning the high ground, the Athenian hoplites rushed in disciplined phalanxes over almost a mile of open fields and then attacked the amazed Persian forces at a run. Although the Persians broke through the center of the Greek lines, the Athenians routed the Persian flanks and then turned in, enveloping the invaders in a deadly trap. In a few hours it was all over. Six thousand Persians lay dead, while fewer than 200 Athenians were buried in the heroes' grave that still marks the Marathon plain. The Persians retreated to their ships and sailed for the Bay of Phalerum near Athens, hoping to attack the city itself before its victorious troops could return. However, the Athenians, though exhausted from the battle, rushed the

The Persian Wars. Greeks fought on both sides in the Persian Wars, while many others remained neutral.

23 miles home in under eight hours, beating the Persian fleet. When the Persians learned that they had lost the race, they turned their ships for Asia.

The almost miraculous victory at Marathon had three enormous consequences for Athens and for Greece in general. First, it established the superiority of the hoplite phalanx as the finest infantry formation in the Mediterranean world. Second, Greeks expanded this belief in military superiority to a faith in the general superiority of Greeks over the "barbarians" (those who spoke other languages). Finally, by proving the value of the citizen army, the victory of the Athenians solidified and enhanced the democratic reforms of Cleisthenes.

Common citizens were determined that the victory won by the hoplite phalanx at Marathon should not be lost to an aristocratic faction at home. To guard against this danger, the Athenian assembly began to practice *ostracism,* a ten-year exile without loss of property, which was imposed on those who threatened to undermine the constitution of Cleisthenes. Each year, every Athenian citizen had the opportunity to write on a potsherd (in Greek, *ostrakon*) the name of the man he most wished to leave Attica. If at least 6,000 citizens voted, the state sent the individual receiving the most votes into temporary exile. No charges or accusations had to be made, much less proven. Anyone who had offended the Athenians or who, by his prominence, seemed a threat to democracy could be ostracized. At the same time, Athenians also began to select their chief officers not simply by direct election but by lot. This practice prevented any individual from rising to power by creating a powerful faction. Themistocles (ca. 528–426 B.C.E.), the son of a noble father and a non-Greek mother, took the lead in using the tools of ostracism and selection by lot to hold the aristocratic factions at bay.

Thermopylae and Salamis

Occupied by problems elsewhere in their vast empire and by the unexpected death of Darius I in 486 B.C.E., the Persians paid little attention to Greece for six years. After Darius's death, his son Xerxes (486–465 B.C.E.) began to amass foodstuffs, weapons, and armies for a land assault on his Greek enemies. Though some Greek states more or less willingly allied themselves with the Persians, the others met in Sparta in 481 B.C.E. to plan resistance. The allies agreed that the Spartans would take command of the combined land and sea forces.

Although larger than those mustered by Athens against Darius, the Greek forces were puny compared with Xerxes' infantry and 1,000 light and highly maneuverable Ionian and Phoenician ships. The Spartan commanders sought a strategic point at which the numerical superiority of the Persian forces would be neutralized. The choice fell on the narrow pass of Thermopylae and the adjacent Euboean strait. While a select force of hoplites held the pass, the Greek fleet, following a strategy devised by the Athenian leader Themistocles, harried the larger Persian one. Neither action produced a Greek victory, but none could have been expected.

At Thermopylae, the Greeks held firm for days against wave after wave of assaulting troops. Finally, Greek allies of the Persians showed them a narrow mountain track by which they were able to attack the Greek position from the rear. Seeing that all was lost, the Spartan king Leonidas (490–480 B.C.E.) sent most of his allies home. Then he and his 300 Spartan equals faced certain death with a casual disdain characterized by the comment made by one Spartan equal. Told that when the Persians shot their arrows, they were so numerous that they hid the sun, the Spartan replied, "Good. If the Persians hide the sun, we shall have our battle in the shade."

While the Persian troops were blocked at Thermopylae, their fleet was being battered by fierce storms in the Euboean straits and harassed by the heavier Greek ships. Here the Greeks learned that in close quarters they could stand up to Xerxes' Phoenician navy. This lesson proved vital a short time later. While the Persian army burned Athens and occupied Attica, Themistocles lured Xerxes' fleet into the narrow strait between Salamis and the mainland. There, the slower Greek vessels bottled up the larger and vastly more numerous enemy ships and cut them to pieces.

After Salamis, Xerxes lost his appetite for fighting Greeks. Without his fleet he could not supply a vast army far from home in hostile territory. Leaving a force to do what damage it could, he led the bulk of his army back to Persia. At Athenian urging, the Greek allies under Leonidas's kinsman Pausanias (d. ca. 470 B.C.E.) met the Persians at Plataea in 479 B.C.E. Once again, hoplite discipline and Greek determination overcame the enemy's numerical superiority. Athenian sea power and Spartan infantry had proven invincible. Soon the Athenians were taking the offensive, liberating the Ionian cities of Asia Minor and, in the process, laying the foundations of an Athenian empire that was every bit as threatening to their neighbors as that of Xerxes.

The Athenian Empire

Sparta, not Athens, should have emerged as the leader of the Greek world after 479 B.C.E. However, the constant threat of a helot revolt and the desire of the members of Sparta's Peloponnesian League to go their separate ways left Sparta too preoccupied with internal problems to fill the power vacuum left by the Persian defeat.

Athens, on the other hand, was only too ready to take the lead in bringing the war home to the Persians. With Sparta out of the picture, the Athenian fleet was the best hope of liberating the Aegean from Persians and pirates. Athenian propaganda emphasized the Persian menace and Ionian solidarity.

The Delian League. Athens accepted control in 478 B.C.E. of what historians have come to call the Delian League, after the island of Delos, a religious center that housed the league's treasury. Athens and some of the states with navies provided ships; others contributed annual payments to the league. Initially, the league pursued the war against the Persians, driving them back along the Aegean and the Black Seas. At the same time, Athens hurriedly rebuilt its defensive fortifications, a move that Sparta and other states correctly interpreted as directed more against them than against the Persians.

Athens's domination of the Delian League ensured its prosperity. Attica, with its fragile agriculture, depended on Black Sea wheat, and the league kept these regions under Athenian control. Since Athens received not only cash "contributions" from league members but also half of the spoils taken in battle, the state's public coffers were filled. The new riches made possible the reconstruction of the city, which had been burned by the Persians, into the most magnificent city of Greece.

The league was too vital to Athenian prosperity to stand and fall with the Persian threat. The drive against the Persian Empire began to falter after a league expedition to Egypt in 454 B.C.E. ended in total defeat. Discouraged by this and other setbacks, the Athenian Callias, acting for the league, apparently concluded a peace treaty with Persia in

449 B.C.E., making the alliance no longer necessary. For a brief moment it appeared that the Delian League might disband. But it was too late. The league had become an empire, and Athens's allies were its subjects.

Athenian Imperialism.   The Athenian empire was an economic, judicial, religious, and political union that was held together by military might. Athens controlled the flow of grain through the Hellespont to the Aegean, ensuring its own supply and heavily taxing cargoes to other cities. Athens controlled the law courts of member cities and used them to repress anti-Athenian groups. Rich and poor Athenian citizens alike acquired territory throughout the empire. The rich took over vast estates confiscated from local opponents of Athenian dominance, while the poor replaced hostile populations in the colonies. Control over this empire depended on the Athenian fleet to enforce cooperation. Athenian garrisons were established in each city, and "democratic" puppet governments ruled according to the wishes of the garrison commanders. Revolt, resignation from the league, or refusal to pay the annual tribute resulted in brutal suppression. Persian tyranny had hardly been worse than Athenian imperialism.

Private and Public Life in Athens

During the second half of the fifth century B.C.E., Athens, enriched by tribute from its over 150 subject states, was a vital, crowded capital that drew merchants, artisans, and laborers from throughout the Greek world. At its height, the total population of Athens and surrounding Attica numbered perhaps 350,000, although probably fewer than 60,000 were citizens—adult males qualified to own land and participate in Athenian politics. Over one-quarter of the total population were slaves. Great landowners, unable to force ordinary freemen to work their estates, had turned to slave labor. Slaves were also vital in mining and other forms of craft and industrial work.

Greek slaves were not distinguished by race, ethnicity, or physical appearance. Anyone could become a slave. Prisoners of war, foreigners who failed to pay taxes, and victims of pirate raids could all end up on the auction blocks of the ancient world. Slaves were as much the property of their owners as land, houses, cattle, and sheep were. Many masters treated their slaves well, but they were under no obligation to do so, and beatings, sexual exploitation, tattooing, starvation, and shackling were all too common.

Metics.   Roughly half of Athens's free population were foreigners—*metoikoi*, or metics. These were primarily Greek citizens of the tributary states of the empire, but they might also be peoples from Africa or from Asia Minor, such as Lydians. The number of metics increased after the middle of the fifth century B.C.E.—both because of the flood of foreigners into the empire's capital and because Athenian citizenship was restricted to persons with two

parents who were of citizen families. Metics could not own land in Attica, nor could they participate directly in politics. They were required to have a citizen protector and to pay a small annual tax. Otherwise, they were free to engage in every form of activity.

Women.   More than half of those born into citizen families were entirely excluded from public life. These were the women, who controlled and directed the vital sphere of the Athenian home but who were considered citizens only for purposes of marriage, transfer of property, and procreation. From birth to death, every female citizen lived under the protection of a male guardian, either a close relative such as a father or brother, or a husband or son. Women spent almost their entire lives in the inner recesses of the home. Fathers arranged marriages, the purposes of which are abundantly clear from the ritualized exchange of words sealing the betrothal:

"I give this woman for the procreation of legitimate children."
"I accept."
"And [I give a certain amount as] dowry."
"I am content."

A wife had no control over her dowry, which passed to her son. In the event of divorce or the death of her husband, the woman and her dowry returned to her father. An honorable Athenian woman stayed at home and managed her husband's household. Only the poorest citizens sent their wives and daughters to work in the marketplace or the fields. For women, even the most casual contact with other men without permission was strictly forbidden, although men were expected to engage in various sorts of extramarital affairs. In the words of one Athenian male, "Hetairai we have for our pleasure, mistresses for the refreshment of our bodies, but wives to bear us legitimate children and to look after the house faithfully." The household, as Athenians never tired of repeating, was the foundation of all society.

Freedom in Community.   Male control over women may have resulted in part from fear. Women were identified with the forces of nature, which included both positive forces such as fertility and life and negative forces such as chaotic irrationality, which threatened civilization. These two poles were epitomized by the cult of Dionysus. He was the god of wine, lifeblood, and fertility, but he was also the deity whose female devotees, the *maenads*, were portrayed as worshipping him in a state of frenzied savagery that could include tearing children and animals limb from limb.

The male citizens of fifth-century B.C.E. Athens were free to an extent previously unknown in the world. But Athenian freedom was freedom *in* community, not freedom *from* community. The essence of their freedom lay in their participation in public life, especially self-government, which was their passion. This participation was always within a complex network of familial, social, and religious connections and obligations. Each person belonged to a

▲ Greek vase painting showing women weaving on a loom.

activities in Athens. However, the aristocracy was still strong, and most of the popular leaders of the century came from the ranks of old wealth and influence. Still, sovereignty lay not with these aristocrats but with the demos—the people.

In theory the adult male citizens of Athens were its sovereigns. Since the time of Solon, they had formed the *ekklesia,* or assembly. On particularly solemn occasions, as many as 6,000 citizens might convene in the *pnyx,* the meeting place of the assembly. They also made up the large juries, always composed of several hundred citizens, who decided legal cases less on law than on the political merits of the case and the quality of the orators who pleaded for each side. Such large bodies were too unwieldy to deal with the daily tasks of government. Therefore, control of these tasks fell to the council, or *boule,* composed of 500 members selected by lot by the tribes; the magistrates, who were also chosen by lot; and ten military commanders or generals, the only major officeholders who were elected rather than chosen at random.

Demagogues. Paradoxically, the resolute determination of Athenian democrats to prevent individuals from acquiring too much power helped to create a series of extraconstitutional power brokers. Since most offices were filled by lot and turned over frequently, real political leadership came not from officeholders but from generals and from popular leaders. These so-called demagogues, while at times holding high office, exercised their power through their speaking skills, informal networks, and knowledge of how to get things done. Demagogues tended to be wealthy aristocrats who acquired this knowledge through their willingness to volunteer on committees or serve as unpaid government workers or in minor elected offices. Governing an empire demanded skill, energy, and experience, but Athenian democracy was formally run by amateurs. Small wonder that the city's public life was dominated by these popular leaders.

Pericles and Athens

For 30 years, one individual dominated Athenian public life: the general Pericles (ca. 495–429 B.C.E.), a great orator and successful military commander who led Athens during the decades of its greatest glory. Athens's system of radical democracy reached its zenith under his leadership, even while Athens's imperial program drew it into a long and fatal war against Sparta, the only state powerful enough to resist it.

Pericles was descended from the Alcmaeonids, a leading Athenian aristocratic family. Nevertheless, as one ancient author put it, he "took his side, not with the rich and the few, but with the many and the poor." Pericles acquired intimate knowledge of government through long service on various public works projects, projects that provided lucrative income to poorer citizens. He was also president of the commission responsible for constructing the great

number of groups: a deme, a tribe, a family, various religious associations, and occupational groups. Each of these communities placed different and even contradictory demands on its members. The impossibility of satisfying all of these demands, of responding to the special interests of each, forced citizens to make hard choices, to set priorities, and to balance conflicting obligations. This process of selection was the essence of Athenian freedom, a freedom that, unlike that of the modern world, was based not on individualism but on a multitude of collectivities. The sum of these overlapping groupings was Athenian society, in which friends and opponents alike were united.

Unity did not imply equality. Even in fifth-century B.C.E. Athens, not all Athenians were socially or economically equal. Most were farmers who looked to military service as a means of increasing their meager income. Others engaged in trade or industry, although metics, with their commercial contacts in their cities of origin, dominated much of these ivory and gold statue of Athena that stood in the Parthenon, the main temple in Athens. He served on the commission that built the Lyceum, or city exercise center, and the Parthenon itself. These enormous projects won him a great popular following while giving him an intimate knowledge of public finance and the details of Athenian government. He enhanced his position further through his great powers of persuasion.

Pericles never ruled Athens. As a general he could only carry out the orders of the ekklesia and the boule, and as a citizen he could only attempt to persuade his fellows. Still, he was largely responsible for the extension of Athenian democracy to all free citizens. Under his influence, Athens abolished the last property requirements for officeholding. He convinced the state to pay those who served on juries, thus making it possible for even the poorest citizens to participate in this important part of Athenian government. But he was also responsible for a restriction of citizenship to those whose mothers and fathers had both been Athenians. Such a law would have denied citizenship to many of the most illustrious Athenians of the sixth century B.C.E., including his own ancestors. The law also prevented citizens of Athens's subject states from developing a real stake in the fate of the empire.

Pericles believed that the Athenian empire had to be preserved at all costs. This policy ultimately drew Athens into deadly conflict with Sparta. The first clash between the two rival powers came around 460 B.C.E. at Megara, which lay between the Peloponnesus and Attica. The Athenians emerged victorious, checking Sparta and absorbing Megara, Aegina, and Boeotia. However, in 446 B.C.E., after the Athenian defeat in Egypt, Megara and Boeotia rebelled, and Sparta invaded the disputed region. Unable to face this new threat at home after the disastrous loss abroad, in 445 B.C.E. the Athenians, under the leadership of Pericles, concluded a peace treaty with Sparta whereby Athens abandoned all of its continental possessions. The treaty was meant to last for 30 years, but it held for only 14.

The two great powers were eager to preserve the peace, but the whole Greek world was a tinderbox ready to burst into flame. The spark came from an unexpected direction. In 435 B.C.E., Corinth and its colony Corcyra on the Adriatic Sea came to blows, and Corcyra sought the assistance of Athens. The Athenians agreed to a defensive alliance with Corcyra and assisted it in defeating its enemy. This assistance infuriated Corinth, an ally of Sparta, and in 432 B.C.E., the Corinthians convinced the Spartans that Athens's imperial ambitions were insatiable. The next year, Sparta invaded Attica, and the Peloponnesian War, which would destroy both great powers, had begun.

The Peloponnesian War

The Peloponnesian War was actually a series of wars and rebellions. Athens and Sparta waged two devastating ten-year

▲ The Delian League and the Peloponnesian War. When Athens turned the Delian League into its own empire, the resulting war pitted the Attica city-state against the combined forces of Sparta and Persia.

wars, from 431 B.C.E. to 421 B.C.E. and then again from 414 B.C.E. to 404 B.C.E. At the same time, cities in each alliance took advantage of the wars to revolt against the great powers, eliciting terrible vengeance from both Athens and Sparta. Within many of the Greek city-states, oligarchs and democrats waged bloody civil wars for control of their governments. Moreover, between 415 and 413 B.C.E., Athens attempted to expand its empire in Sicily, an attempt that ended in disaster. Before it was over, the Peloponnesian War had become an international war, with Persia entering the fray on the side of Sparta. In the end, there were no real victors, only victims.

Initially, Sparta and Athens both hoped for quick victory. Sparta's strength was its army, and its strategy was to invade Attica, devastate the countryside, and force the Athenians into an open battle. Pericles urged Athens to a strategy of conserving its hoplite forces while exploiting its naval strength. Athens was a naval power and, with its empire and control of Black Sea grain, could hold out for years behind its fortifications, the great walls linking Athens to its port of Piraeus. At the same time, the Athenian fleet could launch raids along the coast of the Peloponnesus, thus bringing the war home to the Spartans. Pericles hoped in this way to outlast the Spartans.

The Archidamian War.   The first phase of the war, called the Archidamian War after the Spartan king Archidamus (431–427 B.C.E.), was indecisive. Sparta pillaged Attica but could not breach the great wall nor starve Athens. In 430 B.C.E., the Spartans received unexpected help in the form of plague, which ravaged Athens for five years. By the time it ended in 426 B.C.E., as much as one-third of the Athenian population had died, including Pericles. Still Athens held out, establishing bases encircling the Peloponnesus and urging Spartan helots and allies to revolt.

At Pylos in 425 B.C.E., the Athenian generals Cleon and Demosthenes captured a major force of Spartan equals. The Spartans offset this defeat by capturing the city of Amphipolis on the northern Aegean. The defeated Athenian commander, Thucydides (d. ca. 401 B.C.E.), was exiled for his failure and retired to Spartan territory to write his great history of the war. Exhausted by a decade of death and destruction, the two sides contracted peace in 421 B.C.E. Although Athens was victorious in that its empire was intact, the peace changed nothing, and tensions festered for five years.

Alcibiades and the Sicilian Expedition.   After the peace of 421 B.C.E., Pericles' kinsman Alcibiades (ca. 450–404 B.C.E.) came to dominate the demos. Well-spoken, handsome, and brave but also vain, dissolute, and ambitious, Alcibiades led the city into disaster. Although he was a demagogue who courted popular support, he despised the people and schemed to overturn the democracy. In 415 B.C.E. he urged Athens to expand its empire westward by attacking Syracuse, the most prosperous Greek city of Sicily, which had largely escaped the devastation of the Archidamian War. The expedition went poorly, and Alcibiades, accused at home of having profaned one of the most important Athenian religious cults, was ordered home. Instead, he fled to Sparta, where he began to assist the Spartans against Athens. The Sicilian expedition ended in disaster. Athens lost over 200 ships and 50,000 men. At

---

THE TWO FACES OF ATHENIAN DEMOCRACY

Early in the Peloponnesian War, Thucydides summarized the virtues of Athenian democracy in the speech he ascribes to Pericles in honor of those who died in the first year of the war. By 416 B.C.E., the sixteenth year of the Peloponnesian War, Athenian imperialism no longer even paid lip service to the ideals of democracy or freedom. Thucydides illustrates this in his reconstructed debate between representatives of the Spartan colony of Melos, which had attempted to remain neutral, and representatives of the Athenians, who demanded their surrender and enslavement.

FOCUS QUESTIONS

What limits did the Athenians place on the ideal of democracy?

How did the Athenians justify violence to maintain their empire?

Pericles' Funeral Oration

OUR CONSTITUTION IS CALLED A DEMOCRACY because power is in the hands not of a minority but of the whole people. When it is a question of settling private disputes, everyone is equal before the law; when it is a question of putting one person before another in positions of public responsibility, what counts is not membership of a particular class, but the actual ability which the man possesses. No one, so long as he has it in him to be of service to the state, is kept in political obscurity because of poverty.

The Melian Debate

ATHENIANS: YOU KNOW AS WELL AS WE DO THAT, when these matters are discussed by practical people, the standard of justice depends on the equality of power to compel and that in fact the strong do what they have the power to do and the weak accept what they have to accept.

MELIANS: And how could it be just as good for us to be the slaves as for you to be the masters?

ATHENIANS: You, by giving in, would save yourselves from disaster; we by not destroying you, would be able to profit from you.

MELIANS: So you would not agree to our being neutral, friends instead of enemies, but allies of neither side?

ATHENIANS: No, because it is not so much your hostility that injures us; it is rather the case that, if we were on friendly terms with you, our subjects would regard that as a sign of weakness in us, whereas your hatred is evidence of our power.

Ultimately the Melians rejected Athens's demands, and shortly after the Athenians captured the city, they executed all the men and sold the women and children as slaves.

From Thucydides, *History of the Peloponnesian War.*

the same time, Sparta resumed the war, this time with naval support provided by Persia.

Suddenly, Athens was fighting for its life. Alcibiades soon abandoned Sparta for Persia and convinced the Athenians that if they would abandon their democracy for an oligarchy, Persia would withdraw its support of Sparta. In 411 B.C.E., the desperate Athenian assembly established a brutal, antidemocratic oligarchy, but when the war continued, Athens, amid bitter factionalism, reestablished its democracy. The Persian king renewed his support for Sparta, sending his son Cyrus (ca. 424–401 B.C.E.) to coordinate the war against Athens. Under the Spartan general Lysander (d. 395 B.C.E.), Sparta and its allies finally closed in on Athens. Lysander captured the Athenian fleet in the Hellespont, destroyed it, and severed Athens's vital grain supply. Within months, Athens was entirely cut off from the outside world and starving. In 404 B.C.E., Sparta accepted Athens's unconditional surrender. Athens's fortifications came down, its empire vanished, and its fleet, except for a mere twelve ships, dissolved.

The Peloponnesian War showed not only the limitations of Athenian democracy but the potential brutality of oligarchy as well. More ominously, it demonstrated the catastrophic effects of disunity and rivalry among Greek cities of the Mediterranean.

ATHENIAN CULTURE IN THE HELLENIC AGE

Most of what we today call Greek is actually Athenian. Throughout the Hellenic age (the fifth and early fourth centuries B.C.E., as distinct from the Hellenistic period of roughly the later fourth through second centuries B.C.E.), the turbulent issues of democracy and oligarchy, war and peace, hard choices and conflicting obligations found expression in Athenian culture even as the glory of the Athenian empire was manifested in art and architecture. The great dramatists Aeschylus, Sophocles, and Euripides were Athenian, as were the sculptor Phidias, the Parthenon architects Ictinus and Callicrates, and the philosophers Socrates and Plato. To Athens came writers, thinkers, and artists from throughout the Greek world.

The Examined Life

A primary characteristic of Athenian culture was its critical and rational nature. In heated discussions in the assembly and the agora, the courtroom and the private symposium, Athenians and foreigners drawn to the city no longer looked to the myths and religion of the past for guidance. Secure in their identity and protected by the openness of their radical democracy, they began to examine the past and present and to question the foundations of traditional values. From this climate of inquiry emerged the traditions of moral philosophy and its cousin, history.

The Ionian interest in natural philosophy, the explanation of the universe in rational terms, continued throughout the fifth century B.C.E. But philosophers began also to turn their attention to the human world, in particular to the powers and limitations of the individual's mind and the individual's relationship with society. By the end of his life, the philosopher Heraclitus had become intrigued with the examination of the rational faculties themselves rather than what one could know with them. In part, this meant a search for personal, inner understanding that would lead to proper action within society—in other words, to the search for ethics based in reason. In part, too, such an inquiry led to a study of how to formulate arguments and persuade others through logic.

The Sophists.   In the political world of fifth-century B.C.E. Athens, rhetoric, the art of persuasion, was particularly important because it was the key to political influence. Teachers called sophists ("wise people") traveled throughout Greece, offering to provide an advanced education for a fee. Although the sophistic tradition later gained a negative reputation, teachers such as Gorgias (ca. 485–ca. 380 B.C.E.) and Protagoras (ca. 490–421 B.C.E.) trained young men not only in the art of rhetoric but also in logic. By exercising their students' minds with logical puzzles and paradoxical statements, the sophists taught a generation of wealthy Greeks the powers and complexities of human reason.

Socrates.   The teacher Socrates (ca. 470–399 B.C.E.) was considered by many of his contemporaries as but one more sophist, but he himself reacted against what he saw as the amoral and superficial nature of sophistic education. He was interested in the search for moral self-enlightenment urged by Heraclitus. "Know thyself" was Socrates' plea. An unexamined life, he argued, was not worth living. Socrates refused any pay for his teaching, arguing that he had nothing to teach. He knew nothing, he said, and was superior to the sophists only because he recognized his ignorance while they professed wisdom. Socrates' method infuriated his contemporaries. He would approach individuals who had reputations for wisdom or skill and then, through a series of disarmingly simple questions, force them to defend their beliefs. The inevitable result was that in their own words the outstanding sophists, politicians, and poets of the day demonstrated the inadequacy of the foundations of their beliefs.

Since Socrates refused to commit any of his teaching to writing, we know of him only from the conflicting reports of his former students and opponents. One thing is certain, however: while demanding that every aspect of life be

▲ This bust of Socrates portrays him with the traditional beard of the philosopher. His features display the tradition that this man, whose thoughts were the most beautiful, was nevertheless of remarkably homely appearance.

investigated, Socrates never doubted the moral legitimacy of the Athenian state. Condemned to death in 399 B.C.E. on the trumped-up charges of corrupting the morals of the Athenian youth and introducing strange gods, he declined the opportunity to escape into exile. Rather than reject Athens and its laws, he drank the fatal potion of hemlock given him by the executioner.

Understanding the Past

The philosophical interest in human choices and social constraints found echo in the historical writing of the age.

In particular, two writers established the spectrum of how to understand the past.

Herodotus.   Herodotus (ca. 484–420 B.C.E.), the first historian, was one of the many foreigners who found in Athens the intellectual climate and audience he needed to write an account of the Persian wars of the preceding generation. His book of inquiries, or *historia*, into the origins and events of the conflict between Greeks and Persians is the first true history. Herodotus had traveled widely in the eastern Mediterranean, collecting local stories and visiting famous temples, palaces, and cities. In his study he presents a great panorama of the civilized world at the end of the sixth century B.C.E. Herodotus did not hesitate to report myths, legends, and outrageous tales. His faith in the gods was strong, and he believed that the gods intervene in human affairs. Still, he was more than just a good story-teller. Often, after reporting conflicting accounts, he would conclude, "Both stories are told and the reader may take his choice between them." In other cases, after recounting a particularly farfetched account heard from local informants, he would comment, "Personally, I think this story is nonsense."

As Herodotus explained in his introduction, his purpose in writing was first to preserve the memory of the past by recording the achievements of both Greeks and eastern non-Greeks and second to show how the two came into conflict. It was this concern to explain, to go beyond mere storytelling, that earned Herodotus the designation "father of history." Herodotus was less interested in the mythic dimensions of the conflict than in the human, and his primary concern was the action of individuals under the press of circumstances. Ultimately, the Persian wars became for Herodotus the conflict between freedom and despotism, and he described with passion how different Greek states chose between the two.

Thucydides.   The story of the Peloponnesian War was recorded by a different sort of historian, one who focused more narrowly on the Greek world and on political power. Thucydides had been an Athenian general and a major actor in the first part of the Peloponnesian War until his exile in 425 B.C.E. He began his account at the very outbreak of the conflict, thus writing a contemporary record of the war rather than a history of it. As Herodotus is called the father of history, Thucydides might be called the first social scientist.

For Thucydides the central subject was human society in action. He viewed the Greek states as acting out of rational self-interest. His favorite device for showing the development of such policies was the political set speech in which two opposing leaders attempt to persuade their fellow citizens on the proper course of action. Although fictitious by modern standards, these speeches penetrate to the heart of the tough political choices facing the opposing forces. This hard-nosed approach to political decisions continues to serve as a model to historians and practitioners of power politics.

Still, morality is always just below the surface of Thucydides' narrative. Even as he unflinchingly chronicles the collapse of morality and social order in the face of political expediency, he recognizes that this process will destroy his beloved Athens. In his account of the second phase of the war, Athens acts with the full arrogance of a tyrant. Its overwhelming pride leads it to attack and destroy its weaker neighbors and ultimately to invade Sicily, with disastrous results. In the later, unfinished chapters (Thucydides died shortly after Athens's final defeat), the Peloponnesian War takes on the characteristics of a tragedy. Here Thucydides, the ultimate political historian, shows the deep influence of the dominant literary tradition of his day: Greek drama.

Athenian Drama

Since the time of its introduction by Peisistratus in the middle of the sixth century B.C.E., drama had become popular, not only in Athens but throughout the Greek world. Plays formed part of the annual feast of Dionysus and dealt with mythic subject matter largely taken from the *Iliad* and the *Odyssey*. Three types of plays honored the Dionysian festival. Tragedies dealt with great men who failed because of flaws in their natures. Comedies were more directly topical and political. They parodied real Athenians, often by name, and amused even while making serious points in defense of democracy. Somewhere between tragedies and comedies, satyr plays remained closest to the Dionysian cult. In them, lecherous drunken satyrs, mythical half-man, half-goat creatures, interact with gods and men as they roam in search of Dionysus.

Aeschylus.   Only a handful of the hundreds of Greek plays written in the fifth century B.C.E. survive. The first of the great Athenian tragedians whose plays we know is Aeschylus (525–456 B.C.E.), a veteran of Marathon and an eyewitness of the battle of Salamis. His one surviving trilogy, the *Oresteia,* traces the fate of the family of Agamemnon, the Greek commander at Troy. The three plays of the trilogy explore the chain of violent acts, vengeance, and conflicting obligations that ultimately must be settled by rational yet divinely sanctioned law.

Sophocles.   Aeschylus's younger contemporary Sophocles (496–406 B.C.E.), the most successful of the fifth century B.C.E. tragedians, sought in his mature plays to express human character. He shows how humans make decisions and carry them out, constrained by their pasts, their weaknesses, and their vices, but free nonetheless. Sophocles' message is endurance, acceptance of human responsibility and, at the same time, of the ways of the gods, who overrule people's plans. The heroine of *Antigone,* for whom the play is named, is the sister of Polynices, exiled son of King Oedipus of Thebes. Polynices has died fighting his city, and Creon, its new ruler, commands under penalty of death that Polynices' body be left unburied. This would mean that his soul would never find rest, the ultimate punishment for a Greek. Antigone, with determination and courage equal to her love for her brother, buries Polynices and is entombed alive for her crime. Here the conflict between the state, which claims the total obedience of its people, and the claims of familial love and religious piety meet in tragic conflict. Creon, warned by a prophet that he is offending heaven, orders Antigone's release, but it is too late. Rather than wait for death, she has already hanged herself.

Euripides.   Compared with Aeschylus and Sophocles, Euripides (485–406 B.C.E.) was far more original and daring in his subject matter and treatment of human emotions. His female characters were often wronged and seldom accepted their lot. His plays abound in plot twists and unexpected, violent outbursts. Passion, not reason, rules Euripides' world. His characters are less reconciled to their fates and less ready to accept the traditional gods:

> *Does someone say that there are gods in heaven?*
> *There are not, there are not—unless one chooses*
> *To follow old tradition like a fool.*

Greek Comedy.   Neither passion nor reason but politics rules the world of Greek comedy. Rather than the timelessness of the human condition, Athenian comic playwrights focused their biting satire on the political and social issues of the moment. Particularly, the comic genius Aristophanes (ca. 450–ca. 388 B.C.E.) used wit, imagination, vulgarity, and great poetic sensitivity to attack everything that offended him in his city. In his plays, he mocks and ridicules statesmen, philosophers, rival playwrights, and even the gods. His comedies are full of outrageous turns of plot, talking animals, obscene jokes and puns, and mocking asides. Yet Aristophanes was a deeply patriotic Athenian, dedicated to the democratic system and to the cause of peace. In *Lysistrata,* written in 411 B.C.E., after Athens had renewed the war against Sparta, the women of Greece force their men to make peace by conspiring to refuse them sex as long as war continues. Through the sharp satire and absurd plots of his plays, Aristophanes communicates his sympathy for ordinary people, who must match wits with the charlatans and pompous frauds who attempt to dominate Athens's public life.

The Human Image

The humanity in Greek drama found its parallel in art. In the late sixth century B.C.E., a reversal of the traditional black-figure technique had revolutionized vase painting. Artists had begun to outline scenes on unfired clay and then fill in the background with black or brown glaze. The interior details of the figures were also added in black. The results were a much more lifelike art, a lighter, more natural coloring, and the possibility of more perspective, depth, and molding.

Sculpture reflected the same development toward balance and realism contained within an ideal of human form. The finest bronzes and marbles of the fifth century B.C.E. show freestanding figures whose natural vigor and force, even when they are engaged in strenuous exertion, are balanced by the placidity of their faces and their lack of emotion. The tradition established by the Athenian sculptor Phidias (ca. 500–ca. 430 B.C.E.) sought a naturalism in the portrayal of the human figure, which remained ideal rather than individual.

The greatest sculptural program of the fifth century B.C.E. was that produced for the Athenian acropolis. The reconstruction of the acropolis, which had been destroyed by the Persians, was the culmination of Athenian art. The result was the greatest complex of buildings in the ancient world. One entered the acropolis complex through the monumental *Propylaea,* or gateway, a T-shaped structure approached by a flight of steps. From the top of the steps, one could glimpse both Phidias's great bronze statue of Athena Promachos in the center of the acropolis and, to the right, the Parthenon. As visitors entered the acropolis itself, they passed on the right the small temple of Athena as Victory. Continuing on the Sacred Way, one saw on the left the delicate Erechtheum, which housed the oldest Athenian cults. On the right, visitors were overawed by the Parthenon, a monument as much to Athens as to Athena. Even today, the ruined temple seems a rectangular embodiment of order, proportion, and balance. Every surface, from the floor to the columns to the horizontal beams, curves slightly. The spacing of the columns varies, and each leans slightly inward. Those at the rear are larger than those at the front to compensate for the effect of viewing them from a greater distance. The optical illusion of flatness, regularity, and repetition in the Parthenon was the intended effect.

An illusion, too, was the sense of overwhelming Athenian superiority and grandeur the acropolis was intended to convey. By the time the Erechtheum was completed in 406 B.C.E., however, the Athenian empire was all but destroyed, the city's population was devastated, and its democracy was imperiled. Two years later, Athens surrendered unconditionally to Sparta.

The intellectual and artistic accomplishments of Athens were as enduring as its empire proved ephemeral. Writers and artists alike focused their creative energies on human existence, seeking a proper proportion, order, and meaning, a blend of the practical and ideal, which Athens's political leaders lacked.

FROM CITY-STATES TO MACEDONIAN EMPIRE, 404–323 B.C.E.

The Peloponnesian War touched every aspect of Greek life. The war brought changes to the social and political structures of Greece by creating an enduring bitterness between elites and populace and a distrust of both democracy and traditional oligarchy. The mutual exhaustion of Athens and Sparta left a vacuum of power in the Aegean. Finally, the war raised fundamental questions about the nature of politics and society throughout the Greek world.

Politics After the Peloponnesian War

Over the decades-long struggle, the conduct of war and the nature of politics had changed, bringing new problems for victor and vanquished alike. Lightly armed professional mercenaries willing to fight for anyone who was able to pay gradually replaced hoplite citizen soldiers as the backbone of the fighting forces. As war became more professional and protracted, it also became more brutal. The rise of mercenary armies also meant trouble for democracies such as Athens as well as for Sparta with its class of equals.

Spartan Imperialism. Victory left Sparta no more capable of assuming leadership in 404 B.C.E. than it had been in 478 B.C.E. Years of war had reduced the population of equals to fewer than 3,000. The Spartans proved to be extremely unpopular imperialists. As reward for Persian assistance, Sparta returned the Ionian cities to Persian control. Elsewhere, it established hated oligarchies to rule in a way favorable to Sparta's interests. In Athens, a brutal tyranny of 30 men took control in 404 B.C.E. With Spartan support, they executed 1,500 democratic leaders and forced 5,000 more into exile. The Thirty Tyrants evoked enormous hatred and opposition. Within a year the exiles recaptured the city, restored democracy, and killed or expelled the tyrants.

Similar opposition to Spartan rule emerged throughout the Greek world, shattering the fragile peace created by Athens's defeat. For over 70 years the Greek world boiled in constant warfare. Mutual distrust, fear of any city that seemed about to establish a position of clear superiority, and the machinations of the Persian Empire to keep Greeks fighting each other produced a constantly shifting series of alliances.

Thebes. Persia turned against its former ally when, in 401 B.C.E., Sparta supported an unsuccessful attempt by Cyrus to unseat his brother Artaxerxes II. Soon the unlikely and unstable alliance of Athens, Corinth, Argos, Thebes, and Euboea, financed by Persia, entered a series of vicious wars against Sparta. The first round ended in Spartan victory, due to the shifting role of Persia, whose primary interest was the continued disunity of the Greeks. By 377 B.C.E., however, Athens had reorganized its league and, with Thebes as an ally, was able to break Spartan sea power. The decline of Sparta left a power vacuum that was soon filled by Thebes. Athens, concerned by this new threat, shifted alliances, making peace with its old enemy. However, Spartan military fortunes had so declined that when Sparta attacked Thebes in 371 B.C.E., its armies were destroyed and Spartan power was broken. The next year, Thebes invaded the Peloponnesus and freed Messenia, the foundation of Sparta's economic prosperity. Sparta never recovered. Deprived of its economic base, its body of equals reduced to a mere 800, and its fleet gone, Sparta never regained its historic importance.

Theban hegemony was short-lived. Before long, the same process of greed, envy, and distrust that had devastated the other Greek powers destroyed Thebes. Athens's reconstituted league disintegrated as members opposed Athenian attempts once more to convert a free association of states into an empire. By the 330s B.C.E., all of the Greek states had proven themselves incapable of creating stable political units larger than their immediate polis.

Philosophy and the Polis

The failure of Greek political forms, oligarchy and democracy alike, profoundly affected Athenian philosophers. Plato (ca. 428–347 B.C.E.), an aristocratic student of Socrates, grew up during the Peloponnesian War and had witnessed the collapse of the empire, the brutality of the Thirty Tyrants, the execution of Socrates, and the revival of the democracy and its imperialistic ambitions. From these experiences he developed a hatred for Athenian democracy and a profound distrust of ordinary people's ability to tell right from wrong. Disgusted with public life, Plato left Attica for a time and traveled in Sicily and Italy, where he encountered different forms of government and different philosophical schools. Around 387 B.C.E., he returned to Athens and opened the Academy, a school to provide Athenian youth with what he considered to be knowledge of what was true and good for the individual and the state.

Platonic Forms.   To transmit his teachings, Plato chose the unlikely literary form of the dialogue, in the form of discussions between his teacher, Socrates, and a variety of students and opponents. While Plato shared with his mentor the conviction that human actions had to be grounded in self-knowledge, Plato's philosophy extended much further. His arguments about the inadequacy of all existing forms of government and the need to create a new form of government through the proper education of elite philosopher rulers were part of a complex understanding of the universe and the individual's place in it.

Plato argued that true knowledge is impossible as long as it focuses on the constantly changing, imperfect world of everyday experience. Human beings can have real knowledge only of that which is eternal, perfect, and beyond the experience of the senses, the realm of what Plato called the Forms. We know these Forms from our memories of a previous existence when our spirits had direct contact with the universe of the Forms. When we judge individuals or actions to be true or good or beautiful, we do so not because they are truly virtuous, but because we recognize that they participate in some way in the Idea or Form of truth or goodness or beauty.

According to Plato, the evils of the world, in particular the vices and failures of government and society, result from ignorance of the truth. Most people live as though chained in a cave in which all they can see are the shadows cast by a fire on the walls. In their ignorance they mistake these flickering, imperfect images for reality. Their proper ruler must be a philosopher, one who is not deceived by the shadows. The philosopher's task is to break their chains and turn them toward the source of the light so that they can see the world as it really is.

Aristotelian Empiricism.   Plato's idealist view (in the sense of the Ideas or Forms) of knowledge dominated much of ancient philosophy. However, his greatest student, Aristotle (384–322 B.C.E.), rejected this view in favor of a philosophy rooted in observation of the natural world. Aristotle came from a medical family of northern Greece, and although he was a student in Plato's Academy for almost 20 years, he never abandoned observation for speculation. Systematic investigation and explanation characterize Aristotle's vast work, and his interests ranged from biology to statecraft to the most abstract philosophy. In each field he employed essentially the same method. He observed as many individual examples of the topic as possible and from these specific observations extracted general theories. His theories, whether on the nature of matter, the species of animals, the workings of the human mind, ethics, or the proper form of the state, are distinguished by clarity of logical thinking, precision in the use of terminology, and respect for the world of experience.

In human affairs, Aristotle recommended moderation. Unlike Plato, he did not regard any particular form of government as ideal. Rather, he concluded that the type of government ultimately mattered less than the balance between narrow oligarchy and radical democracy. Consistent with his belief that "virtue lies in a mean," he advocated governments composed of citizens who were neither extremely wealthy nor extremely poor. Moderation was the key to stability and justice. Yet, during the very years that Aristotle was teaching, the vacuum created by the failure of the Greek city-states was being filled by the growing Macedonian monarchy that finally ended a century of Greek warfare and, with it, the independence of the Greek city-states.

▲ A Roman copy of a Greek statue of Aristotle. Many ancient Greek sculptures are known only through Roman copies.

The Rise of Macedon

The polis had never been the only form of the Greek state. Alongside the city-states of Athens, Corinth, Syracuse, and Sparta were more decentralized ethne ruled by traditional hereditary chieftains and monarchs. Macedonia, in the northeast of the mainland, was one such ethnos. Its kings, chosen by the army from within a royal family, ruled in cooperation with nobles and clan leaders. The Macedonian people spoke a Greek dialect, and Macedonian kings and elite identified with Greek culture and tradition. Macedonia had long served as a buffer between the barbarians to the north and the Greek mainland, and its tough farmers and pastoralists were geared to constant warfare. As Athens, Sparta, and Thebes fought each other to mutual exhaustion, Macedonia under King Philip II (359–336 B.C.E.) moved into the resulting power vacuum.

After some early military successes against northern barbarians, Philip, a skillful politician and outstanding military strategist, turned his attention to the south and relentlessly swallowed up one Greek state after another. In 338 B.C.E., Philip achieved a final victory at Chaeronea and established a new league, the League of Corinth. However, unlike all those that had preceded it, this league was no confederation of sovereign states. It was an empire ruled by a king and supported by wealthy citizens whose cooperation Philip rewarded well. This new model of government, a monarchy drawing its support from a wealthy elite, became a fixture of the Mediterranean world for over 2,000 years.

Philip's success was based on his powerful military machine, which combined both Macedonian military tradition and the new mercenary forces that had emerged over the past century in Greece. The heart of his army was the infantry trained in the use of pikes some 14 feet long—4 feet longer than those of the Greek hoplites. Macedonian phalanxes moved forward in disciplined ranks, pushing back their foes, whose shorter lances could not reach the Macedonians. When the enemy were contained, the Macedonian cavalry charged from the flank and cut them to pieces.

No sooner had Philip subdued Greece than he announced a campaign against Persia. He intended to lead a combined Greek force in a war of revenge and conquest to punish the great empire for its invasion of Greece 150 years earlier and its subsequent involvement in the Greek world. Before he could begin, however, he was cut down by an assassin's knife, leaving his 20-year-old son, Alexander (336–323 B.C.E.), to lead the expedition. Within 13 years, Alexander had conquered the world.

The Empire of Alexander the Great

Alexander, envisioning himself a new Achilles, sought to imitate and surpass that legendary hero of the *Iliad*. Alexander's military genius, dedication to his troops, reckless disregard for his own safety, and ability to move both men and supplies across vast distances at great speed enabled him to lead the war machine that Philip had developed on an odyssey of conquest that stretched from Asia Minor to India. In 334 B.C.E., the first year of his campaign, Alexander captured the Greek cities of Asia Minor. Then he continued east. At Gordium, according to legend, he confronted an ancient puzzle, a complex knot tied to the chariot of the ancient king of that city. Whoever could loosen the knot, the legend said, would become master of Asia. Alexander solved that puzzle, as he did all of his others, with his sword. Two months later, he defeated the Persian king Darius III at Issus and then headed south toward the Mediterranean coast and Egypt. After his victories there, he turned again to the north and entered Mesopotamia. At Gaugamela in 331 B.C.E., he defeated Darius a second, decisive time. Shortly afterward, Darius was murdered by the remnants of his followers. Alexander captured the Persian capital of Persepolis with its vast treasure and became the undisputed ruler of the vast empire.

The conquest of Persia was not enough. Alexander pushed on, intending to conquer the whole world. His armies marched eastward, subduing the rebellious Asian provinces of Bactria and Sogdiana. He negotiated the Khyber Pass from what is now Afghanistan into the Punjab, crossed the Indus River, and defeated the local Indian king. Everywhere he went, he reorganized or founded cities, entrusting them to loyal Macedonians and other Greeks and settling them with veterans of his campaigns, and then pushed on toward the unknown. On the banks of the Hyphasis River in what is now Pakistan, his Macedonian warriors finally halted. Worn out by years of bloody conquest and exhausting travel, they refused to go

further. "If there is one thing above all others a successful man should know," their spokesman told Alexander, "it is *when to stop*." Furious but impotent, Alexander led his troops back to Persepolis in 324 B.C.E. Although Alexander was keenly disappointed, no mortal had ever before accomplished such a feat of conquest.

Binding Together an Empire

Alexander is remembered as a greater conqueror than ruler, but his plans for his reign, had he lived to complete them, might have won him equal fame. Unlike his Macedonian followers, who were interested mainly in booty and power, he recognized that only by merging local and Greek peoples and traditions could he forge a lasting empire. Even while founding cities on the Greek model throughout his empire, he carefully respected the local social and cultural traditions of the conquered peoples and encouraged his companions to marry the daughters of local elites. Whether his program of cultural and social amalgamation could have succeeded is a moot point. In 323 B.C.E., less than two years after his return from India, he died at Babylon at the age of 32.

The empire did not outlive the emperor. Vicious fighting soon broke out among his generals and his kin. Alexander's

▼ The Empire of Alexander the Great. Alexander's conquests united Eurasia from Greece to India into a cultural and, briefly, a political unity.

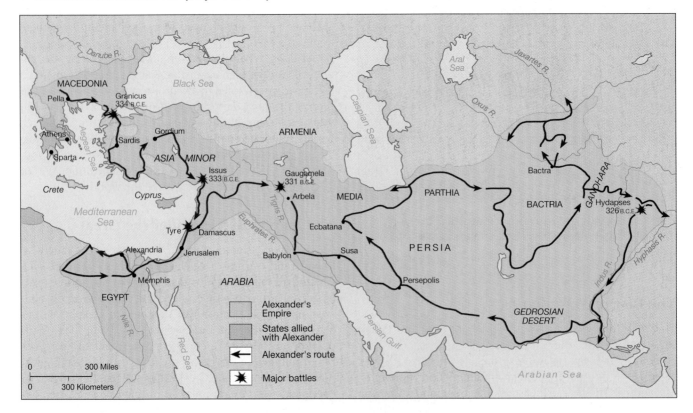

wife Roxane and son Alexander IV (323–317 B.C.E.) were killed, as were all other members of the royal family. The various units of the empire broke apart into separate kingdoms and autonomous cities in which each ruler attempted to continue the political and cultural tradition of Alexander in a smaller sphere. Alexander's empire became a shifting kaleidoscope of states, kingdoms, and cities, dominated by priest-kings, native princelings, and territorial rulers, all vying to enhance their positions while preserving a relative balance of power. By 275 B.C.E., three large kingdoms dominated Alexander's former domain. The most stable was Egypt, which Ptolemy I (323–285 B.C.E.), one of Alexander's closest followers, acquired on Alexander's death and which he and his descendants ruled until Cleopatra VII (51–30 B.C.E.) was defeated by the Roman Octavian in 31 B.C.E. In the east, the Macedonian general Seleucus (246–226 B.C.E.) captured Babylon in 312 B.C.E., and he and his descendants ruled a vast kingdom reaching from what is today western Turkey to Afghanistan. However, whittled away over time by its neighbors, the Seleucid kingdom gradually shrank to a small region of northern Syria before it fell to Rome in 64 B.C.E. After 50 years of conflict, Antigonus Gonatas (276–239 B.C.E.), the grandson of another of Alexander's commanders, secured Macedon and Greece. His Antigonid successors ruled the kingdom until it fell to the Romans in 168 B.C.E.

Alexander's conquests brought Greek traditions of urban organization to a wide area, replacing indigenous ruling elites with Hellenized dynasties. But Alexander's successors never integrated this Greek culture and the more ancient indigenous cultures of their subjects. This failure proved fatal for the Hellenistic kingdoms.

THE HELLENISTIC WORLD

Although vastly different in geography, language, and custom, the Hellenistic kingdoms (so called to distinguish them from the Hellenic civilization of the fifth and early fourth centuries B.C.E.) shared two common traditions. First, great portions of the Hellenistic world, from Asia Minor to Bactria and south to Egypt, had been united at various times by the Assyrian and Persian empires. During these periods they had absorbed much of Mesopotamian civilization, in particular the administrative traditions begun by the Assyrian Tiglath-pileser. Therefore, the Hellenistic kings ruled kingdoms that were already accustomed to centralized government and could rely on the already existing machinery of tax collection and administration to control the countryside. For the most part, however, these kings had little interest in the native populations of their kingdoms beyond the amount of wealth that they could extract from them. Hellenistic monarchs remained Greek and lavished their attentions on the newly created Greek cities, which absorbed vast amounts of the kingdom's wealth.

These cities and their particular form of Greek culture were the second unifying factor in the Hellenistic world. In the tradition of Alexander himself, the Ptolemys, Seleucids, and Antigonids cultivated Greek urban culture and recruited Greeks for their most important positions of responsibility. Alexander had founded over thirty-five cities during his conquests. The Seleucids established almost twice as many throughout their vast domain, even replacing the ancient city of Babylon with their capital, Seleucia, on the Tigris. In Egypt, the Ptolemys replaced the ancient capital of Memphis with the new city of Alexandria. These cities became the centers of political control, economic consumption, and cultural diffusion throughout the Hellenistic world.

Urban Life and Culture

The Hellenistic kingdoms lived in a perpetual state of warfare with one another. Kings needed Greek soldiers, merchants, and administrators and competed with their rivals in offering Greeks all the comforts of home. Hellenistic cities were Greek in physical organization, constitution, and language. They boasted an agora, or marketplace, temples to the Greek gods and goddesses, theaters, baths, and, most important, a *gymnasion*, or combination sports center and school for young men. Sophocles' tragedies played to enthusiastic audiences in an enormous Greek

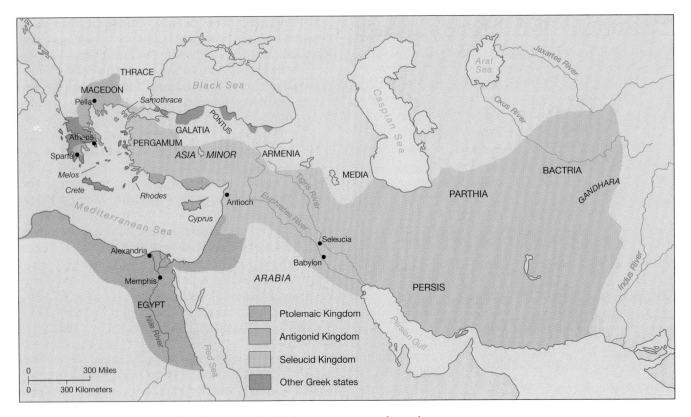

▲ The Hellenistic Kingdoms. Alexander's generals split his empire among themselves,
creating three major kingdoms sharing a common Greek culture.

theater in what is today Ai Khanoum on the Oxus River in Afghanistan, and the rites of Dionysus were celebrated in third-century B.C.E. Egypt with processions of satyrs, maenads, free wine for all, and a golden phallus 180 feet long. These Greeks were drawn from throughout the Greek-speaking world, and in time a universal Greek dialect, *koine*, became the common language of culture and business.

For all their Greek culture, Hellenistic cities differed fundamentally from Greek cities and colonies of the past. Not only were they far larger than any earlier Greek cities, but their government and culture were different from those of other cities or colonies. Colonies had been largely independent poleis. The Hellenistic cities were never politically sovereign. The regional kings maintained firm control over the cities, even while working to attract Greeks from the mainland and the islands to them. This policy weakened the political significance of Greek life and culture. While these cities were in theory democracies, kings firmly controlled city government, and participation in the city councils and magistracies became the affair of the wealthy.

At the same time, Hellenistic cities were much less closed than were the traditional poleis of the Hellenic world. In the new cities of the east, Greeks from all over were welcomed as soldiers and administrators regardless of their city of origin. By the second century B.C.E., Greeks no longer identified themselves by their city of origin but as "Hellenes," that is, Greeks. Native elites could also become Greeks by adopting Greek language and culture.

Women in Public Life

The great social and geographical mobility that was possible in the new cities extended to women as well as men. No longer important simply as transmitters of citizenship, women began to assume a greater role in the family, in the economy, and in public life. Marriage contracts, particularly in Ptolemaic Egypt, emphasized the theoretical equality of husband and wife. In one such contract, the husband and wife were enjoined to take no concubines or male or female lovers. The penalty for the husband was loss of the wife's dowry; for the wife the punishment was divorce. Since women could control their own property, many engaged in business, and some became wealthy and influential.

The most powerful women in Hellenistic society were queens, especially in Egypt, where the Ptolemys adopted the Egyptian tradition of royal marriages between brothers and sisters. Arsinoë II (ca. 316–270 B.C.E.) ruled as an equal with her brother-husband Ptolemy II (286–246 B.C.E.). She inaugurated a tradition of powerful female monarchs that ended only with Cleopatra VII, the last independent ruler of Egypt, who successfully manipulated the Roman generals Julius Caesar (100–44 B.C.E.) and Mark Antony (81–30 B.C.E.) to maintain Egyptian autonomy.

Just as monarchs competed with one another in creating Greek cities, they vied in making their cities centers of Greek culture. Socially ambitious and newly wealthy citizens supported poets, philosophers, and artists and endowed gymnasia and libraries.

Alexandria

The most vibrant center of this rich complex of social change and culture was Alexandria in Egypt. Alexander the Great had founded it after having himself crowned pharaoh in the ancient capital of Memphis in 331 B.C.E. After Alexander's death, Ptolemy I made it not only his political and commercial center but the cultural center for Greek art, science, and scholarship for the whole world. In time, the library at Alexandria housed half a million book-rolls, including all of the great classics of Greek literature. Generations of poet-scholars edited and commented on the classics, in the process inventing literary criticism and preserving much of what is known about classical authors.

Hellenistic Literature

Hellenistic writers were not simply book collectors or critics. They also developed new forms of literature, including the romance, which often recounted imaginary adventures of Alexander the Great, and the pastoral poem, which the Sicilian Theocritus (ca. 310–250 B.C.E.) developed out of popular shepherd songs. Callimachus (ca. 305–ca. 240 B.C.E.) was the master of the short, witty epigram. Throughout antiquity, he was considered a model, more frequently quoted than any other poet but Homer. His influence on Roman poets, including Virgil and Ovid, was essential. Alexandria was able to attract the greatest scholars and poets of the Hellenistic world, but its greatest playwright, Menander (342–292 B.C.E.) refused to leave his native Athens for the rewards of Ptolemaic patronage. Menander's gift was for comedy, but it was a new type of comedy quite removed from the politically biting and often vulgar humor of Aristophanes. Menander wrote with great poetic skill and artistry some 100 wildly complicated, good-natured plays. More than any other ancient poet or playwright, he draws a sympathetic image of ordinary men and women.

Art and Architecture

Political rivalry also encouraged architectural and artistic rivalry, as kings competed for the most magnificent Hellenistic cities. Temples, porticoes, and public buildings grew in size and ornamentation, and Hellenistic architects and planners combined these buildings in harmonious urban ensembles, sometimes using natural hills and slopes to create elegant terraced vistas.

Freestanding statues and magnificent murals and mosaics adorned the public squares, temples, and private homes of Hellenistic cities. While artists continued the traditions of the Hellenic age, they displayed more freedom in portraying tension and restlessness as well as individuality in the human form. Sculptors demonstrated their skill in the portrayal of drapery that was tightly folded or fell naturally across the human form. The Nike (Victory) from Samothrace (ca. 200 B.C.E.) and the Aphrodite from Melos, known more commonly as the Venus de Milo (ca. 120 B.C.E.), are supreme examples of Hellenistic sculptural achievement.

Hellenistic Philosophy

Philosophy, too, flourished in the Hellenistic world, but in directions different from those initiated by Plato and Aristotle, who were both deeply committed to political involvement in the free polis. Instead, Cynics, Epicureans, and Stoics turned inward, advocating types of morality that were less directly tied to the state and society. These philosophies appealed to the rootless Greeks of the Hellenistic east, who were no longer tied by bonds of religion or patriotism to any community.

Cynics. The Cynic tradition, established by Antisthenes (ca. 445–ca. 365 B.C.E.), a pupil of Socrates, and Diogenes of Sinope (d. ca. 320 B.C.E.), taught that excessive attachment to the things of this world was the source of evil and unhappiness. An individual achieves freedom by renouncing material things, society, and pleasures. The more one has, the more one is vulnerable to the whims of fortune. The Cynics' goal was to reduce their possessions, connections, and pleasures to the absolute minimum. "I would rather go mad than enjoy myself," Antisthenes said.

Epicureans. Like the Cynics, the Epicureans sought freedom, but from pain rather than from the conventions of ordinary life. Epicurus (341–270 B.C.E.) and his disciples have often been attacked for their emphasis on pleasure. "You need only possess perception and be made of flesh, and you will see that pleasure is good," Epicurus wrote. But this search for pleasure was not a call to sensual indulgence. Pleasure was to be pursued rationally, with awareness that today's pleasure could mean tomorrow's suffering. The real goal was to reduce desires to those that were simple and attainable. Therefore Epicureans urged retirement from politics, retreat from public competition, and concentration instead on friendship and private enjoyment. For Epicurus, reason properly applied illuminated how best to pursue pleasure. The

▲ The *Nike*, or Winged Victory, is an outstanding example of Hellenistic sculpture. It was found in fragments on the island of Samothrace in the Aegean Sea in 1863. The head and arms were never discovered. The statue is now in the Louvre in Paris.

traditional image of the Epicurean as an indulgent sensualist is a gross caricature. As Epicurus advised one follower, an Epicurean "revels in the pleasure of the body—on a diet of bread and water."

Stoics. The Stoics also followed nature, but rather than leading them to retire from public life, it led them to greater participation in it. Stoic virtue consisted in applying reason to one's life in such a way that one knowingly lived in conformity to nature. Worldly pleasures, like worldly pain, had no particular value. Both were to be accepted and endured. Stoics believed that just as the universe is a system in which stars and planets move according to fixed laws, so too was

human society ordered and unified. As the founder of Stoicism, Zeno (ca. 335–ca. 263 B.C.E.), expressed it, "All men should regard themselves as members of one city and people, having one life and order." According to the Stoics, every person had a role in the divinely ordered universe, and all roles were of equal value. True happiness consisted in freely accepting one's role, whatever it was, while unhappiness and evil resulted from attempting to reject one's place in the divine plan.

Cynicism, Epicureanism, and Stoicism all emphasized the importance of reason and the proper understanding of nature. Hellenistic understanding of nature was one area in which Greek thinkers were influenced by the ancient Near Eastern traditions brought to them through the conquests of Alexander.

Mathematics and Science

Particularly for mathematics, astronomy, and engineering, the Hellenistic period was a golden age. Ptolemaic Egypt became the center of mathematical studies. Euclid (ca. 300 B.C.E.), whose *Elements* was the fundamental textbook of geometry until the twentieth century, worked there, as did his student Apollonius of Perga (ca. 262–ca. 190 B.C.E.), whose work on conic sections is one of the greatest monuments of geometry. Both Apollonius and his teacher were as influential for their method as for their conclusions. Their treatises follow rigorous logical proofs of mathematical theorems, which established the form of mathematical reasoning to the present day. Archimedes of Syracuse (ca. 287–212 B.C.E.) corresponded with the Egyptian mathematicians and made additional contributions to geometry, such as the calculation of the approximate value of pi, as well as to mechanics, arithmetic, and engineering. Archimedes was famous for his practical application of engineering, particularly to warfare, and legends quickly grew up about his marvelous machines with which he helped Syracuse defend itself against Rome.

Mathematical Astronomy. Many mathematicians, such as Archimedes and Apollonius, were also mathematical astronomers, and the application of their mathematical skills to the exact data collected by earlier Babylonian and Egyptian empirical astronomers greatly increased the understanding of the heavens and the earth. Archimedes devised a means of measuring the diameter of the sun, and Eratosthenes of Cyrene (ca. 276–194 B.C.E.) calculated the circumference of the earth to within 200 miles. Aristarchus of Samos (ca. 270 B.C.E.) theorized that the sun and fixed stars were motionless and that the earth moves around the sun. His theory was rejected by contemporaries. Hipparchus of Nicea (ca. 146–127 B.C.E.) placed the earth at the center of the universe. With slight adjustments made 300 years later by Ptolemy of Alexandria, Hipparchus's earth-centric theory remained predominant until the sixteenth century.

Medicine.   Like astronomy, Hellenistic medicine combined theory and observation. In Alexandria, Herophilus of Chalcedon (ca. 270 B.C.E.) and Erasistratus of Ceos (ca. 260 B.C.E.) conducted important studies in human anatomy. The Ptolemaic kings provided them with condemned prisoners, whom they dissected alive; thus they were able to observe the functioning of the organs of the body. The terrible agonies inflicted on their experimental subjects were considered to be justified by the argument that there was no cruelty in causing pain to guilty men to seek remedies for the innocent.

Cultural Resistance.   For all of their vitality, the Hellenistic cities remained parasites on the local societies. No real efforts were made to merge the two and to develop a new civilization. Some ambitious members of the indigenous elites tried to adopt the customs of the Greeks; others plotted insurrection. The clearest example of these conflicting tensions was that of the Jewish community. Early in the second century B.C.E., a powerful Jewish faction, which included the High Priest of Yahweh, supported Hellenization. With the assistance of the Seleucid king, this faction set up a gymnasion in Jerusalem where Jewish youths and even priests began to study Greek and participate in Greek culture. Some even underwent painful surgery to reverse the effects of circumcision so that they could pass for Greeks in naked athletic contests. This rejection of tradition infuriated a large portion of the Jewish population. When the Seleucids finally attempted to introduce pagan cults into the temple in 167 B.C.E., open rebellion broke out and continued intermittently until the Jews gained independence in 141 B.C.E.

This violent opposition was repeated elsewhere from time to time, especially in Egypt and Persia, where, as in Judea, old traditions of religion and monarchy provided rallying points against the transplanted Greeks. In time the Hellenistic kingdoms' inability to bridge the gap between Greek and indigenous populations proved fatal. In the east, the non-Greek kingdom of Parthia replaced the Seleucids in much of the old Persian Empire. In the west, continuing hostility between kingdoms and within kingdoms prepared the way for their progressive absorption by the new power to the west: Rome.

Conclusion

IN THE FIFTH CENTURY B.C.E., the rugged slopes, fertile plains, and arid islands of the Greek world gave rise to characteristic forms of social, political, and cultural organization that have reappeared in varying forms wherever Western civilization has taken root. In Athens, which emerged from the ruins of the Persian invasion as the most powerful and dynamic state in the Hellenic world, the give-and-take of a direct democracy challenged men to raise fundamental questions about the relationship between individual and society, freedom and absolutism, gods and mortals. At the same time, this society of free males excluded the majority of its inhabitants—women, foreigners, and slaves—from participation in government and fought a long and ultimately futile war to hold together an exploitive empire.

The interminable wars among Greek states ultimately left the Greek world open to conquest by a powerful semi-Greek monarchy that went on to spread Athenian culture throughout the known world. Freed from the particularism of individual city-states, Hellenistic culture became a universal tradition emphasizing the individual rather than the community of family, tribe, or religious association. Yet this universal Hellenistic cultural tradition remained a thin veneer, hardly assimilated by the masses of the ancient world. Its proponents, except for Alexander the Great, never sought a real synthesis of Greek and barbarian tradition. Such a synthesis would begin only with the coming of Rome.

QUESTIONS FOR REVIEW

1. Why did Athens become Greece's greatest power in the wake of the Persian wars?
2. What social concerns and cultural accomplishments were expressed in Greek philosophy, drama, and art?
3. What does the Peloponnesian War reveal about weaknesses and divisions in Greek culture?
4. What factors explain Alexander the Great's success in expanding his empire?
5. What changes did Greek culture experience as it was carried eastward with the creation of the Hellenistic kingdoms?

DISCOVERING WESTERN CIVILIZATION ONLINE

You can obtain more information about classical and Hellenistic Greece at the websites listed below. See also the companion website that accompanies this text: www.ablongman.com/kishlansky, which contains an online study guide and additional resources.

War and Politics in the Fifth Century B.C.E.

www.livius.org/persia.html
Links to articles on many aspects of ancient Persian history.

www.pbs.org/empires/thegreeks/
A Public Broadcasting System site devoted to ancient Greece.

www.indiana.edu/~kglowack/athens/
An excellent site devoted to Athens.

www.multimania.com/sdelille/gdpa.html
A site developed by Sven Delille on the Peloponnesian War.

www.stoa.org/diotima/
A site devoted to women and gender in antiquity.

www.museum.upenn.edu/Greek_World/
A University of Pennsylvania Museum online exhibit devoted to ancient Greek society.

history.boisestate.edu/westciv/alexander/
Dr. Ellis L. Knox's page devoted to Alexander the Great.

The Hellenistic World

www.perseus.tufts.edu/GreekScience/Students/Jesse/CLOCK1A.html
A history of clocks in the Hellenistic world.

www.mcs.drexel.edu/~crorres/Archimedes/contents.html
A site devoted to Archimedes and Hellenistic science.

SUGGESTIONS FOR FURTHER READING

General Reading

John Boardman, Jasper Griffin, and Oswyn Murray, *Greece and the Hellenistic World* (New York: Oxford University Press, 1988). An excellent survey of Greek history by a series of experts.

Pierre Vidal-Naquet, *The Black Hunter: Forms of Thought and Forms of Society in the Greek World* (Baltimore: The Johns Hopkins University Press, 1998). A brilliant exploration of Greek society and politics approached through its margins, its contradictions, and its oppositions.

War and Politics in the Fifth Century B.C.E.

Sue Blundell, *Women in Ancient Greece* (Cambridge, Mass.: Harvard University Press, 1995). A good place to start for an understanding of women in classical Greece.

John Manuel Cook, *The Persian Empire* (New York: Schocken, 1983). The standard history of Persia from the perspective of history and archaeology.

M. I. Finley, *Democracy Ancient and Modern,* 2nd ed. (New Brunswick, N.J.: Rutgers University Press, 1985). A valuable essay on Athenian democracy by a leading historian of antiquity.

Charles W. Fornara and Loren J. Samons II, *Athens from Cleisthenes to Pericles* (Berkeley: University of California Press, 1991). Detailed survey of the development of Athenian democracy and empire.

Lisa Kallet, *Money and the Corrosion of Power in Thucydides: The Sicilian Expedition and Its Aftermath* (Berkeley: University of California Press, 2002). A focused study of corruption in a crucial aspect of the Peloponnesian War.

Helen King, *Hippocrates' Woman: Reading the Female Body in Ancient Greece* (New York: Routledge, 1998). A study of Greek medical theory concerning women and women's bodies.

W. K. Lacey, *The Family in Classical Greece* (Ithaca, N.Y.: Cornell University Press, 1984). An account of ordinary life in the Greek world.

G. E. M. de St. Croix, *The Origins of the Peloponnesian War* (Ithaca, N.Y.: Cornell University Press, 1972). An interpretation of the Peloponnesian War that is broader than the title indicates.

Athenian Culture in the Hellenic Age

J. Boardman, *Greek Art,* 3rd ed. (New York: Thames & Hudson, 1985). A handbook introduction by period.

W. Burkert, *Greek Religion* (Cambridge, Mass.: Harvard University Press, 1985). A general survey of the topic.

Simon Goldhill, *Reading Greek Tragedy* (New York: Cambridge University Press, 1986). A general introduction to Athenian tragedy.

W. K. C. Guthrie, *History of Greek Philosophy,* Vol. 3 (New York: Cambridge University Press, 1971). This volume covers the Sophists.

From City-States to Macedonian Empire, 404–323 B.C.E.

A. B. Bosworth, *Conquest and Empire* (New York: Cambridge University Press, 1988). A scholarly but readable account of Alexander the Great.

The Hellenistic World

Peter Green, *Alexander to Actium: The Historical Evolution of the Hellenistic Age* (Berkeley: University of California Press, 1990). Broad examination of the Hellenistic period.

Peter Green, ed., *Hellenistic History and Culture* (Berkeley: University of California Press, 1993). A stimulating series of articles and debates on Hellenistic civilization.

CHAPTER 4

EARLY ROME AND THE ROMAN REPUBLIC, 800–146 B.C.E.

THE VISUAL RECORD

ETERNAL ROME

FIVE MILES FROM ITS MOUTH, the Tiber River snakes in a lazy S around the first highlands that rise from the marshes of central Italy. These weathered cliffs, separated by tributary streams, look down on the river valley that broadens to over a mile and a half wide, the first and only natural ford for many miles. Only three promontories—the Capitoline, Palatine, and Aventine—are separate hills. The others, the Quirinal, Viminal, Caelian, Oppian, and Esquiline, are actually spurs of the distant Apennines. Gradually, the pastoral villages that had been founded on these hills spread down to the valleys between them, united, and grew to a city whose name was synonymous with empire for over 2,000 years.

Rome wasn't built in a day. The earliest Roman villages were found on the Palatine, from whose heights the picture seen here was taken and which remained throughout Rome's history the favored residential area. The Capitoline with its steep cliffs, which begin at the extreme left of the photograph, served as an acropolis, the religious center of the community. Here were found not only temples but also the state archives and the city mint beside the temple of Juno the Admonisher, *Juno Moneta* (hence our word *money*). The Capitol, so the Romans thought, was indestructible and became a symbol of the eternal city. As Romans established colonies across Italy and throughout the Mediterranean, the colonies too had their hill temples, their so-called capitols.

The area in the center of the photograph between the Palatine and Capitoline was originally a low, marshy burial ground. In the seventh century B.C.E., Etruscan kings drained the marshes, making it possible to pave the area and turn it into a public meeting place, or forum. The Forum became the heart of the city. Through it ran the Sacred Way, the road that cuts diagonally from left to right in the photograph. At the south end, to the right of the photograph, was the marketplace, which bustled with shops and businesses. To the north, where the domed church of Saints Luca and Magartina now stands, was the Comitium, the meeting place of the citizens' assembly. Just below it still stands the Curia, the meeting place of the Roman Senate, which survives because it was converted into a Christian church in the seventh century

C.E. Here too temples and monuments rose to meet religious and public needs.

As Rome grew from a simple city to an empire, the Forum reflected these changes. Simple Etruscan architecture gave way to the Greek style of building. Marble replaced brick and stucco. Near the Curia, the golden milestone marked the point from which all distances were measured and to which all roads of the empire led. By the time of Julius Caesar and Augustus, Rome had replaced its Forum, just as it had replaced its republican constitution. Caesar had begun and Augustus completed new forums, known collectively as the Forum of the Caesars, which lay beyond the trees at the upper right of the picture. Their successor Trajan (98–117 C.E.) would build a still greater one just beyond it. Still, for centuries of Romans and for the Western societies that succeeded them, the narrow space encompassing the Capitoline, the Palatine, and the Forum was the center of the city and the world.

LOOKING AHEAD

This chapter begins with a survey of the western Mediterranean and charts the gradual expansion of Roman power from but another Italian village at the site of this forum to the dominant power in the western Mediterranean. As its power expanded abroad, social and economic tensions grew at home, and from this tension arose a new culture, deeply indebted to Greek and Etruscan traditions but deeply original in its political forms and social organization.

THE WESTERN MEDITERRANEAN TO 509 B.C.E.

Civilization came late to the western Mediterranean, carried in the ships of Greeks and Phoenicians. While the great floodplain civilizations of Mesopotamia and Egypt and the Greek communities of the eastern Mediterranean were developing sophisticated systems of urban life and political organization, western Europe and Africa knew only the scattered villages of simple farmers and pastoralists. These populations, such as the Ligurians of northern Italy, were the descendants of Neolithic peoples only remotely touched by the developments in the East. The West was rich in metals, however, and an indigenous Bronze Age culture developed slowly between 1500 and 1000 B.C.E., spreading widely north of the Alps and south into Italy and Spain. By the twelfth century B.C.E., workshops in northern Italy were producing bronze spearheads, swords, and axes both for local use and for export to Crete, Naxos, Corfu, and Mycenae. At the same time, southern Italians were importing bronze knives and ornaments from Greece. In addition to finished weapons and other objects, the Eastern cities sought in Italy and Spain unworked bronze, silver bullion, tin, and iron.

Sometime around the year 1000 B.C.E., a new, distinctive iron-using civilization first appeared in northern Italy. These Villanovans, so called for a major archaeological discovery of this civilization at Villanova near Bologna, differed from earlier Italian peoples in their use of iron, in the practice of cremating their dead and burying their ashes in large urns, and in the greater size and complexity of their settlements.

No one knows whether the Villanovans were new arrivals in Italy or simply the descendants of previous inhabitants. However, around this same time, small groups of people did begin to infiltrate Italy from the east and the north, occupying the mountainous terrain of the Apennines and pushing the indigenous society westward. These new arrivals shared no common organization or identity, but all spoke related Indo-European languages that we call *Italic*, including Latin. These newcomers were warriors. Like the Dark Age Greeks, they soon developed the art of making iron weapons, which gave them a decided advantage over the older inhabitants of the peninsula. By 800 B.C.E. they were in firm control of the mountainous region of central Italy and threatened the coastal societies of the west and south.

Carthage: The Merchants of Baal

Also around 800 B.C.E., Phoenicians arrived in the West from the regions of Tyre, Sidon, and Byblos. They established a series of bases along the route to and from Spain on the coast and on the islands of Corsica, Sicily, Ibiza, and Motya in the Mediterranean and at Utica and Carthage on the coast of North Africa. Carthage was initially no more than a small anchorage for ships. Gradually, however, Carthage established itself as the center of an expanding Phoenician presence in the western Mediterranean.

The city was perfectly situated to profit from both the land and the sea. Its excellent double harbor made it an ideal port. Here ships could lie at rest, protected from storms as well as from enemies by a narrow 70-foot entrance to the sea that could be closed with iron chains. The city was equally protected on land, situated on a narrow isthmus and surrounded by massive walls. As long as Carthage controlled the sea, its commercial center was secure from any enemies.

By the middle of the sixth century B.C.E., Carthage was the center of a real empire. But in contrast with the Athenian empire of the following century, Carthage was much more successful at integrating other cities and peoples into its mercenary military and thus sharing the burden of warfare. This multiethnic empire endured for three centuries, proving far more stable than any of those created by the Greeks.

Although superficially similar to many Greek cities, the Punic (from *Puni* or *Poeni,* the Roman name for the Carthaginians) state differed profoundly in the relationship between citizen and state. Ordinary citizens had little involvement and, apparently, little interest in government, and officials consistently came from among the wealthy and powerful merchant aristocracy. According to Aristotle, however, the aristocracy treated the rest of the population generously, sharing with it profits of its commercial and imperial wealth. Thus the class pressures that created the Greek tyrants never emerged in Carthage.

The Gods of Carthage. The gods of Carthage were local variations of the Phoenician gods, especially Baal Hammon, equated with the ancient supreme god, Kronos, a cruel tyrant who devoured his children. Tanit, goddess of fertility, assumed an importance equal to that of Baal Hammon.

According to hostile Greek and Roman sources, all Carthaginian citizens were obligated to sacrifice their firstborn sons. The sacrifice of children constituted the most important and, to their Greek and barbarian neighbors, the most repulsive aspect of Punic culture. The basic reliability of these reports was dramatically confirmed in 1922, when archaeologists excavated the first of several sites containing urns filled with the remains of hundreds of children. In areas excavated from later periods, these bones are mixed with the bones of sacrificed animals.

Stable, prosperous, and devout, Carthage was the master of the western Mediterranean. But its dominion was not undisputed. From the sixth century B.C.E., the Punic empire felt the pressure of ambitious Greek cities that were eager to gain a share of the West's riches.

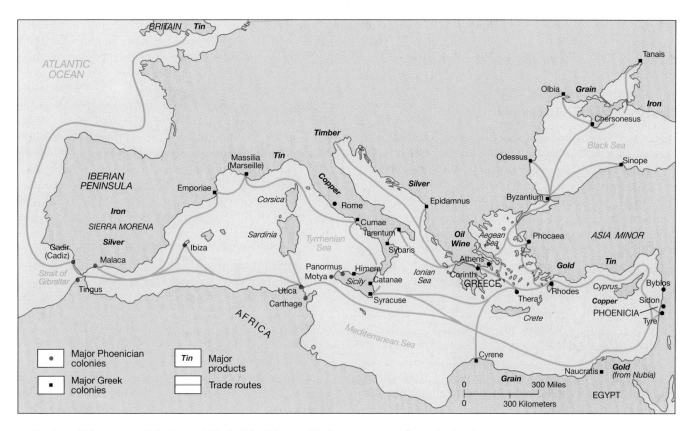

▲ Greek and Phoenician Colonies and Trade. The Western Mediterranean was first colonized by Phoenicians and Greeks who together controlled trade throughout the region.

The Western Greeks

The Greek arrival in the west was the result of a much more complex process than the trading policy of the Phoenicians. As we saw in Chapter 2, toward the end of the Dark Age, commerce, overpopulation, and civic tension sent Greek colonists out in all directions. In the eighth century B.C.E., Crete, Rhodes, Corinth, Argos, Chalcis, Eretria, and Naxos all established colonies in Sicily and southern Italy.

In the seventh century B.C.E., Syracuse became the greatest city of Sicily and one of the most prosperous cities of the Greek world. Greek colonies spread slowly up the boot of Italy, known as Greater Greece, in pursuit of trade and arable land. By the last quarter of the seventh century B.C.E., the autonomous Greek colonies began to encroach on the Carthaginian empire's sphere of influence. Around 631 B.C.E., Greeks from Thera founded a colony at Cyrene in North Africa. The Greek city of Phocaea in Asia Minor established a colony at Marseille around 600 B.C.E.

Both commercial rivalry and open warfare characterized the relationship between Greeks and Phoenicians in the western Mediterranean. In the course of the sixth century B.C.E., Greeks in Sicily attempted to expel the Phoenicians from the island. In the fifth century B.C.E., Syracuse, under its tyrant Gelon (ca. 540–478 B.C.E.), threatened both Punic and Greek cities on the island. In an attempt to defend its colonies, in 480 B.C.E. Carthage launched an enormous force to support Gelon's Greek enemies. The attack took place, probably not coincidentally, at the same moment that Xerxes invaded Greece. At the battle of Himera—fought, we are told, on the same day as the battle of Salamis—the Syracusans soundly defeated the Carthaginians.

Gelon's victory at Himera ushered in a period of prosperity and cultural achievement in Sicily. The tyrants of Syracuse, enriched with the spoils of victory, created a court whose magnificence, wealth, and generosity won admiration throughout the Greek world. This prosperity continued after the elimination of the tyranny in midcentury, and in 415 B.C.E., Syracuse was able to withstand Athens's attempt at conquest. (See Chapter 3, p. 53.)

A far more serious threat appeared in 410 B.C.E., when a new Carthaginian army arrived in Sicily seeking revenge. The Carthaginians rapidly captured and destroyed Himera, extending the boundaries of Punic Sicily. This invasion initiated a century of inconclusive conflict between Syracuse and Carthage.

Early on in their struggle with the Sicilian Greeks, the Carthaginians found allies in the third major civilization of the west. These were the Etruscans, who in the seventh century B.C.E. dominated the western part of central Italy, known as Etruria. The region today is Tuscany; its name derives from *Tusci*, the Roman term for this early people.

Italy's First Civilization

Etruscan civilization was the first great civilization to emerge in Italy. The Etruscans have long been regarded as a people whose origins, language, and customs are shrouded in mystery. However, in recent years, archaeologists have demonstrated that the Etruscans originated in western Italy with an indigenous cultural tradition that was apparently overwhelmed by the chaos of the twelfth-century B.C.E. crisis and the migration of Indo-Europeans from the north. This tradition shares much with Eastern civilizations, such as the importance of underworld gods, fertility cults, and the high status of women. And while the Etruscan language appears to be unrelated to any other language, bilingual inscriptions and careful analysis have enabled scholars to read many of the extant Etruscan texts.

Etruscan civilization coalesced slowly in Etruria over the course of the seventh century B.C.E. from diverse groups sharing a similar cultural and linguistic tradition. In the mid-sixth century B.C.E., in the face of Greek pressure from the south, 12 of these groups united in a religious and military confederation. Over the next 100 years the confederation expanded north into the Po Valley and south to Campania. Cities, each initially ruled by a king, were the centers of Etruscan civilization, and everywhere the Etruscans spread, they either improved on existing towns or founded new ones. Towns in the north included Bologna, Parma, Modena, Ravenna, Milan, and Mantua; in the south there were Nola, Nuceria, Pompeii, Sorrento, and Salerno. The Etruscan confederation remained loose and never developed into a centralized empire. Etruscan kings assumed power in conquered towns, but between the sixth and fifth centuries B.C.E., Etruscan kingship gave way to oligarchic governments, much as Greek monarchies had a bit earlier. In the place of kings, aristocratic assemblies selected magistrates, often paired together or combined into "colleges" to prevent individuals from seizing power. These republican institutions provided the foundation for later Roman republican government.

An Archaic Society. The remnants of an ancient civilization, the Etruscans retained throughout their history social and cultural traditions that had long since vanished elsewhere in the Mediterranean. Society was divided sharply into two classes, lords and servants. The lords' wealth was based on the rich agricultural regions of Etruria where grain grew in abundance and on the equally rich deposits of copper and iron. The vast majority of the population were actual slaves, working the lands and mines of the aristocracy.

The aristocrats were aggressive and imaginative landowners. They developed hydraulic systems for draining marshes, produced a wine that was famous throughout the Mediterranean, and put their slaves to work in mines and in smelting. Still, they were largely absentee landlords, spending much of their time in the towns that characterized Etruscan civilization. These cities, with their massive walls, enclosed populations of as many as 20,000. Although little remains of their largely wooden houses and other buildings, their tombs were furnished with the wares of everyday life, including benches, beds, ornaments, utensils, and vessels and platters of Etruscan and Corinthian manufacture, providing a vivid image of how the Etruscans lived.

The most striking aspect of Etruscan life to Greek contemporaries and to later Romans was the elevated status of Etruscan women. As in the much earlier Minoan civilization, women played an active, public role in society. Unlike honorable Greek women, Etruscan women took part in banquets, attended and even occasionally presided over dances, concerts, and sporting events, and were active in political life. Greeks such as Aristotle regarded the public behavior of Etruscan women as lewd. When a king died, his successor had to be designated and consecrated by the Etruscan queen to establish his legitimacy. To later Romans, this practice was shocking.

Etruscan Dominance. While the Etruscans were consolidating their hegemony in western Italy, they were at the same time establishing their maritime power. From the seventh to the fifth centuries B.C.E., Etruscans controlled the Italian coast of the Tyrrhenian Sea as well as Sardinia, from which their ships could reach the coast of what is today France and Spain. Attempts to extend farther south into Greek southern Italy and toward the Greek colonies on the modern French coast brought the Etruscans and the Greeks into inevitable conflict. Etruscan cities fought sporadic sea battles against Greek cities in the waters of Sicily as well as off the coasts of Corsica and Etruria.

Common hostility toward the Greeks as well as complementary economic interests soon brought the Etruscans into alliances with Carthage. Toward the end of the sixth century B.C.E., Etruscan cities including Rome signed a series of pacts with Carthage that created military alliances against the Phocaeans and Syracuse. Etruscan fleets were victorious over the Phocaeans, driving them from Corsica, but they were no match for Syracuse. In 474 B.C.E., shortly after the battle of Himera, the Syracusan fleet destroyed that of the Etruscans off Cumae.

Cumae marked the beginning of Etruscan decline. Through the fifth century B.C.E., Etruscan cities lost control of the sea to the Greeks. Around the same time, Celts from north of the Alps invaded and conquered the Po Valley.

And to the south, Etruscans saw their inland territories progressively slipping into the hands of their former subjects, the Romans, who had begun to acquire the commercial, political, and military expertise that would drive their long rise to dominance.

FROM CITY TO EMPIRE, 509–146 B.C.E.

What manner of people were these Romans who, from obscure origins, came to rule an empire? Their own answer would have been simple: They were farmers and soldiers, simple people accustomed to simple, straightforward actions. Throughout their long history, Romans liked to refer to the clear-cut models provided by their semilegendary predecessors: Cincinnatus, the farmer, called away to the supreme office of dictator in time of danger, then returning to his plow; Horatius Cocles, the valiant warrior who held back an Etruscan army on the Tiber bridge until it could be demolished and then, despite his wounds, swam across the river to safety; Lucretia, the wife who chose death after dishonor. These were myths, but they were important myths to Romans, who preferred concrete models to abstract principles.

Later Romans liked to imagine the history of their city as one predestined by the gods for greatness. Some liked to trace the origins of Rome to Romulus and Remus, twin sons of the war god Mars and a Latin princess. According to legend, the children, after having been thrown into the Tiber River, were raised by a she-wolf. Other Romans, having absorbed the Homeric traditions of Greece, taught that the founder of Rome was Aeneas, son of the goddess of love, Aphrodite, and the Trojan Anchises, who had wandered west after the fall of Troy. All agreed that Rome had been ruled by kings, who underwent a steady decline in ability and morals until the last, Tarquin the Proud, was expelled by outraged Latins. These legends tell much about the attitudes and values of later Romans. They tell nothing about the actual origins of the city or its rise to greatness.

Latin Rome

Civilization in Italy meant Etruria to the north and Greater Greece to the south. In between lay Latium, a marshy region punctuated by hills on which a sparse population could find protection from disease and enemies. This population was an amalgam of aboriginal Ligurians and the more recently arrived Latins and Sabines, who lived a pastoral life in small, scattered villages.

The Alban Hills south of the Tiber were a center of Latin population. Sometime in the eighth century B.C.E., roughly 40 Latin villages formed a loose confederation, the Alban League, for military and religious purposes. Not long afterward, in the face of an expanding Etruscan

confederation from the north and Sabine penetration from the east, the Albans established a village on the steep Palatine hill to the north. The Palatine was one of several hills overlooking a natural ford on the Tiber. This Alban village, called Roma Quadrata, was soon joined by other Latin and Sabine settlements on nearby hills. By the end of the eighth century B.C.E., seven Latin villages along the route from the Tiber to Alba had formed a league for mutual defense and shared religious cults.

Early Roman society was composed of households; clans, or *gentes;* and village councils, or *curiae* (sing. *curia*). The male head of each household, the *paterfamilias,* had the power of life and death over its members and was responsible for the proper worship of the spirits of the family's ancestors, on whom continued prosperity depended. Within some villages these families were grouped into gentes, which claimed descent from a semimythical ancestor.

▼ On the Etruscan sarcophagus of Larthia Scianti, a matron reclines as at a banquet. Much of our knowledge of the first Italian civilization comes from the elaborate paintings and statuary found in Etruscan cemeteries.

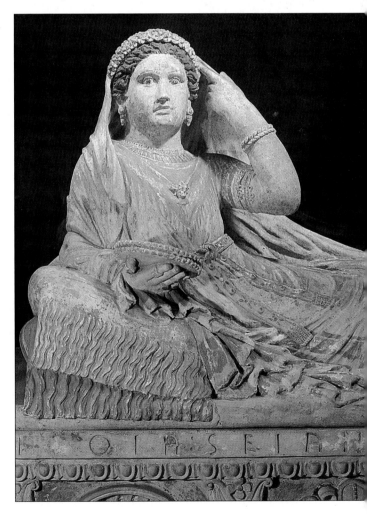

Male members of village families formed councils, which were essentially religious organizations but also provided a forum for public discussion. These curiae tended to be dominated by gentes, but all males could participate, including those who belonged to the *plebians* or *plebs,* that is, families that were not organized into gentes. Later, the leaders of the gentes called themselves *patricians* ("descendants of fathers") and claimed superiority to the plebs, or common people.

Important plebeian and patrician families increased their power through a system of clientage, which remained a fundamental aspect of social and political organization throughout Roman history. Clients were free men who depended on the protection of a more powerful individual or family and who owed various services, including political support, in return for this protection.

Villages themselves grouped together for military and voting purposes into ethnic *tribus,* or tribes, each composed of a number of curiae. Each curia supplied a contingent of infantry, and each tribe cooperated to supply a unit of horsemen to the Roman army.

Assemblies of all members of the curiae expressed approval of major decisions, especially declaration of war and the selection of new kings, and thus played a real if limited political role. More powerful although less formal was the role of the Senate (assembly of elders), which was composed of heads of families. The Senate's power derived from the individual importance of its members and from its role in selecting a candidate for king, who was then presented to the assembly of the curiae for approval.

Kings served as religious leaders, the primary means of communication between gods and humans. Through the early Latin period, royal power remained fundamentally religious and limited by the Senate, curiae, gentes, and families.

The seven villages that made up primitive Rome developed independently of their Etruscan and Greek neighbors. Initially, Romans lived in thatched huts, tended their flocks on the hillsides, and maintained their separate village identities. By the seventh century B.C.E., they had begun fortifications and other structures indicating the beginnings of a dynamic civic life. This independent course of development changed in the middle of the seventh century B.C.E., when the Etruscans overwhelmed Latium and absorbed it into their civilization. Under its Etruscan kings, Rome first entered civilization.

Etruscan Rome

The Etruscans introduced in Latium, especially in Rome, their political, religious, and economic traditions. Etruscan city organization partially replaced Latin tribal structures. Etruscan kings and magistrates ruled Latin towns, increasing the power of traditional Latin kingship. The kings not only were religious leaders, but also led the army, served as judges, and held supreme political power.

As Latium became an integral part of the Etruscan world, the Tiber became an important commercial route. For the first time, Rome began to enter the wider orbit of Mediterranean civilization. The town's population swelled with the arrival of merchants and artisans.

Urban Growth.   As Rome's importance grew, so did its size. Etruscan engineers drained the marshes into a great canal flowing to the Tiber, thus opening the lowlands between the hills to settlement. This in turn allowed them to create and pave the Forum. The Etruscans constructed a series of vast fortifications encircling the town. Under Etruscan influence, the fortified Capitoline hill, which served much like a Greek acropolis, became the cult center with the erection of the temple to Jupiter, the supreme god; Juno, his consort; and Minerva, an Etruscan goddess of craftwork who was similar to Athena. In its architecture, religion, commerce, and culture, Latin Rome was deeply indebted to its Etruscan conquerors.

As important as the physical and cultural changes brought by the Etruscans was their reorganization of the society. As in Greece, this restructuring was tied to changes in the military. The Etruscans had learned from the Greeks the importance of hoplite tactics, and King Servius Tullius (578–534 B.C.E.) introduced this system of warfare into Rome. This led to the abolition of the earlier curia-based military and political system in favor of one based only on property holding. Weakening the traditional Latin social units, the king divided Roman society into two groups: property owners and others. Landowners who were wealthy enough to provide armed military service were organized into five classes and ranked according to the quality of their arms and hence their wealth. Each class was further divided into military units called *centuries*. Members of these centuries constituted the centuriate assembly, which replaced the older curial assemblies for such vital decisions as the election of magistrates and the declaration of war.

The constitution and operation of this centuriate assembly ensured control by the most conservative forces within the society. Small centuries of wealthy well-armed cavalrymen and fully armed warriors outnumbered the more modestly equipped but more numerous centuries. Likewise, men over the age of 47, although in a minority, controlled over half the centuries in each class. Since votes were counted not by individuals but by centuries, this ensured within the assembly the domination of the rich over the poor, the older over the younger. The remainder of the society was the *infra classem* (literally "under class"), who owned no property and were thus excluded from military and political activity.

With this military and political reorganization came a reconstruction of the tribal system. Servius Tullius abolished the old tribal organization in favor of geographically organized tribes into which newcomers could easily be incorporated. Henceforth, while the family remained powerful, involvement in public life was based on property and geography. Latins, Sabines, Ligurians, and Etruscans could all be active citizens of the growing city.

Class Divisions. While the old tribal units and curiae declined, divisions between the patricians and the plebeians grew more distinct. During the monarchy, the patricians came to compose an upper stratum of wealthy nobles. They forbade marriage outside their own circle, forming a closed, self-perpetuating group that monopolized the Senate, religious rites, and magisterial offices. Although partially protected by the kings, the plebeians, whether rich or poor, were pressed into a second-class status and denied access to political power.

In less than two centuries the Etruscans transformed Rome from a small collection of wood and reed villages into a prosperous, unified urban center that played an important role in the economic and political life of central Italy. They laid the foundations of a free citizenry, incorporating Greek models of military and social organization. The transformations brought about by the Etruscan kings became an enduring part of Rome. The Etruscans themselves did not. Just as the hoplite revolution in Greece saw the end of most Hellenic monarchies, around the traditionally reported date of 509 B.C.E. the Roman patricians expelled the last Etruscan king, Tarquin the Proud, and established a republic.

Rome and Italy

Just as in Rome, monarchy was giving way to oligarchic republics across Etruria in the sixth century B.C.E. Rome was hardly exceptional. However, the establishment of the Roman republic coincided roughly with the beginning of the Etruscan decline, allowing Rome to assert itself and to develop its Latin and Etruscan traditions in unique ways.

The Early Republic. The patrician oligarchy had engineered the end of the monarchy, and patricians dominated the offices and institutions of the new republic at the expense of the plebs, who, in losing the king, lost their only defender. Governmental institutions of the early republic developed within this context of patrician supremacy.

Characteristic of republican institutions was that at every level, power was shared by two or more equals who were elected for fixed terms. This practice of shared power was intended to ensure that magistrates would consult with each other before making decisions and that no individual could achieve supreme power at any level. Replacing the king were the two *consuls*, each elected by the assembly for a one-year term. Initially, only the consuls held the *imperium*, the supreme power to command, to execute the law, and to impose the death penalty. Only in

moments of grave crisis might a consul, with the approval of the Senate, name a single *dictator* with extraordinary absolute power for a very brief period, never more than six months. In time, other magistracies developed to perform specialized functions. *Praetors*, who in time also exercised the imperium, administered justice and defended the city in the absence of the consuls. *Quaestors* controlled finances. *Censors* assigned individuals their places in society, determined the amount of their taxes, filled vacancies in the Senate, and negotiated contracts for public construction projects. A variety of military commanders directed wars against neighboring cities and peoples under the imperium of the consuls. In all their actions these officeholders consulted with each other and with the Senate, which was composed of roughly 300 powerful former magistrates. The centuriate assembly functioned as the legislative organ of the state, but it continued to be dominated by the oldest and wealthiest members of society.

Patricians, Plebs, and Public Law. During the early republic, wealthy patricians, aided by their clients, monopolized the Senate and the magistracies. Successful magistrates rose through a series of increasingly important offices, which came to be known as the *cursus honorum,* to the position of consul. Censors selected from among former magistrates in appointing new senators, thus ensuring that the Senate would be dominated by the patrician elite. Patricians also controlled the priesthoods, positions which they held for life. With political and religious power came economic power. The poorer plebs in particular found themselves sinking into debt to wealthy patricians, losing their property, and with it the basis for military service and political participation. In the courtroom, in the temple, in the assembly, and in the marketplace, plebeians found themselves subjected to the whims of an elite from which they were excluded.

The plebs began to organize in response to patrician control. On several occasions in the first half of the fifth century B.C.E., the whole plebeian order withdrew a short distance from the city, refusing to return or to serve in the military until conflicts with the patricians were resolved. In time, the plebs created their own assembly, the Council of the Plebs, which enacted laws that were binding on all plebeians. This council founded its own temples and elected magistrates called *tribunes,* whose persons were declared sacred to the gods. The tribunes protected the plebs from arbitrary patrician power. Anyone who harmed the tribunes, whether patrician or plebeian, could be killed by the plebs without trial. With their own assembly, magistracies, and religious cults, the plebeians were well on the way to creating a separate republic. This conflict between the plebeians and the patricians, known as the Struggle of Orders, threatened to tear Roman society apart just as pressure from hostile neighbors placed Rome on the defensive.

Political Expansion. Roman preeminence in Latium had ended with the expulsion of the last king. The Etruscan town of Veii just north of the Tiber began periodic attacks against Rome. To the south, the Volscians had begun to expand northward into the Litis and Trerus valleys. This military pressure from the outside forced the patricians to seek a compromise with the plebeians. One of the first victories won by the plebs around 450 B.C.E. was the codification of basic Roman law, the Law of the Twelve Tables, which recognized the basic rights of all free citizens. The new law was posted publicly so that all could have access to it. Around the same time, the state began to absorb the plebeian political and religious organizations intact. Gradually, priesthoods, magistracies, and thus the Senate were opened to plebeians. The consulship was the last prize finally won by the plebs in 367 B.C.E. In 287 B.C.E., as the result of a final secession of the plebs, the decisions of the plebeian assembly became binding on all citizens, patrician and plebeian alike.

Bitter differences at home did not prevent patricians and plebs from presenting a united front against their enemies abroad. By the beginning of the fourth century B.C.E., the united patrician-plebeian state was expanding its rule both northward and southward. Roman legions, commanded by patricians but formed of the whole spectrum of property-owning Romans, reestablished Roman preeminence in Latium and then began a series of wars that brought most of Italy under Roman control. In 396 B.C.E., Roman forces captured and destroyed Veii and shortly afterward conquered the rest of southern Etruria. In the south, Roman and Latin forces turned back the Volscians. In 390 B.C.E., Rome suffered a temporary setback at the hands of the Gauls, or Celts, of northern Italy, who raided southward and sacked much of the city before being bought off with a large tribute payment. Even this event had a silver lining. The damage to Rome was short lived, but the Gauls had dealt a deathblow to the Etruscan cities of the north, clearing the way for later Roman conquest. By 295 B.C.E., Rome had secured its rule as far north as the Po Valley. In the south, Roman infantry and persistence proved the equal of professional Greek armies. Rome won a war of attrition against a series of Hellenistic commanders, the last of whom was the Greek king Pyrrhus of Epirus (319–272 B.C.E.). Pyrrhus, regarded as the greatest tactician of his day, won a number of victories that proved more costly to him than to his Roman opponents. In 275 B.C.E., after losing two-thirds of his troops in these "Pyrrhic victories," he withdrew to Sicily. By 265 B.C.E., Rome had absorbed the Hellenistic cities of the south.

Roman conquest benefited patrician and plebeian alike. While the patricians acquired wealth and power, the plebeians received a prize of equal value: land. After the capture of Veii, for example, the poor of Rome received shares of the conquered land. Since landowning was a prerequisite for military service, this distribution created still more peasant soldiers for further expeditions. Still, while the constant supply of new land did much to diffuse the tensions between orders, it did not actually resolve them. Into the late third century B.C.E., debt and landlessness remained major problems, creating tensions in Roman society. Probably not more than half of the citizen population owned land by 200 B.C.E.

Incorporating the Conquered. The Roman manner of treating conquered populations, radically different from anything seen before, also contributed to Rome's success. In war, no one could match the Roman legions for ruthless, thorough destruction. Yet no conquerors had ever shown themselves so generous in victory. After Rome crushed the Latin revolt of 338 B.C.E., virtually all of the Latins were incorporated into the Roman citizenry. Later colonies founded outside of Latium were given the same status as Latin cities. Other, more distant conquered peoples were considered allies and were required to provide troops but no tribute to Rome. In time, they too might become citizens.

The implications of these measures were revolutionary. By extending citizenship to conquered neighbors and by offering the future possibility to allies, Rome tied their fate to its own. Rather than potentially subversive subjects, conquered populations became strong supporters. Thus, in contrast to the Hellenistic cities of the east, where Greeks jealously guarded their status from the indigenous population, Rome's colonies acted as magnets, drawing local populations into the Roman cultural and political orbit. Greeks were scandalized by the Roman tradition of giving citizenship even to freed slaves. By the end of the fourth century B.C.E., some of the sons of these freedmen were finding a place in the Senate. Finally, in all of its wars of conquest, Rome claimed a moral mandate. Romans went to great lengths to demonstrate that theirs were just wars, basing their claims on alleged acts of aggression by their enemies, on the appeal to Rome by its allies, and, increasingly, by presenting themselves as the preservers and defenders of Greek traditions of freedom. Both these political and propagandistic measures proved successful. Between 265 and 91 B.C.E. few serious revolts shook the peace and security of Italy south of the Po.

Benevolent treatment of the conquered spurred further conquest. Since subject cities and peoples did not pay tribute, the only way for Rome to benefit from its conquests or to exercise its authority was to demand and use troops. By 264 B.C.E., all of Italy was united under Roman hegemony. Roman expansion finally brought Rome into conflict with the great Mediterranean power of the west: Carthage.

Rome and the Mediterranean

Since its earliest days, Rome had allied itself with Carthage against the Greek cities of Italy. The zones of interest of the two cities had been quite separate. Carthage was a sea empire, whereas Rome was a land-based power without a navy. The Greeks, aspiring to power on land and sea, posed a threat to both Rome and Carthage. However, once Rome had conquered the Greek cities to the south, it became enmeshed in the affairs of neighboring Sicily, a region with well-established Carthaginian interests. There, in 265 B.C.E., a group of Italian mercenary pirates in Messina, threatened by Syracuse, requested Roman assistance. The Senate refused, but the plebeian assembly, eager for booty, exercised its newly won right to legislate for the republic and accepted. Shortly afterward, the Romans invaded Sicily, and Syracuse turned to its old enemy, Carthage, for assistance. The First Punic War had begun.

The First Punic War.   This war, which lasted from 265 to 241 B.C.E., was a costly, brutal, and drawn-out affair that Rome won by dint of persistence and methodical calculation rather than strategic brilliance. Rome invaded and concluded an alliance with Syracuse in 263 B.C.E. The war rapidly became a sea war. Rome had little previous naval experience but quickly learned the rules of the game and then rewrote them to its own advantage. Taking a wrecked Carthaginian ship as a model, Roman builders constructed twenty fast ships propelled by roughly 200 oarsmen to ram and sink opposing ships. Rome also built 100 larger ships with crews of 300, manned by Roman allies. Unaccustomed to fighting at sea, Roman engineers turned sea battles into land battles by placing on their ships heavy gangplanks that could be dropped onto enemy ships. The gangplanks were equipped with a heavy iron spike to secure them to the enemy's deck. This allowed a contingent of legionnaires to march onto the enemy ship and fight as though on dry land.

With these innovations the Romans won impressive initial victories but still could not deliver a knockout blow in either Sicily or North Africa for over 20 years. Finally, in 241 B.C.E., Rome forced the Carthaginian commander, Hamilcar Barca (ca. 270–229 B.C.E.), to surrender simply because the Romans could afford to build one more fleet than he. Carthage paid a huge indemnity and abandoned Sicily. Syracuse and Messina became allies of Rome. In a break with tradition, Rome obligated the rest of Sicily to pay a true tribute in the form of a tithe (one-tenth) of their crops. Shortly after that, Rome helped itself to Sardinia as well, from which it again demanded tribute, not simply troops. Rome had established an empire.

During the next two decades, Roman legions defeated the Ligurians on the northwest coast, the Celtic Gauls south of the Alps, and the Illyrians along the Adriatic coast. At the same time, Carthage fought a bitter battle against its own mercenary armies, which it had been unable to pay off after its defeat. Carthage then began the systematic creation of an empire in Spain. Trade between Carthage and Rome reached the highest level in history, but trade did not create friendship—only a wary peace. On both sides, powerful leaders saw the treaty of 241 B.C.E. as just a pause in a fight to the death. Hamilcar Barca

▲ The Punic Wars. Rome's three wars against Carthage resulted in both its dominance of the western Mediterranean and the start of an empire outside of Italy.

had his nine-year-old son Hannibal swear to be Rome's eternal enemy. Fearful and greedy Romans insisted that Carthage had to be destroyed for the security of Rome. They were particularly disturbed by the growth of Carthage's Spanish empire, even though Hamilcar Barca assured the Senate that he was simply trying to raise funds to pay off Carthage's indemnity.

Securing Western Hegemony.   After Hamilcar's death, Carthaginian successes in Spain, led by Hamilcar's son-in-law Hasdrubal (d. 221 B.C.E.) and his son Hannibal (247–183 B.C.E.), finally provoked Rome to war in 218 B.C.E. As soon as this Second Punic War had begun, Hannibal began an epic march north out of Spain, along the Mediterranean coast, and across the Alps. In spite of great hardships he was able to transport over 23,000 troops and approximately 18 war elephants into the plains of northern Italy.

Hannibal's brilliant generalship brought victory after victory to the Carthaginian forces. In the first engagement, on the Trebia River in the Po Valley, the Romans lost 20,000 men, two-thirds of their army. Carthaginian success encouraged the Gauls to join the fight against the Romans. Initially, Italian, Etruscan, and Greek allies remained loyal, but after Rome's catastrophic defeats at

Lake Trasimene in Etruria in 217 B.C.E. and especially at Cannae in 216 B.C.E., a number of Italian colonies and allies, namely the cities of Capua and Syracuse, went over to the enemy. In the east, Philip V of Macedon (238–179 B.C.E.) made a treaty with Carthage in the hope of taking Illyria (today the coast of Croatia) from a defeated Rome.

As commanders chosen by the patrician-dominated Senate failed to stop the enemy, the Roman plebs became increasingly dissatisfied with the way the oligarchy was conducting the war. In 217 B.C.E., following the battle of Lake Trasimene, the Senate named the capable general Quintus Fabius Maximus (d. ca. 203 B.C.E.) dictator. He used delaying tactics successfully to slow the Carthaginians. The popular assembly, impatient for a decisive victory, elected a second dictator, thus effectively canceling the position of Quintus Fabius Maximus. The next year, popular pressure forced the election of Gaius Terentius Varro as consul. Varro quickly led the army to the greatest defeat in Roman history at Cannae. There, Hannibal surrounded and annihilated Varro's numerically superior army.

Three things, however, saved the Roman state. First, while some important allies and colonies defected, the majority held firm. Rome's traditions of sharing the fruits of victory with its allies, extending the rights of Roman citizenship, and protecting central and southern Italy against its enemies proved stronger than the appeals of Hannibal. Although he was victorious time and again, without local support Hannibal could not hold the terrain and cities he won. New allies such as Syracuse, which fell in 212 B.C.E., were forcibly returned to the Roman camp. Fabius resumed his delaying tactics, and gradually Hannibal's victories slipped from his hands.

The second reason for Rome's survival was the tremendous social solidarity that all classes and factions of its population showed during these desperate years. In spite of the internal tensions between patricians and plebeians, their ultimate dedication to Rome never faltered. Much of this loyalty was due to the Roman system of strong family and patronage ties. Kinsmen and clients answered the call of their patriarchs and patrons to bounce back repeatedly from defeat. Roman farmer-soldiers stood firm.

The third reason for Rome's ultimate success was Publius Cornelius Scipio (236–184 B.C.E.), also known as Scipio the Elder, a commander who was able to force Hannibal from Italy. Scipio, who earned the title Africanus for his victory, accomplished this not by attacking Hannibal directly, but by taking the war home to the enemy, first in Spain and then in Africa. In 210 B.C.E., Scipio arrived in Spain and rapidly captured the city of Cartagena (New Carthage). Within four years he destroyed Punic power in Spain. Riding the crest of popular enthusiasm at home, he raised a new army and in 204 B.C.E. sailed for Africa. His victories there drew Hannibal home, where at Zama in 202 B.C.E. the Roman commander destroyed the Carthaginian army. Zama put an end to both the Second Punic War and Carthaginian political power. Saddled with a huge indemnity and forced to abandon all of its territories and colonies to Rome, Carthage was reduced to a small portion of the North African coast. It had become in effect a Roman subject.

The Final Destruction. Still, this humiliating defeat was not enough for Rome. While some Roman senators favored allowing Carthage to survive as a means of keeping the Roman plebs under senatorial control, others demanded destruction. Chief among them was the censor Marcus Porcius Cato, known as Cato the Elder (234–149 B.C.E.), who ended every speech with "Carthage must be destroyed." Ultimately, trumped-up reasons were found to renew the war in 149 B.C.E. In contrast to the desperate, hard-fought campaigns of the Second Punic War, the Third was an unevenly matched slaughter. In 146 B.C.E., Scipio Aemilianus (184–129 B.C.E.), or Scipio the Younger, the adopted grandson of Scipio the Elder, overwhelmed Carthage and sold its few survivors into slavery. As a symbolic act of final destruction, he then had the site razed, plowed, and cursed. Carthage's fertile hinterland became the property of wealthy Roman senators.

Expansion into the Hellenistic East. In the same year that Carthage was destroyed, Roman armies destroyed Corinth, a second great center of Mediterranean commerce. This victory marked the culmination of Roman imperialist expansion eastward into the Greek and Hellenistic world, which had begun with the conquest of Illyria. This expansion was not simply the result of Roman imperialist ambitions. The Hellenistic states, in their constant warring and bickering, had drawn Rome into their conflicts against their neighbors. Greek states asked the Roman Senate to arbitrate their disputes. Pergamum requested military assistance against Macedonia. Appealing to Rome's claims as "liberator," cities pressed the Senate to preserve their freedom in the face of aggressive expansion by their more powerful neighbors. In a series of intermittent, uncoordinated, and sporadic engagements, Rome did intervene, although its real focus was on its life-and-death struggle with Carthage.

Roman intentions may not have been conquest, but Roman intervention upset the balance of power in the Hellenistic world. The price of Roman arbitration, intervention, and protection was loss of independence. Gradually, the Roman shadow fell over the eastern Mediterranean.

The treaty that Philip V of Macedon concluded with Carthage during the Second Punic War provided an initial excuse for war, one that was seized on more eagerly by the plebeian assembly than by the Senate. Shortly after its victory at Zama, Rome provoked Philip to war and then easily

POLYBIUS DESCRIBES THE SACK OF NEW CARTHAGE

In the following selection, the Greek historian Polybius, who was a close friend of the adopted grandson of Scipio Africanus, describes the Roman capture of New Carthage (Carthago Nova) in Spain in 210 B.C.E. during the Second Punic War. Before a siege, Romans offered their enemies generous terms, but once the siege had begun, they offered none. The passage shows the combination of brutality and thoroughness with which the Romans liquidated those who defied them.

FOCUS QUESTIONS

Why did Scipio order his troops to kill everyone they found on entering the city? What incentives did Roman citizens have to fight in the Punic Wars?

SCIPIO, WHEN HE JUDGED THAT a large enough number of troops had entered the town, let loose the majority of them against the inhabitants, according to the Roman custom; their orders were to exterminate every form of life they encountered, sparing none, but not to start pillaging until the word was given to do so. This practice is adopted to inspire terror, and so when cities are taken by the Romans you often see not only the corpses of human beings but dogs cut in half and the dismembered limbs of other animals, and on this occasion the carnage was especially frightful because of the large size of the population.

Scipio himself with about 1000 men pressed on toward the citadel. Here [the Carthaginian commander] Margo at first put up some resistance, but as soon as he knew for certain that the city had been captured he sent a message to plead for his safety, and handed over the citadel. Once this had happened the signal was given to stop the slaughter and the troops then began to pillage the city. When darkness fell . . . Scipio . . . recalled the rest of his troops from the private houses of the city and ordered them through the military tribunes to collect all the spoils in the marketplace, each maniple bringing its own share. . . . Next day all the booty . . . was collected in the marketplace, where the military tribunes divided it among their respective legions, according to the Roman custom. . . . All those who have been detailed to collect the plunder then bring it back, each man to his own legion, and after it has been sold, the tribunes distribute the proceeds equally among all.

From Polybius, The Rise of the Roman Empire.

---

defeated him in 197 B.C.E., proclaiming the freedom of the Greek cities and withdrawing from Greece. In 189 B.C.E., the Seleucid Antiochus III (223–187 B.C.E.) of Syria suffered the same fate, and Rome declared the Greek cities in Asia Minor that he had controlled free. The Greeks venerated the Roman commander, Titus Quinctius Flamininus (228–174 B.C.E.), as a god—the first Roman to be accorded this eastern honor.

In reality, the control of the freed cities lay in the hands of local oligarchs who were favorable to Rome. In 179 B.C.E. Philip's son Perseus (179–168 B.C.E.) attempted to stir up democratic opposition to Rome within the cities. This time, Rome responded more forcefully. The Macedonian kingdom was divided into four republics governed by their own senates and magistrates selected from among the local aristocrats. In Epirus, 70 cities were destroyed, and 150,000 people were sold into slavery. This harsh punishment prompted other Greek cities to react with panic even to the mere threat of Roman retribution. When the citizens of Rhodes heard that the Senate was contemplating declaring war on them, they quickly executed all of their anti-Roman fellows.

The final episode of Rome's expansionist drama unfolded during the Third Punic War. When Rome resumed its war with Carthage in 149 B.C.E., several Greek cities attempted once more to assert their autonomy from the hated oligarchies established by Rome. Retribution was swift. Roman legions crushed the rebel forces, and, as an example to all, Corinth was razed and its population was enslaved.

In the west, in northern Italy, Spain, and Africa, Roman conquest had been direct and complete. Tribal structures had been replaced by Roman provinces governed by former magistrates or proconsuls. In the east, Rome preferred to work through the existing political hierarchies. Still, Rome cultivated its image as protector of Greek liberties against the Macedonian and Seleucid monarchies and preferred indirect control to annexation. Its power was no less real for being indirect.

By 146 B.C.E., the Roman republic controlled the whole rim of the Mediterranean from Rhodes in the east across Greece, Dalmatia, Italy, southern Gaul, Spain, and North Africa. Even Syria and Egypt, although nominally independent, had to bow before Roman will. This subjugation

C H R O N O L O G Y	
THE ROMAN REPUBLIC	
509 B.C.E.	Expulsion of last Etruscan king; beginning of Roman Republic
ca. 450 B.C.E.	Law of the Twelve Tables
396 B.C.E.	Rome conquers southern Etruria
295 B.C.E.	Rome extends rule north to Po Valley
265–241 B.C.E.	First Punic War
264 B.C.E.	All of Italy under Roman control
218–202 B.C.E.	Second Punic War
149–146 B.C.E.	Third Punic War; Carthage is destroyed

had been graphically demonstrated in 168 B.C.E., when the Seleucid Antiochus IV (175–164 B.C.E.) invaded the kingdom of the Egyptian ruler Ptolemy VI (180–145 B.C.E.) and besieged Alexandria. The Ptolemys had long before made a treaty with Rome, and the Senate sent an envoy to Antiochus with written instructions to withdraw immediately from Egypt. The king replied that he would like to consult before making a decision. The Roman envoy immediately drew a circle around Antiochus, ordering him to give an answer before he stepped out of the ring. Such directness was unknown in the world of Hellenistic diplomacy. After a moment's hesitation the deeply shocked Antiochus replied that he would do whatever the Romans demanded. Through perseverance and determination, Rome had risen from obscurity to become the greatest power the West had ever known. The republic had endured great adversity. It would not survive prosperity.

REPUBLICAN CIVILIZATION

Territorial conquest, the influx of unprecedented riches, and exposure to sophisticated Hellenistic civilization ultimately overwhelmed earlier Roman civilization. This civilization had been created by stubborn farmers and soldiers who valued authority, simplicity, and piety above all else. This unique culture was the source of strength that led Rome to greatness, but its limitations prevented the republic from resolving its internal social tensions and the external problems caused by the burden of empire.

Farmers and Soldiers

The ideal Roman farmer was not the great estate owner of the Greek world, but the smallholder, the dirt farmer of central Italy. Typical farm families, with holdings of perhaps as little as 10 acres, raised grain, beans, and hogs for their own consumption. In addition, they cultivated vineyards and olive groves for cash crops. But the most important crop of Roman farms was citizens. "From farmers come the bravest men and the sturdiest soldiers," wrote Cato the Elder. Nor was the ideal Roman soldier the gallant cavalryman but rather the solid foot soldier. Cavalry—composed of wealthy citizens who made up the elite equestrian order—and especially allies provided reconnaissance and protected Roman flanks. The main fighting force, however, was the infantry. Sometime in the early republic the Greek phalanx was transformed into the Roman legion, a flexible unit composed of 30 companies of 120 men each, armed with javelins and short swords.

Constant training, careful preparation, and painstaking execution characterized every aspect of Roman military expeditions. Wars were won as much by engineering feats as by feats of arms. Engineers constructed bridges, siege machines, and catapults. By the time of the late republic, Roman armies on the march could construct identical camps each night, quickly building a strong square fort 2,150 feet on a side. Within the camp, every unit had exactly the same location for its quarters, as did the commander and paymaster. The chain of command was rigidly maintained from the commander, a Roman consul, through military tribunes and centurions, two of whom commanded each company of 120 men.

These solid, methodical troops, the backbone of the republican armies that conquered the Mediterranean, were among the victims of that conquest. The pressures of constant international warfare were destroying the farmer-soldiers whom the traditionalists loved to praise. When the Roman sphere of interest had been confined to central Italy, farmers could do their planting in spring, serve in the army during the summer months, and return home to care for their farms in time for harvest. When Rome's wars became international expeditions lasting for years, many soldiers, unable to work their lands while doing military service, had to mortgage their farms in order to support their families. When they returned, they often found that during their prolonged absences they had lost their farms to wealthy aristocratic moneylenders. While aristocrats amassed vast landed estates worked by imported slaves, ordinary Romans and Italians lacked even a family farm capable of supporting themselves and their families. Without land they and their sons were excluded from further military service and sank into the growing mass of desperately poor, disenfranchised citizens.

The Roman Family

In Roman tradition, the *paterfamilias* was the master of the family—which in theory included his wife, children, and slaves—over whom he exercised the power of life and death. This authority lasted as long as he lived. Only at his

▲ One of a series of Roman mosaics illustrating tasks appropriate to the months of the year. Here two laborers are using an olive press with a horizontal screw for the December olive pressing.

death did his sons, even if they were long grown and married, achieve legal and financial independence. The family was the basic unit of society, of the state.

Although not kept in seclusion as in Greece, Roman women theoretically never exercised independent power in this male-dominated world. Before marriage, a Roman girl was subject to the authority of her father. When she married, her father traditionally transferred legal guardianship to her husband, thus severing her bonds to paternal family. A husband could divorce his wife at will, returning her and her dowry to her father. However, wives did exercise real though informal authority within the family. Part of this authority came from their role in the moral education of their children and the direction of the household. Part also came from their control over their dowries. Widows might exercise even greater authority in the raising of their children.

Paternal authority over children was absolute. Not all children born into a marriage became members of the family. The Law of the Twelve Tables allowed defective children to be killed for the good of the family. Newborn infants were laid on the ground before the father, who decided whether the child should be raised. By picking up a son, he accepted the child into the family. Ordering that a daughter be nursed similarly signified acceptance. If there were too many mouths to feed or the child was simply unwanted, the father could command that the infant be killed or abandoned. Abandoned children might be adopted by childless couples.

Nor were all sons born into Roman families. Romans made use of adoption for many purposes. Families without heirs could adopt children. Powerful political and military figures might adopt promising young men as their political heirs. These adopted sons held the same legal rights as the father's natural offspring and thus were integral members of his family.

Slaves, too, were members of the family. On the one hand, slaves were property without personal rights. On the other, they might live and work alongside the free members of the family, worship the family gods, and enjoy the protection and endure the authority of the paterfamilias. In fact, the authority of the paterfamilias was roughly the same over slave and free members of the family. If he desired, he could sell the free members of the family into slavery.

The center of everyday life for the Roman family was the *domus*, the family house whose architectural style had developed from Etruscan traditions. Visitors entered through the front door into the *atrium*, a central courtyard containing a collecting pool into which rainwater for household use flowed from the roof through terra-cotta drains. In niches or on shelves stood wax or terra-cotta busts of ancestors and statues of the household gods. Around the atrium, openings gave on to workrooms, storerooms, bedrooms, offices, and small dining rooms.

Social Effects of Expansion

In the wake of imperial conquests, the Roman family and its environment began to change in ways that were disturbing to many of the oligarchy. Some women, perhaps in imitation of their more liberated Hellenistic sisters, began to take a more active role in public life. One example is Cornelia, a daughter of Scipio Africanus. After her husband's death in 154 B.C.E., she refused to remarry, devoting herself instead to raising her children, administering their inheritance, and directing their political careers.

Some married women, too, escaped the authority of their husbands. Fewer and fewer fathers transferred authority over their daughters to their husbands. Instead, daughters remained under their father's authority as long as he lived. This meant that on the father's death, they became independent persons, able to manage their own affairs without their husbands' consent or interference. Although some historians believe that sentimental bonds of affection may have increased between many husbands and wives and parents and children as legal bonds loosened, it also meant that the wife's relationship to her children was weakened. Roman mothers had never been legally related to their children. Wives and mothers were not fully part of their husbands' families. Their brother's families, not their own children, were their natural heirs. Just as adoption created political bonds, marriage to daughters sealed alliances between men. However, when these alliances fell apart or more advantageous ones presented themselves, fathers could force their daughters to divorce their husbands and to marry someone else. Divorce became increasingly common in the second century B.C.E. More and more, wives were temporary visitors in their husbands' homes.

Not every Roman family could afford its own domus, and in the aftermath of the imperial expansion, housing problems became acute for the poor. In Rome and other towns of Italy, shopkeepers lived in small houses attached to their shops or in rooms behind their workplaces. Peasants who were forced off their land and into cities found shelter in multistory apartment buildings, an increasingly common sight in the cities of the empire. In these cramped structures, families crowded into small, low rooms about ten feet square. In Roman towns throughout Italy, simple dwellings, luxurious mansions, shops, and apartment buildings existed side by side. The rich and the poor rubbed shoulders every day, producing a friction that threatened to burst into flame.

Roman Religion

Romans worshipped many gods, the more the better. Every aspect of daily life and work was the responsibility of individual powers, or *numina*. Every man had his *genius* or personal *numen*, just as every woman had her *juno*. Each family had its household powers, the *lares familiares*, whose proper worship was the responsibility of the pater-familias. The *Vesta* was the spirit of the hearth fire. The *lares* were the deities of farmland, the domus, and the guardians of roads and travelers. The *penates* guarded the family larder or storage cupboard. These family spirits exercised a binding power, a *religio*, on the Romans, and the pious Roman householder recognized these claims and undertook the *officia*, or duties, to which the spirits were entitled. These basic attitudes of religion, piety, and office lay at the heart of Roman reverence for order and authority. They extended to other traditional Roman and Latin gods such as Jupiter, the supreme god; Juno, his wife; Mars, the god of war; and the two-faced Janus, spirit of gates and new beginnings.

Outside the household, worship of the gods and the reading of the future in the entrails of sacrificed animals, the flight of birds, or changes in weather were the responsibilities of colleges of priests. Roman priests did not, as did those in the Near East, form a special caste but rather were important members of the elite who held priesthoods in addition to other public offices. Religion was less a matter of personal relationship with the gods than a public, civic activity that bound society together. State-supported cults with their colleges of priests, Etruscan- and Greek-style temples, and elaborate ceremonies were integral parts of the Roman state and society. The world of the gods reflected that of mortals. As the Roman mortal world expanded, so did the divine.

Romans were quick to identify foreign gods with their own. Thus Zeus became Jupiter, Hera became Juno, and Aphrodite became Venus.

Still, the elasticity of Roman religion could stretch just so far. With the empire came not only the cults of Zeus, Apollo, and Aphrodite to Rome but that of Dionysus as well. Unlike the formal public cults of the other Greek deities, which were firmly in the control of authorities, that of Dionysus was largely outside state control. Women, in the tradition of the maenads, controlled much of the ecstatic and overtly sexual rituals associated with the god. Following the Second Punic War, the cult of Dionysus, known in Latin as Bacchus, spread rapidly in Italy. At its secret rites, or *Bacchanalia*, men and women were rumored to engage in every kind of sexual act.

In 186 B.C.E., the Senate decreed the cult of Bacchus a conspiracy and ordered an inquiry. The consul Spurius Postumius Albinus, acting on the false testimony of a former prostitute, began a brutal persecution. Rituals were banned, priests and adherents were arrested, and rewards were offered to informants, who provided lurid and fanciful accounts of what had taken place at the Bacchanalia. Hundreds of people were imprisoned, and greater numbers were executed. The Senate ordered all shrines to Bacchus destroyed and Bacchanalia banned throughout Italy. Perhaps more than any other episode, the suppression of the Bacchic cult showed the oligarchy's fear of the changes sweeping Roman civilization.

Republican Letters

As Rome absorbed foreign gods, it also absorbed foreign letters. From the Etruscans the Romans adopted and adapted the alphabet, the one in which most Western languages are written to this day. Early Latin inscriptions are largely funeral monuments and some public notices such as the Law of the Twelve Tables. The Roman high priest responsible for maintaining the calendar of annual feasts also prepared and updated annals, short accounts of important religious and secular events of each year. However, before the third century B.C.E., apart from extravagant funerary eulogies carefully preserved within families, Romans had no apparent interest in writing or literature as such. The birth of Latin letters began with Rome's exposure to Greek civilization.

Greek Historians of Rome.   Early in the third century B.C.E., Greek authors had begun to pay attention to expanding Rome. The first serious Greek historian to focus on this new Western power was Timaeus (ca. 356–ca. 260 B.C.E.), who spent most of his productive life in Athens. There he wrote a history of Rome up to the Pyrrhic war, interviewing Roman and Greek witnesses to gain an understanding of this Italian city that had defeated a Hellenistic army. Polybius (ca. 200–ca. 118 B.C.E.), the greatest of the Greek historians to record Rome's rise to power, gathered his information firsthand. As one of a thousand eminent Greeks deported to Rome for political investigation, he became a close friend of Scipio Aemilianus and accompanied him on his Spanish and African campaigns. Polybius's history is both the culmination of the traditions of Greek historiography and its transformation, since it centers on the rise of a non-Greek power to rule "almost the whole inhabited world."

The Origins of Latin Literature. At the same time that Greeks began to take Rome seriously, Romans themselves became interested in Greece, in particular in the international Hellenistic culture of the eastern Mediterranean. The earliest Latin literary works were clearly adaptations if not translations of Hellenistic genres and texts. Already in 240 B.C.E., plays in the Greek tradition were said to have been performed in Rome. The earliest extant literary works, ironically for the sober image of the Roman farmer-soldier, are the plays of Plautus (ca. 254–184 B.C.E.) and Terence (186–159 B.C.E.), lightly adapted translations of Hellenistic comedies.

Scheming servants, mistaken identities, bedroom farces, young lovers, and lecherous elders make up the plots of the Roman plays. The authors of these comedies experimented with and transformed Greek literature. Plautus, in particular, while maintaining superficially the Greek settings of his plays, actually creates a world that is more Roman than Greek. References to Roman laws, magistrates, clients, and social situations abound, as do humorous derogatory comments on Greek mores. Terence, although remaining closer to Greek models, Romanized his material through the creation of an elegant, natural style. His plays rapidly became classics, influencing subsequent generations of Latin authors, who worked to create a literary language separate from but equal to Greek.

THE CRISIS OF ROMAN VIRTUE

Rome's rise to world power within less than a century profoundly affected every aspect of republican life. Magistrates operating far from senatorial control in conquered provinces exercised power and found opportunities for enrichment never before seen. Successful commanders, honored and even deified by Eastern cities, felt the temptation to ignore the strict requirements of senatorial accountability. During the time of a provincial command, it was said, one had to make three fortunes: the first to pay off the bribes it took to get the office, the second to pay off the jury that would investigate corruption after the command had expired, and a third to live on for the rest of one's life. Provincial commanders enriched themselves through extortion, collusion with dishonest government contractors and tax collectors, and wholesale bribe-taking. Ordinary citizens, aware of such abuses, felt increasingly threatened by the wealthy and powerful.

In the second century B.C.E., Romans found themselves in a dilemma as the old and the new exerted equal pressures. These tensions led to almost a century of bitter civil strife and ultimately to the disintegration of the republic. The complex interaction of these tensions can best be seen in the life of one man, Marcus Porcius Cato.

Cato the Elder is often presented as the preserver of the old traditions, in contrast to Scipio Aemilianus, destroyer of Carthage and proponent of Hellenism in the Roman world. True, as censor, fighting against conspicuous consumption, and as self-conscious defender of the past, Cato cast himself in the mold of the traditional Roman. And Scipio, with his love of Hellenism and his political career defined more by personal achievement than traditional magistracies, represented a new type of Roman. But if the division between old and new, between Cato and Scipio, had been so clear-cut, the dilemma of republican Rome would not have been so great. As it was, Cato reflected in himself this contradictory clash of values. Like the two-faced god Janus, whom he invoked in all his undertakings, Cato was the stern censor, the guardian and proponent of traditional Roman virtue, as well as the new Roman of shrewd business acumen, influence, and power unimaginable to the simple farmers he professed to admire.

Cato was born in the Latin town of Tusculum in 234 B.C.E. and grew to maturity on a family estate in Sabine territory. He came of age just at the start of the Second Punic War and distinguished himself in campaigns against

▼ A memorial sculpture of Cato the Elder and his wife. Cato defended the ancient Roman traditions even as he himself was deeply influenced by the changes sweeping Rome.

Hannibal in Italy and Syracuse in Sicily. In between campaigns he became even more famous for his eloquence in pleading legal cases. His talents and energy brought him to the attention of powerful members of the senatorial aristocracy, under whose patronage he came to Rome. There he began to rise through the offices of military tribune, quaestor, and ultimately consul and censor.

This first-generation senator became the spokesman for the traditional values of Rome, for severity and simplicity, for honesty and frugality in private and public life. Cato ridiculed Greek philosophy and education, and he glorified his own simple farm life, the care he took in the management of his estates and of his extended *familia*, and his working in his fields side by side with his slaves.

Actually, Cato, as much as anyone else, was deeply involved in the rapid changes brought about by the empire. He may have worked along with his slaves, but as soon as they grew old, he sold them to the state to avoid having to support them, something no conscientious paterfamilias would ever have done. Although he led the battle to prevent senators from participating in commerce, he was perhaps the first of that body to diversify his holdings and investments. He bought up land, hot baths, and mineral deposits. Although he avoided conspicuous consumption himself, as consul and censor he was responsible for many of the sumptuous building projects in Rome through which ordinary Romans first experienced the luxuries of the Hellenistic world. While scorning Greek culture, he worked bits of Greek authors even into his attacks on Greek civilization.

Cato was neither duplicitous nor hypocritical. He was simply typical. Many senators agreed with him that the old values were slipping away and, with them, the foundation of the republic. Many feared that personal ambition was undermining the power of the oligarchy. Yet these same people could not resist exploiting the changed circumstances for their own benefit.

Conclusion

ROME HAD COME A LONG WAY since its origin as an outpost of the Alban League. At first overshadowed by its more civilized neighbors to the north and south, it had slowly and tenaciously achieved independence from and then domination over its more ancient neighbors. It absorbed or adapted ideas and institutions from the Etruscans, Greeks, and others with whom it came into contact. Rome's great success was largely due to Roman authoritarianism as well as to its genius for creative adaptation, flexibility, and thoroughness and its willingness to give those it conquered a stake in Roman victory. Until the middle of the second century B.C.E. this formula had served the republic well. After the final destruction of Carthage, however, an isolated and fearful oligarchy appeared unwilling or unable to broaden the base of those participating in the Roman achievement. The result was a century of conflict and civil war that destroyed the republican empire.

QUESTIONS FOR REVIEW

1. Why might the Greeks have been surprised by certain characteristics of Carthaginian and Etruscan society?
2. What social, political, and military practices made possible the expansion of Rome from a collection of villages into a power that ultimately destroyed Carthage in the Punic Wars?
3. How were family and household life organized in the domus of the Roman Republic?
4. Why were Romans like Cato the Elder concerned by the changes that accompanied the expansion of Roman international power?

DISCOVERING WESTERN CIVILIZATION ONLINE

You can obtain more information about early Rome at the websites listed below. See also the companion website that accompanies this text: www.ablongman.com/kishlansky, which contains an online study guide and additional resources.

General Websites

www.providence.edu/dwc/rome.htm
A course web page with links to every aspect of Roman history and civilization.

www.history.evansville.net/rome.html
An excellent website dedicated to Roman history.

www.tourismtunisia.com/togo/carthage/carthage.html
A brief introduction to Carthage.

Republican Civilization

www.utexas.edu/depts/classics/faculty/Riggsby/RepGov.html
A detailed explanation of the republican constitution of Rome.

SUGGESTIONS FOR FURTHER READING

Primary Sources

Many of the works of Polybius, Livy, Cato, Caesar, Cicero, and other Roman authors are available in English translation from Penguin Books. *Roman Civilization Selected Readings, Vol. I: The Republic* (1951) by Naphtali Lewis and Meyer Reinhold contains a wide selection of documents with useful introductions.

The Western Mediterranean to 509 B.C.E.

Graeme Barker and Tom Rasmussen, *The Etruscans* (Oxford: Blackwells Publishers, 2000). An introduction to Etruscan studies and history.

Serge Lancel, *Carthage: A History* (Oxford: Blackwell's Publishers, 1997). A basic introduction.

From City to Empire, 509–146 B.C.E.

Mary Beard and Michael Crawford, *Rome in the Late Republic* (Ithaca, N.Y.: Cornell University Press, 1985). A short interpretative essay on the crisis of the late republic.

John Boardman, Jasper Griffin, and Oswyn Murray, *The Oxford History of the Roman World* (New York: Oxford University Press, 2001). A balanced collection of essays on all aspects of Roman history and civilization.

K. R. Bradley, *Slavery and Society at Rome* (New York: Cambridge University Press, 1994). An account of the place of slavery in the Roman world.

P. A. Brunt, *Social Conflicts in the Roman Republic* (New York: W. W. Norton, 1971). Analyzes the continuing struggle between patricians and plebeians until the end of the republic.

Tim Cornell, *The Beginnings of Rome, 1000–264 B.C.* (New York: Routledge, 1995). A new look at the origins of Rome.

Michael Crawford, *The Roman Republic* (Cambridge, Mass.: Harvard University Press, 1978). A modern survey of the republican period, emphasizing political history.

Republican Civilization

Geza Alfoldy, *The Social History of Rome* (Berlin: Walter de Gruyter, 1988). A survey of Rome that emphasizes the relationship between social structure and politics.

Suzanne Dixon, *The Roman Mother* (Norman: University of Oklahoma Press, 1988). A balanced view of Roman mothers in law and in society.

Erich S. Gruen, *The Hellenistic World and the Coming of Rome,* 2 vols. (Berkeley: University of California Press, 1984). A detailed history of the Hellenistic world, presenting Rome's gradual and unintended rise to dominance in it.

Sarah B. Pomeroy, ed., *Women's History and Ancient History* (Chapel Hill: University of North Carolina Press, 1991). The place to begin for the history of women in antiquity.

The Crisis of Roman Virtue

Alan E. Astin, *Cato the Censor* (New York: Oxford University Press, 1978). An excellent biography of Cato that also analyzes his writings.

IMPERIAL ROME, 146 B.C.E.–192 C.E.

THE VISUAL RECORD

THE ALTAR OF AUGUSTAN PEACE

IN 27 B.C.E., OCTAVIAN, KNOWN TO HISTORY as the Emperor Augustus, emerged as the absolute ruler of a Roman world tired of bloodshed. In 13 B.C.E., a grateful (and ingratiating) Senate decreed that Augustus be honored by the construction of an altar dedicated to the new goddess of peace, Pax, erected on the field long-sacred to her opposite, Mars, the god of war. Pax was one of Augustus's favorite divinities and the cornerstone of his political program. In return for abandoning all hopes of republican government, Augustus promised harmony, prosperity, and, above all, peace. More than any other surviving monument, the Altar of Augustan Peace, in its design and in the ideology of its elaborate carved friezes, embodies Augutus's vision of that peace.

The style of the Roman Pantheon, a 20-by-24-foot marble rectangle standing more than three feet tall and surrounded on three sides by a U-shaped counter, revived a form common hundreds of years earlier. Augustus, whose transformation of the Roman state and society was so radical that it has been rightly termed a revolution, was always careful to present the most daring innovations as restorations of ancient republican tradition.

To reach the altar, a visitor must climb a short flight of steps and enter through an enclosure wall erected of massive rectangular slabs of marble. The lower course of the external walls is decorated with delicate, intricately intertwined acanthus plants, a symbol of peaceful abundance that came to be intimately associated with Augustan art. The upper course contains exquisitely carved friezes representing the stories of the two mythical founders of Rome: Romulus, the abandoned child nursed by a she-wolf, and Aeneas, the legendary Trojan warrior who wandered the Mediterranean in obedience to the gods until he arrived at the site of Rome. On the sides of the wall are images of processions. On the south, Augustus and his family prepare to celebrate the cult of the goddess of peace. On the north side magistrates and ordinary Roman citizens carry gifts, either to Augustus or to the Augustan Peace—it was really the same thing.

On the far side of the enclosure, the side most visible to passing Romans, the visitor encounters on the right the goddess Roma and on the left the goddess Pax herself. She sits upon a stone ledge amid lush flowers and plants. At her feet a sheep grazes and a cow reclines, the very image of prosperity and contentment. Pax holds two happy infants in her lap on whom she gazes with love.

Domesticity, abundance, fruitfulness, and the simplicity of an earlier time: this is the image of the Augustan Peace that the emperor and his advisors sought to create. This was to be the new reality of Rome restored, a vision so compelling that subsequent generations referred to the empire of Augustus, the Roman Empire, simply as the *Pax Romana*. And yet, our translation of pax as peace unconsciously accepts Augustus's perspective: to thousands of victims of the empire, a better translation would be pacification. A Roman critic at the end of the first century put it: "They created a desert and called it peace."

LOOKING AHEAD

This chapter explores the consequences of Roman imperial expansion throughout the Mediterranean, the long and violent crises that led to civil war and the end of the republic, and the new forms of government, society, and culture that were imperial Rome.

THE PRICE OF EMPIRE, 146–121 B.C.E.

Roman victory defeated the republic. Roman conquest of the Mediterranean world and the establishment of the Roman Empire spelled the end of the republican system. Roman society could not withstand the tensions caused by the enrichment of the few, the impoverishment of the many, and the demands of the excluded populations of the empire to share in its benefits. Traditional Roman culture could not survive the attraction of Hellenistic civilization with its wealth, luxuries, and individualistic values. Finally, Roman government could not restrain the ambitions of its oligarchs or protect the interests of its ordinary citizens. The creation of a Mediterranean empire brought in its wake a century of revolutionary change before new and stable social, cultural, and political forms were achieved in the Roman world.

Winners and Losers

Rome had emerged victorious in the Punic and Macedonian wars, but the real winners were the members of the oligarchy, the *optimates* (the "best"), as they called themselves, whose wealth and power had grown beyond all imagining. These optimates included roughly 300 senators and magistrates, most of whom had inherited wealth, political connections, and long-established clientages. Since military command and government of the empire were entrusted to magistrates who were answerable only to the Senate of which they were members, the empire was essentially their private domain.

But new circumstances created new opportunities for many others. Italian merchants, slave traders, entrepreneurs, and bankers, many of lowly origin, poured into the cities of the East in the wake of the Roman legions. These newly enriched Romans constituted a second elite and formed themselves into a separate order, that of the *equites,* or equestrians, who were distinguished by their wealth and honorific military service on horseback but were connected with the old military elite. Since the Senate did not create a government bureaucracy to administer the empire, equestrian tax farmers became essential to provincial government. Companies of these *publicans,* or tax collectors, purchased the right to collect rents on public land, tribute, and customs duties from provincials. Whatever they collected beyond the amount contracted for by Roman officials was theirs to keep. Publicans regularly bribed governors and commanders to allow them to gouge the local populations with impunity and on occasion even obtained Roman troops to help them make their collections. Gradually, some of these "new men," their money "laundered" through investments in land, managed to achieve lower magistracies and even move into the senatorial order. Still, the upper reaches of office were closed to all but a tiny minority. By the end of the Punic Wars, only some 25 families could hope to produce consuls.

The losers in the wars included the vanquished who were sold into slavery by the tens of thousands; the provincials who bore the Roman yoke; the Italian allies who had done so much for the Romans; and even the citizen farmers, small shopkeepers, and free artisans of the republic. All four groups suffered from the effects of empire, and over the next century, all resorted to violence against the optimates.

Slave Revolts.   The slaves revolted first. Thousands of them, captured in battle or taken after victory, flooded the Italian and Sicilian estates of the wealthy. Estimates vary, but in the first century B.C.E. the slave population of Italy

◀ Roman slaves sifting grain. Roman victories in the Punic and Macedonian wars brought a huge influx of slaves from the conquered lands. Slaves were pressed into service on the estates and plantations of wealthy landowners.

was probably around two million, fully one-third of the total population. This vastly expanded slave world overwhelmed the traditional role of slaves within the Roman familia. Rural slaves on absentee estates enjoyed none of the protections afforded traditional Roman servants. Cato sold off his slaves when they reached old age; others simply worked them to death. Many slaves, born free citizens of Hellenistic states, found such treatment unbearable. Slaves rose up against their masters in Sicily in 135 B.C.E. and again a generation later and in southern Italy between 104 and 101 B.C.E. The most serious slave revolt occurred in Italy between 74 and 71 B.C.E. Gladiators—professional slave fighters trained for Roman amusement—revolted in Capua. Under the competent leadership of the Thracian gladiator Spartacus, over 100,000 slaves took up arms against Rome. Ultimately, eight legions, more troops than had met Hannibal at Zama, were needed to put down the revolt. All slave revolts succumbed to the superior strength and discipline of the Roman legions, and retribution was always terrible. After the defeat of Spartacus, crucified rebels lined the road from Rome to Naples.

Provincial Revolts. Revolts profoundly disturbed the Roman state, all the more because it was not just slaves who revolted. In many cases, poor free peasants and disgruntled provincials rose up against Rome. The most significant provincial revolt was that of Aristonicus, the illegitimate half-brother of Attalus III (ca. 138–133 B.C.E.) of Pergamum, a Roman client state. Attalus had left his kingdom to Rome at his death. In an attempt to assert his right to the kingdom, Aristonicus armed slaves and peasants and attacked the Roman garrisons. The hellenized cities of Asia Minor remained loyal to Rome, but this provincial uprising, the first of many over the centuries, lasted more than three years, from 133 to 130 B.C.E. In 88 B.C.E., the king of Pontus led a revolt against Romans in Asia Minor, a revolt that spread to Greece before it was quelled.

Revolts by slaves and provincials were disturbing enough. Revolts by Rome's Italian allies were much more serious. After the Second Punic War, these allies, on whose loyalty Rome had depended for survival, found themselves badly treated and exploited. Government officials used state power to undermine the position of the Italian elites. At the same time, Roman aristocrats used their economic power to drive the Italic peasants from their land, replacing them with slaves. Fregellae, south of Rome, revolted in 125 B.C.E. A broader and more serious revolt took place between 91 and 89 B.C.E. after the Senate blocked an attempt to extend citizenship to the allies. During this so-called Social War (from *socii*, the Latin word for allies), almost all the Italian allies rose against Rome. These revolts differed from those in the provinces in that the Italian elites as well as the masses aligned themselves against the Roman oligarchy. Even some ordinary Roman citizens joined the rebel forces against the powerful elite.

Optimates and Populares

The despair that could lead ordinary Roman citizens to armed rebellion grew from the social and economic consequences of conquests. While aristocrats amassed vast landed estates worked by cheap slaves, ordinary Romans often lacked even a family farm capable of supporting them and their families. Many found their way to Rome, where they swelled the ranks of the unemployed, crowded into shoddily constructed tenements, and lived off the public subsidies.

While many senators bemoaned the demise of the Roman farmer-soldier, few were willing to compromise their own privileged position to help. In the face of the oligarchy's unwillingness to deal with the problem, the tribune Tiberius Gracchus (ca. 163–133 B.C.E.) in 133 B.C.E. attempted to introduce a land-reform program that would return citizens to agriculture. Gracchus was the first of the *populares,* political leaders appealing to the masses. His motives were probably a mixture of compassion for the poor, concern over the falling numbers of citizens who had the minimum amount of land to qualify for military service, and personal ambition.

Tiberius Gracchus. During the previous century, great amounts of public land had illegally come into private hands. With the support of reform-minded aristocrats and commoners, Gracchus proposed a law that would limit the amount of public land an individual could hold to about 312 acres. He also proposed a commission to distribute to landless peasants the land recovered by the state as a result of the law. Because many senators who illegally held vast amounts of public land strongly opposed the measure, it faced certain failure in the Senate. Gracchus therefore took it to the plebeian assembly, where it was assured support from the rural poor. Moreover, he further influenced the assembly to depose one of the tribunes who threatened to veto it. The law passed, but Gracchus's maneuvering lost him many of his aristocratic supporters, who feared that a popular democracy led by a demagogue was replacing the senatorial oligarchy.

Also in 133 B.C.E., Gracchus introduced another bill that called for the royal treasury of the kingdom of Pergamum, bequeathed to Rome by Attalus III, to be used to help citizens receiving land to purchase livestock and equipment. These laws, which challenged the Senate's traditional control over finance and foreign affairs, angered the conservative elite; but as long as Gracchus held office, he was protected from any sort of attack by the traditional immunity accorded to tribunes. It was no secret, however, that the Senate planned to prosecute him as soon as his one-year term expired. To escape this fate, he appealed to the assembly to reelect him for an unprecedented second consecutive term. To his opponents this appeal smacked of an attempt to make himself sole ruler, a democratic tyrant

THE REFORMS OF TIBERIUS GRACCHUS

In the following passage, the romanized Greek Appian of Alexandria (ca. 95–ca. 165 C.E.), drawing on earlier but now lost records, describes the positions of the two factions in the dispute over the land reform Tiberius Gracchus introduced in 133 B.C.E.

FOCUS QUESTIONS

How had wealthy Romans acquired vast amounts of public land? Why did the wealthy see Gracchus as so great a threat?

TIBERIUS SEMPRONIUS GRACCHUS, an illustrious man, eager for glory, a most powerful speaker, and for these reasons well known to all, delivered an eloquent discourse while serving as tribune, lamenting the fact that the Italians, a people so valiant in war and related in blood to the Romans, were declining little by little into pauperism and paucity of numbers without any hope of remedy. He inveighed against the multitude of slaves as useless in war and never faithful to their masters, and adduced the recent calamity brought upon the masters by their slaves in Sicily. . . . After speaking thus he again brought forward the law providing that nobody should hold more than 500 *iugera* of public domain. But he added a provision to the former law, that [two] sons of the occupiers might each hold one-half that amount and that the remainder should be divided among the poor by three elected commissioners, who should be changed annually.

This was extremely disturbing to the rich because, on account of the commissioners, they could no longer disregard the law as they had done before; nor could they buy from those receiving allotments, because Gracchus had provided against this by forbidding such sales. They collected together in groups, and made lamentation, and accused the poor of appropriating their fields of long standing, their vineyards, and their buildings. Some said they had paid the price of the land to their neighbors. Were they to lose the money with the land? Others said the graves of their ancestors were in the ground, which had been allotted to them in the division of their fathers' estates. Others said that their wives' dowries had been expended on these estates, or that the land had been given to their own daughters as dowry. . . . All kinds of wailing and expressions of indignation were heard at once. On the other side were heard the lamentations of the poor—that they were being reduced from competence to extreme poverty, and from that to childlessness, because they were unable to rear their offspring. They recounted the military services they had rendered, by which this very land had been acquired, and were angry that they should be robbed of their share of the common property. . . . Emboldened by numbers and exasperated against each other they kindled incessant disturbances, and waited eagerly for the voting of the new law, some intending to prevent its enactment by all means, and others to enact it at all costs.

on the Greek model. A group of senators and their clients, led by one of Gracchus's own cousins, broke into the assembly meeting at which the election was to take place and murdered the tribune and 300 of his supporters.

Gaius Gracchus.   The optimates in the Senate could eliminate Tiberius Gracchus, but they could not so easily eliminate the movement he had led. In 123 B.C.E., his younger brother, Gaius Sempronius Gracchus (153–121 B.C.E.), became tribune. During his two one-year terms he initiated an even broader and more radical reform program. Tiberius had been concerned only about poor citizens. Gaius attempted to broaden the citizenry and to shift the balance of power away from the Senate. Alarmed by the revolt at Fregellae, he attempted to extend citizenship to all Latins and to improve the status of Italian allies by extending to them the right to vote in the assembly. To check the power of senatorial magistrates in the provinces, he transferred to the equestrians the right to investigate provincial corruption. This move brought the wealthy equestrian order into politics as a counterbalance to the Senate. Gaius also improved the supply and distribution of grain in Rome and other Italian cities to benefit the urban poor. He reestablished his brother's land distribution project, extended participation to Latins and Italians, and encouraged colonization as a means to provide citizens with land. Finally, to protect himself and his party from the anticipated reaction of the Senate and to prepare to avenge his brother's death, he pushed through a law stipulating that only the people could condemn a citizen to death.

Gaius's program was extraordinary for several reasons. First, it was exactly that: a program, the first comprehensive attempt to deal with the problems facing Roman society. Second, it proposed a basic shift of power, drawing the equestrian order for the first time into the political arena opposite the Senate and making the assembly rather than the Senate the initiator of legislation. Finally, it offered a solution to the problem of the allies that, although rejected at the time, was finally adopted some 20 years later. In the short run, however, Gaius's program was a failure. In 121 B.C.E., he was not reelected for a third term and thus lost the immunity of the tribunate. Recalling his brother's fate, he armed his supporters. Once more the Senate acted, ordering the consul to take whatever measures he deemed necessary. Gaius and some 3,000 of his supporters died.

The deaths of Tiberius and Gaius Gracchus marked a new beginning in Roman politics. Not since the end of the monarchy had a political conflict been decided with personal violence. The whole episode provided a model for future attempts at reform. Reformers would look not to the Senate or the aristocracy but to the people, from whom they would draw their political power. The experience of the Gracchi also provided a model for repression of other reform programs: violence.

THE END OF THE REPUBLIC

With the Gracchi dead and the core of their reforms dismantled, the Senate appeared victorious against all challengers. At home the masses of ordinary Roman citizens and their political leadership were in disarray. The conquered lands of North Africa and the Near East filled the public coffers as well as the private accounts of Roman senators and publicans. In reality, Rome had solved neither the problem of internal conflict between rich and poor nor that of how to govern its enormous empire. The apparent calm ended when revolts in Africa and Italy exposed the fragility of the Senate's control and ushered in an ever increasing spiral of violence and civil war.

The Crisis of Government

In 112 B.C.E., the Senate declared war against Jugurtha (ca. 160–104 B.C.E.), a North African client state king, who, in his war against a rival, had killed some Roman merchants in the Numidian city of Cirta. The war dragged on for five years amid accusations of corruption, incompetence, and treason. Finally, in 107 B.C.E., the people elected as consul Gaius Marius (157–86 B.C.E.), a "new man" who had risen through the tribunate, and entrusted to him the conduct of the war. To raise an army, Marius ignored property qualifications and enlisted many impoverished Romans, arming them at public expense. Although recruiting of landless citizens had probably taken place before, no one had done it in such an overt and massive manner. Senators looked on Marius's measure with great suspicion, but the poor citizen recruits, who had despaired of benefiting from the land reforms proposed by the Gracchi, looked forward to receiving a grant of land at the end of their military service. Marius quickly defeated Jugurtha in 106 B.C.E.

In the following year, Celtic and Germanic barbarians crossed the Alps into Italy. Although technically disqualified from further terms, Marius was elected consul five times between 104 and 100 B.C.E. to meet the threat. During this period he continued to recruit soldiers from among the poor and, on his own authority, extended citizenship to allies. To his impoverished soldiers, Marius promised land, but after his victory in 101 B.C.E., the Senate refused to give farms to veterans. As a result, Marius's armies naturally shifted their allegiance away from the Roman state and to their popular commander. Soon this pattern of loyalty became the norm. Politicians forged close bonds with the soldiers of their armies. Individual commanders, not the state or the Senate, ensured that their recruits received their pay, shared in the spoils of victory, and obtained land on their retirement. In turn, the soldiers became fanatically devoted to their commanders. Republican armies had become personal armies, potent tools in the hands of ambitious politicians.

The Civil Wars. The outbreak of the Social War in 91 B.C.E. marked the first use of these armies in civil war. Both Marius and the consul Lucius Cornelius Sulla (138–78 B.C.E.) raised armies to fight the Italians, who were pacified only after Roman citizenship was extended to all Italians in 89 B.C.E. The next year, Mithridates VI (120–63 B.C.E.), the king of Pontus, took advantage of the Roman preoccupation in Italy to invade the province of Asia. As soon as the Italian threat receded, Sulla, as the representative of the optimates, raised an army to fight Mithridates. Marius, as leader of the populares who favored reform, attempted to have Sulla relieved of command. Sulla marched on Rome, initiating a bloody civil war. In the course of this war, Rome was occupied three times, once by Marius and twice by Sulla. Each commander ordered mass executions of his opponents and confiscated their property, which he then distributed to his supporters.

Ultimately, Sulla emerged victorious and ruled as dictator from 82 to 79 B.C.E., using this time to shore up senatorial power. He doubled the size of the Senate to 600, filling the new positions with men drawn from the equites. He reduced the authority of tribunes and returned jury courts from the equites to the senators. To weaken the military power of magistrates, he abolished the practice of assigning military commands to praetors and consuls. Rather, they were to be held by proconsuls, or former magistrates, who would serve for one year as provincial governors.

In 79 B.C.E., his reforms in place, Sulla stepped down to allow a return to oligarchic republican rule. Although his changes bought a decade of peace, they did not solve the fundamental problems dividing optimates and populares. If anything, his rule had proved that the only real political option was a dictatorship by a powerful individual with his own army. During the last generation of the republic, idealists continued their hopeless struggle to prop up the dying republican system while more forward-thinking generals fought among themselves for absolute power.

Republican Crisis. Marcus Tullius Cicero (106–43 B.C.E.) reflected the strengths and weaknesses of the republican tradition in the first century B.C.E. Although cultivated, humane, and dedicated to the republican constitution, he was also ambitious, blind to the failings of the optimates, a poor judge of character, and out of touch with the political realities of his time. Like Cato in an earlier age, he was a "new man," the son of a wealthy equestrian who provided his children with the best possible education both in Rome and in Athens and Rhodes. In Greece, Cicero developed a lifelong attachment to Stoic philosophy and developed the oratory skills necessary for a young Roman destined for public life. After returning to Rome, Cicero quickly earned a reputation for his skills as a courtroom orator.

At the same time, he began his climb up the political ladder by championing popular causes while protecting the interests of the wealthy and soliciting the assistance of young optimates. Cicero identified firmly with the elite, hoping that the republic could be saved through the harmonious cooperation of the equestrian and senatorial orders. Neither group was interested in following his program, but most considered him a safer figure than military strongmen like Sulla, who sought high office. In 63 B.C.E., Cicero was elected consul, the first "new man" to hold the office in over 30 years. The real threat to the existence of the republic was posed by the ambitions of powerful military commanders: Pompey (106–48 B.C.E.), Crassus (ca. 115–53 B.C.E.), and Julius Caesar (100–44 B.C.E.).

Pompey and Crassus, both protégés of Sulla, rose rapidly and unconstitutionally through a series of special proconsular commands by judicious use of fraud, violence, and corruption. Pompey first won public acclaim by commanding a victorious army in Africa and Spain. On his return to Rome in 70 B.C.E., he united with Crassus, who had won popularity for suppressing the Spartacus rebellion. Together, they worked to dismantle the Sullan constitution to the benefit of the populares. In return, Pompey received an extraordinary command over all of the coasts of the Mediterranean, in theory to suppress piracy but actually to give him control over all of the provinces of the empire. When, in 66 B.C.E., King Mithridates of Pontus again attacked Greece, Pompey assumed command of the provinces of Asia. His army not only destroyed Mithridates but continued on and conquered Armenia, Syria, and Palestine, acquiring an impressive retinue of client kings and increasing the income from the provinces by some 70 percent.

While Pompey was extending the frontiers of the empire to the Euphrates, Crassus, whose wealth was legendary—"no one should be called rich," he once observed, "who is not able to maintain an army on his income"—was consolidating his power. He allied himself with Julius Caesar, a young, well-connected orator from one of Rome's most ancient patrician families, who nevertheless promoted the cause of the populares. The Senate feared the ambitious and ruthless Crassus. It was to block the election of Crassus's candidate Catiline (Lucius Sergius Catilina, ca. 108–62 B.C.E.) to the consulate in 63 B.C.E. that the Senate elected Cicero instead. Catiline soon joined a conspiracy of Sullan

veterans and populares, but Cicero quickly uncovered and suppressed the conspiracy and ordered Catiline's execution.

The First Triumvirate. When Pompey returned from Asia in triumph in 62 B.C.E., he expected to find Italy convulsed with the Catiline revolt and in need of a military savior in the tradition of Sulla. Instead, thanks to Cicero's quick action, all was in order. Although he never forgave Cicero for stealing his glory, Pompey disbanded his army and returned to private life, asking only that the Senate approve his organization of the territories he had conquered and grant land to his veterans. The Senate refused. In response, Pompey formed an uneasy alliance with Crassus and Caesar. This alliance was known as the First Triumvirate, from the Latin for "three men." Caesar was elected consul in 59 B.C.E. and the following year received command of the province of Cisalpine Gaul in northern Italy.

Pompey and Crassus may have thought that this command would remove the ambitious young man from the political spotlight. Instead, Caesar, who has been called, with only some exaggeration, "the sole creative genius ever produced by Rome," used his province as a staging ground for the conquest of a vast area of western Europe to the mouth of the Rhine. His brilliant military skills beyond the Alps and his dedication to his troops made Caesar immensely popular with his legions. His ability for self-promotion ensured that this popularity was matched at home, where the populares eagerly received news of his Gallic wars. In 53 B.C.E., Crassus died leading an army in Syria, leaving Pompey and the popular young Caesar to dispute supreme power. As word of Caesar's military successes increased his popularity at Rome, it also increased Pompey's suspicion of his younger associate. Finally, in 49 B.C.E., Pompey's supporters in the Senate relieved Caesar of his command and ordered him to return to Italy.

Return he did, but not as commanded. Rather than leave his army, as ordered, on the far side of the Rubicon River, which marked the boundary between his province of Cisalpine Gaul and Italy, Caesar marched on Rome at the head of his legions. This meant civil war, a vicious bloodletting that convulsed the whole Mediterranean world. In 48 B.C.E., Caesar defeated Pompey in northern Greece. Pompey was assassinated shortly afterward in Egypt. Still, the wars went on between Pompey's supporters and Caesar until 45 B.C.E., when, with all his enemies defeated, Caesar returned to Rome.

The Second Triumvirate. In Rome, unlike Sulla, Caesar showed his opponents clemency as he sought to heal the wounds of war and to undertake an unprecedented series of reforms. He enlarged the Senate to 900 and widened its representation, appointing soldiers, freedmen, provincials, and above all wealthy men from the Italian towns. He increased the number of magistracies to broaden participation in government, founded colonies at

Carthage and Corinth, and settled veterans in colonies elsewhere in Italy, Greece, Asia, Africa, Spain, and Gaul.

Still, Caesar made no pretense of returning Rome to republican government. In early 44 B.C.E., although serving that year as consul together with his general Mark Antony (ca. 81–30 B.C.E.), Caesar had himself declared perpetual dictator. This move was too much for some 60 die-hard republican senators. On 15 March, a group led by two enemies whom Caesar had pardoned, Cassius Longinus and Marcus Junius Brutus, assassinated him as he entered the Senate chamber.

Cicero rejoiced when he heard of the assassination, clear evidence of his political naïveté. The republic was dead long before Caesar died, and the assassination simply returned Rome to civil war, a war that destroyed Cicero himself. Antony, Marcus Lepidus (d. 12 B.C.E.), another of Caesar's generals, and Caesar's grandnephew and adopted son Octavian (63 B.C.E.–14 C.E.), who took the name of his great uncle, soon formed the Second Triumvirate to destroy Caesar's enemies. After a bloody purge of senatorial and equestrian opponents, including Cicero, Antony and Octavian set out after Cassius and Brutus, who had fled into Macedonia. At Philippi in 42 B.C.E., Octavian and Antony defeated the armies of the two assassins (or, as they called themselves, liberators), who preferred suicide to capture.

After the defeat of the last republicans at Philippi, the members of the Second Triumvirate began to look suspiciously at one another. Antony took command of the East, protecting the provinces of Asia Minor and the Levant from the Parthians and bleeding them dry in the process. Lepidus received Africa, and Octavian was left to deal with the problems of Italy and the west.

Initially, Octavian had cut a weak and unimposing figure. He was only 18 when he was named adopted son and heir in Caesar's will. He had no military or political experience and was frequently in poor health. Still, he had the magic of Caesar's name with which to inspire the army, he had a visceral instinct for politics and publicity, and he combined these with an absolute determination to succeed at all costs. Aided by more competent and experienced commanders, notably Marcus Agrippa (ca. 63–12 B.C.E.) and Gaius Maecenas (ca. 70–8 B.C.E.), he began to consolidate his power at the expense of his two colleagues. Lepidus attempted to gain a greater share in the empire but found that his troops would not fight against Octavian. He was forced out of his position and allowed to retire in obscurity, retaining only the honorific title of pontifex maximus.

Antony, to meet his ever-growing demand for cash, became dependent on the Ptolemaic ruler of Egypt, the clever and competent Cleopatra. For her part, Cleopatra

▼ The Career of Julius Caesar. Caesar's military career, first against the Gauls and Germans and then against his Roman rivals, took him as far west as the Rhine and east through Greece to Egypt.

manipulated Antony in order to maintain the integrity and independence of her kingdom. Octavian seized the opportunity to portray Antony as a traitor to Rome, a weakling controlled by an Oriental woman who planned to move the capital of the empire to Alexandria. Antony's supporters replied with propaganda of their own, pointing to Octavian's humble parentage and his lack of military ability. The final break came in 32 B.C.E. Antony, for all his military might, could not attack Italy as long as the despised Cleopatra was with him. Nor could he abandon her without losing her financial support. Instead, he tried to lure Octavian to a showdown in Greece. His plan misfired. Agrippa forced him into a naval battle off Actium in 31 B.C.E. in which Antony was soundly defeated. He and his Egyptian queen committed suicide, and Octavian ruled supreme in the Roman Empire.

A Life Worth Leading

Mere survival was a difficult and elusive goal through the last decades of the republic. Still, some members of the elite sought more. They tried to make sense of the turmoil around them and formulate a philosophy of life and a model of personal conduct. By now, the members of Rome's elite were in full command of Greek literature and philosophy, which they studied and adapted to their needs, creating a distinctive Latin cultural tradition. The most prominent figure in the late republic is Cicero, who combined his active life as lawyer and politician with an abiding devotion to Stoic philosophy. In the Stoics' belief in divine providence, morality, and duty to one's allotted role in the universe, Cicero found a rational basis for his deeply committed public life. In a series of written dialogues, Cicero presented Stoic values in a form that created a Latin philosophical language that was freed from slavish imitation of Greek. He also wrote a number of works of political philosophy, particularly *The Republic* and *The Laws*, in conscious imitation of Plato's concern for the proper order of society. For Cicero, humans and gods were bound together in a world governed not simply by might but by justice. The universe, while perhaps not fully intelligible, was nonetheless rational, and reason had to be the basis for society and its laws.

These same concerns for virtue are evident in the writings of the great historians of the late republic, Sallust (86–ca. 34 B.C.E.) and Livy (59 B.C.E.–17 C.E.). Sallust was a supporter of Julius Caesar, who had written his own stylistically powerful histories of the Gallic and Civil Wars. For Sallust, as well as for his younger contemporary, Livy, the chaos of civil war was the direct result of moral corruption and decline that followed the successes of the empire. For Sallust, the moral failing was largely that of the Senate and its members, who trampled the plebs in their quest for power and personal glory. Livy, who was much more conservative, condemned plebeian demagogues as well as

power-hungry senators. Only those aristocratic conservatives who, like Cato, had stood for the ancient Roman traditions merited praise. In the second century B.C.E., the Greek historian Polybius had been fascinated with the rise of the Roman Republic to world supremacy. A century later the Roman historians were even more fascinated with its decline.

A different kind of morality dominated the work of Lucretius (ca. 100–55 B.C.E.), the greatest poet of the late republic. Just as Cicero had molded Stoicism into a Roman civic philosophy, Lucretius presented Epicurean materialist philosophy as a Roman alternative to the hunger for power, wealth, and glory. In his great poem *On the Nature of Things*, Lucretius presented the Epicurean's thoroughly physical understanding of the universe. He described its atomic composition, the evolution of humans from brutish beginnings to civilization, and the evil effects not only of greed and ambition but also of religion. All that exists is material reality, he believed. He also believed that religion, whether the state-supported cults of ancient Rome or the exotic cults introduced from the East, played on mortal fear of death, a fear that was irrational and groundless. "Death is nothing to us," Lucretius wrote. "It is only the natural fulfillment of life. A rational, proportional enjoyment of life is all that matters. Sorrow and anxiety come from but an ignorant emotionalism."

Emotion was precisely the goal of another poetic tradition of the late republic, that of the *neoteric* or new-style poets, especially Catullus (ca. 84–ca. 54 B.C.E.). Avoiding politics and moralistic philosophy, these poets created short, striking lyric poems that, although inspired by Hellenistic poetry, combine polished craftsmanship with a direct realism that is without precedent. Roughly two dozen of Catullus's poems are addressed to his lover:

> My lady says that she wants to marry no one so much as me,
> Not even should Jupiter himself ask her.
> So says she. But what a woman says to her eager lover
> Should be written in the wind and rushing water.

One of the most striking differences between such Latin poetry and its Greek antecedents is the reality and individuality of the persons and relationships expressed.

The same interest in the individual affected the way artists of the late republic borrowed from Greek art. Since Etruscan times, Romans had commemorated their ancestors in wax or wooden busts displayed in the atria of their homes. Hellenistic artists concentrated on the ideal, but Romans cherished the individual. The result was portraiture that caught the personality of the individual's face, even while portraying him or her as one of a type. Statues of the ideal nude, the armored warrior, or the citizen in his simple toga followed the proportions and conventions of Hellenistic sculpture. The heads, however, depict unique individuals who represent the last generation of the Roman Republic.

THE AUGUSTAN AGE AND THE *PAX ROMANA*

It took Octavian two years after his victory at Actium in 31 B.C.E. to eliminate remaining pockets of resistance and to work out a system to reconcile his rule with Roman constitutional traditions while not surrendering any of his power. That power rested on three factors: his immense wealth, which he used to secure support; his vast following among the surviving elites as well as among the populares; and his total command of the army. It also rested on the exhaustion of the Roman people, who were eager, after decades of civil strife, to return to peace and stability. Remembering the fate of Julius Caesar, however, Octavian had no intention of rekindling opposition by establishing an overt monarchy. Instead, in 27 B.C.E. he returned the republic from his own charge to the Senate and the people of Rome. In turn the Senate decreed him the title of Augustus, meaning "exalted."

This meant that Augustus, as Octavian was now called, continued to rule no less strongly than before, but he did so not through any autocratic office or title—he preferred to be called simply the "first citizen," or *princeps*—but by preserving the form of the traditional Roman magistracies. For four years he rested his authority on consecutive terms as consul, and after 23 B.C.E. he held a life position as tribune. The Senate granted him proconsular command of the provinces of Gaul, Spain, Syria, and Egypt, the major sources of imperial wealth and the locations of more than three-quarters of the Roman army. Later, the Senate declared his *imperium*, or command, of these "imperial" provinces superior to that of any governors of other provinces. Thus Augustus, through the power of the plebeian office of tribune, stood as the permanent protector of the Roman people. As simultaneously either consul or proconsul, he held the command of the army, the basis of the ancient patrician authority. He was the first and greatest emperor.

The Senate's formalities deceived no one. Augustus's power was absolute. However, by choosing not to exercise it in an absolutist manner, he forged a new constitutional system that worked well for himself and his successors. By the end of his reign, few living persons could remember the days of the republic, and fewer still mourned its passing. Under Augustus and his successors the empire enjoyed two centuries of stability and peace, the *Pax Romana*, or "Peace of Rome."

The Empire Renewed

Cicero had sought in vain a concord of the orders, a settlement of the social and political frictions of the empire through the voluntary efforts of a public-minded oligarchy. What could not happen voluntarily, Augustus imposed from above, reforming the Roman state, society, and culture.

The Senate. Key to Augustus's program of renewal was the Senate, which he made, if not a partner, then a useful subordinate in his reform. He gradually reduced the number of senators, which had grown to over 1,000, back down to 600. In the process, he eliminated the unfit and incompetent as well as the impoverished and those who failed to show the appropriate reverence toward the princeps. At the same time, he made membership hereditary, although he continued to appoint individuals of personal integrity, ability, and wealth to the body. Most conspicuous among the "new men" to enter the Senate under Augustus were the wealthy leaders of Italian cities and colonies. These small-town notables formed the core of Augustus's supporters and worked most closely with him to renew the Roman elite.

Augustus also shared with the Senate the governance of the empire, although again not on an equal footing. The Senate named governors to the peaceful provinces, while Augustus named commanders to the frontier imperial provinces where the bulk of the legions were stationed. Senators themselves served as provincial governors and military commanders. The Senate also functioned as a court of law in important cases. Still, the Senate remained

C H R O N O L O G Y
THE END OF THE REPUBLIC

135–81 B.C.E.	Revolts against the republic
133–121 B.C.E.	Gracchi reform programs
107 B.C.E.	Gaius Marius elected consul
91–82 B.C.E.	Social War and Civil War (Marius vs. Sulla)
82–79 B.C.E.	Sulla rules as dictator
79–27 B.C.E.	Era of civil wars
63 B.C.E.	Cicero elected consul; First Triumvirate (Pompey, Crassus, Caesar)
59 B.C.E.	Caesar elected consul
45 B.C.E.	Caesar defeats Pompey's forces
44 B.C.E.	Caesar is assassinated; Second Triumvirate (Mark Antony, Lepidus, Octavian)
42 B.C.E.	Octavian and Mark Antony defeat Cassius and Brutus at Philippi
31 B.C.E.	Octavian defeats Mark Antony and Cleopatra at Actium
27 B.C.E.	Octavian is declared Augustus

▲ This idealized marble portrait statue of the emperor Augustus addressing his army was found in the villa of Livia, wife of Augustus, at Prima Porta in Rome. The carvings on his breastplate recall a diplomatic incident during his reign.

a creature of the emperor, seldom asserting itself even when asked to do so by Augustus or his successors and competing within its own ranks to see who could be first to do the emperor's bidding.

The Equites. Augustus undertook an even more fundamental reform of the equites, the wealthy businessmen, bankers, and tax collectors who had vied with the senatorial aristocracy since the reforms of Tiberius Gracchus. After Actium, many equites found themselves proscribed—sentenced to death or banishment—and had their property confiscated. Augustus began to rebuild their ranks by enrolling a new generation of successful merchants and speculators who became the foundation of his administration. Equestrians formed the backbone of the officer corps of the army, of the treasury, and of the greatly expanded imperial administration. The equestrian order was open at both ends. Freedmen and soldiers who acquired sufficient wealth moved into the order, and the most successful and accomplished equestrians were promoted into the Senate.

The Army. The land crisis had provoked much of the unrest in the late republic, and after Actium, Augustus had to satisfy the needs of the loyal soldiers of his 60 legions. Drawing on his immense wealth, acquired largely from the estates of his proscripted enemies, he pensioned off 32 legions, sending them to colonies that he purchased for them throughout the empire. The remaining 28 legions became a permanent professional army stationed in imperial provinces. In time, the normal period of enlistment became fixed at 20 years, after which time Augustus provided the legionnaires with land and enough cash to settle in among the notables of their colonies. After 5 C.E., the state assumed the payment of this retirement bonus. Augustus established a small elite unit, the praetorian guard, in and around Rome as his personal military force. Initially, the praetorians protected the emperors; in later reigns, they would make them.

These measures created a permanent solution to the problem of the citizen-soldier of the later republic. Veteran colonies—all built as model Roman towns with their central forum, baths, temples, arenas, and theaters as well as their outlying villas and farms—helped to romanize the far provinces of the empire. These colonies, unlike the independent colonies of Greece in an earlier age, remained an integral part of the Roman state. Thus romanization and political integration went hand in hand, uniting through peaceful means an empire that had first been acquired by arms. Likewise, ambitious provincials, through service as auxiliaries and later as citizens, acquired a stake in the destiny of Rome.

Not every citizen, of course, could find prosperity in military service and a comfortable retirement. The problems of urban poverty in Rome continued to grow. By the time of Augustus, the capital city had reached a population of perhaps 600,000 people. A tiny minority relaxed in the comfortable homes built on the Palatine. Tens of thousands more crammed into wooden and brick tenements and jostled each other in the crowded, noisy streets. Employment was hard to find, since free men had difficulty competing against slaves. The emperors, their power as tribunes making them protectors of the poor, provided over 150,000 resident citizens with a basic dole of wheat brought from Egypt. The emperors also built aqueducts to provide water to the city. In addition, they constructed vast public recreation centers. These included both the sumptuous baths, which were combination bathing facilities, health clubs, and brothels, and arenas such as the Colosseum, where 50,000 spectators could watch gladiatorial displays, and the Circus Maximus, where a quarter of the city's population could gather at once to watch chariot races. Such mass gatherings replaced the plebeian assemblies of the republic as the occasions on which the populace could express its will. Few emperors were foolish enough to ignore the wishes that the crowd roared out in the Circus.

Divine Augustus. Augustus's renewal of Rome rested on a religious reform. In 17 B.C.E. he celebrated three days of sacrifices, processions, sacred games, and theater performances, known as the secular games. After the death of Lepidus in 12 B.C.E., Augustus assumed the office of pontifex maximus and used it to direct a reinvigoration of Roman religion. He restored numerous temples and revived ancient Roman cults. He established a series of public religious festivals, reformed priesthoods, and encouraged citizens to participate in the traditional cults of Rome. His goals in all these religious reforms were twofold. After decades of public authority controlled by violence and naked aggression, he was determined to restore the traditions of Roman piety, morality, sacred order, and faith in relationship between the gods and Roman destiny. An equally important goal was Augustus's promotion of his own cult. His adoptive father, Julius Caesar, had been deified after his death, and Augustus benefited from this association with a divine ancestor. His own genius, or guiding spirit, received special devotion in temples throughout the West dedicated to "Rome and Augustus." In the East, he was worshipped as a living god. In this manner, the emperor became identical with the state, and the state religion was closely akin to emperor worship. After his death, Augustus and virtually all of the emperors after him were worshipped as official deities in Rome itself.

Closely related to his fostering of traditional cults was Augustus's attempt to restore traditional Roman virtues, especially within the family. Like the reformers of the late republic, he believed that the declining power of the paterfamilias was at the root of much that was wrong with Rome. To reverse the trend and to restore the declining population of free Italians, Augustus encouraged marriage, procreation, and the firm control of husbands over wives. He imposed penalties for those who chose not to marry and bestowed rewards on those who produced large families. He enacted laws to prevent women from having extramarital affairs and even exiled his own daughter and granddaughter for promiscuity.

Poetry and Patronage. Augustus actively patronized those writers who shared his conservative religious and ethical values and who might be expected to glorify the princeps, and he used his power to censor and silence writers whom he considered immoral. Chief among the favored were the poets Virgil (70–19 B.C.E.) and Horace (65–8 B.C.E.). Through their poetry in praise of the emperor, these poets conferred immortality on Augustus.

Horace celebrated Augustus's victory at Actium, his reform of the empire, and reestablishment of the ancient cults that had brought Rome divine favor. In Horace's poems, Augustus is almost a god. His deeds are compared to those of the great heroes of Roman legend and judged superior. Interspersed with the poems praising Augustus are poems of great beauty praising the love of both boys and girls and the enjoyment of wine and music. To Horace, the glories of the new age inaugurated by Augustus with the secular games of 17 B.C.E. included not only the splendor of empire but also the enjoyment of privileged leisure.

Virgil began his poetic career with pastoral poems celebrating the joys of rural life and the bitterness of the loss of lands in the Civil Wars. Later, under the patronage of Maecenas and Augustus, Virgil turned directly to glorifying Augustus and the new age. The ultimate expression of this effort was the *Aeneid,* an epic that was consciously intended to serve for the Roman world the role of the Homeric poems in the Greek.

As he reworked the legend of Aeneas—a Trojan hero who escaped the destruction of the city, wandered throughout the Mediterranean, and ultimately came to Latium—Virgil presented a panoramic history of Rome and its destiny. Unlike the Homeric heroes, Achilles and Odysseus, who were driven by their own search for glory, Aeneas was driven by his piety, that is, his duty toward the gods and his devotion to his father. Aeneas had to follow his destiny, which was the destiny of Rome, to rule the world in harmony and justice. In the midst of his wanderings, Aeneas (like Odysseus before him) entered the underworld to speak with his dead father. There he saw a vision of Rome's greatness to come. He saw the great heroes of Rome, including Augustus, "son of a god," and he was told of the particular mission of Rome.

> Let others fashion in bronze more lifelike, breathing images
> Let others (as I believe they will) draw living faces from marble
> Others shall plead cases better and others will better
> Track the course of the heavens and announce the rising stars.
> Remember, Romans, your task is to rule the peoples
> This will be your art: to teach the habit of peace
> To spare the defeated and to subdue the haughty.

The finest of the poets who felt the heavy hand of Augustus's disfavor was Ovid (43 B.C.E.–17 C.E.), the great Latin poet of erotic love. In *Art of Love* and *Amores* he cheerfully preached the art of seduction and adultery. He delighted in poking irreverent fun at everything from the sanctity of Roman marriage to the serious business of warfare. In his great *Metamorphoses,* a series of artfully told myths, he parodied the heroic epic, mocking with grotesque humor the very material that Virgil used to create the *Aeneid.* By 8 C.E., Augustus had had enough. He exiled the witty poet to Tomis, a miserable frontier post on the Black Sea. There, Ovid spent the last nine years of his life, suffering from the harsh climate, the danger of nomadic attacks, and, most of all, the pain of exile from the center of the civilization he loved. Exactly what offense he committed is not clear. Perhaps for Augustus what was most intolerable was that, in spite of the emperor's efforts to foster an immortal poetic tradition glorifying the Roman virtues, Ovid was clearly appreciated by his contemporaries as the greatest poet of the age.

Augustus's Successors

Horace and Virgil may have made Augustus's fame immortal. His flesh was not. The problem of succession occupied him throughout much of his long reign and was never satisfactorily solved. Since the princeps was not a specific office, but a combination of offices and honors held together by military might and religious aura, formal dynastic succession was impossible. Instead, Augustus attempted to select a blood relative as successor, include him in his reign, and have him voted the various offices and dignities that constituted his own position.

Unfortunately, Augustus outlived all of his first choices. His nephew and adopted son Marcellus, to whom he married his only child Julia, died in 23 B.C.E. He then married Julia to his old associate Agrippa and began to groom him for the position, but Agrippa died in 12 B.C.E. Lucius and Gaius, the sons of Julia and Agrippa, also died young. Augustus's final choice, his stepson Tiberius (14–37 C.E.), proved to be a gloomy and unpopular successor but nevertheless was a competent ruler under whom the machinery of the empire functioned smoothly. The continued orderly functioning of the empire even under the subsequent members of Augustus's family—the mad Gaius, also known as Caligula (37–41), the bookish but competent Claudius (41–54), and initially under Nero (54–68)—is a tribute to the soundness of Augustus's constitutional changes and the vested interest that the descendants of Augustus's military and aristocratic supporters had in them.

Nero was more than even they could bear, however. Profligate, vicious, and paranoid, Nero divided his time between murdering his relatives and associates—including his mother, his aunt, his wife, his tutors, and eventually his most capable generals—and squandering his vast wealth on mad attempts to gain recognition as a great poet, actor, singer, and athlete. (When he competed in games, other contestants wisely lost.) Finally, in 68 C.E., the exasperated commanders in Gaul, Spain, and Africa revolted. Once more, war swept the empire. Nero slit his own throat, and in the next year, the "Year of the Four Emperors," four men in quick succession won the office, only to lose their lives just as quickly. Finally, in 70 C.E., Vespasian (69–79 C.E.), the son of a "new man," who had risen through the ranks to the command in Egypt, secured the principate and restored order.

The first emperors had rounded off the frontiers of the empire, transforming the client states of Cappadocia, Thrace, Commagene, and Judaea in the east and Mauritania in North Africa into provinces. Claudius presided over the conquest of Britain in 43 C.E. These emperors introduced efficient means of governing and protecting the empire and tied together its inhabitants, roughly 50 million in the time of Augustus, in networks of mutual dependence and common interest. Augustus established peaceful relations with the Parthian empire, which permitted unhampered trade between China, India, and Rome. In the west, after a disastrous attempt to expand the empire to the Elbe ended in the loss of three legions in 9 C.E., the frontier was fixed at the Rhine. In the east, the northern border stopped at the Danube. The deserts of Africa, Nubia, and southern Arabia formed what many in the first century C.E. saw as the "natural" southern boundaries of the empire.

When Vespasian's troops fought their way into Rome in vicious hand-to-hand street fighting, the populace watched with idle fascination. The violence of 69 C.E., unlike that of the previous century, involved mostly professional legions and their commanders. The rest of the empire sat back to watch. In a few restive regions of the empire, some Gauls, the Batavians along the Rhine, and diehard Jewish rebels tried to use the momentary confusion to revolt, but by and large the empire remained stable. This stability was the greatest achievement of Augustus and his immediate successors.

The emperors of the Flavian dynasty, Vespasian and his sons and successors Titus (79–81) and Domitian (81–96), were stern and unpretentious provincials who restored the authority and dignity of their office, although they also did away with most of the trappings of republican legitimacy that Augustus and his immediate successors had used. They solidified the administrative system, returned the legions to their fairly permanent posts, and opened the highest reaches of power to provincial elites as never before. After the Flavian emperors, the Antonines (96–193)—especially Trajan (98–117), Hadrian (117–138), and Antoninus Pius (138–161)—ruled for what has been termed "the period in the history of the world during which the human race was most happy and prosperous."

Breaking the Peace. Not all was peaceful in this period, however. Trajan initiated a new and final expansion of the imperial frontiers. Between 101 and 106 he conquered Dacia (modern Romania). He resumed war with the Parthians, conquering the provinces of Armenia and Mesopotamia by 116. During the second century the Palestinian Jews revolted in 115–117 and again in 132–135. The emperor Hadrian put down this second revolt and expelled the surviving Jews from Judaea. Along both the eastern and western frontiers, legions had to contend with sporadic border incidents. Within the borders, however, a system of Roman military camps, towns, and rural states constituted a remarkably heterogeneous and prosperous civilization.

Administering the Empire. The imperial government of this vast empire was as oppressive as it was primitive. Taxes, rents, forced labor service, military levies and requisitions, and outright extortion weighed heavily on its subjects. To a considerable extent, the inhabitants of the empire continued to be governed by the indigenous elites whose cooperation Rome won by giving them broad autonomy. Thus, Hellenistic cities continued to manage their own affairs under the supervision of essentially amateur Roman governors.

▲ The Roman Empire, 14 and 117 C.E. At its fullest extent, the Roman Empire included the entire Mediterranean and Black Sea worlds and all of western Europe, as well as the ancient civilizations of Egypt and Mesopotamia.

Local town councils in Gaul, Germany, and Spain supervised the collection of taxes, maintained public works projects, and kept the peace. In return for their participation in Roman rule, these elites received Roman citizenship, a prize that carried prestige, legal protection, and the promise of further advancement in the Roman world.

In those imperial provinces that were controlled directly by the emperor, the army was much more in evidence, and the professional legions were the ultimate argument of imperial tax collectors and imperial representatives, or *procurators*. Moreover, as the turmoil of the Year of the Four Emperors amply demonstrated, the military was the ultimate foundation of imperial rule itself. Still, soldiers were as much farmers as fighters. Legions usually remained in the same location for years, and veterans' colonies sprang up around military camps.

Finally, much of the governing of the empire was done by the vast households of the Roman elite, particularly that of the princeps. Freedmen and slaves from the emperor's household often governed vast regions, oversaw imperial estates, and managed imperial factories and mines. The descendants of the old Roman nobility might look down their noses at imperial freedmen, but they obeyed their orders.

The empire worked because it rewarded those who worked with it and left alone those who paid their taxes and kept quiet. Local elites, auxiliary soldiers, and freedmen could aspire to rise to the highest ranks of the power elite. As provincials were drawn into the Roman system, they were also drawn into the world of Roman culture. Proper education in Latin and Greek, the ability to hold one's own in philosophical discussion, and the absorption

CHRONOLOGY

THE ROMAN EMPIRE

Julio-Claudian Period, 27 B.C.E.–68 C.E.	Augustus (27 B.C.E.–14 C.E.)
	Tiberius (14–37 C.E.)
	Caligula (37–41)
	Claudius (41–54)
	Nero (54–68)
Year of the Four Emperors, 69 C.E.	
Flavian Period, 69–96	Vespasian (69–79)
	Titus (79–81)
	Domitian (81–96)
Antonine Period, 96–192	Trajan (98–117)
	Hadrian (117–138)
	Antoninus Pius (138–161)
	Marcus Aurelius (161–180)
	Commodus (180–192)

of Roman ways, including styles of dress, recreation, and religious cults, all were essential for ambitious provincials. Thus, in the course of the first century C.E., the disparate portions of the empire competed, not to free themselves from the Roman yoke, but to become Roman themselves.

RELIGIONS FROM THE EAST

The same openness that permitted the spread of Latin letters and Roman baths to distant Gaul and the shores of the Black Sea provided paths of dissemination for other, distinctly un-Roman religious traditions. For many in the empire, the traditional rituals offered to the household gods and the state cults of Jupiter, Mars, and the other official deities were insufficient foci of religious devotion. Many educated members of the elite were actually vaguely monotheistic. Many others in the empire sought personal, emotional bonds with the divine world.

As noted in Chapter 4, in the second century B.C.E. the Roman world had been caught up in the emotional cult of Dionysus, an ecstatic, personal, and liberating religion entirely unlike the official Roman cults. Again in the first century C.E., so-called mystery cults—that is, religions promising immediate personal contact with a deity that would bring immortality—spread throughout the empire. Some were officially introduced into Rome as part of its open polytheism. These included the Anatolian Cybele or great mother-goddess cult, which was present in Rome from the late third century B.C.E. Devotees underwent a ritual in which they were bathed in the blood of a bull or a ram, thereby obtaining immortality. The cult of the Egyptian goddess Isis spread throughout the Hellenistic world and to Rome in the republican period. From Persia came the cult of Mithras, the ancient Indo-Iranian god of light and truth, who, as bringer of victory, found special favor with Roman soldiers and merchants eager for success in this life and immortality beyond the grave. Generally, Rome tolerated these alien cults as long as they could be assimilated into, or at least reconciled in some way with, the cult of the Roman gods and the genius of the emperor.

Jewish Resistance

With one religious group this assimilation was impossible. The Jews of Palestine had long refused any accommodation with the polytheistic cults of the Hellenistic kingdoms or with Rome. Roman conquerors and emperors, aware of the problems of their Hellenistic predecessors, went to considerable lengths to avoid antagonizing this small and unusual group of people. When Pompey seized Jerusalem in 63 B.C.E., he was careful not to interfere in Jewish religion and even left Judaea under the control of the Jewish high priest. Later, Judaea was made into a client kingdom under the puppet Herod. Jews were allowed to maintain their monotheistic cult and were excused from making sacrifices to the Roman gods.

Still, the Jewish community remained deeply divided about its relationship with the wider world and with Rome. At one end of the spectrum were the Sadducees, a party composed largely of members of priestly families, who enjoyed considerable influence with their foreign rulers. They were staunch defenders of the ancient Jewish law, or *Torah*, but not to the exclusion of other later religious and legal traditions. They were willing to work with Rome and even adopt some elements of Hellenism, as long as the services in the temple could continue.

At the other end of the spectrum were the Hasidim, those who rejected all compromise with Hellenistic culture and collaboration with foreign powers. Many expected the arrival of a messiah, a liberator who would destroy the Romans and reestablish the kingdom of David. One party within the Hasidim were the Pharisees, who practiced strict dietary rules and rituals to maintain the separation of Jews and Gentiles (literally, "the peoples," that is, all non-Jews). The Pharisees accepted the writings of the Hebrew prophets along with the Torah and abided by a still larger body of orally transmitted law, the "tradition of the elders." The most prominent figure in this movement was Hillel (ca. 30 B.C.E.–10 C.E.), a Jewish scholar from Babylon who came to Jerusalem as a teacher of the law. He began a tradition of legal and scriptural interpretation that, in an expanded version centuries later, became the Talmud. Hillel was also a moral teacher who taught peace and love, not revolt. "Whatever is hateful to you, do not to your fellow man: this is the whole Law; the rest is mere commentary," he taught.

For all their insistence on purity and separation from other peoples, the Pharisees did not advocate violent revolt against Rome. They preferred to await divine intervention. Another group of Hasidim, the Zealots, were less willing to wait. After 6 C.E., when Judaea, Samaria, and Idumaea were annexed and combined into the province of Judaea and administered by imperial procurators, the Zealots began to organize sporadic armed resistance to Roman rule. As ever, armed resistance was met with violent suppression. Throughout the first century C.E., clashes between Roman troops and Zealot revolutionaries grew more frequent and more widespread.

The Origins of Christianity

The already complex landscape of the Jewish religious world became further complicated by the brief career of Joshua ben Joseph (ca. 6 B.C.E.–30 C.E.), known to history as Jesus of Nazareth and to his followers as Jesus the Messiah or the Christ. Jesus came from Galilee, an area known as a Zealot stronghold. However, while Jesus preached the imminent coming of the kingdom, he did so in an entirely nonpolitical manner. He was, like many popular religious leaders, a miracle worker. When people flocked around him to see his wonders, he preached a message of peace and love of God and neighbor. His teachings were entirely within the Jewish tradition and closely resembled those of Hillel. However, while many contemporary religious leaders announced the imminent coming of the messiah, Jesus' closest followers, the apostles and disciples, began to think that he himself was the messiah and expected him to restore the kingdom of Israel.

For roughly three years, Jesus preached in Judaea and Galilee, drawing large, excited crowds. Many of his followers pressed him to lead a revolt against Roman authority and reestablish the kingdom of David, even though he insisted that the kingdom he would establish was not of this world. Other Jews saw his claims as blasphemy and his assertion that he was the king of Jews, even if a heavenly one, as a threat to the status quo. Jesus became more and more a figure of controversy, a catalyst for violence. Ultimately, the Roman procurator, Pontius Pilate, decided that Jesus posed a threat to law and order. Pilate, like other Roman magistrates, had no interest in the internal religious affairs of the Jews. However, he was troubled by anyone who had the potential for causing political disturbances, no matter how unintentional. Pilate ordered Jesus scourged and put to death by crucifixion, a common Roman form of execution for slaves, pirates, thieves, and noncitizen troublemakers.

Spreading the Faith. The cruel death of Jesus ended the popular agitation he had stirred up, but it did not deter his closest followers. They soon announced that three days after his death, he had risen and had appeared to them numerous times over the next few weeks. They took this resurrection as proof of his claims to be the messiah and confirmation of his promise of eternal life to those who believed in him. Soon a small group of his followers, led by Peter (d. ca. 64 C.E.), formed another Jewish sect—preaching and praying daily in the temple. New members were initiated into this sect, which soon became known as Christianity—through baptism, a purification rite in which the initiate was submerged briefly in flowing water. They also shared a ritual meal in which bread and wine were distributed to members. Otherwise, they remained entirely within the Jewish religious and cultural tradition, and hellenized Jews and pagans who wished to join the sect had to observe strict Jewish law and custom.

Christianity spread beyond its origin as a Jewish sect because of the work of one man, Paul of Tarsus (ca. 5–ca. 67 C.E.). Although Paul was an observant Jew, he was part of the wider cosmopolitan world of the empire and from birth enjoyed the privileges of Roman citizenship. He saw Christianity as a separate tradition, completing and perfecting Judaism but intended for the whole world.

Paul set out to spread his message, crisscrossing Asia Minor and Greece and even traveling to Rome. Wherever he went, Paul won converts and established churches, called *ecclesiae,* or assemblies. Everywhere Paul and the other disciples went, they worked wonders, cast out demons, cured

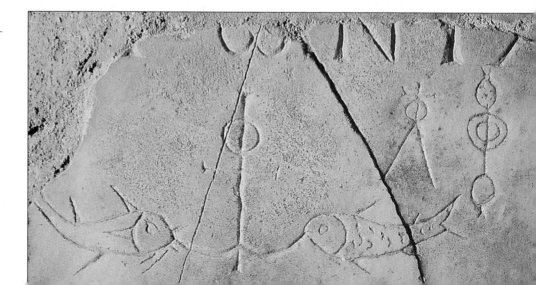

▶ A Roman tombstone inscribed with some of the earliest examples of Christian symbols. The anchor represents hope, while the fish recall Jesus' words "I will make you fishers of men."

illnesses, and preached. Paul's teachings, while firmly rooted in the Jewish historical tradition, were radically new. God had created the human race, he taught, in the image of God and destined it for eternal life. However, by the deliberate sin of the first humans, Adam and Eve, humans had lost eternal life and introduced evil and death into the world. Even then, God did not abandon his people but began, through the Jews, to prepare for their eventual redemption. That salvation was accomplished by Jesus, the son of God, through his faith, a free and unmerited gift of God to his elect. Through faith, the Christian ritual of baptism, and participation in the church, men and women could share in the salvation offered by God, Paul said.

How many conversions resulted from Paul's theological message and how many resulted from the miracles he and the other disciples worked will never be known, but another factor certainly played a part in the success of conversions. That was the courage Christians showed in the face of persecution.

Even Rome's elasticity and tolerance of new religions could be stretched only so far. The Christians' belief in the divinity of their founder was no problem. Their offer of salvation to those who participated in their mysteries was only normal. But their stubborn refusal to acknowledge the existence of the other gods and to participate in the cult of the genius of the emperor was intolerable. Christianity was an aggressive and successful cult, attracting followers throughout the empire. It was viewed not as religion, but as subversion. Beginning during Nero's reign, Roman officials sporadically rounded up Christians, destroyed their sacred scriptures, and executed those who refused to sacrifice to the imperial genius. But instead of decreasing the cult's appeal, persecution only aided it. For those who believed that death was birth into a new and better life, martyrdom was a reward, not a penalty. The strength of their convictions convinced others of the truth of their religion.

Christian Institutions. As the number of Christians increased in the face of persecution, the organization and teaching of this new faith began to evolve. A hierarchy developed within the various communities that Paul and the other apostles established. The leader of each community was the bishop, an office derived from the priestly leader of the Jewish synagogue, who was responsible for both charity and the Torah. Assisted by *presbyters* (priests), deacons, and deaconesses, bishops assumed growing responsibilities as expectations for the second coming receded. These responsibilities included presiding over the *eucharist,* or ritual meal, that was the center of Christian worship, as well as enforcing discipline and teaching.

Christian teaching focused on the Gospels, accounts of Jesus' life written toward the end of the first century; letters, or Epistles; and narratives and visionary writings by his early disciplines and their immediate successors. In their preaching, bishops connected these texts to the tradition of Jewish Scriptures, explaining that the life of Jesus was the completion and fulfillment of the Jewish tradition. Over centuries, certain Gospels and Epistles and one book of revelation came to be regarded as authoritative and, together with the version of Jewish Scripture that was in use in Greek-speaking Jewish communities, constituted the Christian Bible. In the second and third centuries, the Christian message began to be challenged. Hellenistic moral philosophers and Roman officials condemned Christianity as immoral and, because of its rejection of the cult of the emperor and the gods of Rome, atheistic. Neoplatonists found the teachings of Christianity philosophically naive. Even within the Christian community, different groups held different views. Monatists argued that Christians were obligated to fast and abstain from marriage until the second coming. Dualist Gnostics interpreted the Christian message as a secret wisdom, or *gnosis,* which, combined with baptism, freed men and women from their fates.

Bishops defended the faith and determined what was correct. By the end of the first century, episcopal (from the Greek word for bishop) authority was understood to derive from the bishops' status as successors of the apostles. Bishops of the churches that had been established directly by the apostles in Jerusalem, Antioch, Alexandria, and Rome—termed *patriarchates*—claimed special authority over other, less ancient communities. Gradually, the exalted position of the bishop and his assistants led to a distinction between the clergy and the laity, the rank and file of Christians. At the same time, women, who had played central roles in Jesus' ministry, were excluded from positions of authority within the clergy. In this process, the Christian community came to resemble closely the Roman patriarchal household, a resemblance that increased the appeal of the new sect to nonbelievers.

Although Christianity spread rapidly through the eastern Mediterranean in the first and second centuries, it remained a minor irritation in the eyes of the empire's rulers. Its fundamental role in the transformation of the Roman world would not become clear until the third and fourth centuries.

GEOGRAPHICAL TOUR

A Tour of the Empire

Each town in the sprawling empire, from York in the north of Britain to Dura Europos on the Euphrates, was a center of Roman culture, or *Romanitas,* in provinces that were still closely tied to local provincial traditions. Each boasted a forum where locals conducted business and government affairs. Each had an arena for gladiatorial games, baths, a racetrack, and a theater where Greek and Latin plays entertained the populace. Temples to the Capitoline Jupiter and to the deified emperors adorned the cities. Aqueducts brought fresh water from distant springs into the heart of the cities.

Connecting these towns was a network of well-maintained roads frequented by imperial administrators, merchants, the idle rich, and soldiers. Beginning in 120, the roads of the empire saw a most unusual traveler: the emperor Hadrian, who traveled them to conduct an extraordinary inspection of the length and breadth of his empire (see **Map A**). Hadrian, the adopted son and heir of Trajan, had received an excellent Greek education and was an accomplished writer, poet, connoisseur, and critic. Still, he had spent most of his early career as a successful field commander and administrator in Dacia and the lower Danube. Years of military experience had made Hadrian very aware of the potential weaknesses of the vast Roman borders, and his primary interest was to inspect those military commands that were most critical for imperial stability.

The Western Provinces

Thus Hadrian set out westward, traveling first through the provinces of Gaul, prosperous and pacific regions long integrated into the Roman world (see **Map B**). Gaul was known for its good food, its pottery manufacture, and its comfortable, if culturally slightly backward, local elites. Much of Gaul's prosperity came from supplying the legions guarding the Rhine-Danube frontier, and it was across the Rhine toward Germany where the legions faced the barbarians of "Free Germany," that Hadrian was headed. Legions stationed at Xanten, Cologne, and Trier (see **Map B**) were far removed from the Mediterranean world that formed the heart of the empire. The dark forests, cold winters, and crude life made Germany a hardship post. Hadrian threw himself into the harsh camp life of Germany in order to bolster discipline and combat

▼ **Map A. The Roman Empire at the Time of Hadrian.** Hadrian's empire was a well-ordered world of provinces governed by a vast bureaucracy and held together by a common culture and the power of the imperial army.

readiness. He shared rough field rations, long marches, and simple conditions with his troops.

From Germany, Hadrian traveled down the Rhine through what is today Holland and then crossed over to Britain. Here, too, defense was utmost on his mind. Celts from the northern, unconquered portion of the island had been harassing the romanized society to the south. The emperor ordered the erection of a great wall over 50 miles long across Britain from coast to coast. South of the wall, Roman Britain was studded with hundreds of Roman villas, ranging from simple country farmhouses to vast mansions with more than 60 rooms. Over a hundred towns and villages were large enough to boast walls, ranging from London with a population of roughly 30,000 to numerous settlements of between 2,000 and 10,000 inhabitants.

No sooner had he put things straight in Britain than Hadrian returned to Gaul, paused in Nîmes in the south (see **Map B**), and then headed south toward his native Spain (see **Map C**). By the second century C.E., Spain was even more thoroughly romanized than most of Gaul, having been an integral part of the empire since the Second Punic War. It was also far richer. Spanish mines yielded gold, iron, and tin, and Spanish estates produced grain and cattle. Since the reign of Vespasian, the residents of Spanish communities had been given some of the rights of Roman citizens, making them eligible for military service, a value even greater to the empire than Spain's mineral wealth. Problems with military service brought Hadrian to Spain. The populace was becoming increasingly resistant to conscription, a universal phenomenon, and Hadrian's presence strengthened the efforts of recruiters.

The Eastern Provinces

Hadrian soon set sail for the provinces of Asia (see **Map D**). There he was in the heart of the Hellenistic world, so central to the empire's prosperity. Its great cities were centers of manufacture, and its ports were the vital links in Mediterranean trade. As in Hellenistic times, these cities were the organizing principle of the region; local senates were largely self-governing, and rivalries among cities prevented the creation of any sort of provincial identities. In Asia, Hadrian worked with individual communities, showering honors and privileges on the most cooperative and founding new communities in the Anatolian hinterland. The last activity was particularly important because, for all of the civilized glory of urban Asia, the rural areas remained strongly tied to traditions that neither Greeks nor Romans had managed to weaken. The empire remained two worlds: one urban, hellenized, mercantile, and collaborationist; the other rural, traditional, exploited, and potentially separatist.

In 125, Hadrian left Asia for Greece (see **Map E**), where he participated in traditional religious cults. Greek culture continued to be vital for Rome, and by participating in the

▲ **Map B. The Provinces of Gaul.** Gaul was a vast agricultural region supplying legions posted along the Rhine River.

▲ **Map C. Spain.** Roman Spain was a major source of gold, iron, and tin as well as a vital agricultural region.

rituals of Achaea and Athens, the emperor placed himself in the traditions of the legendary Heracles and Philip of Macedon. Finally, in 127, Hadrian returned to Rome via Sicily, a prosperous amalgam of Greek and Latin cultures dominated by vast senatorial estates, or *latifundia*.

This restless emperor spent less than 12 months in Rome before setting out again, this time for Africa. There, as in Germany, his concern was the discipline and preparedness of the troops guarding the rich agricultural areas and thriving commercial centers of the coast from the marauding nomads on the edges of the desert. Shortly after that, he was again in Athens to dedicate public works projects he had undertaken as well as an altar to himself. From Greece he headed east, again crossing Asia and this time moving into Cappadocia and Syria (see **Map A**). His concerns here were again defense, but against a powerful civilized Parthian empire, not barbarian tribes.

Moving southward, Hadrian stopped in Jerusalem, where he dedicated a shrine to Jupiter Capitolinus on the site of the destroyed Jewish temple before heading to Egypt for an inspection trip up the Nile (see **Map F**). Egypt remained the wealthiest Roman province and the most exploited. Since Augustus, Egypt had been governed directly by the imperial household, its agricultural wealth from the Nile Delta going to feed the Roman masses. At the same time, Alexandria continued to be one of the greatest cultural centers of the Roman world. This culture, however, was a fusion of Greek and Egyptian traditions, constantly threatening to form the basis for a nationalist opposition to Roman administrators and tax collectors. Hadrian sought to defuse this powder keg by disciplining administrators and by founding a new city, Antinopolis, which he hoped would create a center of loyalty to Rome.

Hadrian finally returned to the imperial residence on the Palatine in 131. He had spent over ten years on the road and had no doubt done much to strengthen and preserve the *Pax Romana*. Still, to the careful observer the weaknesses of the empire were as evident as its strengths. The frontiers were vast and constantly tested by a profusion of hostile tribes and peoples. Roman citizens from Italy, Gaul, and Spain were increasingly unwilling to serve in such far-flung regions. As a result, the legions were manned by progressively less romanized soldiers, and their battle readiness and discipline, poorly enforced by homesick officers, declined dangerously. In the more civilized eastern provinces, corrupt local elites, imperial governors, and officials siphoned off imperial revenues destined for the army to build their personal fortunes. Also, in spite of centuries of hellenization and Roman administration, city and countryside remained culturally and politically separated. Early in the second century, such problems were small clouds on the horizon, but in the following century they would grow into a storm that would threaten the very existence of the empire.

▲ **Map D. Asia.** Asia remained for Rome the center of Hellenistic civilization with its populous cities and vital trade routes.

▲ **Map E. Italy and Greece.** Italy, although economically dependent on the rest of the empire, was the vital center of the empire, while Greece was honored more for its glorious past than its present importance.

▲ **Map F. Egypt.** Throughout the Roman period,. Egypt was the breadbasket of the empire, supplying Rome and other cities with essential grain.

The Culture of Antonine Rome

Annius Florus, a poet friend of Hadrian, commenting on the emperor's exhausting journeys, wrote:

I do not want to be Caesar,
To walk about among the Britons,
To endure the Scythian hoar-frosts.

To this, Hadrian replied:

I do not want to be Florus,
To walk about among taverns,
To lurk about among cook-shops.

Like the other members of his dynasty, Hadrian enjoyed an easy familiarity with men of letters, and like other men of letters of the period, Florus was a provincial, an African drawn from the provincial world to the great capital. Another provincial, Rome's greatest historian, Cornelius Tacitus (ca. 56–ca. 120), recorded the history of the first century of the empire. Tacitus wrote to instruct and to edify his generation and did so in a style characterized by irony and a sharp sense of the differences between public propaganda and the realities of power politics. His picture of Germanic and British societies served as a warning to Rome against excessive self-confidence and laxity.

Tacitus's contemporaries, Plutarch (ca. 46–after 119) and Suetonius (ca. 69–after 122), were biographers rather than historians. Plutarch, who wrote in Greek, composed *Parallel Lives,* a series of character studies in which he compared an eminent Greek with an eminent Roman. Suetonius also wrote biographies, using anecdotes to portray character. Suetonius's biographies of the emperors fall short of the literary and philosophical qualities of Plutarch's character studies and far short of Tacitus's histories. Suetonius delighted in the rumors of private scandals that surrounded the emperors and used personal vice to explain public failings.

In the later second century, Romans in general preferred the study and writing of philosophy, particularly Stoicism, over history. The most influential Stoic philosopher of the century was Epictetus (ca. 55–135), a former slave who taught that people could be free by the control of their will and the cultivation of inner peace. Like the early Stoics, Epictetus taught the universal brotherhood of humankind and the identity of nature and divine providence. He urged his pupils to recognize that dependence on external things was the cause of unhappiness and therefore they should free themselves from reliance on material possessions, public esteem, and all other things prized by the worldly.

The philosophy of Epictetus found its most eager pupil in an emperor. Marcus Aurelius (161–180) reigned during a period when the stresses glimpsed by Hadrian were beginning to show in a much more alarming manner. Once more, the Parthians attacked the eastern frontier, while in Britain and Germany, barbarians struck across the borders. In 166, a confederation of barbarians known as the Marcomanni crossed the Danube and raided as far south as northern Italy. A plague, brought west by troops returning from the Parthian front, ravaged the whole empire. Like his predecessor Hadrian, Aurelius felt bound to endure the Scythian hoar-frosts rather than luxuriate in the taverns of Rome. He spent virtually the whole of his reign on the Danubian frontier, repelling the barbarians and shoring up the empire's defenses.

Throughout his reign, Aurelius found consolation in the Stoic philosophy of Epictetus. In his soldier's tent at night he composed his *Meditations,* a volume of philosophical musings. Like the slave, the emperor sought freedom from the burden of his office in his will and in the proper understanding of his role in the divine order. He called himself to introspection, to a constant awareness, under the glories and honors heaped upon him by his entourage, of his true human nature: "A poor soul burdened with a corpse."

Aurelius played his role well, dying in what is today Vienna, far from the pleasures of the capital. However, his Stoic philosophy did not serve the empire well. For all his emphasis on understanding, Aurelius badly misjudged his son Commodus (180–192), who succeeded him. Commodus, whose chief interest was in being a gladiator, saw himself as the incarnation of Heracles and appeared in public clad as a gladiator and as consul. As Commodus sank into insanity, Rome was once more convulsed by purges and proscriptions. Commodus's assassination in 192 did not end the violence. The *Pax Romana* was over.

Conclusion

THE HAPHAZARD CONQUEST OF THE MEDITERRANEAN WORLD threw Roman republican government, traditional culture, and antagonistic social groups into chaos. The result was a century and a half of intermittent violence and civil war before a new political and social order headed by an absolute monarch established a new equilibrium. During the following two centuries, a deeply hellenized Roman civilization tied together the vast empire by incorporating the wealthy and powerful of the Western world into its fluid power structure while brutally crushing those who would not or could not conform. The binding force of the Roman empire was great and would survive political crises in the third century as great as those that had brought down the republic 300 years before.

QUESTIONS FOR REVIEW

1. How were rifts in Roman society widened by Rome's expansion into an empire?
2. In what ways were the life and thought of Cicero indicative of an age characterized by civil conflict and the collapse of republican traditions?
3. How was religious reform an important part of Augustus's efforts to restore stability to Roman society?
4. What did the Flavian and Antonine emperors do to keep Rome's vast empire intact and in relative peace?
5. How did Paul of Tarsus transform the teachings of Jesus of Nazareth from an outgrowth of Judaism into a separate spiritual tradition?

DISCOVERING WESTERN CIVILIZATION ONLINE

You can obtain more information about imperial Rome at the websites listed below.
See also the companion website that accompanies this text:
www.ablongman.com/kishlansky, which contains an online study guide and
additional resources.

General Websites

ancienthistory.about.com/cs/gracchi/
An introduction to the Gracchi with links to other sites.

www.iath.virginia.edu/pompeii/page-1.html
A site devoted to the Roman city of Pompeii, which was destroyed by Mount Vesuvius in 79 C.E.

The End of the Republic

johara.web.wesleyan.edu/CCIV274links.html
Dr. Jim O'Hara's web page devoted to the end of the Roman republic.

www.utexas.edu/depts/classics/documents/Cic.html
A site dedicated to Cicero, including texts of his orations and a bibliography.

vergil.classics.upenn.edu/
A site dedicated to providing resources and teaching materials on Virgil.

The Augustan Age and the *Pax Romana*

www.carthage.edu/outis/augustus.html
A web page devoted to the Emperor Augustus with links to archaeology and art of the Augustan Age.

www.unicaen.fr/rome/anglais/geographique/planbis.html
A point and click map of the city of Rome during the empire.

corinth.sas.upenn.edu/corinth.html
A computer reconstruction of Roman Corinth.

SUGGESTIONS FOR FURTHER READING

Primary Sources

Major selections of the works of Caesar, Cicero, Tacitus, Plutarch, Suitonius, and Marcus Aurelius are available in English translation from Penguin Books. *Roman Civilization Selected Readings, Vol. II: The Empire* (1951) by Naphtali Lewis and Meyer Reinhold contains a wide selection of documents with useful introductions.

The Price of Empire

Mary Beard and Michael Crawford, *Rome in the Late Republic* (Ithaca, N.Y.: Cornell University Press, 1985). An analysis of the political processes of the late republic as part of the development of Roman society, not simply the decay of the republic.

Henrik Mouritsen, *Plebs and Politics in the Late Roman Republic* (Cambridge: Cambridge University Press, 2001). A study of the political role of the masses in the last years of the republic.

The End of the Republic

Robert Gurval, *Actium and Augustus: the Politics and Emotions of Civil War* (Ann Arbor: University of Michigan Press, 1998). Important study of the end of the republic.

A. J. Langguth, *A Noise of War: Caesar, Pompey, Octavian, and the Struggle for Rome* (New York: Simon & Schuster, 1994). An account of the era of the Civil Wars and the end of the republic.

The Augustan Age and the *Pax Romana*

Philippe Ariès and Georges Duby, eds., *History of Private Life, Vol. 1: From Pagan Rome to Byzantium* (Cambridge, Mass.: Harvard University Press, 1986). Essays on the interior private life of Romans and Greeks by leading French and British historians.

J. B. Campbell, *The Emperor and the Roman Army* (New York: Oxford University Press, 1984). Essential for understanding the military's role in the Roman empire.

Albrecht Dihle, *Greek and Latin Literature of the Roman Empire: From Augustus to Justinian* (New York: Routledge, 1994). A survey of classical literature.

Karl Galinsky, *Augustan Culture* (Princeton: Princeton University Press, 1998). An important study of the cultural world of Augustus.

Judith P. Hallett, *Fathers and Daughters in Roman Society and the Elite Family* (Princeton, N.J.: Princeton University Press, 1984). A study of indirect power exercised by elite women in the Roman world as daughters, mothers, and sisters.

J. E. Lendon, *Empire of Honour: The Art of Government in the Roman World* (Oxford: Oxford University Press, 2001). A provocative study of Roman despotism and the support it enjoyed from the ruling classes of the provinces.

D. A. West and A. J. Woodman, *Poetry and Politics in the Age of Augustus* (New York: Cambridge University Press, 1984). An exploration of the cultural program of Augustus.

Religions from the East

Schuyler Brown, *The Origins of Christianity: A Historical Introduction of the New Testament,* Rev. ed. (Oxford: Oxford University Press, 1993). A balanced and comprehensive introduction to early Christianity.

Ramsay MacMullen, *Paganism in the Roman Empire* (New Haven, Conn.: Yale University Press, 1981). A description of the varieties and levels of pagan religion in the Roman world.

Geographical Tour: A Tour of the Empire

Peter Garnsey and Richard Saller, *The Roman Empire: Economy, Society, and Culture* (Berkeley: University of California Press, 1987). A topical study of imperial administration, economy, religion, and society, arguing the coercive and exploitive effects of Roman civilization on the agricultural societies of the Mediterranean world.

Fergus Millar, *Rome, the Greek World, and the East: The Roman Republic and the Augustan Revolution* (Chapel Hill: University of North Carolina Press, 2000). A collection of essays by a leading historian surveying Rome's rise to empire.

THE TRANSFORMATION OF
THE CLASSICAL WORLD

- THE VISUAL RECORD: A Bride's Trousseau
- THE CRISIS OF THE THIRD CENTURY
- THE EMPIRE RESTORED

- IMPERIAL CHRISTIANITY
- A PARTING OF THE WAYS

A BRIDE'S TROUSSEAU

VENUS, ASSISTED BY MYTHICAL SEA CREATURES and *erotes*, or cupids, beautifies herself on the central panel of a magnificent silver chest that made up part of a fourth-century Roman bride's trousseau. On the top, the bride, Projecta, and her groom, Secundus, are depicted within a wreath held by two more cupids. Along the base, Projecta, mirroring Venus, completes her own toilette while torchbearers and handmaidens perform for her the tasks of the mythical beings attending to Venus. The iconography and the execution of this sumptuous object— composed of solid silver with silver gilt and measuring almost two feet by one foot—testify to the high status of the bride and her deep attachment to the ancient classical traditions of Greco-Roman culture. Projecta and Secundus were Roman aristocrats, and their marriage was part of Roman rituals of class, wealth, and power as ancient as the goddess on the marriage chest.

Yet, within the thorough paganism of the symbolism and the lavish expense of the workmanship, the Latin inscription engraved on the rim across the front of the lid confronts the viewer with how utterly changed the Roman world had become. It reads, "Secundus and Projecta, live in Christ." In spite of the elaborate pagan symbolism of the casket, Secundus and Projecta were Christians, but they apparently saw nothing improper about commemorating their marriage in the age-old manner of their pagan ancestors. A bride could live in Christ and still be Venus.

Such was the world of late antiquity. By the time Projecta married Secundus, the once persecuted Christian sect was not only legal but well on its way to becoming the established religion in the empire. Formerly a religion of hellenized Jews and freed slaves, it was attracting converts from among the highest classes of Roman society. And yet, while some stern religious teachers might condemn the ancient traditions of Roman religion, and while around the very time of Projecta's marriage the pagan images of divine Victory were being removed from the Roman Senate, aristocratic families, Christian as well as pagan, continued the ancient cultural traditions without a sense of betrayal or contradiction. Rome appeared as eternal and serene as Venus herself.

But the Projecta casket has more to tell us. It was found, along with over 60 other exquisite objects and 70 pounds of silver plate, on the Esquiline hill in Rome, where it had been hastily buried to hide it from some catastrophe. The probable catastrophe is not hard to guess: In 410, when Projecta would have been an elderly woman, the barbarian Visigoths sacked and pillaged Rome for three days, raping Roman women and looting them of such treasures as this marriage chest.

Yet these barbarians were themselves Christians, while the city of Rome had remained a pagan stronghold. Moreover, the Visigoths were an officially designated Roman army reacting to the failure of the state to provide them with what they saw as their due. Such contrasts of paganism and Christianity, barbarity and Roman culture, were integral parts of a new Roman world, one that was characterized by radical transformations of Roman and barbarian culture that took place in the two centuries following the death of Marcus Aurelius in 180. Accelerating this process of change and transformation was the combination of events that are collectively referred to as the crisis of the third century.

LOOKING AHEAD

This chapter follows the profound political and social transformations that turned both the Roman Empire and its barbarian neighbors into radically new societies with different political, religious, and social organizations. By the sixth century, the eastern half of the empire had become profoundly Hellenized, while the western half had disintegrated into numerous Romano-barbarian kingdoms without losing its close identity with Rome.

THE CRISIS OF THE THIRD CENTURY

From the reign of Septimius Severus (193–211) to the time of Diocletian (284–305), both internal and external challenges shook the Roman Empire. The empire survived, but its social, political, and economic structures were radically transformed.

Sheer size was a fundamental problem for the empire. Haphazard expansion in many regions—to the north and west, for instance—overextended the frontiers. The labor and resources needed to maintain this vast territory strained the economic system of the empire. Like a thread stretched to the breaking point, the thin line of border garrisons and forts was ready to snap.

The economic system itself was part of the reason for this strain on resources. For all of its commercial networks, the economy of the empire remained tied to agriculture. To the aristocrats of the ancient world, agriculture was the only honorable source of wealth. The goal of the successful merchant was to liquidate his commercial assets, buy estates, and rise into the leisured landholding elite. As a result, liquid capital for either investment or taxation was always scarce.

The lack of sophistication seen in commercial and industrial business practice characterized the financial system of the empire as well. Government had always been conducted on the cheap. The tax system of the empire had never been very efficient at tapping into the real wealth of the aristocracy. Each individual city made its own collective assessments. Individuals eager to win the gratitude of their local communities were expected to provide essential services from their own pockets. Even with the vast wealth of the empire at its disposal, the government never developed a system of public debt—that is, a policy of borrowing against future revenues. As a result, the only way to solve short-term cash-flow problems was to debase the coinage by using more copper and less silver. This practice became epidemic in the third century, when the price of a bushel of wheat rose over 200 percent.

The failure of the empire to develop a stable political base complicated its economic problems. In times of emergency, imperial control relied on the personal presence and command of the emperor. As the empire grew, it became impossible for this presence to be felt everywhere. Moreover, the empire never developed either a regular system of imperial succession or an adequate power base. Control of the army, which was the ultimate source of imperial power, was possible only as long as the emperor could lead his armies to victory.

Enrich the Army and Scorn the Rest

Through much of the late second and third centuries, emperors failed dismally to lead their armies to victory. The barely romanized provincials in the military bore the brunt of these attacks. When the emperors selected by the distant Roman Senate failed to win victory, frontline armies unhesitatingly raised their own commanders to the imperial office. These commanders set about restructuring the empire in favor of the army. They opened important administrative posts to soldiers, expanded the army's size, raised military pay, initiated expensive building programs in frontier settlements, and in general introduced authoritarian military discipline throughout society. To finance these costly measures, the new military government confiscated senatorial wealth, introduced new forms of taxation, and increasingly debased the coinage.

The Rise of the Military. With their first rise in real income, soldiers in the provinces could improve their standard of living while in service and buy their way into provincial elites on retirement. Free-spending soldiers and imperial extravagance helped the bleak settlements on the edges of military camps grow into prosperous cities with all the comforts of the older parts of the empire.

For the first time, capable soldiers could hope to rise to the highest levels of public power, regardless of their birth. One extraordinarily successful soldier was Publius Helvius Pertinax. Born the son of a freed slave in the north of Italy (Liguria) in 126, he abandoned a career as a schoolteacher to enter the military. By the time he was 50, his success as a military commander won for him the office of consul. He then held a series of military, civil, and proconsular positions in Syria, Britain, Italy, and Africa before returning to Rome. When the Emperor Commodus was murdered in 192, the palace guard proclaimed Pertinax emperor—the first emperor who had not come from the privileged senatorial class.

Economic Disaster. Soon, however, the military control of the empire turned into a nightmare even for the provinces and their armies. Exercising their newly discovered power, armies raised and then destroyed pretender after pretender, offering support to whichever imperial candidate promised them the greatest riches. Pertinax, the first of these soldier-emperors, was murdered by his soldiers less than three months after becoming emperor. The army's incessant demands for higher pay led emperors to lower the amount of silver in the coins with which the soldiers were paid. But the less the coins were worth, the more of them were necessary to purchase goods. And the more goods cost, the less valuable was the soldiers' salary. Such drastic inflation wrecked the economic stability of the empire and spurred the army on to greater and more impossible demands for raises. Emperors who could not meet the demands were killed by their troops. In fact, the army was much more effective at killing emperors than enemies. Between 235 and 284, 17 of the 20 more or less legitimate emperors were assassinated or killed in civil war.

► This cameo was made to the order of Shapur I after the capture of Valerian during the great battle near Antioch in 260. The symbolic scene has Shapur seizing Valerian simply by grasping his hand.

External Threats.

The crisis of the third century did not result only from economic and political instability within the empire. Rome's internal crises coincided with an increase of attacks from outside the empire. In Africa, Berber tribes harassed the frontiers. The Sassanid dynasty in Persia threatened Rome's eastern frontier. When the Emperor Valerian (253–260) attempted to prevent the Persian king of kings Shapur I from seizing Roman Mesopotamia and Armenia, he was captured and held prisoner for the rest of his life.

The greatest danger to Rome came not from the south or east, but from the west. There, along the Rhine, various Germanic tribes known collectively as the Franks and the Alemanni began raiding expeditions into the empire. Along the lower Danube and in southern Ukraine, the Gothic confederation raided the Balkans and harassed Roman shipping on the Black Sea.

An Empire on the Defensive

The central administration of the empire simply could not deal effectively with the numerous barbarian attacks. Left on their own, regional provincial commanders at times even headed separatist movements. Provincial aristocrats who despaired of receiving any help from distant Rome often supported these pretenders. One such commander was Postumus, whom the armies of Spain, Britain, and Gaul proclaimed emperor. His nine-year separatist reign (ca. 258–268) was the longest and most stable of that of any emperor, legitimate or otherwise, throughout this whole troubled period.

Political and military instability had devastating effects on the lives of ordinary people. Citizenship had been extended to virtually all free inhabitants of the empire in 212, but that right was a formality given simply to enlarge the tax base, since only citizens paid inheritance taxes. Society became sharply divided into the privileged *honestiores*—senators, municipal gentry, and the military—and the increasingly burdened *humiliores*—everyone else. The humiliores suffered the most from the tax increases because, unlike the honestiores, they could neither bribe their way out of them nor intimidate tax collectors with private armies. They were also frequent targets of extortion by the military and of violence perpetrated by bandits.

Slave and peasant bandits, rustlers, and even pirates played an ambivalent role in society. Often they terrorized the countryside, descending from the hills to attack villages or travelers. However, at times they also protected peasants from greedy tax collectors and military commanders. In Gaul and Spain, peasants and local leaders organized armed resistance movements, termed *Bacaudae*, to withstand the exorbitant demands of tax collectors. In the first centuries of the empire, bandits operated primarily in peripheral areas that had been recently and poorly subjugated to Roman rule. In the late second and third centuries they became an increasing problem in Italy itself.

The Barbarian Menace

Compounding the internal violence that threatened to destroy the Roman Empire were the external attacks of the Germanic barbarians. These attacks reflected changes within the Germanic world as profound as those within the empire. Between the second and fifth centuries the Germanic world was transformed from a mosaic of small, decentralized, agricultural tribes into a number of powerful military tribal confederations capable of challenging Rome itself. We cannot understand the impact of the barbarians on the empire without understanding the social and political organization and the transformation of these people living beyond the frontier.

Germanic Society. The Germanic peoples typically inhabited small villages organized into patriarchal households, which were integrated into clans, which in turn composed tribes. For the most part, clans governed themselves, and except in war, tribal leaders had little authority over their followers. In the second century, many tribes had kings, but they were religious rather than political leaders.

Germanic communities lived by farming, but cattle raising and especially warfare carried the highest social prestige. Men measured their status by the number of cattle they owned and by their martial ability. Women took care of agricultural chores and household duties. Like the number of cattle, the number of wives showed a man's social position. Polygyny was common among chiefs.

Warfare defined social groupings, and warriors dominated public life. Only within the clan was fighting inappropriate.

But rival clans within the same tribe dealt with one another brutally. Conflict took the form of the feud, and each act of aggression was repaid in kind. If an individual within a clan had a grievance with an individual within another clan, all his kinsmen were obliged to assist him. Thus a single incident could result in a continuous escalation of acts of revenge.

Feuding and Peacemaking. Clans in other tribes were fair game for raiding, looting, and conquering. Individuals, clans, and tribes built their wealth and reputations on warfare. The more successful a tribe was in warfare, the more clans it attracted and the greater its position became in the barbarian world.

The practice of feuding, especially within the tribe, had enormous costs. Families were decimated, and strong warriors who were needed to defend the tribe from outside attack faced constant danger from members of their own tribe. Tribal leaders attempted to reduce hostilities by establishing payments called *wergeld* in place of the blood vengeance demanded in reparation for crimes. Such wergeld, normally paid in cattle or slaves, was voluntary,

---

TACITUS ON THE GERMANS

At the end of the first century C.E. *Tacitus wrote a brief account of the Germanic peoples living beyond the frontiers, in part to inform Romans about the neighboring people and in part to criticize the morals and practices of Roman society. In general, his information, although selective and filtered through Roman culture, appears quite accurate.*

FOCUS QUESTIONS

What, according to Tacitus, are the various types of executive and legislative power among the Germanic peoples? Why was the feud so important in this society?

THEY PICK THEIR KINGS ON THE BASIS of noble birth, their generals on the basis of bravery. Nor do their kings have limitless or arbitrary power, and the generals win favor by the example they set if they are energetic, if they are distinguished, if they fight before the battle-line, rather than by the power they wield. But no one except the priests is allowed to inflict punishment with death, chains, or even flogging, and the priests act not, as it were, to penalize and at the command of the general, but, so to speak, at the order of the god, who they believe is at hand when they are waging war. . . . The nobles make decisions about lesser matters, all freemen about things of greater significance, with this proviso, nonetheless, that

those subjects, of which ultimate judgment is in the hands of the mass of people, receive preliminary consideration among the nobles. . . . When the crowd thinks it opportune, they sit down fully armed. Silence is demanded by the priests, who then also have the right of compulsion. Soon the king or the chieftains are heard, in accordance with the age, nobility, glory in war, and eloquence of each, with the influence of persuasion being greater than the power to command. If a proposal has displeased them, they show their displeasure with a roar; but if it has won favor, they bang their *frameae* [spears] together; the most prestigious kind of approval is praise with arms. . . . There is an obligation to undertake the personal feuds as well as the friendships of one's father or blood-relative; but the feuds do not continue without possibility of settlement, for even murder is atoned for by a specific number of cattle and sheep and the entire family accepts the settlement, with advantage to the community, since feuds are the most dangerous when joined with freedom.

From Tacitus, Germany.

since the right of vengeance was generally recognized, and the unity of the tribe remained precarious.

Tribes also attempted to reinforce unity through religious cults involving shared myths of common ancestry and rituals intended to underline group cohesion. Drinking was the most important of these rituals. When not fighting, Germanic warriors spent much of their time drinking beer together at the table of their war leader. Because it provided the readiest means of preserving grain, beer was a staple of the Germanic diet. Communal beer drinking was also a way of uniting potentially hostile neighbors. Not surprisingly, it could also lead to drunken brawls that reopened the very feuds drinking bouts were intended to end. These feuds could in turn lead to the hiving off of irreconcilable factions, which might in time form their own tribes.

Warrior Bands. In contrast to the familial structure of barbarian society stood another warrior group that cut across kindred and even tribal units. This was the warrior band, called in Latin the *comitatus*. Some young warriors formed personal bonds with particularly able leaders and pledged them absolute loyalty. In return the leaders were obligated to lead their warriors to victory and to share with them the spoils of war. These warrior societies, far from being the basic units of a larger tribal military force, were organized for their own plunder and fighting. While they might be a valuable aid in intertribal warfare, they could also shatter the fragile peace by conducting raids on neighbors, thus bringing whole tribes into internal conflict. Successful warrior leaders might draw sufficient numbers of followers and conquer so many other groups that in time the band would become a new tribe.

Roman Influence in the Barbarian World

Intratribal and intertribal violence produced a rough equilibrium of power and wealth as long as small Germanic tribes lived in isolation. The presence of the Roman Empire, felt both directly and indirectly in the barbarian world, upset this equilibrium. Unintentionally, Rome itself helped to transform the Germanic tribes into the major threat to the imperial system.

The Lure of Roman Culture. The direct presence of Roman merchants extended only about a 100 miles beyond the frontiers into "free Germany." However, the attraction of Roman luxury goods and the Romans' efforts to establish friendly Germanic buffer zones along the borders drew even distant tribes into the Roman imperial system. Across the barbarian world, tribal leaders and comitatus leaders sought the prestige that Roman goods brought them. Roman provincial commanders encouraged these leaders to enter into commercial arrangements with the Romans. In exchange for their cattle, which the Romans needed for their troops, the Germanic leaders received gold and grain. This outside source of wealth greatly in-

creased economic disparity within Germanic society. In addition, some leaders made treaties with Rome, thus receiving the advantage of Roman support, which other tribal leaders lacked. In return for payments of gold and foodstuffs, chieftains of these "federated" tribes agreed to oppose tribes that were hostile to Rome and to prevent young hotheads of their own tribes from raiding across the frontier. Some chiefs supplied warriors for the Roman army. Others even led their comitatus into Roman service. By the late third century the Roman army included Franks, Goths, and Saxons serving as far away from their homes as Egypt. Such "imperial Germans" moved back and forth between the Roman and barbarian worlds, using each as a foundation for increased power in the other and obscuring the cultural and political differences between the two.

The West Germanic Revolution. The effects of contact between barbarians and Romans reached far and wide throughout the empire and beyond the frontier. Along the Rhine and Danube the result was the so-called West Germanic Revolution. To survive in a time of constant warfare, tribes had to become armies. The armies needed a united and effective leadership. Among most of the western Germanic peoples, the tradition of the older tribal king was abandoned. A new kind of nonroyal chieftain emerged as the war leader of the people and as the representative of the war god Woden. In the later second and third centuries the turmoil resulted in the formation of new tribes and tribal confederations: the Marcomanni, the Alemanni, and the Franks. By the end of the second century this internal barbarian transformation spilled over into the empire in the form of the Marcomannian wars and the Saxon, Frankish, and Alemannic incursions into the western provinces.

The Gothic Confederation. Around the same time, along the Oder and Vistula rivers to the north, a group later known as the Goths began their slow consolidation around a royal family. The Goths were unique in that their kings exercised more military authority than was usual for a Germanic tribe. These kings formed the nucleus of a constantly changing barbarian group. A Goth was not necessarily a biological descendant of the small second-century tribe living along the shore of the Baltic. Anyone who fought alongside the Gothic king was a Goth.

Between the second and fourth centuries, the bearers of this Gothic royal tradition began to filter to the south and east, ultimately transferring their model of barbarian organization to the area of present-day Kiev in southern Ukraine. This move was not so much a physical migration of thousands of people across Europe as the gradual confederation under Gothic leadership of various Germanic, Slavic, and Scythian peoples living around the Black Sea. By the early third century, this Gothic confederation was strong enough to challenge Roman supremacy in the region. These first Gothic wars in the east were even more devastating than the later wars in the west.

THE EMPIRE RESTORED

By the last decades of the third century, the empire seemed in danger of crumbling under combined internal and external pressure. That it did not was largely due to the efforts of the soldier-emperor Aurelian (270–275), who was able to repulse the barbarians, restore the unity of the empire, and then set about stabilizing the internal imperial structure.

Diocletian, the God-Emperor

Diocletian (284–305), a Dalmatian soldier who had risen through the ranks to become emperor, completed the process of stabilization and reorganization of the imperial system begun by Aurelian. The result was a regime that in some ways increased imperial power and in other ways simply did away with the pretenses that had previously masked the emperor's true position.

No longer was the emperor *princeps,* or "first citizen." Now he was *dominus,* or "lord," the term of respect used by slaves in addressing their masters. He also assumed the title of *Iovius,* or Jupiter, thus claiming divine status, and demanded adoration as a living god. Diocletian recognized that the empire was too large and complex for one man to rule. To solve the problem, he divided the empire into eastern and western parts, each part to be ruled by both an augustus and a junior emperor, or caesar. Diocletian was augustus in the east, supported by his caesar, Galerian. In the west the rulers were the augustus Maximian and his caesar, Constantius.

The Tetrarchy.   In theory this tetrarchy, or rule by four, provided for regular succession. The caesars, who were married to daughters of the augusti, were to succeed them. Although from time to time subsequent emperors would rule alone, Diocletian's innovation proved successful and enduring. The empire was divided administratively into eastern and western parts until the death of Julius Nepos, the last legitimate emperor in the west, in 480.

In addition to this constitutional reform, Diocletian enacted or consolidated a series of measures to improve the functioning of the imperial administration. He reorganized and expanded the army, approximately doubled the number of provinces, separated their military and civil administration, and greatly increased the number of bureaucrats to administer them. He attempted to stem runaway inflation by increasing the amount of silver in coins and fixing maximum prices and wages throughout the empire. He restructured the imperial tax system, basing it on payments in goods and produce in order to distribute the burden more equitably on all citizens and to avoid problems of currency debasement.

A Militarized Society.   The pillar of Diocletian's success was his victorious military machine. He was effective because, like the barbarian chieftains who had turned their tribes into armies, he militarized society and led this military society to victory. Like Diocletian himself, his soldiers were drawn from provincial marginal regions. They showed tremendous devotion to their god-emperor. By the time of Diocletian's reign, a career such as that of Pertinax had become the rule for emperors rather than the exception.

The career of Aurelius Gaius, an obscure provincial officer, is typical of that of soldiers of Diocletian's army. Gaius was born in a Galatian village in what is today Turkey. He served in infantry and cavalry units in Pannonia and then in Gaul near Strasbourg, advancing through the ranks from simple recruit to cavalryman, adjutant, and finally centurion in Diocletian's personal guard. He traveled the length and breadth of the empire with Diocletian and fought outside the empire in Persia, North Africa, and Numidia. Compared to that of Pertinax, Gaius's career reflects the differences between a successful career at the end of the second century and one at the end of the third. Unlike Pertinax, Gaius served his entire career within the military. Diocletian had largely ended the tradition of mixing civil and military offices. Furthermore, Gaius traveled far and wide but spent very little time in Gaul and none in Britain. The extreme west of the empire was increasingly irrelevant to the interests of the central government. Nor did Gaius visit Italy or Greece, the centers of the old classical world. For him, as for Diocletian, the periphery of the empire had become its center; the center was increasingly marginal to the program of the empire.

Fiscal Reform.   Some aspects of Diocletian's program, such as the improvement of the civil administration and the military, were successful. Others, such as the reform of silver currency and wage and price controls, were dismal failures. One effect of the fiscal reforms was to bind *colons,* or hereditary tenant farmers, to their lands, since they were forbidden to leave the villages where they were registered to pay their taxes. In this practice lay the origins of European serfdom. Another effect was the gradual destruction of the local city councils, since their members, the *decurions,* were held personally responsible for the payment of local assessments whether or not they could be collected from the other inhabitants. In time this led to the dissolution of local civil government.

All of these measures were designed to marshal the entire population in the monumental task of preserving *Romanitas.* Central to this task was the proper reverential attitude toward the divine emperors who directed it. One group seemed stubbornly opposed to this heroic effort: the Christians. In 298, an incident occurred that seemed to confirm their subversive attitude. At a sacrifice in the presence of Diocletian, the Roman priests were unable to obtain the desired favorable omens; they attributed their failure to the

▶ The Empire Under Diocletian, 284–305. Under pressure from external enemies, Rome pulled back from parts of western Europe, the Balkans, and Mesopotamia.

presence of Christians, who were crossing themselves to ward off demons. Such blasphemous conduct—it might be compared, for instance, to desecrating the flag at a modern public assembly—led to the launching of the Great Persecution, which formally began in 303 and lasted sporadically until 313. It resulted in the death of hundreds of Christians who refused to sacrifice to the pagan gods.

Constantine, the Emperor of God

In 305, in the midst of the Great Persecution, Diocletian and his co-augustus Maximian took the extraordinary step of abdicating in favor of their caesars, Galerius and Constantius. This abdication was intended to provide for an orderly succession. Instead, the sons of Constantius and Maximian, Constantine (306–337) and Maxentius (306–312), drawing on the prejudice of the increasingly barbarian armies toward hereditary succession, set about wrecking the tetrarchy. In so doing, they plunged the empire once more into civil war as they fought over the western half of the empire.

Victory and Conversion. Victory in the west came to Constantine in 312, when he defeated and killed Maxentius in a battle at the Mulvian Bridge outside Rome. Constantine attributed his victory to a vision telling him to paint on the shields of his soldiers. For pagans, this symbol ♀ was the solar emblem of the cult of the Unconquered Sun. For Christians, it was the Chi-Rho, ☧, formed from the first two letters of the Greek word for Christ. The next year, in Milan, Constantine rescinded

the persecution of Christians and granted Christian clergy the same privileges that pagan priests enjoyed. Constantine himself was not baptized until near death, a common practice in antiquity. However, during his reign, Christianity grew from a persecuted minority to the most favored cult in the empire.

Constantinople. Almost as important as Constantine's conversion to Christianity was his decision to establish his capital in Byzantium, a city founded by Greek colonists on the narrow neck of water connecting the Black Sea to the Mediterranean. He transformed and enriched this small town, calling it the New Rome. Later it was known as Constantinople, the city of Constantine. For the next 11 centuries, Constantinople served as the heart of the Roman and then the Byzantine world. From his new city, Constantine began to transform the empire into a Christian state and Christianity into a Roman state religion.

The Triumph of Christianity

While paganism was being disestablished, Christianity was rapidly becoming the established religion. The effects of Constantine's conversion on the empire and on Christianity were enormous. Constantine made large financial contributions to Christian communities to repay them for their losses during persecutions. He erected rich churches on the model of Roman basilicas, or administrative buildings, and converted temples into Christian places of worship. He gave bishops the authority to act as magistrates within the Christian community. Once the particular objects of persecution, bishops became favored courtiers. Constantine attempted to make himself the de facto head of the Church. He even presided at the Council of Nicaea in 325, at which the assembled bishops condemned the Arian teaching that Jesus as Son of God was not equal to God the Father. Constantine and his successors, with the brief exception of his nephew Julian (r. 361–363), sought to use the cult of the one God to strengthen their control over the empire.

Emperor and Church. Although Constantine himself continued to maintain cordial relations with representatives of all cults and to use ambiguous language that would offend no one when talking about "the deity," his successors were less broad-minded. After Constantine's death in 337, they began restricting paganism. In 341, pagan sacrifice was banned, and by 355 the temples had been closed and the death penalty for sacrificing to pagan gods had been decreed, although not enforced.

Imperial control over Christianity was strong, but not total. One of the most powerful Christian successors to Constantine, Theodosius I (347–395), met his match in Ambrose (339–397), the bishop of Milan. In 390, the emperor, angered by riots in the Greek city of Thessalonica, ordered a general massacre of the population. Ambrose dared to excommunicate, or ban, the emperor from his church in Milan until Theodosius did public penance for that brutal act. Eventually, the emperor acquiesced, acknowledging that even he was subject to the rule of God as interpreted by the bishops. The incident was often cited later by church leaders to define the relationship between religious and secular authority.

Conversion. Although imperial support was essential to the spread of Christianity in the fourth century, other factors encouraged conversion as well. Christian miracles, particularly that of exorcism, or casting out of demons, won many converts. The ancient world was believed to be filled with daimons, supernatural creatures whose power for good or ill no one doubted. Every village had its possessed persons—mad men and women, troubled youths, and hate-filled citizens. Wandering Christian preachers seemed more competent than others to deal with these tormentors, proving that their God was more powerful than the spirits and that their message was worthy of a hearing.

Over the course of the fourth century, the number of Christians rose from 5 to 30 million. Imperial support, miracles, and preaching could not, by themselves, account for this phenomenal growth. Physical coercion played a large part. The story was told that in one town, on imperial command, all of the local temples were destroyed and "a great number" of leading pagans who refused conversion were tortured to death. The remaining pagan population converted. Whether or not the story is true, it illustrates the essential role that naked force often played in the process of conversion. Conversion—by whatever method—also suited the emperors, who saw a unified cult as an essential means of bolstering their position.

IMPERIAL CHRISTIANITY

The religion to which Constantine converted had matured institutionally and intellectually since its origins as a reform movement within Judaism. By the late third century, Christian communities existed throughout the empire, each headed by a bishop who was considered divinely guided and answerable only to his flock and to God. These bishops replaced pagan philosophers as sources of wisdom and authority. In the west, the bishop of Rome, termed the pope, had acquired the position of first among equals, a position that was at times acknowledged by the eastern patriarchates as well, out of respect for the successor of Peter and Paul and bishop of the ancient capital. However, the Church as a whole was divided on fundamental questions of belief, and the growing importance of Christianity in the Roman Empire added to the gravity of these divisions. The two most contentious issues were, in the Greek-speaking regions of the empire, the nature of Christ, and in the Latin-speaking provinces, the extent to which individuals could earn their salvation through their own virtue.

▼ A painting of Christ from a catacomb ceiling. The catacombs were underground passages near Rome used by the early Christians as cemeteries, for funeral and memorial services, and as places of refuge during times of persecution.

Divinity, Humanity, and Salvation

Jesus, the savior or Christ, was at the heart of Christian belief, but individual Christian communities interpreted the nature of Christ differently as they attempted to reconcile their faith with the intellectual traditions of late antiquity. Christian Scriptures spoke of the Father, the Son, and the Spirit. Yahweh was generally accepted as the Father and Christ as the Son; the Spirit was understood to be the continuing presence of God sent by Jesus after his resurrection and ascension.

Christology. Generally, Christians saw God as a Trinity, at once one and three. But the relationship among the three was a source of endless debate, particularly for Greek-speaking Christians attempting to reconcile their faith with the Neoplatonic ideas of successive emanations from God to creation, which were incorporated into the Christian understanding of the Trinity. Was Christ just a man, chosen by God as a divine instrument, or was he God? If he was God, had he simply appeared to be human? These were not trivial or academic questions for Christians, since the possibility of salvation depended on their answer. Throughout the eastern half of the empire, ordinary people were ready to fight not only with words, but even with weapons to defend their positions.

Throughout the so-called Christological controversies—which began in the early third century and continued through the fifth—Christian groups ranged from those who asserted that Christ was entirely human to those who saw him as entirely divine, or one with God. Others held views between these extremes, claiming that Christ had both human and divine aspects. The Monarchians emphasized the oneness of God by arguing that the Trinity represented three activities, although God possessed only one substance. The Gnostics, who also saw Jesus as God, argued that Jesus had only appeared to be human but in reality was only divine. Emphasizing the humanness of Jesus were the Adoptionists, who explained that Jesus was a man to whom God sent his spirit at baptism.

Origen of Alexandria. The first Christian intellectual to undertake a systematic exposition of the Trinity was the great Alexandrine theologian Origen (185–254). In all of his teachings, Origen moved Christian teaching from a literal to a symbolic understanding of Scripture and gave it a sound philosophical foundation by synthesizing the Neoplatonic tradition with Christianity. His trinitarian teachings insisted on the co-eternality of the Son with the Father, but, drawing as he did on Neoplatonic ideas of emanations, he seemed to subordinate the Son to the Father and to make the Spirit a creation of the Son. In the generations following Origen, the controversy continued, particularly between those who taught the equality of the persons of the Trinity and those who, like the Alexandrine theologian Arius (ca. 250–336), insisted that Jesus was not equal to God the Father but was a lesser divinity created by God. By the time of Constantine the issue of whether or not Jesus was one with God threatened to destroy the unity of Christianity. To settle the controversy, the emperor commanded the bishops of the entire Church to assemble at Nicaea in 325. At the emperor's urging, the council condemned the teachings of Arius and adopted the term *homousion*, "of one being," to describe the equality of the Father and the Son.

The Council of Nicaea did not end the Christological controversy. For almost a century, Arians continued to win adherents to their denial of the divinity of Christ, even among the Christian emperors who succeeded Constantine. Before the Arian tradition finally died out within the empire, missionaries spread it to the barbarian Goths beyond the frontiers. Similarly, at the other extreme, Monophysites in Egypt and Syria argued that Christ had only one nature—the divine. A century after Nicaea, another council was held at Chalcedon in 451 to resolve the issue. Following the recommendation of the bishop of Rome, Pope Leo I (440–461), the bishops at Chalcedon agreed that in the one God there were three divine persons: the Father, the Son, and the Spirit. However, the second person of the Trinity, the Son, had two natures: one fully human, the other fully divine. The Chalcedon formulation established the orthodox, or "right-believing," position, and the full weight of the imperial machinery worked to impose it on all. In Egypt and Palestine the decree was greeted with outrage. Mobs of monks and laity rioted in the streets to oppose the "unclean synod of Chalcedon." Two centuries later, the ease with which Islam was able to conquer these regions from the empire resulted in part from their deep alienation from Orthodox teachings imposed by Constantinople.

Although a western bishop had provided the formula for Chalcedon, Latin Christians were not as deeply concerned with the Christological debates as were the easterners. For westerners, the great question was less the nature of God than the mechanism of salvation and the role of humans in the salvational process. An attempt to answer this and other key doctrinal questions was provided by a man who, more than any other individual, would set the course of western Christianity and political philosophy for the next thousand years: Augustine of Hippo.

Augustine of Hippo. Augustine (354–430) was born into a well-off North African family in the town of Tagaste and was quickly drawn into the good life and upward mobility that were available to bright young provincials in the fourth century. In his *Confessions*, the first psychological autobiography, Augustine describes how his skills in rhetoric took him to the provincial capital of Carthage and then on to Rome and finally Milan, the western imperial

▲ The Spread of Christianity. Christian churches appeared first in the major cities of the empire and spread only gradually into the countryside, in part due to the establishment of monasteries.

residence, where he gained fame as one of the foremost rhetoricians of the empire.

Connections as well as talent contributed to his rise to fame. Although his mother was a Christian, Augustine was not baptized at birth, and while in Carthage, he joined the Manichees, a dualist sect that taught that good and evil were caused by two different ultimate principles and that salvation was possible. As a protégé of the Manichees, Augustine gained introductions to the leading pagan aristocrats of his day.

While in Milan, Augustine came into contact with kinds of people he had never encountered in Africa, particularly Neoplatonists and Christians. The most important of these was Ambrose, bishop of Milan. The encounter with a spiritual philosophy and a Christianity that was compatible with it profoundly changed the young professor. After a period of agonized searching, Augustine converted to the new religion. Abandoning his Italian life, he returned to the North African town of Hippo to found a monastery where he could devote himself to reading the Scriptures. However, his neighbors were determined to harness the intellectual talents of their brilliant native son. When their bishop died, they forcibly seized Augustine and made him their bishop.

Augustine spent the remainder of his life as bishop of this small provincial town, but his reputation as spokesperson for the Christian tradition spread throughout the empire. As a professor of rhetoric he had become an expert in debate, and much of his episcopal career was spent in refuting opponents within the Church as well as dealing with traditional pagans who blamed the problems of the empire on the new religion. Christians, they claimed, had abandoned the traditional gods and the traditional Roman virtues and justice that had made Rome great.

In responding to these attacks, Augustine elaborated a new Christian understanding of human society and the individual's relationship to God, which dominated Western thought for the next 15 centuries. His views were set forth in several works: *Confessions, On the Trinity,* and *City of God.* He rejected elitist attempts to identify the true Church with any earthly community. Likewise, he rejected the claim of pagans that the Roman tradition was the embodiment of true virtue. Instead, he argued that the true members of God's elect necessarily coexisted in the world with sinners. No earthly community, not even the empire or the visible Church, was the true "city of God." Earthly society participated in the true Church, the "city of God," through the sacraments and did so quite apart from the individual worthiness of the recipients or even of the ministers of these rites. Belief that the presence of sinners within the Church blocked the plan of salvation or that responsibility for salvation lay with the individual was to deny the omnipotence of God.

According to Augustine, salvation was free, a gift not earned by virtuous lives but freely granted by God to the elect. In this way, Augustine argued for a distinction between the visible Christian empire and the Christian community. Earlier, the pharisaic Jew Paul had determined that Christianity would survive Judaism even as the latter was being destroyed by Rome. Now Augustine, the Roman rhetorician, determined that Christianity would survive the Roman Empire just as it was disintegrating into barbarian kingdoms. Even as Augustine lay dying in Hippo, the city was under siege by barbarian Vandals.

The Call of the Desert

At the same time that intellectuals like Augustine were attempting to explain Christian doctrine, less intellectual but equally determined men and women were searching for a different way of living Christ's message. This was the hermit, monk, or recluse, who taught less by his or her words than by his or her life, a life that was often so unusual that even the most ignorant and worldly citizen of the late empire could recognize in it the power of God. Beneath the apparent eccentricity, however, lay a fundamental principle: the radical rejection of society's values in favor of absolute dedication to God's.

Shortly after the death of Origen in 254, another Egyptian was undertaking a different path to enduring fame. Anthony (ca. 250–355), a well-to-do peasant, heard the same biblical text that later converted Augustine: "Go, sell all you have and give to the poor and follow me." Anthony was uneducated; it was said that he had been too shy as a boy to attend school. This straightforward peasant did exactly what the text commanded. He disposed of all his goods and left his village for the Egyptian desert. There, for the next 70 years, he sought to follow Christ in a life of constant self-mortification and prayer.

This dropout from civilization deeply touched his fellow Christians, many of whom were disturbed by the abrupt transformation of their religion from persecuted minority to privileged majority. By the time of his death this monk—the word comes from the Greek *monos*, "alone"—found himself the head of a large, loosely knit community of like-minded persons who looked to him as spiritual father, or abbot. Over the next few centuries, thousands rejected the worldliness of civilization and the easy life of the average Christian to lead a monastic life in the wildernesses of the empire.

Monastic Communities

Monasticism took two forms: communal organization and solitary life. Pachomius (ca. 290–346) and Basil the Great (ca. 329–379) in the east and Benedict of Nursia (ca. 480–547) in the west perfected the communal life. Faced with the impossibility of surviving in a harsh environment without cooperation, Egyptian monks banded together into small monastic towns. As many as 2,000 monks lived in these monasteries. They placed themselves under the control of the abbot, who served as spiritual guide and administrator of the community. These men and women sought spiritual perfection through physical self-mortification and through the subordination of their own wills to that of the abbot. Monks drank no wine, ate no meat, used no oil. They spent their days in prayer and work. Abbots organized their monks into houses according to their various crafts, and the surplus of their gardening, baking, basket making, and the like was sold in the villages and towns of Egypt. During the fourth century this monastic tradition spread east to Bethlehem, Jerusalem, Caesarea, and Constantinople and west to Rome, Milan, Trier, Marseille, and Tours. In the following centuries it reached beyond the borders of the empire when Egyptian-style monasticism was introduced into Ireland.

Intellectuals as well as peasants heard the call of monastic life. Chief among the intellectuals was Jerome (ca. 347–420), the greatest linguist of antiquity, who was so impressed by a visit to the monastic communities of the east that he became a priest and founded a monastery in Bethlehem. There, he translated the Bible into Latin. This Latin translation, known as the *Vulgate,* became the standard version of Christian Scripture in the west until the Reformation and, in Roman Catholic countries, until the twentieth century.

In the Greek-speaking world, the definitive form of the monastic community was provided by Basil the Great. Basil had visited the monasteries of Egypt, Palestine, and Syria before founding his own monastery at Pontus near his family estate at Annesi in present-day Turkey. Although he did not write a specific rule for the governance of his monastery, his collection of commentaries and spiritual advice to his followers outlined a form of monastic life in which a day of agriculture, craft work, and care for the sick and the poor was organized within an ordered progression of liturgical prayer. His emphasis on communal life rather than on heroic acts of individual asceticism provided the model for eastern monasticism from his day to the present.

Unlike Anthony of Egypt, Basil was a brilliant and well-educated intellectual who frequently left his monastery to throw himself into the ecclesiastical politics of the empire. By the end of his life, Basil had become bishop of Caesarea. Eastern monastic communities continued this active involvement in political and secular affairs. Monasteries provided the early religious training for most religious leaders. Monks and abbots often involved themselves wholeheartedly in the politics of the empire. Monks rioting in the streets of Constantinople over political issues were a familiar sight for over a thousand years.

In the west, Benedict of Nursia was as influential in structuring communal religious life as Basil was in the east. In time, Benedict became abbot of a small community of monks at Monte Cassino, between Rome and Naples. The rule that he drafted for the governance of his community, while drawn largely from earlier monastic rules circulating in Italy, became the definitive statement of western monasticism. Benedict's rule encouraged moderation and flexibility while emphasizing a life of poverty, chastity, and obedience to an elected abbot. Monks were required to perform some physical labor, and the monastery was intended to be a self-sufficient community. However, the real task of the monk was the continuous praise of God. This consisted of gathering at regular intervals through the day and night for communal prayer. Although Benedict lived and died in obscurity, within two and a half centuries his rule became the universal rule for western monasticism.

Western monasteries, too, provided their share of bishops, but unlike those in the east, western monks remained more isolated from population centers and from direct involvement in public affairs. However, western monasteries were not peripheral to western society and religion. Rather, these rustic communities were centers of religious and economic activity as well as education and learning in the largely rural west. They remained under the authority of the local bishops, who were usually drawn from the lay aristocracy of the empire in the west. Also, western monasteries depended on the political and economic support that they received from lay patrons.

Solitaries and Hermits

Although Anthony had begun as a hermit, he and most Egyptian monks eventually settled into communal lives. Elsewhere, particularly in the desert of Syria, the model of the monk remained the individual hermit. The Syrian desert, unlike that of Egypt, was particularly suitable for such an ascetic life. Here, the desert was milder, an individual could find food in wild roots and water in rain pools, and villages were never too far off. Moreover, the life of the wandering hermit was closely connected to traditional seminomadic lifestyles in the Fertile Crescent. But the Christian hermits who appeared across Syria in late antiquity were unlikely to be mistaken for the familiar Bedouin nomads. The Christian hermits were wild men and women who came down from the mountainsides and galvanized the attention of their contemporaries by their lifestyles. The most famous of the hermits, Simeon Stylites (ca. 390–459), spent 36 years perched at the top of a pillar 50 feet high. Two women, Marana and Cyra, lived 42 years chained in a small open-roofed enclosure.

▲ A gold plaque from a sixth-century Syrian reliquary. The subject is Simeon Stylites on his pillar; the snake represents the vanquished devil. Clients could consult the holy man by climbing up the ladder on the left.

Such people of God, rejecting civilized life in the most overt and radical ways, nevertheless met very real social and cultural needs of the population. Their lack of ties to human society made them the perfect arbitrators in the constant disputes that threatened to disrupt village life. They were individuals of power, whose proven ability to cast out demons and work miracles made them ideal community patrons at a time when traditional power brokers of the village were being lured away to imperial service or provincial cities. The greatest of these holy people, like Simeon Stylites, received as visitors not only local peasants but also emperors and empresses, who eagerly sought their advice.

Unlike the eastern monks, the Syrian hermits of the fourth and fifth centuries had few parallels in the west. Hermits did inhabit the caves and forests of Italy and Gaul, and pious women found solitude as recluses even in the center of Rome. But these westerners did not establish themselves either as independent sources of religious power or as political power brokers. Their monasticism remained a personal religious commitment. When one Roman woman was asked why she remained shut up in her cell, she replied, "I am on a journey." When asked where she was going, she answered simply, "To God."

A PARTING OF THE WAYS

Those who remained in "the world" at the end of the fourth century could hardly take so serene a view of life. Christians and pagans might differ in their explanations for the ills that had befallen the empire, but none could deny their severity. The vulnerability of the Constantinian system became clear shortly after 376, when the Huns, a nomadic horse-riding people from central Asia, swept into the Black Sea region and threw the entire barbarian world once more into chaos. The Huns quickly destroyed the Gothic confederation and absorbed many of the peoples who had constituted the Goths. Others sought protection in the empire. The Visigoths, as they came to be known, were the largest of these groups, and their fate illustrated how precarious existence could be for all the inhabitants of the imperial frontier.

Driven from their lands and thus from their food supply, the Visigoths turned to the empire for assistance. But the Roman authorities treated them as brutally as had the Huns, forcing some to sell their children into slavery in return for morsels of dog flesh. In despair, the Visigoths rose up against the Romans, and against all odds, their desperate rebellion succeeded. They annihilated an imperial army at Adrianople in 378, and the emperor Valens himself was killed. His successor, Theodosius (379–395), was forced to allow the Visigoths to settle along the Danube and to be governed by their own leaders even though they lived within the boundaries of the empire.

Theodosius's treaty with the Visigoths set an ominous precedent. Never before had a barbarian people been allowed to settle as a political unit within the empire. Within a few years the Visigoths were again on the move, traveling across the Balkans into Italy under the command of their chieftain Alaric (ca. 370–410). In 410 they captured Rome and sacked it for three days, an event that sent shock waves throughout the entire empire. The symbolic effect of the Visigoths' victory far exceeded the amount of real damage, which was relatively light. Only after Alaric's death did the Visigoths leave Italy, ultimately settling in Spain and southern Gaul with the emperor's approval.

The Barbarization of the West

Rome did not fall. It was transformed. Romans participated in and even encouraged this transformation. Roman accommodation of the Visigoths set the pattern for subsequent settlement of barbarians in the western half of the empire. By this time, barbarians made up the bulk of the imperial army, and commanders were frequently themselves barbarians. However, these barbarian troops had been integrated into existing Roman military structures. Indeed, these so-called imperial Germans had often proved to be even more loyal to

Rome than were the Roman provincial populations they were to protect. In the late fourth and fifth centuries, emperors accepted whole barbarian peoples as integral parts of the Roman army and settled them within the empire. Usually, the emperors diverted a percentage of tax revenues from the region's estates to support these "guests."

The Visigothic kingdom in southern Gaul and Spain was typical in this respect. Alaric's successor, Ataulf, was extremely eager to win the emperor's approval. He married Galla Placidia, the daughter of the Emperor Theodosius and the sister of Emperor Honorius, in a Roman ceremony in Narbonne in 414. Soon afterward, he established a government at Bordeaux directed by Gallo-Roman aristocrats. Although his opponents soon assassinated him, his successors concluded a treaty with Constantinople in which the Visigoths were recognized as a legitimate, established political presence within the empire. This so-called kingdom of Toulouse endured for almost a century. South of the Pyrenees, the Gothic kingdom of Toledo continued for almost 300 years.

The Visigoths were not the only powerful barbarian people to challenge the empire. The Vandals, who had entered the empire in 406, crossed over into Africa, the richest region of the western empire, and quickly conquered it. Avowed enemies of the empire, the Vandals used their base in North Africa to raid the European coastline and attack Roman shipping. In 455 they sacked Rome much more thoroughly than had the Goths 45 years earlier.

Another threat appeared in the 430s, when the Huns, formerly Roman allies, invaded the empire under their charismatic leader Attila (ca. 406–453). Although defeated in Gaul by a combined army of barbarians under the command of the Roman general Flavius Aetius in 451, they turned toward Italy and penetrated as far as Rome. There, they were stopped not by the rapidly disintegrating imperial forces but by the bishop of Rome, Pope Leo I, who met Attila before the city's gates. What transpired between the two is not known, but Attila's subsequent withdrawal from Italy vastly increased the prestige of the papacy. Now popes not only were successors of Saint Peter and bishops of the principal city of the west, but were replacing the emperor as protector of the city. The foundation of the political power of the papacy was established.

The confederation of the Huns collapsed after the death of Attila in 453, but imperial power did not revive in Italy. A series of incompetent emperors were pushed aside by barbarian generals who assumed power on the peninsula and sought recognition from Zeno, the emperor in the east. However, after the death of the last legitimate western emperor, Julius Nepos, in 480, Zeno conferred the title of patrician on the Ostrogothic king Theodoric. In 489 Theodoric invaded Italy with imperial blessing and established himself as ruler of Italy.

In Gaul, between the Seine and the Loire, the Roman general Flavius Aetius and, after his death, the general

Syagrius continued to represent some imperial presence. But the armies that Aetius and Syagrius commanded consisted entirely of barbarians—particularly Visigoths and Franks—and they represented the interests of local aristocratic factions rather than those of Constantinople. So thoroughly barbarized had these last Roman commanders become in their military command and political control that the barbarians referred to Syagrius as "king of the Romans." Ultimately, in 486, Syagrius was defeated and replaced by the Frank Clovis, son of Syagrius's military commander Childeric, probably with the blessing of the emperor.

Britain met a similar fate. Abandoned by the Roman legions around 407, the Romano-Celtic population in this province concluded a treaty with bands of Saxons and Angles to protect Britain from other barbarian raiders. As had happened elsewhere in the empire, the barbarians came as federated troops and stayed as rulers. Gradually, during the fifth century, Germanic warrior groups conquered much of the island. The Anglo-Saxons pushed the native inhabitants to the west and the north. There, as the Cornish and the *Welsh* (in Anglo-Saxon, Welsh means simply "enemy"), they preserved the Christian religion but largely lost their other Roman traditions.

The New Barbarian Kingdoms

The establishment of barbarian kingdoms within the Roman world meant the end of the western empire as a political entity. However, the emperors in the east and west continued to pretend that all these barbarian peoples, with the exception of the Vandals, were Roman troops commanded by loyal Roman officers who happened to be of barbarian origin. The emperors gave the barbarian kings or war leaders official status within the empire as Roman generals or patricians and occasionally granted them portions of abandoned lands or existing estates. Local Roman elites considered these leaders rude and uncultured barbarians who nevertheless could be made to serve these elites' own interests more easily than better educated imperial bureaucrats.

As a result, the aristocracy of the west, the *maiores*, viewed the decay of the civil government without dismay. This decay was due largely to the poverty of the imperial treasury. In the fifth century, the entire public revenues of the west amounted to little more than the annual incomes of a few wealthy private aristocrats. Managing to escape both taxation and the jurisdiction of public officials, these individuals carved out for themselves vast estates, which they and their families controlled with private armies and which they governed as virtually autonomous lordships. Ordinary freemen, pressed by the remnants of imperial taxation and by barbarians, were forced into accepting the protection and hence control offered by aristocrats, who thereby came to control whole villages and districts.

The primary source of friction between barbarians and provincial elites was religion. Many Goths had converted to Christianity around the time that the Huns had destroyed the Gothic confederation. However, they had chosen the Arian form of Christianity to appease the Arian emperors Constantius and Valens. But the Goths and most other barbarian peoples held to their Arian form of faith long after it had been abandoned in the empire. Therefore, wherever the barbarians settled, they were met with distrust and hostility from the orthodox clergy. In southern Gaul and Italy, this hostility created serious difficulties because during the fifth century, bishops had assumed many of the traditional duties and powers held by provincial Roman administrators.

Although during the fifth century the western aristocracy had largely given up on the civil administration, these wealthy landowners increasingly identified with the episcopacy. In Gaul, bishops were regularly selected from members of the greatest Gallo-Roman senatorial families, establishing veritable episcopal dynasties. In Italy and Spain too, bishops were drawn from the landed aristocracy. These bishops, most of whom were elected after long years of outstanding secular leadership, served as the primary protectors and administrators of their communities, filling the vacuum left by the erosion of other civil offices. They, more than either local civil officials or the Bacaudae, were successful in representing the community before imperial tax collectors or barbarian chieftains.

Thus, in spite of the creation of the barbarian kingdoms, cultural and political leadership at the local level remained firmly in the hands of the aristocracy. Aristocratic bishops, rather than hermits, monopolized the role of mediators of divine power just as their lay brothers, in cooperation with barbarian military leaders, monopolized the role of mediators of secular power.

Barbarian military leaders needed local ties by which to govern the large indigenous populations over whom they ruled. They found cooperation with these aristocrats to be both necessary and advantageous. Thus, while individual land-owners might have suffered in the transition from Roman to barbarian rule, for the most part this transition took place with less disturbance of the local social or political scene than was once thought. During the fifth century the imperial presence simply faded away as barbarian kings came to rule in the name of the emperor. After 480, the emperor resided exclusively in the east. The last western emperors disappeared without serious opposition either from western aristocrats or from their eastern colleagues.

The Hellenization of the East

The eastern half of the empire, in contrast to the west, managed to survive and even to prosper in the fifth and sixth centuries. In the east, beginning in 400, the trends toward militarization and barbarization of the administration were reversed, the strength of the imperial government was reaffirmed, and the vitality and integrity of the empire were restored.

Several reasons account for the contrast between east and west. First, the east had always been more urbanized and

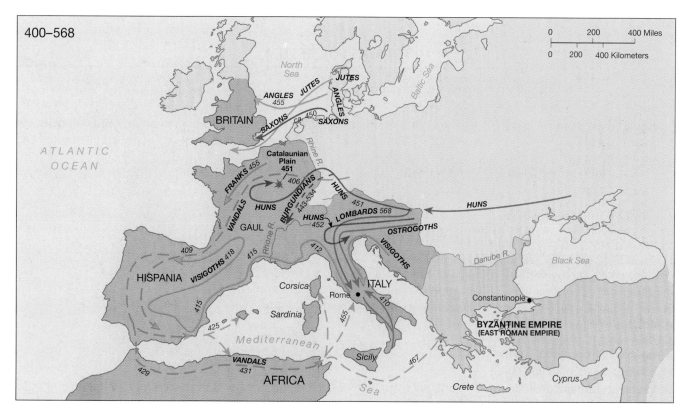

▲ Barbarian Migrations and Invasions. The early cross-border raids of neighboring peoples gave way to migrations of starving and terrified barbarian allies looking for safety in the empire. By the fifth century, large-scale raids by the Huns and Vandals reached throughout the western empire, resulting in permanent settlements.

civilized than the west. It had an old tradition of civil control that antedated the Roman Empire itself. When the decay of Roman traditions allowed regionalism and tribalism to arise in the west, the same decay brought in the east a return to Hellenistic traditions. Second, the east had never developed the tradition of public poverty and private wealth that was characteristic of the west. In the east, tax revenues continued to support an administrative apparatus, which remained in the hands of civilians rather than barbarian military commanders. Moreover, the local aristocracies in the eastern provinces never achieved the wealth and independence of their western counterparts. Finally, Christian bishops, frequently divided over doctrinal issues, never managed to monopolize either sacred power, which was shared by itinerant holy men and monks, or secular power, which was wielded by imperial agents. Thus under the firm direction of its emperors, especially Theodosius and later Zeno, the eastern empire not only survived but prepared for a new expansionist phase under the emperor Justinian.

Conclusion

THE DIVERGENCE IN RELIGIOUS POWER BETWEEN EAST AND WEST was characteristic of the growing differences between the two halves of the Roman Empire at the close of late antiquity. The profound crises—military, social, and economic—that had shaken the empire and the barbarian world in the course of the third century left the west transformed. The new imperial system, based on an absolute ruler and an authoritarian Christianity, held the Roman world together for a few more centuries. Ultimately, however, the two halves of the old Mediterranean empire drifted in different directions as each formed a new civilization from Roman and indigenous traditions.

The east remained more firmly attached not only to Roman traditions of government but also to the much more ancient traditions of social complexity, urban life, and religious culture that stretched back to the dawn of civilization. The emperors continued to rule from Constantinople for another thousand years, but the extent of their authority gradually shrank to little more than the city itself. Furthermore, their empire was so profoundly hellenized in nature that it is properly called Byzantine (from the original name of Constantinople) rather than Roman.

The west experienced a transformation even more profound than that of the east. The triple heritage of late Roman political and military forms, barbarian society, and Christian culture coalesced into a new civilization that was perhaps less the direct heir of antiquity than was that of the east but was all the more dynamic for its distinctiveness. In culture, politics, and patterns of urban and rural life, the west and the east had gone separate ways, and their paths diverged ever more in the centuries ahead.

QUESTIONS FOR REVIEW

1. How did increasing contact between Roman civilization and the Germanic barbarians transform both?
2. How did Constantine's adoption of Christianity and the movement of his capital to Byzantium contribute to the decline of the western empire?
3. How did different views of the divinity of Christ and the means of salvation divide early Christians?
4. What was the attraction of monasticism, and why did it take so many different forms?
5. What were the differences in politics and culture in the eastern and western portions of the empire by the end of the fifth century C.E.?

DISCOVERING WESTERN CIVILIZATION ONLINE

You can obtain more information about the transforming Roman world at the websites listed below. See also the companion website that accompanies this text: www.ablongman.com/kishlansky, which contains an online study guide and additional resources.

The Crisis of the Third Century

ccat.sas.upenn.edu/jod/wola.html
A comprehensive site dedicated to late antiquity by Professor James O'Donnell.

The Empire Restored

www.st.carnet.hr/split/diokl.html
A site devoted to Emperor Diocletian's palace in modern Split.

Imperial Christianity

shsu.edu/~eng_wpf/con-hist.html
Links connecting to sites concerning Constantine.

SUGGESTIONS FOR FURTHER READING

The Crisis of the Third Century

Peter Brown, *The World of Late Antiquity, A.D. 150–750* (New York: Harcourt Brace Jovanovich, 1971). A brilliant essay on the cultural transformation of the ancient world.

A. H. M. Jones, *The Later Roman Empire, 284–602: A Social, Economic and Administrative Survey,* 2 vols. (Baltimore, Md.: Johns Hopkins University Press, 1986). The standard detailed survey of late antiquity by an administrative historian.

Malcolm Todd, *The Early Germans* (Oxford: Blackwell Publishers, 1992). A general introduction to pre-Roman Germanic Society.

The Empire Restored

T. D. Barnes, *The New Empire of Diocletian and Constantine* (Cambridge, Mass.: Harvard University Press, 1982). A current examination of the transformations brought about under these two great emperors.

Ramsay MacMullen, *Paganism in the Roman Empire* (New Haven, Conn.: Yale University Press, 1981). A sensible introduction to the varieties of Roman religion in the imperial period.

Imperial Christianity

G. W. Bowerstock, *Martyrdom and Rome* (New York: Cambridge University Press, 1995). A new look at Christian martyrdom in antiquity.

Peter Brown, *Authority and the Sacred: Aspects of the Christianisation of the Roman* (Cambridge: Cambridge University Press, 1995). A highly readable account of the emergence of Christianity in the Roman world by the leading historian of late antiquity.

W. H. C. Friend, *The Rise of Christianity* (London: Darton, Longman and Todd, 1984). A panoramic survey of Christianity from its origins to the seventh century.

Ramsay MacMullen, *Christianizing the Roman Empire (100–400)* (New Haven, Conn.: Yale University Press, 1984). A view of Christianity's spread from the perspective of Roman history.

A Parting of the Ways

Peter Brown, *The Rise of Western Christendom* (Cambridge, Mass.: Blackwell, 1996). A survey of late antiquity by a master scholar and stylist.

Patrick J. Geary, *The Myth of Nations: The Medieval Origins of Europe* (Princeton: Princeton University Press, 2001). An essay examining the relationship between modern nationalism and ethnic groups in late antiquity.

Judith Herrin, *The Formation of Christendom* (Princeton, N.J.: Princeton University Press, 1987). A history of the transformed Mediterranean world, east and west, to 800 from the perspective of a noted Byzantinist.

Herwig Wolfram, *History of the Goths* (Berkeley: University of California Press, 1988). An ethnologically sensitive history of the formation of the Gothic peoples.

THE CLASSICAL LEGACY IN THE EAST: BYZANTIUM AND ISLAM

- ■ THE VISUAL RECORD: From Temple to Mosque
- ■ THE BYZANTINES

- ■ THE RISE OF ISLAM
- ■ THE BYZANTINE APOGEE AND DECLINE, 1000–1453

FROM TEMPLE TO MOSQUE

FIRST A TEMPLE DEDICATED TO THE SYRIAC GOD HADAD and then to the Roman Jupiter, later the Christian church of Saint John, and finally a mosque, the Great Mosque of Damascus in Syria bears testimony to the great civilizations that have followed one another in the Near East. Like the successive houses of worship, each civilization rose on the ruins of its predecessor, incorporating and transforming the rich legacy of the past into a new culture. Little of the pagan and Christian structures is visible, although the mosque owes much to both, as does the civilization it represents.

Nothing remains of the pre-Roman structure. In the first century C.E. the Romans rebuilt the temple to include an outer enclosure measuring 1,233 by 1,000 feet with four monumental gateways. In the interior was a porticoed court marked by four corner towers. Monumental portals,

or gateways, in the east and west walls provided access to the inner court through triple doorways. In the center of the court stood a structure housing the statue of Jupiter.

Around the time of Constantine, the Roman temple was converted into a Christian church dedicated to Saint John the Baptist. Apparently, a portion of the interior porticoed court, which measured roughly 517 by 318 feet, was enclosed to provide a space for worshippers. Two of the four towers were raised to serve as bell towers.

For a time after Damascus fell to the Arabs in 635, Christians and Muslims shared the church. However, the Muslim population of the city grew rapidly, and by 705, Damascus was the capital of a vast, expanding Muslim empire, which would soon stretch from the Pyrenees to the Indus River. The caliph al-Walid (705–715) wanted a place of prayer befitting his capital's glory. He invited the Christian community to choose a site for another church. When they refused, he expelled them and hired Greek architects to adapt the structure to Muslim worship. They demolished the interior walls of the church, leaving only the ancient walls of a porticoed court and the tower at each of the four corners. These four Christian towers

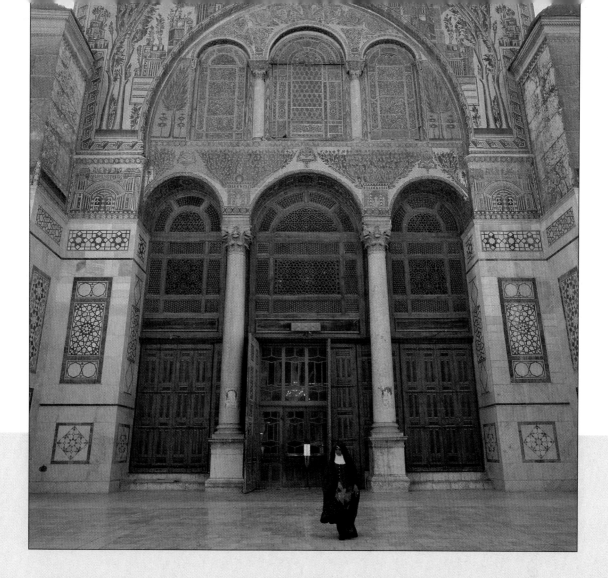

became the first minarets, towers from which Muslim religious leaders call the faithful to prayer five times each day. Al-Walid employed the finest artists available to cover the walls of the mosque with mosaics.

During the preliminary work, an underground chapel was said to have been found, containing a chest with a human head. On the chest was written, "This is the head of John, son of Zacharias." Al-Walid had the sacred relic placed under one of the pillars and a monument erected over it. To this day the shrine survives in the mosque, a symbol of the continuity among Judaism, Christianity, and Islam.

This moment of artistic and religious cooperation was brief. Only a few years later, in 717, al-Walid's successor subjected Constantinople to the most fearful siege it would endure for 500 years. Still, the continuity of religious worship and the common taste for classical art show how deeply both the caliphate and the empire were bound together in the common heritage of late antiquity, of which both were the true heirs.

LOOKING AHEAD

This chapter traces the fates of these two heirs of Mediterranean civilization, Byzantium and Islam, from the sixth to the fifteenth centuries. Inspired by central religious visions, they developed their common heritages into religious, artistic, and social forms that contrast with western Europe's path.

THE BYZANTINES

At the end of the fifth century C.E., the eastern empire of Theodosius and Zeno had escaped the fate that its western counterpart had suffered at the hands of the Germanic peoples. Wealthier and more urbanized than the west, its population had also been accustomed to centralized government for more than a thousand years. Still, the long-term survival of the eastern empire seemed far from certain.

Little unified the empire of Constantinople. The population of the capital split into two rival political factions, whose violent conflicts often threatened the stability of the government. These rival groups, organized militarily and politically, controlled the Circus, or Hippodrome, where the games and chariot races that were the obsession of the city's population took place. These factions took their names, the Greens and the Blues, from their circus colors. When these two factions joined forces with the army, they were powerful enough to create or destroy emperors. Beyond Constantinople the empire's population consisted of the more or less hellenized peoples of Asia Minor, Armenians, Slavs, Arabs, Syrians, Egyptian Copts, and others. Unlike western Europe, the east was still a world of cities, which were centers of commerce, industry, and Hellenistic culture. But the importance of these urban centers began to decline in favor of the rural peasant world, which not only constituted the source of its great wealth but also fed the empire and provided generations of tough soldiers to protect it from its enemies.

Finally, the eastern empire was more divided than unified by its Christianity. Rivalry among the great cities of Antioch, Alexandria, Jerusalem, Rome, and Constantinople was expressed in the competition among their bishops, or patriarchs. The official "right teaching," or orthodox, faith of Constantinople and its patriarch was bitterly opposed by "deviant," or heterodox, bishops of other religious traditions, around which developed separatist ethnic political movements. By the time of Justinian (527–565), emperors were obsessed with maintaining absolute authority and imposing uniformity on their empire.

Justinian and the Creation of the Byzantine State

Strong-willed, restless, and ambitious, Justinian is remembered as "the emperor who never slept." Although his goals were essentially conservative, his attempts to return to the past and restore the territory, power, and prestige of the ancient Roman Empire created a new world. With the assistance of his dynamic wife Theodora, his great generals Belisarius and Narses, his brilliant jurist Thibonian, his scientists Anthemius of Tralles and Isidorus of Miletus, and his brutally efficient administrator and tax collector John of Cappadocia, he remade the empire.

Spurred on by Theodora, in 532 Justinian checked the power of the Circus factions by brutally suppressing a riot that left 30,000 dead in the capital city. Belisarius

◄ A mosaic from the church of San Vitale in Ravenna. The emperor Justinian, along with secular and ecclesiastical officials, is shown bringing an offering to the church. The halo around his head signifies the sacred nature of the imperial office.

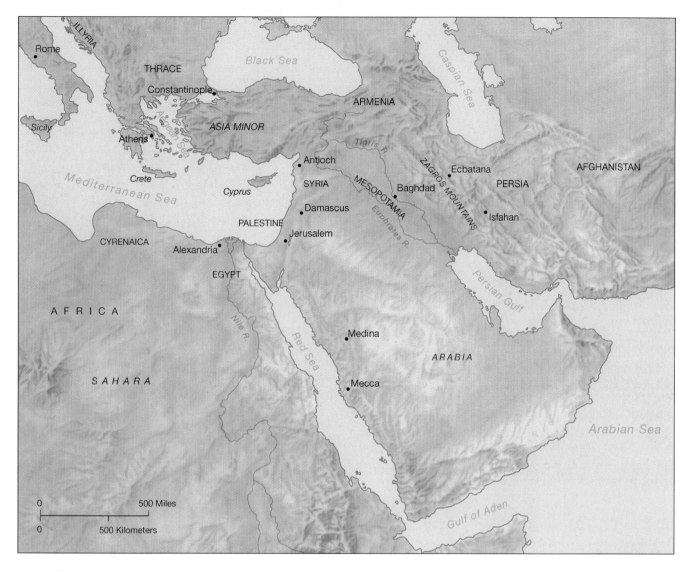

▲ The Eastern Mediterranean. The Arabian Peninsula was peripheral to the Roman and Persian empires until the seventh century when the new Islamic faith suddenly emerged from Arabia to overwhelm its more ancient neighboring empires.

and Narses recaptured North Africa from the Vandals, Italy from the Ostrogoths, and part of Spain from the Visigoths, restoring for one last moment some of the geographical unity of the empire of Augustus and Constantine. Tribonian revised and organized the existing codes of Roman law into the *Justinian Code*, a great monument of western jurisprudence that remains today the foundation of most of Europe's legal systems. Anthemius and Isidorus combined their knowledge of mathematics, geometry, kinetics, and physics to build the Church of the Holy Wisdom (Hagia Sophia) in Constantinople, one of the largest and most innovative churches ever constructed. This structure was as radical as it was simple. In essence it is a huge rectangle, 230 by 250 feet, above which a vast dome 100 feet in diameter rises to a height of 180 feet and seems to float, suspended in air. Less well appreciated were the achievements of John of

Cappadocia, who was able to squeeze the empire's population for the taxes to pay for these conquests, reforms, and building projects.

Ultimately, Justinian's spectacular achievements came at too high a price. He left his successors an empire that had been virtually bankrupted by the costs of his wars and his building projects, was bitterly divided by his attempts to settle religious controversies, and was poorly protected on its eastern border, where the Sassanid Empire was a constant threat. Most of Italy and Spain soon returned to barbarian control. In 602 the Sassanid emperor Chosroes II (d. 628) invaded the empire, capturing Egypt, Palestine, and Syria and threatening Constantinople itself. In a series of desperate campaigns, the emperor Heraclius (610–641) turned back the tide and crushed the Sassanids, but it was too late. A new power, Islam, had emerged in the deserts of Arabia. This new power was to challenge and ultimately absorb

THE JUSTINIAN CODE

In 533, the commission appointed by the emperor Justinian completed the Digest, *the most important section of his great Code, the most influential legal text in European history. In his preface, Justinian explains his reason for ordering the codification and reveals the image of imperial power that would be the cornerstone of the Byzantine state for almost a thousand years.*

FOCUS QUESTIONS

How does Justinian present himself to his subjects? How does Justinian relate conquest and justice?

IN THE NAME OF OUR LORD JESUS CHRIST. The emperor Caesar Flavius Justinianus, conqueror of the Alemanni, Goths, Franks, Germans, Antes, Alani, Vandals, and Africans, pious, happy, and glorious, conqueror and vanquisher, to young men desirous of learning the law, greeting.

Imperial majesty should not only be adorned with military might but also graced by laws, so that in times of peace and war alike the state may be governed aright and so that the Emperor of Rome may not only shine forth victorious on the battlefield, but may also by every legal means cast out the wickedness of the perverters of justice, and thus at one and the same time prove as assiduous in upholding the law as he is triumphant over his vanquished foes.

This double objective we have achieved with the blessing of God through our utmost watchfulness and foresight. The barbarian races brought under our yoke know well our military achievements; and Africa also and countless other provinces bear witness to our power having been after so long an interval restored to the dominion of Rome and to our Empire by our victories which we have gained through the inspiration of Divine guidance. Moreover, all these peoples are now also governed by laws which we ourselves have promulgated or compiled.

When we had elucidated and brought into perfect harmony the revered imperial constitutions which were previously in confusion, we turned our attention to the immense mass of ancient jurisprudence. Now, by the grace of Heaven, we have completed this work of which even we at one time despaired like sailors crossing the open sea.

From Justinian, *The Digest of Roman Law: Theft, Rapine, Damage and Insult.*

---

both the Sassanids and much of the eastern Roman Empire. As a result, the east became increasingly less Roman and more Greek—or, specifically, more *Byzantine*, a term derived from the original name of Constantinople, Byzantium.

For over 700 years the Byzantine Empire played a major role in Western history. From the seventh through tenth centuries, when most of Europe was too weak and disorganized to defend itself against the expansion of Islam, the Byzantines stood as the bulwark of Christianity. When organized government had virtually disappeared in the west, the Byzantine Empire provided a model of a centralized bureaucratic state ruled according to principles of Roman law. When, beginning in the fourteenth century, western Europeans began once more to appreciate the heritage of Greek and Roman art and literature, they turned to Constantinople. There, the manuscripts of Greek writers such as Plato and Homer were available to contribute to a rebirth of classical culture in the west. The Slavic north, caught between the Latin Christians and the Muslims, sought its cultural and religious orientation in the liturgical culture of Byzantine orthodoxy. Perhaps most important, when urban civilization had all but disappeared from the

rest of Europe, Greeks and Latins could still look "to The City," *eis ten polin,* or, as the Turks pronounced it, Istanbul.

Emperors and Individuals

The classic age of Byzantine society, roughly from the eighth through the tenth centuries, has been described as "individualism without freedom." Individuals and small family groups stood as isolated units in a society characterized, until the mid-eleventh century, by the direct relationship between an all-powerful emperor and citizens of all ranks.

Governing Byzantium. In part, this individualism resulted from the Byzantine form of government. The Byzantine state was, in theory and often in fact, an autocracy. Since the time of Diocletian, all members of society were subjects of the emperor, who alone was the source of law. How a person became emperor remained, as it had been in the Roman Empire, more a question of military power than of constitutional succession. Although in theory the emperor was elected by the Senate, army, and people of

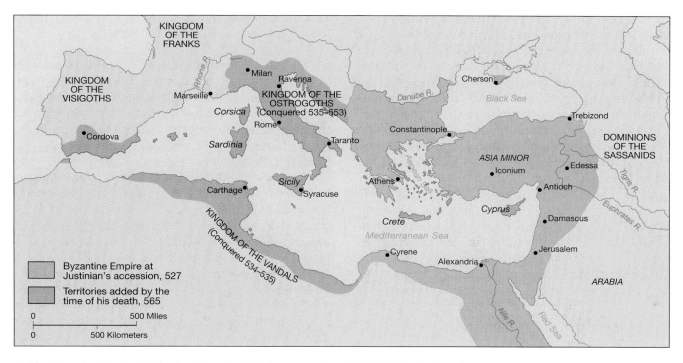

▲ The Byzantine Empire Under Justinian. Justinian's reconquests of North Africa, Italy, and
the coast of Spain severely strained the empire's resources.

Constantinople, emperors generally selected their own successors and had them crowned in their own lifetimes.

As long as the empire remained a civilian autocracy, it was even possible for a woman to rule, either as regent for a minor son or as sovereign. Irene (780–802), widow of Leo IV (725–780), ruled first as regent for her son Constantine VI (780–797). However, when her son reached his majority, she had him blinded and deposed, and she ruled alone from 797 to 802, not merely as the *basilissa*, or wife of the emperor, but as the *basileus*—emperor. In the eleventh century the empire was ruled at different times by two sisters, Zoe (1028–1034), daughter of one emperor and widow of another, and Theodora (1042–1056), who was dragged out of a church by an enthusiastic mob and proclaimed empress.

Male or female, emperors were above and beyond their subjects, often quite literally. In the tenth century, a mechanical throne was installed in the main audience room. The throne would suddenly lift the emperor high above the heads of astonished visitors. Like God the Father, with whom he was closely identified in imperial propaganda, the emperor was separated from the people by an unbridgeable gulf.

Thus the traditional corporate bodies of the Roman Empire wasted away or became window dressing for the imperial cult. The Senate gradually ceased to play any autonomous role, and its powers were officially abolished in the ninth century.

The Circus factions, which in the sixth century had the power to make or break emperors, met the same fate. From autonomous political groups, they too gradually became no more than participants in imperial ceremonies. By the tenth century, the Greens and the Blues were simply officially constituted groups whose role was to praise the emperor by mouthing traditional formulas on solemn occasions.

Bureaucracy and Army.   Although the emperor was the source of all authority, the actual administration of the empire was carried out by a vast bureaucracy composed of military and civilian officers. The empire was divided into roughly 25 provinces, or *themes*. The soldiers in each theme were also farmers, rather than full-time warriors. Each soldier received a small farm by which to support himself and his family. Soldiers held their farms as long as they served in the army. When a soldier retired or died, his farm and his military obligation passed to his eldest son. These farmer-soldiers were the backbone of both the imperial military and the economic system. They not only formed a regular, native, locally based army, but they also kept much of Byzantine agriculture in the hands of small free peasants rather than great aristocrats. The themes were governed by military commanders, or *strategoi*, who presided over both civilian and military bureaucrats.

In contrast to the military command of the themes, the central administration, which focused on the emperor and the imperial family, was wholly civil. The most important positions at court were occupied by eunuchs, castrated men who offered a number of advantages to imperial administration. Eunuchs often directed imperial finance, served as prime ministers, directed the vast bureaucracy, and even undertook military commands. Because they could not have descendants, there was no danger that they would attempt to turn their offices into hereditary positions or that they would plot and scheme on behalf of their children. Moreover, since the sacred nature of the emperor required physical perfection, eunuchs could not aspire to replace their masters on the throne. Finally, although at times their influence with the emperor made them immensely powerful, eunuchs were feared and despised by the general population. Therefore, they had little likelihood of building autonomous power bases outside of imperial favor. The extensive use of eunuchs was one of the keys to the survival of absolutist authority in the empire. Thus imperial authority was preserved at a time when both Islamic and Latin states were experiencing a progressive erosion of central power to the benefit of ambitious aristocratic families.

Families and Villages

A godlike emperor and a centralized bureaucracy left little room for the development of the hierarchies of private patronage, lordship, and group action that were characteristic of western Europe. In the Byzantine Empire, aristocrat and peasant were equal in their political powerlessness. Therefore, Byzantine society tended to be organized at the lowest level, that of the nuclear family. Daily life focused on the protective enclosure of the private home, which served as both shelter and workplace. Professional and craft associations continued to exist as they had in antiquity, but they were not autonomous professional groups intended to protect the interests of their members. Instead, they were fostered and controlled by imperial officials to regulate and tax urban industry.

Rural Life. The countryside, which was the backbone of Byzantine prosperity into the eleventh century, was also a world with limited horizontal and vertical social bonds. Villages were the basic elements in the imperial system. The village court handled local affairs and tax assessments, but it in turn dealt directly with the imperial bureaucracy. Occasionally, villages might unite against imperial tax collectors, but villagers normally dealt with each other and with outside powers as wary individuals. Most peasants, whether they were landowners, peasant soldiers, or renters, survived on the labor of their own family and perhaps one or two slaves. Large cooperative undertakings, as in Islamic lands, and the use of communal equipment, as became the rule in the west, were unknown. Individual families worked their own fields, which were usually enclosed by protective stone or brick walls. Byzantine peasants would have agreed

with the saying in the poem by New Englander Robert Frost: "Good fences make good neighbors."

Urban Life. Like the villages, Byzantine towns were isolated in location and activities. The mountainous terrain of Greece and Asia Minor contributed to this isolation, cutting off ready overland communication among communities and forcing them to turn to the sea. In this respect, Constantinople was ideally situated to develop into the greatest commercial center of the west, at its height boasting a population of over one million. Because of Constantinople's strategic location on the Bosporus, that slim ribbon of water uniting the Black and Mediterranean Seas, all of the products of the empire and those of the Slavic, Latin, and Islamic worlds, as well as Oriental goods arriving overland from central Asia, had to pass through the city. Silks, spices, and precious metals were loaded onto ships at Trebizond and then transported south to Constantinople. Baltic amber, slaves, and furs from the Slavic world were carried down the Dnepr River to the Black Sea and then to the capital. There, all goods passing to the north or south had to be unloaded, assessed, and subjected to a flat import-export tariff of 10 percent.

The empire's cities were centers for the manufacture of luxury goods that were in demand throughout the Islamic and Christian worlds. Imperial workshops in Constantinople and closely regulated workshops in Corinth and Thebes produced fine silks, brocades, carpets, and other luxury products that were marketed throughout the Mediterranean, again subject to the state's customary 10 percent tax.

As vital as maritime commerce was to the empire, most Byzantines despised the sea. They feared it as a source of pirates, sudden storms, and hidden dangers. Moreover, particularly among the elite, commerce was considered demeaning. Never great mariners, Byzantines were largely content to allow others—first Syrians and Slavs and later Italians—to monopolize the empire's commerce.

A Foretaste of Heaven

The cultural cement that bound emperor and subjects together was Orthodox Christianity. The Islamic capture of Alexandria, Jerusalem, and Antioch had removed the centers of regional religious particularism from the empire. The barbarian domination of Italy had isolated Rome and reduced its influence. These two processes left Constantinople as the only remaining patriarchate in the empire and thus the undisputed center of Orthodox Christianity. However, like virtually every other aspect of Byzantine society and culture, the patriarch and the Orthodox faith he led were subordinated to the emperor.

In theory patriarchs were elected, but in reality emperors appointed them. Patriarchs in turn controlled the various

▲ The Byzantine Empire in 814. By the ninth century, the empire had lost all its territories but Asia Minor, Greece, the boot of Italy, and the islands of Sardinia and Sicily.

levels of the Church hierarchy, which included metropolitans, bishops, and the local clergy. This ecclesiastical structure reflected and reinforced the organization of the state bureaucracy. Local priests were drawn from the peasant society of which they were a part. They were expected to be married and to live much like their neighbors. Bishops, metropolitans, and patriarchs were recruited from monasteries and remained celibate. They were, so to speak, spiritual eunuchs who represented the emperor.

The essence of Orthodox religion was the liturgy, or ceremonies, of the Church, which provided, it was said, a foretaste of heaven. Adoration of God and veneration of the emperor went hand in hand as the cornerstone of imperial propaganda. Ecclesiastical and court processions ensured that order and stability reigned in this world as a reflection of the eternal order of the next.

Iconoclasm

The one aspect of religious life that was not entirely under imperial control was monasticism. Since the time of the desert fathers, monastic communities had been an essential part of Christianity. From the sixth century, numerous monastic communities were founded throughout the empire, and by the eleventh century there were at least 300 monasteries within the walls of Constantinople alone. Monasteries were often wealthy and powerful. Moreover, their religious appeal, often based on the possession of miracle-working religious images, or icons, posed an independent source of religious authority that was at odds with the imperial centralization of all aspects of Byzantine life.

Beginning with Emperor Leo III, the Isaurian (717–741), the military emperors who had driven back Islam sought to curtail the independence of monastic culture and particularly the cult of icons that was an integral part of it. These emperors and their supporters, termed *iconoclasts* (literally, "breakers of images"), objected to the mediating role of sacred images in worship. Monasteries, with their miracle-working icons, became particular targets of imperial persecution. They were closed, their estates were confiscated, and their monks were forced to marry. Imperial agents destroyed icons, statues, and illustrated manuscripts and painted over frescoes in churches. The defenders of icons—*iconodules*, or image venerators—were imprisoned, tortured, and even executed. Most bishops, the army, and much of the non-European population of the empire supported the iconoclast emperors, but monks, the lesser clergy, and the majority of the populace, particularly women, violently resisted the destruction of their beloved images.

For more than a century, the iconoclast dispute raged. Finally, in 843, the Empress Theodora (842–858), who ruled during the minority of her son, ended the persecution and restored image veneration. Monasteries reopened and regained much of their former wealth and prestige. Images

▲ The icon of Jesus from the Monastery of St. Catherine at Mt. Sinai, Egypt, dates from the first half of the sixth century and is one of the earliest Byzantine icons still in existence.

were brought out of hiding or new ones were created, and they resumed their role in the eastern Christian church.

The iconoclastic struggle deeply affected Byzantium's relations with the west. Christians in western Europe, and particularly the popes of Rome, never accepted the iconoclast position. The popes considered the iconoclast emperors heretics and looked increasingly to the Frankish Carolingian family for support against them and the Lombards of Italy. In this manner the Franks first entered Italian politics and began, with papal support, to establish themselves as a rival imperial power in the west, which culminated in the coronation of Charlemagne in 800.

Although Byzantium lost Italy and the city of Rome, the empire survived and even flourished. Between the sixth and ninth centuries, the reduced but still vital Roman Empire in the East developed a distinctive political and cultural tradition. The Byzantine system was based on imperial absolutism buttressed by a powerful religious tradition and an effective bureaucracy that dealt directly with individual subjects on behalf of the emperor.

THE RISE OF ISLAM

Arabs lived on the fringes of the Byzantine and Sassanid empires. Trade routes had carried people from the Fertile Crescent and Egypt across northern Arabia for centuries. By the sixth century C.E., Arabic-speaking peoples from the Arabian Peninsula had spread through the Syrian Desert as far north as the Euphrates.

The northern borders of Arabia along the Red Sea had formed Roman provinces that even produced an emperor, Philip the Arab (244–249). Hira, to the south of the Euphrates, became a Sassanid puppet principality that, although largely Christian, often provided the Persians with auxiliaries. Within both the Byzantine and Sassanid empires the distinction between Arab and non-Arab populations was blurred. Except for the Arabic language and a hazy idea of common Arabic kinship, nothing differentiated Arabs from their neighbors.

This was dramatically changed by an obscure merchant in the Arabian city of Mecca, who embarked on a career that would transform the world. Through faith, Muhammad (ca. 570–632) united the tribes of the Arabian Peninsula and propelled them on an unprecedented mission of conquest. Within a century of Muhammad's death, the world of Islam—a word that means "submission to the will of God"—included all of the ancient Near East and extended from the Syr Darya (formerly the Jaxartes) River in Asia south into the Indian subcontinent, west across the African coast to the Atlantic, north through Spain, and along the Mediterranean coast to the Rhone River. Just as their faith combined elements of traditional Arab worship with Christianity and Judaism, the Arabian conquerors and their subject populations created a vital civilization from a mix of Arabian, Roman, Hellenistic, and Sassanid traditions.

Arabia Before the Prophet

Southern Arabia, with relatively abundant rainfall and fertile soils, was an agricultural region long governed by monarchs. Here was the kingdom of Saba, the Sheba of the Bible, which had existed since the tenth century B.C.E. During the fifth century C.E., the kings of the Yemen had extended their influence north over the Bedouin tribes of central Arabia in order to control and protect the caravan trade between north and south. In the late sixth century, however, Ethiopian and then Persian conquerors destroyed the Arabian kingdom of the Yemen and absorbed it into their empires. The result was a power vacuum that left central Arabia and its trade routes across the deserts in confusion.

Bedouin Society.   The interior of the Arabian Peninsula was much less directly affected by the great empires to the north or the Arabian kingdoms to the south. Waterless steppes and seas of shifting sand dunes had long defeated Roman and Persian or Sassanid efforts to control the Arabic Bedouin. These nomads roamed the peninsula in search of pasturage for their flocks. Theirs was a life of independence, simplicity, and danger.

Although they acknowledged membership in various tribes, the Bedouin's real allegiance was to much narrower circles of lineages and tenting groups. As in the Germanic tribes of Europe, kin relationships rather than formal governmental systems protected individuals through the obligation for vengeance and blood feud. In the words of a pre-Islamic poet, "Blood for blood—wiped out were the wounds, and those who had gained a start in the race profited not by their advantage." Tribal chieftains, called *sheikhs*, chosen from ruling families, had no coercive power, either to right wrongs or to limit feuds. They served only as arbitrators and executors of tribal consensus. The patriarch of each family held final say over his kin. He could ignore the sheikh and go his own way.

The individual was unimportant in Bedouin society. Private land ownership was unknown, and flocks and herds were often held in common by kindred. The pastoral economy of the Bedouin provided meat, cheese, and wool. Weapons, ornaments, women, and livestock could be acquired through exchange at the market towns around desert oases. More commonly, these goods and women were taken in raids against other tribes, caravans, and settlements or by exacting payments from weaker neighbors in return for protection. Raids, often launched in defense of family honor, were also the means of increasing prestige and glory in this warrior society. Prizes won in battle were lightly given away as signs of generosity and marks of social importance.

Some of the Arabs of the more settled south, as well as inhabitants of towns along caravan routes, were Christian or Jewish. As farmers or merchants, these groups were looked down upon by the nomadic Bedouin, most of whom remained pagan. Although they recognized some important gods and even a high god usually called Allah, Bedouin worshiped local tribal deities, who were often thought of as inhabiting a sacred stone or spring. Worship involved gifts and offerings and played only a small part in nomadic life. Far more important was commitment to the tribe, expressed through loyalty to the tribal cult and through unity of action against rival tribes.

Harams. Rivalry and feuding among tribes could be set aside at a mutually accepted neutral site, which might grow up around a religious sanctuary. A sanctuary, or *haram*, which was often on the border between tribal areas, was founded by a holy man not unlike the Christian holy men of the Syrian Desert. The holy man declared the site and surrounding area neutral ground on which no violence could take place. Here, enemies could meet under truce to settle differences under the direction of the holy

man or his descendants. Merchant communities sprang up within the safety of these sites, since the sanctuary gave them and their goods protection from their neighbors.

Mecca was just such a sanctuary, around whose sacred black rock, or Ka'bah, a holy man named Qusayy established himself and his tribe, the Quraysh, as its guardians sometime early in the sixth century. In the next century, under the patronage of the Quraysh, Mecca grew into an important commercial center. Through religious, diplomatic, and military means, Quraysh organized camel caravans, which could safely cross the desert from the Yemen in the south to Iran and Syria in the north. During the early seventh century, when increased hostilities between the Byzantine and Sassanid empires severed the direct trading links between the empires, the Quraysh network became the leading commercial organization in northern Arabia. Still, its effectiveness remained tied to the religious importance of Mecca and the Ka'bah. When Muhammad, a descendant of Qusayy, began to preach his monotheistic message, he was seen as a threat to the survival of his tribe and his city.

Muhammad, Prophet of God

More is known about Muhammad's life than about the lives of Moses, Jesus, Buddha, or any of the other great religious reformers of history. Still, Muhammad's adherents quickly wrapped his early years in a protective cloak of pious stories, making it difficult to discern truth from legend. A member of a lesser branch of the Quraysh, Muhammad was an orphan raised by relatives. At about age 20, he became the business manager for Khadijah, a wealthy widow whom he later married. This marriage gave him financial security among the middle ranks of Meccan merchants. In his thirties, he began to devote an increasing amount of time to meditation, retiring to the barren, arid mountains outside the city. There, in the month of Ramadan in the year 610, he reported a vision of a man who told him: "O Muhammad! Thou art the Messenger of God."

Preaching Islam. Khadijah, to whom he confided his revelation in fear and confusion, became his first convert. Within a year he began preaching openly. His early teachings stressed the absolute unity of God, the evils of idolatry, and the threat of divine judgment. Further revelations to Muhammad were copied word for word in what came to be the Qur'an, or Koran. These messages offered Arabs a faith founded on a book. In their eyes, this faith was both within the tradition of the Christianity and Judaism of their neighbors and superior to them. The Qur'an was the final revelation and Muhammad the last and greatest prophet. To Muslims—the term means "true believers"— Muhammad is simply the Prophet.

Muslims believe that Allah's revelation emphasized, above all, his power and transcendence and that the duty of humans is worship. The prayers of Islam, in contrast with those of Christianity and Judaism, are essentially prayers of praise, seldom prayers of petition. This reverential attitude places little premium on scriptural interpretation or theological speculation. Muslims regard the whole Qur'an as the exact and complete revelation of God, literally true and forming a unified whole, though revelations contained in it came at various times throughout the Prophet's life. It is the complete guide for secular and religious life, the fundamental law of conduct for Islamic society. The Prophet emphasized constantly that he was simply God's messenger and merited no special veneration or worship. For this reason, Muslims have always rejected the label *Muhammadan,* which nonbelievers often apply to them. Muslims are not followers of Muhammad but of the God of Abraham and Jesus, who chose to make the final and complete revelation of his power and his judgment through the Prophet.

Initially, such revelations of divine power and judgment neither greatly bothered nor influenced Mecca's merchant elite. Muhammad's earliest adherents, such as his cousin 'Ali ibn Abi (ca. 600–661), came from his own clan and from among the moderately successful members of the Meccan community—the "nearly haves" rather than the "have-nots," as one scholar put it. Elite clans such as the Umayya, who controlled the larger Quraysh tribe, saw little to attract them to the upstart. But soon Muhammad began to insist that those who did not accept Allah as the only God were damned, as were those who continued to venerate the sorts of idols on which Mecca's prosperity was founded. With this proclamation, toleration gave way to hostility. Muhammad and his followers were ostracized and even persecuted.

The Hijra. Around 620, some residents of Medina, a smaller trading community populated by rival pagan, Jewish, and Islamic clans and racked by internal political dissension, approached the Prophet and invited him to govern the community in order to end the factional squabbles. Rejected at home, he answered their call. On 24 September 622, Muhammad and one supporter secretly made their way from Mecca to Medina. This short journey of less than 300 miles, known as the Hijra, was destined to change the world.

The Triumph of Islam

The Hijra marked the beginning of the Islamic dating system in the way that the birth of Jesus began the Christian dating system. The Hijra also marked the Prophet's shift from preaching to action. He organized his followers from Mecca and Medina into the Umma, a community that transcended the old bonds of tribe and clan. He set about

turning Medina into a haram like Mecca, with himself as founding holy man and the Umma as his new family. But this was not to be a haram or indeed a family like any other. Muhammad was not merely a sheikh whose authority rested on consensus. He was God's messenger, and his authority was absolute. His goal was to extend this authority far beyond his adopted town of Medina to Mecca and ultimately to the whole Arab world.

First, he gained firm control of Medina at the expense of its Jewish clans. He had expected these monotheists to embrace his teachings. Instead, they rejected the unlettered Arab's attempt to transform Judaic and Christian traditions into an Arab faith. Rejection was their undoing. The Prophet expelled them in the name of political and religious unity. Those who were not expelled were executed.

Return to Mecca. Muhammad then used this unified community to attack the Quraysh where they were most vulnerable—in their protection of camel caravans. Inability to destroy the upstarts or protect its trading network cost the Quraysh tribe much of its prestige. More and more members of Meccan families and local tribes converted to Islam. In 629, Muhammad and 10,000 warriors marched on Mecca and captured the city in a swift and largely bloodless campaign.

During the three years between Muhammad's triumphant return to Mecca and his death, Islam moved steadily toward becoming the major force in the Arabian Peninsula. The divine revelations increasingly took on legal and practical dimensions as Muhammad was forced to serve not just as Prophet, but as political leader of a major political and economic power. The Umma had become a sort of supertribe, open to all individuals who would accept Allah and his Prophet. The invitation was extended to women as well as to men.

Women in Early Islam. Islam brought a transformation of the rights of women in Arabian society. This did not mean that they achieved equality with men any more than they did in any premodern civilization, east or west. Men continued to dominate Islamic society, in which military prowess and male honor were so valued. Women remained firmly subordinate to men, who could have up to four wives, could divorce them at will, and could keep women segregated from other men. When in public, Islamic women in many regions adopted the Syriac Christian practice of wearing a veil that covered all of the face but the eyes. Islam did, however, forbid female infanticide, a common practice in pre-Islamic society. Brides, not their fathers or other male relatives, received the dowry from their husbands, thus making marriage more a partnership than a sale. All wives had to be treated equally. If a man was unable to do so, he had to limit himself to a single wife. Islamic women acquired inheritance and property rights and had protection against mistreatment in marriage. Although they remained second-class in status, at least women had a status, recognized and protected within the Umma.

An Arabian Faith.   The rapid spread of Islam within the Arab world can be explained by a number of religious and material factors. Men may have been attracted by the sensuous vision of the afterlife promised to believers. Paradise was presented as a world of refreshing streams and leafy bowers, where redeemed men would lie on divans, eat exotic foods served by handsome youths, and be entertained by beautiful virgins called Houris, created especially for them by Allah. Probably more compelling than the description of heaven was the promise of the torments awaiting nonbelievers on the day of judgment: "For the wrongdoers we have prepared a fire which will encompass them like the walls of a pavilion. When they cry out for a drink they shall be showered with water as hot as melted brass, which will scald their faces. Evil shall be their drink, dismal their resting-place."

The concrete attractions of Islam in this world included both economic prosperity and the opportunity to continue a lifestyle of raiding and warfare in the name of Allah. Muhammad won over the leaders of the Quraysh by making Mecca the sacred city of Islam and by retaining the Ka'bah, cleansed of idols, as the center of Islamic pilgrimage.

Muhammad's message spread to other tribes through diplomatic and, occasionally, military means. The divisive nature of Bedouin society contributed to his success. Frequently, factions within other tribes turned to Muhammad for mediation and support against their rivals. In return for his assistance, petitioners accepted his religious message. Since the Qur'an commanded Muslims to destroy idol worship, conversion provided the occasion for holy wars (*jihads*) of conquest and profitable raids against their still-pagan neighbors. Converts showed their piety by sending part of their spoils as alms to Medina. The Qur'an permitted Christians and Jews living under the authority of Islamic communities to continue to practice their faith, but they were forced to pay a head tax that was shared among members of the Umma.

The Spread of Islam

Muhammad died in the summer of 632 after a short illness, leaving no successor and no directions concerning the leadership of the Umma. Immediately, his closest and most influential followers selected Abu Bakr (632–634), the fourth convert to Islam, to be caliph, or successor of the Prophet. Abu Bakr and, after his death two years later, the caliph 'Umar (634–644) faced formidable obstacles. Within the Umma, tensions between the early Medina followers of the Prophet and the Meccan elite were beginning to surface. A more critical problem was that the tribes

which had accepted the Prophet's leadership believed that his death freed them from their treaty obligations. Now they attempted to go their own ways. Some sent emissaries to announce that, while they would remain Muslims, they would no longer pay alms. Others attempted to abandon Islam altogether.

To prevent the collapse of the Umma, Abu Bakr launched a war of reconversion. Purely by chance, this war developed into wars of conquest that reached far beyond the Arab world. Commanded by Khalid ibn al-Walid (d. 642), the greatest early Islamic general, Muslim forces defeated tribe after tribe and brought them back into the Umma. But long-term survival demanded expansion. Since Muslims were forbidden to raid fellow believers and raids were an integral part of Bedouin life, the only way to keep recently converted Bedouin in line was to lead them on military expeditions against non-Muslims. Arab armies could move men and supplies quickly across the arid wastes, crush their enemies, and then retreat back into the desert, beyond the reach of Byzantine and Sassanid forces. Under Abu Bakr, Muslim expansion covered all of Arabia. Under 'Umar, Islam conquered Iran, Iraq, Syria, and Egypt.

The swift and total collapse of the Sassanid Empire and a major portion of the Byzantine Empire astounded contemporaries, not least the Muslims themselves. Their success seemed to be irrefutable proof that Muhammad's message was indeed from God. By 650, Islam stretched from Egypt to Asia Minor, from the Mediterranean to the Indus River.

Another factor that contributed to the Muslims' phenomenal success was the protracted fighting between the Byzantine and Sassanid empires as well as internal divisions within the Byzantine world. For over two decades (ca. 602–628) Egypt, Palestine, and Syria had been under Persian control. Although the Byzantine emperor Heraclius eventually reconquered them, these provinces had not yet recovered from the decades of warfare, and within them a whole generation had grown up with no experience of Byzantine government.

In addition, the reimposed Byzantine yoke was widely resented because of profound cultural differences between Greeks and the inhabitants of Syria, Iraq, and Egypt. Many looked on the Byzantines not as the liberators but as the enemy. Syria and Egypt had always been different from the rest of the Roman world. Although their great cities of Antioch and Alexandria had long been centers of Hellenistic learning and culture, the hinterlands of each enjoyed ancient cultural traditions that were totally alien to their urban neighbors. In Syria, this rural society was Aramaic and Arabic speaking. In Egypt, it was Coptic. With the steady decay of urban life and the rising demands on the rural economy, these local differences rose to greater prominence. Eventually, these peculiarities coalesced around religious traditions sustained by liturgies

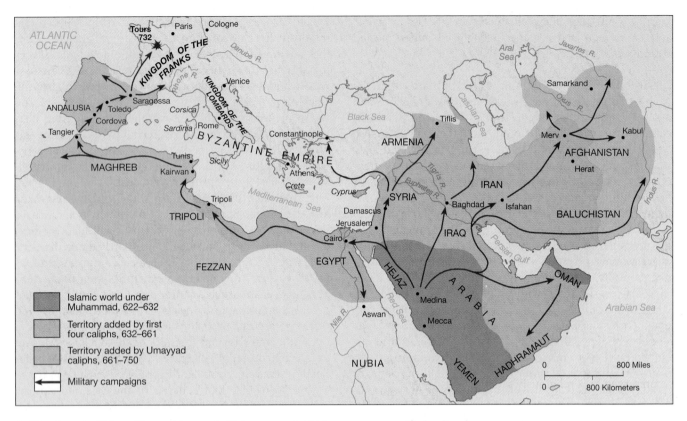

▲ The Spread of Islam. The rapid spread of Islam created within a century a unified cultural and economic zone from India to the Atlantic Ocean within.

that were in the vernacular and sharply at odds with the Orthodox Christianity of Constantinople.

These profound cultural, ethnic, and social antagonisms were largely fought out in the sphere of doctrine, particularly over the nature of Jesus Christ. The form of Christianity that the emperors sought to impose, defined at the Council of Chalcedon in 451, insisted that Jesus was only one person but had two complete natures, one fully human, the other entirely divine. Such a distinction rested less on the language of the New Testament than on the Greek philosophical tradition. To the Syrian and Egyptian communities this position was heresy. "Anathema to the unclean Synod of Chalcedon!" wrote one Egyptian monk. Closer to the Jewish tradition of the transcendence of God, the Syriac and Egyptian Monophysite (meaning "one nature") Christians insisted that Christ had but a single nature and it was divine.

The two groups vented their intense hatred of each other in riots, murders, and vicious persecutions directed by zealous emperors. As a result, for many Christians of the Near East, the arrival of the Muslims, whose beliefs about the unity and transcendence of God were close to their own and who promised religious toleration and an end to persecution, was seen initially as a divine blessing.

Many Christians and Jews in Syria, Palestine, Egypt, and North Africa shared this view of the Muslim conquest as liberation rather than enslavement. Jews and Christians may have been second-class citizens in the Islamic world, but at least they had a defined place. Conquered populations were allowed to practice their religion in peace. Their only obligation was to pay a head tax to their conquerors, a burden that was considerably less onerous than the money exacted by Byzantine tax collectors.

The Byzantines' defeat of the Sassanids indirectly facilitated the Muslims' conquest of Iraq. When the Bedouin realized that the Persians were too weakened to protect their empire against raiders, they intensified their attacks. Soon, recent converts to Islam, too late to profit from the conquests of Syria and Egypt, were spearheading the conquest. By 650 the great Sassanid Empire had disappeared, and the Byzantine Empire had lost Egypt, Syria, Mesopotamia, Palestine, portions of Asia Minor, and much of North Africa. During the reigns of Constantine IV (668–685) and Leo III (717–741), Constantinople itself faced besieging Muslim fleets. Each time, it survived only through the use of a secret weapon, so-called Greek fire, an explosive liquid that burst into flame when sprayed by siphons onto enemy ships. Although the city itself survived, the Muslim conquests reduced the once vast empire to little more than Greece, western Asia Minor, southern Italy, and the Balkans.

Authority and Government in Islam

Conquering the world for Islam proved easier than governing it. What had begun as a religious movement within Arabian society had created a vast multinational empire in which Arabs were a tiny minority. Nothing in the Qur'an, nothing in Arabian experience, provided a blueprint for empire. Thus, the Muslims' ability to consolidate their conquests is even more remarkable than the conquests themselves. Within the first decades following the Prophet's death, two models of governance emerged, models that continue to dominate Islamic politics to the present.

The Umma. The first model was that of pre-Islamic tribal authority. The Umma could be considered a supertribe, governed by leaders whose authority came from their secular power as leaders of the superior military and economic elements within the community. This model appealed particularly to the Quraysh and local tribal leaders who had exercised authority before Muhammad. The second model was that of the authority exercised by the Prophet. In this model, the Umma was more than a supertribe, and its unity and purity had to be preserved by a religiously sanctioned rule exercised by a member of the Prophet's own family. This model was preferred by many of the more recent converts to Islam, especially the poor. Governance under each of the two models was attempted successively in the seventh and eighth centuries.

Regardless of their disagreements on the basis of political authority, both groups adopted the administrative systems of their conquered lands. Byzantine and Sassanid bureaucracy and government, only slightly adjusted, became the models for government in the Islamic world until the twentieth century. In Syria and Egypt, Byzantine officials and even churchmen were incorporated into the government, much as had happened in Europe following the Germanic conquests. For example, John of Damascus (ca. 676–ca. 754), a Christian theologian venerated as a saint, served as the caliph's chief councilor. His faithfulness to the Islamic government and opposition to Byzantine imperial iconoclasm earned him the title of "cursed favorer of Saracens [Muslims]" from the Byzantine emperor.

Likewise, the Muslims left intact the social structures and economic systems of the empires they conquered. Lands remained in the hands of their previous owners. Only state property or, in the Sassanid Empire, that of the Zoroastrian priesthood became common property of the Muslim community. The monastery of Saint Catherine on Mount Sinai, for example, founded by the emperor Justinian around 540, survived without serious harm and still shelters Orthodox monks today.

The Last Orthodox Caliphs. The division of the spoils of conquest badly divided the Umma and precipitated the first crisis in the caliphate. Under 'Umar, two groups received most of the spoils of the conquests. First were the earliest followers of the Prophet, who received a disproportionate share of revenues. Second were the conquerors themselves, who were often recent converts from tribes on the fringes of Arabia. After 'Umar's death, his successor 'Uthman (d. 656), a member of the powerful Umayya clan of Mecca, attempted to consolidate control over Islam by Quraysh elite. He began to reduce the privileges of early converts in favor of the old Meccan elite. At the same time, he demanded that revenue from the provinces be sent to Medina. The result was rebellion, both within Arabia and in Egypt. 'Uthman's only firm support lay in distant Syria, ruled by members of his own clan. Abandoned at home and abroad, he was finally murdered as he sat reading the Qur'an in his home.

In spite of 'Uthman's unpopularity, his murder sent shock waves throughout the Umma. The fate of his successor, Muhammad's beloved son-in-law and nephew 'Ali (656–661), had an even more serious effect on the future of Islam. Although chosen as fourth caliph, 'Ali was immediately charged with complicity in 'Uthman's murder and was strongly opposed by the Umayyad commander of Syria. To protect himself, 'Ali moved the caliphate from Arabia to Iraq, but in 661, 'Ali was murdered by supporters of his Umayyad rivals. Still, the memory of the "last orthodox caliph" remained alive in the Islamic world, especially in Iraq and Iran. Centuries later, a tradition developed in Baghdad that legitimate leadership of Islam could come only from the house of 'Ali. Adherents to this belief developed into a political and religious sect known as *Shi'ism*. Although frequently persecuted as heretical by the majority of Muslims, Shi'ism remains a potent minority movement within the Islamic world today.

Umayyad and 'Abbasid Caliphates

The immediate effect of 'Ali's death, however, was the triumph of the old Quraysh and in particular the Umayyads, who established at Damascus in Syria a caliphate that lasted a century. The Umayyads made no attempt to base their rule on spiritual authority. Instead, they ruled as secular leaders, attempting to unite the Islamic empire through an appeal to Arab unity. Profits from this state went entirely to the Quraysh and members of Arabian tribes, who formed the backbone of the early Umayyad army, monopolized high administration, and acquired rich estates throughout the empire.

Umayyad Caliphate. The Umayyads extended the Islamic empire to its farthest reaches. In the north, armies from Syria marched into Anatolia and were stopped only in 677 by the Byzantine fleet before Constantinople itself.

In the east, Umayyad armies pressed as far as the Syr Darya River on the edge of the Chinese Tang empire. In the south and southwest, the general Tariq ibn Ziyad (d. ca. 720) conquered the Mediterranean coast of Africa and in 711 crossed over the strait near the Rock of Gibraltar (the name comes from the Arabic *jabal Tariq*, "Tariq's mountain") and quickly conquered virtually the entire Iberian peninsula. Soon raiding parties had ventured as far north as the Loire Valley of what is today France. There they were halted by the Frankish commander Charles Martel in 732. Much of Spain, however, remained under Islamic control until 1492.

The Umayyad caliphate's external success in conquering failed to extend to its dealings with the internal tensions of the Umma. The Umayyads could not build a stable empire on the twin foundations of a tiny Arabian elite and a purely secular government taken over from their Byzantine predecessors. Arabs as well as Jews, Zoroastrians, and Christians converted in great numbers. Not all Muslim commanders looked favorably on such conversions. Far from practicing "conversion by the sword," as was often the case in Christian missionary activity, Muslim leaders at times discouraged the spread of Islam among the non-Arabs they had conquered. The reason was simple. Christians and Jews had to pay the head tax imposed on them. If they converted, they no longer paid the tax. In time, this growing population of non-Arab Muslims began to demand a share in the empire's wealth.

The 'Abbasid Revolution.   Not only were the numbers of Muslims increasing, so also was their fervor. Growing numbers of devout Muslims—Arabs and non-Arabs alike—were convinced that leadership had to be primarily spiritual and that this spiritual mandate was the exclusive right of the family of the Prophet. Ultimately, a coalition of dissatisfied Persian Muslims and Arabian religious reformers united under the black banners of the descendants of Muhammad's paternal uncle, 'Abbas (566–ca. 653). In 750, this group overthrew the Umayyads everywhere but in Spain and established a new caliphate in favor of the 'Abbasids.

With the fall of the Umayyad caliphate, Arabs lost control of Islam forever. The 'Abbasids attempted to govern the empire according to religious principles. These were found in the Qur'an and in the *sunnah*, or practices established by the Prophet and preserved first orally and then in the *hadith*, or traditions, which were somewhat comparable to the Christian Gospels. This new empire was to be a universal Muslim commonwealth in which Arabs had no privileged position. "Whoever speaks Arabic is an Arab," ran a popular saying. The 'Abbasids had risen to power as "the group of the saved," and they hoped to make the moral community of Islam the cornerstone of their government, with obedience to 'Abbasid authority an integral part of Islamic belief.

The institutional foundations of the new caliphate, however, like those of the Umayyads, remained firmly in the ancient empires they had conquered. The great caliph Mansur (754–775) moved the capital from Damascus to Baghdad, an acknowledgment of the crucial role of Iraqi and Iranian military and economic strength. The 'Abbasids constructed an autocratic imperial system on the model of their Persian predecessors. With firm control of the military, increasingly composed of slave armies known as Mamluks, the 'Abbasids governed the Islamic empire at its zenith.

Division and Revolt.   Ultimately, however, the 'Abbasids were no more successful than the Umayyads in maintaining authority over the whole Muslim world. By the tenth century, local military commanders, termed *emirs*, took control of provincial governments in many areas while preserving the fiction that they were appointed by the 'Abbasid caliphs. The caliphs maintained the symbolic unity of Islam while the emirs went their separate ways. The majority of Muslims accepted this situation as a necessary compromise. In contrast to the Shi'ites, who continued to look for a leader from the family of 'Ali, the *Sunnis*, as they came to be known, remain to the present the majority group of Muslims. The Sunnis had no fixed theory of government or succession to the caliphate. Instead, they accepted the events of history in a practical manner, secure in the truth of the hadith: "My umma will never agree upon an error."

In the west, the 'Abbasids could not maintain even a facade of unity. The Shi'ites launched sporadic revolts and separatist movements. The most successful was that of 'Ubayd Allah the Fatimid (d. 934), who claimed to be the descendant of 'Ali and rightful leader of Islam. In 909, with the support of North African seminomadic Berbers, he declared himself caliph in defiance of the 'Abbasids at Baghdad. In 969, 'Ubayd's Fatimid successors conquered Egypt and established a new city, Cairo, as the capital of their rival caliphate. By the middle of the eleventh century, the Fatimid caliphate controlled all of North Africa, Sicily, Syria, and western Arabia. In Umayyad Spain, although the Muslim population remained firmly Sunni, the powerful emir 'Abd ar-Rahman III (891–961) in 929 also took the title of caliph, thus making his position religious as well as secular. Everywhere, the political and religious unity of Islam was being torn apart.

The Turks.   The arrival in all three caliphates of Muslim peoples who were not yet integrated into the civilization of the Mediterranean world accelerated this disintegration. From the east, Seljuk Turks, long used as slave troops, entered Iraq and in 1055 conquered Baghdad. Within a decade they had conquered Iran, Syria, and Palestine as well. Around the same time, Moroccan Berbers conquered much of North Africa and Spain, while Bedouin raided freely in what are today Libya and Tunisia. These invasions by Muslims from the fringes of the Islamic commonwealth had catastrophic effects on the Islamic world. The Turks, unaccustomed to commerce and to the administrative traditions of the caliphate, divided their empire among their war leaders, displacing traditional landowners and disrupting commerce. The North African Berbers and Bedouin destroyed the agricultural and commercial systems that had survived successive Vandal, Byzantine, and Arabian invasions.

Islamic Civilization

The Islamic conquest of the seventh century brought peace to Iraq and Iran after generations of struggle and set the stage for a major agricultural recovery. In the tradition of their Persian predecessors, the caliphs organized vast irrigation systems, which made Mesopotamia the richest agricultural region west of China. Peasants and slaves raised dates and olives in addition to wheat, barley, and rice. Sophisticated hydraulics and scientific agriculture brought great regions of Mesopotamia and the Mediterranean coast into cultivation for the first time in centuries.

By uniting the Mediterranean world with Arabia and India, the 'Abbasid empire created the greatest trade network that had ever been seen. Muslim merchants met in bustling ports on the Persian Gulf and the Red Sea to trade silks, paper, spices, and horses from China for silver and cotton from India. Gold from the Sudan was exchanged for iron from Persia. Also offered were carpets from Armenia and Tabaristan, what is today Iran, and slaves from western Europe. Many of these luxury goods found their way to Baghdad, known as the marketplace for the world.

The marketplace for ideas was as active as that for merchandise. Within a few generations, descendants of Bedouin established themselves in the great cities of the ancient Near East and absorbed the traditions of Persian, Roman, and Hellenistic civilization. However, unlike the Germanic peoples of western Europe, who quickly adopted the Latin language and Roman Christianity, the Muslims recast Persian and Hellenistic culture in an Arabic form. Even in Iran, where Farsi, or Persian, survived as the majority language, Arabic vocabulary and structure transformed the traditional language. While 'Abassid political unity was falling apart, this new civilization was reaching its first great synthesis.

Science and Faith. In the process, Arabs became the protectors and preservers of Persian and Hellenistic culture. As early as the eighth century, caliphs collected Persian, Greek, and Syriac scientific and philosophical works and had them translated into Arabic. Legal scholars

▲ Muslim astronomers made many advances. They perfected the astrolabe, an instrument used to observe and calculate the positions of heavenly bodies.

concerned with the authenticity of hadith used Greek rationalist methods to distinguish genuine from spurious traditions. Religious mystics called Sufis blended Neoplatonic and Muslim traditions to create new forms of religious devotion. The medical writings of Hippocrates and Galen circulated widely in the Islamic world, and Muslim physicians were by far the most competent and respected in the West through the fifteenth century. Mathematics and astronomy were both practical and theoretical fields. Muslim intellectuals introduced the so-called Arabic numerals from India and, by the tenth century, had perfected the use of the decimal, fractions, and algebra. Although theoretical astronomy was limited to reforming rather than recasting Ptolemaic theory, Muslim astronomers absorbed and continued the highly accurate traditions of Mesopotamian planetary observation. The tables they compiled were more accurate than those known in the Byzantine and Latin worlds.

Philosophy.   Although most Islamic scientists were professional physicians, astronomers, or lawyers, they were also deeply concerned with abstract philosophical questions, particularly those raised by the works of Plato and Aristotle, which had been translated into Arabic. Many sought to reconcile Islam with this philosophical heritage. Ya'qub al-Kindi (d. 873), the first Arab philosopher, noted that "The truth . . . must be taken wherever it is to be found, whether it be in the past or among strange peoples." The Persian physician Ibn Sina (980–1037), known in the West as Avicenna, wrote over a hundred works on all aspects of science and philosophy. He compiled a vast encyclopedia of knowledge in which he attempted to synthesize Aristotelian thought into a Neoplatonic view of the universe. In the next century, the Cordoban philosopher Ibn Rushd (1126–1198), called Averroës in the West, went still further, teaching an authentic Aristotelian philosophy stripped of Neoplatonic mystical trappings. His commentaries on Aristotle were enormously influential even outside the Islamic world. For Christian philosophers of the thirteenth century, Averroës was known simply as "the Commentator."

Christian Invasion.   At the same time that Muslim thought and culture was at its most creative, Islam faced invasion from a new and unaccustomed quarter: Constantinople. In the tenth and early eleventh centuries, the Byzantines pressed the local rulers of northern Syria and Iraq in a series of raids, which reached as far as the border of Palestine. At the end of the eleventh century, western Europeans, encouraged and supported by the Byzantines, captured Jerusalem and established a Western-style kingdom in Palestine that survived for over a century. Once more, Constantinople was a power in the Mediterranean world.

THE BYZANTINE APOGEE AND DECLINE, 1000–1453

During the tenth and eleventh centuries, Byzantium dominated the Mediterranean world for the last time. Imperial armies under the Macedonian dynasty (867–1059) began to recover some lands that had been lost to Islam during the previous two centuries. Antioch was retaken in 969, and for over a century Byzantine armies operated in Syria and pushed to the border of Palestine. By the middle of the eleventh century, Armenia and Georgia, which had formed independent principalities, had been reintegrated into the empire. To the west, Sicily remained in Muslim hands, but southern Italy, which had been subject to Muslim raids and western barbarian occupation, was secured once

more. Byzantine fleets recaptured Crete, cleared the Aegean of Muslim pirates, and reopened the vital commercial sea routes. To the north, missionaries spread not only the Christian religion but also Byzantine culture among the Slavic peoples beyond the frontiers of the empire. The most important missionaries were the brothers Cyril (ca. 827–869) and Methodius (ca. 827–885), who preached to the Khazars and the Moravians. They also invented the Cyrillic alphabet, which they used to translate the Bible and other Christian writings into Slavic. Their missionary activities laid the foundation for the conversion of Serbia, Bulgaria, and Russia. In 1018, Basil II (976–1025) destroyed the Bulgarian kingdom and brought peace to the Balkan Peninsula.

The conquests of the Macedonian dynasty laid the foundation for a short-lived economic prosperity and cultural renaissance. Conquered lands, particularly Anatolia, brought new agricultural wealth. Security of the sea fostered a resurgence of commerce, and customs duties enriched the imperial treasury. New wealth financed the flourishing of Byzantine art and literature. However, just as in the spheres of Byzantine liturgy and court ceremonial, the goal of Byzantine art was to reflect not the transient "reality" of this world but rather the permanent classical values inherited from the past. Thus, rarely in Byzantine art, literature, or religion was innovation appreciated or cultivated.

The language, style, and themes of classical Greek literature, philosophy, and history completely dominated Byzantine culture. Only in rare works such as the popular epic *Digenis Akrites* does something of the flavor of popular Byzantine life appear. The title of the work means roughly "the border defender born of two peoples," for the hero, Basil, was the son of a Muslim father and a Christian Greek mother. The epic consists of two parts, one describing the exploits of the father, a Muslim emir or general, and the other describing those of Digenis Akrites himself, fighting against both Muslims and bandits. The descriptions of his battles, his encounters with wild beasts and dragons, and his heroic death, as well as those of his intelligence, learning, and magnificent palace, are at once part of the Western epic tradition and a reflection of life on the edge of the empire. *Digenis Akrites* is unique for its close relation to popular oral traditions of Byzantine society.

The Disintegration of the Empire

In all domains, however, the successes of the Macedonian emperors set the stage for serious problems. Rapid military expansion and economic growth allowed new elites to establish themselves as autonomous powers and to position themselves between the imperial administration and the people. The constant demand for troops always exceeded the supply of traditional salaried soldiers. In the eleventh century, emperors began to grant imperial estates to great magnates in return for military service. These grants, termed *pronoia*, often included immunity from imperial taxation and the right to certain administrative activities traditionally carried out by the central government. The practice created in effect a largely independent, landed military aristocracy that stood between the peasantry and the imperial government. This policy weakened the centralized state and reduced its income from taxes.

Internal Conflict.   As generals became dissatisfied with the civilian central administration, they began to turn their armies against the emperors, launching over 30 revolts in as many years. To defend itself against both the Muslims without and the generals within, the central government, composed of intellectuals, eunuchs, and urban aristocrats, had to spend vast sums on mercenary armies. These armies, composed largely of Armenians, Germans, and Normans, soon began to plunder the empire they were hired to protect. Further danger came from other, independent Normans who, under their commander Robert Guiscard (ca. 1015–1085), conquered Byzantine Bari and southern Italy and then Muslim Sicily. Soon Guiscard was threatening the empire itself. The hostility between aristocracy and imperial administration largely destroyed the tradition of civilian government. "Do not wish to be a bureaucrat," one general advised his son. "It is not possible to be both a general and a comedian."

Under increasing pressure from local magnates on the one hand and desperate imperial tax collectors on the other, villages began to make deals with powerful patrons who would represent them in return for the surrender of their independence. Through the eleventh and twelfth centuries, the Byzantine peasantry passed from the condition of individualism without freedom to that of collectivism without freedom. Through the same process, landlords and patrons acquired the means to exercise a political role, which ended the state's monopoly on public power.

Commercial Threats.   At the same time that civil war and external pressure were destroying the provincial administration, Byzantine disdain for commerce was weakening the empire's ability to control its income from customs duties. Initially, the willingness to turn over commerce to Italians and others posed few problems. Those who were engaged in actual commerce were for the most part citizens of the empire and were in any case subject to the 10 percent tariffs. However, in the tenth and eleventh centuries, merchants of Amalfi, Bari, and then Venice came to dominate Byzantine commerce. Venetian merchant fleets could double as a powerful navy in times of need, and by the eleventh century the Venetians were the permanent military and commercial power in the Mediterranean. When Robert Guiscard and his Normans threatened the empire, the emperors had to turn to the Venetians for protection and were forced to cede them major economic privileges. The Venetians acquired the right to maintain important self-governing communities

CHRONOLOGY	
THE BYZANTINE EMPIRE AND THE RISE OF ISLAM	
527–565	Reign of Justinian
610	Muhammad's vision
662	The Hijra, Muhammad's journey from Mecca to Medina
726–787	First phase of iconoclast dispute
732	Muslim advance halted by Franks
750	'Abbasids overthrow Umayyads; take control of Muslim world
802–843	Second phase of iconoclast dispute
843	Empress Theodora ends iconoclast persecution; restores image veneration
867–1059	Macedonian dynasty rules Byzantine Empire; begins recovering lands from Muslims
1054	Schism splits churches of Rome and Constantinople
1071	Robert Guiscard captures Sicily and southern Italy
	Battle of Manzikert
	Seljuk Turks defeat Byzantines
1099	First Crusade establishes Latin kingdom in Jerusalem
1221	Genghis Khan leads Mongol army into Persia
1453	Constantinople falls to Ottomans

in major ports throughout the empire and were allowed to pay lower tariffs than the Byzantines paid.

In 1071, the year that Robert Guiscard captured the last Byzantine city in Italy, the empire suffered an even more disastrous defeat in the east. At Manzikert in Anatolia, the emperor Romanus IV (1067–1071) and his unreliable mercenary army fell to the Seljuk Turks, who captured Romanus. The defeat at Manzikert sealed the fate of the empire. Anatolia was lost, and the gradual erosion of the empire in both the west and the east had begun.

The Conquests of Constantinople and Baghdad

At the end of the eleventh century the Comnenian dynasty (1081–1185) briefly halted the political and economic chaos of the empire. Rather than fighting the tendency of the centralized state to devolve into a decentralized aristocratic one, Alexius I Comnenus (1081–1118) tied the aristocracy to his family, thus making it an instrument of imperial government. In the short run the process was successful. He expanded the use of pronoia to strengthen loyal aristocrats and granted them offices in the central administration that had been traditionally reserved for eunuchs. He stabilized Byzantine currency, which was the international exchange medium in the Islamic and Christian worlds and had been dangerously devalued by his predecessors. Still, by the late twelfth century the empire was a vulnerable second-rate power caught between Latin Europe and Islam.

Initially, the Christian West was a more deadly threat than the Islamic East. In the eleventh century, after more than 500 years of economic and political weakness, western Europe was beginning to reach parity with Byzantium. Robert Guiscard and his Normans, who had conquered Sicily and southern Italy, were typical examples of the powerful militaristic aristocracy that was developing in the remains of the old western empire.

Dangers from the West.   The military threat from the West was paralleled by a religious one. In the centuries that Rome had been largely cut off from Constantinople, Western Christianity had developed a number of rituals and beliefs that differed from Orthodox practice. This parting of the ways had already appeared during the iconoclastic controversies of the eighth and ninth centuries. In the eleventh, it was directed by an independent

▼ The Ottoman Empire, ca. 1450. By the mid-fifteenth century the Ottoman Empire had absorbed virtually all of the Byzantine Empire.

and self-assertive papacy in Rome, which claimed supreme authority throughout Christendom.

Disagreements between the patriarchs of Constantinople and the popes of Rome prevented cooperation between the two Christian worlds and led to further deterioration of relationships between Greeks and Latins. These disagreements came to a head in 1054, when the papal representative, or legate, Cardinal Humbert (ca. 1000–1061) met with the patriarch of Constantinople, Michael Cerularius (ca. 1000–1059), to negotiate ecclesiastical control over southern Italy and Sicily. Humbert was arrogant and demanding, Michael Cerularius haughty and uncompromising. Acting beyond his authority, Humbert excommunicated the patriarch and all his followers. The patriarch responded in kind, excommunicating Humbert and all connected with him. This formal excommunication was lifted in the 1960s, but the split between the churches of Rome and Constantinople continues to the present.

Excommunication was probably the least of the dangers the Byzantines faced from the West. The full fury of the often ignorant, greedy, and violent Western society reached the empire when, after the defeat at Manzikert, the emperor Alexius called on Western Christians for support against the Muslims. To his horror, adventurers of every sort, eager to conquer land and wealth in the name of the cross of Jesus, flooded the empire. In a penetrating and often cynical biography of her father, Alexius's daughter Anna (ca. 1093–1148) describes how, as quickly as possible, Alexius hurried these crusaders (from the Latin *cruciata,* "marked with a cross") on to Palestine before they could turn their violence against his empire. Even while recognizing that the crusaders were uncouth and barbarous, the Byzantines had to admit that the Latins were effective. Despite enormous hardships, the First Crusade was able to take advantage of division in the Muslim world to conquer Palestine and establish a Latin kingdom in Jerusalem in 1099.

The Sack of Constantinople.   The crusaders' initial victories and the growth of Latin wealth and power created in Constantinople a temporary enthusiasm for western European styles and customs. The Byzantines soon realized, however, that the Latin kingdom posed a threat not only to Islam but to them as well. While crusaders threatened Byzantine territories, Venetian merchants imposed a stranglehold on Byzantine trade. When emperors granted other Italian towns concessions equal to those of the Venetians, they found that they had simply amplified their problems. Anti-Latin sentiment reached the boiling point in 1183. In the riots that broke out in that year, Italians and other westerners in Constantinople were murdered, and their goods were seized. Just 21 years later, in 1204, a wayward crusade, egged on by Venice, turned aside from its planned expedition to Palestine to capture a bigger prize: Constantinople. After pillaging the city for three days, the westerners established one of their own as emperor and installed a Venetian as patriarch.

The Byzantines did manage to hold onto a portion of their empire centering on Nicaea, and before long the Latins fell to bickering among themselves. In 1261 the ruler of Nicaea, Michael Palaeologus (ca. 1224–1282), recaptured Constantinople with the assistance of the Genoese and had himself crowned emperor in the Hagia Sophia. Still, the empire was fatally shattered, its disintegration into autonomous lordships complete. The restored empire consisted of little more than the district around Constantinople, Thessalonica, and the Peloponnesus. Bulgarians and Serbs had expanded far into the Greek mainland. Most of the rich Anatolian regions had been lost to the Turks, and commercial revenues were in the hands of the Genoese allies. The restored empire's survival for almost 200 years was due less to its own prerogative than to the internal problems of the Islamic world.

Eastern Conquests.   The caliphs of Baghdad, like the emperors of Constantinople, succumbed to invaders from the barbarous fringes of their empire. In 1221 the Mongol prince Temujin (ca. 1162–1227), better known to history as Genghis Khan ("Universal Ruler"), led his conquering army into Persia from central Asia. From there, a portion of the Mongols went north, invading Russia in 1237 and dividing it into small principalities ruled by Slavic princes under Mongol control. In 1258 a Mongol army captured Baghdad and executed the last 'Abbasid caliph, ending a 500-year tradition. The Mongol armies then moved westward, shattering the Seljuk principalities in Iraq, Anatolia, and Syria and turning back only before the fierce resistance of the Egyptian Mamluks.

From the ruins of the Seljuk kingdom arose a variety of small Turkish principalities, or emirates. After the collapse of the Mongol empire, one of these, the Ottoman, began to expand at the expense of both the weakened Byzantine Empire and the Mongol-Seljuk Empire. In the next centuries the Ottomans expanded east, south, and west.

Around 1350, they crossed into the Balkans as Byzantine allies but soon took over the region for themselves. By 1450 the Ottoman stranglehold on Constantinople was complete. The final scene of the conquest, long delayed but inevitable, occurred three years later.

For Greeks and for Italian intellectuals of the Renaissance, the conquest of Constantinople by the Ottomans was the end of an imperial tradition that reached back to Augustus. But Mehmed the Conqueror (1452–1481) could as easily be seen as its restorer. True, the city was plundered by the victorious army. But this was simply the way of war in the fifteenth century. The city, its palaces, and its religious edifices fared better under the Turks than they had under its previous, Christian conquerors. The Latins had placed a prostitute on the patriarch's throne in the Hagia Sophia. Mehmed, after purging the church of its Christian trappings, rededicated it to the worship of the one God. Once more, Constantinople, for centuries a capital without a country, was the center of a great Mediterranean empire.

Conclusion

ALTHOUGH OFTEN DEADLY ENEMIES, the Byzantine and Islamic worlds were both genuine heirs of the great eastern empires of antiquity. The traditions of the Assyrian, Alexandrian, Persian, and Roman empires lived on in their cities, their bureaucracies, and their agricultural and commercial systems. Both also shared the monotheistic religious tradition that had emerged from Judaism. In their schools and libraries they preserved and transmitted the literary and scientific heritage of antiquity. Through Islam the legacy of the West reached East Asia. Through Byzantium the peoples of the Slavic world became heirs of the caesars. The inhabitants of western Europe long viewed the Byzantine and Islamic civilizations with hostility, incomprehension, and fear. Still, in the areas of culture, government, religion, and commerce, the West learned much from its eastern neighbors.

QUESTIONS FOR REVIEW

1. In what ways was Byzantine society characterized by individualism without freedom?
2. How and why did Muhammad both break from tribal and clan traditions and build upon them in creating Islam?
3. How did conflicts within Islam after Muhammad's death divide it spiritually but also contribute to Islam's expansion across Africa and Spain?
4. How did the rapid expansion of Byzantium under the Macedonian dynasty contribute to the empire's slow collapse?

DISCOVERING WESTERN CIVILIZATION ONLINE

You can obtain more information about the classical legacy in the East at the websites listed below. See also the companion website that accompanies this text: www.ablongman.com/kishlansky, which contains an online study guide and additional resources.

The Byzantines

www.fordham.edu/halsall/Byzantium/
A major site with links to every aspect of Byzantine civilization maintained by Paul Halsall.

history.evansville.net/byzantiu.html
An excellent guide to Byzantine studies on the Web.

The Rise of Islam

metmuseum.org/collections/department.asp?dep=14
A guide to the Islamic collection at New York's Metropolitan Museum.

The Byzantine Apogee and Decline

www.metmuseum.org/explore/Byzantium/byzhome.html
A site dedicated to Byzantine art at the Metropolitan Museum.

aggreen.net/church_history/c_histry.html
A site dedicated to Orthodox Christianity with links to Byzantine history and culture.

SUGGESTIONS FOR FURTHER READING

The Byzantines

Joan M. Hussey, *The Orthodox Church in the Byzantine Empire* (New York: Oxford University Press, 1986). An introduction to Orthodox Christianity.

Alexander Kazhdan and Giles Constable, *People and Power in Byzantium* (Washington, D.C.: Dumbarton Oaks, 1982). An imaginative and controversial analysis of Byzantine culture by a Russian Byzantinist and a western medievalist.

Cyril Mango, *Byzantium: The Empire of New Rome* (New York: Scribner's, 1980). An imaginative and provocative reevaluation of the Byzantine world.

John Moorhead, *Justinian* (New York: Macmillan, 1994). A biography of the great emperor.

Warren T. Treadgold, *A Concise History of Byzantium* (New York: St. Martin's Press, 2001). An up-to-date survey of Byzantine history.

The Rise of Islam

Aziz Al-Azmeh, *Arabic Thought and Islamic Societies* (London: Routledge, Chapman & Hall, 1986). A demanding but valuable introduction to Islamic intellectual history.

Albert Hourani, *A History of the Arab Peoples* (New York: Warner Books, 1992). A clear and thoughtful survey of Arab history for nonspecialists.

Hugh Kennedy, *The Prophet and the Age of the Caliphates* (White Plains, N.Y.: Longman, 1986). A valuable summary of the early political history of Islam.

Bernard Lewis, ed., *Islam and the Arab World* (New York: Knopf, 1976). An illustrated collection of essays on Islamic history and culture.

Bernard Lewis, *The Muslim Discovery of Europe* (New York: W. W. Norton, 1985). Views of the West by Muslim travelers.

Roy P. Mottahedeh, *Loyalty and Leadership in an Early Islamic Society* (Princeton, N.J.: Princeton University Press, 1980). An important introduction to the social values and structures of western Iran and southern Iraq in the tenth and eleventh centuries.

G. E. von Grunebaum, *Classical Islam: A History 600–1258* (Chicago: Aldine, 1970). A general introduction to early Islamic history.

The Byzantine Apogee and Decline, 1000–1453

Michael Agold, *The Byzantine Empire 1025–1204* (White Plains, N.Y.: Longman, 1997). A solid recent survey of the Byzantine Empire before the capture of Constantinople by the Latins.

P. M. Holt, *The Age of the Crusades: The Near East from the Eleventh Century to 1517* (White Plains, N.Y.: Longman, 1986). An excellent survey of the political history of the Near East in the later Middle Ages.

THE WEST IN THE EARLY MIDDLE AGES, 500–900

THE VISUAL RECORD

THE CHAPEL AT THE WATERS

THE PALATINE CHAPEL IN AACHEN, now a small German city near the Belgian border, brings together a fascination with the traditions of the Roman past with the creativity of a new epoch. These two strands describe Europe during the early Middle Ages, generally the period between 500 and 900. Aachen was a favorite residence of the Frankish king Charles the Great, or Charlemagne (768–814), who often came there to enjoy its natural hot springs. In time, it came to be his primary residence, the capital of his vast kingdom, which stretched from central Italy to the mouth of the Rhine River. Around 792, Charlemagne commissioned an architect to design a palace complex, one that would rival the great Roman and Byzantine buildings of Italy and Constantinople.

Royal agents scoured Europe for Roman ruins from which columns, precious marble, and ornaments could be salvaged and reused. From these ancient stones, masons raised a complex of audience rooms, royal apartments, baths, and quarters for court officials. The whole ensemble was intentionally reminiscent of the Lateran Palace in Rome, which was the residence of the popes.

The central building of Charlemagne's palace complex was the chapel, a symmetrical octagon 300 feet on its principal axes, modeled on San Vitale in Ravenna. The choice of model was significant. Ravenna had been the former capital of Roman Italy and of Theodoric the Great, the Ostrogothic king whom Charlemagne greatly admired. But although modeled on Roman buildings, the Palatine Chapel was admirably suited to the glorification of Charlemagne.

The building was divided into three tiers. The first tier, on the ground floor, held the sanctuary, where priest and people met for worship. The topmost tier, supported by ancient Roman pillars, represented the heavens. Between the two was a gallery connected by a passage to the royal residence. On this gallery sat the king's throne. From his seat, Charlemagne could look down on the religious services being conducted below. Looking up to where he sat, worshippers were constantly reminded of the king's intermediary position between ordinary mortals and God. This architectural design boldly asserted that Charlemagne was more than a barbarian king. By 805, when the chapel was dedicated, he had made good this assertion. As a contemporary chronicler wrote while in Rome in the year 800:

On the most holy day of Christmas, when the king rose from prayer in front of the shrine of the blessed apostle Peter to take part in the Mass, Pope Leo placed a crown on his head and he was hailed by the whole Roman people. . . . He was now called Emperor and Augustus.

To Charlemagne and to his supporters, this coronation ceremony revived the Roman Empire in the west. Like his chapel in Aa chen (long afterward known as Aix-la-Chapelle, the chapel at the waters), this empire was built on the remains of Roman traditions grafted onto a vigorous tradition of Germanic kinship and society. According to the Byzantines, who looked on Charlemagne and his imperial coronation with alarm, the western empire could not be revived because it had never really ended. According to them, the death of the last western emperor Julius Nepos in 480 had ended the division of the empire. Since then, the Byzantine emperors had pretended that they ruled both east and west. Charlemagne's claims, made through the ceremony in Rome and more subtly in the imperial architecture of his palace, represented to them not a revival of the empire but a threat to its existence.

LOOKING AHEAD

This chapter will trace western Europe's progress toward Aachen, exploring the spectrum of barbarian successor states before concentrating on the unique blend of Roman, Christian, and Frankish institutions and culture that culminated in the Carolingian Empire, an empire whose legacy endured long after its unity dissolved into competing kingdoms and lordships.

151

THE MAKING OF THE BARBARIAN KINGDOMS, 500–750

The existence of a united empire had long been but a dream. In the year 500, Emperor Anastasius I (491–518) could delude himself that he ruled the whole empire of Augustus, Diocletian, and Constantine, both east and west. Never mind that in the east, war against the Persians dragged on. Never mind that along the northern border of the empire the Bulgarians, a new multiethnic barbarian confederation, had begun to raid into the Balkans. Neither of these conflicts, Anastasius contended, threatened the stability of the empire. In the west, the governor who ruled Italy had sworn that he "rejoiced to live under Roman law, which we are prepared to defend by arms." The king of the once troublesome Vandals had concluded a marriage alliance with the Italian governor and seemed ready to accept Roman statecraft. Beyond the Alps, a Roman officer called a *patrician* ruled the regions of the upper Rhone, and a consul controlled Gaul. In Aquitaine and Spain, legitimate, recognized officers of the empire ruled both Romans and barbarians. What need was there to speak of the end of the empire in the West?

This imperial unity was more apparent than real. The Italian governor was the Ostrogothic king Theodoric the Great (493–526), whose Roman title meant less than his Ostrogothic army. The patrician was the Burgundian king Gondebaud (480–516). The Roman officer in Aquitaine and Spain was the Visigothic king Alaric II (485–507), and the Gallic consul was the Frankish king Clovis (482–511). Each of these rulers courted imperial titles and recognition, but none regarded Anastasius as his sovereign.

Italy: From Ostrogoths to Lombards

In the early sixth century, all of the Germanic peoples who were settled within the old Roman Empire acknowledged the Goths as the most successful of the "blond-haired peoples," as the Romans called the barbarians. The Ostrogoths had created an Italian kingdom in which Romans and barbarians lived side by side. The Visigoths ruled Spain and southern Gaul by combining traditions of Roman law and barbarian military might. Yet neither Gothic kingdom endured for more than two centuries.

The Ostrogothic Kingdom. Theodoric the Ostrogoth was the most cultivated, capable, and sophisticated barbarian ruler. He was also the most powerful. Burgundians, Visigoths, and Alemanni looked to him for leadership and protection. Even Clovis, the ambitious Frankish king, usually bowed to his wishes. Theodoric had spent his teenage years as a pampered hostage in Constantinople. There, he had learned to understand and admire Roman ways. Later,

▲ A gold solidus coin bears a portrait of Theodoric. His left hand holds a globe on which stands a personification of victory. The inscription reads "King Theodoric," but the absence of a robe and diadem shows that he was not considered the equal of the emperor.

after he had conquered Italy at the head of his Gothic army, he established a dual government, which respected both the remains of Roman civil administration and Gothic military organization.

Religion as well as government divided Italy's population. The Ostrogoths were Arians; the majority of the Romans were orthodox Christians. Initially, Theodoric made no effort to interfere with the religion of his subjects, stating, "We cannot command the religion of our subjects, since no one can be forced to believe against his will." This religious toleration attracted into his government outstanding Roman intellectuals and statesmen. The Roman Boethius (480–524), while serving in Theodoric's government, was also trying to synthesize the philosophical traditions of Plato and Aristotle. Cassiodorus (ca. 490–ca. 585), a cultivated Roman senator, served as Theodoric's secretary and held important positions in his government before retiring to found monasteries, where he and his monks worked to preserve the literary and philosophical traditions of Rome. Following Theodoric's death in 526, internal conflict over the succession paved the way for a protracted and devastating invasion by the Byzantines, who destroyed not only the Ostrogothic kingdom but also much of what remained of Roman Italy.

Italy was simply too close to Constantinople and too important for the ambitious Emperor Justinian I (527–565) to ignore. Encouraged by his easy victory over

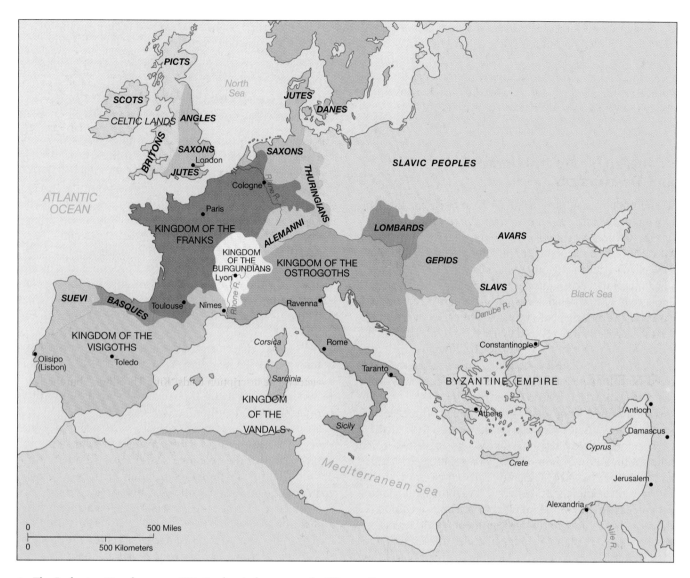

▲ The Barbarian Kingdoms, ca. 526. By the sixth century, the Western Roman Empire had been replaced by smaller kingdoms ruled by barbarian kings granting only nominal recognition to the emperor.

the Vandals, he sent an army into Italy, where he anticipated an easy reconquest of the peninsula. Instead, he got almost 20 years of vicious warfare. Not only were the Goths more formidable foes than he had expected, but when Roman tax collectors arrived with the Roman armies, Justinian found that the Italian people did not greet their "liberators" with open arms. In addition, in the midst of the reconquest a new and terrible disease appeared throughout the Mediterranean world. The plague cut down as much as one third of Europe's population in the next two centuries.

Lombard Conquest. The destruction of Italy by war and disease paved the way for its conquest by the Lombards. As allies in Justinian's army, some members of

this Germanic tribe from along the Danube had learned of the riches of Italy firsthand. In 568, the whole Lombard people left the Carpathian basin to their neighbors, the Avars, and invaded the exhausted and war-torn Italian peninsula. By the end of the sixth century, the Ostrogoths had disappeared, and the Byzantines retained only the heel and toe of the boot of Italy and a narrow strip stretching from Ravenna to Rome. The Byzantine presence in Rome was weak, and by default the popes, especially Gregory the Great (590–604), became the defenders and governors of the city. Gregory organized the resistance to the Lombards, fed the population during famines, and comforted them through the dark years of plague and warfare. A vigorous political as well as spiritual leader, he laid the foundations of the medieval papacy.

The Lombards largely eliminated the Roman tax system under which Italians had long suffered. In the sphere of religion, many of the Lombards initially were Arians, but in the early seventh century the Lombard kings and their followers accepted orthodox Christianity. This conversion paved the way for the unification of the society.

Visigothic Spain: Intolerance and Destruction

Rather than accepting a divided society as did the Ostrogoths or merging into an orthodox Roman culture as did the Lombards, the Visigoths of Gaul and Spain sought to unify the indigenous population of their kingdom through law and religion. Roman law deeply influenced Visigothic law codes and formed an enduring legal heritage to the West. Religious unity was a more difficult goal. The king's repeated attempts to force conversion to Arianism failed and created tension and mistrust. This mistrust proved fatal. In 507, Gallo-Roman aristocrats supported the Frankish king Clovis in his successful conquest of the Visigothic kingdom of Toulouse. Defeat drove the Visigoths deeper into Spain, where they gradually forged a unified kingdom based on Roman administrative tradition and Visigothic kingship.

The long-sought religious unity was finally achieved when King Recared (586–601) and the Gothic aristocracy embraced orthodox Christianity. This conversion further blurred the differences between Visigoths and Roman provincials in the kingdom. It also initiated an unprecedented use of the Church and its ideology to strengthen the monarchy. Visigothic kings modeled themselves after the Byzantine emperors, proclaimed themselves new Constantines, and used Church councils, held regularly at Toledo, as governing assemblies.

Still, the Visigoths continued to distrust anyone who was different, and their suspicion focused especially on the considerable Jewish population, which had lived in Spain since the *Diaspora,* or dispersion, in the first century of the Roman Empire. Almost immediately after Recared's conversion, he and his successors began to enact a series of anti-Jewish measures, culminating in 613 with the command that all Jews accept baptism or leave the kingdom. Although this mandate was never fully carried out, the virulence of the persecution of the Jews grew through the seventh century. At the same time, rivalry within the aristocracy weakened the kingdom and left it vulnerable to attack from without. In 711, Muslims from North Africa invaded and quickly conquered the Visigothic kingdom. While some remnants of the Visigoths held on in small kingdoms in the northwest, most of the population quickly came to terms with their new masters. Jews rejoiced in the religious toleration brought by Islam, and many members of the Christian elite converted to Islam and retained their positions of authority under the new regime.

The Anglo-Saxons: From Pagan Conquerors to Christian Missionaries

The motley collection of Saxons, Angles, Jutes, Frisians, Suebians, and others who came to Britain as federated troops and stayed on as rulers did not coalesce into a united kingdom until almost the eleventh century. Instead, these Germanic warriors carved out small kingdoms for themselves, enslaving the Romanized Britons or driving them into Wales. Although independent, these little kingdoms (their number varied from 5 to as many as 11 at different times) maintained some sort of identity as a group. The king of the dominant kingdom enjoyed some deference from his fellow rulers. Other kings looked to him as first among equals and sought his advice and influence in their dealings with one another. Unlike the Goths, none of these peoples had previously been integrated into the Roman world. Rather than fusing Roman and Germanic traditions, they eradicated the former. Urban life disappeared and, with it, the Roman traditions of administration, taxation, and culture.

In their place developed a world whose central values were honor and glory, whose primary occupation was fighting, and whose economic system was based on plunder and the open-handed distribution of riches. In many ways this Anglo-Saxon world resembled the heroic age of ancient Greece. This was a society dominated by petty kings and their aristocratic war leaders. These invaders were not, like the Goths, just a military elite. They also included free farmers who partly replaced and partly absorbed romanized British peasantry, introducing their language, agricultural techniques, social organization, and folkloric traditions to the southeastern part of the island. These ordinary settlers, much more than the kings and aristocrats, were responsible for the gradual transformation of Britain into England, the land of the Angles.

The Anglo-Saxons were pagans, and although Christianity survived, the relationship between conquered and conquerors did not provide a climate conducive to conversion. Christianity came instead from without. The conversion of England resulted from a two-part effort. The first originated in Ireland, the most western society of Europe and the one in which Celtic traditions had survived little changed for over 1,000 years. Ireland had never formed part of the Roman Empire and so had never developed the forms of urban life and centralized, hierarchical government or religion characteristic of Britain and the Continent. In the fifth century, merchants and missionaries introduced an eastern monastic form of Christianity to Ireland, which adapted easily to the rural tribal organization of Irish society. Although Irish Christianity was entirely orthodox in its beliefs, the isolation of Ireland led to the development of numerous distinctive local practices. Thus, although Ireland had important bishops, the most influential churchmen were powerful abbots of strict ascetic monasteries, closely connected with tribal chieftains, who directed the religious life of their regions. Around 565, the Irish monk Columba (521–597) established a monastery on the island of Iona off the coast of Scotland. From there, wandering Irish monks began to convert northern Britain.

The second effort at Christianizing Britain began with Pope Gregory the Great. In 596, he sent the missionary Augustine (known as Augustine of Canterbury to distinguish him from the bishop of Hippo) to attempt to convert the English. Augustine laid the foundations for a hierarchical, bishop-centered church based on the Roman model. In time, the pagan king Ethelbert and much of his southwest kingdom of Kent accepted Christianity, and the pope named Augustine archbishop of Canterbury.

As Irish missionaries spread south from Iona and Roman missionaries moved north from Canterbury, their efforts created in England two opposing forms of orthodox Christianity. One was Roman, episcopal, and hierarchical. The other was Celtic, monastic, and decentralized. The Roman and Celtic churches agreed on basic doctrines. However, each had its own calendar of religious feasts and its own rituals. King Oswy of Northumbria (d. 670) called an episcopal meeting, or synod, in 664 at Whitby to settle the issue. After hearing arguments from both sides, Oswy accepted the customs of the Roman Church, thus allying himself and ultimately all of Anglo-Saxon England with the centralized, hierarchical form of Christianity, which could be used to strengthen his monarchy.

During the century and a half following the Synod of Whitby, Anglo-Saxon Christian civilization blossomed. Contact with the Continent and especially with Rome increased. The monasteries of Monkwearmouth and Jarrow became centers of learning, culminating in the writings of Bede (673–735), the greatest scholar of his century. His history of the English church and people is the finest historical work of the early Middle Ages.

By the eighth century, England itself had begun to send Christian missionaries to the Continent to convert their still-pagan Germanic cousins. Until the late eighth and ninth centuries, when the Germanic Vikings began to attack Anglo-Saxon settlements, England furnished the Continent with many of its leading thinkers and scholars.

The Franks: An Enduring Legacy

In the fourth century, various small Germanic tribes along the Rhine coalesced into a loose confederation known as the Franks. A significant group of them, the Salians, made the mistake of attacking Roman garrisons and were totally defeated. The Romans resettled the Salians in a largely abandoned region of what is now Belgium and Holland. There, they formed a buffer to protect Roman colonists from other Germanic tribes and provided a ready supply of recruits for the Roman army. During the fourth and fifth centuries, these Salian Franks and their neighbors assumed an increasingly important role in the military defense of Gaul and began to spread out of their "reservation" into more settled parts of the province. Although many high-ranking Roman officers of the fourth century were Franks, most were neither conquerors nor members of the military elite. Rather, they were soldier-farmers who settled beside the local Roman peoples they protected.

In 486, Clovis, leader of the Salian Franks and commander of the barbarized Roman army, staged a successful coup (possibly with the approval of the Byzantine emperor), defeating and killing Syagrius, the last Roman commander in the West. Although Clovis ruled the Franks as king, he worked closely with the existing Gallo-Roman aristocracy as he consolidated his control over various Frankish factions and over portions of Gaul and Germany that were held by other barbarian kingdoms. Clovis's early conversion to orthodox Christianity helped to ensure the effectiveness of this Gallo-Roman cooperation. Clovis converted, hoping that God would give him victory over his enemies and that his new faith would win the support of the Roman aristocracy in Gaul. The king's baptism convinced many of his subjects to convert as well and paved the way for the assimilation of Franks and Romans into a new society. This Frankish society became the model for European social and political organization for over 1,000 years.

The mix of Frankish warriors and Roman aristocrats spread rapidly across western Europe. Clovis and his successors absorbed the Visigothic kingdom of Toulouse, the Thuringians, and the kingdom of the Burgundians and expanded Frankish hegemony through modern Bavaria and south of the Alps into northern Italy. Unlike other barbarian kingdoms such as those of the Huns or Ostrogoths, which evaporated almost as soon as their great founders died, the Frankish synthesis was enduring. Although the dynasty established by Clovis, called the Merovingian after a legendary ancestor, lasted only until the mid-eighth century, the Frankish kingdom was the direct ancestor of both France and Germany.

After Clovis's death in 511, his kingdom was divided among his four sons. For the next 200 years, the heart of the Frankish kingdom, the region between the Rhine and Loire Rivers, was often divided into the kingdoms of Neustria, Burgundy, and Austrasia, each ruled by a Merovingian king. The outlying regions of Aquitaine and Provence to the south and Alemania, Thuringia, and Bavaria to the east were governed by Frankish dukes appointed by the kings. Still, the Frankish world was never as divided as Anglo-Saxon England. In the early eighth century, a unified Frankish kingdom reemerged as the dominant force in Europe.

LIVING IN THE NEW EUROPE

The substitution of Germanic kings for imperial officials made few obvious differences in the lives of most inhabitants of Italy, Gaul, and Spain. The vast majority of Europeans were poor farmers whose lives centered on their villages and fields. For them the seasons in the agricultural year, the burdens of rent and taxation, and the frequent poor harvests, food shortages, famines, and epidemics were more important than empires and kingdoms. Nevertheless, fundamental if imperceptible changes were transforming daily life at every level of society. The slaves and semifree peasants of Rome gradually began to form new kinds of social groups and to practice new forms of agriculture as they merged with the Germanic warrior-peasants. Elite Gallo-Roman landowners came to terms with their Frankish conquerors, and these two groups began to coalesce into a single unified aristocracy. In the same way that Germanic and Roman society began to merge, Germanic and Roman traditions of governance united between the sixth and eighth centuries to create a powerful new kind of medieval kingdom.

Creating the European Peasantry

Three fundamental changes transformed rural society during the early Middle Ages. First, Roman slavery virtually disappeared. Second, the household emerged as the primary unit of social and economic organization. Third, Christianity spread throughout the rural world. Economics, not ethics, destroyed Roman slavery. In the kind of slavery that was typical of the Roman world, large gangs of slaves were housed in dormitories and directed in large-scale operations by overseers. This form of slavery demanded a highly organized form of estate management and could be quite costly, since slaves had to be fed and housed year-round. Since slaves did not always reproduce at a rate sufficient to replace themselves, the supply had to be replenished from elsewhere. However, as the empire ceased to expand, the supply of fresh captives dwindled. As cities shrank, many markets for agricultural produce disappeared, making market-oriented large-scale agriculture less profitable. Furthermore, the Germanic societies that settled in the West had no tradition of gang slavery.

As a result, from the sixth through the ninth centuries, owners abandoned the practice of keeping gangs of slaves in favor of the less complicated practice of establishing slave families on individual plots of land. The slaves and their descendants cultivated these plots, made annual payments to their owners, and also cultivated the undivided portions of the estate, the fruits of which went directly to the owner. Thus slaves became something akin to sharecroppers. Gradually, they began to intermarry with hereditary tenant farmers and others who, though nominally free, found themselves in an economic situation much like that of slaves. By the ninth century, the distinction between slaves who had acquired traditional rights to their farms, or *manses,* and free peasants who held and worked manses belonging to others was blurred. By the tenth and eleventh centuries, peasant farmers throughout much of Europe were subject to the private justice of their landlords, no matter whether their ancestors had been slave or free. Although not slaves in the classical sense, the peasantry had fused into a homogeneous unfree population.

Rural Households

The division of estates into separate peasant holdings contributed to the second fundamental transformation of European peasant society: the formation of the household. Neither the Roman tradition of slave agriculture nor the Germanic tradition of clan organization had encouraged the household as the basic unit of society. Now individual slaves and their spouses were placed on manses, which they and their children were expected to cultivate. The household had become the basic unit of Western economy.

The household was more than an economic unit, however. It was also the first level of government. The head of the household, whether slave or free, male or female—women, particularly widows, were often heads of households—exercised authority over its other members. This authority made the householder a link in the chain of the social order, which stretched from the peasant hovel to the royal court. Households became the basic form of peasant life, but not all peasants could expect to establish their own household. The number of manses was limited, a factor that condemned many men and women to life within the household of a more fortunate relative or neighbor.

Peasant life centered on the house, the village, and the field. Peasant houses often consisted simply of two or three rooms in which dwelt both the human and animal members of the household. The rhythm of peasant life was tied to the agricultural cycle, which had changed little since antiquity. Although women and men worked together on the harvest, peasants normally divided labor into male and female tasks. Husbands and sons worked in the fields. Wives and daughters tended chickens, prepared the dark bread that was the staple of their diet, spun, and wove.

Peasant culture, like peasant society, experienced a fundamental transformation during the early Middle Ages: the peasantry became Christian. In antiquity, Christianity had been an urban phenomenon. The term for the rural population had been synonymous with "unbelievers." They were called pagans, that is, the inhabitants of the countryside, or *pagus.* The spread of Christianity throughout the rural world began in earnest in the sixth century, when bishops and monks began to replace the peasant's traditional agrarian cults with Christian feasts, rituals, and beliefs.

FROM SLAVE TO QUEEN

Queen Balthild (d. ca. 680), an Anglo-Saxon woman captured and sold into slavery in Francia, became the wife of Clovis II, king of Neustria and Burgundy (639–657). Her career, including her regency for her son Clothar III and her eventual forced retirement to the monastery she had founded at Chelles, is typical of the complex role and reputation early medieval queens enjoyed. This lauda- tory account, which was probably written by a nun at Chelles, hints that Balthild had been forced into the convent by those opposed to her political role.

FOCUS QUESTIONS

What roles of a queen does this passage illustrate? What reforms did Balthild attempt to introduce in Frankish society?

DIVINE PROVIDENCE CALLED HER from across the seas. She, who came here as God's most precious and lofty pearl, was sold at a cheap price. Erchinoald, a Frankish magnate and most illustrious man, acquired her, and in his service the girl behaved most hon- orably. She gained such happy fame that, when the said lord Erchinoald's wife died, he hoped to unite himself to Balthild, that faultless virgin, in a matronal bed. But when she heard this, she fled and most swiftly took herself out of his sight. Thereafter it happened, with God's approval, that Balthild, the maid who escaped marriage with a lord, came to be es- poused to Clovis, son of the former king Dagobert. Thus by virtue of her humility she was raised to a higher rank.

She acted as a mother to the princes, as a daughter to priests, and as a most pious nurse to children and adoles- cents. She distributed generous alms to everyone. She guarded the princes' honor by keeping their intimate counsels secret. In accordance with God's will, her hus- band King Clovis migrated from the body and left his sons with their mother. Immediately after him her son Clothar

took up the kingdom of the Franks, maintaining peace in the realm. Then, to promote peace, by command of Lady Balthild with the advice of the other elders, the people of Austrasia accepted her son Childeric as their king and the Burgundians were united with the Franks. And we believe, under God's ordinance, that these three realms then held peace and concord among themselves because of Lady Balthild's great faith. She proclaimed that no payment could be exacted for receipt of a sacred rank. Moreover, she ordained that yet another evil custom should cease, namely that many people determined to kill their children rather than nurture them, for they feared to incur the pub- lic exactions which were heaped upon them by custom, which caused great damage to their affairs.

It was her holy intention to enter the monastery of reli- gious women which she had built at Chelles. But the Franks delayed much for love of her and would not have permitted this to happen except that there was a commo- tion made by the wretched Bishop Sigobrand whose pride among the Franks earned him his mortal ruin. Indeed, they formed a plan to kill him against her will. Fearing that the lady would act heavily against them, and wish to avenge him, they suddenly relented and permitted her to enter the monastery.

From The Life of the Blessed Queen Balthild.

Christianity penetrated more deeply into rural society with the systematic establishment of parishes, or rural churches. By the ninth century, this parish system began to cover Europe. Bishops founded parish churches in the vil- lages of large estates, and owners were obligated to set aside one-tenth of the produce of their estates for the maintenance of the parish church. The priests who staffed these churches came from the local peasantry and received a basic education in Latin and in Christian ritual from their predecessors and from their bishops. The continuing pres- ence of priests in each village had a profound effect on the daily lives of Europe's peasants.

Creating the European Aristocracy

At the same time that a homogeneous peasantry was emerging from the blend of slaves and free farmers, a

homogeneous aristocracy was evolving out of the mix of Germanic and Roman traditions. In Germanic society, the elite had owed its position to a combination of inherited status and wealth, perpetuated through military com- mand. Families who produced great military comman- ders were thought to have a special war-luck granted by the gods. The war-luck bestowed on men and women of these families a near-sacred legitimacy. This legitimacy made the aristocrats largely independent of their kings. In times of war, kings might command, but otherwise, the extent to which they could be said to govern aristo- crats was minimal.

The Roman aristocracy was also based on inheritance, but of land rather than leadership. During the third and fourth centuries, Roman aristocrats' control of land ex- tended over the people who worked that land. At the same time, great landowners were able to free themselves from provincial government. Like their Germanic counterparts, Roman aristocrats acquired a sacred legitimacy, but within the Christian tradition. They monopolized the office of bishop and became identified with the sacred and political traditions associated with the Church.

In Spain and Italy, the religious differences separating Arians and orthodox Christians impeded the fusion of the Germanic and Roman aristocracies. In Gaul, the conversion of Clovis and his people facilitated the rapid blending of the two worlds. North of the Loire River, where the bulk of the Franks had settled, Roman aristocrats soon became Franks. By the mid-sixth century the descendants of Bishop Remigius of Reims, who had baptized Clovis, had Frankish names and considered themselves Franks. Still, the Roman aristocratic tradition of great landholders became an integral part of the identity of the Frankish elite.

In the late sixth century, this northern Frankish aristocracy found its own religious identity and legitimacy in the Irish monasticism introduced by Saint Columbanus (543–615) and other wandering monks. At home in Ireland these monks had been accustomed to working not with kings but with leaders of clans. In Gaul, they worked closely with the Frankish aristocrats, who encouraged them to build monasteries on their estates. Eventually, these monasteries amassed huge landholdings and became major economic and political centers headed by aristocrats who abandoned secular life for the cloister.

South of the Loire River, conditions were decidedly different. Here, Irish monasticism was less important than episcopal office. The few Frankish and Gothic families who had settled in the south were rapidly absorbed into the Gallo-Roman aristocracy, which drew its prestige from control of local religious and secular power. Latin speech and Roman culture distinguished these "Romans," regardless of their ancestry.

Aristocratic Lifestyle

Aristocratic life was similar whether north or south of the Loire, in Anglo-Saxon England, Visigothic Spain, or Lombard Italy. Aristocratic family structures were loosely knit clans that traced descent from important ancestors through either the male or the female line. Clans jealously guarded their autonomy against rival clans and from royal authority.

Feasting and Fighting. The aristocratic lifestyle focused on feasting, hospitality, and the male activities of hunting and warfare. In southern Europe, great nobles lived in spacious villas, often surrounded by solid stone fortifications, an inheritance of Roman traditions. In the north, Frankish and Anglo-Saxon nobles lived in great wooden halls, richly decorated but lacking fortifications. During the fall and winter, aristocratic men spent much of their time hunting deer and wild boar in their forests.

Hunting was not merely sport. Essentially, it was preparation for war, the activity of the summer months. In March, as soon as the snows of winter had begun to melt and roads had become passable, aristocrats gathered their retainers, who had enjoyed their winter hospitality, and marched to war. The enemy varied. It might be rival families with whom feuds were nursed for generations. It might be raiding parties from a neighboring region. Or the warriors might join a royal expedition led by the king and directed against a rival kingdom. Whoever the enemy was, warfare brought the promise of booty and glory.

Women in Aristocratic Society. Within this aristocratic society, women played a wider and more active role than had been the case in either Roman or barbarian antiquity. In part, women's new role was due to the influence of Christianity, which recognized the distinct—though always inferior—rights of women, fought against the barbarian tradition of allowing chieftains numerous wives, and acknowledged women's right to lead a cloistered religious life. In addition, the combination of Germanic and Roman familial traditions permitted women to participate in court proceedings, to inherit and dispose of property, and, if widowed, to serve as tutors and guardians for their minor children. Finally, the long absence of men at the hunt, at the royal court, or on military expeditions left wives in charge of the domestic scene for months or years at a time. The religious life in particular opened to aristocratic women possibilities of autonomy and authority that had previously been unknown in the West. Saint Hilda of Whitby (614–680), an Anglo-Saxon princess, for example, established and ruled a religious community that included both women and men. It was in Hilda's community that the Synod of Whitby took place, and Hilda played an active role, advising the king and assembled bishops.

Governing Europe

The combination in the early Middle Ages of the extremes of centralized Roman power and fragmented barbarian organization produced a wide variety of governmental systems. At one end of the spectrum were the politically fragmented Celtic and Slavic societies. At the other end were the Frankish kingdoms, in which descendants of Clovis, drawing on the twin heritages of Roman institutions and Frankish tradition, attempted not simply to reign but to rule.

Kings and Aristocrats. Rulers and aristocrats both needed and feared each other. Kings had emerged out of the Germanic aristocracy and could rule only in cooperation with aristocrats. Aristocrats were concerned primarily with maintaining and expanding their own spheres of control and independence. They perceived royal authority as a threat. Still, they needed kings. Strong kings brought victory against external foes and thus maintained the flow of booty to the aristocracy. Aristocrats in turn redistributed the spoils of war among their followers to preserve the bonds of warrior society. Thus, under capable kings, aristocrats were ready to cooperate, not as subjects but as partners.

As the successors of Germanic war leaders and late Roman generals, kings were primarily military commanders. During campaigns and at the annual "Marchfield," when the free warriors assembled, the king was all-powerful. At those times he could cut down his enemies with impunity. At other times the king's role was strictly limited. His direct authority extended only over the members of his household and his personal warrior band.

Royal Justice. The king's role in administering justice was similarly ambivalent. He was not the source of law, which was held to be simply the customs of the past, nor was he responsible for enforcing this customary law. Enforcement was the duty of individuals and families. Only if they wished did they bring their grievances to the king or his agents for arbitration or judgment. However, even though they could not formally legislate, kings effectively molded law and legal procedure by collecting, selecting, clarifying, and publishing customary laws. Clovis presents a model for such legislative activity in the compilation of Salic law made during his reign. Visigothic and Anglo-Saxon kings of the seventh through tenth centuries did the same.

As heirs of Roman governmental tradition, kings sought to incorporate these traditions into their roles. By absorbing the remains of local administration and taxation, kings acquired nascent governmental systems. Through the use of written documents, Roman scribes expanded royal authority beyond the king's household and personal following. Tax collectors continued to fill royal coffers with duties collected in markets and ports.

Finally, by assuming the role of protector of the Church, kings acquired the support of educated and experienced ecclesiastical advisers and the right to intervene in disputes involving clergy and laity. Further, as defenders of the Church, kings could claim a responsibility for the preservation of peace and the administration of justice—two fundamental Christian (but also Roman) tasks.

Royal Administration. Early medieval kings had no fixed capitals from which they governed. Instead, they were constantly on the move, supervising their kingdoms and consuming the produce of their estates. Since kings could not be everywhere at once, they were represented locally by aristocrats who enjoyed royal favor. In the Frankish world these favorites were called *counts*, and their districts were called *counties*. In England, royal representatives were termed *ealdormen*, and their regions were known as *shires*. Whether counts or ealdormen,

these representatives were military commanders and judicial officers drawn from aristocratic families close to the king. Under competent and effective kings, partnership with these aristocratic families worked well. Under less competent rulers and during the reigns of minors, these families often managed to turn their districts into hereditary, almost autonomous regions. The sphere of royal authority thus shrank or expanded in large measure in response to the individual qualities of the king.

THE CAROLINGIAN ACHIEVEMENT

The Merovingian dynasty initiated by Clovis presided over the synthesis of Roman and Germanic society. It was left to the Carolingians who followed to forge a new Europe. In the seventh century, members of the new aristocracy were able to take advantage of royal minorities and dynastic rivalries to make themselves into virtual rulers of their small territories. By the end of the century, the kings had become little more than symbolic figures in the Frankish kingdoms. The real power was held by regional strongmen called *dukes*. The most successful of these aristocratic factions was that led by Charles Martel (ca. 688–741) and his heirs, known as the Carolingians.

Charles Martel. This family had risen to prominence in the seventh century by controlling the office of mayor of the palace in Austrasia, the highest court official who advised the king as spokesman for the aristocracy. The Carolingians increased their influence by marrying their sons to daughters of other aristocratic families. In the late seventh century, they extended their control to include Neustria and Burgundy as well as Austrasia. By the second quarter of the eighth century, Charles Martel, while not king, was the acknowledged ruler of the Frankish kingdom.

Charles Martel was ruthless, ambitious, and successful. He crushed rivals in his own family, subdued competing dukes, and united the Frankish realm. He was successful in part because he molded the Frankish cavalry into the most effective military force of the time. His mounted, heavily armored warriors were extremely effective but very costly. He financed them with property confiscated from his enemies. In return for oaths of absolute fidelity he gave his followers, or vassals, estates, which they held as long as they served him faithfully. With this new army he practiced a scorched-earth policy against his opponents that left vast areas of Provence and Aquitaine desolate for decades.

Charles Martel looked beyond military power to the control of religious and cultural institutions. He supported Anglo-Saxon missionaries such as Boniface (ca. 680–755), who were trying to introduce on the Continent the Roman form of Christianity they knew in England.

This hierarchical style of Christianity served Carolingian interests in centralization, especially since Charles appointed his loyal supporters as bishops and abbots. Missionaries and Frankish armies worked hand in hand to consolidate Carolingian rule.

The ecclesiastical policy that proved most crucial to later Carolingians was Charles's support of the Roman papacy. Charles caught the attention of Pope Gregory III (731–741) in 732, after a battle near Tours in which Charles defeated a Muslim force that was attempting to continue the northward expansion of Islam. A few years later, when the pope needed protection from the Lombards to maintain his central Italian territories, he sought and obtained help from the Frankish leader.

Pippin III. The alliance with the papacy solidified during the lifetime of Charles's son Pippin (ca. 714–768).

This bronze equestrian statue of a king dates from the ninth century. The rider wears the typical Frankish attire of hose, tunic, and long riding cloak. The subject is often identified as Charlemagne or his grandson Charles the Bold.

Pippin inherited his father's power, but since he was not of the royal Merovingian family, he had no right to the title of king. No Frankish tradition provided a precedent by which a rival family might displace the Merovingians. Pippin turned instead to the pope, seeking legitimacy in religious authority. In a carefully orchestrated exchange between Pippin and Pope Zacharias (741–752), the latter declared that the individual who exercised the power of king ought also to have the title. Following this declaration the last Merovingian was deposed, and in 751 a representative of the pope anointed Pippin king of the Franks.

The alliance between the new dynasty and the papacy marked the first union of royal legitimacy and ecclesiastical sanction in European history. Frankish, Gothic, and Anglo-Saxon kings had been selected on secular criteria. Kings combined royal descent with military power. Now the office of king required the active participation of the Church. The new Frankish kingship led Europe into the first political, social, and cultural restructuring of the West since the end of the Roman Empire.

Charlemagne and the Renewal of the West

Pippin's son Charlemagne was the heir of the political, religious, and social revolutions begun by his grandfather and father. Charlemagne was a large man, over six feet tall, with piercing eyes, a robust physique, and a restless spirit. To his intimates he was a generous lord constantly surrounded by friends. To his enemies he was the man of iron—the grim and invincible warrior clad head to foot in steel, sweeping all before him. He was a conqueror, but he was also a religious reformer, a state builder, and a patron of the arts. As the leader of a powerful, united Frankish kingdom for over 40 years, Charlemagne changed the West more profoundly than anyone since Augustus.

Almost every spring, Charlemagne assembled his Frankish armies and led them against internal or external enemies. He subdued the Aquitainians and Bavarians, conquered the kingdom of the Lombards and assumed the title of king of the Lombards, crushed the Saxons, annexed the Spanish region of Catalonia, and destroyed the vast Pannonian kingdom of the Avars. In wars of aggression his armies were invincible. Not only were they better armed and mounted, but their ability to transport men and matériel great distances was unmatched.

War booty fueled Charlemagne's renewal of European culture. As a Christian king he considered it his duty to reform the spiritual life of his kingdom and to bring it into line with his concept of the divinely willed order. To achieve this goal, he needed a dedicated and educated clergy. Most of the native clergy were poorly educated and indifferent in their observance of the rules of religious life. Charlemagne set about creating a reformed, educated clergy.

▲ Charlemagne's Empire, 814. Either directly or indirectly. Charlemagne ruled a vast empire that included almost all of the Western Roman Empire except for Spain and Britain.

The Carolingian Renaissance

Charlemagne recruited leading intellectuals from England, Spain, Ireland, and Italy to the royal court to lead a thorough educational program. The architect of his cultural reform, Alcuin of York (ca. 732–804), directed a school for young lay and ecclesiastical aristocrats in the king's palace and encouraged the king to finance a wide variety of educational programs. Charlemagne supported schools in great monasteries such as Fulda and St. Gall for the training of young clerics and laymen. These schools needed books. Charlemagne's educational reformers scoured Italy for fading copies of works by Virgil, Horace, and Tacitus with the same determination that his builders hunted antique marbles and columns for his chapel. Alcuin and others corrected and copied classical texts that had been corrupted by generations of haphazard transmission. The earliest extant manuscripts of virtually all classics of Roman antiquity date from the late eighth or early ninth century. Caroline minuscule, the new style of handwriting that was developed to preserve these texts, was so clear and readable that during the Renaissance, humanists adopted it as their standard script.

Ironically, Charlemagne, who fostered this blossoming of learning and who himself studied a number of subjects under the guidance of Alcuin, never mastered the art of writing. He could read, but according to Einhard, a contemporary biographer of Charlemagne, the emperor "used to keep writing-tablets and notebooks under the pillows on his bed, so that he could try his hand at forming letters during his leisure moments; but, although he tried very hard, he had begun too late in life and he made little progress."

The reformers of this era laid the necessary foundation for what has been called the Carolingian Renaissance. Their successors in the ninth century built on this foundation to make creative contributions in theology, philosophy, and historiography and to some extent in literature. The pursuit of learning was not a purely clerical affair. In the later ninth century, great aristocrats were highly literate and collected their own personal libraries. Count Everard of Friuli, who died in 866, left an estate that included over 50 books, among them works by Augustine, histories, saints' lives, and seven law books. Elite women participated fully in the Carolingian Renaissance. One example is the noblewoman Dhuoda, who composed a manual of instruction for her son.

Educational reform went hand in hand with reform of ecclesiastical institutions. Charlemagne and his son Louis the Pious (814–840) worked to establish the Benedictine rule as the norm for monastic life and to reform the parish clergy. The goal was a purified and organized clergy performing its essential role of celebrating Christian ritual and praying for the Frankish king. At the same time, the monasteries were to provide competent clerics to serve the royal administration at every level. These reforms were expensive. The fiscal reorganization of ecclesiastical institutions was as far-reaching as their cultural reform. For the first time, Frankish synods or councils made *tithing* mandatory, specifying that one tenth of all agricultural harvests was to go to the maintenance of church buildings, support of the clergy, and care of the poor. Monasteries flourished.

Carolingian Government

Charlemagne recognized that conquest alone could not unify his enormous kingdom with its vast differences in languages, laws, customs, and peoples. The glue that held it together was loyalty to him and to the Roman Church. He appointed as counts throughout Europe members of the great Frankish families who had been loyal to his family for generations. Thus he created what might be termed an "imperial aristocracy" that was truly international in scope. In addition to supervising the royal estates in their counties, each spring these counts led the local military contingent, which included all the free men of the county. Counts also presided over local courts, which exercised jurisdiction over the free persons of the county. The king maintained his control over the counts by sending teams of emissaries, or *missi dominici*, composed of bishops and counts to examine the state of each county.

Charlemagne recognized that while his representatives might be drawn from Frankish families, he could not impose Frankish legal and cultural traditions on all his subjects. The only universal system that might unify the kingdom was Roman Christianity. Unity of religious practices, directed by the reformed and educated clergy, would provide spiritual unity. Furthermore, since the clergy could also participate in the administration of the kingdom, they could guarantee administrative unity as well. Carolingian monarchs did not intend the enriched and reformed Church to be independent of royal authority; it was rather to be an integral part of the Carolingian system of government. However, at least some of the educated clerics and lay aristocrats who participated in the system formed a clear political ideology based on Augustinian concepts of Christian government. They attempted to educate Charlemagne and his successors to the duties of a king: maintaining peace and providing justice.

Carolingian government was no modern bureaucracy or state system. It was a mobile palace that included the royal household and ecclesiastical and secular aristocrats. The laymen and clerics who served the king were tied to him by personal oaths of loyalty rather than by any sense of dedication to a state or nation. Still, the attempts at governmental organization were far more sophisticated than anything that the West had seen for four centuries or would see again for another four. The system of counts and missi provided the most effective system of government before the thirteenth century and served as the model for subsequent medieval rulers.

The size of Charlemagne's empire approached that of the old Roman Empire in the West. Only Britain, southern Italy, and parts of Spain remained outside Frankish control. With the reunification of most of the West and the creative adaptation of Roman traditions of culture and government, it is not surprising that Charlemagne's advisers began to compare his empire to that of Constantine. This comparison was accentuated by Charlemagne's conquest of Lombard Italy and his protection of Pope Leo III—a role traditionally played by the Byzantine emperors. By the end of the eighth century, the throne in Constantinople was held by a woman. Irene (752–802) was powerful and capable, but Western male leaders considered her unfit by reason of her sex for such an office. All these factors finally converged in one of the most momentous events in Western political history: Charlemagne's imperial coronation on Christmas Day in the year 800.

Historians debate the precise meaning of this event, particularly since Charlemagne was said to have remarked afterward that he would never have entered St. Peter's Basilica in Rome had he known what was going to happen. Presumably, he meant that he wished to be proclaimed emperor by his Frankish people rather than by the pope, since this is how he had his son Louis the Pious acclaimed emperor in 813. Nevertheless, the imperial coronation of 800 subsequently took on great significance. Louis attempted to make his imperial title the sole basis for his rule, and for the next thousand years, Germanic kings traveled to Rome to receive the imperial diadem and title from the pope. In so doing, they inadvertently strengthened papal claims to enthrone—and at times to dethrone—emperors.

Carolingian Art

The same creative adaptation of the classical heritage that gave birth to a new Western empire produced a new Western art. The artistic traditions of the barbarian world consisted almost entirely of the decoration of small, portable objects such as weapons, jewelry, and, after conversion, manuscripts. Barbarian art was essentially nonrepresentational and consisted primarily of elaborate interlaced geometric forms of great sophistication.

For Charlemagne and his reformers, such abstract art was doubly inappropriate. Not only was it too distant from the Roman heritage that they were trying to emulate, but it could not be used for instruction or propaganda. Therefore, Charlemagne invited Italian and Byzantine artists and artisans to his kingdom to teach a form of representational art that would decorate as well as educate. However, these southern traditions were no more slavishly followed by northern artists than were Roman political traditions wholly taken over by Charlemagne's government. The synthesis of Mediterranean and northern artistic traditions produced a dynamic plastic style of representation in which figures seem intensely alive and active. These figures, which appear in manuscript illuminations, ivories, and bas-reliefs, are often arranged in narrative cycles that engage the mind as well as the eye.

GEOGRAPHICAL TOUR

Europe in the Ninth Century

The Carolingian Empire stretched from the Baltic Sea to the Adriatic and linked, through a network of commerce and exchange, the Germanic and Slavic worlds of the north, the Islamic world of Spain and the Near East, and the Mediterranean world of Byzantium. Carolingian kings rebuilt roads, bridges, and ports to facilitate trade. Charlemagne also reformed Western currency, abandoning gold coinage in favor of the more easily obtainable and liquid silver.

Silver was the medium of exchange at the northern ports of Durstede near the mouth of the Rhine and Quentovic near modern Etaples, where Frankish merchants haggled with Anglo-Saxon and Danish traders over cloth, furs, and amber from the Baltic. Merchants along the Slavic frontier and down the Danube dealt primarily in human commodities. Great slave trains passed from these regions into the Rhine region. In Verdun, young boys were castrated at "eunuch factories" before being sent down the Rhone River to the cities of lower Provence, where they were sold to Muslim agents from Spain and North Africa. Jewish and Greek merchants supplied the Frankish church and aristocracy with luxury goods from Constantinople and the East. The travels of such a merchant in the early ninth century might begin with a short trip from Quentovic to the English coast and then continue clockwise around the Frankish world (see **Map A**).

▼ **Map A. Europe in the Ninth Century.** In the course of the ninth century, individual kingdoms developed across Europe.

▲ **Map B. England.** Anglo-Saxon England was divided into a shifting number of small kingdoms ruled by rival dynasties.

England

A continental visitor in England (see **Map B**) would be well treated. In 796, Charlemagne had written to King Offa of Mercia (757–796), offering English merchants protection in his kingdom. Offa, the only king whom Charlemagne referred to as "brother," ruled a prosperous southeast England. Charlemagne's letter indicates that Mercia's prosperity owed much to trading, in which Anglo-Saxon woolens and silver were exchanged for wine, oil, and other products of the Continent.

Mercian supremacy did not long survive Offa. In the constant warfare among Anglo-Saxon kingdoms during the first half of the ninth century, Mercia fell to Wessex (see **Map B**). The cycle of rise and fall of little kingdoms might have continued had the Vikings not come onto the scene. These Scandinavian raiders had been harassing the coast since 786. However, they did not pose a serious threat to England until 865, when a great Viking army interested not in raiding but in conquest landed north of the Humber River. All but one of the Anglo-Saxon kingdoms were destroyed.

The surviving king, Alfred of Wessex (870–899), reorganized his army, established a network of fortifications, created a navy, and thus temporarily halted the Viking

conquest. Still, he realized that his military achievement could be consolidated only by the transformation of his political base. Few of Alfred's contemporaries saw him as the savior of England. He had first to win the loyalty of people in his own kingdom and then attract that of Anglo-Saxons outside it.

Alfred won support by reforming the legal and cultural foundations of his kingdom. His legal reforms aimed to reassure subjects of the various Anglo-Saxon kingdoms of equal treatment. At the same time, they emphasized the importance of oaths of loyalty and the gravity of treason. Finally, Alfred inaugurated a religious and cultural program to extend literacy and learning so that his people might better understand and follow God's word. Because, by this time, Latin was almost entirely unknown in England, Alfred and his reformers used the vernacular Anglo-Saxon. Alfred encouraged the translation of the greatest books of the Christian tradition into Anglo-Saxon, even translating some of them himself. By the time Alfred died in 899, southern England was united under Wessex leadership. The north, from the Thames to Chester, was occupied and colonized by Danes. In this region, known as the *Danelaw*, the Vikings settled down as farmers and slowly merged with the local population.

Scandinavia

Scandinavians in England were merchants as well as raiders. They sold furs, amber, and fish for English silver and cloth. A merchant who was interested in the northern trade might depart England from York and travel down the Ouse and the Humber to the North Sea (see **Map B**). To make this passage, he might sail with a Scandinavian merchant Viking in his longboat, that supreme expression of Viking culture. These magnificent ships, over 70 feet long, were fast, flexible, and easily maneuverable. A merchant's journey would begin with passage across the Channel, followed by a two-day sail north along the coast of Jutland to the mouth of the Eider (see **Map C**). From here, travelers could cross the peninsula to Hedeby at the head of the Slie Fjord on the Baltic. After a few days a serious trader would press on, passing the Swedish archipelago, out past Oland and Gotland, through the narrow straits where Stockholm now stands, to Birka, the greatest port of Scandinavia. Here Danes, Swedes, Franks, Frisians, Anglo-Saxons, Balts, Greeks, and Arabs met to trade furs, ivory, and amber for weapons, fine English cloth, silver, and gold. Like England, Scandinavia had long been an area of Frankish commercial and political interest. The Saxons had previously formed a buffer between the Scandinavians and the Frankish world, but Charlemagne's conquests had brought the two societies into direct contact.

Norse Society. Scandinavian society resembled Germanic society of the first century. It was composed of

◄ **Map C. Scandinavia.** Fleeing political consolidation at home, Scandinavian Vikings raided and settled into Russia and Ukraine, west to Iceland and the British Isles, down the Atlantic coast, and even into the Mediterranean.

three social classes. At the top were wealthy chiefs, or *jarlar* (earls), who had numerous servants, slaves, and free retainers. At the bottom were *thralls*, or bondsmen. In between were peasant freeholders, who formed the bulk of the population. Military ability and political cunning were equally prized in women and men. In this society, women enjoyed considerable freedom and authority that shocked observers from other cultures. An Arab merchant who visited Hedeby reported that women could claim the right to divorce whenever they wished. In the ninth century, however, internal developments began to threaten the traditional independence of men and women alike, contributing to the Scandinavian expansion into the rest of Europe.

Royal Consolidation. Scandinavian kings were traditionally selected by groups of earls and exercised a position more as first among equals than as ruler. However, around the end of the eighth century, Scandinavian kings began to consolidate power at home and to look to the wealthy Anglo-Saxon and Frankish worlds as sources of

booty and glory. Earls and royal pretenders, threatened or displaced by the kings, also began to go *viking*—that is, raiding—to replace abroad what they had lost at home.

Vikings. The directions in which Northmen went viking depended on the region of Scandinavia from which they came. Swedes looked eastward, trading with the Slavic world and Byzantium. Norwegians looked to Ireland and Scotland and later to Greenland, Iceland, and North America. The Danes tended to focus on England and the Frankish empire (see **Map C**).

Swedish merchant Vikings, known as the *Rus'*, traveled down the Volga, Dvina, and Dnepr rivers as far as the Black and Caspian seas in search of furs and slaves (see **Map C**). There they met the trading routes of the Byzantine Empire and the caliphate of Baghdad. Rus'-fortified trading settlements at Novgorod, Smolensk, and Kiev (see **Map C**) became the nuclei of a Slavic-Scandinavian political unit to which the Rus' eventually gave their name: Russia.

Norwegians began their viking in Europe's western islands in the late eighth century. Ireland, until then undisturbed by either Roman or Germanic invaders, was the first victim. Other Norwegians raided south along the coast of the Frankish kingdom, Spain, and even into the Mediterranean, where they made forays into Provence, North Africa, and Italy (see **Map C**). The political consolidation in Norway under Harold Finehair (860–933), which culminated in 872, led more Norwegians to go viking. Earls who objected to Harold's consolidation went abroad to maintain their freedom. Some settled in the Faroe Islands; others colonized Iceland.

The southernmost Scandinavians, the Danes, were most intimately familiar with the Frankish and Anglo-Saxon realms. Some of these Vikings, led by Danish kings, colonized whole areas such as Northumbria and the region at the mouth of the Seine. It was this latter region that later became Normandy—land of the Northmen.

▲ **Map D. The Slavic World.** In the ninth century new kingdoms appeared in the Slavic world under the influence of Vikings, Franks, Byzantine missionaries, Magyar raiders, and local chieftains.

▼ An example of the animal style common in the Celtic-Germanic art of the early Middle Ages, this wooden animal head is the terminal of a post from a seventh-century Viking ship.

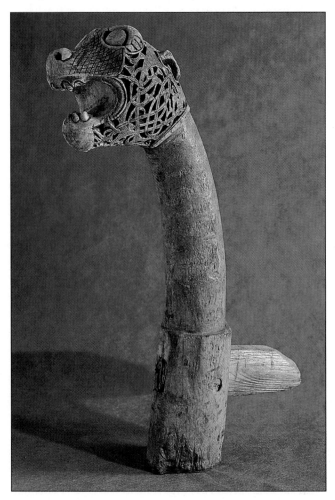

The Slavic World

A merchant in Scandinavia might join an expedition of Swedish Rus' to cross the Baltic Sea and enter the Slavic world (see **Map D**) in search of ermine and slaves. The Carolingians' effects were felt, both in merchant activity and in the presence of imperialist armies and missionaries. The Slavic world of the ninth century was a rapidly changing amalgam of Germanic and Slavic peoples whose ultimate orientation—north to Scandinavia, east to Constantinople, or west to Aachen—was an open question.

Slavic Origins. The development of Slavic society and culture was quite similar to that of the Germans. In the sixth century, Slavic tribes had begun to filter westward. In the seventh century, a Frank named Samo (d. ca. 660) organized a brief but powerful confederation of Slavs in the area between the Sudeten Mountains and the eastern Alps.

Conversion of the Slavs. In the following century, the Great Moravian Empire developed out of Slavic tribes along the March River (see **Map D**). Both the Byzantine and Carolingian empires sought to bring Moravia into their spheres of influence. In the middle of the ninth century, Frankish, Italian, and Greek missionaries began to compete to organize a Christian church in this Slavic empire. In 852, a Slavic prince, particularly suspicious of the Franks, turned to the Greeks. He encouraged the missionary efforts of Cyril and Methodius, who translated liturgical texts into Slavonic, laying the basis for a Slavic church, and began the tradition of Slavic literacy.

The promising beginning made by the two brothers was short lived, as the Franks feared an independent Slavic church. In 864, the Carolingian king Louis the German (843–876) conquered Moravia. Methodius, who had been appointed archbishop of Moravia and Pannonia by the pope, was imprisoned in a German monastery. The Frankish hegemony lasted only a few decades. In 895, a new steppe people, the Magyars, or Hungarians, swept into Pannonia as had the Huns and Avars before them. These new invaders destroyed the Franks' puppet Moravian empire and split the Slavic world in two: the northern and southern Slavs. The Magyar kingdom (see **Map D**) proved to be a greater threat to the Franks than did the Slavs or Avars. Not only did the Magyars conquer Pannonia as far as the Enns River, but for 50 years they raided deep into the Carolingian empire.

Muslim Spain

The Slavic world was not only in contact with the Christian societies of Byzantium and the West. Muslim merchants used Arab gold to buy furs and slaves from Rus' traders at settlements along the Dnepr. A Spanish merchant might depart from Kiev and, to avoid the Magyars, travel down the Dnepr to the Black Sea, past Constantinople, and then across the length of the Mediterranean to Al-Andalus, as the Muslims called Spain (see **Map E**).

After the disintegration of the Umayyad caliphate (see Chapter 7, pp. 141–142), the last Umayyad, 'Abd ar-Rahman I (731–788), made his way to Spain, where in 756 he established an independent emirate. Under the centralized control of the Umayyad emirs, the economic and cultural life of urban Spain, which had stagnated under the Visigoths, experienced a renaissance as vital as that taking place across the Pyrenees in the Frankish empire.

The Umayyad Emirate. To secure the emirate, 'Abd ar-Rahman and his successors had to overcome internal division and external aggression. The Spanish population included an elite minority of Arabs, recently arrived Syrians, North African Berbers, converted Spaniards, Christian Spaniards, and Jews. In addition, Frankish aggression and Scandinavian Vikings continually harassed Al-Andalus.

In the short run, 'Abd ar-Rahman secured control by brute force. Relying on a professional army composed mainly of slaves, the emirs crushed revolts mounted by various Muslim factions. They strengthened a series of semiautonomous districts, or marches, commanded by military governors as buffers against the Frankish kingdom to the north. Finally, they established a line of guard posts along the coast to protect themselves against the Northmen. In the long run, the emirs sought stability in religion and law. They presented themselves as the champions and defenders of Islam and cultivated the study and application of Islamic law as a source of justice and social order.

The economic prosperity of Al-Andalus was based on an enlightened system of agriculture, which included the introduction of oranges, rice, sugarcane, and cotton from the eastern Mediterranean. Complementing agriculture was a renewed urban life bolstered by vigorous trade to the north, east, and south. In the ninth and tenth centuries, Spain was the most prosperous region of Europe and one of the wealthiest areas of the Muslim world.

In this climate of security and prosperity developed the most sophisticated and refined culture in the West. Arabic poetry and art developed in a manner exactly the opposite of that in the Carolingian world. Poetry, visual art, and architecture deemphasized physical forms and encouraged abstraction and meditation. Such abstract contemplative art did not develop in Western Christendom for centuries.

AFTER THE CAROLINGIANS: FROM EMPIRE TO LORDSHIPS

Alien, dynamic, and potentially threatening neighbors surrounded the Carolingian kingdom. To the west was Anglo-Saxon England; to the east were the Slavic and Byzantine worlds. Scandinavia lay to the north, and Al-Andalus threatened to the south. In the later ninth and

▼ **Map E. Spain.** Under the Umayyad emirs. Spain prospered as a center of agriculture, trade, and mixed Islamic, Jewish and Christian cultures.

tenth centuries, the Frankish kingdom collapsed, owing in part to the actions of these neighbors but primarily to the kingdom's own internal weaknesses.

Charlemagne, despite his imperial title, had remained dependent on his traditional power base, the Frankish aristocracy. For them, learned concepts of imperial renovation meant little. They wanted wealth and power. Under Charlemagne, the empire's prosperity and relative internal peace had resulted largely from continued successful expansion at the expense of neighbors. Its economy had been based on plunder and the redistribution of war booty among the aristocracy and wealthy churches. As wars of conquest under Charlemagne gave place to defensive actions against Magyars, Vikings, and Saracens, the supply of wealth dried up. Aristocratic supporters were rewarded with estates within the empire and thus became enormously wealthy and powerful.

Disintegration of the Empire

Competition among Charlemagne's descendants as well as grants to the aristocracy weakened central authority. By fate rather than by design, Charlemagne had bequeathed a united empire to his son Louis the Pious (814–840).

▼ The Division of Charlemagne's Empire. Internal tensions, dynastic competition, and external pressures led to the disintegration of Charlemagne's empire and the emergence of what would become France and Germany.

Charlemagne had intended to follow Frankish custom and divide his estate among all his sons, but only Louis survived him. Louis's three sons, in contrast, fought one another over their inheritance, and in 843 they divided the empire among them. The eldest son, Lothair (840–855), who inherited his father's imperial title, received an unwieldy middle portion that stretched from the Rhine south through Italy. Louis the German (840–876) received the eastern portions of the empire. The youngest son, Charles the Bald (840–877), was allotted the western portions. In time, the western kingdom became France, and the eastern kingdom became the core of Germany. The middle kingdom, which included modern Holland, Belgium, Luxembourg, Lorraine (or Lotharingia, from "Lothair"), Switzerland, and northern Italy, remained a disputed region into the twentieth century.

The disintegration of the empire meant much more than its division among Charlemagne's heirs. In no region were his successors able to provide the degree of peace and public control that he had established. The Frankish armies, designed for wars of aggression, were too clumsy and slow to deal with the lightning raids of Northmen, Magyars, and Saracens. The constant need to please aristocratic supporters made it impossible for kings to prevent aristocrats from absorbing free peasants and churches into their economic and political spheres. Increasingly, these magnates were able to transform the offices of count and bishop into inherited familial positions. They also determined who would reign in their kingdoms and sought kings who posed no threat to themselves.

Most aristocrats saw this greater autonomy as their just due. Only dukes, counts, and other local lords could organize resistance to internal and external foes at the local level. They needed both economic means and political authority to provide protection and maintain peace. These resources could be acquired only at the expense of royal power. Therefore, during the late ninth and tenth centuries, much of Europe found its equilibrium at the local level as public powers, judicial courts, and military authority became the private possession of wealthy families.

Emergence of France and Germany

Ultimately, new royal families emerged from among these local leaders. The family of the counts of Paris, for example, gained enormous prestige from the fact that they had led the successful defense of the city against the Vikings from 885 to 886. For a time they alternated with Carolingians as kings of the West Franks. After the ascension of Hugh Capet in 987, they entirely replaced the Carolingians.

In a similar manner, the eastern German kingdom, which was divided into five great duchies, began to elect non-Carolingians as kings. In 919, the dukes of this region elected as their king Duke Henry of Saxony (919–936), who had proven his abilities fighting the Danes and Magyars. Henry's son, Otto the Great (936–973), proved to be a strong ruler who subdued the other dukes and definitively crushed the Magyars. In 962, Otto was crowned emperor by Pope John XII (955–964), thus reviving the empire of Charlemagne, though only in its eastern half. However, the dukes of this eastern kingdom chafed constantly at the strong control the Ottonians attempted to exercise at their expense. Although the empire Otto reestablished endured until 1806, he and his successors never matched the political or cultural achievements of the Carolingians.

By the tenth century, the early medieval kingdoms, based on inherited Roman notions of universal states and barbarian traditions of charismatic military leadership, had all ended in failure. After the demise of the Carolingian empire, the West began to find stability at a more local but also more permanent level. However, the local nature of Western society did not mean that the Roman and Carolingian traditions were forgotten. Carolingian religious reform, classical learning, and political ideology were preserved in the following centuries.

Cluny

Church reform took on a new life in 909 with the foundation of the monastery of Cluny in eastern France. Cluniac monks, drawn from the lesser aristocracy, were God's shock troops, fighting evil with their prayers with the same vigor that their secular cousins fought the enemy with their swords. Cluny, inspired by the monastic program of Louis the Pious and granted immunity from secular interference, became the center of an extraordinary expansion of Benedictine monasticism throughout the West.

The revival of classical learning that was begun in Carolingian schools, although hampered by the new wave of invasions that began in the latter ninth century, continued in centers such as St. Gall, Auxerre, and Corvey. During the late ninth and tenth centuries, Western Christian civilization spread to the north and east. By the year 1000, Scandinavia, Poland, Bohemia, and even Hungary had become Christian kingdoms with national churches whose bishops were approved by the pope. Among the aristocracy, just as all restraints on this warrior elite seemed to have been thrown off, a gradual process of transformation of their material and mental world began. Encouraged by Cluniac monasticism and by episcopal exhortations, nobles began to consider limiting their violence against one another and placing it instead in the service of Christendom.

Conclusion

ALTHOUGH THE MAGYAR, VIKING, AND SARACEN RAIDS contributed to the disintegration of the Carolingian empire, their role was secondary. The internal dynamics of the Frankish world and its unresolved social and political tensions were the essential causes of the collapse of the Carolingian synthesis.

In the long run, however, the Carolingian synthesis left a powerful and enduring legacy. At the start of the Middle Ages in the West, a variety of Germanic kingdoms experimented with a whole spectrum of ways to reconcile the twin elements of barbarian and Roman tradition. The Ostrogoths attempted to preserve the two as separate entities and soon vanished. The Visigoths sought unification through coercion and found themselves isolated and weakened. In England, Germanic invaders sought to replace Roman traditions entirely. Only the Franks found a lasting means of amalgamating Roman and Germanic societies.

The key elements of this synthesis were orthodox Christianity, Roman administration, and Frankish military kingship. Between 500 and 800, these three elements coalesced into a vital new civilization. Although the political structure created by Charlemagne did not survive his grandsons, the Frankish model proved enduring in every other respect. The cultural renaissance laid the foundation of all subsequent European intellectual activities. The alliance between the Church and monarchy provided the formula for European kings for almost a thousand years. The administrative system with its central and local components, its counts and its missi, its diplomas and capitularies, provided the model for later medieval government in England and on the Continent. The idea of the Carolingian Empire, the symbol of European unity, has never entirely disappeared from the West.

QUESTIONS FOR REVIEW

1. What social and political forces encouraged division within the various Gothic, Anglo-Saxon, and Frankish kingdoms?
2. How did the household and the parish provide new units for organizing European society?
3. How did the aristocracy evolve out of Germanic and Roman traditions, and how was the aristocracy both a support and a threat to the kingdoms of the early Middle Ages?
4. What were Charlemagne's achievements?
5. Why did Charlemagne's empire not outlive him for long?

DISCOVERING WESTERN CIVILIZATION ONLINE

You can obtain more information about the West in the early middle ages at the websites listed below. See also the companion website that accompanies this text: www.ablongman.com/kishlansky, which contains an online study guide and additional resources.

General Websites

http://labyrinth.georgetown.edu/
Labyrinth is the central website for all medieval studies.

The Making of the Barbarian Kingdoms

www.wmich.edu/medieval/rawl/keynes1/home.htm
A comprehensive bibliographical site on Anglo-Saxon civilization created and maintained by Simon Keynes.

metmuseum.org/collections/department.asp?dep=17
A look at some of the Metropolitan Museum's collection of medieval art, including migration period jewelry.

Living in the New Europe

loki.stockton.edu/~ken/wharram/wharram.htm
A site devoted to exploring a lost medieval village from Roman times to the high Middle Ages.

The Carolingian Achievement

ccat.sas.upenn.edu/jod/map.html
A site with links to centers of Carolingian renaissance culture.

After the Carolingians

bubl.ac.uk/link/v/vikingarchaeology.htm
A site devoted to Viking society and archaeology.

ishi.lib.berkeley.edu/history155/slides/kingship/index.html
Interactive explorations of ninth through eleventh century images of kings.

SUGGESTIONS FOR FURTHER READING

The Making of the Barbarian Kingdoms, 500–750

Richard Phillip Abels, *Alfred the Great: War, Kingship, and Culture in Anglo-Saxon England* (London: Longman, 1998). An introduction to the England of King Alfred.

James Campbell, ed., *The Anglo-Saxons* (Oxford, England: Phaidon, 1982). A collection of essays on Anglo-Saxon England by an outstanding group of archaeologists and historians.

Walter Pohl, ed. with Helmut Reimitz, *Strategies of Distinction: The Construction of Ethnic Communities, 300–800* (Leiden: Brill, 1998). An important collection devoted to early medieval ethnicity.

Ian Wood, *The Merovingian Kingdoms 450–751* (London: Longman, 1994). Excellent survey of early Frankish history with an emphasis on government.

Living in the New Europe

Lisa M. Bitel, *Land of Women: Tales of Sex and Gender from Early Ireland* (Ithaca: Cornell University Press, 1998). An intelligent and well-written look at women in early medieval Ireland.

Suzanne Fonay Wemple, *Women in Frankish Society: Marriage and the Cloister 500–900* (Philadelphia: University of Pennsylvania Press, 1981). A pioneering study of women in the early Middle Ages.

The Carolingian Achievement

Heinrich Fichtenau, *The Carolingian Empire: The Age of Charlemagne* (Toronto: University of Toronto Press, 1957). A classic reevaluation of the weaknesses of the Carolingian empire.

Paul Fouracre, *The Age of Charles Martel* (New York: Longman, 2000). An exploration of the Frankish world in the early eighth century.

Rosamond McKitterick, *The Frankish Kingdoms Under the Carolingians, 751–987* (New York: Longman, 1983). A very detailed study of Carolingian history with an emphasis on intellectual developments.

Rosamond McKitterick, ed., *The New Cambridge Medieval History, c. 700–c. 900*, vol. II (Cambridge: Cambridge University Press, 1995). An excellent collective history of all aspects of Europe in the eighth and ninth centuries.

Geographical Tour: Europe in the Ninth Century

Geoffrey Barraclough, ed., *Eastern and Western Europe in the Middle Ages* (New York: Harcourt Brace Jovanovich, 1970). Essays by specialists on eastern Europe and its relationship to the West.

Roger Collins, *Early Medieval Spain: Unity in Diversity 400–1000* (New York: St. Martin's Press, 1983). A balanced survey of Visigothic and Islamic Spain.

F. Donald Logan, *The Vikings in History* (New York: HarperCollins, 1991). General introduction to the Vikings.

After the Carolingians: From Empire to Lordships

Heinrich Fichtenau, *Living in the Tenth Century: Studies in Mentalities and Social Orders* (Chicago: University of Chicago Press, 1990). A brilliant evocation of the quest for order on the Continent following the dissolution of the Carolingian Empire.

Timothy Reuter, *Germany in the Early Middle Ages, 800–1056* (New York: Longman, 1991). A readable, original survey of early German history by a British scholar who is thoroughly knowledgeable about current German scholarship.

THE HIGH MIDDLE AGES, 900–1300

- THE VISUAL RECORD: The Royal Tombs at Fontevrault
- THE COUNTRYSIDE

- MEDIEVAL TOWNS
- THE INVENTION OF THE STATE

THE ROYAL TOMBS AT FONTEVRAULT

IN THE MONASTIC CHURCH OF FONTEVRAULT, a double monastery of monks and nuns in western France ruled by a powerful abbess, reposes the body of the most powerful and influential woman of the twelfth century: Eleanor of Aquitaine (1122–1204), heiress of one of the greatest principalities of France, wife of two kings, and mother of two more. The life-size polychrome figure, executed shortly after her death, reclines peacefully, her hands holding a book, but the serenity of her repose masks the turbulence of her life. Beside her lie her husband Henry II of England (1154–1189) and their son Richard the Lion-Hearted (1189–1199). The paths that brought Eleanor, Henry, and Richard to Fontevrault tell much about the world of the High Middle Ages.

At her father's death, Eleanor became the most coveted heiress in Europe. The French king Louis VII promptly married her to secure her vast holdings in the south and west. He divorced her in 1152 for failing to provide him with a male heir. She immediately married Henry, the count of Anjou and, from 1150, duke of Normandy. Their marriage united the west of France. Eleanor also bore Henry eight children, four of them boys, much to the chagrin of her former husband. When Henry became King Henry II of England in 1154, he and Eleanor together ruled a vast region of Europe, from Scotland to south-central France, often called the Angevin Empire.

Eleanor and Henry directed the most exciting and creative court in Europe, a court that moved around constantly. However, Eleanor felt most at home in her native Poitiers. Her court became a center of literary production, and her patronage was responsible for the flourishing of French romances and Provençal love lyrics.

Henry was one of the greatest figures in the development of English royal power. He attempted to rule his wife's lands with an iron hand. He also sought to exclude his sons from real authority. The sons, in turn, spent much of their time in revolt against their father, often with the assistance of their mother.

Henry then imprisoned Eleanor in the convent at Fontevrault, where she remained under lock and key for more than 15 years. After Henry's death, their son Richard the Lion-Hearted freed Eleanor. She governed the Angevin realm while Richard went off to battle, and when he was taken hostage on his return from the Third Crusade, it was

Eleanor who collected the ransom that paid for his liberty. Richard died in 1199 while besieging a castle. Eleanor's youngest son John succeeded to the throne, and she retired voluntarily to Fontevrault, where she died in 1204.

Eleanor's life spanned the age of feudal lordships and the creation of the medieval state. Her youth was spent in a world in which great feudal nobles like her father had dominated public life. Her middle years saw western Europe find its own voice as it developed a vibrant culture under the domination of vast, eclectic interlocking lordships, principalities, and kingships such as the Angevin Empire. But she lived on into a world dominated by kings who relied on a growing world of merchants, bankers, professional soldiers, and bureaucrats to create a smaller but more cohesive and ultimately more powerful centralized monarchy. Eleanor was at home in the first world, and she helped to create and dominate the second. The third was alien to her, and her death at Fontevrault came in good time.

LOOKING AHEAD

This chapter analyzes the world of Eleanor, the peasants whose fields and villages were ultimately the source of the aristocracy's wealth, the knights and ladies who made up the courts of Henry and Eleanor, and the monastic reform movements that introduced new religious values to Europe. It also visits the emerging cities of western and central Europe to understand the rebirth of commerce and trade and with it the urban society and culture it made possible. Finally, it traces the development of medieval monarchies, the new political powers created by men such as Henry II.

THE COUNTRYSIDE

From the tenth through the thirteenth centuries, enormous transformations recreated the rural landscape of Europe. The most significant changes concerned the peasantry, but they are difficult to chronicle, since the common people seldom left any record of their thoughts or lives.

By the tenth century, the population of Europe was growing, and with this increase came new forms of social organization and economic activity. Between the years 1000 and 1300, Europe's population almost doubled, from approximately 38 million to 74 million. Various reasons have been proposed for this growth: less warfare and raiding, the decline of slavery, gradually improving agricultural techniques and equipment, and possibly a slowly improving climate.

During the tenth century, the great forests that had covered most of Europe began to be cut back as population spread out from the islands of cultivation. From around 1100, in the north of Germany and in what is today Holland, enterprising peasants began to drain marshes, a slow process of creating new land that would continue into the present century. This progress was not everywhere linear. In England, for example, forests actually gained on plow-land after the Norman Conquest of 1066. By the mid twelfth century, however, the acrid smoke from slash-and-burn clearing of the forest could be smelled all across Europe.

The Peasantry: Serfs and Freemen

The peasants who engaged in the opening of this internal frontier were the descendants of the slaves, unfree farmers, and petty free persons of the early Middle Ages. In the east along the frontier of the Germanic empire, in the Slavic world, in Scandinavia, in southern Gaul, in northern Italy, and in the reconquered portions of Christian Spain, they were free persons who owned land, entered into contracts with magnates, and remained responsible for their own fates. Across much of northwestern Europe, in particular in France in the eleventh century, the various gradations in status disappeared, and the peasantry formed a homogeneous social category loosely described as serfs. Although they were not slaves in a legal sense, their degraded status, their limited or nonexistent access to public courts of law, and their enormous dependency on their lords left them in a situation similar to that of those Carolingian slaves settled on individual farmsteads in the ninth century. Each year, peasants paid their lords certain fixed portions of their meager harvests. In addition, they had to work a certain number of days on the *demesne*, or reserve of the lord, the produce of which went directly to him for his use or sale. Finally, they were required to make ritual payments symbolizing their subordination.

Most peasants led lives of constant insecurity. They were poorly housed, clothed, and fed; subject to the constant scrutiny of their lords; and defenseless against natural or human-made disasters. Their homes were typically small one- or two-room shacks constructed of mud and wood and shared with their most valuable domestic animals. These huts usually had no windows and, until the sixteenth century, no chimneys. Smoke from the open hearth escaped through a hole in the roof.

Peasants' houses were clustered in villages on manors or large estates. In some parts of Europe this was the result of their lord's desire to keep a close eye on his labor supply. Beginning in the tenth century in central Italy and elsewhere, lords forced peasants to abandon isolated farmsteads and traditional villages and to move into small, fortified settlements. In these new villages, peasants were obligated to have disputes settled in the lord's court, to grind their grain in the lord's mill, and to bake their bread in the lord's oven—all primary sources of revenue for the lord. The same sort of monopoly applied to the Church. Villagers had to contribute a tenth of their revenues to the Church and to make donations in order to receive the sacraments. In some villages, these payments may have actually gone to the Church, but usually they too went to the lord.

Each morning men went out to their fields, which surrounded the village. In some villages, each peasant householder held thin strips of widely scattered land, while pasturage and woodland were exploited in common. Such an open-field system allotted all peasant households a portion of all the different sorts of land. In other villages, each household tended a unified parcel of land. Such closed fields generally corresponded with greater divergences in wealth within the village and encouraged more independence.

Agricultural Innovation. Agricultural technology gradually changed the ways that peasants worked their land and the amount of food they could produce. Instead of a light plowshare that simply cut a furrow, a heavier plow with a moldboard—a curved iron plate attached above the plowshare to lift and turn the soil, depositing it to one side of the furrow—spread across Europe. It increased production in the heavy-soil areas north of the Alps and in bottom lands. The moldboard plow with wheels was often pulled by several pairs of oxen, which made it too expensive for the ordinary farmer working alone. The new plow thus promoted cooperative organization of the work of plowing and reliance on the open-field system of land tenure.

With the introduction of new technology for plowing came new systems of crop rotation. Traditionally, farmers divided their land into two parts, one planted, the other plowed (usually twice) but allowed to remain fallow. Around the eighth century, some peasants began to introduce a three-field system: one-third of the land was planted in autumn with wheat or rye, one-third remained fallow, and one-third was planted in spring with barley, rye, or a leguminous crop such as beans or peas that added nutrients to the soil. As this innovation became standard after the year 1000, the result was a greatly increased yield, a minimal increase in labor, and an improved diet.

While the men worked the fields, women took charge of the domestic tasks. These included carding wool, spinning, weaving, caring for the family's vegetable garden, bearing and raising children, and brewing the thick, soup-like beer that was a primary source of carbohydrates in the peasant diet. During harvest, women worked in the fields alongside the men.

Beer, black bread, beans, cabbage, onions, and cheese made up the typical peasant diet. Meat was a rarity and usually came from pigs. Only in northern Europe, where the shortage of winter fodder necessitated culling herds each winter, did peasants occasionally enjoy beef. Inadequate agricultural methods and inefficient storage systems left the peasantry in constant threat of famine.

Negotiating Freedom. The expansion of arable land offered new hope and opportunities to peasants. Population growth, as rapid as it was between the tenth and twelfth centuries, did not keep up with the increasing demand for laborers in newly settled areas of Europe. Lords were often willing to make special arrangements with groups of peasants to encourage them to bring new land under cultivation. From the beginning of the twelfth century, peasant villages acquired from their lord the privilege to deal with him and his representatives collectively rather than individually. Villages purchased the right to control petty courts and to limit fines imposed by the lord's representative. Peasants acquired protection from arbitrary demands for labor and extraordinary taxes.

These good times did not last forever. Gradually, during the late twelfth and thirteenth centuries, the labor market stagnated. Europe's population—particularly in France, England, Italy, and western Germany—began to reach a saturation point. As a result, lay and ecclesiastical lords found that they could profit more by hiring cheap laborers than by demanding customary services and payments from their serfs. They also found that their serfs were willing to pay for increasing privileges.

Peasants could purchase the right to marry without the lord's consent, to move to neighboring manors or nearby towns, and to inherit. They acquired personal freedom from their lord's jurisdiction, transformed their servile payments into payments of rent for their manses, purchased their own land, and commuted their labor services into annual or even one-time payments. In other words, they began to purchase their freedom. This free peasantry benefited the emerging states of western Europe, since kings and towns could extend their legal and fiscal jurisdictions over these persons and their lands at the expense of the nobility. Governments thus encouraged the extension of freedom and protected

peasants from their former masters. By the fourteenth century, serfs were a rarity in many parts of western Europe.

This is not to say that these freed serfs and their descendants necessarily gained prosperity. Freedom often meant freedom from the protection that lords had provided. It meant the freedom to fail and even to starve. Some free peasants were able to participate in the emerging world of cash-crop farming and to tie into a growing trend toward agricultural specialization. Others, by the fourteenth century, roamed the countryside trying to survive, occasionally becoming the source of political and social turmoil.

Even as western serfs were acquiring a fragile freedom, the free peasants in much of eastern Europe and Spain were losing it. In much of the Slavic world, through the eleventh century, peasants lived in large, roughly territorial communes of free families. Gradually, however, princes, churches, and aristocrats began to build great landed estates. By the thirteenth century—under the influences of western and Byzantine models and of the Mongols, who dominated much of the Slavic world from 1240—lords began to acquire political and economic control over the peasantry. In Hungary during the twelfth century, free peasants and unfree servants merged to form a stratum of serfs subordinated to the emerging landed aristocracy and the lesser nobility composed of free warriors. A similar process took place in parts of Spain. In all of these regions the decline of the free peasantry accompanied the decline of public authority to the benefit of independent nobles. The aristocracy rose on the backs of the peasantry.

The Aristocracy: Warriors and Heiresses

Beginning in the late tenth century, writers of legal documents began to use an old term in a novel manner to designate certain powerful free persons who belonged neither to the old aristocracy nor to the peasantry. The term was *miles*, which in classical Latin meant "soldier." As it was used in the Middle Ages, we would translate it as "knight." The knightly function gradually came to entail a certain status and lifestyle.

The center of the knightly lifestyle was northern France. From there the ideals of knighthood, or chivalry, spread out across Europe, influencing aristocrats as far east as Byzantium. The essence of this lifestyle was fighting. Through warfare this aristocracy had maintained or acquired its freedom, and through warfare it justified its privileges. The origins of this small elite (probably nowhere more than two percent of the population) were diverse. Many of its members were descended from the old aristocracy of the Carolingian age. They traced descent through the male line. Inheritance was usually limited to the eldest sons, and daughters were given a dowry but did not share in inheritance. Younger sons had to find service with some great lord or live in the household of their older brothers. Even the eldest sons who became heads of households could not dispose of family property without consulting their kinsmen.

Such noble families, proud of their independence and ancestry, maintained their position through complex kin networks, mutual defense pacts with other nobles, and control of castles, from which they could dominate the surrounding countryside. By the twelfth century, nobles lived safely behind the castle walls, often even independent of the local counts, dukes, and kings. This lesser nobility absorbed control of such traditionally public powers as justice, peace, and taxation.

Aristocratic Education. For the sons of such nobles, preparation for a life of warfare began early, often in the entourage of a maternal uncle or a powerful lord. Boys learned to ride, to handle heavy swords and shields, to manage a lance on horseback, and to swing an ax with deadly accuracy. They also learned lessons about honor, pride, and family tradition. The feats of ancestors or heroes, celebrated in such works as the *Song of Roland* and the legends of King Arthur, were sung by traveling minstrels at the banqueting table and provided models of knightly action. The culmination of this education for English and French nobles came in a ceremony of knighting. An adolescent of age 16 to 18 received a sword from an older, experienced warrior. No longer a "boy," he now became a "youth," ready to enter the world of fighting for which he had trained.

A youth was a noble who had been knighted but who had not married or acquired land either through inheritance or as a reward from a lord for service and thus had not yet established his own "house." He led the life of a warrior, joining in promising military expeditions and amusing himself with tournaments—mock battles that often proved as deadly as the real thing—in which one could win an opponent's horses and armor as well as renown. Drinking, gambling, and lechery were other common activities. This was an extraordinarily dangerous lifestyle, and many youths did not survive to the next stage in a knight's life, that of acquiring land, wife, honor, and his own following of youths.

The period between childhood and maturity was as dangerous for noblewomen as for men. Marriage was the primary form of alliance between noble houses, and the production of children was essential to the continued prosperity of the family. Therefore, the daughters of the nobility were generally brought up for marriage and procreation. They were usually married at around age 16 and then were expected to produce as many children as possible. Given the primitive knowledge of obstetrics and hygiene, bearing children was even more dangerous than bearing a lance. Many noblewomen died in childbirth, often literally exhausted by frequent successive births. Although occasionally practiced, contraception

was condemned both by the Church and by husbands eager for offspring.

In this martial society, the official political and economic status of women declined considerably. Because they were considered unable to participate in warfare, in northern Europe women were also frequently excluded from inheritance, estate management, courts, and public deliberations. This at least was the theory, although we know that many individual women continued to control property, manage estates, and testify in court.

Still, the most powerful women were widows who had borne sons and who could play a major part in raising them. Such women were not uncommon. If a noblewoman was able to bear children successfully, she stood an excellent chance of surviving her husband, who was probably at least 15 years her senior and whose military pursuits placed him in constant danger. Such women, experienced in management by years of directing the households of their husbands, well connected by kinship, and experienced in court intrigue from years of attending assemblies in the company of their husbands and sons, could often hold their own with their male counterparts. Their support and alliances were actively sought by aristocrats, kings, and churches.

However, such a role was not likely to endear her to her male contemporaries. For all their martial valor, medieval men feared women and female sexuality. They mistrusted the representative of another lineage who was essential to the continuance of their own. Both secular tradition and Christian teaching portrayed women as devious, sexually demanding temptresses often responsible for the corruption and downfall of men. Many men felt threatened by the aggressive sexual stereotype. They resented the power wielded by wealthy widows and abbesses.

Land and Loyalty. The noble lifestyle required wealth, and wealth meant land. The nobility was essentially a society of heirs who had inherited not only land but also the serfs who worked their manors. Lesser nobles acquired additional property from great nobles and from ecclesiastical institutions in return for binding contracts of mutual assistance. This tradition was at least as old as the Carolingians, who granted their followers land in return for military service. In later centuries, counts and lesser lords continued this tradition, exchanging land for support. Individual knights became *vassals* of lay or ecclesiastical magnates, swearing fealty or loyalty to the lord and promising to defend and aid him. In return, the lord swore to protect his vassal and granted him a means of support by which the vassal could maintain himself while serving his lord. Usually, this grant, termed a *fief*, was a parcel of productive land and the serfs and privileges attached to it, which the vassal and his heirs could hold as long as they provided the designated service to the lord.

by kinship, regional alliances, personal bonds of fealty, and the surviving elements of Carolingian administration inherited by counts and dukes. In much of Europe the society of the eleventh and twelfth centuries was one of intensely local autonomous powers in which public order and political authority were spread as widely as ever in European history.

The Church: Saints and Monks

The religious needs of the peasantry remained those that their pre-Christian ancestors had known: fertility of land, animals, and women; protection from the ravages of climate and the warrior elite; and supernatural cures for the ailments and disabilities of their harsh life. The cultural values of the nobility retained the essentials of the Germanic warrior ethos, including family honor, battle, and display of status. The rural Church of the high Middle Ages met the needs of both, although it subtly changed them in the process.

Most medieval people, whether peasants or lords, lived in a world of face-to-face encounters, a world in which abstract creeds counted for little. In this world, religion meant primarily action, and the essential religious actions were the liturgical celebrations performed by the clergy. Although many of the parish priests had received only rudimentary instruction from their predecessors and had minimal knowledge of Latin and theology, such intellectual shortcomings were not important. Ordinary lay people just wanted priests who would not extort them by selling the sacraments, would not seduce their wives and daughters, and would remain in the village to perform the rituals necessary to keep the supernatural powers well disposed toward the community.

The most important of these supernatural powers was not some distant divinity but the saints—local, personal, even idiosyncratic persons. During their lives, saintly men and women had shown that they enjoyed God's special favor. After their deaths they continued to be the link between the divine and earthly spheres. Through their bodies, preserved as relics in the monasteries of Europe, they continued to live among mortals even while participating in the heavenly court. Thus they could be approached and won over through offerings, bribes, oaths, and rituals of supplication and submission. Praying and fasting, petitioners pilgrimaged to a saint's tomb, normally found in a monastery, and kept vigil there, beseeching the saint for protection. Some saints attracted national or even international pilgrimages. As the recipients of gifts to the saints, monastic communities became wealthy and powerful.

Monastic Culture.   In addition to orchestrating the cult of saints, monasteries also took responsibility for the cult of the ordinary dead. In particular, monastic communities

▲ A knight and a lady in a fifteenth-century garden. The ideals of chivalry and courtly love glorified women in literature and song, but in real life the subordinate status of women reflected the values of a martial society.

Individual lords often had considerable numbers of vassals, who might also be the vassals of other lay and secular lords. The networks formed vital social and political structures. In some unusual situations—as in England immediately after the Norman Conquest and in the Latin Kingdom of Jerusalem, founded in 1099—these structures of lords and vassals constituted systems of hierarchical government. Elsewhere, individuals often held fiefs from, and owed service to, more than one lord, and not all of the individuals in a given county or duchy owed their primary obligation to the count or duke. Likewise, often most of a noble's land was owned outright rather than held in fief, thus making the feudal bond less central to his status. As a result, these bonds—anachronistically called *feudalism* by French lawyers of the sixteenth and seventeenth centuries—constituted just one more element of a social system tied together

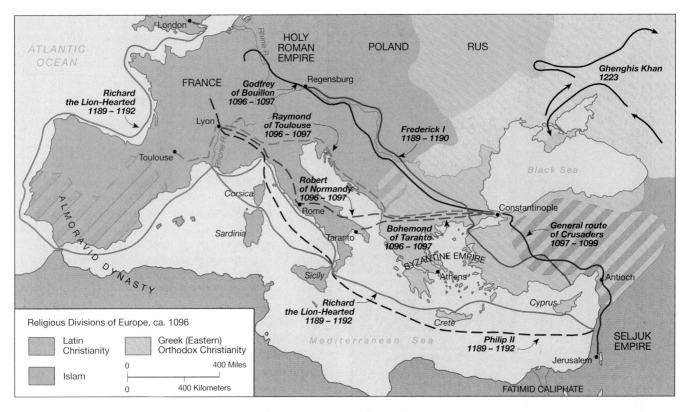

▲ The Crusades. The wars to conquer and protect the Latin Kingdom of Jerusalem brought
Western Christians into violent contact with the Islamic and Orthodox worlds.

commemorated and prayed for members of noble families
who, through donations of land, had become especially associated with the monastic community. Association with
such monasteries through gifts and exchanges of property,
and particularly through burial in the monastic cemetery,
provided the surest means of continuing noble families'
honor and prestige into the next world. Across Europe,
noble families founded monasteries on their own lands or
invited famous abbots to reorganize existing monasteries.

Supported by both peasants and nobles, Benedictine
monasteries reached their height in the eleventh and
twelfth centuries. Within their walls developed a religious culture, the essence of which was the passionate
pursuit of God. The goal was not simply salvation but
perfection, and this required discipline of the body
through a life of voluntary chastity and poverty and discipline of the spirit through obedience and learning. The
Benedictine's life moved to the rhythm of the divine office, the ancient series of eight hours each day when the
monks put aside work, study, or rest and assembled in
the monastic church for the communal chanting of
prayers, psalms, and hymns.

Monasteries were communities that specialized in
prayer and therein found their social justification. They
were also enormously rich and powerful. The monastery
of Cluny, in saving souls through prayer, became the first
international organization of monastic centers, with

abbeys and dependent communities, called priories,
throughout Europe. The abbots of Cluny were among the
most powerful and influential people of the eleventh and
twelfth centuries, considered to be the equals of kings,
popes, and emperors. To remain in form for the strenuous
liturgical commemoration of living and dead patrons,
Cluniac monks largely abandoned the tradition of manual
work, leaving such mundane activities to their thousands
of serfs and lay agents.

Monastic Reform. The Cluniac monks' comparative
luxury and concentration on liturgy to the neglect of other
spiritual activities led some monastic reformers to call for a
return to simplicity, separation from the rest of society, and
a deeper internal spirituality. Chief among these groups
were the Cistercians, who, under the dynamic leadership
of Bernard of Clairvaux (1090–1153), spread their rigorous ascetic form of monasticism from England to the
Vienna woods. The Cistercians built monasteries in the
wilderness and discouraged the kinds of close ties with
secular society that the Cluniacs had established.
Paradoxically, by establishing themselves in remote areas,
organizing their estates in an efficient manner, and gaining
a great reputation for asceticism, the Cistercians also became enormously wealthy and successful leaders in the
economic changes taking place in the twelfth and thirteenth centuries.

The rural Church not only served the lay population but worked to transform it. Although monks and bishops were spiritual warriors, most abhorred bloodshed among Christians and sought to limit the violence of aristocratic life. This attitude combined altruistic and selfish motives, since Church property was often the focus of aristocratic greed. The decline of public power and the rise of aristocratic autonomy and violence were particularly marked in southern France. There, beginning in the tenth century, churchmen organized the Peace of God and the Truce of God, movements that attempted to protect peasants, merchants, and clerics from aristocratic violence and to limit the times when warfare was allowed. During the eleventh century, the goals of warfare were shifted from attacks against other Christians to the defense of Christian society. This redirection produced the Crusades, religious wars of conquest authorized by popes and directed against Europe's non-Christian neighbors.

Crusaders: Soldiers of God

The Crusades left a complex and troubling legacy in world civilization. Between 1096 and 1272, waves of zealous and adventuresome European Christians set out to do battle with the Muslims. Eight main crusades were launched, each lasting from one to four years, except the Seventh Crusade (1248–1254), which dragged on longer. The First Crusade originated in 1095, when Pope Urban II (1088–1099), hoping to direct noble violence away from Christendom, urged Western knights to use their arms to free the Holy Land from Muslim occupation. In return, he promised to absolve them from all of the punishment due for their sins in this life or the next. After terrible hardships the crusaders succeeded in taking Jerusalem in 1099 and established a Latin Kingdom in Palestine. For over two centuries, bands of Western warriors went on armed pilgrimages to defend this precarious kingdom. The Second Crusade (1145–1149) ended in defeat and disaster at the hands of Seljuk Turks in Asia Minor. In 1187 the Muslim commander Saladin recaptured Jerusalem, causing Emperor Frederick Barbarossa and the kings of France and England, Philip II Augustus and Richard the Lion-Hearted, to embark on the Third Crusade (1187–1192). This crusade also failed, but Richard signed a peace treaty with Saladin. On his way home, the English king was captured and imprisoned in Austria until his mother, Eleanor, could

---

POPE URBAN II SUMMONS A CRUSADE

In 1095, Pope Urban II convened a Church council in Clermont, France. The primary focus of the council was to establish peace within the Christian community, but at the same time he launched his appeal for aid to the Byzantine Empire, thus launching what would be the First Crusade. We do not have his exact words but this version of his sermon was preserved by Fulcher of Chartres, a cleric who participated in the crusade and who was present at the council.

FOCUS QUESTIONS

What effects does Urban hope the crusade will have within Christian society? What rewards does he promise those who participate?

NOW THAT YOU, O SONS OF GOD, have consecrated yourselves to God to maintain peace among yourselves more vigorously and to uphold the laws of the Church faithfully, there is work to do. As most of you have been told, the Turks, a race of Persians, who have penetrated within the boundaries of the Byzantine Empire even to the Mediterranean to the Bosporus, in occupying more and more of the lands of the Christians, have overcome them, already victims of seven battles, and have killed and captured them, have overthrown churches, and have laid waste God's kingdom. Concerning this affair I, with suppliant prayer—not I, but the Lord—exhort you, heralds of Christ, to persuade all of whatever class, both knights and footmen, both rich and poor, in numerous edicts, to strive to help expel that wicked race from our Christian lands before it is too late. I speak to those present, I send word to those not here, moreover, Christ commands it. Remission of sins will be granted for going thither, if they end a shackled life either on land or in crossing the sea, or in struggling against the heathen. I, being vested with that gift from God, grant this to those who go. Let those who are accustomed to wage private wars wastefully even against Believers, go forth against the Infidels in a battle worthy to be undertaken now and to be finished in victory. Nor, let those, who until recently existed as plunderers, be soldiers of Christ; not let those who until recently existed as plunderers, against brothers and relations, rightly fight barbarians; now let those who recently were hired for a few pieces of silver, win their eternal reward.

Edward Peters, ed., *The First Crusade. The Chronicle of Fulcher of Chartres and Other Source Materials* (Philadelphia: University of Pennsylvania Press, 1971), pp. 30–31.

raise the ransom to buy his freedom. Five subsequent crusades accomplished little.

The Idea of the Crusade

Although military failures, the Crusades appealed particularly to younger sons and knights who hoped to acquire in the East the status that constricting lineages denied them in the West. Other such holy wars were directed against the Muslims in Spain, the Slavs in eastern Europe, and even heretics and political opponents in France and Italy.

The Crusades were brutal and vicious, and the crusaders were often motivated as much by greed as by piety. Doubts about the spiritual significance of such wars contributed to their decline. So, too, did the rise of centralized monarchies, whose rulers usually viewed the Crusades as wasteful and futile. The age of the Crusades passed with the age of the independent warrior aristocracy.

In the eleventh and twelfth centuries, peasants, lords, and monks made up the great majority of Europe's population and lived together in mutual dependence, sharing involvement in the rhythm of the agrarian life. From the later part of the twelfth century, however, this rural world became increasingly aware of a different society: that of the growing cities and towns of Europe, whose citizens moved to the newer rhythms of commerce and manufacture.

MEDIEVAL TOWNS

To the traditional rural mind, towns seemed somehow immoral. Nobles disdained urban society for its lack of respect for aristocracy and its disinterest in their cult of violence. Still, as rude warriors were transformed into courtly nobles, these nobles were drawn to urban luxuries and became indebted to urban moneylenders to maintain their "gracious" lifestyles. For many peasants, towns were refuges from the hopelessness of their normal lives. "Town air makes one free," they believed, and many serfs fled the land to try their fortunes in the nearby towns.

Italian Cities

Urban life had never ceased in Italy, which had maintained its urban traditions and ties with the Mediterranean world since antiquity. Although urban populations had shrunk in late antiquity and they were dominated by their bishops, who exercised secular and ecclesiastical lordship, the towns of the Italian peninsula had continued to play commercial and political roles and to attract not only runaway serfs but even nobles, who maintained fortified towers within the town walls.

The coastal cities of Amalfi, Bari, Genoa, and especially Venice had continued to play important roles in commerce both with the Byzantines and with the new Muslim societies. For Venice this role was facilitated by its official status as a part of the Byzantine Empire, which gave it access to Byzantine markets. With nothing of their own to trade but perhaps salt and, in Venice, glass, these cities acted as go-betweens for the transport of eastern spices, silks, and ivories, which they exchanged for Western iron, slaves, timber, grain, and oil. To protect their merchant ships, Italian coastal cities developed their own fleets, and by the eleventh century they were major military forces in the Mediterranean. Venice's fleet became the primary protector of the Byzantine Empire and was thereby able to win more favorable commercial rights than those enjoyed by Greek merchants.

Merchants and Capitalists.   As the merchants of the Italian towns penetrated the markets at the western end of the great overland spice routes connecting China, India, and central Asia with the Mediterranean, they established permanent merchant colonies in the East. When expedient, they did not hesitate to use military force to win concessions.

For the Italians, who had no scruples about trading with Muslims, the Crusades were primarily economic opportunities. Only the Italians had the ships and the expertise to transport the crusaders by sea, the only option that offered hope of success, and then to bring them supplies once they were in Palestine. Crusaders paid the Italian merchants handsomely for their assistance and also granted them economic and political rights in the Palestinian port cities such as Tyre and Acre. The culmination of this relationship between northern crusaders and Italians was the Fourth Crusade, which, short on funds, was sidetracked by the Venetians into capturing and sacking Constantinople, a blow from which the Byzantine Empire never recovered. Venice emerged as the undisputed Mediterranean power.

By the thirteenth century, Italian merchants had spread far beyond the Mediterranean. The great merchant banking houses of Venice, Florence, and Genoa had established offices around the Mediterranean and Black seas; south along the Atlantic coast of Morocco; east into Armenia and Persia; west to London, Bruges, and Ghent; and north to Scandinavia. Some individual merchants, the Venetian Marco Polo (1254–1324), for example, traded as far east as China.

These international commercial operations required more sophisticated systems of commercial law and credit. Italian merchants responded by developing double-entry bookkeeping, limited-liability partnership, commercial insurance, and international letters of exchange. Complex commercial affairs also required a system of credit and interest-bearing loans, an idea that was abhorrent to traditional rural societies. Churchmen condemned borrowing and lending at credit, but bankers found ways of hiding interest payments in contracts, thus allowing lender and seller to participate in the growing world of credit-based transactions.

Underlying the expanding commercial developments was a basic change: a new mentality that considered commerce an honorable occupation. Since antiquity, aristocrats had considered only warfare and agriculture to be worthy pursuits. The strength of the Italian towns was that they were able to throw off the rural, aristocratic value system. The Italian passion for commerce spread from the seacoasts to the towns throughout Italy and from there to Marseille, Barcelona, and other cities in southern Europe. By the twelfth century, wealthy citizens, whether descended from successful merchants or from landed aristocrats, were indifferently termed magnates. The rest of the town's population were called *populars*. The difference between the two was essentially economic.

Communal Government. In the eleventh and early twelfth centuries, many Italian towns bought off or expelled their traditional lords such as counts and bishops, thus allowing the magnates and populars of these cities to create their own governing institutions or communes. Within many towns the magnates formed their own corporation—the society of knights—to protect their privileged position. Families of nobles and magnates, whose cultural values were similar to those of the rural aristocracy, competed with each other for honor and power. Feuds fought out between noble families and their vassals in city streets were frequent events in Italian towns.

Opposing the magnates were popular corporations—the society of the people—which sought to rein in the violent and independent-minded nobles. Each of these popular organizations, dominated by the prominent leaders of craft and trade associations, had its own elected officers and its own military, headed by a "captain of the people," who might command as many as 1,000 troops against the magnates.

To tip the scales in their favor, differing parties frequently invited outside powers into local affairs. The greatest outside contenders for power in the Italian cities were the Germanic empire and the papacy. Most towns had an imperial faction (named Ghibelline after Waiblingen castle, which belonged to the family of the emperor Frederick II), bitterly opposed by a papal faction (in time called Guelph after the Welf family, which opposed Frederick's family). Eventually, the Guelphs became the party of the wealthy who were eager to preserve the status quo, and the Ghibellines became the party of those out of power.

To maintain civic life in spite of these conflicts, cities established complex systems of government in which officers were selected by series of elections and lotteries designed to prevent any one faction from seizing control.

▼ Medieval Trade Networks. Italian, Flemish, and German merchants tied northern and southern Europe to the eastern Mediterranean and beyond through networks of trade routes and markets that crossed religious, cultural, and political boundaries.

Sovereignty lay with the *arengo,* or assembly, which included all adult male citizens. Except in very small communes this body was too large to function efficiently, so most communes selected a series of working councils. The great council might be as large as 400; an inner council had perhaps 24 to 40 members. Generally, executive authority was vested in consuls, whose numbers varied widely and who were chosen from various factions and classes. When these consuls proved unable to overcome the partisan politics of the factions, many towns turned to hiring *podestas,* nonpolitical professional city managers from outside the community. These were normally magnates from other communes who had received legal educations and who served for relatively short periods. In Modena, for example, they served for six months. They were required to bring with them four judges, 24 cavalrymen, and sergeants and grooms to help maintain order. They could not have any relatives in Modena, could not leave town without permission of the great council, and could not eat or drink with local citizens lest they be drawn into factional conflicts.

Northern Towns

Merchant and manufacturing towns also developed along the Baltic and North Seas and the English Channel. Scandinavian fish and timber, Baltic grain, English wool, and Flemish cloth circulated by sea around Scandinavia, Lithuania, northern Germany, Flanders, and England, linking them in a common economic network.

The earliest of these interrelated communities were the cloth towns of Flanders, Brabant, and northern France. Chief among them were Ghent, Bruges, and Ypres and the wool-exporting towns of England, particularly London. In the eleventh century, Flanders, lacking the land for large-scale sheep grazing and facing a growing population, began to specialize in the production of high-quality cloth made from English wool. At the same time, England, which experienced an economic and population decline following the Norman Conquest, began to export the greater part of its wool to Flanders to be worked. The need for water to power looms and to wash the woolen cloth during production tended to concentrate this industry along waterways. By the late eleventh century, the production of wool cloth began to develop from a cottage occupation into Europe's first major industry. Now manufacture was concentrated in towns, and men replaced women at the looms. Furthermore, production was closely regulated and controlled by a small group of extremely wealthy merchant-drapiers (cloth makers).

Concentration of capital, specialization of labor, and increase of urban population created vibrant, exciting cities that were essentially composed of three social orders. At the top were wealthy patricians, the merchant-drapiers. Their agents traveled to England and purchased raw wool, which they then distributed to weavers and other master craftsmen. These craftsmen—often using equipment rented from the patricians—carded, dyed, spun, and wove the wool into cloth. Finally, the finished cloth was returned to the patricians, whose agents then marketed it throughout Europe. Through their control of raw materials, equipment, capital, and distribution the merchant-drapiers controlled the cloth trade and thus the economic and political life of the Flemish wool towns. Through their closed associations, or guilds, they controlled production and set standards, prices, and wages. They also controlled communal government by monopolizing urban councils.

At the bottom of urban society were the unskilled and semiskilled artisans, called "blue nails" because constant work with dye left their fingers permanently stained. These poorly paid workers led an existence that was more precarious than that of most peasants. In the early fourteenth century, the temporary interruption of grain shipments from northern Germany to Ypres left thousands dead of starvation. Small wonder that from the thirteenth century on, "blue nails" were increasingly hostile to patricians. Sporadic rebellions and strikes spread across Flanders, Brabant, and northern France. Everywhere, they were ruthlessly suppressed. The penalty for organizing a strike was death.

Between the patricians and the workers stood the masters, the skilled craftsmen who controlled the day-to-day production of cloth and lesser crafts. They organized into guilds to protect themselves from competition. The masters often leased their looms or other equipment from the merchant-drapiers and received from them raw materials and wages to be distributed to their workers.

The Fairs of Champagne

Tying together the northern and southern commercial worlds were the great fairs of Champagne. Six times during the year, the towns of Champagne—particularly Troyes and Provins—swelled with exotic crowds of merchants from Flanders, England, Scandinavia, Germany, Brabant, Spain, and Italy. Rich and poor people from the surrounding countryside also poured into the towns as merchants from north and south met to bargain and trade under the protection of the local counts.

Northern merchants offered cloth, which was known by the name of the town in which it was made. From Italy came merchants of great Italian trading companies to purchase northern cloth for resale throughout the Mediterranean. Southern merchants brought silks, sugar, salt, alum (a chemical that was essential in cloth manufacture), and, most important, spices to trade at the fairs. Medieval cooks gloried in the use of spices, of which they knew over 200. The liberal use of exotic spices may have served as a preservative, and spices probably hid the taste of half-rotten food. But the use of spices was primarily a part of the conspicuous consumption by which the rich displayed their wealth and status.

In addition to the trade in cloth and spices, leather from Spain, iron from Germany, copper and tin from Bohemia, salted or smoked fish and furs from Scandinavia, and local wines, cheeses, and foodstuffs also changed hands under the watchful eyes of fair officials, who supervised weights, measures, and currency exchanges. The fair staff also provided courts to settle disagreements among merchants. These great international exchanges connected the financial and marketing centers of the south with the manufacturing and trading communities of the north, tying the northern world to the south more effectively than had any system since the political institutions of the Roman Empire.

Scholasticism and Urban Intellectual Life

The urban world of the twelfth and thirteenth centuries created forms of religious and cultural expression particularly suited to it. The cathedral schools shifted away from monastic education to an education aimed more at participation in the affairs of the world. Young men were taught the essential urban skills of writing, computation, and law.

The Medieval University.   In the late eleventh and early twelfth centuries, the pace of urban intellectual life quickened. The combination of population growth, improved agricultural productivity, political stability, and educational interest culminated in what has been called the renaissance of the twelfth century. Bologna and Paris became the undisputed centers of the new educational movements. Bologna specialized in the study of law, while Paris became the leader in the study of liberal arts and theology. Students at Bologna organized a *universitas,* or guild of students, the first true university. The law students, many of them adults from wealthy backgrounds, controlled every aspect of the university from the selection of administrators to the exact length of professors' lectures. Professors and administrators were fined if they broke any of the regulations.

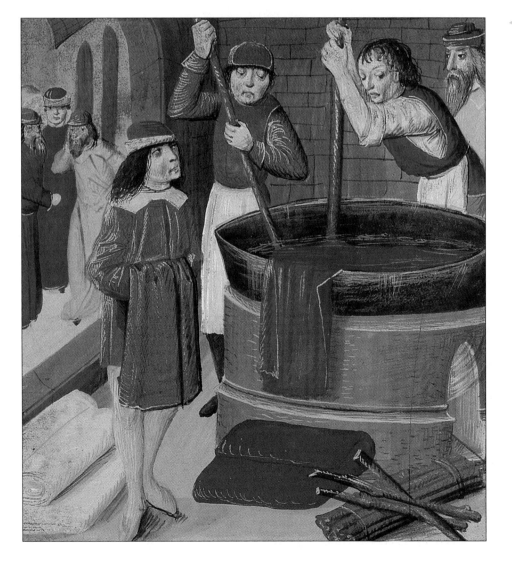

◁ As towns grew, the numbers and types of jobs grew as well. In this fifteenth-century Flemish manuscript illumination, a master of the dyer's guild supervises as men of the guild dye cloth.

◁ This illustration from a fourteenth-century manuscript shows Henry of Germany delivering a lecture to university students in Bologna.

In the early twelfth century, students from across Europe flocked to Paris to study with the greatest and most original intellect of the century, Peter Abelard (1079–1142). Brilliant, supremely self-assured, and passionate, Abelard was in his early twenties when he arrived in Paris and quickly took the intellectual community by storm. He ridiculed the established teachers, bested them in open debate, and established his own school, which drew the best minds of his day. Abelard's intellectual method combined the tools of legal analysis perfected in Bologna with Aristotelian logic and laid the foundation of what has been called the Scholastic method. Logical reasoning, Abelard believed, could be applied to all problems, even those concerning the mysteries of faith.

So great was Abelard's reputation that an ambitious local cleric engaged him to give private instruction to his brilliant niece, Heloise. Soon Abelard and Heloise were having an affair. When Heloise became pregnant, the two were secretly married. Fearing to harm his clerical career, Abelard refused to make the marriage public, preferring to protect his career rather than Heloise's honor. Her outraged uncle hired thugs, who broke into Abelard's room and castrated him. After Abelard recovered from his mutilation, he and Heloise both entered monasteries, and Abelard spent years as the abbot of a small monastery in Brittany. In 1136, he returned to teach in Paris, where he

quickly drew new attacks, this time led by Bernard of Clairvaux, who accused him of heresy. Abelard was convicted by a local council and forced to burn some of his own works. He sought protection from his persecutors in the monastery of Cluny, where he died in 1142.

Although Abelard met tragedy in his personal and professional life, the intellectual ferment that he had begun in Paris continued long after him. By 1200, education had become so important in the city that the universitas, or corporation of professors, was granted a charter by King Philip Augustus, who guaranteed its rights and immunities from the control of the city. Unlike that at Bologna, the University of Paris remained a corporation of masters rather than of students. It was organized like other guilds into masters; bachelors, who were similar to journeymen in other trades; and students, who were analogous to apprentices.

Students began their studies at around age 14 or 15 in the faculty of arts. After approximately six years, they received a bachelor of arts degree, which was a prerequisite to enter the higher faculties of theology, medicine, or law. After additional years of reading and commenting on specific texts under the supervision of a master, they received the title of master of arts, which gave them the license to teach anywhere within Christian Europe. During their years of study, students also enjoyed a spirited life that revolved around the taverns and brothels that filled the student district, or Latin Quarter. Drunken brawls were frequent, and relationships between students and townspeople were often strained because students enjoyed legal immunity from city laws.

The intellectual life of the universities through the thirteenth and fourteenth centuries was dominated by Aristotelian thought. The introduction of the works of Aristotle into the West between 1150 and 1250 created an intellectual crisis every bit as profound as that of the Newtonian revolution of the seventeenth century or the Einsteinian revolution of the twentieth. For centuries, Western thinkers had depended on the Christianized Neoplatonic philosophy of Origen and Augustine. Aristotle was known in the West only through his basic logical treatises, which in the twelfth century, thanks in large part to the work of Peter Abelard, had become the foundation of intellectual work. Logic, or dialectic, was seen as the universal key to knowledge, and the university system was based on its rigorous application to traditional texts of law, philosophy, and Scripture.

The Aristotelian Challenge. Beginning in the late twelfth century, Christian and Jewish scholars began translating Aristotle's treatises on natural philosophy, ethics, and metaphysics into Latin. Suddenly, Christian intellectuals who had already accepted the Aristotelian method were brought face to face with Aristotle's conclusions: a world without an active, conscious God, a world in which everything from the functioning of the mind to the nature of matter could be understood without reference to a divine creator. Further complicating matters, the texts arrived not from the original Greek, but normally through Latin translations of Arabic translations accompanied by learned commentaries by Muslim and Jewish scholars, especially by Averroës, the greatest Aristotelian philosopher of the twelfth century.

As the full impact of Aristotelian philosophy began to reach churchmen and scholars, reactions varied from condemnation to whole-hearted acceptance. To many, it appeared that there were two irreconcilable kinds of truth, one knowable through divine revelation and the other through human reason. Scholasticism attempted to bridge the gap by using reason to deepen one's understanding of that which is accepted on faith.

One Parisian scholar who refused to accept the dichotomy of faith and reason was Thomas Aquinas (1225–1274), a professor of theology and the most brilliant intellect of the High Middle Ages. Aquinas refused to accept the possibility that human reason, which was a gift from God, led necessarily to contradictions with divine revelation. His *Summa Against the Gentiles* (1259–1264) and his incomplete *Summa of Theology* (1266–1273) sought to defend the integrity of human reason and to reconcile it with divine revelation. Properly applied, the

principles of Aristotelian philosophy could not lead to error, he argued. However, human reason unaided by revelation could not always lead to certain conclusions. Questions about such matters as the nature of God, creation, and the human soul could not be resolved by reason alone. In developing his thesis, Aquinas recast Christian doctrine and philosophy, replacing their Neoplatonic foundation with an Aristotelian base. Although not universally accepted in the thirteenth century, Aquinas's synthesis came to dominate Christian intellectual life for centuries.

Preaching and Poverty. Aquinas was a member of a new religious order, the Dominicans, who along with the Franciscans appeared in response to the social and cultural needs of the new urbanized, monetized European culture. Benedictine monasticism was ideally suited to a rural, aristocratic world but had little place in the bustling cities of Italy, Flanders, and Germany. In these urban, commercial environments, Christians were more concerned with the problems of living in the world than escape from it. Lay persons and clerics alike were concerned with the growing wealth of ecclesiastical institutions, and across southern Europe especially, individual reformers attacked the wealthy lifestyles of monks and secular clergy as un-Christian.

Torn between their own involvement in a commercial world and an inherited Christian-Roman tradition that looked on commerce and capital as degrading, reformers called for a return to what they imagined to have been the life of the primitive Church, one that emphasized both individual and collective poverty. The poverty movement attracted great numbers of followers, many of whom also criticized clerical morality and questioned the value of sacraments and the priesthood. Although many reformers were condemned as heretics and were sporadically persecuted, the reform movement continued to grow and threatened to destroy the unity of Western Christendom.

The people who preserved the Church's unity aimed at reforming the Church from within. Francis of Assisi (1182–1226), the son of a prosperous Italian merchant, rejected his luxurious life in favor of one of radical poverty and service to others. He was a man of piety, simplicity, humility, and joy. As he wandered about, preaching repentance, he drew great numbers of followers from all ranks, especially from the urban communities of Italy. Convinced of the importance of obedience, Francis asked Pope Innocent III to approve the way of life he had chosen for himself and his followers. The pope granted his wish, and the Order of Friars Minor, or Franciscans, grew by thousands, drawing members from as far away as England and Hungary.

Francis insisted that his followers observe strict poverty, both individually and collectively. The order could not own property, nor could its members even touch money. They were expected to beg for their food as they traveled

▲ An altarpiece depicting Saint Francis of Assisi with six scenes from his life. His hands show the stigmata—symbolic marks that represent the wounds Christ received on the cross.

from town to town, preaching, performing manual labor, and serving the poor. Francis did not approve of women followers leading such a life but insisted that they pursue radical poverty within cloistered convents that were often within the walls of towns.

In time, the expansion of the order and its involvement in preaching against heresy and in education brought about compromises with Francis's original ideals. The Franciscans needed churches in which to preach, books with which to study, and protection from local bishops. Most of the friars accepted these changes. These, the so-called conventuals, were bitterly opposed by the spirituals, or rigorists, who sought to maintain the radical poverty of their founder. In the fourteenth century this conflict led to a major split in the order and ultimately to the condemnation of the spirituals as heretics.

The order of friars founded by Dominic (1170–1221) also adopted a rule of strict poverty, but their primary focus was on preaching. This order emphasized intellectual activity and higher education and spoke out against heresies. Thus the Dominicans too gravitated toward the cities of western Europe and especially toward its great universities. These new orders of preachers, highly educated, enthusiastic, and eloquent, began to formulate for the urban laity of Europe a new vision of Christian society, a society not only of peasants, lords, and monks, but also of merchants, artisans, and professionals. Their central organizations and their lack of ties to the rural aristocracies also made them the favorite religious orders of the increasingly powerful centralized monarchies.

THE INVENTION OF THE STATE

The disintegration of the Carolingian Empire in the tenth century left political power fragmented among a wide variety of political entities. In general, these were of two types. The first, the papacy and the empire, were elective traditional structures that claimed universal sovereignty over the Christian world, based on a sacred view of political power. The second, largely hereditary and less extravagant in their religious and political pretensions, were the limited kingdoms that arose within the old Carolingian world or on its borders.

The Universal States: Empire and Papacy

The Frankish world east of the Rhine River had been less affected than the kingdom of the West Franks by the onslaught of Vikings, Magyars, and Saracens. The eastern Frankish kingdom, a loose confederacy of five duchies—Saxony, Lorraine, Franconia, Swabia, and Bavaria—had preserved much of the Carolingian religious, cultural, and institutional traditions. In 919, Duke Henry I of Saxony (919–936) was elected king, and his son Otto I (936–973) laid the foundation for the revival of the empire. Otto inflicted a devastating defeat on the Magyars in 955, subdued the other dukes, and tightened his control over the kingdom. He accomplished this largely through the extensive use of bishops and abbots, whom he appointed as his agents and sources of loyal support. In 951, Otto invaded and conquered Lombardy. Eleven years later, he entered Rome, where he was crowned emperor by the pope.

The Medieval Empire. Otto, known to history as "the Great," had established the main outlines of German imperial policy for the next 300 years. This policy included conflict with the German aristocracy, reliance on bishops and abbots as imperial agents, and preoccupation with Italy. His successors, both in his own Saxon dynasty (919–1024) and in the succeeding dynasties, the Salians (1024–1125) and the Staufens (1138–1254), continued this tradition. Magnates elected the German kings, who were then consecrated as emperors by the pope. Royal fathers were generally able to bring about the election of their sons, and in this manner they attempted to turn the kingship into a hereditary office. However, the royal families could not manage to produce male heirs in each generation, and so the magnates continued to exercise real power in royal elections.

The magnates' ability to expand their own power and autonomy at the expense of their Slavic neighbors to the east also contributed to the weakness of the German monarchy. In the 1150s, for example, Henry the Lion (ca. 1130–1195), Duke of Bavaria and Saxony, carved out an autonomous principality in the Slavic areas between the Elbe and the Vistula, founding the major trading towns of Lübeck and Rostock. It was the goal of every great aristocratic family to extend its own independent lordship.

To counter such aristocratic power, emperors looked to the Church both for the development of the religious cult of the emperor as "the Anointed of the Lord" and as a source of military and political support. While the offices of count and duke had become hereditary within the great aristocracy, the offices of bishop and abbot remained public charges to which the emperor could appoint loyal supporters. Since these ecclesiastics had taken vows of celibacy, the emperor did not fear that they would attempt to pass their offices on to their children. Moreover, churchmen tended to be experienced, educated administrators who could assist the emperor in the administration of the empire. Like the Carolingians, the Saxon and Salian emperors needed a purified, reformed Church that was free of local aristocratic control to serve the interests of the emperor. This imperial church was the cornerstone of the empire.

The laymen on whom the emperor could rely, particularly from the eleventh century, were trusted household serfs whom the emperors used as their agents. Although unfree, these ministerials were entrusted with important military commands and given strategic castles throughout the empire. Despised by the freeborn nobility, they tended at first to be loyal supporters of the emperor. In the twelfth century, they adopted the chivalric ideals of their aristocratic neighbors and took advantage of conflicts between emperor and pope to acquire autonomy. As old noble families died out, ministerial families replaced them as a new hereditary aristocracy.

Otto the Great had entered Italy to secure his southern flank. His successors became embroiled in Italian affairs until, in the thirteenth century, they abandoned Germany altogether. As emperors, they had to be crowned by the pope. This was possible only if they controlled Rome. Moreover, the growing wealth of northern Italian towns was an important source of financial support if Lombardy could be controlled. As the emperors were drawn further into papal and Italian politics, frequently with disastrous results, Germany became merely a source of men and matériel with which to fight the Lombard towns and the

▲ The Empire of Otto the Great, ca. 963. The Ottonian Empire included not only Germany but Slavic lands to the east and disputed regions such as Lorraine to the west.

pope. From the eleventh through the thirteenth centuries, emperors granted German princes autonomy in return for their support.

The Papacy. The early successes of this imperial program created the seeds of its own destruction. Imperial efforts to reform the Church resulted in a second, competing claimant to universal authority: the papacy. In the later tenth and early eleventh centuries, emperors had intervened in papal elections, deposed and replaced corrupt popes, and worked to ensure that bishops and abbots would be educated, competent churchmen. The most effective reformer was Emperor Henry III (1039–1056), who undertook to reform the Church both in Germany and in Rome. When three rivals claimed the papacy, Henry called a synod, or meeting of bishops, which deposed all three and installed the first of a series of German popes.

The most impressive was Henry's own cousin, Leo IX (1049–1054), who traveled widely in France, Germany, and Italy. Leo condemned simony, the practice of buying Church offices, and fostered monastic reforms such as that of Cluny. He also encouraged the efforts of a group of young reformers drawn from across Europe.

Investiture and Reform.   In the next decades these new, more radical reformers began to advocate a widespread renewal of the Christian world, led not by emperors but by popes. These reformers pursued an ambitious set of goals. They sought to reform the morals of the clergy and in particular to eliminate married priests. They tried to free churches and monasteries from lay control both by forbidding lay men and women from owning churches and monasteries and by eliminating simony. They particularly condemned "lay investiture," the practice by which kings and emperors appointed bishops and invested them with the symbols of their office. Finally, they insisted that the pope, not the emperor, was the supreme representative of God on earth and as such had the right to exercise a universal sovereignty.

Every aspect of the reform movement met with strong opposition throughout Europe. Emperor Henry IV (1056–1106) clashed head-on with Pope Gregory VII (1073–1085) over the emperor's right to appoint and to install or invest bishops in their offices. This investiture controversy changed the face of European political history. For the first time, public opinion played a crucial role in politics, and for the first time the idea of the separate spheres of church and state began to emerge in European political theory.

In the end, the conflict weakened both the empire and the papacy. In 1075 the emperor Henry IV, supported by many German bishops, attempted to depose Gregory. In return, Gregory excommunicated and deposed Henry, freed the German nobility from their obligations to him, and encouraged them to rebel. As anti-imperial strength grew, Henry took a desperate gamble. Crossing the Alps in the dead of winter in 1077, he arrived before the castle of Canossa in northern Italy, where Gregory was staying. Dressed as a humble penitent, Henry stood in the snow, asking the pope for forgiveness and reconciliation. As a priest, the pope could not refuse, and he lifted the excommunication. Once more in power, Henry resumed appointing bishops. In 1080, Gregory again excommunicated and deposed Henry, but this time the majority of the German nobles and bishops remained loyal to the emperor, and Henry marched on Rome. Deserted by most of his clergy, Gregory fled to southern Italy and died in Salerno in 1085.

Henry did not long enjoy his victory. Gregory's successors rekindled the opposition to Henry and even convinced Henry's own son to join in the revolt. The conflict ended only in 1122, when Emperor Henry V (1106–1125) and Pope Calixtus II (1119–1124) reached an agreement known as the Concordat of Worms, which differentiated between the royal and spiritual spheres of authority and allowed the emperors a limited role in episcopal election and investiture. This compromise changed the nature of royal rule in the empire, weakening the emperors and contributing to the long-term decline of royal government in Germany.

The decline that began with the investiture controversy continued as emperors abandoned political power north of the Alps to pursue their ambitions in Italy. Frederick I Barbarossa (1152–1190) gained the support of the German princes for his largely futile efforts in northern Italy by granting them extraordinary privileges. His successors continued his policy of focusing on Italy with no better success. In 1230, Frederick II (1215–1250) conceded to each German prince sovereign rights in his own territory. From the thirteenth to the nineteenth centuries, these princes ruled their territories as independent states, leaving the office of emperor a hollow title.

The investiture controversy ultimately compromised the authority of the pope as well as that of the emperor. First, the series of compromises beginning with the Concordat of Worms established the potent Western idea of separate spheres of authority for secular and religious government. Second, although in the short run popes were able to exercise enormous political influence, from the thirteenth century they were increasingly unable to make good their claims to absolute authority.

The Pinnacle of Papal Power.   Papal power was based on more than Scripture. Over the centuries the popes had acquired large amounts of land in central Italy and in the Rhone Valley, which formed the nucleus of the Papal States. Moreover, in every corner of Europe, bishops and clergy were, at least in theory, agents of papal programs. Church courts also claimed jurisdiction over all clerics, regardless of the nature of the legal problem, and over all baptized Christians in such fundamental issues as legitimacy of marriages, inheritances, and oaths.

During the pontificate of Innocent III (1198–1216) the papacy reached the height of its power. Innocent made and deposed emperors, excommunicated kings, summoned a crusade against heretics in the south of France, and placed whole countries such as England and France under interdict, that is, the suspension of all religious services, when rulers dared to contradict him. Still, he found time to support Francis of Assisi and Dominic and, in 1215, to call the Fourth Lateran Council, which culminated the reforms of the past century.

At the council, more than 1,200 assembled bishops and abbots, joined by great nobles from across Europe, defined fundamental doctrines such as the nature of the Eucharist, ordered annual confession of sins, and detailed procedures for the election of bishops. They also mandated a strict lifestyle for clergy and forbade their participation in judicial procedures in which accused persons had to undergo

C H R O N O L O G Y
PROMINENT POPES AND RELIGIOUS FIGURES OF THE HIGH MIDDLE AGES

1049–1054*	Pope Leo IX
1073–1085	Pope Gregory VII
1088–1099	Pope Urban II
1098–1179	Hildegard of Bingen
1119–1124	Pope Calixtus II
1170–1221	Saint Dominic
1182–1226	Saint Francis of Assisi
1198–1216	Pope Innocent III
1225–1274	Saint Thomas Aquinas
1294–1303	Pope Boniface VIII

*Dates for popes are dates of reign.

painful ordeals, such as grasping a piece of red-hot iron and carrying it a prescribed distance to prove their innocence. More ominously, the council also mandated that Jews wear special identifying markings on their clothing—a sign of the increasing hostility that Christians felt toward the Jews in their midst.

During the thirteenth century, the papacy continued to perfect its legal system and its control over clergy throughout Europe. However, politically the popes were unable to assert their claims to universal supremacy. This was true both in Italy, where the communes in the north and the kingdom of Naples in the south resisted direct papal control, and in the emerging kingdoms north of the Alps, where monarchs successfully intervened in Church affairs. The old claims of papal authority rang increasingly hollow. When Pope Boniface VIII (1294–1303) attempted to prevent the French king Philip IV (1285–1314) from taxing the French clergy, boasting that he could depose kings "like servants" if necessary, Philip proved him wrong. Philip's agents hired a gang of adventurers, who kidnapped the pope, plundered his treasury, and released him a broken, humiliated wreck. He died three weeks later. The French king who had engineered Boniface's humiliation represented a new political tradition: the medieval nation-state.

The Nation-States: France and England

The office of king was less pretentious than that of emperor. As the Carolingian world disintegrated, a variety of kingdoms had appeared in France, Italy, Burgundy, and Provence. Kingship was well established in England and northern Spain, and powerful chieftains were consolidating royal power at the expense of their aristocracies in Scandinavia, Poland, Bohemia, and Hungary. The claims of

kings were much more modest than those of emperors or popes. Kings laid claim to a limited territory; they were only one of many representatives of God on earth; and finally, they were far from absolute rulers. During the tenth and eleventh centuries, the powers of justice, coinage, taxation, and military command, once considered public, had been usurped by aristocrats and nobles. Kings needed the support of these magnates, and often—as in the case of France—these dukes and counts were wealthier and more powerful than the kings. Still, between the tenth and fourteenth centuries, some monarchies, especially those of France and England, developed into powerful, centralized, and vigorous kingdoms. In the process they gave birth to what has become the modern state.

France: Biology, Bureaucracy, and Sanctity. In 987, when Hugh Capet was elected king of the West Franks, no one suspected that his successors would become the most powerful rulers of Europe, for they were relatively weak magnates whose only real power lay in the region between Paris and Orléans. The dukes of Normandy, descendants of Vikings whose settlement had been recognized by Frankish kings, ruled their duchy with an authority of which the kings could only dream. Less than a century later, Duke William of Normandy expanded his power even more by conquering England. In the twelfth century, the English kings ruled the Angevin Empire, a vast collection of hereditary lands on both sides of the English Channel. Other nobles, such as the counts of Flanders and the counts of Poitou, also seemed more impressive than the house of Hugh Capet. Nevertheless, under Hugh's successors, the kingdom of France became the most powerful monarchy in Europe and the center of European learning, architecture, and art.

The medieval French monarchy owed its creation in large part to biology and bureaucracy. Between 987 and 1314, every royal descendant of Hugh Capet (after whom the dynasty was called the Capetian) left a male heir—an extraordinary record for a medieval family. During the same period, by comparison, the office of emperor was occupied by men from no fewer than nine families. By simply outlasting the families of their great barons, the Capetian kings were able to absorb lands when other families became extinct. This success was not just the result of luck. Kings such as Robert the Pious (996–1031) and Louis VII (1137–1180) risked excommunication to divorce wives who had not produced male heirs. In 1152, Louis had his marriage to the richest heiress of the twelfth century, Eleanor of Aquitaine (1122–1204), annulled in part because she had given him no sons. With the annulment he also lost the chance to absorb her territories of Aquitaine and Poitou. A few months later, Eleanor married Count Henry of Anjou (1133–1189), who two years later became King Henry II of England. Imagine Louis's chagrin when Eleanor produced four sons with Henry, in the process making the English kings the greatest magnates in France.

The Capetians' long run of biological luck, combined with the practice of having a son crowned during his father's lifetime and thus being firmly established before his father's death, was only part of the explanation for the Capetian success. The Capetians also wisely used their position as consecrated sovereigns to build a power base in the Ile de France (the region around Paris) and among the bishops and abbots of the kingdom and then to insist on their feudal rights as the lords of the great dukes and counts of France. It was this foundation that Louis VII's son Philip II (1180–1223) used to create the French monarchy.

Philip II was known to posterity as Augustus, or the aggrandizer, because through his ruthless political intrigue and brilliant organizational sense he more than doubled the territory he controlled and more than quadrupled the revenue of the French crown. Through marriage he acquired Vermandois, the Amienois, Artois, and Valois. He later absorbed Flanders and set the stage for the absorption of the great county of Toulouse by his son Louis VIII (1223–1226) in the aftermath of the crusade against the dualist Albigensian heretics launched by Pope Innocent III. Philip's greatest coup, however, was the confiscation of all the continental possessions of the English King John (1199–1216), the son of Henry II and Eleanor of Aquitaine. Although John was sovereign in England, as lord of Normandy, Anjou, Maine, and Touraine, he was technically a vassal of King Philip. When John married the fiancée of one of his continental vassals, the outraged vassal appealed to Philip in his capacity as John's lord. Philip summoned John to appear before the royal court, and when he refused to do so, Philip ordered him to surrender all of his continental fiefs. This meant war, and one by one, John's continental possessions fell to the French king. Philip's victory over John's ally the emperor Otto IV (1198–1215) at Bouvines in 1214 sealed the English loss of Normandy, Maine, Anjou, Poitou, and Touraine.

To govern these vast regions, Philip needed an effective administrative system. Using members of families from the old royal demesne, he set up administrative officials called *baillis* and *seneschals*, nonfeudal salaried agents who collected his revenues and represented his interests. The baillis in particular, who were drawn from commoner families and often had received their education at the University of Paris, were the foundation of the French bureaucracy, which grew in strength and importance through the thirteenth century. By governing the regions of France according to local traditions but always with an eye to the king's interest, these bureaucrats did more than anyone else to create a stable, enduring political system.

Philip's grandson Louis IX (1226–1270) fine-tuned this administrative machine and, through his own piety, endowed it with the aura of sanctity. Generous, brave, and capable, Louis took seriously his obligation to provide justice for the poor and protection for the weak. A disastrous crusade, the so-called Seventh Crusade (1248–1254), which ended in his capture and ransom in Egypt, convinced Louis that his failure was punishment for his sins and those of his government. When he returned to France, he dispatched investigators to correct abuses by baillis and other royal officials and restored property that had been unjustly confiscated by his father's agents during the Albigensian Crusade. In addition he established a permanent central court in Paris to hear appeals from throughout the kingdom. In 1270, Louis attempted another crusade and died in an epidemic in Tunis. The goodwill and devotion that Louis won from his subjects were a precious heritage that benefited his successors for centuries.

The growth of royal power transformed the traditional role of the aristocracy. As the power and wealth of the French kings increased, the ability of the nobles to maintain their independence decreased. Royal judges undermined lords' control over the peasantry. Royal revenues enabled kings to hire warriors rather than relying on traditional feudal levies. At the same time, the increasing expenses of the noble lifestyle forced all but the wealthiest aristocrats to look for sources of income beyond their traditional estates. Increasingly, they found this in royal service. Thus, in the thirteenth century the nobility began to lose some of its independence to the state.

England: Conquest, Accounting, and Cooperation. A very different path brought the English monarchy to a level of power similar to that of the French by the end of the thirteenth century. While France was made by a family and its bureaucracy, the kingdom that was originally forged by Alfred and his descendants was transformed by the successors of William the Conqueror.

When King Edward the Confessor (1042–1066) died, three claimants disputed the succession. Anglo-Saxon sources insist that Edward and his nobles had chosen Earl Harold Godwinson (ca. 1022–1066) over Duke William of Normandy and the Norwegian king Harold III (1045–1066). William insisted that Edward had designated him and that years before, when Earl Harold had been shipwrecked on the Norman coast and befriended by the duke, he had sworn an oath to assist William in gaining the crown. Harold of Norway and William sailed for England. Harold Godwinson defeated the Norwegian's army and killed the king, but he met his end shortly afterward on the bloody field of Hastings, and William the Conqueror secured the throne.

William's England was a small, insular kingdom that had been united by Viking raids little more than a century before. Hostile Celtic societies bordered it to the north and west. Still, it had important strengths. First, the king of the English was not simply a feudal lord, a first among equals—he was a sovereign. Second, Anglo-Saxon government had been participatory, with the freemen of each shire taking part in court sessions and sharing the responsibilities of government. Finally, the king had agents, or *reeves*, in each shire

(shire reeves, or sheriffs) who were responsible for representing the king's interests, presiding over the local court, and collecting royal taxes and incomes.

This ability to raise money was the most important aspect of the English kingship for William the Conqueror and his immediate successors, who remained thoroughly continental in interest, culture, and language (the first English king to speak English fluently was probably King John). England was seen primarily as a source of revenue. To tap this wealth, the Norman kings transformed rather than abolished Anglo-Saxon governmental traditions, adding Norman feudal bonds and administrative control to Anglo-Saxon kingship.

William preserved English government while replacing Anglo-Saxon officers with his continental vassals, chiefly Normans and Flemings. He rewarded his supporters with land confiscated from the defeated Anglo-Saxons, but he was careful to give out land only in fief. In contrast to continental practice, in which many lords owned vast estates outright, in England all land was held directly or indirectly by the king. Because he wanted to know the extent of his new kingdom and its wealth, William ordered a comprehensive survey of all royal rights. The recorded account, known as the Domesday Book, was the most extensive investigation of economic rights since the Merovingians abandoned the late Roman tax rolls.

William and his successors needed an efficient system of controlling England when they were away. To this end, they developed the royal court, an institution inherited from their Anglo-Saxon predecessors, into an efficient system of fiscal and administrative supervision. The most important innovation was the use of a large checkerboard, or exchequer, which functioned like a primitive computer to audit the returns of their sheriffs. Annual payments were recorded on long rolls of parchment called pipe rolls, the first continuous accounting system in Europe. These improved accounting methods produced the most efficient and prosperous royal administration in Europe.

In the first half of the twelfth century, almost two decades of warfare over the succession greatly weakened royal authority, but Henry II (1154–1189) reestablished central power by reasserting his authority over the nobility and through his legal reforms. Using his continental wealth and armies, he brought the English barons into line, destroyed private castles, and reasserted his rights to traditional royal incomes. He strengthened royal courts by expanding royal jurisdiction at the expense of Church tribunals and of the courts of feudal lords.

Henry's efforts to control the clergy led to one of the epic clashes of the investiture struggle. The archbishop of Canterbury, Thomas à Becket (ca. 1118–1170), although a personal friend of Henry, refused to accept the king's claim to jurisdiction over clergy. For six years, Becket lived in exile on the Continent and infuriated Henry by his stubborn adherence to the letter of Church law. He was allowed to return to England in 1170, but that same year he was struck down in his own cathedral by four knights eager for royal favor. The king did penance but, unlike the German emperors, ultimately preserved royal authority over the English Church.

Henry's program to assert royal courts over local and feudal ones was even more successful, laying the foundation for a system of uniform judicial procedures throughout the kingdom: the common law. In France, royal agents observed local legal traditions but sought always to turn them to the king's advantage. In contrast, Henry's legal system simplified and cut through the complex tangle of local and feudal jurisdictions concerning land law. Any free person could purchase, for a modest price, a letter, or writ, from the king ordering the local sheriff to impanel a jury to determine whether that person had been recently dispossessed of an estate, regardless of that person's legal right to the property. The procedure was swift and efficient. If the jury found for the plaintiff, the sheriff immediately restored the property, by force if necessary. While juries may not have meted out justice, they did resolve conflicts, and they did so in a way that protected landholders. These writs became enormously successful and expanded the jurisdiction of royal courts.

Henry's son John may have made the greatest contribution to the development of the English state by losing Normandy and most of his other continental lands. Loss of these territories forced English kings to concentrate on ruling England, not on their continental territories. Moreover, John's financial difficulties, brought about by his unsuccessful wars to recover his continental holdings, led him to such extremes of fiscal extortion that his barons, prelates, and the townspeople of London revolted. In June 1215 he was forced to accept the "great charter of liberties," or *Magna Carta,* a conservative feudal document demanding that he respect the rights of his vassals and of the burghers of London. The great significance of the document was its acknowledgment that the king was not above the law.

John and his weak, ineffective son Henry III (1216–1272), although ably served by royal judges, were forced by their failures to cede considerable influence to the great barons of the realm. Henry's son Edward I (1272–1307), a strong and effective king who conquered Wales, defended the remaining continental possessions against France, and expanded the common law, found that he could turn baronial involvement in government to his own advantage. By summoning his barons, bishops, and representatives of the towns and shires to participate in a "parley," or "parliament," he could raise more funds for his wars. Like similar Spanish, Hungarian, and German assemblies of the thirteenth century, these assemblies were occasions to consult, to present royal programs, and to extract extraordinary taxes for specific projects. They were also opportunities for those who were summoned to petition the king for redress of grievances. However, since the growing wealth of the towns and countryside made their financial support essential, these groups came to anticipate that they had a right to be consulted and to consent to taxation.

Through a system of royal courts and justices employing local juries and a tradition of representative parliaments, this forced self-government, coupled with an exacting system of accounting, increased the power of the English monarchy. By 1300, France, with its powerful royal bureaucracy, and England, with its courts and accountants, were the most powerful states in the West.

Conclusion

BY 1300, EUROPE HAD ACHIEVED A LEVEL OF POPULATION DENSITY, economic prosperity, cultural sophistication, and political organization greater than at any time since the Roman Empire. Across Europe a largely free peasantry cultivated a wide variety of crops, both for local consumption and for growing commercial markets, while landlords sought increasingly rational approaches to estate management and investment. In cities and ports, merchants, manufacturers, and bankers presided over an international commercial and manufacturing economy that connected Scandinavia to the Mediterranean Sea. In schools and universities, students learned the skills of logical thinking and disputation while absorbing the traditions of Greece and Rome in order to prepare themselves for careers in law, medicine, and government. In courts and palaces, nascent bureaucracies worked to expand the rule of law over recalcitrant nobles, to keep the peace, and to preserve justice. Finally, after almost a thousand years of political, economic, and intellectual isolation, western Europe had become once more a dominant force in world civilization.

QUESTIONS FOR REVIEW

1. How did the different social roles of peasants, knights, and clergymen interact and complement each other?
2. In what ways did life in the urban world pose a threat to the values and priorities of aristocrats and churchmen?
3. How were the pope and the emperor both dependent on each other and in conflict?
4. Why would Europe's medieval kings ultimately be more successful than the emperor or the papacy in establishing strong, centralized states?

DISCOVERING WESTERN CIVILIZATION ONLINE

You can obtain more information about the High Middle Ages at the websites listed below. See also the companion website that accompanies this text: www.ablongman.com/kishlansky, which contains an online study guide and additional resources.

General Websites

www.georgetown.edu/labyrinth/subjects/women/women.html
Links to resources on medieval women.

www.fordham.edu/halsall/medweb/
Professor Paul Halsall's links to the medieval world.

The Countryside

www.castlesontheweb.com/
An entire website dedicated to castles, abbeys, and medieval churches.

Medieval Towns

www.dur.ac.uk/~dla0www/c_tour/tour.html
A virtual tour of Durham's cathedral.

www.philippe-auguste.com/uk/index.html
A site featuring medieval Paris at the end of the twelfth century.

geocities.com/Athens/Academy/8636/Toledo.html
A site devoted to the city of Toledo in the Middle Ages with an emphasis on its Jewish history links to other related Spanish sites.

The Invention of the State

philae.sas.upenn.edu/French/caroly.html
A hypertext site devoted to Capetian France (in French).

www.georgetown.edu/labyrinth/subjects/british_isles/england/england.html
Labyrinth links to medieval English history and civilization.

http://www.erlangerhistorikerseite.de/ma_fenster.html
Links to medieval Germany sites (in German).

SUGGESTIONS FOR FURTHER READING

The Countryside

Frederic Cheyette, *Ermengard of Narbonne* (Ithaca: Cornell University Press, 2001). An evocative account of Provençal society in the eleventh and twelfth centuries.

Georges Duby, *The Knight, the Lady, and the Priest: The Making of Modern Marriage in Medieval France* (New York: Pantheon, 1984). A short study of the conflict between lay and religious social values in medieval France.

Richard W. Kauper, *Chivalry and Violence in Medieval Europe* (Oxford: Oxford University Press, 2001). A comprehensive look at the relationship between chivalry and medieval violence.

Jonathan Riley-Smith, ed., *The Oxford Illustrated History of the Crusades* (Oxford: Oxford University Press, 2001). A comprehensive, collectively authored introduction to Crusade history.

Medieval Towns

Hilde de Ridder-Symoens, ed., *A History of the University in Europe, Vol. 1: Universities in the Middle Ages* (Cambridge: Cambridge University Press, 1991). A multi-authored comprehensive history of medieval universities to 1500.

Barbara A. Hanawalt and Kathryn L. Reuerson, eds., *City and Spectacle in Medieval Europe* (Minneapolis: University of Minnesota Press, 1994). Essays on urban ritual and culture in the Middle Ages.

Robert S. Lopez, *The Commercial Revolution of the Middle Ages, 950–1350* (New York: Cambridge University Press, 1971). An excellent survey of medieval commercial history.

Joseph H. Lynch, *The Medieval Church: A Brief History* (London and New York: Longman, 1992). A short introduction to medieval Church history.

David Nicholas, *The Growth of the Medieval City* (New York: Addison-Wesley Longman, 1997). A survey of the diversity of medieval urban development from late antiquity to the 1330s.

The Invention of the State

Thomas N. Bisson, ed., *Cultures of Power: Lordship, Status, and Process in Twelfth-Century Europe* (Philadelphia: University of Philadelphia Press, 1995). Important collection of essays on medieval lordship.

M. T. Clanchy, *England and Its Rulers, 1066–1272* (New York: B & N Imports, 1983). A good survey of English political history.

Horst Fuhrmann, *Germany in the High Middle Ages, c. 1050–1200* (New York: Cambridge University Press, 1986). A fresh synthesis of German history by a leading German historian.

Bernard F. Reilly, *The Medieval Spains* (Cambridge: Cambridge University Press, 1993). Comprehensive survey of the social, political, and cultural history of the medieval Iberian peninsula.

Joseph R. Strayer, *On the Medieval Origins of the Modern State* (Princeton, N.J.: Princeton University Press, 1970). A very brief but imaginative account of medieval statecraft by a leading French institutional historian.

10

THE LATER MIDDLE AGES, 1300–1500

- THE VISUAL RECORD: Webs of Stone and Blood
- POLITICS AS A FAMILY AFFAIR

- LIFE AND DEATH IN THE LATER MIDDLE AGES
- THE SPIRIT OF THE LATER MIDDLE AGES

THE VISUAL RECORD

WEBS OF STONE AND BLOOD

LIKE A DELICATE BASKET OF WOVEN STONE, the Gothic vaulting in the choir of Saint Vitus Cathedral in Prague encloses and unifies the sacred space over which it floats. In a similar manner, the great aristocratic families of the fourteenth and fifteenth centuries spun webs of estates, hereditary principalities, and fiefs across Europe. In art as in life, dynamic individuals reshaped the legacy of the past into new and unexpected forms.

In France, where Gothic architecture originated in the twelfth century, architects had long used stone springers and vaults, but only to emphasize verticality and lift the eyes of the faithful to the heavens. Through the thirteenth and fourteenth centuries, French architects vied with one another to raise their vaults ever higher but never rethought the basic premise of their design. Peter Parler (1330–1399), the architect of Saint Vitus, approached the design of his cathedral in a novel way. He used intersecting vaults not simply for height but to bind together the interior space of the edifice in a net of intersecting stone arches. This ability to rethink the architectural heritage of the past marked Peter Parler as the greatest architectural genius of the fourteenth century. Emperor Charles IV (1355–1378), the head of the most successful web-spinning aristocratic family of the late Middle Ages, recognized Parler's talent and enlisted him in making the Bohemian capital one of the most splendid cities of Europe.

Along with his innovations in architecture, Peter Parler also opened new directions in sculpture. Again breaking with French tradition, in which sculptors sought to present their subjects as ideal types, Parler concentrated on realism and individual portraiture in his work. The carved heads of Bohemia's kings, queens, prelates, and princes that peer down from the ambulatory of Saint Vitus are real people with their blemishes, their virtues, and their vices marked in their faces. Parler's own portrait bust also appears among those of kings and queens.

Parler was 23 when Charles IV, then king of Bohemia and soon to be Holy Roman Emperor, invited him to complete his great Prague cathedral, which had been begun by a French architect and modeled on the great cathedrals of France. With Charles's patronage, Parler modified the building program to incorporate his original vision of architecture and portraiture. He went on to direct the construction of churches, bridges, and towers in Prague and throughout Bohemia. Within a generation, Parler's students had spread his refinement of Gothic architecture and sculpture throughout the Holy Roman Empire. Parler, the weaver of stone, and Charles, the weaver of politics, were emblematic of their age.

LOOKING AHEAD

This chapter explores the tensions, crises, and creativity of Parler's age. It examines the rise of Central Europe as a central stage of cultural and political action, follows the disasters of the Hundred Years' War, the Black Death, and the Great Schism, and reviews the religious, artistic, and literary creativity of the later Middle Ages.

POLITICS AS A FAMILY AFFAIR

Like those of his architect, Charles's roots were in the Rhineland and his cultural inspiration was in France. The ancestral estates of his family, the house of Luxembourg, lay on the banks of the Moselle River. Between 1250 and 1350, the Luxembourg family greatly expanded its political and geographical powers by involving itself in the dynastic politics of the decaying Holy Roman Empire. During the fourteenth century, Charles of Luxembourg (later Emperor Charles IV) controlled a patchwork of lands that included Luxembourg, Brabant, Lusatia, Silesia, Moravia, Meissen, and Brandenburg. His daughter married Richard II of England. A son succeeded him as king of Bohemia, and another obtained the Hungarian crown.

Such fragmented and shifting territorial bases were typical of the great families of the fourteenth and fifteenth centuries. Everywhere, family politics threatened the fragile institutional developments of the thirteenth century, but this was especially true in the empire. Aristocrats competed for personal power and used public office, military command, and taxing power for private ends. What mattered was neither territorial boundaries nor political divisions but marriage alliances, kinship, and dynastic ambitions.

The Struggle for Central Europe

In addition to the Luxembourgs, four other similarly ambitious families competed for dominance in the empire. First were the Wittelsbachs, the Luxembourgs' chief competitors. The Wittelsbachs had originated in Bavaria but had since spread across Europe. In the west the Wittelsbachs had acquired Holland, Hainaut, and Frisia; in the east they temporarily held Tyrol and Brandenburg. Next were the Habsburgs, allies of the Luxembourgs, who had begun as a minor comitial family in the region of the Black Forest. They expanded eastward, acquiring Austria, Tyrol, Carinthia, and Carniola. When Rudolf I of Habsburg (1273–1291) was elected emperor in 1273, Otakar II, king of Bohemia (1253–1278) and head of the powerful Premysl family, dismissed Rudolf as "poor." Compared with the Premysls, perhaps he was. At its height, the Premysl family controlled not only Bohemia but also Moravia, Austria, and a miscellany of lands stretching from Silesia in the north to the Adriatic Sea. Finally, the house of Anjou, descendants of Charles of Anjou, the younger brother of the French king Louis IX, who had become king of Naples, created a similar eastern network. Charles's son Charles Robert secured election as king of Hungary in 1310. His son Louis (1342–1382) added the crown of Poland (1370–1382) to the Hungarian crown of Saint Stephen. The protracted wars and maneuvers that these families conducted for dominance in the empire resembled nothing so much as the competition that had taken place three centuries earlier for dominance in feudal France.

Eastern Expansion. For over a century, not only great princes but also monks, adventurers, and simple peasants streamed into the kingdoms and principalities of eastern Europe. Since the early thirteenth century, the Teutonic orders had used the sword to spread Christianity along the Baltic coast. By the early fourteenth century, these knight-monks had conquered Prussia and the coast as far east as the Narva River, now well within Russia, where they reached the borders of the Christian principality of Novgorod. The pagan inhabitants of these regions had to choose between conversion and expulsion. When they fled, their fields were turned over to land-hungry German peasants. Long wagon trains of pioneers snaked their way across Germany from the Rhineland, Westphalia, and Saxony to this new frontier. There they were able to negotiate advantageous contracts with their new lords, guaranteeing them greater freedom than they had known at home.

By the fifteenth century, religious and secular German lords had established a new agrarian economy, modeled on western European estates, in regions that were previously unoccupied or sparsely settled by the indigenous Slavic peoples. This economy specialized in the cultivation of grain for export to the west. Each fall, fleets of hundreds of ships sailed from Gdansk and Riga to the ports of the Netherlands, England, and France. Returning flotillas carried Flemish cloth and tons of salt, for preserving food, as far as Novgorod. The influx of Baltic grain into Europe caused a decline in domestic grain prices and a corresponding economic slump for landlords throughout the fourteenth and fifteenth centuries.

Central European Kingdoms. Farther south, the Christian kingdoms of Poland, Bohemia, and Hungary beckoned different sorts of westerners. Newly opened silver and copper mines in Bohemia, Silesia, southern Poland, and Hungarian Transylvania needed skilled miners, smelters, and artisans. Many were recruited from the overpopulated regions of western Germany. East-west trade routes developed to export these metals, giving new life to the Bohemian towns of Prague and Brno, the Polish cities of Kraków and Lwów, and Hungarian Buda and Bratislava. Trade networks reached south to the Mediterranean via Vienna, the Brenner Pass, and Venice. To the north, trade routes extended to the Elbe River and the trading towns of Lübeck and Bremen. The Bavarian towns of Augsburg, Rothenburg, and Nuremberg flourished at the western end of this network. To the east, Lwów became a trading center connecting southern Russia with the west.

The wealth of eastern Europe, its abundant land, and its relative freedom attracted both peasants and merchants. The promise of profitable marriages with eastern royalty

▲ Central and Eastern Europe, ca. 1378. In the fourteenth century, Europe was dominated by rival dynasties holding far-flung territories.

drew ambitious aristocrats. Continually menaced by one another and by the aggressive German aristocracy to the west, the royal families of Poland, Hungary, and Bohemia were eager to make marriage alliances with powerful aristocratic families from farther afield. Through such a marriage, for example, Charles Robert of Anjou became king of Hungary after the extinction of that realm's ancient royal dynasty. Similarly, Charles Robert's son Louis inherited the Polish crown in 1370 after the death of Casimir III, the last king of the Polish Piast dynasty. Nobles of the eastern European kingdoms were pleased to confirm the election of such outsiders. The elections prevented powerful German nobles from claiming succession to the Bohemian, Hungarian, and Polish thrones. At the same time, the families of the western European aristocracy did not have sufficiently strong local power bases to challenge the autonomy of the eastern nobility.

Charles IV (1347–1378) was typical of these restless dynasts. His grandfather, Emperor Henry VII (1308–1313), had arranged for his son John of Luxembourg to marry Elizabeth (d. 1330), the Premysl heiress of Bohemia, and thus acquire the Bohemian crown in 1310. John was king in name only. He spent most of his career fighting in the dynastic wars of the empire and of France. However, by mastering the intricate politics of the decaying Holy Roman Empire, he arranged the deposition of the Wittelsbach emperor Louis IV (1314–1347) and secured the election of Charles as king of the Romans, that is, heir of the empire, in 1346. The following year the Bohemian crown passed to Charles.

Although born in Prague, Charles had spent most of his youth in France, where he was deeply influenced by French culture. On his return to Prague in 1333, however, he rediscovered his Czech cultural roots. As king of

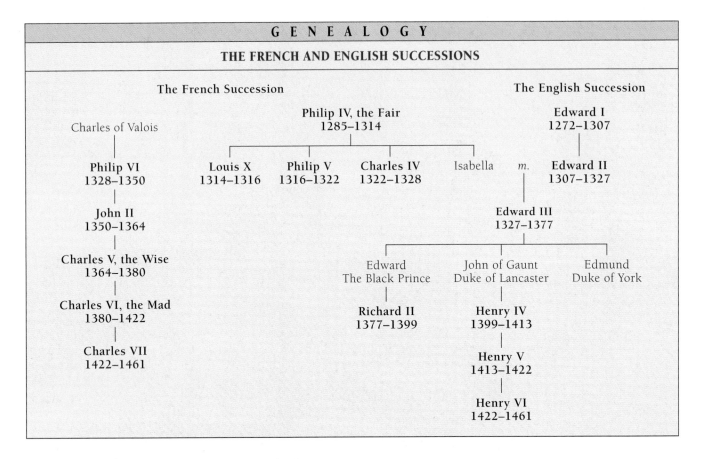

Bohemia, he worked to make Prague a cultural center by combining French and Czech traditions. He imported artisans, architects, and artists to transform and beautify his capital. In 1348 he founded a university in Prague, the first in the empire, modeled on the University of Paris. Keenly interested in history, Charles provided court historians with the sources necessary to write their histories of the Bohemian kingdom.

Charles took a more active role in this cultural renewal than perhaps any European king since Alfred of England, fostering a literary renaissance in both Latin and Czech. Although he had forgotten his native Czech during his long stay in France, he soon learned to read and write it as well as French, German, Italian, and Latin. He authored a number of religious texts, fostered the use of the Czech language in religious services, and initiated a Czech translation of the Bible. He even composed his own autobiography, perhaps the first lay person to do so in medieval Europe.

The effects of Charles's cultural policies were far-reaching—but in directions he never anticipated. His interests in Czech culture and religious reform bore unexpected fruit during the reign of his son Sigismund, king of Germany (1410–1437), Bohemia (1419–1437), and Hungary (1387–1437) and Holy Roman Emperor (1433–1437). During Sigismund's reign, Czech religious and political reformers came into open conflict with the

powerful German-speaking minority at the University of Prague. Led by the theologian Jan Hus (ca. 1372–1415), this reform movement ultimately challenged the authority of the Roman Church and became the direct predecessor of the great Reformation of the sixteenth century.

Even while building up his beloved city of Prague, Charles was dismantling the Holy Roman Empire. By the fourteenth century, the title of emperor held little political importance, although as an honorific title it was still bitterly contested by the great families of the empire. Charles sought to end such disputes and at the same time to solidify the autonomy of the kingdoms such as Bohemia against the threats of future imperial candidates. In 1356 he issued the "Golden Bull," an edict that officially recognized what had long been the reality, namely, that the various German princes and kings were autonomous rulers. The bull also established the procedure by which future emperors would be elected. Thereafter, the emperor was chosen by seven great princes of the empire without the consultation or interference of the pope—a tradition of interference that dated to the coronation of Charlemagne. The procedure made disputed elections less likely, but it acknowledged that the office itself was less significant.

The same process that sapped the power of the emperor also reduced the significance of the princes. The empire fragmented into a number of large kingdoms and duchies such as Bohemia, Hungary, Poland, Austria, and Bavaria in the east and over 1,600 autonomous principalities, free towns, and sovereign bishoprics in the west. The inhabitants of these territories, often ruled by foreigners who had inherited sovereign powers through marriage, organized themselves into estates—political units of knights, burghers, and clergy—to present a united front in dealing with their prince. The princes, in turn, did not enjoy any universally recognized right to rule and were forced to negotiate with their estates for any powers they actually enjoyed.

The disintegration of the empire left political power east of the Rhine widely dispersed for over 500 years. While this meant that Germany did not become a nation-state until the nineteenth century, decentralization left late medieval Germany as a fertile region of cultural and constitutional creativity. In this creative process, the office of emperor played no role. After the Habsburg family definitively acquired the imperial office in 1440, the office of emperor ceased to have any role in Germany. Rather, the office became one of the building blocks of the great multinational Habsburg empire of central Europe, an empire that survived until 1918.

A Hundred Years of War

The political map of western Europe was no less a patchwork quilt of family holdings than was the empire. In the Iberian Peninsula, power struggles and futile wars engaged the three Christian monarchies of Castile, Aragon, and Portugal. Only with the marriage of Ferdinand of Aragon and Isabella of Castile in 1469 did something like a unified Spain begin to emerge from this world of family rivalries.

Similar struggles threatened to overwhelm the feudal monarchies of France and England in the fourteenth and fifteenth centuries. In both kingdoms, weakening economic climates and demographic catastrophe exacerbated dynastic crises and fierce competition.

Three long-simmering disputes triggered the series of campaigns collectively termed the Hundred Years' War. The first issue was conflicting rights in Gascony in southern France. Since the mid-thirteenth century, the kings of England had held Gascony as a fief of the French king. Neither monarchy was content with this arrangement, and for the next 75 years, kings quarreled constantly over sovereignty in the region.

The second point of contention was the close relationship between England and the Flemish cloth towns, which were the primary customers for English wool. Early in the fourteenth century, Flemish artisans rose up in a series of bloody revolts against the aristocratic cloth dealers who had long monopolized power. The count of Flanders and the French king supported the wealthy merchants; the English sided with the artisans.

The third dispute concerned the royal succession in France. Charles IV (1322–1328), the son of Philip IV, the Fair, died without an heir. The closest descendant of a French king was the grandson of Philip the Fair, King Edward III of England (1327–1377). However, Edward was the son of Philip's daughter Isabella. The French aristocracy, which did not want an English king to inherit the throne and unite the two kingdoms, pretended that according to ancient Frankish law, the crown could not pass through a woman. Instead, they preferred to give the crown to a cousin of the late king, Philip VI (1328–1350), who became the first of the Valois kings of France. At first, the English voiced no objection to Philip's accession, but in 1337, when the dispute over Gascony again flared up and Philip attempted to confiscate the region from his English "vassal" Edward III, the English king declared war on Philip. Edward's stated goal was not only to recover Gascony but also to claim the crown of his maternal grandfather.

Chivalry and Warfare.   Though territorial and dynastic rivalries were the triggers that set off the war, its deeper cause was chivalry. The elites of Europe were both inspired by and trapped in a code of conduct that required them not only to maintain their honor by violence but also to cultivate violence to increase that honor. This code had been appropriate in a period of weak kingship, but by the late thirteenth century the growth of courts and royal power in France and in England left little room for private vengeance and vendettas. Nobles were now more often royal retainers than knights errant traveling about the countryside righting wrongs. Government was increasingly an affair of lawyers and bureaucrats, war an affair of professionals. Yet kings and nobles alike still agreed with the sentiment expressed by a contemporary poet: "The glory of princes is in their pride and in undertaking great peril." By the fourteenth century, only war provided sufficient peril.

Edward III of England and his rival Philip VI of France both epitomized the chivalrous knight. Both gloried in luxurious living and conspicuous consumption. Captivated by the romantic tales of King Arthur and the Round Table, in 1344 Edward organized a four-day-long round table celebration at which he entertained the most outstanding nobles in England with jousting contests, minstrels, and expensive gifts. A few years later, Edward organized the Order of the Garter, a select group of nobles who were to embody the highest qualities of chivalry. For a ruler like Edward, obsessed with knightly glory, war with France was the ideal way to win honor and fame.

In spite of his chivalric ideals, Edward was practical when it came to organizing and financing his campaigns. Philip shared Edward's ideals but lacked his rival's practicality and self-assurance. Before his elevation to the throne, Philip had been a valiant and successful warrior, fond of jousting, tournaments, and lavish celebrations. After his coronation he continued to act like a figure from a knightly romance, surrounding himself with aristocratic advisers who formed the most brilliant court of Europe, dispensing the royal treasure to his favorites, and dreaming of leading a great crusade to free the Holy Land. However, as the first French king in centuries who was elected rather than born into the right of succession, he treated the magnates from whose ranks he had come with excessive deference. He hesitated to press them for funds and deferred to them on matters of policy even while missing opportunities to raise other revenue from towns and merchants. Finally, although a competent warrior, Philip was no match in strategy or tactics for his English cousin.

Still, the sheer size and wealth of France should have made it the favorite in any war with England. Its population of roughly 16 million made it by far the largest and most densely populated kingdom in Europe. It was a major producer of cereal, wines, and cloth. The Flemish cloth towns, subdued by Philip in 1328, were the most industrialized area of Europe. England, by contrast, was a small, sparsely populated kingdom of under 5 million, and its economy was much less tied into international trade.

At the start of the war, Philip could rely on an income roughly three to five times greater than that of Edward. His greater income was matched by greater expenses, however, and he had no easy way to raise extraordinary funds for war. In contrast, the English king could use Parliament as an efficient source of war subsidies. Edward could also extract great sums from taxes on England's wool exports. Even after the invasion of France, Philip had to resort to manipulation of the coinage, confiscation of Italian bankers' property, and a whole range of nuisance taxes to finance his campaigns.

War was expensive. In spite of chivalrous ideals, nobles no longer fought as vassals of the king but as highly paid mercenaries. The nature of this service differed greatly on the two sides of the Channel. In France, the tactics and personnel had changed little since the twelfth century. The core of any army was the body of heavily armored nobles who rode into battle with their lords, supported by lightly armored knights. Behind them marched infantrymen recruited from towns and armed with pikes. Although the French also hired mercenary Italian crossbowmen, the nobles despised them and never used them effectively.

In contrast, centuries of fighting against Welsh and Scottish enemies had sharpened the English armies and their tactics. The great nobles continued to serve as heavily armored horsemen, but professional companies of foot soldiers raised by individual knights made up the bulk of the army. These professional companies consisted largely of pikemen and, most important, longbowmen. Although it was not as accurate as the crossbow, the English longbow had a greater range. Moreover, when massed archers fired volleys of arrows into enemy ranks, they proved extremely effective against enemy pikemen and even lightly armored cavalry.

English Successes. The first real test of the two armies came at the Battle of Crécy in 1346. When an overwhelmingly superior French force advanced against the English army, the English massed their archers on a hill and rained arrows down on the French cavalry, which attacked in a glorious but suicidal manner. The English victory was total. By midnight they had repelled 16 assaults, losing only 100 men while killing over 3,000 French. The survivors, including Philip VI, fled in disorder. Strangely enough, the French learned nothing from the debacle. In 1356, Philip's successor John II (1350–1364) rashly attacked an English army at Poitiers and was captured. In 1415, the French blundered in a different way at Agincourt. This time, most of the heavily armored French knights dismounted and attempted to charge the elevated English position across a muddy field. Barely able to walk and unable to rise if they fell, all were captured. Out of fear that his numerically inferior army would be overwhelmed if the French recovered their breath, the English king ordered over 1,500 French nobles and 3,000 ordinary soldiers killed. English losses were fewer than 100.

Pitched battles were not the worst defeats for the French. More devastating were the constant raiding and systematic destruction of the French countryside by the English companies. The relief effort launched by Pope Benedict XII (1334–1342) in 1339 gives some idea of the scale of destruction. Papal agents, sent to aid victims of the English invasion, paid out over 12,000 pounds—the equivalent of one-third of the English annual royal income—to peasants in just one region of northern France.

Raiding and pillaging continued for decades, even during long truces between the French and English kings. During periods of truce, unemployed free companies of French and English mercenaries roamed the countryside, supporting themselves by banditry while awaiting the renewal of more formal hostilities. Never had the ideals of chivalric conduct been so far distant from the brutal realities of warfare.

The French kings were powerless to prevent such destruction, just as they were unable to defeat the enemy in open battle. Since the kings were incapable of protecting their subjects or winning in battle, the "silken thread binding together the kingdom of France," as one observer put it, began to unravel, and the kingdom that had been so painstakingly constructed by the Capetian monarchs began to fall apart. Not only did the English make significant territorial conquests, but the French nobles began behaving much like those in the Holy Roman Empire, carving out autonomous lordships. Private warfare and castle building, never entirely eradicated even by Louis IX and Philip IV, increased as royal government lost its ability to control the nobility. Whole regions of the kingdom slipped entirely from royal authority. Duke Philip the Good of Burgundy (1396–1467) allied himself with England against France and profited from the war to form a far-flung lordship that included Flanders, Brabant, Luxembourg, and Hainaut. By the time of his death, he was the most powerful ruler in Europe. Much of the so-called Hundred Years' War was actually a French civil war.

The battle of Agincourt (1415) was one of the great battles of the Hundred Years' War. The heavily armored French cavalry met defeat at the hands of a much smaller force of disciplined English pikemen and longbowmen.

During this century of war, the French economy suffered even more than the French state. Trade routes were broken, and commerce declined as credit disappeared. French kings repeatedly seized the assets of Italian merchant bankers in order to finance the war. Such actions made the Italians, who had been the backbone of French commercial credit, extremely wary about extending loans in the kingdom. The kings then turned to French and Flemish merchants, extorting from them forced loans that dried up capital that might otherwise have been returned to commerce and industry. Politically and economically, France seemed doomed.

Joan of Arc and the Salvation of France.   The flower of French chivalry did not save France. Instead, at the darkest moment of the long and bloody struggle, salvation came at the hands of a simple peasant girl from the county of Champagne. By 1429, the English and their Burgundian allies held virtually all of northern France, including Paris. Now they were besieging Orléans, the key to the south. The heir to the French throne, the dauphin, was the weak-willed and uncrowned Charles VII (1422–1461). To him came Joan of Arc (1412–1431), an illiterate but deeply religious girl who bore an incredible message of hope. She claimed to have heard the voices of saints ordering her to save Orléans and have the dauphin crowned according to tradition at Reims.

Charles and his advisers were more than skeptical about this brash peasant girl who announced her divinely ordained mission to save France. Finally convinced of her sincerity, if not of her ability, Charles allowed her to accompany a relief force to Orléans. The French army, its spirit buoyed by the belief that Joan's simple faith was the work of God, defeated the English and ended the siege. This victory led to others, and on 16 July 1429, Charles was crowned king at Reims.

After the coronation, Joan's luck began to fade. She failed to take Paris, and in 1431 she was captured by the Burgundians, who sold her to the English. Eager to get rid of the troublesome girl, the English had her tried as a heretic. Charles made no move to save her, even though she had saved his kingdom. She was burned at the stake in Rouen on 30 May 1431.

Despite Joan's inglorious end, the tide had turned. The French pushed the English back toward the coast. In the final major battle of the war, fought at Formigny in 1450, the French used a new and telling weapon to defeat the English: gunpowder. Rather than charging the English directly, as they had done so often before, they mounted cannon and pounded the English to bits. Gunpowder completed the destruction of the chivalric traditions of warfare begun by archers and pikemen. By 1452, English continental holdings had been reduced to the town of Calais. The continental warfare of more than a century was over.

The English Wars of the Roses.   Though war on the Continent had ended, warfare in England was just beginning. In some ways, the English monarchy had suffered even more from the Hundred Years' War than had the French. At the outset, English royal administration had been more advanced than that of the French. The system of royal agents, courts, and parliaments had created the expectation that the king could preserve peace and provide justice at home while waging successful and profitable wars abroad. As the decades dragged on without a decisive victory, the king came to rely on the aristocracy, enlisting its financial assistance by granting these magnates greater power at home.

War created powerful and autonomous aristocratic families with their own armies. Under a series of weak kings these families fought among themselves. Ultimately, they took sides in a civil war to determine the royal succession. For 30 years, from 1455 to 1485, supporters of the house of York, whose badge was the white rose, fought the rival house of Lancaster, whose symbol was the red rose. The

English Wars of the Roses, as the conflict came to be called, finally ended in 1485, when Henry Tudor of the Lancastrian faction defeated his opponents. He inaugurated a new era as Henry VII (1485–1509), the first king of the Tudor dynasty.

LIFE AND DEATH IN THE LATER MIDDLE AGES

The violence and pageantry of late medieval life played out against a backdrop of extraordinary social upheaval. By the end of the thirteenth century, population growth in the West had strained available resources to the breaking point. All arable land was under cultivation, and even marginal moorland, rocky mountainsides, and plains were being pressed into service to feed a growing population. At the same time, kings and nobles demanded ever higher taxes and rents to finance their wars and extravagant lifestyles. The result was a precarious balance in which a late frost, a bad harvest, or hungry mercenaries could mean disaster. Part of the problem could be alleviated by importing grain from the Baltic or from Sicily, but this solution carried risks of its own. Transportation systems were too fragile to ensure regular supplies, and their rupture could initiate a cycle of famine, disease, and demographic collapse. Population began to decline slowly

▼ Spread of the Black Death. Spread by merchants and travelers, the plague killed more than a third of Europe's population within five years.

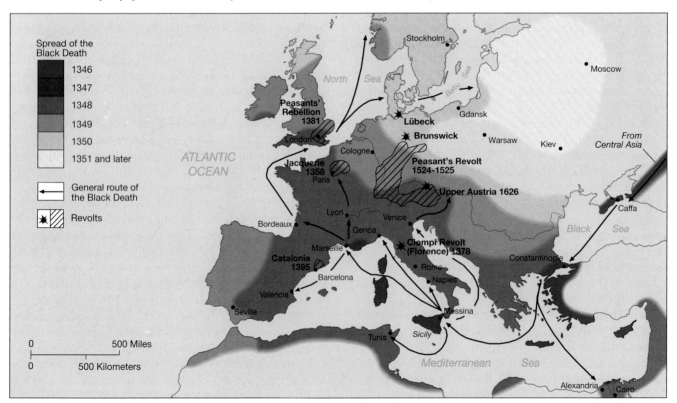

around 1300, and the downturn became catastrophic within 50 years. Between 1300 and 1450, Europe's population fell by more than 30 percent. It did not recover until the seventeenth century.

Dancing with Death

Between 1315 and 1317, the first great famine of the fourteenth century, triggered by crop failures and war, struck Europe. People died by the thousands. Urban workers, because they were chronically undernourished, were particularly hard hit. In the Flemish cloth town of Ypres, whose total population was less than 20,000, the town ordered the burial of 2,794 paupers' corpses within a five-month period. Although this was the greatest famine in medieval memory, it was not the last. The relatively prosperous Italian city of Pistoria, for example, recorded 16 different famines and food shortages in the fourteenth and fifteenth centuries. Disease accompanied famine. Crowded and filthy towns, opposing armies with their massed troops, and overpopulated countrysides provided fertile ground for the spread of infectious disease. Moreover, the greatly expanded trade routes of the thirteenth and fourteenth centuries, which carried goods and grain between East and West, also provided highways for deadly microbes. At Pistoria again, local chroniclers of the fourteenth and fifteenth centuries reported 14 years of sickness, fevers, epidemic, and plague.

Between 1347 and 1352, from one-half to one-third of Europe's population died from a virulent combination of bubonic, septicemic, and pneumonic plagues, known to history as the Black Death. The disease, carried by the fleas of infected rats, traveled the caravan routes from central Asia. It arrived in Messina, Sicily, aboard a merchant vessel in October 1347. From there the Black Death spread up the boot of Italy and then into southern France, England, and Spain. By 1349 it had reached northern Germany, Portugal, and Ireland. The following year the Low Countries, Scotland, Scandinavia, and Russia fell victim.

Plague victims died horribly. Soon after being bitten by an infected flea, they developed high fever, began coughing, and suffered excruciatingly painful swellings in the lymph nodes of the groin or armpits. These swellings were known as *buboes,* from which the disease took its name. In the final stages the victims began to vomit blood. The bubonic form of the disease usually killed within five days. The septicemic form, which attacked the blood, was swifter and deadlier. People infected by the airborne pneumonic form usually died in less than three days—in some cases, within a matter of hours.

Plague was all the more terrifying because its cause, its manner of transmission, and its cure were totally unknown until the end of the nineteenth century. Preachers saw the plague as divine punishment for sin. Ordinary people frequently accused Jews of causing it by poisoning drinking water. The medical faculty of Paris announced that it was the result of the conjunction of the planets Saturn, Jupiter, and Mars, which caused a corruption of the surrounding air.

Responses to the plague were equally varied. In many German towns, terrified Christian citizens looked for outside scapegoats and slaughtered the Jewish community. Cities, aware of the risk of infection although ignorant of its process, closed their gates and turned away outsiders. Individuals with means fled to country houses or locked themselves in their homes to avoid contact with others. Nothing worked. As devastating as the first outbreak of the plague was, its aftershocks were even more catastrophic. Once established in Europe, the disease continued to return roughly once each generation. The last outbreak of the plague in Europe was the 1771 epidemic in Moscow that killed 60,000.

The Black Death, along with other epidemics, famines, and war-induced shortages, affected western Europe much more than eastern Europe. The culminating effect of these disasters was a darker, more somber vision of life than that of the previous centuries. This vision found its expression in the Dance of Death, an increasingly popular image in art. Naked, rotting corpses dance with great animation before the living. The latter, depicted in the dress of all social orders, are immobile, surprised by death, reluctant but resigned.

Although no solid statistics exist from the fourteenth century, the plague certainly killed more people than all of the wars and famines of the century. It was the greatest disaster ever to befall Europe. The Black Death touched every aspect of life, hastening a process of social, economic, and cultural transformation that was already under way. The initial outbreak shattered social and economic structures. Fields were abandoned, workplaces stood idle, international trade was suspended. Traditional bonds of kinship, village, and even religion were broken by the horrors of death, flight, and failed expectations. "People cared no more for dead men than we care for dead goats," wrote one survivor. Brothers abandoned brothers, wives deserted husbands, and terror-stricken parents refused to nurse their own children.

Nothing had prepared Europe for this catastrophe. No teaching of the Church or its leaders could adequately explain it, and in spite of desperate attempts to fix the blame on Jews or strangers, no one but God could be held responsible. Survivors stood alone and uncertain before a new world. Across Europe, moralists reported a general lapse in traditional ethics, a breakdown in the moral codes. The most troubling aspect of this breakdown was what one defender of the old order termed "the plague of insurrection" that spread across Europe. This plague was brought on by the dimming of the hopes held by the survivors of the Black Death.

► A page from the fourteenth-century psalter and prayer book of Bonne of Luxembourg, Duchess of Normandy. The three figures of the dead shown here contrast with three living figures on the facing page of the psalter to illustrate a moral fable.

The Plague of Insurrection

Initially, even this darkest cloud had a silver lining. Lucky survivors of the plague soon found other reasons to rejoice. Property owners, when they finished burying their dead, discovered that they were far richer in land and goods. At the other end of the social spectrum, the plague had eliminated the labor surplus. Peasants were suddenly in great demand. For a time, at least, they were able to negotiate substantially higher wages and an improved relationship with landlords.

These hopes were short lived. The rise in expectations produced by the redistribution of wealth and the labor shortage created new tensions. Landlords sought laws forcing peasants to accept pre-plague wages and tightened their control over serfs to prevent them from fleeing to cities or other lords. At the same time, governments attempted to benefit from laborers' greater prosperity by imposing new taxes. In cities, where the plague had been particularly devastating, the demographic decline sharply lowered demand for goods and thus lowered the need for manufacturing and production of all kinds. Like rural landowners, master craftsmen sought legislation to protect their incomes. New laws reduced production by restricting access to trades and increased masters' control over the surviving urban laborers. Social mobility, once a characteristic of urban life, slowed to a halt. Membership in guilds became hereditary, and young apprentices and journeymen had little hope of ever rising to the level of independent master craftsmen.

These new tensions led to violence when kings added their demands for new war taxes to the landlords' and masters' attempts to erase the peasants' and workers' recent gains. The first revolts took place in France, where peasants and townspeople, disgusted with the incompetence of the nobility in their conduct of the war against England, feared that their new wealth would be stolen from them by corrupt and incompetent aristocrats.

The Jacquerie. In 1358, to ransom King John II from the English, the French government attempted to increase taxes on the peasantry. At the same time, local nobles increased their rents and demands. Peasants in the area of Beauvais, north of Paris, fearing that they would lose their modest gains of the previous ten years, rebelled against their landlords. The revolt—known as the Jacquerie for the archetypical French peasant, Jacques Bonnehomme—was a spontaneous outburst directed against the nobility, whom the peasants saw as responsible for all their ills. Without real leadership or program, peasants attacked as many nobles as they could find, killing men, women, and children and burning their homes and castles. The peasants' brutality deeply shocked the upper classes, whose own violence was constrained within the bounds of the chivalric code. Because the Church largely supported the power structure, the uprising was also strongly anticlerical. Churches were burned, and priests were killed. Success bred further attacks, and the disorganized army of peasants began to march south toward Paris, killing, looting, and burning everything associated with the despised nobility.

In the midst of this peasant revolt, Etienne Marcel (ca. 1316–1358), a wealthy Parisian cloth merchant, led an uprising of Parisian merchants, which sought to take control of royal finances and force fiscal reforms on the dauphin, the future Charles V. Although initially the rebels were primarily members of the merchant and guild elite, Marcel soon enlisted the support of the radical townspeople against the aristocracy. He even made overtures to the leaders of the Jacquerie to join forces. For a brief time it appeared that the aristocratic order in France might succumb. However, in the end, peasant and merchant rebels were no match for professional armies. The Jacquerie met its end at Meaux, outside Paris, where an aristocratic force cut the peasants to pieces. Survivors were systematically hunted down and hanged or burned alive. The Parisian revolt met a similar fate. Aristocratic armies surrounded the city and cut off its food supply. Marcel was assassinated, and the dauphin Charles regained the city.

The English Peasants' Revolt and Urban Uprisings. The French revolts set the pattern for similar uprisings across Europe. Rebels were usually relatively prosperous peasants or townspeople whose economic situations were threatened by aristocratic attempts to turn back the clock to the period before the Black Death. In 1381, English peasants, reacting to new and hated taxes, rose in a less violent but more coordinated revolt known as the Great Rebellion. Peasant revolts took place in the northern Spanish region of Catalonia in 1395 and in Germany throughout the fourteenth and fifteenth centuries. The largest was the great Peasants' Revolt of 1524. Although always ruthlessly suppressed, European peasant uprisings continued until the peasant rebellion of 1626 in upper Austria. These outbursts indicated not necessarily the desperation of Europe's peasantry, but the new belief that they could change their lives for the better through united action.

Urban artisans imitated the example of their rural cousins. Although there had been some uprisings in the Flemish towns before the Black Death, revolts of townspeople picked up momentum in the second half of the fourteenth century. The town rebels were generally independent artisans and small tradesmen who wanted to break the control of the powerful guilds. The one exception to this pattern was the Ciompi revolt of 1378 in Florence, in which the wool workers forced recognition of two guilds of laborers alongside the powerful guilds of masters. The workers and artisans controlled city government until 1382, when mercenaries hired by the elite surrounded the workers' slums and crushed them in bloody house-to-house fighting. In spite of the brutal suppression and ultimate failure of popular revolts, they became permanent if intermittent features on the European social landscape. The legacy of the Jacquerie was seen 431 years later in the storming of the Bastille.

Living and Dying in Medieval Towns

Population decline, war, and class conflict in France and the Low Countries fatally weakened the vitality of the commercial and manufacturing system of northwestern Europe. These same events reduced the market for Italian goods and undermined the economic strength of the great Italian cities. The Hundred Years' War bankrupted many of Florence's greatest banking houses, such as the Bardi and Peruzzi, that lent to both French and English kings. Commercial activity declined as well. In the 1330s, Venice had sent between four and nine trading galleys to Flanders each year; by the 1390s the city was sending only three to five. Genoa, which had earlier led in the trade with the cloth towns of the north, saw the economic activity of its port decline by roughly one-third to one-half during the same period. While Italians did not disappear from northern cities, they no longer held a near monopoly on northern trade.

Economic Shifts. The setbacks of the Italians worked to the advantage of German towns in the disintegrating empire. Along the Baltic Sea, in Scandinavia, and in northern Germany, towns such as Lübeck, Lüneburg, Visby, Bremen, and Cologne formed a commercial and political alliance to control northern trade. During the second half of the fourteenth century this Hanseatic League—the word *Hansa* means "company"—monopolized the northern grain trade and forced Denmark to grant its members exclusive rights to export Scandinavian fish throughout Europe. Hanseatic merchants established colonies from Novgorod to London to Bruges and even Venice. They carried dried and salted fish to Prague and supplied grain from Riga to England and France.

English towns also profited from the decline of Flanders and France. The population decline of the fourteenth century led many English landowners to switch from traditional farming to sheep raising, since pasturing sheep required few workers and promised cash profits. While surviving peasants were driven off the land and forced to beg for a living, lords produced more wool than ever before. However, instead of exporting the wool to Flanders to be made into cloth, the English began to make cloth themselves. Protected by high tariffs on imports and low duties on exports, England had become a major exporter of finished cloth by the middle of the fifteenth century.

Poverty and Crime.   The new social and economic circumstances of European towns accentuated the gulf between rich and poor. The streets and markets of fifteenth-century towns bustled with the sights and sounds of rich

▼ Breaking on the wheel was a particularly gruesome punishment inflicted on condemned criminals during the later Middle Ages. The criminal's broken limbs are threaded through the spokes of the wheel and tied with ropes. The mocking executioner holding leftover rope stands at the right. To the left are three seemingly sympathetic spectators.

Hanseatic merchants, Italian bankers, and prosperous local tradesmen. The back alleys and squatter settlements on the edges of these towns teemed with a growing mass of desperate workers and their families. The combination of economic depression, plague, and rural crisis deepened the misery of the growing population of urban poor. Medieval towns responded by developing new means of public assistance and social control.

Traditionally, charity, whether by individuals or organizations, had been a religious act that focused more on the soul of the giver than on the life of the recipient. Hospitals, for example, were all-purpose religious institutions providing lodging for pilgrims, the elderly, and the ill. By the fourteenth century, such pious institutions had become inadequate to deal with the increasing numbers of poor and ill. Towns began to assume control over a centralized system of public assistance. Although men and women who had taken religious vows staffed these institutions, city governments contributed to their budgets and oversaw their finances. Cities also attempted to rationalize the distribution of charity according to need and merit. Antwerp, for example, established a centralized relief service, which distributed badges to those deemed worthy of public assistance. Only people who wore the badges could receive food.

One consequence of poverty was increased crime, which led to repressive measures and harsh punishments. Traditionally, in much of Europe, crimes such as robbery, larceny, and even manslaughter had been punishable by fines and payments to the victim or the victim's heirs. Elsewhere, as in France and England, where corporal punishment had been the normal penalty for major crimes, hanging, blinding, and the loss of a hand or foot had been the most common punishments. During the later Middle Ages, gruesome forms of mutilation and execution became common for a long list of offenses. Petty larceny was punished with whipping, cutting off ears or thumbs, branding, or expulsion. In some towns, robbery of an amount over three pence was punished with death. Death by hanging might be replaced by more savage punishments such as breaking on the wheel. In this particularly brutal torture, the prisoner's limbs and back were first broken with a wagon wheel. Then the criminal was tied to the wheel and left on a pole to die. Drowning, boiling, burning, and burial alive, a particularly common punishment for women, were other frequently used methods of execution.

The frequency of such punishments increased with their severity. In Augsburg, until the middle of the thirteenth century, executions were so rare that the city did not even have a public executioner before 1276. However, in the following two centuries the city fathers increased executions in an attempt to combat a rising crime rate. In 1452 the skulls of 250 hanged persons were found in pits on the gallows hill. At the same time, the bodies of 32 thieves twisted in the wind above.

THE SPIRIT OF THE LATER MIDDLE AGES

In spite of the constant presence of death, Europeans of the later Middle Ages celebrated life with vigor, creativity, and a growing sense of individuality and independence. During the fourteenth century, the Church failed to provide unified leadership. The institutional division of the Church was paralleled by divisions over how to lead the proper Christian life. Many devout Christians developed independent lifestyles that were intended to bring them closer to God without reliance on the Church hierarchy. Some elaborated beliefs that the church branded as heresy. Others called into question the philosophical bases of theological speculation that had developed since the time of Abelard and Aquinas. Finally, the increasing pluralism of European culture gave rise to new literary traditions that both celebrated and criticized the medieval legacy of Christianity, chivalry, and social order.

The Crisis of the Papacy

The universal empire as well as its traditional competitor, the universal Church, declined in the later Middle Ages. The papacy never recovered from the humiliating defeat Pope Boniface VIII suffered at the hands of King Philip the Fair in 1303. The ecclesiastical edifice created by the thirteenth-century popes was shaken to its foundations, first by becoming a virtual appendage of the French monarchy and then by a dispute that for more than 40 years gave European Christians a choice between two, and finally three, claimants to the chair of Saint Peter.

In 1305 the College of Cardinals elected as pope the bishop of Bordeaux. The new pope, who took the name Clement V (1305–1314), was close to Philip IV of France and had no desire to meet the fate of his predecessor, Pope Boniface VIII. Therefore Clement took up residence not in Rome but in the papal city of Avignon on the east bank of the Rhone River. Technically, Avignon was a papal estate within the Holy Roman Empire. Actually, with France just across the river, the pope at Avignon was under French control.

The Avignon Papacy. For the next 70 years, French popes and French cardinals ruled the Church. The traditional enemies of France as well as religious reformers who expected leadership from the papacy looked on this situation with disgust. Critics such as the Italian poet Petrarch accused the Avignon popes and their courtiers of every possible crime and sin, but they were no worse than any other great lords of the fourteenth century. In pursuit of political and financial rewards, they had simply lost sight of their roles as religious leaders.

The popes of Avignon were more successful in achieving their financial goals than in winning political power. Although they attempted to follow an independent course in international affairs, their French orientation eroded their influence in European politics, especially in the Holy Roman Empire. Pope John XXII (1316–1334), one of the most unpleasant and argumentative individuals ever to hold the chair of Peter, tried to block the election of the Wittelsbach Louis of Bavaria as emperor. Louis ignored the pope, invaded Italy, and was proclaimed emperor by the people of Rome. In 1338, the German electors solemnly declared that the imperial office was held directly from God and did not require papal confirmation—a declaration that was later upheld in the Golden Bull. No longer could the popes exert any direct influence in the internal affairs of Europe's states.

Frustrated politically, the Avignon popes concentrated on perfecting the legal and fiscal system of the Church and were enormously successful in concentrating the vast financial and legal power of the Church in the papal office. From the papal court, or *curia*, they created a vast and efficient central bureaucracy whose primary role was to increase papal revenues.

Revenues came from two main sources. The less lucrative but ultimately more critical source was the sale of indulgences. The Church had long taught that sinners who repented might be absolved of their sins and escape the fires of hell. However, they still had to suffer temporal punishment. This punishment, called penance, could take the form of fasting, prayer, or performance of some good deed. Having failed to do penance on earth, absolved sinners would have to endure a period in purgatory before they could be admitted to heaven. However, since the saints had done more penance than was required to make up for the temporal punishments due them, they had established a treasury of merit, a sort of spiritual bank account. The pope was the banker and could transfer some of this positive balance to repentant sinners in return for some pious act such as contributing money to build a new church. These so-called indulgences could be purchased for one's own use or to assist the souls of family members already in purgatory. Papal "pardoners" working on commission used high-pressure sales pitches to sell indulgences across Europe.

The second and major source of papal income was the sale of Church offices, or *benefices*. Popes claimed the right to appoint bishops and abbots to all benefices and to collect a hefty tax for the appointment. Papal appointees often acquired numerous offices and viewed them merely as sources of income, leaving pastoral duties, when they were performed at all, to hired local clergy.

The Great Schism. In 1377, Pope Gregory XI (1370–1378) returned from Avignon to Rome but died almost immediately on arrival. Thousands of Italians, afraid that the cardinals would elect another Frenchman, surrounded the church where they were meeting and demanded an Italian pope. The terrified cardinals elected an Italian, who took the name Urban VI (1378–1389). Once elected, Urban attempted to reform the curia, but he did so in a most undiplomatic way, insulting the cardinals and threatening to appoint enough non-French bishops to their number to end French control of the curia. The cardinals soon left Rome and announced that because the election had been made under duress, it was invalid and Urban should resign. When he refused, they held a second election and chose a Frenchman, Clement VII (1378–1394), who took up residence in Avignon. The Church now had two heads, both with reasonable claims to the office.

The chaos created by this so-called Great Schism divided Western Christendom. In every diocese, when a bishop died, his successor had to be appointed by the pope. But by which pope? To whom did taxes go? Who received the income from the sale of indulgences or benefices? Did appeals in the Church courts go to Rome or to Avignon? More significantly, since each pope excommunicated the supporters of his opponent, everyone in the West was under a sentence of excommunication. Could anyone be saved?

Nothing in Church law or tradition offered a solution to this crisis. Nor did unilateral efforts to settle the crisis succeed. France twice invaded Italy in an attempt to eliminate Urban but failed both times. When Urban and Clement died, cardinals on both sides elected successors. By the end of the fourteenth century, France and the empire were exasperated with their popes, and even the cardinals were determined to end the stalemate.

Conciliarism. Church lawyers argued that only a general council could end the schism. Both popes opposed this "conciliarist" argument because it suggested that an assembly of the Church rather than the pope held supreme authority. However, in 1408, cardinals from both sides summoned a council in the Italian city of Pisa. The council deposed both rivals and elected a new pope. But this solution only made matters worse, since neither pope accepted the council's decision. Europe now had to contend with not two but three popes, each claiming to be the true successor of Saint Peter.

Six years later, the Council of Constance managed a final solution. There, under the patronage of the emperor-elect Sigismund (1410–1437), cardinals, bishops, abbots, and theologians from across Europe met to resolve the crisis. Their goal was not only to settle the schism but also to reform the Church to prevent a recurrence of such a scandal. The participants at Constance hoped to restructure the Church as a limited monarchy in which the powers of the pope would be controlled through frequent councils. The Pisan and Avignon popes were deposed. The Roman pope,

abandoned by all of his supporters, abdicated. Before doing so, however, he formally convoked the council to preserve the tradition that a general council had to be called by the pope. Finally, the council elected as pope an Italian cardinal who was not aligned with any of the claimants. The election of the cardinal, who took the name of Martin V (1417–1431), ended the schism.

The relief at the end of the Great Schism could not hide the very real problems left by over a century of papal weakness. The prestige of the papacy had been permanently compromised. Everywhere, the Church had become more national in character. The conciliarist demand for control of the Church, which had ended the schism, lessened the power of the pope. Moreover, during the century between Boniface VIII and Martin V, new religious movements had taken root across Europe, movements that the political creatures who had occupied the papal office could neither understand nor control. The Council of Constance, which brought an end to the schism, also condemned Jan Hus, the leader of the Czech reform movement and the spiritual founder of the later Protestant reformation of the sixteenth century. The disintegration of the Church loomed ever closer as pious individuals turned away from the organized Church and sought divine help in personal piety, mysticism, or even magic.

Discerning the Spirit of God

When Joan of Arc first appeared before the dauphin in 1429, he feared that she was a witch. Only a physical examination by matrons, which determined that she was a virgin, persuaded him otherwise—witches were believed to have had intercourse with the devil. Everyone in the late Middle Ages was familiar with witches, saints, and heretics. Distinguishing among them was often a matter of perspective.

Witchcraft. Accusations of witchcraft were relatively rare in the Middle Ages. The age of witch-hunts occurred later, in the sixteenth and seventeenth centuries. During the Middle Ages, magic existed in a wide variety of forms, but its definition was fluid, and its practitioners were not always considered evil. Alchemists and astrologers held honored places in society, while simple practitioners of folk religion, medicine, and superstition were condemned, particularly when they were poor women. Witches, believed to have made a contract with the devil, were condemned and persecuted as heretics. Only at the end of the fifteenth century, with the publication of the *Witches' Hammer*, a handbook for inquisitors, did the European witch craze begin in earnest. Earlier, authorities feared more those people who sought their own pacts not with the devil but with God.

Lay Piety. Even as Europeans were losing respect for the institutional Church, people everywhere were seeking closer and more intimate relationships with God. Distrusting the formal institutions of the Church, lay persons and clerics turned to private devotions and to mysticism to achieve union with the divine. Most of these stayed within the Church. Others, among them many female mystics, maintained an ambiguous relationship with the traditional institutions of Christianity. A few, such as the Brethren of the Free Spirit, broke sharply with it.

In the fourteenth and fifteenth centuries a great many pious lay men and women chose to live together to strive for spiritual perfection without entering established religious orders. The Brethren of the Common Life in the Rhineland and Low Countries dedicated themselves to preaching, charity, and a pious life. In the early fifteenth century, an unknown member of the Brethren wrote the *Imitation of Christ,* a book of spiritual direction that remains today the most widely read religious text after the Bible.

Christians of the later Middle Ages sought to imitate Christ and venerated the Eucharist, or communion wafer, which the Church taught was the actual body of Jesus. Male mystics focused on imitating Jesus in his poverty, his suffering, and his humility. Women developed their own form of piety, which focused not on wealth and power but on spiritual nourishment, particularly as provided by the Eucharist. For women mystics, radical fasting became preparation for the reception of the Eucharist, which was often described in highly emotional and erotic terms. After a long period of fasting, Lukardis of Oberweimar (d. 1309) had a vision in which Jesus appeared to her as a handsome youth and blew into her mouth. In the words of her biographer, "She was infused with such sweetness and such inner fruition that she felt as if drunk." From the age of 23, Catherine of Sienna (d. 1380) subsisted entirely on the Eucharist, cold water, and bitter herbs that she sucked and then spat out. For those and other pious women, fasting and devotion to the Eucharist did not mean rejection of the body. Rather, these were attempts to use their senses to approach perfect union with God, who was for them both food and drink.

Heresy and Revolt

Only a thin line separated the saint's heroic search for union with God from the heretic's identification with God. The radical Brethren of the Free Spirit believed that God was all things and that all things would return to God. Such pantheism denied the possibility of sin, punishment, and the need for salvation. Members of the sect were hunted down, and many were burned as heretics. The specter of the Inquisition, the ecclesiastical court system that was charged with ferreting out heretics, hung over all such communities.

John Wycliffe. When unorthodox Christians were protected by secular lords, the ecclesiastical courts were powerless. This was the case with John Wycliffe (ca. 1330–1384), an Oxford theologian who attacked the doctrinal and political bases of the Church. He taught that the value of the sacraments depended on the worthiness of the priest administering them, that Jesus was present in the Eucharist only in spirit, that indulgences were useless, and that salvation depended on divine predestination rather than individual merit. Normally, these teachings would have led him to the stake. But he had also attacked the Church's right to wealth and luxury, an idea whose political implications pleased the English monarchy and nobility. Wycliffe's own exemplary manner of life and his teaching that the Church's role in temporal affairs should be severely limited made him an extremely popular figure in England. Therefore he was allowed to live and teach in peace. Only under Henry V (1413–1422) were Wycliffe's followers, known as Lollards, vigorously suppressed by the state. Before this condemnation took place, however, Wycliffe's teachings reached the kingdom of Bohemia through the marriage of Charles IV's daughter Anne of Bohemia to the English king Richard II. Anne took with her to England a number of Bohemian clerics, some of whom studied at Oxford and absorbed Wycliffe's political and religious teachings, which they then took back to Bohemia.

Jan Hus. In Prague, some of Wycliffe's less radical teachings took root among the theology faculty of the new university, where the leading proponent of Wycliffe's teachings was Jan Hus (1373–1415), an immensely popular young master and preacher. Although Hus rejected Wycliffe's ideas about the priesthood and the sacraments, he and other Czech preachers attacked indulgences and demanded a reform of Church liturgy and morals. They grafted these religious demands onto an attack on German dominance of the Bohemian kingdom. These attacks outraged both the Pisan pope John XXIII (1410–1415) and the Bohemian king Wenceslas IV (1378–1419), who favored the German faction. The pope excommunicated Hus, and the king expelled the Czech faculty from the university. Hus was convinced that he was no heretic and that a fair hearing would clear him. He therefore agreed to travel to the Council of Constance under promise of safe conduct from the emperor-elect Sigismund to defend his position. There, he was tried on a charge of heresy, convicted, and burned at the stake.

News of Hus's execution touched off a revolt in Bohemia. Unlike the peasant revolts of the past, however, this revolt had broad popular support throughout all levels of Czech society. Peasants, nobles, and townspeople saw the attack on Hus and his followers as an attack on Czech independence and national interest by a Church and an empire controlled by Germans. Soon a radical faction known as the Taborites was demanding the abolition of private property and the institution of a communal state. Although moderate Hussites and Bohemian Catholics combined to defeat the radicals in 1434, most of Bohemia remained Hussite through the fifteenth century. The sixteenth-century reformer Martin Luther declared himself a follower of Jan Hus.

Religious Persecution in Spain

Through the thirteenth century, even as kings of England and France expelled Jews from their kingdoms and as they were subjected to sporadic pogroms and massacres in Germany, Jews and Muslims were tolerated on the Iberian Penninsula. This fragile existence was shattered in the fourteenth and fifteenth centuries. The causes were complex: a declining economy, political unrest, Christian triumphalism as the reconquest moved into its last stages, and nascent nationalism all increased intercultural tensions. In 1391, mendicant friars inflamed Aragon with preaching against Jews and caused widespread violent attacks. Thereafter, in towns across Spain Christians rose up in arms against their Jewish neighbors in riots animated both by a hatred of Jews and a protest against the king. Thousands died and thousands more were forced to convert.

The Muslim population fared no better. In the fifteenth century Muslims faced conversion or expulsion, first to Granada and, after that last Muslim principality fell in 1492, to North Africa. Those who resisted were hunted down, their villages destroyed, and their populations dispersed.

In time, even Muslim and Jewish converts (termed respectively *moriscos* and *conversos*) found that Christian baptism was not necessarily a protection. Most moriscos remained secretly faithful to Islam and were ruthlessly persecuted and expelled. Many conversos also continued to practice their faith in secret for generations. However, many descendants of Jewish converts became sincere Christians: their ranks included bishops, inquisitors, and even saints (such as Teresa of Ávila). Nevertheless, Spaniards became obsessed with fears of anyone descended from Jews or Muslims and instituted legal sanctions against anyone who could not prove "purity of blood," that is, who might have Jewish or Muslim ancestors. Such racism has left a terrible heritage into the present.

William of Ockham and the Spirit of Truth

The critical and individualistic approach that characterized religion during the later Middle Ages was also typical of the philosophical thought of the period. The delicate balance between faith and reason taught by Aquinas and other intellectuals in the thirteenth century disintegrated in the fourteenth. As in other areas of life, intellectuals questioned the basic suppositions of their predecessors, directing intellectual activity away from general speculations and toward particular, observable reality.

The person primarily responsible for this new intellectual climate was the English Franciscan William of Ockham (ca. 1300–1349). Excommunicated for his defense of radical poverty, Ockham joined the imperialist cause at the court of Emperor Louis IV. Imperial power, he argued, derived not from the pope but from the people. He believed that people should be free to determine their own form of government and to elect rulers. They should be able to make their choice directly, as in the election of the emperor by electors who represent the people, or implicitly, through continuing forms of government. In either case, Ockham believed, government should be entirely secular and that neither popes nor bishops nor priests should have any role. Ockham went still further. He denied the absolute authority of the pope, even in spiritual matters. Rather, Ockham argued, parishes, religious orders, and monasteries should send representatives to regional synods, which in turn would elect representatives to general councils. Ockham's ideas on Church governance offered the one hope for a solution to the Great Schism that erupted shortly after his death. The Council of Constance, which ended the schism, was the fruit of Ockham's political theory.

As radical as Ockham's political ideas were, his philosophical outlook was even more extreme and exerted a more direct and lasting influence. The Christian Aristotelianism that developed in the thirteenth century had depended on the validity of general concepts called universals, which could be analyzed through the use of logic. Aquinas and others who studied the eternity of the world, the existence of God, the nature of the soul, and other philosophical questions believed that people could reach general truths by abstracting universals from particular, individual cases. Ockham argued that universals were merely names, no more than convenient tags for discussing individual things. He stated that universals had no connection with reality and could not be used to reason from particular observations to general truths. This radical nominalism (from the Latin *nomen*, "name") thus denied that human reason could aspire to certain truth. For Ockham and his followers, philosophical speculation was essentially a logical, linguistic exercise, not a way to certain knowledge.

Just as Ockham's political theory dominated the later fourteenth century, his nominalist philosophy won over the philosophical faculties of Europe. Since he had discredited the value of Aristotelian logic to increase knowledge, the result was, on the one hand, a decline in abstract speculation and, on the other, a greater interest in scientific observation of individual phenomena. In the next generation, Parisian professors, trained in the tradition of Ockham, laid the foundation for scientific studies of motion and the universe

CONVIVENCIA

By the High Middle Ages the position of Jews in western Europe was difficult. They had been expelled from England and from France. In Spain, under a system known as Convivencia, *or living together, they still enjoyed royal protection. However, as this text, known as* Las Siete Partidas, *issued in 1263 by King Alfonso X of Castile and in force through the fourteenth and fifteenth centuries shows, hostility, fueled by unfounded rumors of ritual murder, was making Jewish life increasingly precarious.*

FOCUS QUESTIONS

What beliefs and prejudices led to Christians' intolerance toward Jews? What protections did Jews receive from the king?

JEWS SHOULD PASS THEIR LIVES AMONG CHRISTIANS quietly and without disorder, practicing their own religious rites, and not speaking ill of the faith of Our Lord Jesus Christ, which Christians acknowledge. Moreover, a Jew should be very careful to avoid preaching to, or converting any Christian, to the end that he may become a Jew, by exalting his own belief and disparaging ours. Whoever violates this law shall be put to death and lose all his property. And because we have heard it said that in some places Jews celebrated, and still celebrate Good Friday, which commemorates the Passion of Our Lord Jesus Christ, by way of contempt; stealing children and fastening them to crosses, and making images of wax and crucifying them, when they cannot obtain children; we order that, hereafter, if in any part of our dominions anything like this is done, and can be proved, all persons who were present when the act was committed shall be seized, arrested and brought before the king; and after the king ascertains that they are guilty, he shall cause them to be put to death in a disgraceful manner, no matter how many there may be.

We also forbid any Jew to dare to leave his house or his quarter on Good Friday, but they must all remain shut up until Saturday morning; and if they violate this regulation, we decree that they shall not be entitled to reparation for any injury or dishonor inflicted upon them by Christians.

Saturday is the day on which Jews perform their devotions, and remain quiet in their lodgings, and do not make contracts or transact any business; and for the reason that they are obliged by their religion, to keep it, no one should on that day summon them or bring them into court. Wherefore we order that no judge shall employ force or any constraint upon Jews on Saturday, in order to bring them into court on account of their debts; or arrest them; or cause them any other annoyance; for the remaining days of the week are sufficient for the purpose of employing compulsion against them, and for making demands for things which can be demanded of them, according to law. Jews are not bound to obey a summons served upon them on that day; and, moreover, we decree that any decision rendered against them on Saturday shall not be valid; but if a Jew should wound, kill, rob, steal, or commit any other offense like these for which he can be punished in person and property, then the judge can arrest him on Saturday.

We also decree that all claims that Christians have against Jews, and Jews against Christians shall be decided and determined by our judges in the district where they reside, and not by their old men. And as we forbid Christians to bring Jews into court or annoy them on Saturday; so we also decree that Jews, neither in person, nor by their attorneys, shall have the right to bring Christians into court, or annoy them on this day. And in addition we forbid any Christian, on his own responsibility, to arrest wrong any Jew either in his person or property, but where he has any complaint against him he must bring it before our judges; and if anyone be so bold as to use violence against the Jews, or rob them of anything he shall return them double the value of the same.

Las Siete Partidas, tr. Samuel Parsons Scott (Chicago: Published for the Comparative Law Bureau of the American Bar Association by Commerce Clearing House, Inc., 1931).

that led to the scientific discoveries of the sixteenth and seventeenth centuries.

Vernacular Literature and the Individual

Just as the religious and philosophical concerns of the later Middle Ages developed within national frameworks and criticized accepted authority from the perspective of individual experience, so too did the vernacular (as opposed to Latin) literatures of the age begin to explore the place of the individual within an increasingly complex society. Across Europe, authors reviewed the traditional values of society with a critical eye, reworking and transforming traditional literary genres into statements both personal and profound.

CHRONOLOGY

THE LATER MIDDLE AGES, 1300–1500

1305–1377	Babylonian Captivity (Avignon papacy)
1337–1452	Hundred Years' War
1347–1352	Black Death spreads throughout Europe
1358	Jacquerie revolt of French peasants; Etienne Marcel leads revolt of Parisian merchants
1378	Ciompi revolt in Florence
1380	Death of Catherine of Siena
1378–1417	Great Schism divides Christianity
1381	Great Rebellion of English peasants
1409–1410	Council of Pisa
1414–1417	Council of Constance ends Great Schism
1415	Jan Hus executed
1431	Death of Joan of Arc
1455–1485	English Wars of the Roses

Italy. In Italy, a trio of Tuscan poets, Dante Alighieri (1265–1321), Petrarch (1304–1374), and Boccaccio (1313–1375), not only made Italian a literary language but composed in it some of the greatest literature of all time. Dante, the first and greatest of the three, was born into a modest but respectable Florentine family, entered public life, and in 1301 fell victim to the viciousness of Florentine politics. He was exiled from his beloved city for the remainder of his life. During his exile he wrote philosophical treatises and literary works, which culminated in his *Divine Comedy,* written during the last years of his life.

The *Divine Comedy* is a view of the whole Christian universe, populated with people from antiquity and from Dante's own day. The poem is both a sophisticated summary of philosophical and theological thought at the beginning of the fourteenth century and an astute political commentary on his times. The poet sets this vision within a three-part poetic journey through hell (*Inferno*), purgatory (*Purgatorio*), and heaven (*Paradiso*). In each part, Dante adopts a poetic style appropriate to the subject matter. His journey through hell to witness the sufferings of the damned is described in brutal, immediate language. In purgatory, Dante meets sinners whose punishments will someday end. These he describes in a language of dreams, imagination, and nostalgic recollection. Paradise is portrayed in a symbolic language that is nonphysical and nonrepresentational. In the face of transcendent perfection, human imagery and poetry fail. In his final vision he sees the reflected light of a mystical rose in which the saints are ranked. The *Divine Comedy* is Dante's personal summary of all that is good and bad in medieval culture and politics.

England. Dante had set his great poem within a vision of the other world. Emerging English literature was more firmly rooted in contemporary society. William Langland (ca. 1330–1395) and Geoffrey Chaucer (ca. 1343–1400) both presented images of their social milieu. In *Piers Plowman,* Langland presents society from the perspective of the peasantry. Chaucer's work is much more sophisticated and wide-ranging, weaving together the whole spectrum of late medieval literature and life.

Chaucer placed his tales in the mouths of a group of 30 pilgrims traveling to the tomb of Thomas à Becket at Canterbury. The pilgrims represent different walks of life: a simple knight, a vulgar miller, a lawyer, a lusty widow, a merchant, a squire, a physician, a nun, her chaplain, and a monk, among others. Each pilgrim is at once strikingly individual and representative of his or her profession or station in life. The tales that they tell are drawn from folklore, Italian literature, the lives of the saints, courtly romance, and religious sermons. However, Chaucer played with the tales and their genres in the retelling. He used them to contrast or illuminate the persons and characters of their tellers as well as to comment in subtle and complex ways on the literary, religious, and cultural traditions of which they were part. In his mastery of the whole heritage of medieval culture and his independent use of this heritage, Chaucer proved himself the greatest English writer before Shakespeare.

France. Much of Italian and English literature drew material and inspiration from French, which continued into the fifteenth century to be the language of courtly romance, projecting an unreal world of allegory and nostalgia for a glorious if imaginary past. Popular literature, which developed largely in the towns, often dealt with courtly themes but with a critical and more realistic eye.

In this literary world an extraordinary woman, who was widowed at 25, was able to earn a living for herself and her family with her pen. As a successful woman of letters, Christine de Pisan (1364–ca. 1430) fought the stereotypical medieval image of women as weak, sexually aggressive temptresses. With wit and reason she argued that women could be virtuous and showed the fallacies of traditional antifeminist preaching, poetry, and belief. She appealed to women to develop their own sense of self-worth directly from experience and not to rely on the advice of men, who could not have any direct knowledge of the meaning of being a woman. In her *Hymn to Joan of Arc* she saluted her famous contemporary for her accomplishments, bringing dignity to women, striving for justice, and working for peace in France. Christine's life and writing epitomized the new possibilities and new interests of the fifteenth century. They included an acute sense of individuality, a willingness to look for truth not in the clichés of the past but in actual experience, and a readiness to defend one's views with tenacity. Although an heir of the medieval world, Christine, like her contemporaries, already embodied the attitudes of a new age.

That new age was reflected in a second tradition in fifteenth-century France, that of realist poetry. Around 1453, just as the English troops were enduring a final battering from the French artillery, Duke Charles of Orléans (1394–1465) organized a poetry contest. Each contestant was to write a ballad that began with the contradictory line "I die of thirst beside the fountain." The duke, himself an outstanding poet, wrote an entry that embodied the traditional courtly themes of love and fortune:

> *I die of thirst beside the fountain,*
> *Shaking from cold and the fire of love;*
> *I am blind and yet guide the others;*
> *I am weak of mind, a man of wisdom;*
> *Too negligent, often cautious in vain,*
> *I have been made a spirit,*
> *Led by fortune for better or for worse.*

An unexpected and very different entry came from the duke's prison. The prisoner-poet, François Villon (1432–ca. 1464), was a child of the Paris streets, an impoverished student, a barroom brawler, a killer, and a thief. He was also the greatest realist poet of the Middle Ages, and his poetry won him release from prison. His entry read:

> *I die of thirst beside the fountain,*
> *Hot as fire, my teeth clattering,*
> *At home I am in an alien land;*
> *I shudder beside a glowing brazier,*
> *Naked as a worm, gloriously dressed,*
> *I laugh and cry and wait without hope,*
> *I take comfort and sad despair,*
> *I rejoice and have no joy,*
> *Powerful, I have no force and no strength,*
> *Well received, I am expelled by all.*

The duke focused on the sufferings of love, the thief on the physical sufferings of the downtrodden. The two poets represent the contradictory tendencies of literature in the later Middle Ages. From Prague to Paris, vernacular languages had come into their own everywhere. Poets used their native tongues to express a spectrum of sentiments and to describe a spectrum of emotions and values. The themes and ideas that were expressed ranged from the polished, traditional values of the aristocracy trying to maintain the ideals of chivalry in a new and changed world to the views of ordinary people, by turns reverent or sarcastic, joyful or despondent.

Conclusion

THE LEGACY OF THE MIDDLE AGES was a complex and ambiguous one. The thousand years of synthesis of classical, barbarian, and Christian traditions did not disappear. The bonds holding this world together were not yet broken. But the last centuries of the Middle Ages bequeathed a critical detachment from this heritage, expressed in the revolts of peasants and workers, the preaching of radical religious reformers, the poems of mystics and visionaries, and rising individualism.

QUESTIONS FOR REVIEW

1. What social and political forces prevented both the Holy Roman Emperors and the French kings from uniting the lands they ruled?
2. How did disease transform social relations in fourteenth-century Europe?
3. Why did a division in the papacy mean both political chaos and spiritual fear for Europeans?
4. How did the vernacular literature of Dante, Chaucer, and Christine de Pisan represent a departure from previous literary traditions?

DISCOVERING WESTERN CIVILIZATION ONLINE

You can obtain more information about the later Middle Ages at the websites listed below. See also the companion website that accompanies this text: www.ablongman.com/kishlansky, which contains an online study guide and additional resources.

Politics as a Family Affair

http://lava.ds.arch.tue.nl/gallery/praha/thrad_sv.html
A site devoted to Peter Parler's St. Vitus Cathedral.

http://www.bnf.fr/enluminures/themes/t_1/st_1_02/a102_002.htm
A selection of medieval manuscript illuminations from the French National Library depicting battles from the Hundred Years' War.

Life and Death in the Later Middle Ages

http://dsc.discovery.com/anthology/momentsintime/black death/blackdeath.html
A Discovery Channel "tour" of the Great Plague of the fourteenth century.

The Spirit of the Later Middle Ages

www.avignon.com/anglais/avi003.html
A brief introduction to Avignon and the papal palaces.

SUGGESTIONS FOR FURTHER READING

General Reading

Margaret Aston, *The Fifteenth Century: The Prospect of Europe* (New York: W. W. Norton, 1968). A general survey of the fifteenth century.

Robert Bartlett, *The Making of Europe: Conquest, Colonization, and Cultural Change, 950–1350* (Princeton: Princeton University Press, 1993). A comparative study of Europe's expansion into the Celtic, Islamic, and Slavic worlds in the later Middle Ages.

Johan Huizinga, *The Autumn of the Middle Ages,* tr. Rodney J. Payton and Ulrich Mammitzsch (Chicago: University of Chicago Press, 1996). An important new translation of the classic interpretation of culture and society in the Burgundian court in the later Middle Ages.

Politics as a Family Affair

Geoffrey Barraclough, ed., *Eastern and Western Europe in the Middle Ages* (New York: Harcourt Brace Jovanovich, 1970). An excellent collection of essays on various aspects of eastern European history.

Richard W. Kaeuper, *War, Justice and Public Order: England and France in the Later Middle Ages* (Oxford: Oxford University Press, 1988). A fine analysis of the effects of war in England and France.

Joachim Leuschner, *Germany in the Late Middle Ages* (Amsterdam: Elsevier, 1980). An introduction to late medieval German history.

Jean W. Sedier, *East Central Europe in the Middle Ages, 1000–1500* (Seattle: University of Washington Press, 1994). A comprehensive introduction to the history of eastern Europe.

Life and Death in the Later Middle Ages

Bronislaw Geremek, *The Margins of Society in Late Medieval Paris,* tr. Jean Birrell (Cambridge: Cambridge University Press, 1987). A landmark study of the urban poor in the late Middle Ages.

Edward S. Hunt and James M. Murray, *A History of Business in Medieval Europe, 1200–1550* (Cambridge: Cambridge University Press, 1995). A brief and readable history of medieval business practice.

David Nicholas, *The Growth of the Medieval City: From Late Antiquity to the Early Fourteenth Century* (London and New York: Longman, 1997). A comprehensive survey of medieval towns.

Teofilo F. Ruiz, *Spanish Society 1400–1600* (Harlow: Longman, 2001). A sensitive and original survey of Spanish society at the end of the Middle Ages.

Philip Zieger, *The Black Death* (New York: Sutton Publishing, 1999). A reliable introduction to the plague in the fourteenth century.

The Spirit of the Later Middle Ages

Renate Blumenfeld-Kosinski, ed., Kevin Brownlee, tr. *The Selected Writings of Christine de Pizan: New Translations, Criticism* (New York: Norton, 1997). A selection of de Pizan's works and of scholarship on her. The place to start for learning about her.

Caroline Walker Bynum, *Holy Feast and Holy Fast: The Religious Significance of Food to Medieval Women* (Berkeley: University of California Press, 1987). An imaginative and scholarly examination of the role of food in the spirituality of medieval women.

Eamon Duffy, *The Stripping of the Altars: Traditional Religion in England, 1400–1580* (New Haven: Yale University Press, 1992). A revisionist study of local religion at the end of the Middle Ages.

John Freccero, *Dante and the Poetics of Conversion* (Cambridge, Mass.: Harvard University Press, 1986). A serious and rewarding study of Dante by an acknowledged master.

Malcolm Lambert, *Medieval Heresy: Popular Movements from the Gregorian Reform to the Reformation*, 2nd. ed. (Oxford: Blackwell, 1992). A comprehensive survey of heretical movements from the eleventh to the sixteenth centuries.

Lee Patterson, *Chaucer and the Subject of History* (Madison: University of Wisconsin Press, 1991). A challenging study of Chaucer, the poet's understanding of history, and his relationship to modernity.

CHAPTER 11

THE ITALIAN RENAISSANCE

- THE VISUAL RECORD: A Civic Procession
- RENAISSANCE SOCIETY
- RENAISSANCE ART

- RENAISSANCE IDEALS
- THE POLITICS OF THE ITALIAN CITY-STATES

A CIVIC PROCESSION

I T IS 25 APRIL 1444, the day Venice celebrates its patron, Saint Mark, with a procession around the square that bears his name. Processions are a common form of civic ritual through which a community defines itself. This procession includes the religious orders (the white-clad brothers of the Confraternity of Saint John are passing before us now), the civic leaders seen just behind them, and an entire band filing by on the right. The procession is not staged, as a modern ceremony would be, and this difference is evident in the relaxed attitude of the ordinary citizens who gather in the middle of the square. In the lower left-hand corner, some friars are reading music; at the lower right, members of the confraternity carry their candles negligently.

Yet the painting, *The Procession of the Relic of the Holy Cross* (1496) by Gentile Bellini (ca. 1429–1507), was commissioned to commemorate a miracle rather than a civic procession. On the evening before Saint Mark's day, a visiting merchant and his son were touring the square when the boy accidentally fell and cracked his skull. The doctors who were called to treat him regarded the case as hopeless and advised the father to prepare for his son's death. The next morning, the Brothers of the Confraternity of Saint John paraded their relic, a piece of the true cross on which Jesus was crucified. The merchant (the red-clad figure kneeling just to the right of center where the line of brothers breaks) approached the golden altarpiece containing the relic, knelt, and prayed that Saint Mark would miraculously cure his son. The next day, the boy revived.

The Brothers of Saint John commissioned Bellini to commemorate this event. Bellini came from the most distinguished family of painters in Venice. His father, Jacopo, had studied in Florence and had brought both of his sons into his workshop when they were young boys. Until the age of 30, Gentile and his younger and more famous brother, Giovanni, worked on their father's commissions, learning the difficult craft of painting. Art was very much a family business in fifteenth-century Italy. The large workshops with their master and hordes of apprentices turned out vast canvases with assembly-line precision. The master was first and foremost a businessman who gained the commissions. He then created the composition and sketched it out; his skilled assistants, like the Bellini brothers, worked on the more complex parts; and young apprentices painted backgrounds.

Although *The Procession of the Relic of the Holy Cross* was designed to recreate a central moment in the history of the confraternity, it is not the confraternity that dominates the picture. Miracles were a part of civic life, and each town took pride in the special manifestations of heavenly care that had taken place within it. Thus it is Venice that is the centerpiece of Bellini's canvas. Dominating the painting is the Basilica of San Marco, with its four great horses over the center portico and the winged lion—the city's symbol—on the canopy above the horses. The procession emanates from the duke's palace to the right of the church, and the great flags of

the city flutter everywhere. By the end of the fifteenth century, Venice was one of the greatest powers on earth, the center for international trade and finance. Home to the largest concentration of wealthy families anywhere in Europe, it could well afford the pomp and splendor of its processions.

LOOKING AHEAD

The achievements of God and the achievements of humans blend together in Bellini's painting as they blended together in that era of remarkable accomplishments that historians call the Renaissance. In this chapter, we shall see how philosophy, art, architecture, and literature enjoyed a remarkable development in the Italian city-states and how Renaissance ideals were exported throughout the continent and came to define the age.

217

RENAISSANCE SOCIETY

Perhaps the most surprising result of the Black Death was the way in which European society revived itself in the succeeding centuries. Even at the height of the plague, a spirit of revitalization was evident in the works of artists and writers. Petrarch (1304–1474), the great humanist poet and scholar, was among the first to differentiate the new age in which he was living from two earlier ones: the classical world of Greece and Rome, which he admired, and the subsequent Dark Ages, which he detested. This spirit of self-awareness is one of the defining characteristics of the Renaissance. "It is but in our own day that men dare boast that they see the dawn of better things," wrote Matteo Palmieri (1406–1475).

What was the Renaissance? A French word for an Italian phenomenon, *renaissance* literally means "rebirth." The word captures both the emphasis on humanity that characterized Renaissance thinking and the renewed fascination with the classical world. But the Renaissance was an age rather than an event. There is no moment at which the Middle Ages ended. Late medieval society was artistically creative, socially well developed, and economically diverse. Yet eventually, the pace of change accelerated, and it is best to think of the Renaissance as an era of rapid transitions. Encompassing the two centuries between 1350 and 1550, it passed through three distinct phases. The first, from 1350 to 1400, was characterized by a declining population, the uncovering of classical texts, and experimentation in a variety of art forms. The second phase, from 1400 to 1500, was distinguished by the creation of a set of cultural values and artistic and literary achievements that defined Renaissance style. The large Italian city-states developed stable and coherent forms of government, and the warfare between them gradually ended. In the final period, from 1500 to 1550, invasions from France and Spain transformed Italian political life, and the ideas and techniques of Italian writers and artists radiated to all points of the Continent. Though Renaissance ideas and achievements did spread throughout western Europe, they are best studied where they first developed: on the Italian peninsula.

Cities and Countryside

The Italian peninsula differed sharply from other areas of Europe in the extent to which it was urban. By the late Middle Ages, nearly one in four Italians lived in a town, in contrast to one in ten elsewhere. Not even the plague did much to change this ratio. By 1500, seven of the ten largest cities in the West were in Italy. Naples, Venice, and Milan, each with a population of more than 100,000, led the rest. But it was the numerous smaller towns, with populations nearer to 1,000, that gave the Italian peninsula its urban character. Cities dominated their regions economically, politically, and culturally and served as convenient centers of judicial and ecclesiastical power. The diversified activities of their inhabitants created vast concentrations of wealth, and Italy was the banking capital of the world.

Cities acted as central places around which a cluster of large and small villages was organized. Urban areas, especially the small towns, provided markets for the agricultural produce of the countryside and for the manufactured goods of the urban craft workers. This allowed for the specialization in agricultural and industrial life that increased both productivity and wages. Cities also caught the runoff of rural population, especially the surplus of younger sons and daughters who could not be accommodated on the farms. Cities grew by migration rather than by natural increase. Thus the areas surrounding a city were critical to its prosperity and survival. The urban system was a network of cities encompassed by towns encircled by rural villages. Florence, the dominant city in the region of Tuscany, exemplifies this relationship. Though it possessed two thirds of its region's wealth, Florence contained only 14 percent of the regional population. The surrounding countryside was agriculturally rich, because marketing costs were low and demand for foodstuffs was high. Smaller cities channeled their local produce and trade to Florence.

Although cities may have dominated Renaissance Italy, by present standards they were small in both area and population. A person could walk across fifteenth-century Florence in less than half an hour. In 1427 its population was 37,000, only half its pre-plague size. Most Italian cities contained large fields for agricultural production, and within the outer walls of Florence were gardens and grain fields. Inside the inner city walls the people crowded together into tightly packed quarters. The intensity of the stench from raw sewage, rotting foodstuffs, and animals being brought to slaughter was equaled only by the din of hoofs and wooden cartwheels on the paving stones.

Urban populations were organized far differently than rural ones. On the farms the central distinctions involved ownership of land. Some farmers owned their estates outright and left them intact to their heirs. Others were involved in a sharecropping system by which absentee owners of land supplied working capital in return for half of the farm's produce. A great gulf in wealth separated owners from sharecroppers. Those who owned their land normally lived with surplus; those who sharecropped always lived on the margin of subsistence.

In the city, however, distinctions were based first on occupation, which largely corresponded to social position and wealth. Cities began as markets, and the privilege to participate in the market defined citizens. City governments provided protection for consumers and producers by creating monopolies through which standards for

Largest cities
- ■ 125,000 and over
- ▲ 100,000 to 125,000
- ● 50,000 to 100,000
- ○ 25,000 to 50,000

▲ Largest Cities in Western Europe, ca. 1500. There were as many large cities in the Italian peninsula as in all of the rest of western Europe.

craftsmanship were maintained and profits for craftsmen were guaranteed. These monopolies were called guilds or companies. Each large city had its own hierarchy of guilds. At the top were the important manufacturing groups—clothiers, metalworkers, and the like. Just below them were bankers, merchants, and the administrators of civic and Church holdings. At the bottom were grocers, masons, and other skilled workers. Roughly speaking, all of those within the guild structure, from bottom to top, lived comfortably. Yet the majority of urban inhabitants were not members of guilds. Many managed to eke out a living as wage laborers; many more were simply destitute. As a group, these poor people constituted as much as half of the entire population. Most depended on civic and private charity for their very survival.

The disparities between rich and poor were overwhelming. The concentration of wealth in the hands of an ever-narrowing group of families and favored guilds characterized every large city. One reason for this was the extreme instability of economic life. Prices and wages fluctuated wildly in response to local circumstance. After an epidemic of plague, wages climbed and the prices of consumer goods tumbled. A bad harvest sent food prices skyrocketing. Only those who could stockpile goods in times of plenty and consume them in times of want were safe. Capital was the key to continued wealth. Monopolies ensured the profitability of trade and manufacturing, but only those with sufficient capital could engage in either. In Florence, for example, 10 percent of the families controlled 90 percent of the wealth, with an even more extreme concentration at the top.

Production and Consumption

This concentration of wealth and the way in which it was used defined the Renaissance economy. Economic life is bound up in the relationship between supply and demand. The late medieval economy, despite the development of international banking and long-distance trade, was still an economy of primary producers: Between 70 and 90 percent of Europe's population was involved in subsistence agriculture. Even in Italy, which contained the greatest concentration of urban areas in the world, agriculture predominated. The manufacture of clothing was the only other significant economic activity. Most of what was produced was for local consumption rather than for the marketplace. The relationship between supply and demand was precisely measured by the full or empty stomach. Even in good times, more than 80 percent of the population lived at subsistence level with food, clothing, and shelter their only expenses. Therefore, when we discuss the market economy of the Renaissance, we are discussing the circumstances of the few rather than the many.

The defining characteristic of the early Renaissance economy was population change. Recurring waves of plague kept population levels low for more than a century. In the century between 1350 and 1450, one in every six years was characterized by an unusually high mortality rate. At the end of this period, Florence's population was only a quarter of what it had been at the beginning. This dramatic reduction in population depressed economic growth. The general economy did not revive until the sustained population increase toward the end of the fifteenth century. Until then, in both agriculture and manufacturing, supply outstripped demand.

On the farms, surviving farmers occupied the best land and enlarged their holdings. In the shops, finished products outnumbered the consumers who survived the epidemics. Overproduction meant lower prices for basic commodities, and the decline in population meant higher wages for labor. At the lowest levels of society, survivors found it easier to earn their living and even to create a surplus than had their parents. For a time the lot of the masses improved.

But for investors, such economic conditions meant that neither agriculture nor cloth making was particularly attractive. Expensive investments in land or equipment for sharecropping were paid off in inexpensive grain; high wages for the few surviving skilled workers brought a return in cheap cloth. In such circumstances, consumption was more attractive than investment, but it was not merely the perceived shortage of profitable investment opportunities that brought on the increase in conspicuous consumption during the fifteenth century. In the psychological atmosphere created by unpredictable, swift, and deadly epidemics, luxurious living seemed an appropriate response. Moreover, although tax rates increased, houses and personal property normally remained exempt, making luxury goods attractive investments.

For these reasons the production and consumption of luxuries soared. By the middle of the fourteenth century, Florence was known for its silks and jewelry as much as for its cloth. Venice became a European center for the glass industry, especially for the finely ground glass that was used in eyeglasses. Production of specialty crops such as sugar, saffron, fruits, and high-quality wine expanded. International trade increasingly centered on acquiring Eastern specialties, resulting in a serious outflow of gold and silver that enriched first the Byzantine and then the Ottoman emperors.

The Experience of Life

Luxury helped to improve a life that for rich and poor alike was short and uncertain. Renaissance children who survived infancy found their lives governed by parentage and by gender. In parentage the great divide was between those who lived with surplus and those who lived at subsistence. The first category encompassed the wealthiest bankers and merchants down to those who owned their own farms or engaged in small urban crafts. The vast majority of urban and rural dwellers were members of the second category. About the children of the poor we know very little, other than that their survival was unlikely. If they did not die at birth or shortly afterward, they might be abandoned—especially if female—to the growing number of orphanages in the cities, waste away from lack of nutrition, or fall prey to ordinary childhood diseases. Eldest sons were favored; younger daughters were disadvantaged. In poor families, however, this favoritism meant little more than early apprenticeship to day labor in the city or farm labor in the countryside. Girls were frequently sent out as domestic servants far from the family home.

Childhood.   Children of the wealthy had better chances for survival than did children of the poor. For the better off, childhood might begin with "milk parents," in the home of the family of a wet nurse who would breast-feed the baby through infancy. Only the very wealthy could afford a live-in wet nurse, which would increase the child's chances of survival. Again, daughters were more likely to be sent far from home and least likely to have their nursing supervised. The use of wet nurses not only emancipated parents from the daily care of infants, it also allowed them to resume sexual relations. Nursing women refrained from sex in the belief that it affected their milk.

During the period between weaning and apprenticeship, Renaissance children lived with their families. There was no typical Renaissance family. Nuclear families—that is, parents and their children under one roof—were probably more common than extended families, which might include

ON THE FAMILY

Leon Battista Alberti wrote a number of important tracts that set out the general principles of a subject, including On Architecture, *which was considered the basic text for 300 years. His writings on the family bring insight into the nature of a patriarchal, male-dominated institution.*

FOCUS QUESTIONS

According to Alberti, why is it important for men to look for an "honorable manner" when choosing a wife? What role would Alberti see the wife playing in a marriage?

THEY SAY THAT IN CHOOSING A WIFE ONE LOOKS for beauty, parentage, and riches. . . . Among the most essential criteria of beauty in a woman is an honorable manner. Even a wild, prodigal, greasy, drunken woman may be beautiful of feature, but no one would call her a beautiful wife. A woman worthy of praise must show first of all in her conduct, modesty, and purity. Marius, the illustrious Roman, said in that first speech of his to the Roman people: "Of women we require purity, of men labor." And I certainly agree. There is nothing more disgusting than a coarse and dirty woman. Who is stupid enough not to see clearly that a woman who does not care for neatness and cleanliness in her appearance, not only in her dress and body but in all her behavior and language, is by no means well mannered? How can it be anything but obvious that a bad-mannered woman is also rarely virtuous? We shall consider elsewhere the harm that comes to a family from women who lack virtue, for I myself do not know which is the worse fate for a family, total celibacy or a single dishonored woman. In a bride, therefore, a man must first seek beauty of mind, that is, good conduct and virtue.

In her body he must seek not only loveliness, grace, and charm but must also choose a woman who is well made for bearing children, with the kind of constitution that promises to make them strong and big. There's an old proverb, "When you pick your wife, you choose your children." All her virtues will in fact shine brighter still in beautiful children. It is a well-known saying among poets: "Beautiful character dwells in a beautiful body." The natural philosophers require that a woman be neither thin nor very fat. Those laden with fat are subject to coldness and constipation and slow to conceive. They say that a woman should have a joyful nature, fresh and lively in her blood and her whole being. They have no objections to a dark girl. They do reject girls with a frowning black visage, however. They have no liking for either the undersized or the overlarge and lean. They find that a woman is most suited to bear children if she is fairly big and has limbs of ample length. They always have a preference for youth, based on a number of arguments which I need not expound here, but particularly on the point that a young girl has a more adaptable mind. Young girls are pure by virtue of their age and have not developed any spitefulness. They are by nature modest and free of vice. They quickly learn to accept affectionately and unresistingly the habits and wishes of their husbands.

From Leon Battista Alberti, *On the Family.*

grandparents and other relatives. But the composition of the family changed over the course of the life cycle and included times in which married children or grandparents were present and others when a single parent and small children were the only members. Moreover, even nuclear families commonly contained stepparents and stepchildren as well as domestic servants or apprentices. A child returning to the parental household was as likely to form emotional bonds with older siblings as with parents.

The family was an economic unit as well as a grouping of relatives. Decisions to abandon children, to send them away from the household when very young, or to take in domestic servants were based on economic calculations. In the competition for scarce resources, the way in which children were managed might determine the survival of the family unit. Sons could expect to be apprenticed to a

trade, probably between the ages of 10 and 13. Most, of course, learned the crafts of their fathers, but not necessarily in their father's shop. Sons inherited the family business and its most important possessions—tools of the trade or beasts of labor for the farm. Inheritance customs varied. In some places, only the eldest son received the equipment of the family occupation; in others, like Tuscany, all the sons shared it. Still, in the first 15 years of life, these most-favored children would have spent between one-third and one-half of their time outside the household in which they had been born.

Marriage and the Family. Expectations for daughters centered on their chances of marriage. For a girl, dowry was everything. If a girl's father could provide a handsome one, her future was secure; if not, the alternatives were a convent, which would take a small bequest, or a match lower down the social scale, where the quality of life deteriorated rapidly. Daughters of poor families entered domestic service in order to have a dowry provided by their masters. The dowry was taken to the household of the husband. There, the couple resided until they established their own separate family. If the husband died, it was to his parental household that the widow returned.

Women married in late adolescence, usually around the age of 20. Among the wealthy, marriages were perceived as familial alliances and business transactions rather than love matches. The dowry was an investment on which fathers expected a return, and while the bride might have some choice, it was severely limited. Compatibility was not a central feature in matchmaking. Husbands were, on the average, ten years older than their wives and likely to leave them widows. In the early fifteenth century, about one-fourth of all adult women in Florence were widows.

Married women lived in a state of nearly constant pregnancy. Alessandra Strozzi, whose father was one of the wealthiest citizens of Florence, married at age 16, gave birth to eight children in ten years, and was widowed at age 25. Not all pregnancies produced children. The rates of miscarriages and stillbirths were very high, and abortions and infanticide were not unknown. Only among the families who hovered between surplus and subsistence is there any evidence of attempts to control pregnancies. These efforts, which relied on techniques such as the rhythm method and withdrawal, were not particularly effective. The rhythm method was especially futile because of the misunderstanding of the role of women in conception. It was not yet known that the woman contained an egg that was fertilized during conception. Without this knowledge it was impossible to understand the cycle of ovulation. Practically speaking, family size was limited on the one end by late marriages and on the other by early deaths.

Life experiences differed for males. Men married later—near the age of 25 on the farms, nearer 30 in the cities because of the cost of setting up in trade or on the land. Late marriage meant long supervision under the watchful eye of father or master, an extended period between adolescence and adulthood. The reputation that Renaissance cities gained for homosexuality and licentiousness must be viewed in light of the advanced age at which males married. The level of sexual frustration was high, and its outlet in ritual violence and rape was also high. Many men, even with families, never succeeded in setting up separately from their fathers or older brothers.

Men came of age at 30 but were thought to be old by 50. Thus for men, marriage and parenthood took place in middle age rather than in youth. Valued all their lives more highly than their sisters, male heads of households were the source of all power in their domiciles, in their shops, and in the state. They were responsible for overseeing every aspect of the upbringing of their children. But their wives were essential partners who governed domestic life. Women labored not only at the hearth, but in the fields and shops as well. Their economic contribution to the well-being of the family was critical, both in the dowry they brought at marriage and in the labor they contributed to the household. If their wives died, men with young children remarried quickly. While there were many bachelors in Renaissance society, there were few widowers.

In most cases, death came suddenly. Epidemic diseases, of which plague was the most virulent, struck with fearful regularity. They struck harder at the young—children and adolescents, who were the majority of the population—and hardest in the summer months, when other viruses and bacteria weakened the population. Medical treatment was more likely to hasten death than to prolong life. Lorenzo de Medici's physician prescribed powdered pearls for the Florentine ruler's gout. After that, Lorenzo complained more of stomach pains than of gout. Starvation was rare, less because of food shortage than because the seriously undernourished were more likely to succumb to disease than to famine. In urban areas the government would intervene to provide grain from public storehouses at times of extreme shortage; in the countryside, large landholders commonly exercised the same function.

The Quality of Life

Although life may have been difficult during the Renaissance, it was not unfulfilling. Despite constant toil and frequent hardship, people of the Renaissance had reason to believe that their lives were better than those of their ancestors and that their children's lives would be better still. On the most basic level, health improved and, for those who survived plague, life expectancy increased owing to the relative surplus of grain throughout the fifteenth century and the wider variety of foods consumed. Bread remained the most widely consumed foodstuff, but there was more pork and lamb in the diet of ordinary people in the fifteenth century than there would be for the next 400 years. At the upper levels of society, sweet wine and citrus fruits helped to offset the lack of vegetables. This diversification of diet resulted from improvements in transportation and communication, which brought more goods and services to a growing number of towns in the chain that linked the regional centers to the rural countryside.

The towns and cities also introduced a new sense of social and political cohesiveness. The city was something to which people belonged. In urban areas they could join social groups of their own choosing and develop networks of support that were not possible in rural environments. Blood relations remained the primary social group. Kin were the most likely source of aid in times of need, and charity began at home. Kin groups extended well beyond the immediate family, with both cousins and in-laws laying claim to the privileges of blood. The urban family could also depend on the connections of neighborhood. In some Italian cities, wealth or occupation determined housing patterns. In others, like Florence, rich and poor lived side by side and identified themselves with their small administrative unit and with their local church. Thus they could participate in relationships with others both above and below them in social scale. From their superiors they gained connections that helped their families; from their inferiors they gained devoted clients.

As in the Middle Ages, the Church remained the spatial, spiritual, and social center of people's lives. Though Renaissance society became more worldly in outlook, this worldliness took place within the context of an absorbing devotional life. There was not yet any separation between faith and reason. The Church provided explanations for both the mysterious and the mundane. The clergy performed the rituals of baptism, marriage, and burial that measured the passage of life. Religious symbols also adorned the flags of militia troops, the emblems of guilds, and the regalia of the city itself. The Church preserved holy relics that were venerated for their power to protect the city or to endow it with particular skills and resources. Through its holy days, as much as through its rituals, the Church helped to channel leisure activities into community celebrations.

A growing sense of civic pride and individual accomplishment were underlying characteristics of the Italian Renaissance, enhanced by the development of social cohesion and community solidarity that both Church and city-state fostered. It is commonly held that the Renaissance was both elitist and male dominated, that it was an experience separate from that of the society at large. There can be no question that it was the rich who commissioned works of art or that it was the highly skilled male artisans who executed them. But neither lived in a social vacuum. The Renaissance was not an event whose causes were the result of the efforts of the few or whose consequences were limited to the privileged. In fact, the Renaissance was not an event at all. Family values that permitted early apprenticeships in surrogate households and emphasized the continuity of crafts from one generation to the next made possible the skilled artists of the Renaissance cities. The stress on the production of luxury goods placed higher value on individual skills and therefore on excellence in workmanship. Church and state sought to express social values through representational art. One of the chief purposes of wall murals was to instruct the unlettered in religion, to help them visualize the central episodes in Christian history. The grandiose architecture and statuary that adorned central places were designed to enhance civic pride and communicate the protective power of public institutions.

RENAISSANCE ART

In every age, artistic achievement represents a combination of individual talent and predominant social ideals. Artists may be at the leading edge of the society in which they live, but it is the spirit of that society that they capture in word or song or image. Artistic disciplines also have their own technical development. Individually, Renaissance artists were attempting to solve problems about perspective and three-dimensionality that had defeated their predecessors. But the particular techniques or experiments that interested them owed as much to the social context as they did to the artistic one. For example, the urban character of Italian government led to the need for civic architecture, public buildings on a grand scale. The celebration of individual achievement led to the explosive growth of portraiture. Not surprisingly, major technological breakthroughs were achieved in both areas.

This relationship between artist and social context was especially important in the Renaissance, when artists were closely tied to the crafts and trades of urban society and to the demands of clients who commissioned their work. Although it was the elite who patronized art, it was skilled tradespeople who produced it. Artists normally followed the pattern of any craftsman: an apprenticeship begun as a teenager and a long period of training and work in a master's shop. This form of education gave the aspiring artist a practical bent and a keen appreciation for the business side of art. Studios were identified with particular styles and competed for commissions from clients, especially the Church. Wealthy individuals commissioned art as investments, as marks of personal distinction, and as displays of public piety. Isabella d'Este (1474–1539), one of the great patrons of Renaissance artists, wrote hundreds of letters specifying the details of the works she commissioned. She once sent an artist a thread of the exact dimensions of the pictures she had ordered. Demand for art was high. The vast public works projects needed buildings, the new piazzas (public squares) and palazzos (private houses) needed statuary, and the long walls of churches needed murals.

The survival of so many Renaissance masterpieces allows us to reconstruct the stages by which the remarkable artistic achievements of this era took place. Although advances were made in a variety of fields during the Renaissance, the three outstanding areas were architecture, sculpture, and painting. Modern artists would consider each a separate discipline, but Renaissance artists crossed their boundaries without hesitation. Not only could these artists work with a variety of materials, their intensive and varied apprenticeships taught them to apply the technical solutions of one field to the problems of another. Few Renaissance artists confined themselves to one area of artistic expression, and many created works of enduring beauty in more than one medium. Was Michelangelo's greatest achievement his sculpture of David, his paintings on the ceiling of the Sistine Chapel, or his design for the dome of Saint Peter's? Only a century of interdisciplinary cross-fertilization could have prepared the artistic world for such a feat.

An Architect, a Sculptor, and a Painter

The century that culminated in Michelangelo's extraordinary achievements began with the work of three Florentine masters who deeply influenced one another's development: Brunelleschi (1377–1446), Donatello (1386–1466), and Masaccio (1401–1428). In the Renaissance, the dominant artistic discipline was architecture. Buildings were the most expensive investment patrons could make, and the technical knowledge necessary for their successful construction was immense. The architect not only designed a building, he also served as its general contractor, construction supervisor, and inspector. Moreover, the architect's design determined the amount and the scale of the statuary and decorative paintings to be incorporated. By 1400 the Gothic style of building had dominated western Europe for over two centuries. Its characteristic pointed arches, vaulted ceilings, and slender spires had simplified building by removing the heavy walls that were formerly thought necessary to support great structures. Gothic construction permitted greater height, a characteristic that was especially desirable in cathedrals, which stretched toward the heavens. But although the buildings themselves were simplified, the techniques for erecting them became more complex. By the fifteenth century, architects had turned their techniques into an intricate style. They became obsessed by angular arches, elaborate vaultings and buttresses, and long, pointed spires.

It was Brunelleschi who decisively challenged the principles of Gothic architecture by recombining its basic elements with those of classical structures. Basing his designs on geometric principles, Brunelleschi reintroduced planes and spheres as dominant motifs. His greatest work was the dome on the cathedral in Florence, begun in 1420. His design for the dome was simple but bold. The circular windows are set inside a square of panels, which in turn are set inside a rectangle. Brunelleschi is generally credited with having been the first Renaissance artist to have understood and made use of perspective, though it was immediately put to more dramatic effect in sculpture and painting.

In sculpture, the survival of Roman and Hellenistic pieces, mostly bold and muscular torsos, conveyed the direct influence of classical art. Donatello translated these classical styles into more naturalistic forms. His technique is evident in the long, flowing robes in most of his works, sculpted in the natural fashion in which cloth hung. Donatello revived the free-standing statue, which demanded greater attention to human anatomy because it was viewed from many angles. He also led the revival of

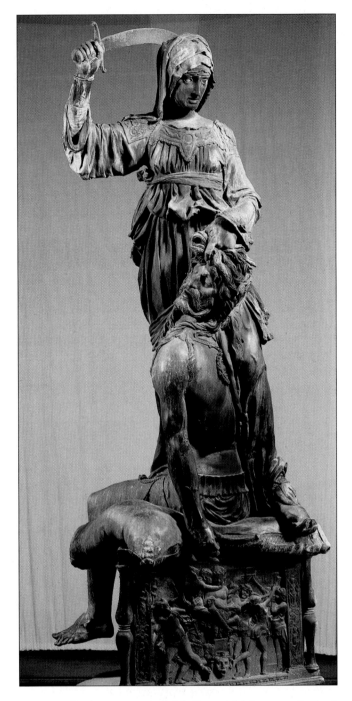

▲ Donatello's bronze statue *Judith Slaying Holofernes* symbolized the Florentines' love of liberty and hatred of tyranny.

the equestrian statue, sculpting the Venetian captain-general Gattamelata for a public square in Padua. This enormous bronze horse and rider (1445–1450) relied on the standpoint of the viewer to achieve its overpowering effect. This use of linear perspective is also seen in Donatello's breathtaking altar scenes of the miracles of Saint Anthony in Padua, which resemble nothing so much as a canvas cast in bronze.

These altar scenes evince the unmistakable influence of the paintings of Masaccio. His frescoes in the Brancacci Chapel in Florence were studied and sketched by all of the great artists of the next generation, who unreservedly praised his naturalism. What most claim the attention of the modern viewer are Masaccio's shading of light and shadow and his brilliant use of linear perspective to create the illusion that a flat surface has three dimensions. Masaccio's work depicted standard Christian themes, but always with a novel approach. In an adoration scene he portrayed a middle-aged Madonna and a dwarfish baby Jesus; in a painting of Saint Peter paying tribute money, he used his own likeness as the face of one of the apostles. His two best-known works are the *Holy Trinity* (1425), which provides the classic example of the use of linear perspective, and the *Expulsion of Adam and Eve* (ca. 1427).

Renaissance Style

By the middle of the fifteenth century, a recognizable Renaissance style had triumphed. The outstanding architect of this period was Leon Battista Alberti (1404–1472), whose treatise *On Building* (1452) remained the most influential work on the subject until the eighteenth century. Alberti consecrated the geometric principles laid down by Brunelleschi and infused them with a humanist spirit. He revived the classical dictum that a building, like a body, should have an even number of supports and, like a head, an odd number of openings. This furthered precise geometric calculations in scale and design.

No sculptor challenged the preeminence of Donatello for another fifty years, but in painting there were many contenders for the garlands worn by Masaccio. The first was Piero della Francesca (ca. 1420–1492), who broke new ground in his concern for the visual unity of his paintings. From portraits to processions to his stunning fresco *The Resurrection* (ca. 1463), Piero concentrated on the most technical aspects of composition. Another challenger was Sandro Botticelli (1445–1510), whose classical themes, sensitive portraits, and bright colors set him apart from the line of Florentine painters with whom he studied. His mythologies of the *Birth of Venus* and *Spring* (ca. 1478) depart markedly from the naturalism inspired by Masaccio.

This concern with beauty and personality is also seen in the paintings of Leonardo da Vinci (1452–1519), whose creative genius embodied the Renaissance ideal of the "universal man." Leonardo's achievements in scientific, technical, and artistic endeavors read like a list of all of the subjects known during the Renaissance. His detailed anatomical drawings and the method he devised for rendering them, his botanical observations, and his engineering inventions (including models for a tank and an airplane) testify to his unrestrained curiosity. His paintings reveal a continuation of the scientific application of mathematics to matters of proportion and perspective. Leonardo's psychological portrait *La Gioconda*

(1503–1506), popularly called the Mona Lisa, is quite possibly the best-known picture in the Western world.

From Brunelleschi to Alberti, from Masaccio to Leonardo da Vinci, Renaissance artists placed a unique stamp upon visual culture. By reviving classical themes, geometric principles, and a spirit of human vitality, they broke decisively from the dominant medieval traditions. Art became a source of individual and collective pride, produced by masters, but consumed by all. Cities and wealthy patrons commissioned great works of art for public display. New buildings rose everywhere, adorned with the statues and murals that still stand as a testimony to generations of artists.

Michelangelo

The artistic achievements of the Renaissance culminated in the creative outpourings of Michelangelo Buonarroti (1475–1564). Poet, sculptor, painter, and architect, Michelangelo imparted his genius to everything he touched. Uncharacteristically, he came from a family of standing in Florentine society. At the age of 14, over the opposition of his father, he was apprenticed to a leading painter and spent his spare time in Florentine churches, copying the works of Masaccio, among others.

In 1490, Michelangelo gained a place in the household of Lorenzo de Medici. He claimed to have taught himself sculpturing during this two-year period, a remarkable feat considering the skills required. In fact, what was unusual about Michelangelo's early development was that he avoided the long years of apprenticeship during which someone else's style was implanted on the young artist. In the Medici household he came into contact with leading Neoplatonists, who taught that humankind was on an ascending journey of perfectibility toward God. These ideas can be seen as one source of the heroic concept of humanity that Michelangelo brought to his work.

In 1496, Michelangelo moved to Rome, where his abilities as a sculptor brought him to the attention of Jacopo Galli, a banker. Galli commissioned a classical work for himself and procured another for a French cardinal, which became the *Pietà*. Although this was his first attempt at sculpting a work of religious art, Michelangelo would never surpass it in beauty or composition. The *Pietà* created a sensation in Rome, and by the time Michelangelo returned to Florence in 1501, at the age of 26, he was already acknowledged as one of the great sculptors of his day. He was immediately commissioned to work on an enormous block of marble that had been quarried nearly a half-century before and had defeated the talents of a series of carvers. He worked continuously for three years on his *David* (1501–1504), a piece that completed the union between classical and Renaissance styles.

Though Michelangelo always believed himself to be primarily a sculptor, his next outstanding work was in the field of painting. In 1508, Pope Julius II summoned

▲ The creation of Adam and Eve, a detail from Michelangelo's frescoes on the ceiling of the Sistine Chapel. The Sistine frescoes had become obscured by dirt and layers of varnish and glue applied at various times over the years. In the 1980s, they were cleaned to reveal their original colors.

Michelangelo to Rome and commissioned him to decorate the ceiling of the small ceremonial chapel that had been built next to the new papal residence. Michelangelo's plan was to portray, in an extended narrative, human creation and those Old Testament events that foreshadowed the birth of the Savior. First, Michelangelo framed his scenes within the architecture of a massive classical temple. In this way he was able to give the impression of having flattened the rounded surface on which he worked. Then, within the center panels, came his fresco scenes of the events of the creation and of human history from the Fall to the Flood. His representations were simple and compelling: the fingers of God and Adam nearly touching, Eve with one leg still emerging from Adam's side, and the half-human snake in the temptation are all majestically evocative.

The *Pietà*, the *David*, and the paintings of the Sistine Chapel were the work of youth. Michelangelo's crowning achievement, the building of Saint Peter's basilica in Rome, was the work of age. The base work of Saint Peter's had already been laid, and drawings for its completion had been made thirty years earlier by Donato Bramante. Michelangelo altered these plans in an effort to bring more light into the church and to provide a more majestic facade outside. His main contribution, however, was the design of the great dome, which centered the interior of the church on Saint Peter's grave. More than the height, it is the harmony of Michelangelo's design that creates the sense of the building thrusting upward like a Gothic cathedral of old. Michelangelo did not live to see the dome of Saint Peter's completed.

Renaissance art served Renaissance society, reflecting both its concrete achievements and its visionary ideals. This art was a synthesis of old and new, building on classical models, particularly in sculpture and architecture, but adding newly discovered techniques and skills. When Giorgio Vasari (1511–1574) came to write his *Lives of the Great Painters, Sculptors, and Architects* (1550), he found over 200 artists worthy of distinction. But Renaissance artists did more than construct and adorn buildings or celebrate and beautify spiritual life. Inevitably, their work expressed the ideals and aspirations of the society in which they lived—the new emphasis on learning and knowledge, on the here and now rather than the hereafter, and, most important, on humanity and its capacity for growth and perfection.

RENAISSANCE IDEALS

Renaissance thought went hand in glove with Renaissance art. Scholars and philosophers searched the works of the ancients to find the principles on which to build a better life. They scoured monastic libraries for forgotten manuscripts, discovering, among other things, Greek poetry, history, the works of Homer and Plato, and Aristotle's *Poetics*. Their rigorous application of scholarly procedures for the collection and collation of these texts was one of the most important contributions of the Renaissance intellectuals who came to be known as humanists. Humanism developed in reaction to an intellectual world that was centered on the Church and dominated by other-worldly concerns. Although humanism was by no means antireligious, it was thoroughly secular in outlook.

Humanists celebrated worldly achievements. Pico della Mirandola's *Oration on the Dignity of Man* (1486) is the best known of a multitude of Renaissance writings influenced by the discovery of the works of Plato. Pico believed that people could perfect their existence on earth because God had endowed humans with the capacity to determine their own fate. This emphasis on human potential found expression in the celebration of human achievement.

Thus humanists studied and taught the humanities, the skills of disciplines such as philology, the art of language, and rhetoric, the art of expression. Though they were mostly lay people, humanists applied their learning to both religious and secular studies. Although most reacted strongly against Scholasticism, they were heavily indebted to the work of medieval churchmen. Nor were they hostile to the Church. Petrarch, Bruni, and Alberti were all employed by the papal court at some time in their careers, as was Lorenzo Valla, the most influential of the humanists. Their interest in human achievement and human potential must be set beside their religious beliefs. As Petrarch stated quite succinctly, "Christ is my God; Cicero is the prince of the language I use."

Humanists and the Liberal Arts

The most important achievements of humanist scholars centered on ancient texts. It was the humanists' goal to discover as much as had survived from the ancient world and to provide texts of classical authors that were as full and accurate as possible.

Studying the Classical World. Although much was already known of the Latin classics, few of the central works of ancient Greece had been recovered. Humanists preserved this heritage by reviving the study of the Greek language and by translating Greek authors into Latin. After the fall of Constantinople in 1453, Italy became the center for Greek studies as Byzantine scholars fled the Ottoman conquerors. Humanists also introduced historical methods in studying texts, establishing principles for determining which of many manuscript copies of an ancient text was the oldest, the most accurate, and the least corrupted by their copyists. This was of immense importance in studying the writings of the ancient Fathers of the Church, many of whose manuscripts had not been examined for centuries. The humanist emphasis on the humanistic disciplines fostered new educational ideals. Along with the study of theology, logic, and natural philosophy, which had dominated the medieval university, humanist scholars stressed the importance of grammar, rhetoric, moral philosophy, and history. They believed that the study of these "liberal arts" should be undertaken for its own sake. This gave a powerful boost to the ideal of the perfectibility of the individual that appeared in so many other aspects of Renaissance culture.

Humanists furthered the secularization of Renaissance society through their emphasis on the study of the classical world. The rediscovery of Latin texts during the late Middle Ages spurred interest in all things ancient. Petrarch, who is rightly called the father of humanism, revered the great Roman rhetorician Cicero above all others. Petrarch's emphasis upon language led to efforts to recapture the purity of ancient Latin and Greek, languages that had become corrupted over the centuries. The leading humanist in the generation after Petrarch was Leonardo Bruni (1370–1444), who was reputed to be the greatest Greek scholar of his day. He translated Plato and Aristotle and did much to advance mastery of classical Greek and foster the ideas of Plato.

Philology and Lorenzo Valla. The study of the origins of words, their meaning, and their proper grammatical usage may seem an unusual foundation for one of the most vital of all European intellectual movements. But philology was, in fact, the humanists' chief concern. This can best be illustrated by the work of Lorenzo Valla (1407–1457). Valla was brought up in Rome, where he was largely self-educated, though according to the prescriptions of the

Florentine humanists. Valla entered the service of Alfonso I, king of Naples, and applied his humanistic training to affairs of state. The kingdom of Naples bordered on the Papal States, and its kings were in continual conflict with the papacy. The pope asserted the right to withhold recognition of the king, a right that was based on the jurisdictional authority supposedly ceded to the papacy by the Emperor Constantine in the fourth century—the so-called Donation of Constantine. Valla settled the matter definitively. Applying historical and philological critiques to the text of the Donation, Valla proved that it could not have been written earlier than the eighth century, 400 years after Constantine's death. He mercilessly exposed words and terms that had not existed in Roman times, such as *fief* and *satrap,* and thus proved beyond doubt that the Donation was a forgery and papal claims based on it were without merit.

Civic Humanism. Valla's career demonstrates the impact of humanist values on practical affairs. Although humanists were scholars, they made no distinction between an active and a contemplative life. A life of scholarship was a life of public service. This civic humanism is best expressed in the writings of Leon Battista Alberti (1404–1472), whose treatise *On the Family* (1443) is a classic study of the new urban values, especially prudence and thrift. Alberti extolled the virtues of "the fatherland, the public good, and the benefit of all citizens." An architect, a mathematician, a poet, a playwright, a musician, and an inventor, Alberti was one of the great virtuosi of the Renaissance.

Alberti's own life might have served as a model for the most influential of all Renaissance tracts, Castiglione's *The Courtier* (1528). Baldesar Castiglione (1478–1529) directed his lessons to the public life of the aspiring elite. It was his purpose to prescribe the characteristics that would make the ideal courtier, who was as much made as born. He prescribed every detail of the education necessary for the ideal state servant, from table manners to artistic attainments. Castiglione's perfect courtier was an amalgam of all that the elite of Renaissance society held dear. He was to be educated as a scholar, he was to be occupied as a soldier, and he was to serve his state as an adviser.

Machiavelli and Politics

At the same time that Castiglione was drafting a blueprint for the idealized courtier, Niccolò Machiavelli (1469–1527) was laying the foundation for the realistic sixteenth-century ruler. No Renaissance work has been more important or more controversial than Machiavelli's *The Prince* (1513). Its vivid prose, its epigrammatic advice—"men must either be pampered or crushed"—and its clinical dissection of power politics have attracted generation after generation of readers. With Machiavelli, for better or worse, begins the science of politics.

Machiavelli came from an established Florentine family. He entered state service and rose to the relatively important office of secretary to the Council of Ten, the organ of Florentine government that was responsible for war and diplomacy. Here, Machiavelli received his education in practical affairs. He was an emissary to Cesare Borgia during his consolidation of the Papal States at the turn of the century and carefully studied Borgia's methods. A tireless correspondent, Machiavelli began to collect materials for various tracts on military matters.

But as suddenly as he rose to his position of power and influence, he fell from it. The militia he had advocated and in part organized was soundly defeated by the Spaniards, and the Florentine republic fell. Machiavelli was summarily dismissed from office in 1512 and was imprisoned and tortured the following year. Released and banished from the city, he retired to a small country estate. Immediately, he began writing what became his two greatest works: *The Prince* (1513) and *The Discourses on Livy* (1519).

Machiavelli has left a haunting portrait of his life in exile, and it is important to understand how intertwined his studies of ancient and modern politics were.

> On the coming of evening, I return to my house and enter my study; and at the door I take off the day's clothing covered with mud and dust, and put on garments regal and courtly; and reclothed appropriately, I enter the ancient courts of ancient men, where, received by them with affection, I feed on that food which only is mine and which I was born for.

The Prince is a handbook for a ruler who would establish a lasting government. It attempts to set down principles culled from historical examples and contemporary events to aid the prince in attaining and maintaining power. By study of these precepts and by their swift and forceful application, Machiavelli believed, the prince might even control fortune itself. What made *The Prince* so remarkable in its day, and what continues to enliven debate over it, is that Machiavelli was able to separate all ethical considerations from his analysis. Whether this resulted from cynicism or from his own expressed desire for realism, Machiavelli uncompromisingly instructed the would-be ruler to be half human and half beast—to conquer neighbors, to murder enemies, and to deceive friends. Steeped in the humanist ideals of fame and *virtù*—a combination of virtue and virtuosity, of valor, character, and ability—he sought to reestablish Italian rule and place government on a stable scientific basis that would end the perpetual conflict among the Italian city-states.

The careers of Lorenzo Valla and Niccolò Machiavelli illustrate how humanists were able to bring the study of the liberal arts into the service of the state. Valla's philological studies had a vital impact on diplomacy; Machiavelli's historical studies were directly applicable to warfare. Humanists created a demand for learning that helps account for the growth of universities, the spread of literacy, and the rise of printing. They also created a hunger for knowledge that characterized intellectual life for nearly two centuries.

THE POLITICS OF THE ITALIAN CITY-STATES

Like studs on a leather boot, city-states dotted the Italian peninsula. They differed in size, shape, and form. Some were large seaports; others were small inland villages. Some cut wide swaths across the plains; others were tiny islands. The absence of a unifying central authority in Italy, resulting from the collapse of the Holy Roman Empire and the papal schism, allowed ancient guilds and confraternities to transform themselves into self-governing societies. By the beginning of the fifteenth century, the Italian city-states were the center of power, wealth, and culture in the Christian world.

This dominion rested on several conditions. First, their geographical position favored the exchange of resources and goods between East and West. A great circular trade encompassed the Byzantine Empire, the North African coastal states, and the Mediterranean nations of western Europe. The Italian peninsula dominated the circumference of that circle. Its port cities, Genoa and Venice especially, became great maritime powers through their trade in spices and minerals. Moreover, just beyond the peninsula to the north lay the vast and populous territories of the Holy Roman Empire. Their continuous need for manufactured goods, especially cloth and metals, was filled by long caravans that traveled from Italy through the Alps. Milan specialized in metal crafts. Florence was a financial capital as well as a center for the manufacture of fine luxury goods. Finally, the city-states and their surrounding areas were agriculturally self-sufficient.

Because of their accomplishments we tend to think of these Italian "city-states" as small nations. Even the term city-state implies national identity. Each city-state governed itself according to its own rules and customs, and each defined itself in isolation from the larger regional or tribal associations that had once prevailed. Italy was neither a nation nor a people.

The Five Powers

Although there were dozens of Italian city-states, by the early fifteenth century five had emerged to dominate the politics of the peninsula. In the south was the kingdom of Naples, the only city-state governed by a hereditary monarchy. Its politics were mired in conflicts over its succession. During the fourteenth century, Naples was ruled successively by French and Hungarian princes. The fifteenth century began with civil warfare between rival claimants of both nations, and it was not until the

▲ Italy, 1494, showing the largest of the city-states. The city-states were among the most wealthy urban areas in the world.

Spaniard Alfonso I of Aragon (1442–1458) secured the throne in 1443 that peace was restored and Naples and Sicily were reunited.

Bordering Naples were the Papal States, whose capital was Rome but whose territories stretched far to the north and lay on both sides of the spiny Apennine mountain chain that extends down the center of the peninsula. Throughout the fourteenth and early fifteenth centuries the territories under the nominal control of the Church were largely independent and included such thriving city-states as Bologna, Ferrara, and Urbino. Even in Rome the weakened papacy had to contend with noble families for control of the city.

The three remaining dominant city-states—Florence, Milan, and Venice—were bunched together in the north. Florence, center of Renaissance culture, was one of the wealthiest cities of Europe before the devastations of the plague and the sustained economic downturn of the late fourteenth century. The city itself was inland, and its main waterway, the Arno, ran to the sea through Pisa, whose subjugation in 1406 was a turning point in Florentine history. Nominally, Florence was a republic, but during the fifteenth century it was ruled in effect by its principal banking family, the Medici.

To the north of Florence was the duchy of Milan, the major city in Lombardy. It, too, was landlocked, cut off from the sea by Genoa. But Milan's economic life was oriented northward to the Swiss and German towns beyond the Alps, and its major concern was preventing foreign invasions. The most warlike of the Italian cities, Milan was a despotism, ruled for nearly two centuries by the Visconti family.

The last of the five powers was the republic of Venice, which became the leading maritime power of the age. Until the fifteenth century, Venice was less interested in securing a landed empire than in dominating a seaborne one. The republic was ruled by a hereditary elite, headed by an elected *doge*, who was the chief magistrate of Venice, and a variety of small elected councils.

The political history of the Italian peninsula during the late fourteenth and early fifteenth centuries is one of unrelieved turmoil. Wherever we look, the governments of the city-states were threatened by foreign invaders, internal conspiracies, or popular revolts. In the 1370s, the Genoese and Venetians fought their fourth war in little more than a century, this one so bitter that the Genoese risked much of their fleet in an unsuccessful effort to conquer Venice itself. At the turn of the century, the Hungarian occupant of the throne of Naples invaded both Rome and Florence. Florence and Milan were constantly at war with each other. Nor were foreign threats the only dangers. In Milan, three Visconti brothers inherited power. Two murdered the third, and then the son of one murdered the other to reunite the inheritance. The Venetians executed one of their military leaders, who was plotting treachery. One or another Florentine family usually faced exile when governments there changed hands. Popular revolts channeled social and economic discontent against the ruling elites in Rome, Milan, and Florence. The revolt of the "Ciompi" (the wooden shoes) in Florence in 1378 was an attempt by poorly paid wool workers to reform the city's exclusive guild system and give guild protection to the wage laborers lower down the social scale. In Milan, an abortive republic was established in reaction against strong-arm Visconti rule.

By the middle of the fifteenth century, however, two trends were apparent amid this political chaos. The first was the consolidation of strong centralized governments within the large city-states. These took different forms but yielded a similar result: internal political stability. The return of the popes to Rome after the Great Schism restored the pope to the head of his temporal estates and began a long period of papal dominance over Rome and its satellite territories. In Milan, one of the great military leaders of the day, Francesco Sforza (1401–1466), seized the reins of power after the failure of the Visconti line. The succession of King Alfonso I in Naples ended a half century of civil war. In both Florence and Venice the grip of the political elite over high offices was tightened by placing greater power in small advisory councils and, in Florence,

by the ascent to power of the Medici family. In sum, this process is known as the rise of signorial rule. The rise of the signories made possible the second development of this period: the establishment of a balance of power within the peninsula.

It was the leaders of the Italian city-states who first perfected the art of diplomacy. Constant warfare necessitated continual alliances, and by the end of the fourteenth century the large city-states had begun the practice of keeping resident ambassadors at the major seats of power. This provided leaders with accurate information about the conditions of potential allies and enemies. Diplomacy was both an offensive and a defensive weapon. This was especially so because the city-states hired their soldiers as contract labor. These mercenary armies, whose leaders were known as *condottieri,* from the name of their contract, were both expensive and dangerous to maintain. If they did not bankrupt their employers, they might desert them or, even worse, turn on them. Thus Francesco Sforza, the greatest *condottiere* of the fifteenth century, gained power in Milan. Sforza's consolidation of power in Milan initially led to warfare, but ultimately it formed the basis of the Peace of Lodi (1454). This established two balanced alliances, one between Florence and Milan and the other between Venice and Naples. These states, along with the papacy, pledged mutual nonaggression, a policy that lasted for nearly 40 years.

The Peace of Lodi did not bring peace. It only halted the long period in which the major city-states struggled against one another. Under cover of the peace the large states continued the process of swallowing up their smaller neighbors and creating quasi-empires. Civilian populations were overrun, local leaders were exiled or exterminated, tribute money was taken, and taxes were levied. Each of the five states either increased its mainland territories or strengthened its hold on them. Venice and Florence especially prospered.

Venice: A Seaborne Empire

Water shaped the destiny of Venice. Facing the Adriatic Sea, the city is formed by a web of lagoons. Through its center snakes the Grand Canal, whose banks were lined with buildings that celebrated its civic and mercantile power. At the Piazza San Marco stood the vast palace of the doge, elected leader of the republic, and the Basilica of Saint Mark, a domed church built in the Byzantine style. At the Rialto were the stalls of bankers and moneylenders. Here, too, were the auction blocks for the profitable trade in European slaves, east European serfs, and battlefield captives who were sold into service to Egypt or Byzantium.

Venice owed its prosperity to trade rather than conquest. Its position at the head of the Adriatic permitted access to the raw materials of both East and West. The rich Alpine timberland behind the city provided the hardwoods necessary for shipbuilding. The inhabitants of the hinterland were steady consumers of grain, cloth, and the new manufactured goods—glass, silk, jewelry, and cottons—that came pouring onto the market in the late Middle Ages.

But the heart of Venetian success lay in the way in which it organized its trade and its government. The key to Venetian trade was its privileged position with the Byzantine Empire. Venice had exchanged with the Byzantines military support for tax concessions that gave Venetian traders a competitive edge in the spice trade with the East. The spice trade was so lucrative that special ships were built to accommodate it. These galleys were constructed at public expense and doubled as the Venetian navy in times of war. By controlling these ships, the government strictly regulated the spice trade. Rather than allow the wealthiest merchants to dominate it, as they did in other cities, Venice specified the number of annual voyages and sold shares in them at auction based on a fixed price. This practice allowed big and small merchants to gain from the trade and encouraged all merchants to find other trading outlets.

Like its trade, Venetian government was also designed to disperse power. Although it was known as the Most Serene Republic, Venice was not a republic in the sense that we use the word; it was rather an oligarchy—a government by a restricted group. Political power was vested in a Great Council whose membership had been fixed at the end of the thirteenth century. All males whose fathers enjoyed the privilege of membership in the Great Council were registered at birth in the Book of Gold and became members of the Great Council when they came of age. From the body of the Great Council, which numbered about 2,500 at the end of the fifteenth century, was chosen the Senate, a council about one-tenth the size, whose members served a one-year term. It was from the Senate that the true officers of government were selected: the doge, who was chosen for life, and members of a number of small councils, who administered affairs and advised the doge. Members of these councils were chosen by secret ballot in an elaborate process by which nominators were selected at random. Terms of office on the councils were extremely short in order to limit factionalism and to prevent any individual from gaining too much power. Though small groups exercised more power in practice than they should have in theory, the Venetian oligarchy was never troubled by either civil war or popular rebellion.

With its mercantile families firmly in control of government and trade, Venice created a vast overseas empire in the East during the thirteenth and fourteenth centuries. Naval supremacy allowed the Venetians to offer protection to strategic outposts in return for either privileges or tribute. But in the fifteenth century, Venice turned westward. In a dramatic reversal of its centuries-old policy, it began a process of conquest in Italy itself. There were several reasons for this new policy. First, the Venetian navy was no longer the unsurpassed power that it once had been. The

Genoese wars had drained resources, and the revival of the Ottoman Turks in the East posed a growing threat that ultimately resulted in the fall of Constantinople (1453) and the end of Venetian trading privileges. Outposts in Dalmatia and the Aegean came under assault from both the Turks and the king of Hungary, cutting heavily into the complicated system by which goods were circulated by Venetian merchants. It was not long before Portuguese competition affected the most lucrative of all the commodities traded by the Venetians: pepper. Perhaps more important, mainland expansion offered new opportunities for Venice. Not all Venetians were traders, and the new industries that were being developed in the city could readily benefit from control of mainland markets. Most decisive of all, opportunity was knocking. In Milan, Visconti rule was weakening, and the Milanese territories were ripe for picking.

Venice reaped a rich harvest. From the beginning of the fifteenth century to the Peace of Lodi, the Most Serene Republic engaged in unremitting warfare. Its successes were remarkable. It pushed out to the north to occupy all the lands between the city and the Habsburg territories; it pushed to the east until it straddled the entire head of the Adriatic; and it pushed to the west almost as far as Milan itself. The western conquests, in particular, brought large populations under Venetian control, which, along with their potential as a market, provided a ready source of taxation. By the end of the fifteenth century, the mainland dominions of Venice were contributing nearly 40 percent of the city's revenue at a cost far smaller than that of the naval empire a century earlier.

Florence: Spinning Cloth into Gold

Florentine prosperity was built on banking and wool. Beginning in the thirteenth century, Florentine bankers were among the wealthiest and most powerful in the world. Initially, their position was established through support of the papacy in its long struggle with the Holy Roman Empire. Florentine financiers established banks in all the capitals of Europe and the East. In the Middle Ages, bankers served more functions than simply handling and exchanging money. Most were also tied to mercantile adventures and underwrote industrial activity. So it was in Florence that international bankers purchased high-quality wool to be manufactured into the world's finest woven cloth.

The activities of both commerce and cloth manufacture depended on external conditions, and so the wealth of Florence was potentially unstable. In the mid-fourteenth century, instability came with the plague that devastated the city. Nearly 40 percent of the entire population was lost in the single year 1348, and recurring outbreaks continued to ravage the survivors. Loss of workers and markets seriously disrupted manufacturing. By 1380, cloth production had fallen to less than a quarter of pre-plague levels. On the heels of plague came wars. The property of Florentine bankers and merchants abroad was an easy target, and in this respect the wars with Naples at the end of the fourteenth century were particularly disastrous. Thirty years of warfare with Milan, interrupted by only a single decade of peace (1413–1423), resulted in total bankruptcy for many of the city's leading commercial families. More significant, the costs of warfare created a massive public debt. Every Florentine of means owned shares in this debt, and the republic was continually devising new methods for borrowing and staving off crises of repayment. Small wonder that the republic turned for aid to the wealthiest banking family in Europe, the Medici.

As befitted a city whose prosperity was based on manufacturing, Florence had a strong guild tradition. The most important guilds were associated with banking and cloth manufacture, but they included the crafts and food processing trades as well. Only guild members could participate in government, electing the nine *Signoria* who administered laws, set tax rates, and directed foreign and domestic policy. Like that of Venice, Florentine government was a republican oligarchy, and like Venice, it depended on rotated short periods in office and selections by lot to avoid factionalism. But Florence had a history of factionalism that was longer than its history of republican government. Its formal structures were occasionally altered so that powerful families could gain control of the real centers of political power, the small councils and emergency assemblies through which the Signoria governed. Conservative leadership drawn from the upper ranks of Florentine society guided the city through the wars of the early fourteenth century. But soon afterward, the leaders of

its greatest families—the Albizzi, the Pazzi, and the Medici—again divided Florentine politics into factions.

The ability of the Medici to secure a century-long dynasty in a government that did not have a head of state is just one of the mysteries surrounding the history of this remarkable family. Cosimo de Medici (1389–1464) was one of the richest men in Christendom when he returned to the city in 1434 after a brief exile. His leading position in government rested on supporters who were able to gain a controlling influence on the Signoria. Cosimo built his party carefully, banishing his Albizzi enemies, recruiting followers among the craftsmen he employed, and even paying delinquent taxes to maintain his voters' eligibility. Most important, emergency powers were invoked to reduce the number of citizens qualified to vote for the Signoria until the majority were Medici backers.

Cosimo was a great patron of artists and intellectuals. He collected books and paintings, endowed libraries, and spent lavishly on his own palace, the Palazzo Medici. Cosimo's position as an international banker brought him into contact with the heads of other Italian city-states, and it was his personal relationship with Francesco Sforza that finally ended the Milanese wars and brought about the Peace of Lodi.

Cosimo's grandson, Lorenzo (1449–1492), held strong humanist values instilled in him by his mother, Lucrezia Tornabuoni, who organized his education. He brought Michelangelo and other leading artists to his garden; he brought Pico della Mirandola and other leading humanists to his table. Lorenzo's power was based on his personality and reputation. His diplomatic abilities were the key to his survival. Almost immediately after Lorenzo came to power, Naples and the papacy began a war with Florence, a war

▼ A view of Florence in 1490.

that was costly to the Florentines in both taxation and lost territory. In 1479, Lorenzo traveled to Naples and personally convinced the Neapolitan king to sign a separate treaty. This restored the Italian balance of power and ensured continued Medici rule in Florence.

There is some doubt whether Lorenzo should be remembered by the title "the Magnificent" that was bestowed on him. His absorption in politics came at the expense of the family's commercial enterprises, which were nearly ruined during his lifetime. Branch after branch of the Medici bank closed as conditions for international finance deteriorated, and the family fortune dwindled. Moreover, the emergency powers that Lorenzo invoked to restrict participation in government changed forever the character of Florentine republicanism, irredeemably corrupting it. There is no reason to accept his enemies' judgment that Lorenzo was a tyrant, but the negative consequences of his rule cannot be ignored. In 1494, two years after Lorenzo's death, the peninsula was plunged into the wars that turned it from the center of European civilization into a satellite region.

The End of Italian Hegemony, 1450–1527

In the course of the Renaissance, western Europe was Italianized. For a century, the city-states dominated the trade routes that connected East and West. Italian manufactures, such as Milanese artillery, Florentine silk, and Venetian glass, were prized above all others. The ducat and the florin, two Italian coins, were universally accepted in an age when every petty prince minted his own. The peninsula exported culture in the same way that it exported goods. Humanism quickly spread across the Alps, aided by the recent invention of printing (which the Venetians soon dominated), and Renaissance standards of artistic achievement were known worldwide and everywhere imitated. The city-states shared their technology as well. The compass and the navigational chart, projection maps, double-entry bookkeeping, eyeglasses, the telescope—all profoundly influenced what could be undertaken. In this spirit, Christopher Columbus, a Genoese seaman, successfully crossed the Atlantic under the Spanish flag, and Amerigo Vespucci, a Florentine merchant, gave his name to the newly discovered continents.

Political and Military Unrest. But it was not in Italy that the rewards of such achievement were enjoyed. There, the seeds of political turmoil and military imperialism, combined with the rise of the Ottoman Turks, were to reap a not unexpected harvest. Under the cover of the Peace of Lodi, the major city-states had scrambled to enlarge their mainland empires. By the end of the fifteenth century, they eyed one another warily. Each expected the others to begin a peninsulawide war for hegemony and took the steps that ultimately ensured the contest. Each shared the dream of recapturing the glory that was Rome. Long years of siege and occupation had militarized the Italian city-states. Venice and Florence balanced their budgets on the backs of their captured territories, Milan had been engaged in constant war for decades, and even the papacy was militarily aggressive.

The Italian Decline. The disunited Italians were not able to meet the challenge of the most remarkable military leader of the age, the Ottoman prince Mehmed II (1451–1481), who conquered Constantinople and Athens and threatened Rome itself. The rise of the Ottomans (whose name is derived from Osman, their original tribal leader) is one of the most compelling stories in world history. Little more than a warrior tribe at the beginning of the fourteenth century, 150 years later the Ottomans had replaced stagnant Byzantine rule with a virile and potent empire. First they gobbled up the towns and cities in a wide arc around Constantinople. Then they fed on the Balkans and the eastern kingdoms of Hungary and Poland. By 1400, they were a presence in all the territory that stretched from the Black Sea to the Aegean; by 1450, they were its master.

Venice was most directly affected by the Ottoman advance. Not only was its favored position in eastern trade threatened, but during a prolonged war at the end of the fifteenth century the Venetians lost many of their most important commercial outposts. Ottoman power closed off the markets of eastern Europe, and by 1480, Venetian naval supremacy was a thing of the past.

Successive popes pleaded in vain for holy wars to halt the advance of the Ottoman Turks. The fall of Constantinople in 1453 was an event of epochal proportions for Europeans; many believed that it foreshadowed the end of the world. Yet it was Italians rather than Ottomans who plunged the peninsula into the wars from which it never recovered.

The Wars of Italy (1494–1529) began when Naples, Florence, and the Papal States united against Milan. At first this alliance seemed little more than another shift in the balance of power. But rather than call on Venice to redress the situation, the Milanese leader, Ludovico Sforza, sought help from the French. An army of French cavalry and Swiss mercenaries, led by Charles VIII of France (1483–1498), invaded the peninsula in 1494. With Milanese support, the French swept all before them. Florence was forced to surrender Pisa, a humiliation that led to the overthrow of the Medici and the establishment of French sovereignty. The Papal States were next to be occupied, and within a year Charles had conquered Naples without engaging the Italians in a single significant battle. Unfortunately, the Milanese were not the only ones who could play at the game of foreign alliances. The Venetians and the pope united and called on the services of King Ferdinand of Aragon and the Holy Roman Emperor. Italy was now a battleground in what became a total European war for dynastic supremacy. The city-states used their foreign allies to settle old scores and to extend their own mainland empires. At the turn of the century, Naples was dismembered. In 1509 the pope conspired to organize the most powerful combination of forces yet known against Venice. All of the mainland possessions of the Most Serene Republic were lost, but by a combination of good fortune and skilled diplomacy, Venice itself survived. Florence was less fortunate, becoming a pawn first of the French and then of the Spanish. The final blow to Italian hegemony was the sack of Rome in 1527 by German mercenaries.

Conclusion

THE SENSE OF LIVING IN A NEW AGE, the spirit of human achievement, and the curiosity and wonderment of writers and artists all characterized the Renaissance. The desire to recreate the glories of Rome was not Machiavelli's alone. It could be seen in the palaces of the Italian aristocracy, in the papal rebuilding of the Holy City, and in the military ambitions of princes. But the legacy of empire, of "ancient and heroic pride," had passed out of Italian hands.

QUESTIONS FOR REVIEW

1. What social and cultural conditions were peculiar to the Italian peninsula, and how might those conditions have contributed to the Renaissance?
2. What were the principal characteristics of the Renaissance style in the visual arts?
3. What is humanism, and why was the study of languages so important to the humanists?
4. In what ways did the ideas of Niccolò Machiavelli reflect the reality of politics in the city-states of Renaissance Italy?

DISCOVERING WESTERN CIVILIZATION ONLINE

You can obtain more information about the Italian Renaissance at the websites listed below. See also the companion website that accompanies this text: www.ablongman.com/kishlansky, which includes an online study guide and additional resources.

Renaissance Society

www.history.evansville.net/renaissa.html#Resources
A site of links to a wide array of subjects relating to the Renaissance. A good starting point.

www.mega.it/eng/egui/epo/secrepu.htm
The history of the Florentine republic with links to major tourist attractions and buildings. Brief biographies of important Florentine citizens can also be found.

www.siue.edu/COSTUMES/COSTUME5_INDEX.HTML
Part of a site devoted to the history of dress. This page shows examples of the clothing worn by different classes as well as in different countries during the fifteenth and sixteenth centuries.

Renaissance Art

www.italian-art.org/frames.html
A pictorial guide to the major artists of the Italian Renaissance and their works. Thumbnail representations lead to links on specific pieces.

www.greatbuildings.com/architects/Leon_Battista_Alberti.html
A page devoted to Alberti's architecture with a brief biography and links to pictures.

www.mega.it/eng/egui/pers/micbuon.htm
A website devoted to Michelangelo with a variety of links to text and images of Renaissance Florence.

www.ibiblio.org/wm/paint/tl/it-ren/
Reproductions of Renaissance art with accompanying text.

SUGGESTIONS FOR FURTHER READING

General Reading

P. Burke, *Culture and Society in Renaissance Italy* (Princeton, N.J.: Princeton University Press, 1999). A good introduction to social and intellectual developments.

J. R. Hale, ed., *A Concise Encyclopedia of the Italian Renaissance* (Oxford: Oxford University Press, 1981). A treasure trove of facts about the major figures and events of the era.

Denys Hay, *The Italian Renaissance* (Cambridge: Cambridge University Press, 1977). The best first book to read, an elegant interpretive essay.

Renaissance Society

Carlo Cipolla, *Before the Industrial Revolution: European Society and Economy, 1000–1700,* 3rd ed. (New York: W. W. Norton, 1994). A sweeping survey of social and economic developments across the centuries.

J. R. Hale, *Renaissance Europe: The Individual and Society* (Berkeley: University of California Press, 1978). A lively study that places the great figures of the Renaissance in their social context.

Margaret L. King, *Women of the Renaissance* (Chicago: University of Chicago Press, 1991). A recent study by a leading women's historian.

Renaissance Art

Howard Hibbard, *Michelangelo* (New York: Harper & Row, 1974). A compelling biography of an obsessed genius.

Michael Levey, *Early Renaissance* (London: Penguin, 1967). A concise survey of art, clearly written and authoritative.

Linda Murray, *High Renaissance and Mannerism* (London: Thames & Hudson, 1985). The best introduction to late Renaissance art.

Renaissance Ideals

Hans Baron, *The Crisis of the Early Italian Renaissance* (Princeton, N.J.: Princeton University Press, 1966). One of the most influential intellectual histories of the period.

George Holmes, *The Florentine Enlightenment,* 2nd ed. (Oxford: Clarendon Press, 1992). A new edition of the best study of intellectual developments in Florence.

Quentin Skinner, *Machiavelli* (Oxford: Oxford University Press, 1981). A brief but brilliant biography.

The Politics of the Italian City-States

Gene Brucker, *Florence, The Golden Age 1138–1737* (Berkeley: University of California Press, 1998). The best single-volume introduction to Florentine history with excellent illustrations.

Frederic C. Lane, *Venice: A Maritime Republic* (Baltimore, Md.: Johns Hopkins University Press, 1973). A complete history of Venice that stresses its naval and mercantile developments.

Charles Stinger, *The Renaissance in Rome* (Bloomington, Ind.: University of Indiana Press, 1998). A thorough account of one of the great ages in the history of Rome.

CHAPTER 12

THE EUROPEAN EMPIRES

- THE VISUAL RECORD: Ptolemy's World
- EUROPEAN ENCOUNTERS
- GEOGRAPHICAL TOUR: Europe in 1500

- THE FORMATION OF STATES
- THE DYNASTIC STRUGGLES

PTOLEMY'S WORLD

FOR OVER 1,000 YEARS, educated Europeans thought of the world as it had been described by Ptolemy in the second century. Most of their knowledge came from guesswork rather than observation. The world was a big place when you had to cross it on foot or by four-legged beast or in small, rickety vessels that hugged the shoreline as they sailed. People without education lived in a world bounded by their farm and their village and thought of neighboring cities as faraway places. There were few experiences to pass from generation to generation, and those that were handed down changed from fact to fancy in the retelling. The people of the Renaissance probably knew less for certain about the planet they inhabited than had the Greeks, and the Greeks knew precious little. But lack of knowledge did not cause confusion. People who lived at the end of the fifteenth century knew enough to conduct their affairs and to dream their dreams.

The map depicts the image of the world that Ptolemy bequeathed, the world that the Renaissance inherited with his calculations and writings. The first thing to notice is that it is shaped as a sphere. Though popular myth held that the world was flat, educated Europeans understood that it was spherical. Ptolemy had shown the earth as an irregular semicircle divided into degrees of longitude, beginning with 0° in the west, where Europe was situated, and progressing to 180° in the east. His construction of latitude was less certain, for less was known (then as now) about the extreme north and south. But Ptolemy did locate an equator, somewhat off center, and he portrayed as accurately as he could what was known of the European landmass. Scandinavia in the north and England and Ireland, set off from the Continent and from each other, are readily visible. The contours of Spain in the southwest are clear, though distorted. Because Ptolemy's world centered on the Mediterranean—literally "sea in the middle of the earth"—it was most accurately reconstructed. Italy, Greece, and Asia Minor are easily recognizable, while France and Spain stretch out of shape like taffy. The size of the Mediterranean is grossly overestimated, its coastline occupying nearly a quarter of the map.

Africa, too, is swollen. It spans the too-wide Mediterranean and then balloons out to cover the entire Southern Hemisphere. Its eastern portions, stretching into Asia, are labeled *terra incognita*—"unknown land." Europe, Africa, and Asia are the only continents. They are watered by a single ocean whose name changes with the languages of its neighboring inhabitants. Most remarkable of all, land covers three quarters of the earth's surface. This was the world as it was known to Europeans in 1400, and this was why the ensuing century would be called the age of exploration.

LOOKING AHEAD

As we shall see in this chapter, using new navigational techniques, advances in ship construction, and a pioneering spirit, Europeans would strike out to both east and west until the globe was circumnavigated, new lands and new peoples encountered, and a sense of living in a new age awakened.

EUROPEAN ENCOUNTERS

The early sixteenth century was an age of exploration in many ways. Knowledge bequeathed from the past created curiosity about the present. Technological change made long sea voyages possible, and the demands of commerce provided incentives. Ottoman expansion on the southern and eastern frontiers of the Continent threatened access to the goods of the East on which Europeans had come to rely. Spices were rare and expensive, but they were not merely luxuries. They had many practical uses. Some acted as preservatives, others as flavorings to make palatable the rotting foodstuffs that were the fare of even the wealthiest Europeans. Some spices were used as perfumes to battle the noxious gases that rose from urban streets and invaded homes and workplaces. The drugs of the East, the nature of which we can only guess at, helped to soothe chronic ill health. The demand for all of these "spices" continued to rise at a greater rate than their supply.

To pay for the spices, Western gold and silver flowed steadily eastward. As supplies of precious metals dwindled, economic growth in Europe slowed. Throughout the fifteenth century, ever-larger amounts of Western specie were necessary to purchase ever-smaller amounts of Eastern commodities. Europe faced a severe shortage of gold and silver, a shortage that threatened its standard of living and its prospects for economic growth. The search was on for new sources of gold.

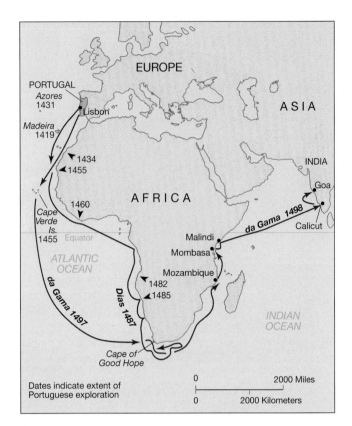

▲ Portuguese explorers moved gradually down the coast of Africa and ultimately reached western India in their search for gold, spices, and slaves.

A Passage to India

It was the Portuguese who made the first dramatic breakthroughs in exploration and colonization. Perched on the southwestern tip of Europe, Portugal was an agriculturally poor and sparsely populated nation. Among its few marketable commodities were fish and wine. However, the Portuguese had long sailed the Atlantic, where they had established bases in the Azores and Madeira islands. Their small ships, known as caravels, were ideal for ocean travel, and their navigators were among the most skillful in the world. Yet they were unable to participate in the lucrative Mediterranean trade in bullion and spices until the expanding power of the Ottomans threatened the traditional eastern sea routes.

Prince Henry the Navigator. In the early fifteenth century, the Portuguese gained a foothold in northern Africa and used it to stage voyages along the continent's unexplored western coast. Like most explorers, the Portuguese were motivated by a mixture of faith and greed. Establishing southern bases would enable them to surround their Muslim enemies while also giving them access to the African bullion trade. The Portuguese navigator Bartolomeu Dias (ca. 1450–1500) summarized these goals

succinctly: "To give light to those who are in darkness and to grow rich." Under the energetic leadership of Prince Henry the Navigator (1394–1460), the Portuguese pushed steadily southward. Prince Henry studied navigational techniques, accumulated detailed accounts of voyages, and encouraged the creation of accurate maps of the African coastline. What was learned on one trip was applied to the next. Soon the Portuguese were a power in the West African trade in slaves and gold ore. Black slaves became a staple of the African voyages, with nearly 150,000 slaves imported in the first fifty years of exploration. Most slaves were used as domestic servants and laborers in Portugal; others were sent to work the lucrative sugar plantations established by Prince Henry on the island of Madeira.

Prince Henry's systematic program paid off in the next generation. By the 1480s, Portuguese outposts had reached almost to the equator, and in 1487, Bartolomeu Dias rounded the tip of Africa and opened the eastern African shores to Portuguese traders. The aim of these enterprises was access to Asia rather than Africa. Dias might have reached India if his crew had not mutinied and forced him to return home. A decade later, Vasco da Gama (ca. 1460–1524) rounded the Cape of Good Hope and crossed into the Indian Ocean. When he returned to

Lisbon in 1499, laden with the most valuable spices of the East, Portuguese ambitions were achieved. Larger expeditions followed, one of which, blown off course, touched the South American coast of Brazil, which was soon subsumed within the Portuguese dominions.

The Asian Trade.   The Portuguese came to the East as traders rather than as conquerors. Building on their experience in West Africa, they developed a policy of establishing military outposts to protect their investments and subduing native populations only when necessary. Their achievements resulted more from determination than from technological superiority. Throughout the East the Portuguese took advantage of local feuds to gain allies, and they established trading compounds that were easily defensible. By the beginning of the sixteenth century, the Portuguese empire spanned both the eastern and western coasts of Africa and the western shores of India. Most important, the Portuguese controlled Ceylon and Indonesia, the precious Spice Islands from which came cloves, cinnamon, and pepper. Almost overnight, Lisbon became one of the trading capitals of the world, tripling in population between 1500 and 1550.

It was northern Europe that was to harvest what Portugal had sown. The long voyages around Africa were costly and dangerous. Portugal produced no valuable commodities and had to exchange bullion for spices. Moreover, the expense of maintaining a far-flung empire ate into the profits of trade at the same time that the increased volume necessary to make the voyages worthwhile drove down spice prices. Between 1501 and 1505, over 80 ships and 7,000 men sailed from Portugal to the East. This vast commitment was underwritten by Flemish, German, and Italian bankers. Soon Antwerp replaced Lisbon as the marketplace for Asian spices. Ironically, it was in the accidental discovery of Brazil rather than in Asia that the Portuguese were rewarded for the enterprise of their explorers.

Mundus Novus

While the bulk of Portuguese resources were devoted to the Asian trade, those of the Spanish kingdom came to be concentrated in the New World. Though larger and richer than its western neighbor, Spain had been segmented into a number of small kingdoms and principalities and divided between Christians and Muslims. Not until the end of the fifteenth century, when the crowns of Aragon and Castile were united and the Muslims were expelled from Granada, could the Spanish concentrate their resources. By then they were far behind in establishing commercial enterprises. With Portugal dominating the African route to India, Queen Isabella of Castile was persuaded by a Genoese adventurer, Christopher Columbus (ca. 1446–1506), to take an interest in a western route. That interest resulted in one of the greatest accidents of history.

Christopher Columbus.   Like all well-informed people of his day, Columbus believed the world was round. He calculated that a westward course would be shorter and less expensive than the path that the Portuguese were breaking around Africa—but he was wrong. He misjudged the size of the globe by a quarter and the distance of the journey by 400 percent. Columbus sailed westward into the unknown in 1492, and on 12 October he landed in the Bahamas, on an island that he named San Salvador. He had discovered a *Mundus Novus*, a New World.

Initially, Columbus's discovery was a disappointment. He had gone in search of a western passage to the Indies and he had failed to return to Spain laden with Eastern spices. Despite his own belief that the islands he had discovered lay just off the coast of Japan, it was soon apparent that he had found an altogether unknown landmass.

▼ This sixteenth-century map of Java and the Moluccas shows European traders bartering for spices. At the upper left, a ship laden with the rich cargo sails for markets in Europe.

Columbus's own explorations and those of his successors continued to focus on discovering a route to the Indies. This was all the more imperative once the Portuguese succeeded in finding the passage around Africa. Rivalry between the two nations intensified after 1500, when the Portuguese began exploring the coast of Brazil. In 1494, the Treaty of Tordesillas had confined Portugal's right to the eastern route to the Indies as well as to any undiscovered lands east of an imaginary line fixed west of the Cape Verde Islands. This entitled Portugal to Brazil. The Spanish received whatever lay west of the line. At the time, few doubted that Portugal had the better of the bargain.

But Spanish-backed explorations soon proved the value of the newly discovered lands. In 1513, Vasco Núñez de Balboa (1475–1517) crossed the Isthmus of Panama and became the first European to view the Pacific Ocean. The discovery of this ocean refueled Spanish ambitions to find a western passage to the Indies.

Ferdinand Magellan. In 1519, Ferdinand Magellan (ca. 1480–1521), a Portuguese mariner in the service of Spain, set sail in pursuit of Columbus's goal of reaching the Spice Islands by sailing westward. His voyage, which he did not live to complete, remains the most astounding of the age. After making the Atlantic crossing, Magellan resupplied his fleet in Brazil. Then his ships began the long southerly run toward the tip of South America, though he had no idea of the length of the continent. After suppressing mutinies and overcoming shipwrecks and desertions, Magellan finally found the straits that still bear his name. By the time Magellan entered the Pacific, he had already lost two ships and much of his crew.

When Magellan finally reached land, first in the Marianas and then in the Philippines, the crew fell prey to natives more aggressive than those they had met in South America. Magellan's foolhardy decision to become involved in a local war cost him his life. It was left to his navigator, Sebastian Elcano (ca. 1476–1526), to complete the journey. In 1522, three years and one month after setting out, Elcano returned to Spain with a single ship and eighteen survivors of the crew of 280. But in his hold were spices of greater value than the cost of the expedition. His return provided practical proof that the world was round, but it also demonstrated that the vastness of the Pacific Ocean made a western passage to the Indies uneconomical. The circumnavigation of Magellan and Elcano brought to an end the first stage of the Spanish exploration of the New World. In 1529, the Spanish crown relinquished its claims to the Spice Islands to the Portuguese for a cash settlement. By then, trading spices was less alluring than mining gold and silver.

The Spanish Conquests

The exploits of Hernando Cortés (1485–1547) opened the next stage of Spanish discovery. The Spanish colonized the New World along the model of their reconquest of Spain. Individuals were given control over land and the people on it in return for military service. The interests of the crown were threefold: to convert the natives to Christianity, to extend sovereignty over new dominions, and to gain profit from the venture. The colonial entrepreneurs had a singular interest: to grow rich. Most of the colonizers came from the lower orders of Spanish society. Even the original captains and governors were drawn from groups, such as younger sons of the nobility, that would have had little opportunity for rule in Castile.

Many of the protective measures taken by the crown to ensure orderly colonization and fair treatment of the natives were ineffective in practice. During the first decades of the sixteenth century, Spanish captains and their followers subdued the Indian populations of the Caribbean Islands and put them to work on the agricultural haciendas they had carved out for themselves. As early as 1498, Castilian women began arriving in the New World. Their presence helped to change the character of the settlement towns from wild frontier garrisons to civilized settlements. Some of the women ultimately inherited huge estates and participated fully in the forging of Spanish America.

Life on the hacienda, however, did not always satisfy the ambitions of the Spanish colonizers. Hernando Cortés was one such conquistador. Having participated in the conquest of Cuba, Cortés sought an independent command to lead an expedition into the hinterland of Central America, where a fabulous empire was rumored to exist. Having gathered a force of 600 men, Cortés sailed across the Gulf of Mexico in 1519 and established a fort at Vera Cruz, where he garrisoned 200 men. He then sank his boats so that none of his company could turn back. With 400 soldiers he marched 250 miles through steamy jungles and over rugged mountains before glimpsing the first signs of the great Aztec civilization. The Aztec empire was a loose confederation of native tribes that the Aztecs had conquered during the previous century. It was ruled by the emperor Montezuma II (1502–1520) from his capital at Tenochtitlán, a marvelous city built of stone and baked clay in the middle of a lake. Invited to an audience with the Aztec emperor, Cortés and his men saw vast stores of gold and silver.

The conquest of the Aztecs took nearly a year and remains an overwhelming feat of arms. Nearly 100,000 natives from the tribes that the Aztecs had conquered supported the Spanish assault. Cortés's cavalry terrified the Aztecs, who had never seen either horses or iron armaments. Cortés also benefited from the Aztec practice of taking battlefield captives to be used in religious sacrifices. This allowed many Spanish soldiers who would otherwise have been killed to be rescued and to fight again.

By 1522, Cortés was master of an area larger than all of Spain. But the cost in native lives was staggering. In 30

THE HALLS OF MONTEZUMA

Bernal Díaz del Castillo (ca. 1492–1581) was one of the soldiers who accompanied Hernando Cortés on the conquest of the Aztecs. Díaz wrote The True History of the Conquest of New Mexico *to refute what he regarded as inaccurate accounts of the conquest. In this passage, he describes the Aztec gods from a Christian point of view and shows how difficult it was for the Europeans to understand the different cultures they were encountering.*

FOCUS QUESTIONS

Díaz describes the Aztec gods as devils and idols. What does this reveal about the Europeans' way of thinking? Why would Cortés want to see Montezuma's gods, and why does Montezuma show them to him?

THEN CORTÉS SAID TO MONTEZUMA . . . . "Your Highness is indeed a great prince, and it has delighted us to see your cities. Now that we are here in your temple, will you show us your gods?"

Montezuma replied that he would first have to consult with his priests. After he had spoken with them, he bade us enter a small tower room, a kind of hall where there were two altars with very richly painted planks on the ceiling. On each altar there were two giant figures, their bodies very tall and stout. The first one, to the right, they said was Uichilobos, their god of war. It had a very broad face with monstrous, horrible eyes, and the whole body was covered with precious stones, gold, and pearls that were stuck on with a paste they make in this country out of roots. The body was circled with great snakes made of gold and precious stones, and in one hand he held a bow and in the other some arrows. A small idol standing by him they said was his page; he held a short lance and a shield rich with gold and precious stones. Around the neck of Uichilobos were silver Indian faces and things that we took to be the hearts of these Indians, made of gold and decorated with many precious blue stones. There were

braziers with copal incense, and they were burning in them the hearts of three Indians they had sacrificed that day. All the walls and floor were black with crusted blood, and the whole place stank.

To the left stood another great figure, the height of Uichilobos, with the face of a bear and glittering eyes made of their mirrors, which they call *tezcal*. It was decorated with precious stones the same as Uichilobos, for they said that the two were brothers. This Tezcatepuca was the god of hell and had charge of the souls of the Mexicans. His body was girded with figures like little devils, with snakelike tails. The walls were so crusted with blood and the floor was so bathed in it that in the slaughterhouses of Castile there was no such stink. They had offered to this idol five hearts from the day's sacrifices. . . .

Our captain said to Montezuma, half laughingly, "Lord Montezuma, I do not understand how such a great prince and wise man as yourself can have failed to come to the conclusion that these idols of yours are not gods, but evil things—devils is the term for them. . . ."

The two priests with Montezuma looked hostile, and Montezuma replied with annoyance, "Señor Malinche, if I had thought that you would so insult my gods, I would not have shown them to you. We think they are very good, for they give us health, water, good seedtimes and weather, and all the victories we desire. We must worship and make sacrifices to them. Please do not say another word to their dishonor."

From Bernal Díaz, *The True History of the Conquest of New Mexico* (1552–1568).

---

years a population of approximately 25 million had been reduced to fewer than 2 million. Most of the loss was due to exposure to European diseases such as smallpox, typhoid, and measles, against which the indigenous peoples had no immunity. Their labor-intensive system of agriculture could not survive the rapid decrease in population, and famine followed pestilence.

This tragic sequence was repeated everywhere the Europeans appeared. In 1531, Francisco Pizarro (ca. 1475–1541) conquered the Peruvian empire of the Incas, vastly extending the territory under Spanish control. A

huge silver mine was discovered in 1545 at Potosí in what is now southern Bolivia, and the gold and silver that poured into Spain in the next quarter century helped to support Spanish dynastic ambitions in Europe. During the course of the sixteenth century, over 200,000 Spaniards migrated across the ocean. Perhaps one in ten were women, who married and set up families. Succeeding generations created huge haciendas built with the forced labor of black African slaves, who proved better able to endure the rigors of mining and farming than did the native peoples.

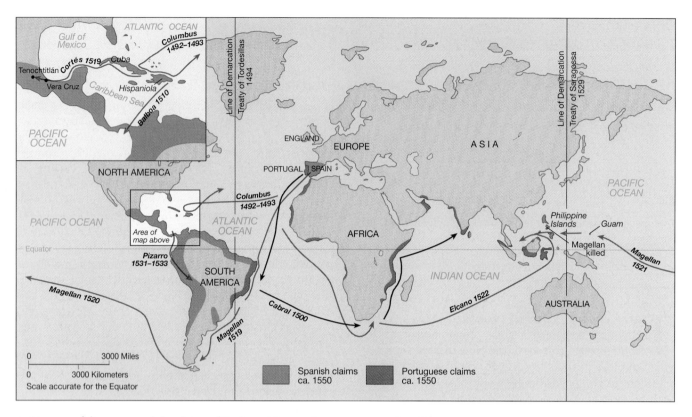

▲ Voyages of discovery and the claims of Spain and Portugal to overseas empires. Pope Alexander VI divided the New World between the two Iberian powers.

The Legacy of the Encounters

By the seventeenth century, long-distance trade had begun to integrate the regions of the world into a single marketplace. Slaves bought in Africa mined silver in South America. The bullion was shipped to Spain, where it was distributed across Europe. Most went to Amsterdam to settle Spanish debts, Dutch bankers having replaced the Italians as the paymasters of Europe. From Holland, some of the silver traveled east to the Baltic Sea, the Dutch lifeline, where vital stores of grain and timber were purchased for home consumption. Even more of this silver was carried to Asia to buy spices in the Spice Islands, cottons in India, or silk in China. Millions of ounces flowed from America to Asia via the European trading routes. On the return voyage, Indian cottons were traded in Africa to purchase slaves for the South American silver mines.

Gold, God, and Glory.　Gold, God, and glory neatly summarized the motives of the European explorers. The gold of Africa and the silver of South America enriched the Western nations. Christian missions arose wherever the European empires touched down: among Africans, Asians, and Amerindians. And glory there was in plenty. The feats of the great discoverers were recounted in story and song.

They were worthy of celebration. In less than 50 years, tenacious European seafarers found passages to the east and

continents to the west. In doing so, they overcame terrors both real and imagined. Sailors to the New World expected to find all manner of horrible creatures. Cyclopes and headless one-legged torsos were popularized in drawings; cannibals and giants were described in realistic detail by the earliest voyagers. Hazardous journeys in uncharted waters took their toll in men and ships. The odds of surviving a voyage of discovery were no better than those of surviving the plague. No wonder mutiny was a constant companion of discovery.

Yet all of these fears and inhibitions were overcome. So, too, were technological problems. Advances in navigational skills, especially in dead reckoning and later in calculating latitude from the position of the sun, were essential preconditions for covering the distances that were to be traveled. Ship designs became more sophisticated. The magnetic compass and the astrolabe were indispensable tools. Better maps and charts fueled both ambitions and abilities. It was a mapmaker who named the newly found continents after Amerigo Vespucci (1451–1512), the Italian explorer who voyaged to Brazil for the Portuguese. It may have been an accident that Columbus found the New World, but it was no coincidence that he was able to land in the same place three more times.

Nor was it happenstance that European forces conquered the peoples they encountered in both east and west. Generations of warfare against Muslims had honed the skills of Christian warriors. European ships were sturdily built and armed with cannons that could be used on land or at sea. Soldiers were well-equipped and battle-tested. Military leaders were trained and experienced in the arts of siege and the tactics of divide and conquer.

European Reflections.   Riches and converts, power and glory, all came in the wake of exploration. But in the process of discovering new lands and new cultures, Europe also learned something of its own aspirations. Early Portuguese voyagers went in quest of the mythical Prester John, a saintly figure who was said to rule a heaven on earth in the middle of Africa. The first children born on Madeira were named Adam and Eve, though this slave plantation of sugar and wine was an unlikely Garden of Eden. The optimism of those who searched for the fountain of youth in the Florida swamps was not only that they would find it there, but that a long life was worth living. Contact with the cultures of the New World also forced a different kind of thinking about life in the old one. The supposed customs of strange lands provided the setting for one of the great works of English social criticism, Sir Thomas More's *Utopia* (1516).

Europe also discovered and revealed a darker side of itself in the age of exploration. Accompanying the boundless optimism and assertive self-confidence that made so much possible was a tragic arrogance and callous disregard toward native peoples. Portuguese travelers described Africans as "dog-faced, dog-toothed people, satyrs, wild men, and cannibals." Such attitudes helped to justify enslavement. Though they encountered heritages that were in some ways richer than their own, few Westerners harbored any appreciation of them. The Portuguese spice trade did not depend on da Gama's indiscriminate bombardment of the port of Calicut. In this and other unfortunate episodes the destruction was wanton. It revealed the rapaciousness, greed, and cruelty of many European conquerors. These were the impulses of the Crusades rather than of the Renaissance.

▼ Contact with cultures of the New World forced Europeans into a different way of thinking about the old world. In this detail from *The Cognoscenti*, a seventeenth-century Flemish painting, English scholars and navigators examine European encounters with new lands and new cultures.

GEOGRAPHICAL TOUR

Europe in 1500

Just as the map of the world was changing as a result of the voyages of discovery, so the map of Europe was changing as a result of the activities of princes. The early sixteenth century was the age of the prince, the first great stage of nation building that would last for the next 300 years. The New Monarchies, as they are sometimes called, consolidated territories that were divided culturally, linguistically, and historically. The states of Europe are political units that were forged by political means: by diplomacy, by marriage, and most commonly by war. The national system that we take for granted when thinking about Europe is a relatively recent development. Before we can observe its beginnings, we must first have a picture of Europe as it existed in 1500 (see **Map A**). At that time it was composed of nearly 500 distinct political units.

Europe is a concept rather than a clear-cut geographical unit. The vast plain that stretches from the Netherlands to the steppes of Russia presents few natural barriers to migration. Tribes had been wandering across this plain for thousands of years, slowly settling into the more fertile lands to practice their agriculture. Only in the south did geographical forces stem the flow of humanity. The Carpathian Mountains created a basin for the settlement of Slavic peoples that ran down to the Black Sea. The Alps provided a boundary for French, Germanic, and Italian settlements. The Pyrenees defined the Iberian peninsula, with a mixture of African and European peoples.

▼ **Map A. Europe in 1500.** While the western part of Europe had taken on its modern features, central and eastern Europe continued to change their boundaries.

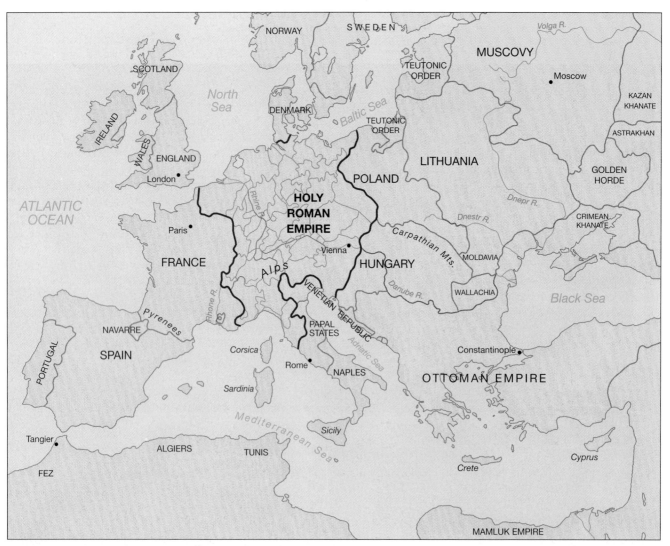

Boundaries of Eastern Europe

In the east, three great empires had created the political geography that could be said to define a European boundary: the Mongol, the Ottoman, and the Russian. During the early Middle Ages, Mongol warriors had swept across the Asian steppes and conquered most of central and southern Ukraine. By the sixteenth century, the Mongol empire was disintegrating, its lands divided into a number of separate states called khanates. The khanate of the Crimea, with lands around the northern shores of the Black Sea, created the southeastern border of Europe (see **Map B**).

The Ottoman territories defined the southern boundary. By 1450, the Ottomans controlled all of Byzantium and Greece, dominating from the Black Sea to the Aegean. Fifty years later, they had conquered nearly all the lands between the Aegean and the Adriatic Seas. A perilous frontier was established on the Balkan peninsula. There the principalities of Moldavia, Wallachia, Transylvania, and Hungary (see **Map B**) held out against the Ottomans for another quarter of a century before being overrun.

The Russian state defined the eastern boundary of Europe. Russia, too, had been a great territorial unit of the Middle Ages, centered at Kiev in the west and stretching eastward into Asia. The advance of the Mongols in the thirteenth century had contracted the eastern part of Russia. Its western domains had disintegrated under the practice of dividing the ruling prince's inheritance among his sons. In 1500, Europe reached as far east as the principality of Muscovy. There the heritage of East and West mingled. In some periods of history, Russia's ties with the West were most important; at other times, Russia retreated into isolation from Europe.

The northern borders of eastern Europe centered on the Baltic Sea, one of the most important trading routes of the early modern era (see **Map B**). On the northern coasts lay the Scandinavian nations of Sweden, Norway, and Denmark. These loosely confederated nations had a single king throughout the fifteenth century. Denmark, the southernmost of the three, was also the richest and most powerful. On the southern side of the Baltic lay the dominions of the Teutonic Knights, physically divided by the large state of Poland-Lithuania. The Teutonic territories, in the valuable Baltic region of Prussia, had been colonized by German crusaders in the thirteenth century.

Poland-Lithuania comprised an enormous territory that stretched the length of Europe from the Baltic to the Black Sea (see **Map B**). The crowns of these two nations had been joined at the end of the fourteenth century, and their dynastic history was tied up with the nations of Bohemia and Hungary to their west and south. While Bohemia was increasingly drawn into the affairs of central Europe, Hungary remained more eastern in orientation. This was partly because the Bohemians gave nominal allegiance to the Holy Roman Emperor and partly because the Ottoman

▲ **Map B. Eastern Europe Before the Consolidation of Russia.** The Duchy of Lithuania had reached the height of its power and stretched from the Baltic to the Black Sea.

conquests had engulfed a large part of the Hungarian territories. At the end of the fifteenth century, Poland, Lithuania, Bohemia, and Hungary were all ruled by the same family, the Jagiellons.

Mongols and Ottomans to the south, Russians in the east, Scandinavia in the north, Poland-Lithuania in the center, and Hungary in the west—such were the contours of the eastern portion of Europe. Its lands were, on the whole, less fertile than those farther west, and its climate was more severe. It was a sparsely populated region. Its wealth lay in the Baltic fisheries, in the Hungarian and Bohemian silver mines, and in the enormous Russian forests, where wood and its by-products were plentiful. Except in the southern portions of Poland and central Bohemia, the region was agriculturally poor. The eastern territories had been resettled during the population crisis of the early fourteenth century. Then native Slavs were joined by German colonizers from the west and Asian conquerors from the east. This clash of cultures did much to define the political history of eastern Europe.

Central Europe

The middle of the continent was defined by the Holy Roman Empire and was occupied almost entirely by Germanic peoples. In length, the empire covered the territory from the North and Baltic seas to the Adriatic and the Mediterranean,

▶ **Map C.** This map of central Europe shows the boundaries of the Holy Roman Empire.

where the Italian city-states were located. In width, it stretched from Bohemia to Burgundy. Politically, central Europe comprised a bewildering array of principalities, church lands, and free towns. By the end of the fifteenth century, the Holy Roman Empire was an empire in name only. The large states of Brandenburg, Bohemia, and Bavaria resembled the political units of the east. In the south, the Alps provided an effective physical boundary, which allowed the Archduchy of Austria and the Swiss Confederation to follow their own separate paths. Stretching across the center of the empire, from the Elbe River to the North Sea, were a jumble of petty states. Great cities such as Nuremberg and Ulm in the south, Bremen and Hamburg in the north, and Frankfurt and Cologne in the west were free municipalities. Large sections of the northwestern part of the empire were governed by the Church through resident bishops. Further

to the west were the prosperous Low Countries: Holland and its port of Amsterdam, Brabant and its port of Antwerp. In the southwest, the empire extended in some places as far as the Rhone River and included the rich estates of Luxembourg, Lorraine, and Burgundy (see **Map C**).

The riches of the empire made it the focal point of Europe. Nearly 15 million people lived within its borders. Its agriculture varied from the olive- and wine-producing areas in the southwest to the great granaries in its center. Rich mineral deposits and large reserves of timber made the German lands industrially advanced. The European iron industry was centered here, and the empire was the arms manufacturer for the western world. The empire was also a great commercial center, heir to the Hanseatic League of the Middle Ages, and its merchants were replacing the Italians as the leading international bankers.

Like the empire, the Italian peninsula was divided into a diverse collection of small city-states (see **Map C**). During the course of the fifteenth century, five of these had emerged as most powerful (see Chapter 11). In the north were the Duchy of Milan, Florence, and Venice. In the south was Rome, spiritual center of Catholicism and residence of the pope. Though Roman and papal government were separate jurisdictions, in fact their fates were bound together. Papal lands stretched far to the north of Rome, and wars to defend or expand them were Roman as well as papal ventures. The kingdom of Naples, the breadbasket of the Mediterranean, occupied the southernmost part of Italy and included the agriculturally rich island of Sicily.

Western Europe

The Iberian peninsula, the French territories, and the British Isles formed the westernmost borders of Europe (see **Map D**). Separated from France in the north by the Pyrenees, and surrounded by the Atlantic Ocean and the Mediterranean Sea on the west and east, the Iberian peninsula was most influenced by the fact that it is separated from North Africa only by the easily navigable Strait of Gibraltar. During the Middle Ages, the peninsula was overrun by North African Muslims, whom the Spanish called Moors. From the eighth to the fifteenth centuries, Iberian history was dominated by the *reconquista*, the recapture and re-Christianization of the conquered territories. This reconquest was finally completed in 1492, when the Moors were pushed out of Granada and the Jews were expelled from Spain. At the end of the fifteenth century, the Iberian peninsula contained several separate kingdoms. The most important were Portugal on the western coast; Aragon with its Mediterranean ports of Barcelona and Valencia; and Castile, the largest of the Iberian states (see **Map D**). The marriage of King Ferdinand of Aragon and Queen Isabella of Castile in 1469 had joined the crowns of Aragon and Castile, but the two kingdoms remained separate.

The remnants of ancient Gaul were also favored by a maritime location, with coasts on the Mediterranean and the Atlantic. Britain was less than thirty miles from France across the English Channel. Toward the end of the fifteenth century, France was still divided into many smaller fiefs. The royal domain centered on Paris and extended to Champagne in the east and Normandy in the west (see **Map D**). South of this area, however, from Orléans to Brittany, were principalities that had long been contested between England and France. Nor was the rich central plain yet integrated into the royal domain. Agriculturally, French lands were the richest in Europe. France enjoyed both Mediterranean and Atlantic climates, which suited the growing of the widest variety of foodstuffs. Its population of approximately 13 million was second only to that of the Holy Roman Empire.

▲ **Map D.** Western Europe was already consolidated into nation-states.

Across the Channel lay Britain (comprising England, Scotland, and Wales) and Ireland (see **Map D**). Britain had been settled by an array of European colonizers—Romans, Danes, Angles, and Saxons—before being conquered in the eleventh century by the French Normans. From that time, it was protected by the rough waters of the English Channel and the North Sea and allowed to develop a distinct cultural and political heritage. Wales to the west and Scotland to the north were still separate nations at the beginning of the sixteenth century. Both were mountainous lands with harsh climates and few natural advantages. They were sparsely populated. Though Ireland, too, was sparsely populated, it contained several rich agricultural areas that were especially suited for dairying and grazing.

In 1500, Europe exhibited a remarkable diversity of political and geographical forms. Huge states in the east, tiny principalities in the center, and emerging nations in the west seemingly had little in common. There was as yet no state system, and there was no clear group of dominant powers. The western migration of the Germanic peoples appeared to be over, but their consolidation was as yet unimagined. The Iberians struggled to expel the Moors, the Hungarians to hold back the Ottomans. Everywhere one looked were fragmentation and disarray. Yet in less than half a century the largest empire yet known in the West would be formed. States would be consolidated and dynasties established all over the continent. And with the rise of the state would come the dream of dominion, an empire over all of Europe.

THE FORMATION OF STATES

Machiavelli identified the prince as the agent of change in the process of state formation. He believed that the successful prince could bring unity to his lands, security to his borders, and prosperity to his subjects. The unsuccessful prince brought nothing but ruin.

A process as long and as complex as the formation of a state, however, depends on more than the will of an individual. Factors such as geography, population, and natural resources are all important. So, too, are the structures through which human activity is channeled. The ways in which families are organized and wealth is transmitted from generation to generation can result in large estates with similar customs or small estates with varying ones. The manner in which social groups are formed and controlled can mean that power is centralized or dispersed. The beliefs of ordinary people and the way they practice them can define who is a part of a community and who is apart from it. All these elements and many others affected the way in which European states began to take shape at the end of the fifteenth century. Despite these complexities, we should not lose sight of the simple truth of Machiavelli's observations. In the first stages of the consolidation of European nations the role of the prince was crucial.

Indeed, in the middle of the fifteenth century there were many factors working against the formation of large states in Europe. The most obvious involved simple things such as transportation and communication. The distance that could be covered quickly was very small. In wet and cold seasons, travel was nearly impossible. Similarly, directives from the center to the localities were slow to arrive and slower still to be adopted. Large areas were difficult to control and to defend. Communication was not only subject to the hazards of travel. Distinct languages or dialects, a principal feature of small states, contributed to separate cultures. Customary practices, common ancestry, and shared experiences helped to define a sense of community through which small states defined themselves.

To these natural forces that acted to maintain the existence of small units of government were added invented ones. To succeed, a prince had to establish supremacy over a number of rivals. For the most part, states were inherited. In some places it was customary to follow the rule of primogeniture, inheritance by the eldest son. In others, estates were split among sons or among children of both sexes. Some traditions, like the French, excluded inheritance through women; others, like the Castilian, treated women's claims as equal to men's. Short lives meant prolonged disputes about inheritance. Rulers had to defend their thrones from rivals with strong claims to legitimacy.

Rulers also had to defend themselves from the ambitions of their mightiest subjects. The constant warfare of the European nobility was one of the central features of the later Middle Ages. To avoid resort to arms, princes and peers entered into all manner of alliances, using their children as pawns and the marriage bed as the chessboard. Rulers also faced independent institutions within their states, powerful organizations that had to be won over or crushed. By the end of the fifteenth century, the long process of taming the Church was about to enter a new stage. Fortified towns presented a different problem. They possessed both the labor and the wealth necessary to raise and maintain armies. They also jealously guarded their privileges. Rulers who could not tax their towns could not rule their state. Finally, most kingdoms had assemblies representing the propertied classes, especially in matters of taxation. Some, like the English Parliament and the Spanish Cortes, were strong; others, like the Imperial Diet and the French Estates-General, were weak. But everywhere, they posed an obstacle to the extension of the power of princes.

In combination, these factors slowed and shaped the process of state formation. But neither separately nor together were they powerful enough to overcome it. The fragmentation of Europe into so many small units of government made some consolidation inevitable; and as the first large states took shape, the position of smaller neighbors grew ever more precarious.

This was especially true by the end of the fifteenth century because of the increase in the destructive power of warfare. Technological advances in cannonry and in the skills of gunners and engineers made medieval fortifications untenable. The fall of Constantinople was as much a military watershed as it was a political one. Gunpowder decisively changed battlefield tactics. It made heavy armor obsolete and allowed for the development of a different type of warfare. Lightly armored horses and riders not only could inflict more damage on one another, but were now mobile enough to be used against infantry. Infantry armed with long pikes or small muskets became the crucial components of armies that were growing ever larger. Systems of supply were better, sources of small arms were more available, and the rewards of conquest were more tangible. What could not be inherited or married could be conquered.

Eastern Configurations

The interplay of factors that encouraged and inhibited the formation of states is most easily observed in the eastern parts of Europe. There the different paths taken by Muscovy and Poland-Lithuania stand in contrast. At the beginning of the sixteenth century, the principality of Muscovy was the largest European political unit. Muscovy had established itself as the heir to the ancient state of Russia through conquest, shrewd political alliances, and the good fortune of its princes to be blessed with long reigns. Muscovy's growth was phenomenal. Under Ivan III, "the Great" (1462–1505), Muscovy expanded to the north and west. During a long series of wars it annexed Novgorod and large parts of Livonia and Lithuania. Between 1460 and 1530, Muscovy increased its territory by 1.5 million square miles.

A number of factors led to the rise of Muscovy. First, external threats had diminished. The deterioration of the Mongol empire, which had dominated south-central Russia, allowed Ivan to escape the yoke of Mongol rule that the Russian princes had worn for centuries. Second, the fall of Constantinople made Muscovy the heir to eastern Christendom, successor to the Roman and Byzantine empires. Ivan's marriage to Sophia, niece of the last emperor of Byzantium, cemented this connection. Sophia brought both Italian craftsmen and Byzantine customs to the Russian court, helping Ivan open his contacts with the wider world. Third, Ivan the Great was fortunate in having no competitors for his throne. He was able to use other social groups to help administer the new Muscovite territories without fear of setting up a rival to power.

Ivan extended the privileges of his nobility and organized a military class, the members of which received land as a reward for their fidelity. He also developed a new theory of sovereignty that rested on divine rather than temporal power. Traditionally, Russian princes ruled their lands by patrimony. They owned both estates and occupants. Ivan the Great extended this principle to cover all lands to which there was an ancient Russian claim and combined it with the religious authority of the Orthodox Church. Both he and his successors ruled with the aid of able Church leaders, who were normally part of the prince's council.

Ivan the Terrible. What made the expansion of Muscovy so impressive is that land once gained was never lost. The military and political achievements of Ivan the Great were furthered by his son Vasili and his more famous grandson Ivan IV, "the Terrible" (1533–1584). Ivan IV defeated the Mongols on his southeastern border and incorporated the entire Volga basin into Muscovy. But his greatest ambition was to gain a port on the Baltic Sea and establish a northern outlet for commerce. His objective was to conquer Livonia, but in nearly three decades of warfare between Muscovy and Poland-Lithuania, with whom Livonia had allied itself, Muscovy's territorial victories fell short of the real prize. Furthermore, Ivan's northern campaigns seriously weakened the defense of the south. In 1571, the Crimean Tartars advanced from their territories on Muscovy's southwestern border and inflicted

a powerful psychological blow when they burned the city of Moscow. Although the Tartars were eventually driven off Muscovite soil, expansion in both north and south was at an end for the next 75 years.

By the reign of Ivan IV, Muscovite society was divided roughly into three groups: the hereditary nobility, known as the boyars; the military service class; and the peasantry, who were bound to the land. There was no large mercantile presence in Muscovy, and its urban component remained small. The boyars, who were powerful landlords of great estates, owed little to the tsar. They inherited their lands and did not necessarily benefit from expansion and conquest. Members of the military service class, on the other hand, were bound to the success of the crown. Their military service was a requirement for the possession of their estates, which were granted out of lands gained through territorial expansion. Gradually, the new military service class grew in power and prestige, largely at the expense of the older boyars. Ivan IV used members of the military service class as legislative advisers and elevated them in his parliamentary council (the Zemsky Sobor), which also contained representatives of the nobility, clergy, and towns.

Unlike his grandfather, Ivan IV had an abiding mistrust of the boyars. They had held power when he was a child, and it was rumored that his mother had been poisoned by them. It was his treatment of the boyars that earned him the nickname "the Terrible." During his brutal suppression of supposed conspiracies, several thousand families were massacred by Ivan's own orders and thousands more by the violent excesses of his agents. He also forcibly relocated boyar families. This practice made the boyars' situation similar to that of the military service class, whose members owed their fortunes to the tsar. For the first time the boyars were required to perform military service to the tsar.

All of these measures contributed to the breakdown of local networks of influence and power and to a disruption of local governance. But they also made possible a system of central administration, one of Ivan IV's most important achievements. He created departments of state to deal with the various tasks of administration, and this resulted in more efficient management of revenues and of the military. Ivan IV promoted the interests of the military service class over those of the boyars, but he did not destroy the nobility. New boyars were created, especially in conquered territories, and these new families owed their positions and loyalty to the prince. Both boyars and the military benefited from Ivan's policy of binding the great mass of people to the land. Russian peasants had few political or economic rights in comparison to Western peasants, but during the early sixteenth century even the meager rights of Russian peasants were curtailed. The right of peasants to move from the estate of one lord to that of another was suspended, all but binding the peasantry to the land. This serfdom made possible the prolonged absence of military leaders from their estates and contributed to the creation of the military service class. But it also made imperative the costly system of coercing agricultural and industrial labor. In the long term, serfdom retarded economic development by removing the incentive for large landholders to make investments in commerce or to improve agricultural production.

Poland-Lithuania. The growth of an enlarged and centralized Muscovy stands in contrast to the experiences of Poland-Lithuania during the same period. At the end of the fifteenth century, Casimir IV (1447–1492) ruled the kingdom of Poland and the grand duchy of Lithuania. His son Wladislaw II ruled Bohemia (1471–1516) and Hungary (1490–1516). Had the four states been permanently consolidated, they could have become an effective barrier to Ottoman expansion in the south and Russian expansion in the east. But the union of crowns did not mean the union of states or the dominance of any one state.

While the Polish-Lithuanian monarchs enjoyed longevity similar to that of the Muscovites, those who ruled Hungary and Bohemia were not so fortunate. By the sixteenth century, a number of claimants to both crowns existed, and the competition was handled by diplomacy rather than war. The accession of Wladislaw II, for example, was accompanied by large concessions first to the Bohemian towns and later to the Hungarian nobility. The formal union of the Polish and Lithuanian crowns in 1569 also involved the decentralization of power and the strengthening of the rights of the nobility in both countries. In the end, the states split apart. The Russians took much of Lithuania; the Ottomans took much of Hungary. Bohemia, which in the fifteenth century had been ruled more by its nobles than by its king, was absorbed into the Habsburg territories after 1526.

There were many reasons why a unified state failed to develop in east-central Europe. First, wars with the Ottomans and the Russians absorbed resources. Second, the princes faced rivals to their crowns. Though Casimir IV was able to place his son on the thrones of both Bohemia and Hungary, he managed to do so against the powerful claims of the Habsburg princes, who continued to intrigue against the Jagiellons. These contests for power necessitated concessions to leading citizens, which decreased the princes' ability to centralize their kingdoms or to effect real unification among them. The nobility of Hungary, Bohemia, and Poland-Lithuania all developed strong local interests that increased over time. In Bohemia, Wladislaw II was king in name only, and even in Poland the nobility won confirmation of its rights and privileges from the monarchy. War, rivalries for power, and a strong nobility prevented any one prince from dominating this area as the princes of Muscovy dominated theirs.

The Western Powers

As in the east, there was no single pattern to the consolidation of the large western European states. They, too, were internally fragmented and externally imperiled. While England had to overcome the ruin of decades of civil war, France and Spain faced the challenges of invasion and occupation. Western European princes struggled against powerful institutions and individuals within their states. Some they conquered; others they absorbed. Each nation formed its state differently: England by administrative centralization, France by good fortune, and Spain by dynastic marriage. Yet in 1450, few imagined that any one of these states would succeed.

The Taming of England. Alone among European states, England suffered no threat of foreign invasion during the fifteenth century. This island fortress might easily have become the first consolidated European state were it not for the ambitions of the nobility and the weakness of the crown. For 30 years, the English aristocracy fought over the spoils of a helpless monarch. The Wars of the Roses (1455–1485) were as much a free-for-all among the English peerage as they were a contest for the throne between the houses of Lancaster and York. At their center was an attempt by the dukes of York to wrest the crown from the mad and ineffective Lancastrian king Henry VI (1422–1461). All around the edges was the continuation of local and family feuds that had little connection to the dynastic struggle.

Three decades of intermittent warfare had predictable results. The houses of Lancaster and York were both destroyed. Edward IV (1461–1483) succeeded in gaining the crown for the House of York, but he was never able to wear it securely. When he died, his children, including his heir, Edward V (1483), were placed in the protection of their uncle Richard III (1483–1485). It was protection that they did not survive. The two boys disappeared, reputedly murdered in the Tower of London, and Richard declared himself king. Richard's usurpation led to civil war, and he was killed by the forces of Henry Tudor at the battle of Bosworth Field in 1485. By the end of the Wars of the Roses, the monarchy had lost both revenue and prestige, and the aristocracy had stored up bitter memories for the future.

It was left to Henry Tudor to deal with the power of the nobility and the poverty of the monarchy. No English monarch had held secure title to the throne for over a century. Henry Tudor, as Henry VII (1485–1509), put an end to this dynastic instability at once. He married Elizabeth of York, in whose heirs would rest the legitimate claim to the throne. Their children were indisputable successors to the crown. He also began the long process of taming his overmighty subjects. Traitors were hanged, and turncoats were rewarded. He and his son Henry VIII (1509–1547) adroitly created a new peerage, which soon was as numerous as the old feudal aristocracy. These new nobles owed their titles and loyalty to the Tudors. They were favored with offices and spoils and were relied on to suppress both popular and aristocratic rebellions.

The financial problems of the English monarchy were not so easily overcome. In theory and practice, an English king was normally supposed to live "of his own," that is, by relying on the revenues from his own estates rather than on payments from his subjects. The English landed classes had established the principle that only on extraordinary occasions were they to be required to contribute to the maintenance of government. This principle was defended through their representative institution, the Parliament. When the kings of England wanted to tax their subjects, they had first to gain the assent of Parliament. Though Parliaments did grant requests for extraordinary revenue, especially for national defense, they did so grudgingly. The English landed elites were not exempt from taxation, but they were able to control the amount of taxes they paid.

Since the king was dependent on the efficient management of his own estates, English state building required the growth of centralized institutions that could oversee royal lands and collect royal customs. Gradually, medieval institutions such as the Exchequer were supplanted by newer organs that were better able to adjust to modern methods of accounting, record keeping, and enforcement. Henry VII sent ministers to view and value royal lands. He ordered the cataloging and collection of feudal obligations in order to squeeze as much as possible from a not very juicy inheritance. His financial problems limited both domestic and foreign policy.

Not until the middle of the next reign was the English monarchy again solvent. As a result of his dispute with the papacy, Henry VIII confiscated the enormous wealth of the Catholic church and, with one stroke, solved the Crown's monetary problems (see Chapter 13). But the real contribution that Henry and his chief minister, Thomas Cromwell (ca. 1485–1540), made to forming an English state was the way in which this windfall was administered. Cromwell accelerated the process of centralizing government that had begun under Edward IV. He divided administration according to its functions by creating separate departments of state, modeled on courts. These new departments were responsible for record keeping, revenue collection, and law enforcement. Each had a distinct jurisdiction and a permanent trained staff. Cromwell coordinated the work of these distinct departments by expanding the power of the Privy Council, which included the heads of these administrative bodies. Through a long evolution, the Privy Council came to serve as the king's executive body. Cromwell also saw the importance of Parliament as a legislative body. Through Parliament, royal policy could be turned into statutes that had the assent of the political nation. If Parliament was well managed, issues that were potentially controversial could be

▲ Hans Holbein's last portrait of Henry VIII, painted in 1542. Henry made England into one of the world's greatest naval powers but embroiled the kingdom in a series of costly foreign wars. He married six times in an effort to produce a legitimate male heir.

defused. Laws passed by Parliament were more easily enforced locally than were proclamations issued by the king.

The Unification of France. The forces working against the consolidation of a French state were formidable. France was surrounded by aggressive and powerful neighbors with whom it was frequently at war. Its greatest nobles were semi-independent princes who were constant rivals for the throne. French people were primarily loyal to their province and viewed the pretensions of the monarchy with deep suspicion. France was also splintered by profound regional differences. The north and south were divided by culture and by language (the *langue d'oc* in the south and the *langue d'oil* in the north).

The first obstacles to unification that were overcome were the external threats to French security. For over a century the throne of France had been contested by the kings of England. The so-called Hundred Years' War, which was fought intermittently between 1337 and 1453, originated in a dispute over the inheritance of the French crown and English possessions in Gascony in southern France (see Chapter 10). The war was fought on French soil, and by the early fifteenth century, English conquests in north central France extended from Normandy to the borders of the Holy Roman Empire.

The struggle between the kings of England and the kings of France allowed French princes and dukes, who were nominally vassals of the king, to enhance their autonomy by making their own alliances with the highest bidder. When the English were finally driven out of France in the middle of the fifteenth century, the kings of France came into a weakened and divided inheritance.

Nor was England the only threat to the security of the French monarchy. On France's eastern border, in a long arching semicircle, were the estates of the dukes of Burgundy. The kings of France and the dukes of Burgundy shared a common ancestry: both were of the House of Valois. But the two branches of the family grew apart. The original Burgundian inheritance was in the southeast, centered at Dijon. A good marriage and good fortune brought to the first duke the rich northern province of Flanders. For the next hundred years, the aim of the dukes of Burgundy was to unite their divided estates. While England and France were locked in deadly embrace, Burgundy systematically grew, absorbing territory from both the Holy Roman Empire and France. The conquest of Lorraine finally connected the ducal estates in one long, unbroken string. The power of Burgundy threatened its neighbors in all directions. Both France and the empire were too weak to resist its expansion, but the confederation of Swiss towns to the southwest of Burgundy was not. In a series of stunning military victories, Swiss forces repelled the Burgundians from their lands and demolished their armies. Charles the Bold, the last Valois duke of Burgundy, fell at the Battle of Nancy in 1477. His estates were quickly dismembered. France recovered its ancestral territories, including Burgundy itself, and through no effort of its own was now secure on its eastern border.

The king who was most associated with the consolidation of France was Louis XI (1461–1483). He inherited an estate that had been exhausted by warfare and civil strife. More by chance than by plan, he vastly extended the territories under the dominion of the French crown and, more important, subdued the nobility. Louis XI was as cunning as he was peculiar. In an age in which royalty was expressed through magnificence, Louis sported an old felt hat and a well-worn coat. His enemies constantly underestimated his abilities, which earned him the nickname "the Spider." But during the course of his reign, Louis XI gradually won back what he had been forced to give away. Years of fighting both the English and each other left the ranks of the French aristocracy depleted. As blood spilled on the battlefields, the stocks of fathers and sons ran low. Estates to which no male heirs existed fell forfeit to the king. In this manner the crown absorbed Anjou and Maine in the northwest and Provence in the south. More important, Louis XI ultimately obtained control of the two greatest independent fiefs, Brittany and Orléans, by marrying his son Charles to the heiress of Brittany and his daughter Jeanne to the heir of Orléans. When, in 1527, the lands of the duke of Bourbon fell to the crown, the French monarch ruled a unified state.

The French experience demonstrated how a state could be formed without the designs of a great leader. Neither Louis XI nor his son Charles VIII (1483–1498) was a nation builder. Louis's main objective was always to preserve his estate. His good fortune saved him from the consequences of many ill-conceived policies. But no amount of luck could make up for Louis's failure to obtain the Burgundian Low Countries for France after the death of Charles the Bold in 1477. The marriage of Mary of Burgundy to Maximilian of Habsburg was one of the great turning points in European history. It initiated a struggle for control of the Low Countries that endured for over two centuries.

These long years of war established the principle of royal taxation, which was so essential to the process of state building in France. This enabled the monarchy to raise money for defense and for consolidation. Because of the strength of the nobles, most taxation fell only on the commoners, the so-called third estate. The *taille* was a direct tax on property from which the nobility and clergy were exempt. The *gabelle* was a consumption tax on the purchase of salt in most parts of the kingdom, and the *aide* was a tax on a variety of commodities, including meat and wine. These consumption taxes were paid by all members of the third estate, no matter how poor they might be. Although there was much complaint about taxes, the French monarchy established a broad base for taxation and a high degree of compliance long before any other European nation.

Along with money went soldiers, needed to repel the English and to defend the crown against rebels and traitors. Again the French monarchy was the first to establish the principle of a national army, raised and directed from the center but quartered and equipped regionally. From the nobility were recruited the cavalry, from the towns and countryside the massive infantry. Fortified towns received privileges in return for military service to the king. Originally, towns were required to provide artillery, but constant troubles with the nobility had led the kings of France to establish their own store of heavy guns. The towns supplied small arms, pikes, and swords and later pistols and muskets. By the beginning of the sixteenth century, the French monarch could raise and equip an army of his own.

Taxation and military obligation demanded the creation and expansion of centralized institutions of government. This was the most difficult development in the period of state formation in France. The powers of royal agents were constantly challenged by the powers of regional nobles. It is easy to exaggerate the extent of the growth of central control and to underestimate the enduring hold of regional and provincial loyalties. Even the crown's absorption of estates did not always end local privileges and customs. But despite continued regional autonomy, a beginning had been made.

The Marriages of Spain.   Before the sixteenth century there was little prospect of a single nation emerging on the Iberian peninsula. North African Muslims, called Moors, occupied the province of Granada in the south; the stable kingdom of Portugal dominated the western coast. The Spanish peoples were divided among a number of separate states. The two most important were Castile, the largest and wealthiest kingdom, and Aragon, which was composed of a number of quasi-independent regions, each of which maintained its own laws and institutions. Three religions and four languages (not including dialects) widened these political divisions. And the different states had different outlooks. Castile was, above all, determined to rid itself of the Moors in Granada and to convert to Christianity its large Jewish population. Aragon played in the high-stakes game for power in the Mediterranean. It claimed sovereignty over Sicily and Naples and exercised it whenever it could.

A happy teenage marriage brought together the unhappy kingdoms of Castile and Aragon. When Ferdinand of Aragon and Isabella of Castile secretly exchanged wedding vows in 1469, both their homelands were rent by civil war. In Castile, Isabella's brother Henry IV (1454–1474) struggled unsuccessfully against the powerful Castilian nobility. In Aragon, Ferdinand's father, John II (1458–1479), faced a revolt by the rich province of Catalonia on one side and the territorial ambitions of Louis XI of France on the other. Joining the heirs together increased the resources of both kingdoms. Ferdinand took an active role in the pacification of Castile, while Castilian riches allowed him to defend Aragon from invasion. In 1479, the two crowns were united, and the Catholic monarchs, as they were called, ruled the two kingdoms jointly. But the unification of the crowns of Castile and Aragon was not the same as the formation of a single state. Local privileges were zealously guarded, especially in Aragon, where the representative institutions of the towns, the

Cortes, were aggressively independent. The powerful Castilian nobility never accepted Ferdinand as their king and refused him the crown after Isabella's death.

But Ferdinand and Isabella (1479–1516) took the first steps toward forging a Spanish state. Their most notable achievement was the final recovery of the lands that had been conquered by the Moors. For centuries the Spanish kingdoms had fought against the North African Muslims who had conquered large areas of the southern peninsula. The *reconquista* ("reconquest") was characterized by short bursts of warfare followed by long periods of wary coexistence. By the middle of the fifteenth century, the Moorish territory had been reduced to the province of Granada. The final stage of the reconquista began in 1482 and lasted for a decade. It was waged as a holy war and was financed in part by grants from the pope and the Christian princes of Europe. In 1492, Granada finally fell, and the province was absorbed into Castile.

The reconquista played an important part in creating a national identity for the Christian peoples of Spain. To raise men and money for the war effort, Ferdinand and Isabella mobilized their nobility and town governments and created a central organization to oversee the invasion. The conquered territories were used to reward the men who had aided the effort, though the crown maintained control and jurisdiction over most of the province. But the idea of the holy war also had a darker side and an unanticipated consequence. The Jewish population that had lived peacefully in Castile and Aragon became another object of hostility. Many Jews had risen to prominence in government and in skilled professions. Others, who had accepted conversion to Christianity and were known as conversos, had become powerful figures in church and state.

Both groups were now attacked. The conversos fell prey to a special church tribunal created to examine their sincere devotion to Catholicism. This was the Spanish Inquisition, which, though it used traditional judicial practices—torture to gain confessions, public humiliation to show contrition, and burnings at the stake to maintain purity—used them on a scale never before seen. Thousands of conversos were killed, and many more families had their wealth confiscated to be used for the reconquista. In 1492, the Jews were expelled from Spain. Though the reconquista and the expulsion of the Jews inflicted great suffering on victims and incalculable loss to the Castilian economy, both events enhanced the prestige of the Catholic monarchs.

In many ways, Ferdinand and Isabella trod the paths of the medieval monarchy. They relied more on personal contact with their people than on the use of a centralized administration. They frequently dispensed justice personally, sitting in court and accepting petitions from their subjects. Queen Isabella was venerated in Castile, where women's rights to inheritance remained strong. Ferdinand's absences from Aragon were always a source of contention between him and the Cortes of the towns. Yet he was careful to provide regents to preside in his absence and regularly returned to visit his native kingdom.

The joint presence of Ferdinand and Isabella in the provinces of Spain was symbolic of the unity they strove to achieve. Ferdinand made Castilian the official language of government in Aragon and even appointed Castilians to Aragonese posts. He and Isabella actively encouraged the intermarriage of the two aristocracies and the expansion of the number of wealthy nobles who held land in both kingdoms. Nevertheless, these measures did not unify Spain or erase the centuries-long tradition of hostility among the diverse Iberian peoples.

It was left to the heirs of Ferdinand and Isabella to forge together the Spanish kingdoms, and the process was a painful one. The hostility to a foreign monarch that both the Castilian nobility and the Aragonese towns had shown to Ferdinand and Isabella increased dramatically at the accession of their grandson Charles V (1516–1556), who had been born and raised in the Low Countries, where he ruled over Burgundy and the Netherlands. Through a series of dynastic accidents, Charles was heir to the Spanish crown with its possessions in the New World and to the vast Habsburg estates that included Austria. Charles established his rule in Spain gradually. For a time he was forced to share power in Castile and to suppress a disorganized aristocratic rebellion.

Because of his foreign obligations, Charles was frequently absent from Spain. During those periods he governed through regents and royal councils that did much to centralize administration. Though Castile and Aragon had separate councils, they were organized similarly and had greater contact than before. Charles V realized the importance of Spain, especially of Castile, in his empire. He established a permanent bureaucratic court, modeled on that of Burgundy, and placed able Spaniards at the head of its departments. This smoothed over the long periods when Charles was abroad, especially the 13 years between 1543 and 1556.

The most important factor in uniting the Spanish kingdoms, however, was the fact that Charles V brought Spain to the forefront of European affairs in the sixteenth century. Spanish prowess, whether in arms or in culture, became a source of national pride that helped to erode regional identity. Gold and silver from the New World helped to finance Charles's great empire, and he achieved nearly all of the ancient territorial ambitions of the Spanish kingdoms. In Italy, he prosecuted Aragonese claims to Sicily and Naples. In the north, he held on firmly to the kingdom of Navarre, which had been annexed by Ferdinand, and secured Spain's border with France. In the south, he blocked off Ottoman and Muslim expansion. The reign of Charles V ushered in the dawn of Spain's golden age.

THE DYNASTIC STRUGGLES

The formation of large states throughout Europe led inevitably to conflicts among them. Long chains of marriages among the families of the European princes meant that sooner or later the larger powers would lay claim to the same inheritances and test the matter by force. Thus the sixteenth century was a period of almost unrelieved general warfare in Europe. Advances in technology made war more efficient and more expensive—and also more horrible. The use of artillery against infantry increased the number of deaths and maiming injuries, as did the replacement of the arrow by the bullet. As the size of armies increased, so did casualties. The slaughter of French nobility at Pavia in 1525 was the largest in a century; the Turkish sultan, Suleiman the Magnificent, recorded the burial of 24,000 Hungarian soldiers after the battle of Mohacs in 1526.

Power and Glory

The frequency with which offensive war was waged in the sixteenth century raises a number of questions about the militaristic values of the age. Valor remained greatly prized—a Renaissance virtue inherited from the crusading zeal and chivalric ideals of the Middle Ages. Princes saw valor as a personal attribute and sought to do great deeds. Ferdinand of Aragon and Francis I (1515–1547) of France won fame for their exploits in war. Charles the Bold and Louis II of Hungary were less fortunate. Their battlefield deaths led to the breakup of their states. Wars were fought to further the interests of princes rather than the interests of national sovereignty or international Christianity. They were certainly not fought in the interests of their subjects. States were an extension of a prince's heritage. The wars of the sixteenth century were dynastic wars.

The New Monarchs waged war and defended their territories in new ways. Internal security depended on locally raised forces or hired mercenaries. Both required money, which was becoming available in unprecedented quantities as a result of the increasing prosperity of the early sixteenth century and the windfall of gold and silver from the New World. Professional soldiers, of whom the Swiss and Germans were the most noteworthy, sold their services to the highest bidders. Developments in transport and supply enabled campaigns to take place far from the center of a state. Finally, communications were improving. The need for knowledge about potential rivals or allies had the effect of expanding the European system of diplomacy. Resident agents were established in all the European capitals, and they had a decisive impact on war and peace. Their dispatches formed the most reliable source of information about the strengths of armies or the weaknesses of governments, about the births of heirs or the deaths of princes.

Personality also played a part in the international warfare of the early sixteenth century. The three most consistent protagonists—Charles V, Francis I, and Henry VIII—were of similar age and outlook. Each came unexpectedly to his throne in the full flush of youth, eager for combat and glory. The three were self-consciously rivals, each jealous of the others' successes, each triumphant in the others' failures. As the three monarchs aged together, their youthful wars of conquest matured into strategic warfare designed to maintain a continental balance of power.

The Italian Wars

The struggle for supremacy in Europe in the sixteenth century pitted the French House of Valois against the far-flung estates of the Habsburg empire. Yet the wars took place in Italy. The rivalries among the larger Italian city-states proved to be fertile ground for the newly consolidated European monarchies. Both French and Spanish monarchs had remote but legitimate claims to the kingdom of Naples in southern Italy. In 1494, the French king, Charles VIII, took up an invitation from the ruler of Milan to intervene in Italian affairs. His campaign was an unqualified, if fleeting, success. He marched the length of the peninsula, overthrew the Medici in Florence, forced the pope to open the gates of Rome, and finally seized the crown of Naples. The occupation was accomplished without a single great battle and lasted until the warring Italian city-states realized that they had more to fear from the French than from one another. Once that happened, Charles VIII beat a hasty retreat. But the French appetite for Italian territory was not sated. Soon a deal was struck with Ferdinand of Aragon to divide the kingdom of Naples in two. All went according to plan until these thieves fell out among themselves. In the end, Spain wound up with all of Naples, and France was left with nothing but debts and grievances.

Therefore when Francis I came to the French throne and Charles V came to the Spanish, Naples was just one of several potential sources of friction. Not only had Ferdinand betrayed the French in Naples, he had also broken a long-standing peace on the Franco-Spanish border by conquering the independent but French-speaking kingdom of Navarre. Francis could be expected to avenge both slights. Charles, on the other hand, was the direct heir of the dukes of Burgundy. From his childhood he longed for the restoration of his ancestral lands, including Burgundy itself, which had been gobbled up by Louis XI after the death of Charles the Bold. Competition between Francis and Charles became all the more ferocious when Charles's grandfather, the Holy Roman Emperor Maximilian I (1486–1519), died in 1519. Both monarchs launched a vigorous campaign for the honor of succeeding him.

Charles V, who now inherited the Habsburg lands in Austria and Germany, succeeded to this eminent but

▲ Jean Clouet, *Portrait of Francis* I (sixteenth century). Rivalry between Francis and Charles V plunged Europe into decades of war.

empty dignity. His election as Holy Roman Emperor not only aggravated the personal animosity among the monarchs, but added another source of conflict in Italy. When Louis XII (1498–1515) had succeeded to the throne of France, he had laid claim to the duchy of Milan through an interest of his wife's, though he was unable to enforce it. Francis I proved more capable. In 1515, he stunned all of Europe by crushing the vaunted Swiss mercenaries at the battle of Marignano. But the duchy of Milan was a territory under the protection of the Holy Roman Emperor, and it soon appealed for imperial troops to help repel the French invaders. Milan was strategically important to Charles V because it was the vital link between his Austrian and Burgundian possessions. Almost as soon as he took up the imperial mantle, Charles V was determined to challenge Francis I in Italy.

The key to such a challenge was the construction of alliances among the various Italian city-states and most especially with England, whose aid both Charles and Francis sought to enlist in the early 1520s. Henry VII had found foreign alliances a ready source of cash, and he was always eager to enter into them as long as they did not involve raising armies and fighting wars. Henry VIII was made of sterner stuff. He longed to reconquer France and to cut a figure on the European scene. Despite the fact that his initial continental adventures had emptied his treasury without fulfilling his dreams, Henry remained eager for war. He was also flattered to find himself the object of attention of both Valois and Habsburg emissaries. Charles V made two separate trips to London, and Henry crossed the Channel in 1520 to meet Francis I in one of the gaudiest displays of conspicuous consumption that the century would witness, appropriately known as the Field of the Cloth of Gold.

The result of these diplomatic intrigues was an alliance between England and the Holy Roman Empire. English and Burgundian forces would stage an invasion of northern France, while Spanish and German troops would again attempt to dislodge the French from Italy. The strategy worked better than anyone could have imagined. In 1523, Charles's forces gained a foothold in Milan by taking the heavily fortified town of Pavia. Two years later, Francis was ready to strike back. At the head of his own royal guards, he massed Swiss mercenaries and French infantry outside Pavia and made ready for a swift assault. Instead, a large imperial army arrived to relieve the town, and in the subsequent battle, the French suffered a shattering defeat. Francis I was captured.

The victory at Pavia, which occurred on Charles V's twenty-fifth birthday, seemingly made him master of all of Europe. His ally Henry VIII urged an immediate invasion and dismemberment of France and began raising an army to spearhead the attack. But Charles's position was much less secure than it appeared. The Ottomans threatened his Hungarian territories, and the Protestants threatened his German lands. He could not afford a war of conquest in France. His hope now was to reach an agreement with Francis I for a lasting European peace, and for this purpose the French king was brought in captivity to Madrid. Charles's terms, however, led not to peace but to 30 years of warfare.

Charles demanded that Burgundy be returned to him. Though Francis was hardly in a position to bargain, he held out on this issue for as long as possible and secretly prepared a disavowal of the final agreement before it was made. By the Treaty of Madrid in 1526, Francis I yielded Burgundy and recognized the Spanish conquest of Navarre and Spanish rule in Naples. The agreement was sealed by the marriage of Francis to Charles's sister, Eleanor of Portugal. But marriage was not sufficient security for such a complete capitulation. To secure his release from Spain, Francis was required to leave behind as hostages his seven- and eight-year-old sons until the treaty was fulfilled. For three years the children languished in Spanish captivity.

No sooner had he set foot on French soil than Francis I renounced the Treaty of Madrid. Despite the threat that this posed to his children, Francis argued that the terms had been extracted against his will, and he even gained the sanction of the pope for violating his oath. Setting France on a war footing, he began seeking new allies. Henry VIII, disappointed with the meager spoils of his last venture, switched sides. So, too, did a number of Italian city-states, including Rome. Most important, Francis I entered into an alliance with the Ottoman sultan, Suleiman the Magnificent (1520–1566), whose armies were pressing against the southeastern borders of the Holy Roman Empire. In the year following Pavia, the Ottomans secured an equally decisive triumph at Mohacs, which cut Hungary in two and threatened Vienna, the eastern capital of the Habsburg lands. Almost overnight, Charles V had been turned from hunter into hunted. The Ottoman threat demanded immediate attention in Germany, the French and English were preparing to strike in the Low Countries, and the Italian wars continued. In 1527, Charles's unpaid German mercenaries stormed through Rome, sacked the papal capital, and captured the pope. Christian Europe was mortified.

The struggle for European mastery ground on for decades. The Treaty of Cateau-Cambrésis in 1559 brought to a close 60 years of conflict. In the end, the French were no more capable of dislodging the Habsburgs from Italy than were the Habsburgs of forcing the Ottomans out of Hungary. The great stores of silver that poured into Castile from the New World were consumed in the fires of continental warfare. In 1557, both France and Spain declared bankruptcy to avoid foreclosures by their creditors. For the French, the Italian wars were disastrous. They seriously undermined the state's financial base, eroded confidence in the monarchy, and thinned the ranks of the ruling nobility. The adventure begun by Charles VIII in search of glory brought France nearly to ruin. It ended with fitting irony. After the death of Francis I, his son Henry II (1547–1559) continued the struggle. Henry never forgave his father for abandoning him in Spain, and he sought revenge on Charles V, who had been his jailer. He regarded the Treaty of Cateau-Cambrésis as a victory and celebrated it with great pomp and pageantry. Among the feasts and festivities were athletic competitions for the king's courtiers and attendants. Henry II entered the jousting tournament and there was killed.

Conclusion

CHARLES V DIED IN HIS BED. The long years of war made clear that the dream to dominate Europe could only be a dream. He split apart his empire and granted to his brother, Ferdinand I (1558–1564), the Austrian and German lands and the mantle of the Holy Roman Empire. To his son, Philip II (1556–1598) he ceded the Low Countries, Spain and the New World, Naples, and his Italian conquests. In 1555, Charles abdicated all of his titles and retired to a monastery to live out his final days. The cares of an empire that had once stretched from Peru to Vienna were lifted from his shoulders. Beginning with his voyage to Castile in 1517, he had made ten trips to the Netherlands, nine to Germany, seven to Italy, six to Spain, four to France, two to England, and two to Africa. "My life has been one long journey," he told those who witnessed him relinquish his crowns. On 21 September 1558, he rested forever.

QUESTIONS FOR REVIEW

1. What impulses in European society were revealed by the global exploration and conquests of the Portuguese and the Spanish?
2. What qualities characterized the "New Monarchies" and what are some of the best examples of such princely states?
3. How and why did the experience of political and territorial unification differ in England, France, and Spain?
4. How did war between the great European monarchies contribute to unity within each?

DISCOVERING WESTERN CIVILIZATION ONLINE

You can obtain more information about the European empires at the websites listed below. See also the companion website that accompanies this text: www.ablongman.com/kishlansky, which includes an online study guide and additional resources.

European Encounters

www.win.tue.nl/cs/fm/engels/discovery/
A site devoted to all ages of discovery with maps, short biographies, and timelines. There are links to the writings of Columbus, Cortés, and other early voyagers.

www1.minn.net/~keithp/
Everything you ever wanted to know about Christopher Columbus.

www.loc.gov/exhibits/1492
A Library of Congress online exhibit on the causes and consequences of European exploration and expansion.

www.castellobanfi.com/features/story_3.html
A site devoted to the food and drink associated with a long ocean voyage in the fifteenth century.

www.fordham.edu/halsall/sbook1z.html
Dozens of primary sources relating to the voyages of discovery.

The Formation of States

www.archsoc.com/Henry.html
A board game that teaches both history and strategy.

SUGGESTIONS FOR FURTHER READING

General Reading

Denys Hay, *Europe in the Fourteenth and Fifteenth Centuries* (London: Longman, 1966). A good first survey of political history.

David Nicholas, *The Transformation of Europe 1300–1600* (New York: Oxford University Press, 1999). A comprehensive survey that emphasizes continuities between the sixteenth century and the preceding period.

Eugene Rice, *The Foundations of Early Modern Europe, 1460–1559*, 2d ed. (New York: Norton, 1994). An outstanding synthesis.

European Encounters

Felipe Fernandez-Armesto, *Columbus* (Oxford: Oxford University Press, 1991). The best of the recent studies. Reliable, stimulating, and up-to-date.

Lyle McAlister, *Spain and Portugal in the New World, 1492–1700* (Minneapolis: University of Minnesota Press, 1984). The most up-to-date history of the great South American empires.

Dan O'Sullivan, *Age of Discovery, 1400–1550* (London: Longman, 1984). Best short synthetic work.

John Thornton, *Africa and Africans in the Making of the Atlantic World* (Cambridge: Cambridge University Press, 1992). The African effect on the development of the West.

Geographical Tour—Europe in 1500

N. J. G. Pounds, *An Historical Geography of Europe, 1500–1800* (Cambridge: Cambridge University Press, 1990). A remarkable survey of the relationship between geography and history.

Daniel Waley, *Later Medieval Europe* (London: Longman, 1985). A good brief account.

The Formation of States

Jeremy Black, ed., *European Warfare, 1453–1815* (New York: St. Martin's Press, 1999). A collection of scholarly essays on the military developments of the early modern period.

R. J. Knecht, *French Renaissance Monarchy* (London: Longman, 1984). A study of the nature of the French monarchy and the way it was transformed in the early sixteenth century.

J. R. Lander, *Government and Community, England, 1450–1509* (Cambridge, Mass.: Harvard University Press, 1980). A comprehensive survey of the late fifteenth century.

John Lynch, *Spain, 1516–1598: From Nation State to World Empire* (Cambridge, Mass.: Blackwell, 1994). The most up-to-date survey.

J. H. Shennan, *The Origins of the Modern European State, 1450–1725* (London: Hutchinson, 1974). An analytic account of the rise of the state.

The Dynastic Struggles

M. F. Alvarez, *Charles V* (London: Thames & Hudson, 1975). An accessible biography of the most remarkable man of the age.

J. R. Hale, *War and Society in Renaissance Europe* (Baltimore, Md.: Johns Hopkins University Press, 1986). Assesses the impact of war on the political and social history of early modern Europe.

J. J. Scarisbrick, *Henry VIII* (Berkeley: University of California Press, 1968). The definitive biography.

THE REFORM OF RELIGION

- THE VISUAL RECORD: *Sola Scriptura*
- THE INTELLECTUAL REFORMATION
- THE LUTHERAN REFORMATION

- THE PROTESTANT REFORMATION
- THE CATHOLIC REFORMATION

SOLA SCRIPTURA

"IN THE BEGINNING WAS THE WORD, and the Word was with God, and the Word was God." In no other period of European history was this text of the apostle John so appropriate. In the early sixteenth century, Europeans developed an insatiable appetite for hearing and reading the Bible. Scriptures rolled off printing presses in every shape and form, from the great vellum tomes of Gutenberg, pictured here, to pocket Bibles that soldiers carried into battle. They came in every imaginable language. Before 1500 there were 14 complete Bibles printed in German, four each in Italian, French, and Spanish, one in Czech, and even one in Flemish. There were hundreds more editions in Latin, the official Vulgate Bible first translated by Saint Jerome in the fourth century. Separate sections, especially the Psalms and the first books of the Old Testament, were also printed by the thousands. When Martin Luther began his own German translation of the Bible in 1522, it immediately became an international bestseller. In 25 years, it went into 430 editions. It is estimated that 1 million German Bibles were printed in the first half of the sixteenth century, at a time when Europe had a German-speaking population of about 15 million people, 90 percent of whom were illiterate.

Bible owning was no fad. It was but one element in a new devotional outlook that was sweeping the Continent and would have far-reaching consequences for European society during the next 150 years. A renewed spirituality was to be seen everywhere. It was expressed in a desire to change the traditional practices and structures of the Roman Church. It was expressed in a desire to have learned and responsible ministers to tend to the needs of their parishioners. It was expressed in a desire to establish godly families, godly cities, and godly kingdoms. Sometimes it took the form of sarcasm and bitter denunciations; sometimes it took the form of quiet devotion and pious living. It came from within the Roman Church as much as from without.

The inspiration for reform was based on the Word of God. Scholars, following humanist principles, worked on biblical translations in an attempt to bring a purer text to light. Biblical commentary dominated the writings of

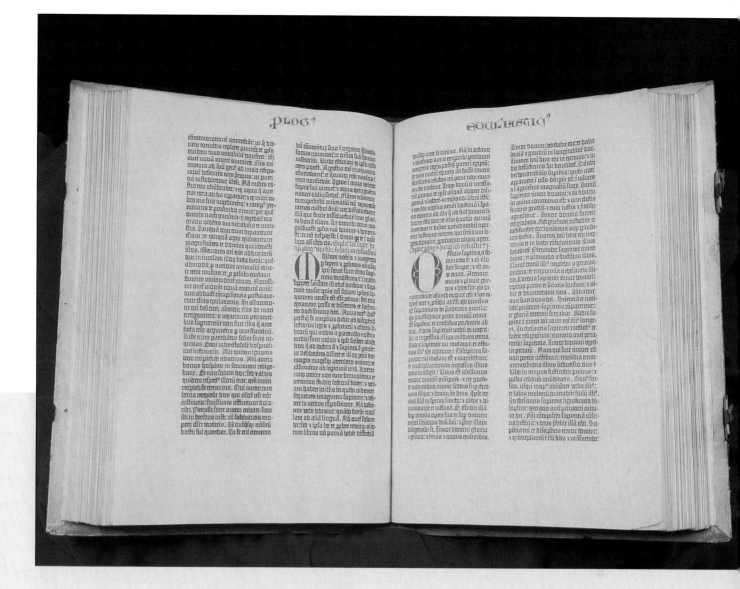

churchmen as never before. Woodcut pictures depicting scenes from the life of Jesus or from the Old Testament were printed in untold quantities for the edification of the unlettered. For the first time, common people could, in their own dwellings, contemplate representations of the lives of the saints. Many of the Bibles that were printed in the vernacular—that is, in the languages spoken in the various European states rather than in Latin—were interleaved with illustrations of the central events of Christian history. Preachers spoke to newly aware audiences and relied on biblical texts to draw out their message. Study groups, especially in urban areas, proliferated so that the literate could read and learn together. Bible reading became a part of family life, one that mothers and fathers could share with their children and their servants.

LOOKING AHEAD

Sola Scriptura—*by the word alone—became the battle cry of religious reform. As we will see in this chapter, in the early decades of the sixteenth century Europeans experienced one of the greatest of all religious rebirths. New Protestant denominations were founded and Roman Catholicism was infused with a spirit of growth and renewal. Figures such as Luther, Calvin, and Ignatius of Loyola were part of the most remarkable generation of religious leaders since the foundation of Christianity.*

THE INTELLECTUAL REFORMATION

In the early sixteenth century, reformers throughout western Europe preached new ideas about religious doctrine and religious practice. At first these ideas took the form of a sustained critique of the Roman Catholic Church, but they soon developed a momentum of their own. Some reformers remained within traditional Catholicism; others moved outside and founded new Protestant churches. Wherever this movement for religious reform, whether Catholic or Protestant, appeared, it was fed by new ideas. And the rapid communication of new ideas was made possible by the development of printing, which appeared in Germany in the late fifteenth century and spread across Europe in the succeeding decades. Yet printing was as much a result as a cause of the spread of ideas. The humanist call for a return to the study of the classics and for the creation of accurate texts, first heard in Italy, aroused scholars and leaders in all of the European states. Their appetite for manuscripts exhausted the abilities of the scribes and booksellers who reproduced texts. Printing responded to that demand.

The Print Revolution

The development of printing did not cause religious reform, but it is difficult to see how reform would have progressed in its absence. The campaign to change the doctrine and practice of Catholicism was waged through the press, as millions of flyers and pamphlets were distributed across Europe to spread the new ideas. One third of all books sold in Germany between 1518 and 1525 were written by Martin Luther.

Printing, one of the true technological revolutions in western history, was not invented. It developed as a result of progress made in allied industries, especially papermaking and goldsmithing. Scholars and university students needed copies of manuscripts. Their need led to the development of a trade in bookselling that flourished in almost every university town. The process of reproduction was slowed by difficulties in obtaining the sheepskins and calfskins on which the manuscripts were written. In the early fifteenth century, copyists began to substitute paper made from linen rags for the expensive vellum skins. A number of German craftsmen experimented with using movable metal type to make exact reproductions of manuscripts on paper. In the 1450s in Mainz, Johannes Gutenberg (ca. 1400–1468) and his partners succeeded and published their famous Bibles.

The association of early printing with goldsmithing resulted from the high level of technical skill that was necessary to create the hard metal stamps from which the softer metal type was produced. Printing was an expensive business. The investment in type and in paper was considerable. Only the press itself was cheap; any corn or wine press could be used to bring the long, flat sheets of paper down on a wooden frame filled with ink-coated metal type. Booksellers initially put up the capital needed to cast the stamps, mold the type, and buy the paper. They bound the printed pages and found the markets to distribute them. At first, sales were slow. Printed books were considered inferior to handwritten manuscripts. Nor at first were printed books less expensive. Buying a Bible such as those printed by Gutenberg was a major investment, equivalent to purchasing a house today. Many printing shops quickly went bankrupt as they misjudged their markets and were unable to pay back their loans.

Still, once it was begun, printing spread like wildfire. By 1480, over 110 towns had established presses, most in Italy and Germany. After that the pace quickened. By the beginning of the sixteenth century, Venice and Paris were the centers of the printing industry; the Paris presses produced over 300 new titles annually. Most of the early printed works were either religious or classical. Bibles, church service books, and the commentaries of the Church Fathers were most common. Cicero topped the list of classical authors.

Printing rapidly came to be a basic part of life. In the first 40 years after the presses were first set up, perhaps as many as 20 million books were produced and distributed. Printing changed the habits of teachers and students, the way in which the state conducted its business, and the methods of legal training and legal proceedings. Compilations of laws could now be widely distributed and more uniformly enforced. Printing had a similar effect on the development of scientific study. The printing press popularized the discoveries of the New World and contributed to the reproduction of more accurate charts and maps, which in turn facilitated further discovery. Printing also helped to standardize language by frequent repetition of preferred usage and spelling. Perhaps most important, printing created an international intellectual community whose ideas could be dispersed the length and breadth of the Continent. The printing press enhanced the value of ideas and of thinking. Nothing could be more central to the reform of religion.

Christian Humanism

Many of the ideas that spread across Europe as the result of the printing revolution originated in Italian humanism (see Chapter 11). The revival of classical literature, with its concern for purity in language and eloquence in style, was one of the most admired achievements of the Renaissance. Students from all over Europe who descended on Italian universities to study medicine and law came away with strong doses of philology, rhetoric, moral philosophy, and the other liberal arts. By the beginning of the sixteenth century, the force of humanism was felt strongly in northern and western Europe, where it was grafted onto the traditional theological teaching. The combination was a new and powerful intellectual movement known as Christian humanism.

The humanism of the north differed from that of the Italian city-states. Although the Italian humanists were certainly Christian, they were interested in secular subjects, especially in mastering classical languages and translating classical texts. Italian humanists had established techniques for the recovery of accurate texts and had developed principles for compiling the scholarly editions that now poured forth from the printing presses. Christian humanists applied these techniques to the study of the authorities and texts of the Church. Most of the new humanists had been trained in Italy, where they devoted themselves to the mastery of Greek and Latin. They had imbibed the idea that scholars, using their own critical faculties, could establish the authority of texts and the meaning of words. Building on the patient work of their predecessors and the advantages offered by printing, this new generation of humanists brought learning to educated men and women throughout Europe.

Christian humanism was a program of reform rather than a philosophy. It aimed to make better Christians through better education. Humanists were especially interested in the education of women. Thomas More (1478–1535) raised his daughters to be among the educated elite of England. Renowned women scholars held places at Italian universities. Humanist educational principles posed an implicit challenge to Roman Catholicism.

Schools had once been the monopoly of the Church, which used them to train clergymen. Literacy itself had been preserved over the centuries so that the gospel could be propagated.

By the sixteenth century these purposes had been transformed. Schools now trained many people who were not destined for careers in the Church, and literacy served the needs of the state, the aristocracy, and the merchant classes. More important, as the humanists perfected their techniques of scholarship, the Church continued to rely on traditional methods of training and traditional texts. The dominant manner of teaching at the schools and universities was known as Scholasticism. Passages of biblical texts were studied through the commentaries of generations of Church Fathers. Rote memorization of the opinions of others was more highly valued than critical thinking. Argument took place by formal disputation of questions on which the Fathers of the Church disagreed. The Vulgate Bible was used throughout western Christendom. It was now a thousand years old.

The Humanist Movement

Many humanist criticisms of Church teaching focused on its failure to inspire individuals to live a Christian life. Humanist writers were especially scathing about popular practices that bordered on superstition, such as pilgrimages to holy places or the worship of relics from the early history of the Church. Such beliefs became the butt of popular humor: "If the fragments [of the Lord's Cross] were joined together they would seem a full load for a freighter. And yet the Lord carried his whole cross." Christian humanists wanted to inspire Christians. As the great Dutch humanist Desiderius Erasmus observed, "To be learned is the lot of only a few; but no one is unable to be a Christian, no one is unable to be pious."

Christian humanism was an international movement. The humanists formed the elite of the intellectual world of the sixteenth century, and their services were sought by princes and peers as well as by the most distinguished universities. In fact, the New Monarchs supported the humanists and protected them from their critics. Marguerite of Navarre, sister of Francis I, was an accomplished writer who frequently interceded on behalf of the leading French humanists. Ferdinand of Aragon, Henry VIII, and the Holy Roman Emperors Maximilian I and Charles V all brought humanists to their courts and aided their projects. Maria of Hungary and Mary and Elizabeth Tudor were trained in humanist principles and participated in humanist literary achievements. This support was especially important for educational reforms. Under the influence of the French humanist Jacques Lefevre d'Étaples (ca. 1455–1536), Francis I established the College de France; under the direction of Cardinal Jiménez de Cisneros, the University of Alcala was founded in Spain. Throughout northern Europe, professorships in Greek and Latin were endowed at universities to help further the study of classical languages.

The centerpiece of humanist reforms was the translation of Christian texts. Skilled in Greek and Latin, informed by scholars of Hebrew and Aramaic, humanist writers prepared new editions of the books of the Bible and of the writings of the early Church Fathers. The Polyglot (literally "many languages") Bible that was produced in 1522 at the University of Alcala took a team of scholars 15 years to complete. They rigorously compared texts of all known biblical manuscripts and established the principle that inconsistencies among Latin manuscripts were to be resolved by reference to Greek texts and difficulties in Greek texts by reference to Hebrew texts. The result was six volumes that allowed scholars to compare the texts. The Old Testament was printed in three parallel columns of Hebrew, Latin Vulgate, and Greek. The New Testament was printed in double columns of Greek and Vulgate. The Greek edition of the Bible and its establishment as a text that was superior to the Vulgate caused an immediate sensation throughout humanist and Church circles.

The Wit of Erasmus

Though the Polyglot Bible contained the first completed Greek edition of the New Testament, it was not the first published one. That distinction belongs to the man whose name is most closely associated with the idea of Christian humanism: Desiderius Erasmus of Rotterdam (ca. 1466–1536). Orphaned at an early age, Erasmus was educated by the Brothers of the Common Life, a lay brotherhood that specialized in schooling children and preparing them for a monastic life. Marked out early by his extraordinary intellectual gifts, Erasmus entered a monastery and was then allowed to travel to pursue his studies, first in France and then in England.

In England, Erasmus learned of new techniques for instructing children both in classical knowledge and in Christian morals, and he became particularly interested in the education of women. While in England, Erasmus composed a short satire, *In Praise of Folly* (1509), a work that became one of the first bestsellers. He also came to realize the importance of recovering the texts of the early Church Fathers.

At the age of 30, Erasmus began the arduous task of learning ancient Greek and devoted his energies to a study of the writings of Saint Jerome, the principal compiler of the Vulgate, and to preparing an edition of the Greek texts of the Bible. Erasmus's translation of the New Testament and his edition of the writings of Saint Jerome both appeared in 1516.

Erasmus devoted his life to restoring the direct connection between the individual Christian and the textual basis of Christian doctrine. Although he is called the father of biblical criticism, Erasmus was not a theologian. He was more interested in the practical impact of ideas than in the ideas themselves. His scathing attacks on the Scholastics, popular superstition, and the pretensions of the traditionalists in the Church and the universities all had the same goal: to restore the experiences of Christ to the center of Christianity. His sarcastic indictment of theologians in his book *In Praise of Folly* illustrates his irreverent attitude toward men of the church:

> As for theologians, perhaps the less said the better on this gloomy and dangerous theme, since they are a style of man who show themselves exceeding supercilious and irritable unless they can heap up six hundred conclusions about you and force you to recant; and if you refuse, they promptly brand you as a heretic—for it is their custom to terrify by their thunderings those whom they dislike.

Though his patrons were the rich and his language was Latin, Erasmus also hoped to reach men and women lower down the social order, those whom he believed the Church had failed to educate. "The doctrine of Christ casts aside no age, no sex, no fortune or position in life. It keeps no one at a distance."

THE LUTHERAN REFORMATION

On the surface, the Roman Catholic Church appeared to be as strong as ever at the beginning of the sixteenth century. Yet everywhere in Europe, the cry was for reform. Reform the venal papacy and its money-sucking bishops.

Reform the ignorant clergy, the sacrilegious priests, the fallen nuns, and the wayward friars. Wherever one turned, one saw abuses. Parish livings were sold to the highest bidder to raise money. This was simony. Rich appointments were given to the kinsmen of powerful Church leaders rather than to those who were most qualified. This was nepotism. Individual clergymen accumulated numerous positions whose responsibilities they could not fulfill. This was pluralism. Some priests who took the vow of chastity lived openly with their concubines. Some mendicants who took the vow of poverty dressed in silk and ate from golden plates.

The Spark of Reform

Europe was becoming more religious. The signs of religious fervor were everywhere. Cities hired preachers to expound the gospel. Pilgrims to the shrines of saints clogged the roadways every spring and summer. Rome remained the greatest attraction, but pilgrims covered the Continent. The shrine of the apostle Saint James at Compostela in Spain was believed to cure the ill. Endowments of masses for the dead increased. Henry VII of England provided money for 10,000 masses to be said for his soul. Even city merchants might bequeath funds for several hundred masses. In the chantries, where such services were performed, there were neither enough priests nor enough altars to supply the demand.

People wanted more from the Church than the Church could possibly give them. Humanists condemned visits to the shrines as superstitious; pilgrims demanded that the relics be made more accessible. Reformers complained of pluralism; the clergy complained that they could not live on the salary of a single office. Civic authorities demanded that the established Church take greater responsibility for good works; the pope demanded that civic authorities help to pay for them.

Contradiction and paradox dominated the movements for reform. Though the most vocal critics of the Church complained that its discipline was too lax, for many ordinary people its demands were too rigorous. The obligations of penance and confession weighed heavily on them. Church doctrine held that sins had to be washed away before the souls of the dead could enter heaven. Until then, they suffered in purgatory. Sins were cleansed through penance, the performance of acts of contrition assigned after confession. But the ordeal of confession kept many people away. "Have you skipped Mass? Have you dressed proudly? Have you thought of committing adultery? Have you insulted or cursed your parents?" These were just a few of the uncomfortable questions that priests were instructed to pose in confession. In towns, merchants were asked about their trading practices, shopkeepers about the quality of their goods. Magistrates were questioned about their attitudes to the

▲ An anonymous caricature of Johann Tetzel, whose sale of an indulgence inspired Martin Luther's Ninety-five Theses. Tetzel answered with 122 theses of his own but was rebuked and disowned by the Catholics.

clergy, intellectuals about their attitudes to the pope. It is hardly surprising that the sale of indulgences became a popular substitute for penance and confession.

The Sale of Indulgences

An indulgence was a portion of the treasury of good works performed by righteous Christians throughout the ages. Indulgences could be granted to people who wanted to atone for their sins. Strictly speaking, an indulgence supplemented penance rather than substituted for it. It was effective only for the contrite—for sinners who repented of their sins. But as the practice of granting indulgences spread, this subtle distinction largely disappeared. The living bought indulgences to cleanse the sins of the dead, and some even bought indulgences in anticipation of sins they had not yet committed.

By the sixteenth century, to limit abuses by local church authorities, only the pope, through his agents, could grant indulgences. Popes used special occasions to offer an indulgence for pilgrimages to Rome or for contributions to special papal projects. Other indulgences were licensed locally, usually at the shrines of saints or at churches that contained relics.

The indulgence controversy was a symptom rather than a cause of the explosion of feelings that erupted in the small German town of Wittenberg in 1517. In that year the pope was offering an indulgence to help finance the rebuilding of Saint Peter's Basilica in Rome. The pope chose Prince Albert of Brandenburg (1490–1545) to distribute the indulgence in Germany, and Albert hired the Dominican friar Johann Tetzel (ca. 1465–1519) to preach its benefits.

Martin Luther Challenges the Church

Enthusiasm for the indulgence spread to the neighboring state of Saxony, where the ruler, Frederick III, the Wise (1463–1525), banned its sale. Frederick's great collection of relics carried their own indulgences, and Tetzel offered unwelcome competition. But Saxons flocked into Brandenburg to make their purchases, and by the end of October, Tetzel was not very far from Wittenberg Castle, where Frederick's relics were housed. On All Saints' Day the relics would be opened to view, and with the harvest done, one of the largest crowds of the year would gather to see them. On the night before, Martin Luther (1483–1546), a professor of theology at Wittenberg University, posted on the door of the castle church ninety-five theses attacking indulgences and their sale.

In so doing, Luther was following the Scholastic tradition of disputation, in which scholars presented propositions, or theses, for open debate with all comers. Luther's theses were controversial, but they were meant to be. Only circumstance moved Luther's theses from the academic to the public sphere. Already there was growing concern among clergy and theologians about Tetzel's blatant sale of indulgences. Hordes of purchasers believed that they were buying unconditional remission of sin. Individual priests and monks began to sound the alarm: an indulgence without contrition was worthless.

Luther's theses focused this concern and finally communicated it beyond the walls of the Church and the university. The theses were quickly translated into German and spread throughout the Holy Roman Empire. Prospective buyers of indulgence became wary; past purchasers became angry. But Prince Albert and the pope needed the income. They could not stand by while sales collapsed and anticlerical and antipapal sentiment grew.

Martin Luther's Faith

Although he was only an obscure German professor, Martin Luther was not a man to challenge lightly. In his youth he had studied for a career in law, but against his father's wishes he entered an Augustinian monastery and was ordained a priest in 1507. He received his doctorate at the university in Wittenberg and was appointed to the theology faculty in 1512. An outstanding teacher, Luther began to be picked for administrative posts and became overseer of 11 Augustinian monasteries. His skills in disputation were widely recognized, and he was sent to Rome to argue a case on behalf of his order. He fulfilled each task beyond expectation.

In all outward appearances, Luther was successful and contented, but beneath this tranquil exterior lay a soul in torment. Despite his devotion, he could not erase his sense of sin; he could not convince himself that he could achieve the righteousness God demanded of him.

Knowledge of his salvation came to Luther through study. His internal agonies led him to ponder over and over again the biblical passages that described the righteousness of God. In the intellectual tradition in which he had been trained, that righteousness was equated with law. The righteous person either followed God's law or was punished by God's wrath. It was this understanding that tormented him. "I thought that I had to perform good works till at last through them Jesus would become a friend and gracious to me." But no amount of good works could overcome Luther's feelings of guilt for his sins. Almost from the moment he began lecturing in 1512, he searched for the key to the freedom of his own soul.

Even before he wrote his Ninety-five Theses, Luther had made the first breakthrough by a unique reading of the writings of Saint Paul. "I pondered night and day until I understood the connection between the righteousness of God and the sentence 'The just shall live by faith.' Then I grasped that the justice of God is the righteousness by which through grace and pure mercy, God justifies us through faith. Immediately I felt that I had been reborn and that I had passed through wide open doors into paradise!" Finally he realized that the righteousness of God was a gift freely given to the faithful. To receive God's righteousness, one had only to believe in God's infinite mercy. It was this belief that fortified Luther during his years of struggle with both civil and Church powers.

Over the next several years, Luther refined his spiritual philosophy and drew out the implications of his newfound beliefs. His religion was shaped by three interconnected tenets. First came justification by faith alone—*sola fide*. An individual's everlasting salvation came from faith in God's goodness rather than from the performance of good works. Sin could not be washed away by penance, and it could not be forgiven by indulgence. Second, faith came only through the knowledge and contemplation of the Word of God—*sola scriptura*. All that was needed to understand the justice and mercy of God was contained in the Bible. Reading the Word, hearing the Word, expounding on and studying the Word—this was the path to faith and through faith to salvation. Third, all who believed in God's righteousness and had achieved their faith through the study of the Bible were equal in God's eyes. The priesthood included all believers. Each followed his or her own calling and found his or her own faith through Scripture. Ministers and preachers could help others to learn God's Word, but they could not confer faith.

Luther's ideas posed a fundamental challenge to the Roman Catholic Church, but it was not Luther alone who initiated the reform of religion. His obsession with salvation was based on the same impulse that had made indulgences so popular. Justification by faith alone provided an alternative to the combination of works and faith that many Roman Catholics found too difficult to fulfill. Luther's insistence that faith comes only through the study of the Word of God was facilitated by the new learning and the invention of printing. The printing press prepared the ground for the dissemination of his ideas as much as it disseminated them. This was a contribution of the Renaissance. Luther's hope for the creation of a spiritual elite, confirmed in their faith and confident of their salvation, readily appealed to the citizens of hundreds of German towns who had already made of themselves a social and economic elite. This was a contribution of the growth of towns. The idea of the equality of all believers meant that all were equally responsible for fulfilling God's commandments. This set secular rulers on an equal footing with the pope at a moment in Western history when rulers were already challenging papal power in matters of both church and state. This was a contribution of the formation of states. For all his painful soul-searching, Luther embodied the culmination of changes of which he was only dimly aware.

From Luther to Lutheranism

The first to feel the seriousness of Luther's challenge to the established order was the reformer himself. The head of Luther's order, a papal legate, and finally the Emperor Charles V all called for Luther to recant his views on indulgences. Luther was excommunicated by Pope Leo X in 1521 and ordered by Charles V to appear before the diet, or assembly, in Worms, Germany, in April of that year. There he gave the same infuriating reply: if he could be shown the places in the Bible that contradicted his views, he would gladly change them. Charles V declared Luther an enemy of the empire. In both Church and state he was now an outlaw.

In fact, during the three years between the posting of his theses and his appearance before the emperor, Luther came to conclusions that were much more radical than his initial attack on indulgences. He came to believe that the papacy was a human rather than a divine invention. Therefore he denounced both the papacy and the general councils of the Church. In his *Address to the Christian Nobility of the German Nation* (1520) he called on the princes to take the reform of religion into their own hands.

But Luther had attracted powerful supporters as well as powerful enemies. Prince Frederick III of Saxony consistently intervened on his behalf, and the delicate international situation forced Luther's chief antagonists to move more slowly than they might have wished. The pope hoped first to keep Charles V off the imperial throne and then to maintain a united front with the German princes against him. Charles V, already locked in his lifelong struggle with the French, needed German military support and peace in his German territories. These factors consistently played into Luther's hands.

While the pope and the emperor were otherwise occupied, Luther refined his ideas and won important converts. As time passed, Luther's reputation grew, not only in Germany, but all over Europe. Between 1517 and 1520, he published 30 works, all of which achieved massive sales. Luther's individual accomplishments were remarkable, but what turned his theology into a movement, which after 1529 came to be known as Protestantism, was the support he received among German princes and within German cities.

Princes and Cities. Individual princes turned to Luther's theology for several reasons. First and foremost was sincere religious conviction. Second were political and economic factors. As German princes worked to centralize their administrations, protect themselves from predatory neighbors, and increase their revenues, they felt the burden of papal exactions. Taxes and gifts flowed south to a papacy dominated by Italians. Luther's call for civil rulers to lead their own churches meant that civil rulers could keep their own revenues.

The Reformation spread particularly well in the German cities, especially those to which the emperor had granted the status of freedom from the rule of any prince. The cities had long struggled with the tension of the separate jurisdictions of state and Church. Much urban property was owned by the Church and so was exempt from taxation and law enforcement, and the clergy constituted a significant proportion of urban populations. Reformed religion stressed the equality of clergy and laity and thus the indisputable power of civil authorities. Paradoxically, it was because the cities contained large numbers of priests that Luther's ideas reached the cities quickly. Many of his earliest students served urban congregations and began to develop doctrines and practices that, though based on Luther's ideas, were adapted to the circumstances of city life. The reform clergy became integrated into the life of the city in a way that the Catholic clergy had not. They married the daughters of citizens, became citizens themselves, and trained their children in the guilds. Moreover, the imperial free cities were also centers of the printing trade and home to many of the most noted humanists who were initially important in spreading Luther's ideas.

Luther's message held great appeal for the middle orders in the towns. While it was necessary for the leader of a state to support reform if it was to survive, in the cities it was the petty burghers, lesser merchants, tradespeople, and artisans who led the movements that ultimately gained the approval of city governments. These groups resented the privileges given to priests and members of religious orders who paid no taxes and were exempt from the obligations of citizenship. The level of anticlericalism, always high in Germany, was especially acute in cities that were suffering economic difficulties. Pressure from ordinary people and petty traders forced town leaders into action. The evangelism of reforming ministers created converts and an atmosphere of reform. Support from members of the ruling oligarchy both mobilized these pressures and capitalized on them. Town governments secured their own autonomy over the Church, tightening their grip on the institutions of social control and enhancing the social and economic authority of their members. Once they became Protestant, city governments took over many of the functions of the religious houses, often converting them into schools or hostels for the poor. Former monks were allowed to enter trades. Former nuns were encouraged to marry. Luther himself married an ex-nun after the dissolution of her convent.

The Appeal for Women.   Religious reform appealed to women as well as men, but it affected them differently. Noblewomen were among the most important defenders of Protestant reformers, especially in states in which the prince opposed it. Marguerite of Navarre (1492–1549), sister of Francis I, frequently intervened with her brother on behalf of individual Lutherans who fell afoul of Church authorities. She created her own court in the south of France and stocked it with both humanists and Protestants. Her devotional poem, *Mirror of the Sinful Soul* (1533), inspired women reformers and was translated into English by Elizabeth I. Mary of Hungary (1505–1558) played a similar role in the Holy Roman Empire. Sister of both Charles V and Ferdinand I, queen of Hungary, and later regent of the Netherlands, she acted as patron to Hungarian reformers. Though Mary was more humanist than Protestant, Luther dedicated an edition of Psalms to her, and she read a number of his works. Her independent religious views infuriated both of her brothers. Bona, wife of Sigismund I of Poland, was especially important in eastern reform. An Italian by birth, Bona (1493–1558) was a central figure in spreading both Renaissance art and humanist learning into Poland. She became one of the largest independent landowners in the state and initiated widespread agricultural and economic reforms. Her private confessor was one of Poland's leading Protestants.

Luther's reforms also appealed to women who were not so highly placed in society. The doctrine of the equality of all believers put men and women on an equal spiritual footing even if it did nothing to break the male monopoly of the ministry. In the private sphere, family life became the center of faith when salvation was removed from the control of the Church. Luther's marriage led him to a deeper appreciation of the importance of the wife and mother in the family's spirituality.

By following humanist teaching on the importance of educating women of the upper orders and by encouraging literacy, the reformers did much that was uplifting. Girls' schools were founded in a number of German cities, and townswomen could use their newly acquired skills in their roles as shopkeepers, family accountants, and teachers of their children. But there were losses as well as gains. The attack on the worship of saints and especially of the Virgin Mary removed female images from religion. Protestantism was male-dominated in a way that Catholicism was not. Moreover, the emphasis on reading the Bible tended to reinforce the image of women as weak and inherently sinful. The dissolution of the convents took away the one institution that valued women's gender and allowed them to pursue a spiritual life outside marriage.

The Spread of Lutheranism

By the end of the 1520s, the empire was divided between cities and states that accepted reformed religion and those that adhered to Roman Catholicism. Large German communities across northern Europe, mostly founded as trading outposts, became focal points for the penetration of reformist ideas. In Livonia, the Teutonic Knights established a Lutheran form of worship that soon took hold all along the shores of the Baltic. Lutheran-inspired reformers seized control of the Polish port city of Gdansk, which they held for a short time, and neighboring Prussia officially established a Lutheran church. Polish translations of Luther's writings were disseminated into Poland-Lithuania, and Protestant communities were established as far south as Krakow.

Merchants and students carried Luther's ideas into Scandinavia, but there the importance of political leaders was crucial. Christian III (1534–1559) of Denmark had been present at the Diet of Worms when Luther made his famous reply to Charles V. Christian was deeply impressed by the reformer, and after a ruinous civil war he confiscated Catholic Church property in Denmark and created a reformed religion under Luther's direct supervision.

Paradoxically, Lutheranism came to Sweden as part of an effort to throw off the yoke of Danish dominance. When Gustav I Vasa (1523–1560) led a successful uprising against the Danes and became king of Sweden, he encouraged the spread of Protestant ideas. The result was a more gradual establishment of Lutheranism in Sweden than in Denmark.

Luther's impact extended into central Europe. Bohemia had had a reforming tradition of its own that antedated Luther. Though the Catholic Church had condemned the teachings of Jan Hus (1373–1415), Hussitism was in fact the all-but-established religion in most parts of Bohemia. Ferdinand the Emperor was bound by law to allow its moderate practice. Hussites had already initiated many of the reforms on which Luther insisted: the Mass was said in Czech, and the Bible had been translated into the vernacular. Hussites believed that communion in both forms was mandated by the Bible. This was the real issue that separated them from Roman Catholics, for the Hussites refused to accept the traditional view that the authority of either the pope or the general council of the Church could alter God's command. On all these issues, Hussites and Lutherans shared a common program. But the Hussites were conservative in almost everything else. While the

◄ The Spread of Lutheranism fro
to Scandinavia, Central Europe,
England. Protestant ideas took h
exclusively in northern Europe.

German communities in Bohemia accepted the core of Lutheran doctrine, most Czechs rejected justification by faith alone and maintained their own practices.

As important as Protestant ideas were in northern and central Europe, they proved most fertile in the Swiss towns of the empire. Here was planted the second generation of reformers, theologians who drew radical new conclusions from Luther's insights. In the east, Huldrych Zwingli (1484–1531) brought reformed religion to the town of Zurich. Educated at the University of Basel and deeply influenced by humanist thought early in his career, Zwingli was a preacher among the Swiss mercenary troops that fought for the empire. In 1516, he met Erasmus in Basel and, under his influence, began a study of the Greek writings of the Church Fathers and of the New Testament. Zwingli was also influenced by reports of Luther's defiance of the pope, for his own antipapal views were already developing. Perhaps most decisively for his early development, Zwingli was stricken by plague in 1519. In his life-and-death struggle he came to a profoundly personal realization of the power of God's mercy.

These experiences became the basis for the reform theology that Zwingli preached in Zurich. He believed that the Church had to recover its earlier purity and to reject the innovations in practices that successive popes and general councils had brought in. He stressed the equality of believers, justification by faith alone, and the sufficiency of the gospel as authority for church practice. He attacked indulgences, penance, clerical celibacy, prayers to the Virgin, statues and images in churches, and a long list of other practices. He regarded the Mass as a commemorative event rather than one that involved the real presence of Christ. His arguments were so effective that the town council adopted them as the basis for a reform of religion.

The principles that Zwingli preached quickly spread to neighboring Swiss states. Practical as well as theological, Zwingli's reforms were carried out by the civil government with which he allied himself. This was not the same as the protection that princes had given to Lutherans. Rather, in the places that came under Zwingli's influence, there was an important integration of church and state. He stressed the divine origins of civil government and the importance of the magistrate as an agent of Christian reform: "A church without the magistrate is mutilated and incomplete." This theocratic idea—that the leaders of the state and the leaders of the church were linked—became the basis for further social and political reform.

THE PROTESTANT REFORMATION

By the middle of the 1530s, Protestant reform had entered a new stage. Luther did not intend to form a new religion; his struggle had been with Rome. His religion was one of protest. Most of his energy was expended in attack and counterattack. The second generation of reformers faced a different task. The new reformers were the church builders who had to systematize doctrine for a generation that had already accepted religious reform. Their challenge was to draw out the logic of reformed ideas and to create enduring structures for reformed churches. The problems they faced were as much institutional as doctrinal. How was the new church to be governed in the absence of the traditional hierarchy? How could discipline be enforced when members of the reformed community went astray? What was the proper relationship between the community of believers and civil authority? Whatever the failings of the Roman Catholic Church, it had ready answers to these critical questions.

Geneva. In the sixteenth ... the dual government of the ...nolic bishop of the town, who ...nt. The Genevans also had their ... traditionally struggled for power ... the 1530s the council had gained ...council confiscated church lands and ...ized the Church's legal powers, and ...and most of his administrators to flee the ... Savoy inevitably followed, and Geneva ...y have been crushed into submission except ...e with neighboring Bern, a potent military ...ng the Swiss towns.

... was saved and was free to follow its own course ...us matters. In 1536 the adult male citizens of the ...ted to become Protestant. But there was as yet no re-...er in Geneva to establish a Protestant program and no ...ar definition of what that program might be.

Martin Luther had started out to become a lawyer and ended up a priest. John Calvin started out to become a priest and ended up a lawyer. The difference tells much about each man. Calvin (1509–1564) was born in France,

the son of a bishop's secretary. His education was based on humanist principles, and he learned Greek and Hebrew, studied theology, and received a legal degree from the University of Orléans. Around the age of 20 he converted to Lutheranism. Francis I was determined to root Protestants out of France, and Calvin fled Paris. Persecution of Protestants continued in France, and one of Calvin's close friends was burned for heresy. These events left an indelible impression on Calvin. In 1535, he left France for Basel, where he wrote and published the first edition of *Institutes of the Christian Religion* (1536), a defense of French Protestants against persecution. Calvin returned briefly to France to wind up his personal affairs and then decided to settle in Strasbourg, where he could retire from public affairs and live out his days as a scholar.

To Calvin, providence guided all human action. He could have no better evidence for this belief than what happened next. War between France and the empire clogged the major highways to Strasbourg. Soldiers constantly menaced travelers, and Protestants could expect the worst from both sides. Therefore Calvin and his companions detoured through Geneva, where Guillaume Farel (1489–1565), one of Geneva's leading Protestant reformers, persuaded Calvin to remain in Geneva and lead its reformation.

THE ETERNAL DECREE

John Calvin was born in France but led the Reformation in the Swiss town of Geneva. He was one of the leaders of the second generation of reformers, whose task was to refine the structure of church doctrine. Calvinism was propounded in the Institutes of the Christian Religion *(1534), from which this section on the doctrine of predestination is taken.*

FOCUS QUESTIONS

According to Calvin, why is everyone contaminated by sin?

What power do humans have over their spiritual destiny?

WE MUST BE CONTENT WITH THIS—that such gifts as it pleased the Lord to have bestowed upon the nature of man he vested in Adam; and therefore when Adam lost them after he had received them, he lost them not only from himself but also from us all. . . . Therefore from a rotten root rose up rotten branches, which sent their rottenness into the twigs that sprang out of them; for so were the children corrupted in their father that they in turn infected their children. . . .

And the apostle Paul himself expressly witnesseth that therefore death came upon all men, because all men have sinned and are wrapped in original sin and defiled with the

spots thereof. And therefore the very infants themselves, since they bring with them their own damnation from their mothers' womb, are bound not by another's but by their own fault. For although they have not as yet brought forth the fruits of their own iniquity, yet they have the seeds thereof inclosed within them; yea, their whole nature is a certain seed of sin, therefore it cannot but be hateful and abominable to God. . . .

Predestination we call the eternal decree of God, whereby he has determined with himself what he wills to become of every man. For all are not created to like estate; but to some eternal life and to some eternal damnation is foreordained. Therefore as every man is created to the one or the other end, so we say that he is predestinate either to life or to death.

From John Calvin, *Institutes of the Christian Religion.*

Calvin's greatest contributions to religious reform came in church structure and discipline. He had studied the writings of the first generation of reformers and accepted without question justification by faith alone and the biblical foundation of religious authority. Like Luther and Zwingli, he believed that salvation came from God's grace. But more strongly than his predecessors he believed that the gift of faith was granted only to some and that each individual's salvation or damnation was predestined before birth. The doctrine of predestination was a traditional one, but Calvin emphasized it differently and brought it to the center of the problem of faith. "Many are called but few are chosen," Calvin quoted from the Bible. Those who were predestined to salvation were obliged to govern; those who were predestined to damnation were obliged to be governed.

Calvin structured the institution of the Genevan church in four parts: the pastors, who preached the Word to their congregations; the doctors, who studied and wrote; the deacons, who oversaw the institutions of social welfare, such as hospitals and schools, run by the church; and finally the elders of the church, who governed the church in all moral matters. They were the most controversial part of Calvin's establishment and the most fundamental. They had the power to discipline. Chosen from among the elite of the city, the 12 elders enforced the strict Calvinist moral code that extended into all aspects of private life. Sexual offenses were the most common. Adultery and fornication were vigorously suppressed, and prostitutes, who had nearly become a recognized guild in the early sixteenth century, were expelled from Geneva.

The structure that Calvin gave to the Genevan church soon became the basis for reforms throughout the Continent. The Calvinist church was self-governing, independent of the state, and therefore capable of surviving and even flourishing in a hostile environment. Expanded in several subsequent editions, *The Institutes of the Christian Religion* became the most influential work of Protestant theology. It had begun as an effort to extend Protestantism to Calvin's homeland, and waves of Calvinist-educated pastors returned to France in the mid-sixteenth century and established churches along Calvinist lines. Calvinism spread north to the Low Countries, where it became the basis for Dutch Protestantism, and east, where it flourished in Lithuania. It reached places untouched by Luther and revitalized reform where Lutheranism had been suppressed. Perhaps its greatest impact was in Britain, where the reformation took place not once but twice.

The English Reformation

The king of England wanted a divorce. Henry VIII had been married to Catherine of Aragon (1485–1536) as long as he had been king, and she had borne him no male heir to carry on his line. She had given birth to six children and endured several miscarriages, yet only one

daughter, Mary, survived. Henry came to believe that this was God's punishment for his marriage. Catherine had been married first to Henry's older brother, who had died as a teenager, and there was at least one scriptural prohibition against marrying a brother's wife. A papal dispensation had been provided for the marriage; now Henry wanted a papal dispensation for an annulment. For three years his case ground its way through the papal courts. Catherine of Aragon was the aunt of the Emperor Charles V, and the emperor had taken her side in the controversy. With imperial power in Italy at its height, the pope was content to hear all of the complex legal and biblical precedents argued at leisure.

By 1533, Henry could wait no longer. He had already impregnated Anne Boleyn (ca. 1507–1536), one of the ladies-in-waiting at his court, and for the child—which Henry was certain would be a boy—to be legitimate, a marriage would have to take place at once. Legislation was prepared in Parliament to prevent papal interference in the decisions of England's courts, and Thomas Cranmer (1489–1556), archbishop of Canterbury, England's highest ecclesiastical officer, agreed to annul Henry's first marriage and celebrate his second. This was the first step in a complete break with Rome. Under the guidance of Thomas Cromwell (ca. 1485–1540), the English Parliament passed statute after statute that made Henry supreme head of the church in England and owner of its vast wealth. Monasteries were dissolved, and a Lutheran service was introduced. On 7 September 1533, Anne Boleyn gave birth not to the expected son, but to a daughter, the future Queen Elizabeth I.

The Church of England. Henry's reformation was an act of state, but the English Reformation was not. There was an English tradition of dissent from the Roman Church that stretched back to the fourteenth century. Anticlericalism was especially virulent in the towns, where citizens refused to pay fees to priests for performing services such as burial. And humanist ideas flourished in England, where Thomas More, John Colet, and a host of others supported both the new learning and its efforts to reform spiritual life. Luther's attack on ritual and the Mass and his emphasis on Scripture and faith echoed the lost Lollard program and found many recruits in London and the northern port towns.

Protestantism grew slowly in England because it was vigorously repressed. Like Francis I and Charles V, Henry VIII viewed actual attacks on the established church as potential attacks on the established state. Henry had earned the title Defender of the Faith from the pope in 1521 for authoring an attack on Luther. The first published English translation of the New Testament, made by William Tyndale in 1525, had to be smuggled into England. As sensitivity to the abuses of the Church grew and Lutheran ideas spread, official persecution sharpened.

Henry's divorce unleashed a groundswell of support for religious change. The king's own religious beliefs remained a secret, but Anne Boleyn and Thomas Cromwell sponsored Lutheran reforms, and Thomas Cranmer put them into practice. Religion was legislated through Parliament, and the valuable estates of the Church were sold to the gentry. These practices found favor with both the legal profession and the landed elites and made Protestantism more palatable among these conservative groups. It was in the reign of Edward VI (1547–1553), Henry's son by his third wife, that the central doctrinal and devotional changes were made. Church service was now conducted in English, and the first two English prayer books were created. The Mass was reinterpreted along Zwinglian lines and became the Lord's Supper, the altar became the communion table, and the priest became the minister. Preaching became the center of the church service, and concern about the education of learned ministers resulted in commissions to examine and reform the clergy.

Beginning in the 1530s, state repression turned against Catholics. Those who would not swear the new oaths of allegiance or recognize the legality of Henry VIII's marriage suffered for their beliefs as the early Protestants had suffered for theirs. Thomas More and over 40 others paid with their lives for their opposition. An uprising in the north in 1536, known as the Pilgrimage of Grace, was suppressed, but Catholicism continued to flourish in England, surviving underground during the reigns of Henry and Edward and reemerging under Mary I (1553–1558).

The Successors of Henry VIII.   Mary Tudor, the first woman to rule England, held to the Catholic beliefs in which her mother, Catherine of Aragon, had raised her, and she vowed to bring the nation back to her mother's church. She reestablished papal sovereignty, abolished Protestant worship, and introduced a crash program of education in the universities to train a new generation of priests. The one thing that Mary could not achieve was restoration of monastic properties and church lands. They had been scattered irretrievably, and any attempt at confiscation from the landed elite would surely have been met with insurrection. Catholic retribution for the blood of their martyrs was not long in coming. Cranmer and three other bishops were burned for heresy.

Nearly 800 Protestants fled the country rather than suffer a similar fate. These Marian exiles, as they came to be called, settled in a number of reformed communities, Zurich, Frankfurt, and Geneva among them. There they imbibed the second generation of Protestant ideas, especially Calvinism, and from there they began a propaganda campaign to keep reformed religion alive in England. It was the Marian exiles who were chiefly responsible for the second English reformation, which began in 1558 when Mary died and her half-sister, Elizabeth I (1558–1603), came to the throne.

Under Elizabeth, England returned to Protestantism, but not the Protestantism that had come before. Even the most advanced reforms during Edward's reign now seemed too moderate for the returning exiles. Against Elizabeth's wishes, the English church adopted the Calvinist doctrine of predestination and the simplification (but not wholesale

◀ Among the Protestant victims executed during the reign of Mary I was Thomas Cranmer. Convicted of heresy, he was burned at the stake in Oxford in 1556.

reorganization) of the structure of the church. But it did not become a model of thoroughgoing reformation. The Thirty-nine Articles (1563) continued the English tradition of compromising points of disrupted doctrine and of maintaining traditional practices wherever possible.

The Reformation of the Radicals

Schism breeds schism. That was the stick with which Catholic Church and civil authorities beat Luther from the beginning. By attacking the authority of the established church and flouting the authority of the established state, he was fomenting social upheaval. But he insisted that his own ideas buttressed rather than subverted authority, especially civil authority under whose protection he had placed the Church. As early as 1525, peasants in Swabia appealed to Luther for support in their social rebellion. They based some of their most controversial demands, such as the abolition of tithes and labor service, on biblical authority. Luther instructed the rebels to lay down their arms and await their just rewards in heaven. But Luther's ideas had a life of their own. He clashed with Erasmus over free will and with Zwingli over the Mass. Toward the end of his life he felt that he was holding back the floodgates against the second generation of Protestant thinkers. Time and again, serious reformers wanted to take one or another of his doctrines farther than he was willing to go himself. The water was seeping in everywhere.

The most dangerous threat to the establishment of an orthodox Protestantism came from groups who were described, not very precisely, as Anabaptists. Though this label—which means, literally, "baptism again"—identified people who practiced adult baptism, it was mainly used to tar religious opponents with the brush of extremism. Anabaptists appeared in a number of German and Swiss towns in the 1520s. Taking seriously the doctrine of justification by faith, Anabaptists argued that only believers could be members of the true church of God. Because baptism was the sacrament through which entry into the church took place, Anabaptists reasoned that it was a sacrament for adults rather than infants. But infant baptism was a core doctrine for both Catholics and Protestants. It symbolized the acceptance of Christ, and without it, eternal salvation was impossible. It was a practical doctrine. Unbaptized infants who died could not be accepted in heaven, and infant mortality was appallingly common.

Thus the doctrine of Anabaptism posed a psychological as well as a doctrinal threat to the reformers. But the practice of adult baptism paled in significance compared to many of the other conclusions that religious radicals derived from the principle of *sola scriptura*—by the Word alone. Some groups argued the case that since true Christians were only those who had faith, all others must be cast out of the church. These true Christians formed small separate sects. Many believed that their lives were guided by the Holy Spirit, who directed them from within.

Some went further and denied the power of civil authority over true believers. Some argued for community of goods among believers and rejected private property. Others literally followed passages in the Old Testament that suggested polygamy and promiscuity.

Wherever they settled, these small bands of believers were persecuted to the brutal extent of the laws of heresy. Catholics burned them, Protestants drowned them, and they were stoned and clubbed out of their communities. There was enough substance in their ideas and enough sincerity in their patient sufferings that they continued to recruit followers as they were driven from town to town, from Germany into the Swiss cities, and from Switzerland into Bohemia and Hungary.

There, on the eastern edges of the empire, the largest groups of Anabaptists finally settled. Though all practiced adult baptism, only some held goods in common or remained pacifist. Charismatic leaders such as Balthasar Hubmaier (1485–1528) and Jacob Hutter (d. 1536) spread Anabaptism to Moravia in southern Bohemia, where they converted a number of nobles to their views. They procured land for their communities, which came to be known as the Moravian Brethren. Independent groups existed in England and throughout northwest Europe, where Menno Simons (1496–1561), a Dutch Anabaptist, spent his life organizing bands of followers who came to be known as Mennonites.

THE CATHOLIC REFORMATION

Like a rolling wave, Protestant reform washed across Europe, but the rock of the Roman Catholic Church endured. Though pieces of the universal church crumbled away in northern Germany, Switzerland, Bohemia, Scandinavia, England, and Scotland, the dense mass remained in southern Germany, Italy, Poland-Lithuania, Spain, France, and Ireland. Catholics felt the same impulses toward a more fulfilling religious life as Protestants and complained of the same abuses of clerical, state, and papal powers. But the Catholic response was to reform the church from within. A new personal piety was stressed, which led to the founding of additional spiritual orders. The ecclesiastical hierarchy became more concerned with pastoral care and initiated reforms of the clergy at the parish level. The challenge of converting other peoples, Asians and Amerindians especially, led to the formation of missionary orders and to a new emphasis on preaching and education. Protestantism itself revitalized Catholicism.

The Spiritual Revival

The quest for individual spiritual fulfillment dominated later medieval Roman Catholicism. Erasmus, Luther, and Zwingli were all influenced by a Catholic spiritual movement known as the New Piety. It was propagated in

Germany by the Brethren of the Common Life, a lay organization that stressed the importance of personal meditation on the life of Christ. *The Imitation of Christ* (1427), the central text of the New Piety, commonly attributed to Thomas à Kempis (1379–1471), was among the most influential works of the later Middle Ages. The Brethren taught that a Christian life should be lived according to Christ's dictates as expressed in the Sermon on the Mount. They instructed their pupils to lead a simple ascetic life with personal devotion at its core. These were the lessons that the young Erasmus found so liberating and the young Luther so stifling.

The New Piety, with its emphasis on a simple personal form of religious practice, was a central influence on Christian humanism. It is important to realize that humanism developed within the context of Catholic education and that many churchmen embraced the new learning and supported educational reform or patronized works of humanist scholarship. The Polyglot Bible was organized by Cardinal Jiménez de Cisneros (1436–1517), Archbishop of Toledo and Primate of Spain. The greatest educational reformer in England, John Colet (1467–1519), was dean of Saint Paul's, London's cathedral church. Without any of his famed irony, Erasmus dedicated his Greek Bible to the pope. The leading Christian humanists remained within the Catholic Church even after many of their criticisms had formed the basis of Protestant reforms.

This combination of piety and humanism imbued the ecclesiastical reforms initiated by church leaders. Archbishop Jiménez de Cisneros, who also served as inquisitor-general of the Spanish Inquisition, undertook a wide-ranging reorganization of Spanish religious life in the late fifteenth century. Though not every project was successful, Jiménez de Cisneros's program took much of the sting out of Protestant attacks on clerical abuse, and there was never a serious Protestant movement in Spain.

The most influential reforming bishop was Gian Matteo Giberti (1495–1543) of Verona. Using his own frugal life as an example, Giberti rigorously enforced vows, residency, and the pastoral duties of the clergy. He founded almshouses to aid the poor and orphanages to house the homeless. In Verona, Giberti established a printing press, which turned out editions of the central works of Roman Catholicism, especially the writings of Augustine.

The most important indication of the reforming spirit within the Roman Church was the foundation of new religious orders in the early sixteenth century. Devotion to a spiritual life of sacrifice was the chief characteristic of the lay and clerical orders that had flourished throughout the Middle Ages. In one French diocese the number of clergy quadrupled in the last half of the fifteenth century. Although the number of entrants to the traditional orders of Franciscans and Dominicans did not rise as quickly, the growth of lay communities such as the Brethren of the Common Life attested to the continuing appeal of Catholic devotionalism.

Devotionalism was particularly strong in Italy, where a number of new orders received papal charters. The Capuchins were founded by the Italian peasant Matteo de Bascio (ca. 1495–1552). He sought to follow the strictest rule of the life of Saint Francis of Assisi, a path that even the so-called Observant Franciscans had found too arduous. In contrast, the Theatines were established by a group of well-to-do Italian priests who also wished to lead a more austere devotional existence than was to be found in the traditional orders. Like the Capuchins, they accepted a life of extreme poverty, in which even begging was only a last resort.

In Spain, Saint Teresa of Ávila (1515–1582) led the reform of the Carmelites. She believed that women had to withdraw totally from the world around them to achieve true devotion. Against the wishes of the male superiors of her order, she founded a convent to put her beliefs into practice and began writing devotional tracts like *The Way of Perfection* (1583). In 1535, Angela Merici (ca. 1474–1540) established the Ursulines, one of the most original of the new foundations, composed of young unmarried girls who remained with their families but lived chaste lives devoted to the instruction of other women.

Loyola's Pilgrimage

At first glance, Saint Ignatius Loyola (1491–1556) seems an unlikely candidate to lead one of the most vital movements for religious reform in the sixteenth century. The thirteenth child of a Spanish noble family, Loyola trained for a military life in the service of Castile. In 1521, he was one of the garrison defenders when the French besieged Pamplona. A cannonball shattered his leg, and he was carried home for a long enforced convalescence. There, he slowly and carefully read the only books in the castle: a life of Christ and a history of the saints. His reading inspired him. Before, he had sought glory and renown in battle. But when he compared the truly heroic deeds of the saints to his own vainglorious exploits, he decided to give his life over to spirituality.

Loyola was not a man to do things by halves. He resolved to model his life on the sufferings of the saints about whom he had read. He renounced his worldly goods and endured a year-long regimen of physical abstinence and spiritual nourishment in the town of Manresa. He deprived himself of food and sleep for long periods and underwent a regimen of seven hours of daily prayer, supplemented by nearly continuous religious contemplation. "But when he went to bed great enlightenment, great spiritual consolations often came to him, so that he lost much of the time he had intended for sleeping." During this period of intense concentration he first began to have visions, which later culminated in a mystical experience in which Christ called Loyola directly to his service.

Like Luther, Loyola was tormented by his inability to achieve grace through penance, but unlike Luther he redoubled his efforts. At Manresa, Loyola encountered the

Rubens's (1577–1640) *The Miracles of Saint Ignatius Loyola*. Founder of the Society of Jesus, Loyola prepared his Jesuit recruits for an active, rather than a contemplative, life.

Imitation of Christ, which profoundly influenced his conversion. He recorded the techniques he used during this vigil in *The Spiritual Exercises*, which became a handbook for Catholic devotion. In 1523, crippled and barefoot, he made a pilgrimage to Jerusalem. He returned to Spain intent on becoming a priest.

By this time, Loyola had adopted a distinctive garb that attracted both followers and suspicion. Twice, the Spanish ecclesiastical authorities summoned him to be examined for heresy. In 1528, he decided to complete his studies in France, where he and a small group of friends eventually decided to form a brotherhood after they became priests. They devoted themselves to the cure of souls and took personal vows of poverty, chastity, and obedience to the pope. On a pilgrimage to Rome, Loyola and his followers

again attracted the attention of ecclesiastical authorities. Loyola explained his mission to them and in 1540 won the approval of Pope Paul III to establish a new holy order, the Society of Jesus.

Loyola's Society was founded at a time when the spiritual needs of the Church were being extended beyond the confines of Europe. Loyola volunteered his followers, who came to be known as Jesuits, to serve in the remotest parts of the world. One disciple, Francis Xavier (1506–1552), made converts to Catholicism in the Portuguese port cities in the East and then in India and Japan. Other Jesuits became missionaries to the New World, where they offered Christian consolation to the Amerindian communities. By 1556, the Society of Jesus had grown from 10 to 1,000, and Loyola had become a full-time administrator in Rome.

Loyola never abandoned the military images that had dominated his youth. He enlisted his followers in military terms. The Jesuits were "soldiers of God" who served "beneath the banner of the Cross." Loyola's most fundamental innovation in these years was the founding of schools to train recruits for his order. Jesuit training was rigorous. Since they were being prepared for an active rather than a contemplative life, Jesuits were not cloistered during their training. Jesuit schools were opened to the laity, and lay education became one of the Jesuits' most important functions. Loyola lived to see the establishment of nearly a hundred colleges and seminaries and the spread of his order throughout the world. He died while at prayer.

The Counter-Reformation

The Jesuits were both the culmination of one wave of Catholic reform and the advance guard of another. They combined the piety and devotion that stretched from medieval mysticism through humanism, diocesan reforms, and the foundations of new spiritual orders. But they also represented an aggressive Catholic response that was determined to meet Protestantism head on and repel it. This was the Church militant. Old instruments such as the Inquisition were revived, and new weapons such as the Index of Prohibited Books were forged. But the problems of fighting Protestantism were not only those of combating Protestant ideas. Like oil and water, politics and religion failed to combine. Emperor Charles V and the hierarchy of the German church demanded thoroughgoing reform of the Catholic Church; the pope and the hierarchy of the Italian church resisted the call. As head of the Catholic Church, the pope was distressed by the spread of heresy in the lands of the empire. As head of a large Italian city-state, the pope was consoled by the weakening of the power of his Spanish rival. Brothers in Christ, pope and emperor were mortal enemies in everything else. Throughout the Catholic states of Germany came the urgent cry for a reforming council of the Church. But the voices were muffled as they crossed the Alps and made their way down the Italian peninsula.

At the emperor's instigation the first serious preparations for a general council of the Church were made in the 1530s. The papacy warded it off. The complexities of international diplomacy were one factor—the French king was even less anxious to bring peace to the empire than the pope was—and the complexities of papal politics were another. The powers of a general council in relation to the powers of the papacy had never been clarified. After the advent and spread of Protestantism, successive popes had little reason to believe that in this gravest crisis of all, a council would be mindful of papal prerogatives. In fact, Catholic reformers were as bitter in their denunciations of papal abuses as Protestants were. The second attempt to arrange a general council of the Church occurred in the early 1540s. Again the papacy warded it off.

CHRONOLOGY	
THE REFORMATION AND THE COUNTER-REFORMATION	
1517	Luther writes his Ninety-five Theses
1521	Luther is excommunicated and declared an enemy of the empire; Henry VIII receives title Defender of the Faith
1523	Zwingli expounds his faith in formal disputation
1533	Henry VIII divorces Catherine of Aragon, marries Anne Boleyn, and breaks with the Church of Rome
1536	Calvin publishes *Institutes of the Christian Religion*
1540	Loyola receives papal approval for Society of Jesus
1545–1563	Council of Trent
1553	Mary I restores Catholicism in England
1563	Elizabeth I enacts the Thirty-nine Articles, which restores Protestantism to England

These factors ensured that when a general council of the Church finally did meet, its task would not be an easy one. The northern churches, French and German alike, wanted reforms of the papacy; the papacy wanted a restatement of orthodox doctrine. Many princes whose states were divided among Catholics and Protestants wanted compromises that might accommodate both. Ferdinand I, King of Bohemia, saw the council as an opportunity to bring the Hussites back into the fold. Charles V and the German bishops wanted the leading Protestant church authorities to offer their own compromises on doctrine that might form a basis for reuniting the empire. The papacy wanted traditional church doctrine reasserted.

The general council of the Church that finally met in Trent from 1545 to 1563 thus had nearly unlimited potential for disaster. It began in compromise—Trent was an Italian town under the government of the emperor—but ended in total victory for the views of the papacy. For all of the papacy's seeming weaknesses (the defections of England and the rich north German territories cut into papal revenues, and Italy was under Spanish occupation) an Italian pope always held the upper hand at the council. Fewer than one-third of the delegates came from outside Italy. The French looked on the council suspiciously and played only a minor role, and the emperor forbade his bishops to attend after the council moved to Bologna.

Yet for all of these difficulties, the councillors at Trent made some real progress. They corrected a number of abuses, of which the sale of indulgences was the most substantive. They formulated rules for the better regulation of parish priests and stressed the obligation of priests and bishops to preach to their congregations. They ordered seminaries to be founded in all dioceses where there was not already a university so that priests could receive sufficient education to perform their duties. They prepared a new modern and uniform Catholic service and centralized and updated the Index of Prohibited Books to include Protestant writings from all over the Continent.

The Council of Trent made no concessions to Protestants, moderate or radical. The councillors upheld justification by faith and works over justification by faith alone. They confirmed the truth of Scripture and the traditions of the Church against Scripture alone. They declared the Vulgate to be the only acceptable text of the Bible and encouraged vast bonfires of Greek and Hebrew Scriptures in an effort to undo the great scholarly achievements of the humanists. They reaffirmed the seven sacraments and the doctrine of the miracle of the Eucharist. They upheld clerical celibacy. The redefinition of traditional Roman Catholicism drew the doctrinal lines clearly and ended decades of confusion. But it also meant that the differences between Catholics and Protestants could now be settled only by the sword.

The Empire Strikes Back

Warfare dominated the reform of religion almost from its beginning. The burnings, drownings, and executions by which both Catholics and Protestants attempted to maintain religious purity were but raindrops compared to the sea of blood that was shed in sieges and on battlefields beginning in the 1530s. The Catholic divisions were clear. The empire continued to be engaged in the west with its archenemy, France, and in the south with the ever-expanding Ottoman Empire. Charles V needed not only peace within his own German realms, but positive support for his offensive and defensive campaigns. He could never devote his full resources to suppressing Protestant dissent.

Yet there was never a united Protestant front to suppress. The north German towns and principalities that accepted Lutheranism in the 1520s had had a long history of warfare among themselves. Princes stored up grievances from past wars and contested inheritances; cities stored up jealousies from commercial rivalries and special privileges. Added to this was the division between Luther and Zwingli over doctrinal issues that effectively separated the German and Swiss components of the Reformation from each other.

Although both the Protestant and the Catholic sides were internally weak, it was the greater responsibilities of Charles V that allowed for the uneasy periods of peace. Each pause gave the Protestant reformers new life. Lutheranism continued to spread in the northern part of the empire, Zwinglian reform in the south. Charles V asked the papacy to convoke a general council and the Protestants to stop evangelizing in new territories. But Protestant leaders were no more capable of halting the

▼ The Religious Divisions of Europe, ca. 1555. Prior to 1520, all of Europe was Roman Catholic.

spread of the Reformation than were Catholics. Thus each violation of each uneasy truce seemed to prove treachery. In 1546, just after Luther's death, both sides raised armies in preparation for renewed fighting. In the first stage of war, Charles V scored a decisive victory, capturing the two leading Protestant princes and conquering Saxony and Thuringia, the homeland of Lutheran reform.

Charles V's greatest victories were always preludes to his gravest defeats. The remaining Protestant princes were driven into the arms of the French, who placed dynastic interests above religious concerns. Again Europe was plunged into general conflict, with the French invading the German states from the west, the Turks from the south, and the Protestant princes from the north. Charles V, now an old and broken man, was forced to flee through the Alps in the dead of winter and was brought to the bargaining table soon after. By the Peace of Augsburg in 1555 the emperor agreed to allow the princes of Germany to establish the religion of their people. Protestant princes would govern Protestant states, and Catholic princes would govern Catholic states. The Peace of Augsburg ended 40 years of religious struggle in Germany.

Conclusion

IN 1547, THE THEN-VICTORIOUS CHARLES V stood at the grave of Martin Luther. He had been buried in the shadow of the church in which he had been baptized, and now other shadows darkened his plot. Imperial troops were masters of all Saxony and were preparing to turn back the religious clock in Luther's homeland. The emperor was advised to have the body exhumed and burned, to carry out 25 years too late the Edict of Worms that had made Luther an outlaw from Church and state. But Charles V was no longer the self-confident young emperor who had been faced down by the Saxon monk on that long-ago day. Popes had come and gone, and his warrior rivals, Francis I and Henry VIII, were both dead. Charles alone survived. He had little stomach for the petty revenge that he might now exact on the man who, more than any other, had ruined whatever hope there might have been for a united empire that was dominant over all of Europe. "I do not make war on dead men," Charles declared as he turned away from the reformer's grave. But the ghosts of Luther and Zwingli, of Calvin and Ignatius of Loyola were not so easily laid. For another century they would haunt a Europe that could do nothing else but make war on dead men.

QUESTIONS FOR REVIEW

1. How did humanism prepare the way for the Reformation?
2. What motivated Martin Luther?
3. What were the differences between the reforming ideas of Luther, Zwingli, and Calvin?

4. How did the Catholic Church respond to the challenges posed by the Protestant Reformation?

DISCOVERING WESTERN CIVILIZATION ONLINE

You can obtain more information about the reform of religion at the websites listed below. See also the companion website that accompanies this text: www.ablongman.com/kishlansky, which includes an online study guide and additional resources.

The Lutheran Reformation

www.wittenberg.de/e/seiten/personen/luther.html
A site devoted to Martin Luther and the city of Wittenberg. Texts of the famous Ninety-five Theses and other of Luther's writings as well as pictures of locations associated with the Lutheran Reformation.

The Protestant Reformation

www.educ.msu.edu/homepages/laurence/reformation/index.htm
The Reformation guide is the best starting place for information about all aspects of the Protestant Reformation. Dozens of links to follow.

www.wsu.edu/~dee/REFORM/REFORM.HTM
A primarily text-based site created by Washington State University, with profiles of key individuals and explanations of the issues at stake.

www.iclnet.org/pub/resources/text/wittenberg/wittenberg-home.html
The home page of Project Wittenberg, containing a large number of texts (including hymns) by Luther and other Reformers.

tudorhistory.org/
A site with links to a variety of subjects relating to England under the Tudors. Biographies of the kings and queens, bibliographies, maps, and documents.

www.mun.ca/rels/hrollmann/reform/pics/pics.html
Contemporary pictures of leading reformers and the
places associated with the Protestant Reformation.
Excellent reproductions, especially from woodcuts.

**Internet Modern History Sourcebook: Reformation
Europe**

www.fordham.edu/halsall/mod/modsbook02.html
Sources for both the Reformation and Counter-
Reformation with links to other valuable sites.

SUGGESTIONS FOR FURTHER READING

General Reading

Euan Cameron, *The European Reformation* (Oxford:
Oxford University Press, 1991). The most up-to-date survey of the Reformation period. Difficult but rewarding.

Hans J. Hillerbrand, ed., *The Oxford Encyclopedia of the
Reformation* (New York: Oxford University Press, 1996).
An enormous reference resource.

Steven Ozment, *The Age of Reform, 1250–1550* (New
Haven, Conn.: Yale University Press, 1980). An important
interpretation of an epoch of religious change.

The Intellectual Reformation

Roland Bainton, *Erasmus of Christendom* (New York:
Charles Scribner's Sons, 1969). Still the best starting point
and most compelling biography.

Adrian Johns, *The Nature of the Book: Print and Knowledge
in the Making* (Chicago: University of Chicago Press,
1998). A major new synthesis.

R. W. Scribner, *For the Sake of Simple Folk* (Cambridge:
Cambridge University Press, 1994). A study of the impact
of the Reformation on common people. Especially good
on the iconography of reform.

The Lutheran Reformation

Roland Bainton, *Here I Stand* (New York: New American
Library, 1968). The single most compelling biography of
Luther.

Alister E. McGrath, *Reformation Thought: An Introduction,*
2d ed. (New York: Basil Blackwell, 1993). A useful general
work that explains the central doctrines of the Protestant
Reformation, from Luther to the radical reformers.

Bernd Moeller, *Imperial Cities and the Reformation* (Durham,
N.C.: Labyrinth Press, 1982). A central work that defines
the connection between Protestantism and urban reform.

Heiko Oberman, *Luther: Man Between God and the Devil*
(New York: Doubleday, 1992). English translation of one

of the best German biographies of Luther. Sets Luther
within the context of late medieval spirituality.

G. R. Potter, *Huldrych Zwingli* (New York: St. Martin's
Press, 1984). A difficult but important study of the great
Swiss reformer.

The Protestant Reformation

William Bousma, *John Calvin* (Oxford: Oxford University
Press, 1988). A study that places Calvin within the context of the social and intellectual movements of the sixteenth century.

Claus-Peter Clasen, *Anabaptism, A Social History,
1525–1618* (Ithaca, N.Y.: Cornell University Press, 1972).
An important study of the Anabaptist movement.

A. G. Dickens, *The English Reformation,* 2d ed. (London:
Batsford, 1989). An update of the classic study of reform
in England.

J. J. Scarisbrick, *The Reformation and the English People*
(Oxford: Blackwell, 1984). A work that argues for the gradual acceptance of Protestantism in the English Reformation.

The Catholic Reformation

Martin D. W. Jones, *The Counter Reformation: Religion and
Society in Early Modern Europe* (Cambridge: Cambridge
University Press, 1995). A readable and reliable account
of the progress of the Counter-Reformation.

W. W. Meissner, *Ignatius of Loyola: The Psychology of a Saint*
(New Haven, Conn.: Yale University Press, 1994). A
searching study of the founding spirit of the Counter-
Reformation.

John W. O'Malley, *Trent and All That: Renaming Catholicism
in the Early Modern Era* (Cambridge, Mass.: Harvard
University Press, 2000). A reexamination of Catholicism
in the century surrounding the Council of Trent.

EUROPE AT WAR, 1555–1648

- THE VISUAL RECORD: The Massacre of the Innocents
- THE CRISES OF THE WESTERN STATES

- THE STRUGGLES IN EASTERN EUROPE
- THE THIRTY YEARS' WAR, 1618–1648

THE MASSACRE OF THE INNOCENTS

"WAR IS ONE OF THE SCOURGES with which it has pleased God to afflict men," wrote Cardinal Richelieu (1585–1642), the French minister who played no small part in spreading the scourge. War was a constant of European society and penetrated to its very core. It dominated all aspects of life. It enhanced the power of the state, it defined gender roles, it consumed lives and treasure and commodities ravenously. War affected every member of society from combatants to civilians. There were no innocent bystanders. Grain in the fields was destroyed because it was food for soldiers; houses were burned because they provided shelter for soldiers. Civilians were killed for aiding the enemy or holding out against demands for their treasure and supplies. Able-bodied men were taken forcibly to serve as conscripts, leaving women to plant and harvest as best they could.

Neither the ancient temple nor the Roman costume can conceal the immediacy of the picture shown here. It is as painful to look at now as it was when it was created over 350 years ago. Painted by Nicolas Poussin (1594–1665) at the height of the Thirty Years' War, the *Massacre of the Innocents* remains a horrifying composition of power, terror, and despair. The cruel and senseless slaughter of the innocent baby that is about to take place is echoed throughout the canvas. In the background between the executioner's legs can be seen a mother clasping her own child tightly and anticipating the fall of the sword. In the background on the right, another mother turns away from the scene and carries her infant to safety. In the foreground strides a mother holding her dead child. She tears at her hair and cries in anguish. To a culture in which the image of mother and child—of Mary and Jesus—was one of sublime peacefulness and joy, the contrast could hardly have been more shocking.

The picture graphically displays the cruelty of the soldier, the helplessness of the child, and the horror of the mother. By his grip on the mother's hair and his foot on the baby's throat, the warrior shows his brute power. The mother's futile effort to stop the sword illustrates her powerlessness. She scratches uselessly at the soldier's back. Naked, the baby boy raises his hands as if to surrender to the inevitable, as if to reinforce his innocence.

To study Europe at war, we must enter a world of politics and diplomacy, of issues and principles, of judgment and error. There can be no doubt that the future of Europe was decisively shaped by this century of wholesale slaughter, during which dynastic and religious fervor finally ran its course. The survival of Protestantism, the disintegration of the Spanish empire, the rise of Holland and Sweden, the collapse of Poland and Muscovy, the fragmentation of Germany—these were all vital transformations the consequences of which would be felt for centuries. We cannot avoid telling this story, untangling its causes, narrating its course, and revealing its outcome.

But neither should we avoid facing its reality. Look again at the painting by Poussin.

LOOKING AHEAD

As we will see in this chapter, warfare in the seventeenth century decisively reshaped power relations of families and states. Protestantism survived after nearly a century of military challenge and the power of the great Habsburg dynasty was finally crushed. In its place rose France, England, and Holland, and a new chapter of European conflict began.

THE CRISES OF THE WESTERN STATES

"Un roi, une foi, une loi"—"One king, one faith, one law." This was a prescription that members of all European states accepted without question in the sixteenth century. Society was an integrated whole, equally dependent on monarchical, ecclesiastical, and civil authority for its effective survival. A European state could no more tolerate the presence of two churches than it could the presence of two kings. But the Reformation had created two churches. The coexistence of Catholics and Protestants in a single realm posed a stark challenge to accepted theory and traditional practice.

The problem proved intractable because it admitted only one solution: total victory. There could be no compromise for several reasons. Religious beliefs were profoundly held. Religious controversy was more than a life-and-death struggle: it was a struggle between everlasting life and eternal damnation. Doomed, too, was the practical solution of toleration. To the modern mind, toleration seems so logical that it is difficult to understand why it took over a century of bloodshed before it came to be grudgingly accepted by the most bitterly divided countries. But toleration was not a practical solution in a society that admitted no principle of organization other than one king, one faith.

The French Wars of Religion

No wars are more terrible than civil wars. The loss of lives and property is staggering, but the loss of communal identity is greater still. Generations pass before societies recover from their civil wars. Such was the case with the French wars of religion.

The Spread of Calvinism and Religious Division. Protestantism came late to France. Not until after Calvin reformed the Church in Geneva and began to export his brand of Protestantism did French society begin to divide along religious lines. By 1560 there were over 2,000 Protestant congregations in France, and their membership totaled nearly 10 percent of the French population. Calvin and his successors achieved their greatest following among the middle ranks of urban society: merchants, traders, and artisans. They also found a receptive audience among aristocratic women, who eventually converted their husbands and children.

However, the wars of religion were brought on by more than the rapid spread of Calvinism. Equally important was the vacuum of power that had been created when Henry II (1547–1559) died in a jousting tournament. Surviving Henry were his extraordinary widow, Catherine de Médicis, three daughters, and four sons, the oldest of whom, Francis II (1559–1560), was only 15 years old. Under the influence of his beautiful young wife, Mary,

▲ Catherine de Médicis (1519–1598), the wife of Henry II of France, was the real power behind the throne during the reigns of her sons Charles IX (1560–1574) and Henry III (1574–1589). Her overriding concern was to ensure her sons' succession and to preserve the power of the monarchy.

Queen of Scots, Francis allowed her relatives, the Guise family, to dominate the great offices of state and to exclude their rivals from power. The Guises controlled the two most powerful institutions of the state: the army and the Church.

The Guises were staunchly Catholic, and among their enemies were the Bourbons, princes of the blood with a direct claim to the French throne but also a family with powerful Protestant members. The revelation of a Protestant plot to remove the king from Paris provided the Guises with an opportunity to eliminate their most potent rivals. The Bourbon duc de Condé, the leading Protestant peer of the realm, was sentenced to death. But five days before Condé's execution, Francis II died, and Guise power evaporated. The new king, Charles IX (1560–1574), was only 10 years old and firmly under the grip of his mother, Catherine de Médicis, who now declared herself regent of France.

Civil War. Condé's death sentence convinced him that the Guises would stop at nothing to gain their ambitions. Force would have to be met with force. Protestants and Catholics alike raised armies, and in 1562, civil war ensued. Because of the tangle of motives among the participants, each side in the struggle had different objectives. Catherine wanted peace and was willing to accept almost any strategy for securing it. At first she negotiated with the Bourbons, but she was ultimately forced to accept the fact that the Guises were more powerful. The Guises wanted to suppress Protestantism and eliminate Protestant influence at court. They were willing to undertake the task with or without the king's express support.

Once the wars began, the leading Protestant peers fled the court, but the position of the Guises was not altogether secure. Henry Bourbon, king of Navarre, was the next in line to the throne should Charles IX and his two brothers die without male heirs. Henry had been raised in the Protestant faith by his mother, Jeanne d'Albret, whose own mother, Marguerite of Navarre, was among the earliest protectors of the Huguenots, as the French Calvinists came to be called.

The inconclusive nature of the early battles might have allowed for the pragmatic solution by Catherine de Médicis had it not been for the assassination of the duc de Guise in 1563 by a Protestant fanatic. This act added a personal vendetta to the religious passions of the Catholic leaders. They encouraged the slaughter of Huguenot congregations and openly planned the murder of Huguenot leaders. Protestants gave as good as they got. In open defiance of Valois dynastic interests, the Guises courted support from Spain, while the Huguenots imported Swiss and German mercenaries to fight in France. Noble factions and irreconcilable religious differences were pulling the government apart.

The Saint Bartholomew's Day Massacre. By 1570, Catherine was ready to attempt another reconciliation. She announced her plans for a marriage between her daughter Margaret and Henry of Navarre, a marriage that would symbolize the spirit of conciliation between the crown and the Huguenots. The marriage was to take place in Paris during August 1572. The arrival of Huguenot leaders from all over France to attend the marriage ceremony presented an opportunity of a different kind to the Guises and their supporters. If leading Huguenots could be assassinated in Paris, the Protestant cause might collapse, and the truce that the wedding signified might be turned instead into a Catholic triumph.

Saint Bartholomew was the apostle whom Jesus described as a man without guile. Ironically, it was on his feast day that the Huguenots who had innocently come to celebrate Henry's marriage were led like lambs to the slaughter. On 24 August 1572 the streets of Paris ran red with Huguenot blood. Although frenzied, the slaughter was inefficient. Henry of Navarre and a number of other important Huguenots escaped the carnage and returned to their urban strongholds. In the following weeks the violence spread from Paris to the countryside, and thousands of Protestants paid for their beliefs with their lives.

One King, Two Faiths

The Saint Bartholomew's Day Massacre was a transforming event in many ways. In the first place, it prolonged the wars. A whole new generation of Huguenots now had an attachment to the continuation of warfare: their fathers and brothers had been mercilessly slaughtered. By itself, the event was shocking enough; in the atmosphere of anticipated reconciliation created by the wedding, it screamed out for revenge. And the target for retaliation

◄ Painting of the Saint Bartholomew's Day Massacre. The massacre began in Paris on 24 August 1572, and the violence soon spread throughout France.

was no longer limited to the Guises and their followers. By accepting the results of the massacre, the monarchy sanctioned it and spilled Huguenot blood on itself. For more than a decade, Catherine de Médicis had maintained a distance between the crown and the leaders of the Catholic movement. That distance no longer existed.

The Theory of Resistance. After Saint Bartholomew's Day, Huguenot theorists began to develop the idea that resistance to a monarch whose actions violated divine commandments or civil right was lawful. For the first time, Huguenot writers provided a justification for rebellion. Perhaps most importantly, a genuine revulsion against the massacres swept the nation. A number of Catholic peers now joined with the Huguenots to protest the excesses of the crown and the Guises. These Catholics came to be called the *politiques*, from their desire for a practical settlement of the wars. They were led by the duke of Anjou, who was next in line to the throne when Charles IX died in 1574 and Henry III (1574–1589) became king.

Against them, in Paris and a number of other towns, the Catholic League was formed, a society that pledged its first allegiance to religion. The League took up where the Saint Bartholomew's Day Massacre left off, and the slaughter of ordinary people who professed the wrong religion continued. Matters grew worse in 1584 when the duke of Anjou died. With each passing year it was becoming apparent that Henry III would produce no male heir. After the duke's death, the Huguenot Henry of Navarre was the next in line for the throne. Catholic Leaguers talked openly of altering the royal succession and began to develop theories of lawful resistance to monarchical power. By 1585, when the final civil war began—the war of the three Henrys, named for Henry III, Henry Guise, and Henry of Navarre—the crown was in the weakest possible position. Paris and the Catholic towns were controlled by the League, and the Protestant strongholds were controlled by Henry of Navarre. King Henry III could not abandon his capital or his religion, but neither could he gain control of the Catholic party. The extremism of the Leaguers kept the politiques away from court; and without the politiques there could be no settlement.

In December 1588, Henry III summoned Henry Guise and Guise's brother to a meeting in the royal bedchamber. There, they were murdered by the king's order. The politiques were blamed for the murders—revenge was taken on a number of them—and Henry III was forced to flee his capital. He made a pact with Henry of Navarre, and together royalist and Huguenot forces besieged Paris. All supplies were cut off from the city, and only the arrival of a Spanish army prevented its fall. In 1589, Catherine de Médicis died, her ambition to reestablish the authority of the monarchy in shambles, and in the same year a fanatic priest gained revenge for the murder of the Guises by assassinating Henry III.

Henry IV. Now Henry of Navarre came into his inheritance. But after nearly 30 years of continuous civil war, it was certain that a Huguenot could never rule France. If Henry was to become king of all France, he would have to become a Catholic king. It is not clear when Henry made the decision to accept the Catholic faith—"Paris is worth a Mass," he reportedly declared—but he did not announce his decision at once. Rather, he strengthened his forces, tightened his bonds with the politiques, and urged his countrymen to expel the Spanish invaders. He finally made his conversion public and in 1594 was crowned Henry IV (1589–1610). A war-weary nation was willing to accept him.

In 1598, Henry proclaimed the Edict of Nantes, which granted limited toleration to the Huguenots. It was the culmination of decades of attempts to find a solution to the existence of two religions in one state. It was a compromise that satisfied no one, but it was a compromise that everyone could accept. "One king, two faiths" was as apt a description of Henry IV as it was of the settlement. Yet neither Henry's conversion nor the Edict of Nantes stilled the passions that had spawned and sustained the French wars of religion. Sporadic fighting between Catholics and Huguenots continued, and fanatics on both sides fanned the flames of religious hatred. Henry IV survived 18 attempts on his life before he was finally felled by an assassin's knife in 1610, but by then he had established the monarchy and brought a semblance of peace to France.

C H R O N O L O G Y	
THE FRENCH WARS OF RELIGION	
1559	Death of Henry II
1560	Protestant duc de Condé sentenced to death
1562	First battle of wars of religion
1563	Catholic duc de Guise assassinated; Edict of Amboise grants limited Protestant worship
1572	Saint Bartholomew's Day Massacre
1574	Accession of Henry III
1576	Formation of Catholic League
1584	Death of duc d'Anjou makes Henry of Navarre heir to throne
1585	War of the three Henrys
1588	Duc de Guise murdered by order of Henry III
1589	Catherine de Médicis dies; Henry III assassinated
1594	Henry IV crowned
1598	Edict of Nantes

The combined territories of the Spanish and Austrian Habsburgs during the reign of Philip II. Charles V had divided his estates to make it easier for them to be governed.

The World of Philip II

While France was caught up in religious strife, Spain, by the middle of the sixteenth century, had achieved the status of the greatest power in Europe. The dominions of Philip II (1556–1598) of Spain stretched from the Atlantic to the Pacific; his continental territories included the Netherlands in the north and Milan and Naples in Italy. In 1580, Philip became king of Portugal, uniting all the states of the Iberian peninsula. With the addition of Portugal's Atlantic ports and its sizable fleet, Spanish maritime power was now unsurpassed. Philip saw himself as a Catholic monarch fending off the spread of heresy. He came to the throne at just the moment that Calvinism began its rapid growth in northern Europe and provided the impetus for the greatest crisis of his reign: the revolt of the Netherlands.

Though Philip's father, Charles V, amassed a great empire, he had begun only as the Duke of Burgundy. Charles's Burgundian inheritance encompassed a diverse territory in the northwestern corner of Europe. The 17 separate provinces of this territory were called the Netherlands, or the Low Countries, because of the flooding that kept large portions of them under water. The Netherlands, one of the richest and most populous regions of Europe, was an international leader in manufacturing, banking, and commerce. In the southern provinces, French was the background and language of the inhabitants; in the northern ones, Germans had settled, and Dutch was spoken.

The Low Countries had accepted the Peace of Augsburg in a spirit of conciliation in which it was never intended. Here, Catholics, Lutherans, Anabaptists, and Calvinists peaceably coexisted. As in France, this situation changed dramatically with the spread of Calvinism. The heavy concentration of urban populations in the Low Countries provided the natural habitat for Calvinist preachers, who made converts across the entire social spectrum. As Holy Roman Emperor, Charles V may have made his peace with Protestants, but as king of Spain he had not. Charles V had maintained the purity of the Spanish Catholic Church through a careful combination of reform and repression.

Philip II intended to pursue a similar policy in the Low Countries. With papal approval, he initiated a scheme to reform the hierarchy of the Church by expanding the numbers of bishops, and he invited the Jesuits to establish schools for orthodox learning. Simultaneously, he strengthened the power of the Inquisition and ordered the enforcement of the decrees of the Council of Trent. The Protestants sought the protection of their local nobles, who, Catholic or Protestant, had their own reasons for opposing the strict enforcement of heresy laws. Provincial nobles and magistrates resented both the policies that were being pursued and the fact that they disregarded local autonomy. Town governors and noblemen refused to cooperate in implementing the new laws.

The Revolt of the Netherlands

The passive resistance of nobles and magistrates was soon matched by the active resistance of the Calvinists. Unable to enforce Philip's policy, Margaret of Parma, his half-sister, whom Philip had made regent, agreed to a limited toleration. But in the summer of 1566, before this toleration could be put into effect, bands of Calvinists unleashed a storm of iconoclasm in the provinces, breaking stained glass windows and statues of the Virgin and the saints, which they claimed were idolatrous. Helpless in the face of determined Calvinists and apathetic Catholics, local authorities could not protect Church property. Iconoclasm gave way to open revolt. Fearing social rebellion, even the leading Protestant noblemen took part in suppressing these riots.

Rebellion and War. In Spain the events in the Netherlands were treated for what they were: open rebellion. Despite the fact that Margaret had already restored order, Philip II was determined to punish the rebels and enforce the heresy laws. A large military force under the command of the Duke of Alba (1507–1582) was sent from Spain as an army of occupation. Alba lured leading Protestant noblemen to Brussels, where he publicly executed them in 1568. He also established a military court to punish participants in the rebellion, a court that came to be called the Council of Blood. The Council handed down over 9,000 convictions, 1,000 of which carried the death penalty. As many as 60,000 Protestants fled beyond Alba's jurisdiction. Alba next made an example of several small towns that had been implicated in the iconoclasm. He allowed his soldiers to pillage the towns at will before slaughtering their entire populations and razing them to the ground. By the end of 1568, royal policy had gained a sullen acceptance in the Netherlands, but for the next 80 years, with only occasional truces, Spain and the Netherlands were at war.

The Protestants Rebel. Alba's policies had driven Protestants into rebellion, and this forced the Spanish government to maintain its army by raising taxes from the provinces that had remained loyal. Soon the loyal provinces were also in revolt, not over religion but over taxation and local autonomy. Tax resistance and fear of an invasion from France left Alba unprepared for the series of successful assaults Protestants launched in the northern provinces during 1572. The Protestant generals established a permanent base in the northwestern provinces of Holland and Zeeland. By 1575, they had gained a stronghold that they would

never relinquish. Prince William of Orange assumed the leadership of the two provinces, which were now united against the tyranny of Philip's rule.

Spanish government was collapsing all over the Netherlands. William ruled in the north, and the States-General, a parliamentary body composed of representatives from the separate provinces, ruled in the south. Margaret of Parma had resigned in disgust at Alba's tactics, and Alba had been relieved of his command when his tactics failed. No one was in control of the Spanish army. The soldiers, who had gone years with only partial pay, now roamed the southern provinces looking for plunder. Brussels and Ghent had both been targets, and in 1576 the worst atrocities of all occurred when mutinous Spanish troops sacked Antwerp. Over 7,000 people were slaughtered, and nearly one-third of the city burned to the ground.

The "Spanish fury" in Antwerp effectively ended Philip's rule over his Burgundian inheritance. The Protestants had established a permanent home in the north. The States-General had established its ability to rule in the south, and Spanish policy had been totally discredited. To achieve a settlement, the Pacification of Ghent of 1576, the Spanish government conceded local autonomy in taxation, the central role of the States-General in legislation, and the immediate withdrawal of all Spanish troops from the Low Countries. This rift among the provinces was soon followed by a permanent split. In 1581, one group of provinces voted to depose Philip II while a second group decided to remain loyal to him. Philip II refused to accept the dismemberment of his inheritance or to recognize the independent Dutch state that now existed in Holland.

Meanwhile, Protestant England under Elizabeth I (1558–1603) had sided with the Dutch Protestants opposing Philip II. During Elizabeth's reign, England and Spain entered a long period of hostility. English pirates raided Spanish treasure ships returning to Europe, and Elizabeth covertly aided both French and Dutch Protestants. Finally, in 1588, Philip decided to invade England. A great fleet set sail from the Portuguese coast to the Netherlands, where a large Spanish army was waiting to be conveyed to England.

The Spanish Armada comprised over 130 ships, many of them the pride of the Spanish and Portuguese navies. They were bigger and stronger than anything possessed by the English, whose forces were largely merchant vessels hastily converted for battle. But the English ships were faster and more easily maneuverable in the unpredictable winds of the English Channel. They also carried guns that could easily be reloaded for multiple firings, whereas the Spanish guns were designed to discharge only one broadside before hand-to-hand combat ensued. With these advantages the English were able to prevent the Armada from reaching port in the Netherlands and to destroy many individual ships as they were blown off course.

Throughout the 1580s and 1590s, Spanish military expeditions attempted to reunite the southern provinces and to

C H R O N O L O G Y
REVOLT OF THE NETHERLANDS
1559	Margaret of Parma named regent of the Netherlands
1566	Calvinist iconoclasm begins revolt
1567	Duke of Alba arrives in Netherlands and establishes Council of Blood
1568	Protestant Count Egmont executed
1572	Protestants capture Holland and Zeeland
1573	Alba relieved of his command
1576	Sack of Antwerp; pacification of Ghent
1581	Catholic and Protestant provinces split
1585	Spanish forces take Brussels and Antwerp
1609	Twelve Years' Truce

▲ The defeat of the immense armada that Philip II sent to invade England in 1588 dealt a serious blow to Spain's standing in Europe.

conquer the northern ones. But Spanish successes in the south were outweighed by the long-term failure of their objectives in the north. In 1609, Spain and the Netherlands concluded the Twelve Years' Truce, which tacitly recognized the existence of the state of Holland. By the beginning of the seventeenth century, Holland was not only an independent state; it was one of the greatest rivals of Spain and Portugal.

THE STRUGGLES IN EASTERN EUROPE

In eastern Europe, dynastic struggles outweighed the problems created by religious reform. Muscovy remained the bulwark of Eastern Orthodox Christianity, immune from the struggles over the Roman faith. Protestantism did spread into Poland-Lithuania, but its presence was tolerated by the Polish state. The spread of dissent was checked not by repression, but by a vigorous Catholic reformation led by the Jesuits. The domestic crises in the East were crises of state rather than of the church. In Muscovy, the disputed succession that followed the death of Ivan the Terrible plunged the state into anarchy and civil war. Centuries of conflict between Poland-Lithuania and Muscovy came to a head with the Poles' desperate gamble

to seize control of their massive eastern neighbor. War between Poland-Lithuania and Muscovy inevitably dominated the politics of the entire region. The Baltic states, most notably Sweden, soon joined the fray.

Kings and Diets in Poland

Until the end of the sixteenth century, Poland-Lithuania was the dominant power in the eastern part of Europe. It was economically healthy and militarily strong. Through its Baltic ports, especially Gdansk, Poland played a central role in international commerce and a dominant role in the northern grain trade. The vast size of the Polish state made defense difficult, and during the course of the sixteenth century it had lost lands to Muscovy in the east and to the Crimean Tartars in the south. But the permanent union with Lithuania in 1569 and the gradual absorption of the Baltic region of Livonia more than compensated for these losses. Matters of war and peace, of taxation, and of reform were placed under the strict supervision of the Polish Diet, a parliamentary body that represented the Polish landed elite. The Diet also carefully controlled religious policy. Roman Catholicism was the principal religion in Poland, but the state tolerated numerous Protestant and Eastern creeds. In the Warsaw Confederation of 1573 the Polish gentry vowed "that we who differ in matters of religion will keep the peace among ourselves."

The biological failure of the Jagiellon monarchy in Poland ended that nation's most successful line of kings. Without a natural heir the Polish nobility and gentry, who officially elected the monarch, had to peddle their throne among the princes of Europe. When Sigismund III (1587–1632) was elected to the Polish throne in 1587, he was also heir to the crown of Sweden. Sigismund accepted the prohibitions against religious repression outlined in the Warsaw Confederation, but he actively encouraged the establishment of Jesuit schools, the expansion of monastic orders, and the strengthening of the Roman Catholic Church.

All of these policies enjoyed the approval of the Polish ruling classes. But the Diet would not support Sigismund's efforts to gain control of the Swedish crown, which he inherited in 1592 but from which he was deposed three years later. If Sigismund triumphed in Sweden, all Poland would get was a part-time monarch. The Polish Diet consistently refused to give the king the funds necessary to invade Sweden successfully. Nevertheless, Sigismund mounted several unsuccessful campaigns against the Swedes that sapped Polish money and manpower.

Muscovy's Time of Troubles

The wars of Ivan the Great and Ivan the Terrible in the fifteenth and sixteenth centuries were waged to secure agricultural territory in the west and a Baltic port in the north. Both objectives came at the expense of Poland-Lithuania. But after the death of Ivan the Terrible in 1584, the Muscovite state began to disintegrate. For years it had been held together only by conquest and fear. Ivan's conflicts with the boyars, the hereditary nobility, created an aristocracy that was unwilling and unable to come to the aid of Ivan's successors. By 1601, the crown was plunged into a crisis of legitimacy known as the Time of Troubles. Ivan had murdered his heir in a fit of anger and left his half-witted son to inherit the throne. This led to a vacuum of power at the center as well as a struggle for the spoils of government. Private armies ruled great swaths of the state, and pretenders to the crown—all claiming to be Dimitri, the lost brother of the last legitimate tsar—appeared everywhere. Ambitious groups of boyars backed their own claimants to the throne. So, too, did ambitious foreigners who eagerly sought to carve up Muscovite possessions.

Muscovy's Time of Troubles was Poland's moment of opportunity. While Muscovy floundered in anarchy and civil war, Poland looked to regain the territory that it had lost to

▼ Eastern Europe (ca. 1550) after the consolidation of Russia and the growth of Poland. The eastern part of Europe was still sparsely populated and economically underdeveloped.

Muscovy over the previous century. Sigismund abandoned war with Sweden to intervene in the struggle for the Russian crown. Polish forces crossed into Muscovy, and Sigismund's generals backed one of the strongest of the false Dimitris, but their plan to put him on the throne failed when he was assassinated. Sigismund used the death of the last false Dimitri as a pretext to assert his own claim to the Muscovite crown. More Polish forces poured across the frontier. In 1610 they took Moscow, and Sigismund proclaimed himself tsar, intending to unite the two massive states.

The Russian boyars, so long divided, now rose against the Polish enemy. The Polish garrison in Moscow was starved into submission, and a native Russian, Michael Romanov (1613–1645), was chosen tsar by an assembly of landholders, the Zemsky Sobor. He made a humiliating peace with the Swedes—who had also taken advantage of the Time of Troubles to invade Muscovy's Baltic provinces—in return for Swedish assistance against the Poles. Intermittent fighting continued for another 20 years. In the end, Poland agreed to peace and a separate Muscovite state but only in exchange for large territorial concessions.

The Rise of Sweden

Sweden's rise to power during the seventeenth century was as startling as it was swift. Until the Reformation, Sweden had been part of the Scandinavian confederation ruled by the Danes. Although the Swedes had a measure of autonomy, they were very much a junior partner in Baltic affairs. Denmark controlled the narrow sound that linked the Baltic Sea with the North Sea, and its prosperity derived from the tolls it collected on imports and exports. When, in 1523, Gustav I Vasa led the uprising of the Swedish aristocracy that ended Danish domination, he won the right to rule over a poor, sparsely populated state with few towns or developed seaports. The Vasas ruled Sweden in conjunction with the aristocracy. Although the throne was hereditary, the part played by the nobility in elevating Gustav I Vasa (1523–1560) gave the nobles a powerful voice in Swedish affairs. Through the council of state, known as the Rad, the Swedish nobility exerted a strong check on the monarch.

Sweden's aggressive foreign policy began accidentally. When in the 1550s the Teutonic Knights found themselves no longer capable of ruling in Livonia, the Baltic seaports that had been under their dominion scrambled for new alliances. Muscovy and Poland-Lithuania were the logical choices, but the town of Reval, an important outlet for Russian trade near the mouth of the Gulf of Finland, asked Sweden for protection. After some hesitation, since the occupation of territory on the southern shores of the Baltic would involve great expense, Sweden fortified Reval in 1560. A decade later, Swedish forces captured Narva, farther to the east, and consolidated Sweden's hold on the Livonian coast. By occupying the most important ports on

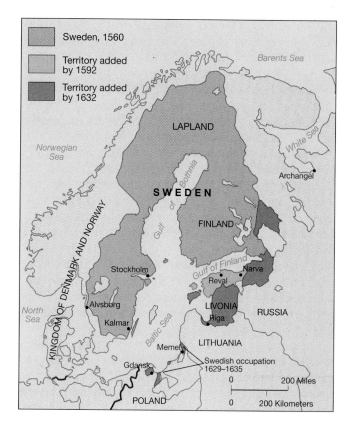

▲ The Rise of Sweden. For the only time in its history, Sweden acquired territories on the European mainland.

the Gulf of Finland, Sweden could control a sizable portion of the Muscovite trade.

Now only two obstacles prevented the Swedes from dominating trade with Muscovy: Archangel in the north and Riga in the south. In the 1580s, the Muscovites established a port at Archangel on the White Sea. With this new port they opened a trading route to the west around northern Scandinavia. Sweden benefited from the White Sea trade by claiming the northern portions of the Scandinavian peninsula that were needed to make the trade secure. In all of their dealings with Muscovy the Swedes sought further privileges at Archangel while laying plans for its conquest. Riga was a problem of a different sort. As the Swedes secured the northern Livonian ports, more of the Muscovy trade moved to the south and passed through Riga, which would have to be captured or blockaded if the Swedes were to control commerce in the eastern Baltic.

Sigismund's aggressive alliance with the Polish Jesuits had persuaded the Swedish nobility that he would undermine their Lutheran church, and Sigismund was deposed in favor of his uncle Charles IX (1604–1611). War between Sweden and Poland resulted from Sigismund's efforts to regain the Swedish crown, and the Swedes used the opportunity to blockade Riga and to occupy more Livonian territory. The Swedish navy was far superior to any force that the Poles could assemble, but on land, Polish forces were masters. The Swedish invasion force suffered a crushing defeat and had to retreat to its coastal enclaves. The Poles now had an opportunity to retake all of Livonia, but, as always, the Polish Diet was reluctant to finance Sigismund's wars. Furthermore, Sigismund had his eyes on a bigger prize. Rather than follow up its Swedish victory, Poland invaded Muscovy.

Meanwhile, the blockade of Riga and the assembly of a large Swedish fleet in the Baltic threatened Denmark. The Danes continued to claim sovereignty over Sweden and took the opportunity of the Polish-Swedish conflict to re-assert it. In 1611, under the energetic leadership of the Danish king Christian IV (1588–1648), Denmark invaded Sweden from both the east and the west. The Danes captured the towns of Kalmar and Alvsborg and threatened to take Stockholm. To end the Danish war, Sweden accepted humiliating terms in 1613, renouncing all claims to the northern coasts and recognizing Danish control of the Arctic trading route.

Paradoxically, these setbacks became the springboard for Swedish success. Fear of the Danes led both the English and the Dutch into alliances with Sweden. These countries all shared Protestant interests, and the English were heavily committed to the Muscovy trade, which was still an important part of Swedish commerce. Fear of the Poles had a similar effect on Muscovy. In 1609 the Swedes agreed to send 5,000 troops to Muscovy to help repel the Polish invasion. In return, Muscovy agreed to cede to Sweden its Baltic possessions. This was accomplished in 1617 and gave Sweden complete control of the Gulf of Finland.

In 1611, during the middle of the Danish war, Charles IX died and was succeeded by his son Gustavus Adolphus (1611–1632), one of the leading Protestant princes of his day. Gustavus's greatest skills were military, and he inherited an ample navy and an effective army. Unlike nearly every other European state, Sweden raised its forces from its own citizens. Gustavus introduced new weapons such as the light mobile gun and reshaped his army into standard-size squadrons and regiments, which were easier to administer and deploy.

The calamitous wars that Gustavus inherited from his father occupied him during the early years of his reign. He was forced to conclude the humiliating peace with the Danes in 1613 and to go to war with the Russians in 1614 to secure the Baltic coastal estates that had been promised in 1609. Gustavus's first military initiative was to resume war with Poland to force Sigismund to renounce his claim to the Swedish throne. In 1621, Gustavus landed in Livonia and in two weeks captured Riga, the capstone of Sweden's Baltic ambitions. Occupation of Riga increased Swedish control of the Muscovy trade and deprived Denmark of a significant portion of its customs duties. Gustavus now claimed Riga as a Swedish port and successfully demanded that ships

sailing from there pay tolls to Sweden rather than Denmark. By the mid-seventeenth century, Sweden ranked among the leading Protestant powers.

THE THIRTY YEARS' WAR, 1618–1648

In time, the isolated conflicts that dotted the corners of Europe were joined together. In 1609, Spain and the Dutch Republic had signed a truce that was to last until 1621. In over 40 years of nearly continuous fighting, the Dutch had carved out a state in the northern Netherlands. They used the truce to consolidate their position and increase their prosperity. Spain had reluctantly accepted Dutch independence, but Philip III (1598–1621), like his father before him, never abandoned the objective of recovering his Burgundian inheritance. By the beginning of the seventeenth century, Philip had good reasons for hope. Beginning in the 1580s, Spanish forces had reconquered the southern provinces of the Netherlands. The prosperous towns of Brussels, Antwerp, and Ghent were again under Spanish control, and they provided a springboard for another invasion.

The Twelve Years' Truce gave Spain time to prepare for the final assault. During this time, Philip III attempted to resolve all of Spain's other European conflicts so that he could then give full attention to a resumption of the Dutch war. Circumstance smiled on his efforts. In 1603, the pacific James I (1603–1625) came to the English throne. Secure in his island state, James I desired peace among all Christian princes. He quickly concluded the war with Spain that had begun with the attempted invasion of the Spanish Armada, and he entered into negotiations to marry his heir to a Spanish princess. In 1610, the bellicose Henry IV of France was felled by an assassin's knife. French plans to renew war with Spain were abandoned with the accession of the eight-year-old Louis XIII (1610–1643).

Bohemia Revolts

The Peace of Augsburg had served the German states well. The principle that the religion of the ruler was the religion of the state complicated the political life of the Holy Roman Empire, but it also pacified it. Though rulers had the right to enforce uniformity on their subjects, in practice many of the larger states tolerated more than one religion. By the beginning of the seventeenth century, Catholicism and Protestantism had achieved a rough equality within the German states, symbolized by the fact that of the seven electors who chose the Holy Roman Emperor, three were Catholic, three were Protestant, and the seventh was the emperor himself, acting as king of Bohemia. This situation was not unwelcome to the leaders of the Austrian Habsburg family who succeeded Emperor Charles V. By necessity the eastern Habsburgs were more

WAR IS HELL

No source has better captured the brutality of the Thirty Years' War than the novel Simplicissimus *(1669). In a series of loosely connected episodes, the hero (whose name means "the simplest of the simple") is snatched from his village to serve in marauding armies whose confrontations with local villagers are usually more horrifying than the episode narrated here.*

FOCUS QUESTIONS

How do the peasants respond to the troopers' actions? What does this passage suggest about the breadth of the average villager's experience?

THESE TROOPERS WERE EVEN NOW READY TO MARCH, and had the pastor fastened by a rope to lead him away. Some cried, "Shoot him down, the rogue!" Others would have money from him. But he, lifting up his hands to heaven, begged, for the sake of the Last Judgment, for forbearance and Christian compassion, but in vain; for one of them rode down and dealt him such a blow on the head that he fell flat, and commended his soul to God. Nor did the remainder of the captured peasants fare any better. But even when it seemed these troopers, in their cruel tyranny, had clean lost their wits, came such a swarm of armed peasants out of the wood, that it seemed a wasps'-nest had been stirred. And these began to yell so frightfully and so furiously to attack with sword and musket that all my hair stood on end; and never had I been at such a merrymaking before: for the peasants of the Spessart and the Vogelsberg are as little wont as are the Hessians and men of the Sauerland and the Black Forest to let themselves be crowed over on their own dunghill. So away went the troopers, and not only left behind the cattle they had captured, but threw away bag and baggage also, and so cast all their booty to the winds lest themselves should become booty for the peasants: yet some of them fell into their hands. This sport took from me well-nigh all desire to see the world, for I thought, if 'tis all like this, then is the wilderness far more pleasant.

From Hans Von Grimmelshausen, *The Adventurous Simplicissimus.*

tolerant than their Spanish kinfolk. The head of their house was elected king of Bohemia and king of Hungary, both states with large Protestant populations.

A Fatal Election.   In 1617, Mathias, the childless Holy Roman Emperor, began making plans for his cousin, Ferdinand Habsburg, to succeed him. Ferdinand was a very devout and very committed Catholic. To ensure a Catholic majority among the electors, the emperor relinquished his Bohemian title and pressed for Ferdinand's election as the new king of Bohemia. The Protestant nobles of Bohemia forced the new king to accept the strictest limitations on his political and religious powers, but once elected, Ferdinand had not the slightest intention of honoring the provisions that had been thrust on him. His opponents were equally strong willed. When Ferdinand violated Protestant religious liberties, a group of noblemen marched to the royal palace in Prague in May 1618, found two of the king's chief advisers, and hurled them out of an upper-story window.

The Defenestration of Prague, as this incident came to be known, initiated a Protestant counteroffensive throughout the Habsburg lands. Fear of Ferdinand's policies led to Protestant uprisings in Hungary as well as Bohemia. The men who seized control of the government declared Ferdinand deposed and the throne vacant. But they had no candidate to accept their crown. Whatever their religion, princes were always uneasy about the overthrow of a lawful ruler. Whoever came to be called king of Bohemia in place of Ferdinand would have to face the combined might of the Habsburgs. When Emperor Mathias died in 1619, Ferdinand succeeded to the imperial title as Ferdinand II (1619–1637), and Frederick V, one of the Protestant electors, accepted the Bohemian crown.

Frederick V, the "Winter King."   Frederick was a sincere but weak Calvinist whose credentials were much stronger than his abilities. His mother was a daughter of Prince William of Orange and his wife, Elizabeth, was a daughter of James I of England. It was widely believed that Elizabeth's resolution that she would "rather eat sauerkraut with a king than roast meat with an elector" decided the issue. No decision could have been more disastrous for the fate of Europe. Frederick ruled a geographically divided German state known as the Palatinate. One hundred miles separated the two segments of his lands, but both were strategically important. The Lower Palatinate bordered on the Catholic Spanish Netherlands and the Upper Palatinate on Catholic Bavaria.

Once Frederick accepted the Bohemian crown, he was faced with a war on three fronts. Ferdinand II had no difficulty enlisting allies to recover the Bohemian crown, since he could pay them with the spoils of Frederick's lands. Spanish troops from the Netherlands occupied the Lower Palatinate, and Bavarian troops occupied the Upper Palatinate. Frederick, by contrast, met rejection wherever he turned. Neither the Dutch nor the English would send more than token aid; both had advised him against breaking the imperial peace. The Lutheran princes of Germany would not enter into a war between Calvinists and Catholics, especially after Ferdinand II promised to protect the Bohemian Lutherans.

At the Battle of the White Mountain in 1620, Ferdinand's Catholic forces annihilated Frederick's army. Frederick and Elizabeth fled to Denmark, and Bohemia was left to face the wrath of Ferdinand, the victorious king and emperor. The retribution was horrible. Mercenaries who had fought for Ferdinand II were allowed to sack Prague for a week. Elective monarchy was abolished, and Bohemia became part of the hereditary Habsburg lands. Free peasants were enserfed and subjected to imperial law. Nobles who had supported Frederick lost their lands and their privileges. Calvinism was repressed and thoroughly

rooted out, consolidating forever the Catholic character of Bohemia. Frederick's estates were carved up, and his rights as elector were transferred to the Catholic duke of Bavaria. The Battle of the White Mountain was a turning point in the history of central Europe, for it forced all Protestant nations to arm for war.

The War Widens

For the Habsburgs, religious and dynastic interests were inseparable. Ferdinand II and Philip III of Spain fought for their beliefs and for their patrimony. Their victory gave them more than they could have expected. Ferdinand swallowed up Bohemia and strengthened his position in the empire. Philip gained possession of a vital link in his supply route between Italy and the Netherlands. Spanish expansion threatened France. The occupation of the Lower Palatinate placed a ring of Spanish armies around France from the Pyrenees to the Low Countries. The French too searched for allies. But French opinion remained divided over which was the greater evil: Spain or Protestantism.

The Danes Respond.   Frederick, now in Holland, refused to accept the judgment of battle. He lobbied for a grand alliance to repel the Spaniards from the Lower Palatinate and to restore the religious balance in the empire. Though his personal cause met with little sympathy, his political logic was impeccable, especially after Spain again declared war on the Dutch. A grand Protestant alliance—secretly supported by the French—brought together England, Holland, a number of German states, and Denmark. It was the Danes who led this potentially powerful coalition. In 1626, a large Danish army under the command of King Christian IV engaged imperial forces on German soil. But Danish forces could not match the superior numbers and the superior leadership of the Catholic mercenary forces under the command of the ruthless and brilliant Count Albrecht von Wallenstein (1583–1634). In 1629, the Danes withdrew from the empire and sued for peace.

If the Catholic victory at the White Mountain in 1620 threatened the well-being of German Protestantism, the Catholic triumph over the Danes threatened its survival. More powerful than ever, Ferdinand II was determined to turn the religious clock back to the state of affairs that had existed when the Peace of Augsburg was concluded in 1555. He demanded that all lands that had then been Catholic but had since become Protestant must now be returned to the Catholic fold. He also proclaimed that because the Peace of Augsburg made no provision for the toleration of Calvinists, they would no longer be tolerated in the empire. These policies together constituted a virtual revolution in the religious affairs of the German states, and they proved impossible to impose. Ferdinand succeeded in only one thing: he united Lutherans and Calvinists against him. Moreover, the costs of the war were heavy even for the victors. Wallenstein, who had over 130,000 men in

C H R O N O L O G Y	
THE THIRTY YEARS' WAR	
1618	Defenestration of Prague
1619	Ferdinand Habsburg elected Holy Roman Emperor; Frederick of the Palatinate accepts the crown of Bohemia
1620	Catholic victory at battle of the White Mountain
1621	End of Twelve Years' Truce; war between Spain and Netherlands
1626	Danes form Protestant alliance under Christian IV
1627	Spain declares bankruptcy
1630	Gustavus Adolphus leads Swedish forces into Germany
1631	Sack of Magdeburg; Protestant victory at Breitenfeld
1632	Protestant victory at Lützen; death of Gustavus Adolphus
1635	France declares war on Spain
1640	Portugal secedes from Spain
1643	Battle of Rocroi; French forces repel Spaniards
1648	Peace of Westphalia

arms, would no longer take orders from anyone, and Ferdinand II was forced to dismiss him from service.

Protestant Gains. In 1630, King Gustavus Adolphus of Sweden decided to enter the German conflict to protect Swedish interests. While Gustavus Adolphus struggled to construct his alliance, imperial forces continued their triumphant progress. In 1631, they besieged, captured, and put to the torch the town of Magdeburg. Perhaps three-fourths of the 40,000 inhabitants of the town were brutally slaughtered. The sack of Magdeburg marked a turning point in Protestant fortunes. It gave the international Protestant community a unifying symbol that enhanced Gustavus's military efforts. Brandenburg and Saxony joined Gustavus Adolphus, allowing him to open a second front in Bohemia. In the autumn of 1631, this combination overwhelmed the imperial armies. Gustavus won a decisive triumph at Breitenfeld, while the Saxons occupied Prague.

Gustavus Adolphus lost no time in pressing his advantage. While Ferdinand II pleaded with Wallenstein to again lead the imperial forces, the Swedes marched west to the Rhine, easily conquering the richest of the Catholic cities and retaking the Lower Palatinate. In early 1632, Protestant forces plundered Bavaria, but Wallenstein resumed his command and chose to chase the Saxons from Bohemia rather than the Swedes from Bavaria. Not until the winter of 1632 did the armies of Gustavus and Wallenstein finally meet. At the Battle of Lutzen the Swedes won the field but lost their beloved king. Wounded in the leg, the back, and the head, Gustavus Adolphus died. In less than two years he had decisively transformed the course of the war and the course of Europe's future. Protestant forces now occupied most of central and northern Germany.

The Long Quest for Peace

The final stages of the war involved the resumption of the century-old struggle between France and Spain. When the Twelve Years' Truce expired in 1621, Spain again declared war on the Dutch. Dutch naval power was considerable, and the Dutch took the war to the far reaches of the globe, attacking Portuguese settlements in Brazil and in the East and harassing Spanish shipping on the high seas. In 1628, the Dutch captured the entire Spanish treasure fleet as it sailed from the New World. Spain had declared bankruptcy in 1627, and the loss of the whole of the next year's treasure from America exacerbated an already catastrophic situation.

These reversals, combined with the continued successes of Habsburg forces in central Europe, convinced Louis XIII and his chief minister, Cardinal Richelieu, that the time for active involvement in European affairs was now at hand. Throughout the early stages of the war, France had secretly aided anti-Habsburg forces. Gustavus Adolphus's unexpected success dramatically altered French calculations.

▶ Gustavus Adolphus of Sweden, shown at the battle of Breitenfeld in 1631. The battle was the first important Protestant victory of the Thirty Years' War. Gustavus died on the battlefield at Lützen in the following year.

Now it was evident that the Habsburgs could no longer combine their might, and Spanish energies would be drained off in the Netherlands and central Europe. The time had come to take an open stand. In 1635, France declared war on Spain.

France took the offensive first, invading the Spanish Netherlands. In 1636, a Spanish army struck back, pushing to within 25 miles of Paris before it was repelled. Both sides soon began to search for a settlement, but pride prevented them from laying down their arms. Spain toppled first. Its economy in shambles and its citizens in revolt over high prices and higher taxes, it could no longer maintain its many-fronted war. The Swedes again defeated imperial forces in Germany. The Dutch destroyed much of Spain's Atlantic fleet in 1639, and the Portuguese rose up against the union of crowns that had brought them nothing but expense and the loss of crucial portions of their empire. In 1640, the Portuguese regained their independence. In 1643, Spain gambled once more on a knockout blow against the French. But at the Battle of Rocroi, exhausted French troops held out, and the Spanish invasion failed.

By now, the desire for peace was universal. Most of the main combatants had long since perished: Philip III, ever optimistic, in 1621; Frederick V, an exile to the end, in 1632; Gustavus Adolphus, killed at Lutzen in the same year; Wallenstein, murdered by order of Ferdinand II in 1634; Ferdinand himself in 1637; and Louis XIII in 1643, five days before the French triumph at Rocroi. Those who succeeded them did not have the same passions, and after so many decades the longing for peace was the strongest emotion on the Continent.

▼ The Peace of Westphalia, 1648, recognized the new boundaries of European states that included an independent Portugal and United Netherlands. It also recognized the growth of the Ottoman Empire into the Balkans.

In 1648 a series of agreements, collectively known as the Peace of Westphalia, established the outlines of the political geography of Europe for the next century. Its focus was on the Holy Roman Empire, and it reflected Protestant successes in the final two decades of war. Sweden gained further territories on the Baltic, making it master of the north German ports. France, too, gained in territory and prestige. It kept the vital towns in the Lower Palatinate through which Spanish men and matériel had moved, and though it did not agree to come to terms with Spain immediately, France's fear of encirclement was at an end. The Dutch gained statehood through official recognition by Spain and through the power they had displayed in building and maintaining an overseas empire.

Territorial boundaries were reestablished as they had existed in 1624, giving the Habsburgs control of both Bohemia and Hungary. The independence of the Swiss cantons was now officially recognized as were the rights of Calvinists to the protection of the Peace of Augsburg, which again was to govern the religious affairs of the empire. Two of the larger German states were strengthened as a counterweight to the emperor's power. Bavaria was allowed to retain the Upper Palatinate, and Brandenburg, which ceded some of its coastal territory to Sweden, gained extensive territories in the east. The emperor's political control over the German states was also weakened. German rulers were given independent authority over their states and the imperial diet, rather than the emperor, was empowered to settle disputes. Thus weakened, future emperors ruled in the Habsburg territorial lands with little ability to control, or influence, or even arbitrate German affairs. The judgment that the Holy Roman Empire was neither holy, nor Roman, nor an empire was now irrevocably true.

Conclusion

THE PEACE OF WESTPHALIA put the pieces of the map of European states back together. Protestantism and Catholicism now coexisted, and there was to be little further change in the geography of religion. The northwest of Europe—England, Holland, Scandinavia, and the north German states—was Protestant; the south was Catholic. The empire of the German peoples was now at an end, and the Austro-Hungarian empire was at a beginning. Holland and Sweden had become international powers; Spain and Denmark faded from prominence. Muscovy began a long period of isolation from the West as it attempted to restore a semblance of government to its people.

The costs of the century of nearly continuous warfare were horrific. The population of Germany fell from 15 million in 1600 to 11 million in 1650. The armies brought destruction of all kinds in their wake. Plague again raged in Europe; the town of Augsburg lost 18,000 inhabitants in the early 1630s. Famine, too, returned to a continent that 50 years earlier had been self-sufficient in grain. The war played havoc with all of the economies that it touched. Inflation, devaluation of coinage, and huge public and private debts were all directly attributable to the years of fighting. Furthermore, the toll taken on the spirit of generations that never knew peace is incalculable.

QUESTIONS FOR REVIEW

1. How was Henry IV able to bring peace to France after decades of civil war?
2. What were the political and religious connections between the Armada launched against England by Philip II and the revolt of the Netherlands?
3. How did Sweden rise to become one of Europe's great powers in the first half of the seventeenth century?
4. How did religion help spark and spread the Thirty Years' War?
5. What were the effects of the Peace of Westphalia on political arrangements in the heart of Europe?

DISCOVERING WESTERN CIVILIZATION ONLINE

You can obtain more information about Europe at war at the websites listed below.
See also the companion website that accompanies this text:
www.ablongman.com/kishlansky, which includes an online study guide and
additional resources.

The Crises of the Western States

www.fordham.edu/halsall/mod/modsbook1.html#Conflict
Links to documents on the French wars of religion, the invasion of the Spanish Armada, and the Thirty Years' War.

www.ibiblio.org/wm/paint/tl/north-ren/
Links to pictures and portraits from the late sixteenth and early seventeenth centuries.

www.ibiblio.org/wm/paint/auth/bruegel/death.jpg
A web page depicting Peter Brueghel's *Triumph of Death*, one of the most evocative paintings of the destruction wrought by warfare in early modern Europe.

The Thirty Years' War, 1618–1648

www.yale.edu/lawweb/avalon/westphal.htm
The full text of the Treaty of Westphalia that ended the Thirty Years' War.

SUGGESTIONS FOR FURTHER READING

General Reading

M. S. Anderson, *The Origins of the Modern European State System, 1494–1618* (London: Longman, 1998). A survey of developments stressing war and diplomacy across all of Europe.

Richard Bonney, *The European Dynastic States, 1494–1660* (Oxford: Oxford University Press, 1991). The most up-to-date introduction to the period by a noted historian of France.

Geoffrey Parker, *Europe in Crisis, 1598–1648* (Oxford: Blackwells, 2001). Compelling study of European states in the early seventeenth century.

The Crises of the Western States

Susan Brigden, *New Worlds, Lost Worlds: The Rule of the Tudors, 1485–1603* (New York: Viking, 2001). The latest volume in the new Penguin History of Britain series.

Mack Holt, *The French Wars of Religion, 1562–1629* (Cambridge: Cambridge University Press, 1995). The wars of religion seen in a long perspective.

Jonathan Israel, *The Dutch Republic and the Hispanic World, 1606–1661* (Oxford: Clarendon, 1986). A panoramic survey of the stormy relations between empire and republic.

John Lynch, *Spain, 1516–1598: From Nation State to World Empire* (Cambridge, Mass.: Blackwell, 1994). The most up-to-date survey.

Geoffrey Parker, *Philip II* (Boston: Little, Brown, 1978). The best introduction.

Michael Roberts, *Gustavus Adolphus and the Rise of Sweden* (London: English Universities Press, 1973). A highly readable account of Sweden's rise to power.

Penry Williams, *The Later Tudors* (Oxford: Oxford University Press, 1995). A recent survey in the Oxford history of England.

The Struggles in Eastern Europe

David Kirby, *Northern Europe in the Early Modern Period: The Baltic World, 1492–1772* (London: Longman, 1990). The best single volume on Baltic politics.

Maureen Perrie, *Pretenders and Popular Monarchisms in Early Modern Russia* (Cambridge: Cambridge University Press, 1995). Recent scholarship on the Time of Troubles, focusing on the royal impostors.

Michael Roberts, *The Swedish Imperial Experience* (Cambridge: Cambridge University Press, 1979). Reflections on Swedish history by the preeminent historian of early modern Sweden.

The Thirty Years' War

Ronald G. Asch, *The Thirty Years' War: The Holy Roman Empire and Europe, 1618–1648* (New York: St. Martin's Press, 1997). A narrative survey of this complicated conflict.

J. H. Elliott, *Richelieu and Olivares* (Cambridge: Cambridge University Press, 1984). A comparison of statesmen and statesmanship in the early seventeenth century.

Geoffrey Parker, ed., *The Thirty Years' War*, 2d ed. (London: Routledge, 1997). A revised edition of the standard survey of the conflict.

CHAPTER 15

THE EXPERIENCES OF LIFE IN EARLY MODERN EUROPE, 1500–1650

- ■ THE VISUAL RECORD: Haymaking
- ■ ECONOMIC LIFE
- ■ SOCIAL LIFE
- ■ PRIVATE AND COMMUNITY LIFE

THE VISUAL RECORD

HAYMAKING

I T IS SUMMER IN THE LOW COUNTRIES. The trees are full, the meadows are green, and bushes hang heavy with fruit. The day has dawned brightly for haymaking. Yesterday, the long meadow was mowed. Today, the hay will be gathered, and the first fruits and vegetables of the season will be harvested. From throughout the village, families come together in labor. Twice each summer, the grass is cut, dried, and stacked. Some of it will be left in the fields for the animals until autumn; some will be carried into large lofts and stored for the winter.

This scene of communal farming was repeated with little variation throughout Europe in the sixteenth century. The village we are viewing is fairly prosperous. We can see at least three horses (still a luxury for farmers) and a large wheeled cart. The houses of the village also suggest comfort. The one at the far right is typical. It contains one floor for living and a loft for storage. The chimney separates a kitchen in the back from the long hall where the family works, sleeps, and entertains itself. The bed—it is not uncommon for there to be only one for the whole family—is probably located near the fireplace. It will be restuffed with straw after the harvest. The spinning wheel probably stands near the single window, which is covered by oiled animal skin, since glass is still much too expensive for use in rural housing. The long end of the hall, farthest from heat and light, will be home to the family's animals once winter sets in. But now, in summer, it is a luxurious space where children can play or parents can claim a little privacy.

The church, easily distinguished by its steeple and arched doorway, is made of brick. The steeple has 16 windows, probably all set with expensive glass and some even with stained glass. The church would have been built over several generations at considerable cost to the villagers. Even the most prosperous houses in the far meadow are all made of timber and thatch, and only the village well, in the middle of the picture, and the chimneys of the houses show any other sign of brick.

In the center of the scene are a large number of laborers. Four men with pitchforks load the cart while two women sweep the hay that falls back into new piles. Throughout the field, men and women, distinguished only by their clothing, rake hay into large stacks for successive loadings of the cart. At least 25 individuals work at these tasks. Men perform the heaviest work of loading the haycart and hammering the scythes; men and women share all the other

298

work. Although no children appear in the scene, some are undoubtedly at work picking berries and beans.

The scenes of physical labor remind us that the life of ordinary people in the sixteenth century was neither romantic nor despondent, neither quaint nor primitive. It had its own joys and sorrows, its own triumphs and failures. Inevitably, we compare it to our experiences and contrast it to our comforts. By our standards, a sixteenth-century prince endured greater material hardships than a twentieth-century slum resident. There was no running water, no central heating, no lavatories, no electricity. There was no relief for toothache, headache, or numbing pain. Travel was dangerous and exhausting. There was no protection from the open air, and many nights were spent on the bare ground. Waiting for winds to sail was more tedious and uncertain than waiting for planes to fly. Entertainment was sparse and the court jester was no match for stereo and video. But though we cannot help but be struck by these differences, we must not judge life in sixteenth-century Europe by our own standard of living. We must exercise our historical imagination if we are to appreciate the conditions of early modern European society.

LOOKING AHEAD

In this chapter, we will examine the social and economic conditions of early modern European society, dominated as it was by extreme change, and often, hardship. We will see how population growth put pressure on the European economy and how the rich became richer as food prices rose. We will also see how European governments were overwhelmed by changes they could only dimly perceive.

ECONOMIC LIFE

There was no typical sixteenth-century European. Language, custom, geography, and material conditions separated people in one place from those in another. Contrasts between social groups were more striking still. A Muscovite boyar had more in common with an English nobleman than either had with his own country's peasants. A Spanish goldsmith and a German brass maker lived remarkably similar lives when compared to the life of a shepherd anywhere in Europe. No matter how carefully historians attempt to distinguish between country and town life, between social or occupational groups, or between men and women, they are still smoothing out edges that are very rough, turning individuals into aggregates, and sacrificing the particular for the general.

One distinctive sixteenth-century experience that all groups shared, though they could only dimly perceive it, was change. In general, one generation improved on the situation of the last. Agriculture increased; more land was cleared, more crops were grown, and better tools were crafted. On the negative side, irreplaceable resources were lost as more trees were felled, more soil was eroded, and more fresh water was polluted. These changes and dynamic transformations in economic and social conditions affected everyday life in the sixteenth century.

Rural Life

In the sixteenth century, as much as 90 percent of the European population lived on farms or in small towns in which farming was the principal occupation. Villages were small and relatively isolated. They might range in size from a hundred families, as was common in France and Spain, to fewer than 20 families, which was the average size of Hungarian villages. These villages, large or small, prosperous or poor, were the bedrock of the sixteenth-century state. Surplus peasant population fed the towns' insatiable need for laborers and the crowns' for soldiers. The manor, the parish, and the rural administrative district were the institutional infrastructures of Europe. Each organized the peasantry for its own purposes. Manorial rents supported the lifestyle of the nobility; parish tithes supported the works of the Church; and local taxes supported the power of the state. Rents, tithes, and taxes easily absorbed more than half of the wealth produced by the land.

To survive on what remained, the village community had to be self-sufficient. In good times there was enough to eat and some to save for the future. Hard times meant hunger and starvation. One in every three harvests was bad; one in every five was disastrous. Between one-fifth and one-half of the grain harvested had to be saved as seed for the next planting season. When hunger was worst, people faced the agonizing choice of eating or saving their "seed corn."

The Sixteenth-Century Household. Hunger and cold were the constant companions of the average European. In Scandinavia and Muscovy, winter posed as great a threat to survival as starvation did. Everywhere in Europe, homes were inadequate shelter against the cold and damp. Most were built of wood and roofed in thatch. Inside walls were patched with dried mud, and windows were few and narrow. Piled leaves or straw covered the ground and acted as insulation. The typical house was one long room with a stone hearth at the end. The hearth provided both heat and light and belched forth soot and smoke through a brick chimney.

People had relatively few household possessions. The essential piece of furniture was the wooden chest, which was used for storage. A typical family could keep all of its belongings in the chest, which could then be buried or carried away in time of danger. The chest had other uses as well. Its flat top served as a table or bench or a raised surface on which food could be placed. Tables and stools were becoming more common during the sixteenth century, though chairs were still a great luxury. In areas in which spinning, weaving, or other domestic skills were an important part of the family's economy, a long bench was propped against the wall, usually beneath a window. Bedsteads were also becoming more common as the century wore on. They raised the straw mattresses off the ground, keeping them warmer and drier. All other family possessions related to food production. Iron spits and pots, or at least metal rings and clamps for wooden ones, were treasured goods that were passed from generation to generation. Most other implements were wooden. Long-handled spoons, boards known as trenchers used for cutting and eating, and one large cup and bowl were the basic stock of the kitchen. The family ate from the long trencher and passed the bowl and cup. Knives were essential farm tools that doubled for kitchen and mealtime duty, but forks were still a curiosity.

The scale of life was small, and its pace was controlled by nature: up at dawn, asleep at dusk, long working hours in summer, short ones in winter. For most people the world was bounded by the distance that could be traveled on foot. Those who stayed all their lives in their rural villages may never have seen more than a hundred other people at once. Their wisdom, handed down through generations, was of the practical experience that was necessary to survive the struggle with nature.

Reliance on Agriculture. Peasant life centered on agriculture. Technology and technique varied little across the Continent, but there were significant differences depending on climate and soil. Across the great plain, the breadbasket that stretched from the Low Countries to Poland-Lithuania, the most common form of crop growing was still the three-field rotation system. In this method, winter crops such as wheat or rye were planted in one field; spring crops such as barley, peas, or beans were planted in another; and the third field was left fallow. More than 80 percent of what was grown on the farm was consumed on the farm. In most parts of Europe, wheat was a luxury crop, sold at market rather than eaten at home. Wheat bread was prized for its taste, texture, and white color. Rye and barley were the staples for peasants. These grains were cheaper to grow, had higher yields, and could be brewed as well as baked. Most was baked into the coarse black bread that was the mainstay of the peasant diet. Two to three pounds a day for an adult male was an average allotment when grain was readily available. Beer and gruels of grain and skimmed milk or water flavored with fruit juice supplemented peasant fare. In one form or another, grain provided over 75 percent of the calories in a typical diet.

The warm climate and dry weather of Mediterranean Europe favored a two-crop rotation system. With less water and stronger sunlight, half the land had to be left fallow each year to restore its nutrients. Here, fruit, especially grapes and olives, was an essential supplement to diet. With smaller cereal crops, wine replaced beer as a beverage. The fermentation of grapes and grain into wine and beer also provided convenient ways of storing foodstuffs. Wine and olive oil were also luxury products and were most commonly exchanged for meat, which was less plentiful on southern European farms.

Animal husbandry was the main occupation in the third agricultural area of Europe, the mountainous and hilly regions. Sheep, the most common animal, provided the raw material for almost all clothing. Their skins were used for parchment and as window coverings, and they were a ready source of inexpensive meat. In western Europe, their wool was the main export of both England and Spain. Sheep could graze on land that was unsuitable for grain growing, and they could be sheared twice a year to provide a surplus of wool. Pigs were prevalent in woodland settlements. They foraged for food and were kept, like poultry, for slaughter. Oxen were essential as draft animals. In the dairying areas of Europe, cattle produced milk, cheese, and butter; in Hungary and Bohemia, the great breeding center of the Continent, they were raised for export; almost everywhere else, they were used as beasts of burden.

◁ Grain Supply and Trade in Sixteenth-Century Europe. There were two distinct trading routes in northern Europe centering on the Baltic Sea and in southern Europe centering on the Mediterranean Sea.

Most agricultural land was owned not by those who worked it, but by lords who let it out in various ways. The land was still divided into manors, and the manor lord, or *seigneur*, was still responsible for maintaining order, administering justice, and arbitrating disputes. Lords were not necessarily individual members of the nobility; in fact, the lords were more commonly the Church or the state. In western Europe, peasants generally owned between one-third and one-half of the land they worked; eastern European peasants owned little if any land. But by the sixteenth century, almost all peasants enjoyed security of tenure on the land they worked. In return for various forms of rents, they used the land as they saw fit and could hand it down to their children. Rents were only occasionally paid in coin, though money rents became more common as the century progressed. More frequently, the lord received a fixed proportion of the land's yield or received labor from the peasant. Labor service was being replaced by monetary payments in northern and western Europe, but it continued in the east. German and Hungarian peasants normally owed two or three days' labor on the lord's estate each week, while Polish peasants might owe as much as four days. Labor service tied the peasants to the land they worked. Eastern European peasants were less mobile than peasants in the west, and as a result, towns were fewer and smaller in the east.

Though the land in each village was set out in large fields so that crops could be rotated, families owned their own pieces within the field, usually in scattered strips. There were also large common fields used as pasture, as well as common woodlands where animals foraged, fuel was gathered, and game was hunted. Villagers disputed frequently over rights to sticks and branches of trees and over the number of sheep or cows that could be grazed in the meadows, especially when resources were scarce.

Farm work was ceaseless toil. Six or seven times a year, farmers tilled the fields to spread animal manure below the surface of the soil. Although most villages possessed metal plows, the team of draft animals was the single essential component for farming. The births of foals and calves were more celebrated events than the births of children; the death of an ox or a horse was a catastrophe. Calamities lurked everywhere, from rain and drought to locusts and crows. Most farms could support only one family at subsistence level, and excess sons and daughters had to fend for themselves, either through marriage in the village or by migration to a town.

Town Life

In the country, people worked to the natural rhythm of the day and season. In the town, the bell tolled every hour. In the summer, the laborers gathered at the town gates at four in the morning, in the winter at seven. The bell signaled the time for morning and afternoon meals as well as the hour to lay down tools and return home. Wages were paid for hours worked—seven in winter, as many as sixteen in midsummer.

The Heart of Commerce. In all towns, an official guild structure organized and regulated labor. Rules laid down the requirements for training, the standards for quality, and the conditions for exchange. Only those who were officially sanctioned could work in trades, and each trade could perform only specified tasks.

While the life of the peasant community turned on self-sufficiency, that of the town turned on interdependence. The town was one large marketplace in which the circulation of goods dictated the residents' survival. Men and women in towns worked as hard as people on farms, but town dwellers generally received a more varied and more comfortable life in return. This is not to suggest that hunger and hardship were unknown in towns. Urban poverty was endemic and grew worse as the century wore on. In most towns, as much as one quarter of the entire population might be destitute, living on casual day labor, charity, or crime. But the institutional network of support for the poor and homeless was stronger. The urban poor fell victim more often to disease than to starvation.

Towns were distinguished by the variety of occupations that existed within them. The preparation and exchange of food dominated small market towns. Peasants would bring in their finest produce for sale and exchange it for vital manufactured goods such as iron spits or pots for cooking. In smaller towns, there was as much barter as sale; in larger places, money was exchanged for commodities. Women dominated the food trades in most market towns, trading, buying, and selling in the shop fronts that occupied the bottom story of their houses. In these small towns, men divided their time between traditional agricultural pursuits—there were always garden plots and even substantial fields attached to towns—and manufacturing. Almost every town made and distributed to the surrounding area some special product that drew to the town the wealth of the countryside.

The Workforce. In larger towns, the specialization of labor was more intense, and wage earning was more essential. Large traders dominated the major occupations such as baking, brewing, and cloth manufacture, leaving distribution in the hands of the family economy, where there might still be a significant element of bartering. Piecework handicrafts became the staple for less prosperous town families, who prepared raw materials for the large manufacturers or finished products before their sale. Metalworking or glassworking normally took place in one quarter of the town, brewing or baking in another. Each craft required long years of technical training, which was handed down from parents to children.

In large towns there were also specialized trades that women performed. There were 55 midwives in Nuremberg in the middle of the sixteenth century, and a board of women chosen from among the leading families of the town supervised their work. Nursing the sick also seems to have been an exclusively female occupation. So, too, was prostitution, which was officially sanctioned in most large towns in the early sixteenth century. There were official brothels, which were subject to taxation and government control. Public bathhouses served as unofficial brothels for the upper ranks of urban society. They, too, were regulated, especially after the first great epidemic of venereal disease in the early sixteenth century.

Most town dwellers, however, lived by unskilled labor. The most lucrative occupations were strictly controlled, so people who flocked to towns in search of employment usually hired themselves out as day laborers, hauling and lifting goods onto carts or boats or delivering water and food. After the first decades of the century, the supply of laborers exceeded the demand, and town authorities were constantly attempting to expel the throngs of casual workers. The most fortunate of such workers might succeed in becoming servants.

Domestic service was a critical source of household labor. Even families who were on the margins of subsistence employed servants to undertake innumerable household tasks, which allowed parents to pursue their primary occupations. Domestics were not apprentices, though they might aspire to become apprentices to the trade followed in the family with whom they lived. If they had kinship bonds in the town, apprenticeship was a likely outcome. But more commonly, domestics remained household servants, frequently changing employers in hope of more comfortable housing and better food.

Just as towns grew by the influx of surplus rural population, they sustained themselves by the import of surplus agricultural production. Most towns owned vast tracts of land, which they leased to peasants or farmed by hired labor. The town of Nuremberg controlled 25 square miles of forest and farmlands; the region around Toledo was inhabited by thousands of peasants who paid taxes and rents to city landlords. All towns had municipal storehouses of grain to preserve their inhabitants from famine during harvest failures. The diet of even a casual laborer would have been envied by an average peasant. Male grape pickers in Stuttgart received meat, soup, vegetables, wine, and beer; females got soup, vegetables, milk, and bread. In addition they received their wages. It is hardly surprising that towns were enclosed by thick walls and defended by armed guards.

Economic Change

Over the course of the sixteenth century, the European population increased by about one-third, much of the growth taking place in the first 50 years. Rough estimates suggest the rise to have been from about 80 million to 105 million. Patterns of growth varied by region. The population of the eastern part of Europe seems to have increased more steadily across the century, whereas in western Europe there was a population explosion in the early decades. The population of France may have doubled between 1450 and 1550, from 10 million to 20 million, before the wars of religion reversed the trend at the end of the century. The population of England nearly doubled between 1500 and 1600 from more than 2 million to more than 4 million. Europe had finally recovered from the devastation of the Black Death, and by 1600 its population was greater than it had ever been. Demographic growth was even more dramatic in the cities. In 1500, only four cities had populations greater than 100,000; in 1600 there were eight. Fifteen large cities more than doubled their populations. London experienced a phenomenal 400 percent increase.

The rise in population dramatically affected the lives of ordinary Europeans. In the early part of the century, the first phase of growth brought prosperity. Because there was uncultivated land that could be plowed and enough commons and woodlands to be shared, population increase was a welcome development. Even when rural communities began to reach their natural limits, opportunity still existed in the burgeoning towns and cities. At first the cycle was beneficial. Surplus on the farms led to economic growth in the towns. Growth in the towns meant more opportunities for people on the farms.

The first waves of migrants to the towns found opportunity everywhere. Apprenticeships were easy to find, and the shortage of casual labor kept wages at a decent rate. For a short while, rural families could send their younger sons and daughters to the towns and could purchase a few luxury goods for themselves.

This window of opportunity could not remain open forever. With more mouths to feed, more crops had to be planted, and new fields were carved from less fertile areas. In some villages, land was taken from the woodlands or scrublands that were used for animal forage and domestic fuel. In Spain, the land that was reclaimed came at the expense of land used for sheep grazing. This damaged both the domestic and foreign wool trade. It also reduced the amount of fertilizer that was available for enriching the soil. In England and the Low Countries, large drainage projects were undertaken to reclaim land for crops. In the east, so-called forest colonies sprang up, clearing space in the midst of woodlands for new farms.

By midcentury the window of opportunity shut more firmly on people who were attempting to enter the urban economy. Town governments tightened apprenticeship requirements. Guilds raised fees for new entrants and designated only a small number of places where their goods could be purchased. Most apprenticeships were limited to patrimony: one son for each full member. Such restrictions meant that newly arrived immigrants could enter only the less profitable small crafts.

As workers continued to flood into the towns, real wages began to fall, not only among the unskilled but throughout the workforce. A black market in labor developed to take

▲ Population Density in Europe, ca. 1600. Most people lived in the western part of the continent on its coastal areas.

advantage of the surplus population. In terms of purchasing power, the wages of a craftsman in the building trade in England fell by half during the sixteenth century. Peasants in the French region of Languedoc who hired out for farm labor lost 56 percent of their purchasing power during the century. Grape pickers, among the least skilled agricultural laborers, endured declines up to 300 to 400 percent.

The fall in real wages took place against a backdrop of inflation that has come to be called the Price Revolution. Over the course of the century, cereal prices increased between fivefold and sixfold, and prices of manufactured goods increased between twofold and threefold. Most of the rapid increase came in the second half of the century, a result of both population growth and the import of precious metals from the New World. Sixteenth century governments understood little about the relationship between money supply and prices. Gold and silver from America

flooded the international economy, raising commodity prices. As prices rose, so did the deficits of the state, which was the largest purchaser of both agricultural and manufactured goods. With huge deficits, states began to devalue their coins in the mistaken belief that this would lower their debt. But debased coinage resulted in still higher prices, and higher prices resulted in greater debt. The Price Revolution was felt throughout the Continent and played havoc with government finances, international trade, and the lives of ordinary people.

A 500 percent inflation in agricultural products over a century is not much by modern standards. Compounded, the rate averages less than 2 percent a year. But the Price Revolution did not take place in a modern society or within a modern market economy. In the sixteenth century, this level of rising prices disrupted everything. In the Spanish town of Seville, almost all buildings were rented on 99-year leases to the families who lived and worked in them. This was a fairly common practice throughout Europe. It meant that a landlord who rented a butcher shop and living quarters in 1501 could not raise the rent until 1600! Similarly, lords frequently held the right to purchase agricultural produce at specified prices. That system, similar to today's commodity market, helped both lords and peasants plan ahead, but it assumed steady prices.

Therefore, an enduring increase of prices created profound social dislocation and threw into turmoil all groups and sections of the European economy. Some people became destitute; others became rich beyond their dreams. The towns were particularly hard hit, for they exchanged manufactured goods for food and so suffered when grain prices rose faster than those of other commodities. Landholders who derived their income from rents were squeezed; those who received payment in kind reaped a windfall of more valuable agricultural goods. As long as ordinary peasants consumed what they raised, the nominal value of commodities did not matter. But if some part of their subsistence was obtained by labor, they were in grave peril.

There was now an enormous incentive to produce a surplus for market and to begin to specialize in particular grains that were in high demand. Every small scrap of land that individual peasant families could bring under cultivation would now yield foodstuffs that could be exchanged for manufactured goods that had been unimaginable luxuries a generation earlier. The tendency for all peasants to hold roughly equivalent amounts of land abruptly ceased. The fortunate could now become prosperous by selling their surplus. The unfortunate found ready purchasers for their strips and common rights.

The beneficial cycle now turned vicious. Those who had sold out and left the land looking for prosperity in the towns were forced to return to the land as agrarian laborers. In western Europe, they became the landless poor, seasonal migrants without the safety net of rooted communal life. In eastern Europe, labor service enriched the landed nobility, who were able to sell vast stores of grain in the export market. Poland-Lithuania became a major supplier of cereals to northern Europe. But agricultural surplus from the east could not make up for the great shortfall in the west. By the end of the sixteenth century, the western European states faced a crisis of subsistence.

SOCIAL LIFE

The basic assumption of sixteenth century European society was inequality. The group, rather than the individual, was the predominant unit in society. The first level of the social order was the family and the household, then came the village or town community, and finally the gradations of ranks and orders of society at large. Each group had its own place in the social order, and each performed its own essential function. Society was the sum of its parts.

This traditional social organization was severely tested over the course of the sixteenth century. Economic change reshaped ideas of mobility and drew sharper distinctions between rural and urban life. The growth of towns challenged beliefs about the primacy of agricultural production and the subordinate nature of trade and commerce. The rise to new wealth and prominence of some social groups challenged traditional elites' hold on power and prestige. The transformation of landholding patterns in the villages challenged the stability of rural communities. The rising numbers of poor people challenged the institutions of charitable relief and posed the threat of crime and disorder. Eventually, these developments led to bloody confrontations between social groups.

Social Constructs

Hierarchy was the dominant principle of social organization in the sixteenth century. The hierarchy of masters, journeymen, and apprentices dominated trades; trades themselves existed in a hierarchy. Civic government was a hierarchy of officials led by the elite of councillors and mayors. Among the peasants was the hierarchy of freeholder, laborer, and leaseholder, as well as the more flexible social hierarchy among the ancient and prosperous families and the newer and struggling ones. The family itself was hierarchically organized, with the wife subordinate to her husband, the children to their parents, and the apprentices and servants to their master and mistress. Hierarchy was a principle of orderliness that helped to govern social relations. It is tempting to approach hierarchy through wealth, but the ranks of the nobility cannot be explained by gradations of wealth among nobles, and there were many rich town dwellers who were not members of the governing elite.

Status rather than wealth determined the social hierarchy of the sixteenth century. It conferred privileges and exacted responsibilities according to rank. Status was everywhere apparent. It was confirmed in social conventions such as bowing and hat doffing. In towns and cities, the clothing people were allowed to wear, even the foods they were allowed to eat, reflected status. Status was signified by titles, not just in the ranks of the nobility, but even in ordinary communities of masters and mistresses, goodmen and goodwives, squires and ladies, the English equivalents of a wide variety of European titles. The acceptance of status was an everyday, unreflective act. Inequality was an unquestioned fact of life.

Images that people used to describe both the natural world and their social world reinforced the functional nature of hierarchy. The most elaborate image was that of the Great Chain of Being, a description of the universe in which everything had a place, from God at the top to inanimate objects such as rocks and stones at the bottom. Complex accounts of the Chain listed the nine orders of angels, the multiple ranks of humans, even the degrees of animals and plants, from which lions emerged as kings of the jungle. For ordinary people the Great Chain of Being expressed the belief that all life was interconnected, that every link was a part of a divinely ordered universe and was as necessary as every other.

The second metaphor that was used to describe society stressed this notion of interdependency even more strongly. This was the image of the Body Politic, in which the head ruled, the arms protected, the stomach nourished, and the feet labored. In the state, the king was the head, the church was the soul, the nobles were the arms, the artisans were the hands, and the peasants were the feet. Like the Chain of Being, the Body Politic was a profoundly conservative concept of social organization that precluded the idea of social mobility.

Social Structure

The Great Chain of Being and the Body Politic were static concepts of social organization. But in the sixteenth century, European society was in a state of dynamic change. Fundamentally, all European societies were divided between nobles and commoners, though relationships between the two orders differed from place to place.

The Nobles. Nobility was a legal status that conferred certain privileges on its holders and passed by inheritance from one generation to the next. Each rank had its own privileges, and each was clearly demarcated from the next. The coat of arms was a universally recognized symbol of rank and family connection. Though various systems of title were in use across the Continent, the hierarchy of prince, duke, earl, count, and baron was roughly standard.

Because rulers conferred these titles on individuals, elevating some to higher ranks and others from commoner to noble, the nobility was a political order as well as a social one. Political privileges were among the nobility's most important attributes. In many countries, the highest offices of the state and the military were reserved for members of the nobility. Noblemen were also granted rights of political participation in the deliberative bodies of the state. In England, the peerage was defined as all those who were summoned to the House of Lords. In most parts of central Europe, the nobility alone composed the diets that advised the monarch.

Finally, members of the nobility held economic privileges, a result both of their rank and of their role as lords on the lands they owned. In almost every state, the nobility was exempt from most kinds of taxation. The interests of the nobles conflicted directly with those of the ruler, and the larger the number of tax exemptions for the nobility, the stronger was its power in relation to the monarch. Tax exemptions of the nobility were most extensive in eastern and central Europe. There, the crowns were elective rather than hereditary, allowing the nobles to bargain their support. As

Polish agriculture developed into an export industry, exemption from internal tolls and customs gave the nobility a competitive advantage over merchants in the marketing of goods. The nobility in western Europe enjoyed fewer immunities but not necessarily less valuable ones.

Privileges implied obligations. Initially, the nobility was the warrior caste of the state, and its primary obligations were to raise, equip, and lead troops into battle. Much of the great wealth that nobles possessed was at the service of the ruler during times of war, and war was a perpetual activity. By the sixteenth century, the military needs of the state had far surpassed the military power of its nobility. Warfare had become a national enterprise that required central coordination. Nobles became administrators as much as warriors, though it is fair to say that many did both. The French nobility came to be divided into the nobility of the sword and the nobility of the robe—that is, warriors and officeholders.

Nobles also had the obligation of governing at both the national and the local level. At the discretion of the ruler, they could be called to engage in any necessary occupation, no matter how disruptive to their economic or family affairs. They administered their estates and settled the disputes of their tenants. In times of want, they were expected to provide for the needy. The obligation of good lordship was implicitly understood, if not always explicitly carried out, between lord and peasant.

Town Elite and Gentry. The principal distinction in sixteenth-century society was between lord and commoners, but it was not the only one. A new social group was emerging in the towns—a group that had neither the legal nor the social privileges of nobility but performed many of the same functions. The towns remained a separate unit of social organization in most states, enjoying many of the same political and economic privileges as the nobility. Representatives of the towns met with the nobles and the king and were the most important part of the national deliberative assemblies, like the English Parliament or the French estates. Towns were granted legal rights to govern their own citizens, to engage in trade, and to defend themselves by raising and storing arms. Though they paid a large share of most taxes, towns also received large tax concessions.

As individuals, members of the town elite held no special status in society at large. Some were among the richest people in the state, but they had to devise their own systems of honor and prestige. In Venice the *Book of Gold* distinguished the local elite from the ranks of ordinary citizens. In France and Spain, some of the highest officers of leading towns were granted noble status. In England, wealthy guild members could become knights, a rank just below noble status. German burghers, as prosperous townsmen were called, remained caught between noble and common, despised from above because they worked with their hands, envied from below for their wealth and

Georges de La Tour, *The Fortune Teller.* In the painting, which serves as a warning to the naive about the wicked ways of the world, a fashionably dressed young innocent is drawn into the snare of the wily fortune teller.

comfort. In Wurtenberg, the nobility withdrew from the towns and sought the status of free knights.

In rural society the transformation of agricultural holdings in many places also created a group that fit uncomfortably between lords and commoners. The accumulation of larger and larger estates, by purchase from the nobility, the state, or the church, made lords—in the sense of landowners with tenants—of many who were not lords in rank. They received rents and dues from their tenants, administered their estates, and preserved the so-called moral economy that sustained the peasants during hard times. In England, this group came to be known as the gentry, and there were parallel groups in Spain, France, and the Holy Roman Empire. The gentry aspired to the privileges of the nobility. In England, members of the gentry had the right to have a coat of arms and could be knighted. But knighthoods were not hereditary and did not confer membership in the House of Lords. In Spain, the caballeros and hidalgos gained noble privileges but were still of lower status than the grandees.

Social stratification also marked rural communities. In many German villages, a principal distinction was made between those who held land in the ancient part of the settlement—the Esch—and those who held land in those areas into which the village had expanded. The Esch was normally the best land. But interestingly, the holders of the Esch were tied to the lord of the estate, while holders of the less desirable lands were free peasants. Here, freedom

to move from place to place was less valued than was the right to live in the heart of the village.

Just the opposite set of values prevailed in English villages, where freeholders were in the most enviable position. They led the movements to break up the common fields for planting and were able to initiate legal actions against their lord. Whenever village land was converted to freehold, unfree tenants would go into debt to buy it. Increasingly, French peasants came to own the land they farmed. They protested against the very title of villein, claiming that its older association with serfdom discouraged others from trading with those so labeled. The distinction between free and unfree went even further in Muscovy, where thousands of starving laborers sold themselves into slavery.

In towns, the order of rank below the elite pertained as much to the kind of work that one performed as it did to the level at which the work was undertaken. The critical division in town life was between those who had the freedom of the city—citizens—and those who did not. Citizenship was restricted to membership in certain occupations and was closely regulated. It could be purchased, but most citizenship was earned by becoming a master in one of the guilds. Only males could be citizens. In Germany, the feminine equivalent for the word that denoted a male citizen meant prostitute! But women who were married to citizens enjoyed their husbands' privileges, and widows of citizens could pass the privileges to their new husbands when they remarried.

Social Change

In the sixteenth century, social commentators believed that change was transforming the world in which they lived. In 1600, a Spanish observer blamed the rise of the rich commoners for the ills of the world. An Englishman commenting on the rise of the gentry could give no better definition of its status than to say that a gentleman was one who lived like a gentleman. In France, the challenge that the new nobility of the robe posed to the old nobility of the sword poisoned relations between these two segments of the ruling elite. The military service class in Muscovy, who were of more use to the Muscovite princes than the traditional landed nobility, posed an even greater threat to the privileges of the boyars.

The New Rich. Pressures on the ruling elites of European society came from above as well as below. The expansion of the state and the power of the prince frequently came as a result of direct conflict with the nobility. Only in east central Europe did the consolidation of the state actually enhance the privileges of the traditional noble orders, and these were areas in which towns were small and urban elites were weak.

Many factors promoted social change during the course of the sixteenth century. First, population increase necessitated an expansion of the ruling orders. With more people to govern, there had to be more governors who could perform the military, political, and social functions of the state. Second, opportunities to accumulate wealth expanded dramatically with the Price Revolution. Traditionally, wealth was calculated in land and tenants rather than in the possession of liquid assets such as gold and silver. But with the increase in commodity prices, surplus producers could rapidly improve their economic position. Moreover, state service became a source of unlimited riches. The profits to be made from tax collecting, officeholding, or the law could easily surpass those to be made from landholding. And the newly rich clamored for privileges.

The New Poor. Social change was equally apparent at the bottom of the social scale, but here it could not be so easily absorbed. The continuous growth of population created a group of landless poor who squatted in villages and clogged the streets of towns and cities. Rough estimates suggest that as many as one-quarter of all Europeans were destitute. This was a staggering figure in great cities, amounting to tens of thousands in London or Paris.

Traditionally, local communities cared for their poor. Widows, orphans, and the handicapped, who would normally constitute over half of the poor in a village or town, were viewed as the "deserving poor," worthy of the care of the community through the Church or private almsgiving. Catholic communities such as Venice created a system of private charity that paralleled the institutions of the Church. Though Protestant communities took charity out of the control of the Church, they were no less concerned about the plight of the deserving poor. In England a special tax, the poor rate, supported the poor. Perhaps the most elaborate system of all existed in the French town of Lyon. There, all the poor were registered and given identity cards. Each Sunday, they would receive a week's worth of food and money. Young girls were provided with dowries, and young boys were taught crafts. But this enlightened system was for the deserving poor only.

Charity was an obligation of the community, but as the sixteenth century wore on, the number of destitute people grew beyond the ability of the local community to care for them. Many of those who now begged for alms fell outside the traditional categories of the deserving poor. They were men and women who were capable of working but incapable of finding more than occasional labor. They left their native communities in search of employment and thus forfeited their claims on local charity. Most wound up in the towns and cities, where as strangers they had no claim on local charity. Poor mothers abandoned their newborn infants on the steps of foundling hospitals or the houses of the rich.

The problem of crime complicated the problems of poverty and vagrancy. Increasing population and increasing wealth equaled increasing crime; the addition of the poor to the equation aggravated the situation. The poor, outsiders to the community without visible means of support, were the easiest targets of official retribution. Throughout the century, numerous European states passed vagrancy laws. In England, the poor were whipped from village to village until they were returned home. Both Venetian and Dutch vagrants were regularly rounded up for galley service. Vagrants in Hungary were sold into slavery. Sexual offenses were criminalized, especially bastardy, since the birth of illegitimate children placed an immediate burden on the community. Prostitutes, who had long been tolerated and regulated in towns, were now persecuted. Rape increased. Capital punishment was reserved for the worst crimes—murder, incest, and grand larceny being most common—but, not surprisingly, executions were carried out mostly on outsiders to the community.

Peasant Revolts

The economic and social changes of the sixteenth century had serious consequences. Most telling was the upswing of violent confrontations between peasants and their lords. Across Europe and with alarming regularity, peasants took up arms to defend themselves from what they saw as violations of traditional rights and obligations. Peasant revolts were not hunger riots. Though they frequently occurred in periods of want, they were not desperate attacks against warehouses or grain silos. Nor

Agrarian Changes.   It is essential to realize that while peasants revolted against their lords, at bottom their anger and frustration were caused by agrarian changes that could be neither controlled nor understood. As population increased and market production expanded, many of the traditional rights and obligations of lords and peasants became oppressive. One example is that of forest rights. On most estates the forests surrounding a village belonged to the lord. Commonly, the village had its own woodlands in which animals foraged and fuel and building material were available. As population increased, new land was put under the plow, and grain fields pressed up against the forest. There were more animals in the village, and some of them were let loose to consume the young sprouts and saplings. Soon there was not enough food for the wild game that was among the lord's most valuable property. So the game began to feed on the peasants' crops, which were now placed so appetizingly close to the forests. It was a capital crime for a peasant to kill wild game, but neither could the peasants allow the game to consume their crops.

A similar conflict arose over enclosing crop fields. An enclosure was a device—normally a fence or hedge that surrounded an area—to keep a parcel of land separate from the planted strips of land owned by the villagers. It could be used for grazing animals or raising a specialty crop for the market. But an enclosure destroyed the traditional form of village agriculture whereby decisions on which crops to plant were made communally. It became one of the chief grievances of the English peasants. But while enclosures broke up the old field system in many villages, they were a logical response to the transformation of land ownership that had already taken place. As more and more land was accumulated by fewer and fewer families, it made less and less sense for them to work widely scattered strips all over the village. If a family could consolidate its holdings by swaps and sales, it could gain an estate that was large enough to be used for both crops and grazing. An enclosed estate allowed wealthy farmers to grow more luxury crops for market or to raise only sheep on a field that had once been used for grain.

Enclosure was a process that both lord and rich peasant undertook, but it drove the smallholders from the land and was thus a source of bitter resentment for the poorer peasants. It was easy to protest the greed of the lords who, owning the most land, were the most successful enclosers. But enclosures resulted more from the process whereby villages came to be characterized by a very small elite of large landholders and a very large mass of smallholders and landless poor. It was an effect rather than a cause.

From Hungary to England, peasant revolts brought social and economic change into sharp relief. A call for a crusade against Ottoman advances in 1514 provided the opportunity for Hungarian peasants to revolt against their noble landlords. Thousands dropped their plowshares and grasped the sword of a holy war. But, in fact, war against

▲ *Feeding the Hungry* by Cornelius Buys, 1504. A maidservant is doling out small loaves to the poor and the lame at the door of a wealthy person's home. The poor who flocked to the towns were often forced to rely on charity to survive.

did those who took part in the revolts form an undisciplined mob. Most revolts chose leaders, drew up petitions of grievances, and organized the rank and file into a semblance of military order. Leaders were literate—drawn more commonly from among the lower clergy or minor gentry than from the peasantry—political demands were moderate, and tactics were sophisticated. But peasant revolts so profoundly threatened the social order that they were met with the severest repression.

the Ottomans did not materialize. Instead, the mobilized peasants, under the leadership of disaffected army officers and clergymen, issued grievances against the labor service that they owed to their lords as well as numerous violations of customary agricultural practices. Their revolt turned into a civil war and was crushed with great brutality. In eastern England, Ket's Rebellion centered on peasant opposition to enclosure. The rebels occupied Norwich, the second largest city in the realm, but their aspirations were for reform rather than revolution. They, too, were crushed by well-trained forces.

Uprising in Germany.   The complexity of these problems is perhaps best revealed in the series of uprisings that are known collectively as the German Peasants' War. It involved tens of thousands of peasants, and it combined a whole series of agrarian grievances with an awareness of the new religious spirit preached by Martin Luther. Luther condemned both lords and peasants—the lords for their rapaciousness, the peasants for their rebelliousness. Though he had a large following among the peasants, his advice that earthly oppressions be passively accepted was not followed. The Peasants' War was directed against secular and ecclesiastical lords, and the rebels attacked both economic and religious abuses. The combination of demands, such as the community's right to select its own minister and the community's right to cut wood freely, attracted a wide following in the villages and small towns of southern and central Germany. The printed demands of the peasantry, the most famous of which was the Twelve Articles of the Peasants of Swabia (1525), helped to spread the movement far beyond its original bounds. The peasants organized themselves into large armies led by experienced soldiers, but ultimately, movements that refused compromise were ruthlessly crushed.

At base, the demands of the peasantry addressed the agrarian changes that were transforming German villages. Population growth was creating more poor villagers who could only hire out as laborers but who demanded a share of common grazing and woodlands. Because the presence of these poor people increased the taxable wealth of the village, they were advantageous to the lord. But the strain they placed on resources was felt by both the subsistence and surplus farmers. Tensions within the village were all the greater in that the landless members were the kin of the landed. If they were to be settled properly on the land, then the lord would have to let the village expand. If they were to be kept on the margins of subsistence, then the more prosperous villagers would have to be able to control their numbers and their conduct. In either case, the peasants needed more direct responsibility for governing the village than existed in their traditional relationship with their lord. Therefore, the peasants of Swabia demanded release of the village peasantry from the status of serfs. They wanted to be allowed to move off the land, to marry out of the village without penalty, and to be free of the death taxes that further impoverished their children. They also wanted stable rents fixed at fair rates, a limit placed on labor service, and a return to the ancient customs that governed relations between lords and peasants. All of these proposals were backed by an appeal to Christian principles of love and charity. They were profoundly conservative.

The demands of the German peasants reflected a traditional order that no longer existed. In many places, the rents and tithes that the peasants wanted to control no longer belonged to the lords of the estates. They had been sold to town corporations or wealthy individuals who purchased them as an investment and expected to realize a fair return. Most tenants did enjoy stable and fixed rents, but only on their traditional lands. As they increased their holdings, perhaps to keep another son in the village or to expand production for the market, they were faced with the fact that rents were higher and land was more expensive than it had been before. Marriage fines, death duties, and labor service were oppressive, but they balanced the fact that traditional rents were very low. In many east German villages, peasants willingly increased their labor service for a reduction in their money rents. It was hardly likely that they could have both. If the peasants were being squeezed, and there can be little doubt that they were, it was not only the lords who were doing the squeezing. The Church took its tenth, the state increased its exactions, and the competition for survival and prosperity among the peasants themselves was ferocious. Peasants were caught between the jaws of an expanding state and a changing economy. When they rebelled, the jaws snapped shut.

PRIVATE AND COMMUNITY LIFE

The great events of the sixteenth century—the discovery of the New World, the consolidation of states, the increasing incidence and ferocity of war, and the reform of religion—all had a profound impact on the lives of ordinary people. However slowly and intermittently these developments penetrated to isolated village communities, they were inextricably bound up with the experiences and world view of all Europeans.

The Family

Sixteenth-century life centered on the family, the primary kinship group. European families were predominantly nuclear, composed of a married couple and their children. In western Europe, a small number of families contained the adult siblings of the family head, uncles and aunts who had not yet established their own families. This pattern was more common in the east, especially in Hungary and Muscovy, where taxation was based on households and thus encouraged extended families. Yet, however families were composed, kinship had a wider orbit than just parents and children. In-laws, step relations, and cousins were considered part of the kin group and could be called on for support in a variety of contexts from charity to employment and business partnerships. In towns, such family connections created large and powerful clans.

In a different sense, family was lineage, the connections between preceding and succeeding generations. This was an important concept among the upper ranks of society, in which ancient lineage, genuine or fabricated, was a valued component of nobility. Even in peasant communities, however, lineage existed in the form of the strips in the field that were passed from generation to generation and named for the family that owned them.

The family was also an economic unit. It was the basic unit for the production, accumulation, and transmission of wealth. Occupation determined the organization of the economic family. Every member of the household had his or her own functions that were essential to the survival of the unit. Tasks were divided by gender and by age, but there was far more intermixture than is traditionally assumed. On farms, women worked at nearly every occupation with the exception of mowing and plowing. In towns, they were vital to the success of shops and trades, though they were denied training in the skilled crafts. As laborers, they worked in the town fields—for little more than half the wages of men performing the same tasks—and in carrying and delivering goods and materials. Children contributed to the economic vitality of the household from an early age.

Finally, the family was the primary unit of social organization. It was in the family that children were educated and the social values of hierarchy and discipline were taught. Authority in the family was strictly organized in a set of three overlapping categories. At the top was the husband, head of the household, who ruled over his wife, children, and servants. All members of the family owed obedience to the head. Children owed obedience to their parents, male or female. Similarly, servants owed obedience to both master and mistress. Male apprentices were under the authority of the wife, mother, and mistress of the household. The importance of the family as a social unit was underscored by the fact that people who were not attached to families attracted suspicion in sixteenth-century society. Single men were often viewed as potential criminals, single women as potential prostitutes.

Though the population of Europe was increasing in the sixteenth century, families were not large. Throughout northern and western Europe, the size of the typical family was two adults and three or four children. Late marriages and breast-feeding helped to control family size. The first restricted the number of childbearing years; the second increased the space between pregnancies. Women married around age 25, men slightly later. Most women could expect about 15 fertile years and seven or eight pregnancies if neither they nor their husband died in the interim. Only three or four children were likely to survive beyond the age of ten. In her fertile years, a woman was constantly occupied with infants. If she used a wet nurse, as many women in the upper ranks of society did, then she was likely to have 10 or 12 pregnancies during her fertile years and correspondingly

▶ *Peasant Family* (ca. 1640), a realistic scene of peasant life in France by the genre painter Louis Le Nain.

more surviving children. Constant pregnancy and child care may help explain some of the gender roles that men and women assumed in the sixteenth century. Biblical injunctions and traditional stereotypes help explain others. Whether a woman was pregnant or not, her labor was a vital part of the domestic economy, especially until the first surviving children were strong enough to assume their share. The woman's sphere was the household. On the farm, she was in charge of the preparation of food, the care of domestic animals, the care and education of children, and the manufacture and cleaning of the family's clothing. In towns, women supervised the shop that was part of the household. They sold goods, kept accounts, and directed the work of domestics or apprentices.

The man's sphere was the public one: the fields in rural areas, the streets in towns. Men plowed, planted, and did the heavy reaping work of farming. They made and maintained essential farm equipment and had charge of the large farm animals. They marketed surplus produce and made the few purchases of equipment or luxury goods. Men performed the labor service that was normally due the lord of the estate, attended the local courts in various capacities, and organized the affairs of the village. In towns, men engaged in heavy labor, procured materials for craft work, and marketed their product if it was not sold in the household shop. Only men could be citizens of the towns or full members of most craft guilds, and only men were involved in civic government.

This separation of men and women into the public and the domestic spheres meant that marriage was a blending of complementary skills. Each partner brought to the marriage essential knowledge and abilities that were fundamental to the economic success of the union. Except in the largest towns, nearly everyone was married for at least a part of his or her life. Remarriage was more common for men than for women, however, because a man continued to control the family's property after the death of his wife, whereas a widow might have only a share of it after bequests to children or provisions for apprentices.

While male roles were constant throughout the life cycle, as men trained for and performed the same occupations from childhood to death, female roles varied greatly depending on the situation. While under the care of fathers, masters, or husbands, women worked in the domestic sphere; once widowed, they assumed the public functions of head of household. Many women inherited shops or farmland; most became responsible for the placement and training of their children. But because of the division of labor on which the family depended and because of the inherent social and economic prejudices that segregated public and domestic roles, widows were particularly disadvantaged.

Communities

The family was part of a wider community. On the farm, this community was the rural village; in the town, it was the ward, quarter, or parish in which the family lived. Community life must not be romanticized. Interpersonal violence, lawsuits, and feuds were common in both rural and urban communities. Like every other aspect of society, the community was socially and economically stratified, gender roles were segregated, and resources were inequitably divided. But the community was also the place where people found their social identity. It provided marriage partners for its families, charity for its poor, and a local culture for all of its inhabitants.

Identities and Customs.   The two basic forces that tied the rural community together were the lord and the priest. The lord set conditions for work and property ownership that necessitated common decision making on the part of the village farmers. The lord's presence, commonly in the form of an agent, could be both a positive and a negative force for community solidarity. Use of the common lands, the rotation of labor service, and the form in which rents in kind were paid were all decisions that had to be made collectively. Village leadership remained informal, though in some villages, headmen or elders bargained with the lord's agent or resolved petty disputes among the villagers. Communal agreement was also expressed in communal resistance to violations of custom or threats to the moral economy. All these forms of negotiation fused individual families into a community. So, too, in a different way did the presence of the parish priest or minister, who attended all the pivotal events of life—birth, marriage, and death. The church was the only common building of the community; it was the only space that was not owned outright by the lord or an individual family. The scene of village meetings and ceremonies, it was the center of both spiritual and social life. The parish priest served as a conduit for all the news of the community and the focal point for the village's festive life.

Communities were also bound together by their own social customs. In rural parishes, there was the annual perambulation, a walk around the village fields that usually occurred before planting began. It was led by the priest, who blessed the fields as the village farmers followed.

In towns, ceremonial processions were far more elaborate. Processions might take place on saints' days in Catholic communities or on anniversaries of town liberties. The order of the march, the clothing worn by the participants, and the objects displayed reflected the strict hierarchies of the town's local organizations.

Weddings and Festivals.   Not all ceremonial occasions were so formal. The most common ceremony was the wedding, a public event that combined a religious rite and a community procession with feasting and festivity. It took different forms in different parts of Europe and in different social groups. Many couples were engaged long before they were married, and in many places it was the engagement that was most important to the individuals and the wedding that was most important to the community. Traditional weddings involved the formal transfer of property, an important event in rural communities where the ownership of strips of land or common rights concerned everyone. The bridal dowry and the groom's inheritance were formally exchanged during the wedding, even if both were small. The public procession, "the marriage in the streets," as it was sometimes called in towns, proclaimed the union throughout the community.

Other ceremonies were equally important in creating a shared sense of identity within the community. In both town and countryside, the year was divided by a number of festivals that defined the rhythm of toil and rest. They coincided with both the seasonal divisions of agricultural life and the central events of the Christian calendar. Christmas and Easter were probably the most widely observed Christian holidays, but Carnival, which preceded Lent, was a frenzied round of feasts and parties that resulted in a disproportionate number of births nine months later. The twelve days of Christmas were only loosely attached to the birth of Jesus and were even abolished by some Protestant churches. The rites of May, which celebrated the rebirth of spring, were filled with sexual play among the young adults of the community. All Hallows' Eve was a celebration for the community's dead. Their spirits wandered the village on that night, visiting kin and neighbors.

In addition to feasting, dancing, and play, festivals often included sports, such as soccer or wrestling, which served to channel aggressions. At such times, village elders would also arbitrate disputes, and marriage alliances or property transactions would be arranged.

Festivals further cemented the political cohesion of the community. Seating arrangements signaled the hierarchy of the community, and public punishment of offenders reinforced deference and social and sexual mores. Youth groups or the village women might band together to shame a promiscuous woman or to place horns on the head of a cuckolded husband. These forms of community ritual worked not only to punish offenders but also to reinforce the social and sexual values of the village as a whole.

Popular Beliefs and the Persecution of Witches

Ceremony and festival are reminders that sixteenth-century Europe was still a preliterate society. Despite the introduction of printing and the millions of books that were produced during the period, the vast majority of Europeans conducted their affairs without the benefit of literacy. Outside a small circle of intellectuals, there was little effective knowledge about either human or celestial bodies. The mysteries of the sun, moon, and stars were as deep as those of health and sickness. But this does not mean that ordinary people lived in a constant state of terror and anxiety. They used the knowledge they did have to

form a view of the universe that conformed to their experiences and responded to their hopes.

Magical Practices. These beliefs blended Christian teaching and folk wisdom with a strong strain of magic. Popular belief in magic could be found everywhere in Europe, and it operated in much the same way as science does today. Only skilled practitioners could perform magic. It was a technical subject that combined expertise in the properties of plants and animals with theories about the composition of human and heavenly bodies. It had its own language, a mixture of ancient words and sounds with significant numbers and catch phrases. Magicians specialized. Alchemists worked with rocks and minerals, astrologers with the movement of the stars. Witches were thought to understand the properties of animals especially well.

Magical practices appealed to people at all levels of society. The wealthy favored astrology and paid handsomely to discover which days and months were the most auspicious for marriages and investments. The poorest villagers sought the aid of herbalists to help control the constant aches and pains of daily life. Sorcerers and wizards were called on in more extreme circumstances, such as a threatened harvest or matters of life and death. These magicians competed with the remedies offered by the Church. Special prayers and visits to the shrines of particular saints were believed to have similar curative value. Magical and Christian beliefs were often practiced simultaneously. In some French villages, for example, four-leaf clovers were considered especially powerful if they were found on a particular saint's day. It was not until the end of the century, when Protestant and Catholic leaders condemned magical practices and began a campaign to root them out, that magic and religion came into conflict.

Magical practices served a variety of purposes. Healing was the most common, and many "magical" brews were effective remedies for the minor ailments for which they were prescribed. Most village magicians were women because it was believed that women had unique knowledge and understanding of the body. Magic was also used for predictive purposes. Certain charms and rituals were believed to have the power to affect the weather, the crops, and even human events. As always, affairs of the heart were as important as those of the stomach. Magicians advised the lovesick on potions and spells that would gain them the object of their desires. Finally, it was believed that magic had the power to alter the course of nature and could be used for both good and evil purposes.

The Witchcraft Craze. Magic for evil was black magic, or witchcraft. Witches were believed to possess special powers that put them into contact with the devil and the forces of evil, which they could then use for their own purposes. Belief in the prevalence of good and evil spirits was Christian as well as magical. But the Church had gradually consigned the operation of the devil to the afterlife and removed his direct agency from earthly affairs. Beginning in the late fifteenth century, church authorities began to prosecute large numbers of suspected witches. By the end of the sixteenth century, there was a continent-wide witch craze. Confessions were obtained under torture, as were further accusations.

Witches were usually women, most often unmarried or widowed. In a sample of more than 7,000 cases of witchcraft prosecuted in early modern Europe, over 80 percent of the defendants were women. There is no clear explanation for why women fulfilled this important and powerful role. Belief in women's special powers over the body through their singular ability to give birth is certainly one part of the explanation, for many stories about the origins of witches suggest that they were children fathered by the devil and left to be raised by women. This sexual element of union with the devil and the common belief that older women were sexually aggressive combined to threaten male sexual dominance. Witches were

THE DEVIL'S DUE

Evidence of the supernatural world abounded for the people of premodern Europe. Natural disasters such as plague and human disasters such as war promoted fear of witchcraft. When the world seemed out of balance and the forces of good retreated before the forces of evil, people sought someone to blame for their troubles. Witches were an obvious choice. Accused witches were most commonly women on the margins of society. Once brought before the authorities, many admitted their traffic with Satan, especially under torture. The Witch Hammer is a set of detailed instructions for the rooting out of witches, including procedures to induce their confessions.

FOCUS QUESTIONS

What is the point of torture, punishment, or investigation? Is the suspected witch seen as being in control of his or her magic?

THE METHOD OF BEGINNING AN EXAMINATION BY TORTURE IS AS FOLLOWS: First, the jailers prepare the implements of torture, then they strip the prisoner (if it be a woman, she has already been stripped by other women, upright and of good report). This stripping is lest some means of witchcraft may have been sewed into the clothing—such as often, taught by the Devil, they prepare from the bodies of unbaptized infants, [murdered] that they may forfeit salvation. And when the implements of torture have been prepared, the judge, both in person and through other good men zealous in the faith, tries to persuade the prisoner to confess the truth freely; but, if he will not confess, he bids attendants make the prisoner fast to the strappado or some other implement of torture. The attendants obey forthwith, yet with feigned agitation. Then, at the prayer of some of those present, the prisoner is loosed again and is taken aside and once more persuaded to confess, being led to believe that he will in that case not be put to death.

But if, neither by threats nor by promises such as these, the witch cannot be induced to speak the truth, then the jailers must carry out the sentence, and torture the prisoner according to the accepted methods, with more or less of severity as the delinquent's crime may demand. And,

while he is being tortured, he must be questioned on the articles of accusation, and this frequently and persistently, beginning with the lighter charges—for he will more readily confess the lighter than the heavier. And, while this is being done, the notary must write down everything in his record of the trial—how the prisoner is tortured, on what points he is questioned, and how he answers.

And note that, if he confesses under the torture, he must afterward be conducted to another place, that he may confirm it and certify that it was not due alone to the force of the torture.

But, if the prisoner will not confess the truth satisfactorily, other sorts of tortures must be placed before him, with the statement that, unless he will confess the truth, he must endure these also. But, if not even thus he can be brought into terror and to the truth, then the next day or the next but one is to be set for a *continuation* of the tortures—not a *repetition*, for they must not be repeated unless new evidence be produced. . . .

And during the interval, before the day assigned, the judge, in person or through approved men, must in the manner above described try to persuade the prisoner to confess, promising her (if there is aught to be gained by this promise) that her life shall be spared.

The judge shall see to it, moreover, that throughout this interval guards are constantly with the prisoner, so that she may not be left alone; because she will be visited by the Devil and tempted into suicide.

From The Witch Hammer.

also believed to have peculiar physical characteristics. A group of Italian witches, male and female, were distinguished by having been born with a caul, that is, a membrane around their heads that was removed after birth. Accused witches were strip-searched to find the devil's mark, which might be any bodily blemish. Another strand of explanation lies in the fact that single women existed on the fringes of society, isolated and exploited by the community at large. Their occult abilities thus became a protective mechanism that gave them a function within the community while they remained outside it.

It is difficult to know how important black magical beliefs were in ordinary communities. Most of the daily magic that was practiced was a mixture of charms, potions, and prayers that mingled magical, medical, and Christian beliefs. Misfortunes that befell particular families or social groups were blamed on the activities of witches. The campaign of the established churches to root out magic was directed largely against witches. The churches transposed witches' supposed abilities to communicate with the devil into the charge that they worshiped the devil. Because there was such widespread belief in the presence of diabolical spirits and in the capabilities of witches to control them, Protestant and Catholic church courts could easily find witnesses to testify in support of the charges against individual witches. Over 100,000—perhaps several times that many—condemned witches in Europe were burned, strangled, drowned, or beheaded. Yet wherever sufficient evidence exists to understand the circumstances of witchcraft prosecutions, it is clear that the community itself was under some form of social or economic stress rather than that there was any increase in the presence or use of witches.

Conclusion

POPULATION GROWTH, ECONOMIC DIVERSIFICATION, and social change characterized life in sixteenth-century Europe. It was a century of extremes. The poor were getting poorer, and the rich were getting richer. The early part of the century has been called the golden age of the peasantry; the later part has been called the crisis of subsistence. At all levels of the social scale, the lives of grandparents and grandchildren were dramatically different. For surplus producers, the quality of life improved throughout the century. The market economy expanded. Agricultural surplus was exchanged for more land and a wider variety of consumer goods. Children could be given an education, and domestic and agricultural labor was cheap and plentiful. For subsistence producers, the quality of life eroded. In the first half of the century, their diet contained more meat than it would for the next 300 years. Their children could be absorbed on new farms or sent to towns where there was a shortage of both skilled and unskilled labor. But gradually, the outlook turned bleak. The land could support no more new families, and the towns needed no more labor. As wages fell and prices rose, peasants in western Europe were caught between the crushing burdens of taxation from lord, state, and church and the all-too-frequent catastrophes of poor harvests, epidemic disease, and warfare. In eastern Europe, the peasantry was tied to the land in a new serfdom, which provided minimum subsistence in return for the loss of freedom and opportunity. When peasants anywhere rose up against these conditions, they were cut down and swept away like new-mown hay. The witch-hunts of the sixteenth and early seventeenth centuries reflected troubled times, a pervasive misogyny, and a misguided effort to eliminate the cause of the troubles.

QUESTIONS FOR REVIEW

1. What physical forces and social customs shaped the everyday life of Europe's rural population?
2. What was the nature of demographic change in the sixteenth century, and what was its impact on the European economy?
3. How are the terms "stratification," "hierarchy," and "status" useful for understanding social relations in early modern Europe?
4. How were the different roles of men and women within the family reflected in the different lives of men and women in the wider community?

DISCOVERING WESTERN CIVILIZATION ONLINE

You can obtain more information about life in early modern Europe at the websites listed below. See also the companion website that accompanies this text: www.ablongman.com/kishlansky, which include an online study guide and additional resources.

Social Life

www.fordham.edu/halsall/mod/modsbook04.html
A site with links to sources, pictures, and accounts of everyday life in early modern Europe. A good place to start.

www.fordham.edu/halsall/mod/17france-soc.html
Documents illustrating social conditions in early modern France.

Private Life

Womenshistory.about.com/cs/witches
This site offers historical information about witches and witchcraft in Europe and America and includes links to related sites.

www.englishhistory.net/tudor/life.html
Part of a comprehensive site on Tudor England, this section on life in Tudor England offers information on topics including food and drink, pastimes and entertainment, and mental illness.

SUGGESTIONS FOR FURTHER READING

General Reading

Henry Kamen, *European Society, 1500–1700* (London: Hutchinson, 1984). A general survey of European social history.

Peter Laslett, *The World We Have Lost: Further Explored* (New York: Scribners, 1984). One of the pioneering works on the family and population history of England.

Robert Mandrou, *Introduction to Modern France* (New York: Harper & Row, 1977). Explores a variety of subjects in French social history from the mental to the material world.

Economic Life

Judith Bennett, *Ale, Beer, and Brewsters: Women's Work in a Changing World* (Oxford: Oxford University Press, 1996). An important study of the role of women in one of the most traditional trades.

Fernand Braudel, *Civilization and Capitalism: The Structures of Everyday Life* (New York: Harper & Row, 1981). Part of a larger work filled with fascinating detail about the social behavior of humankind during the early modern period.

Social Life

Peter Blickle, *The Revolution of 1525* (Baltimore, Md.: Johns Hopkins University Press, 1981). A provocative interpretation of the causes and meaning of the German Peasants' War.

Michael Bush, *Noble Privilege* (New York: Holmes & Meier, 1983). An analytic account of the types of privileges enjoyed by the European nobility, based on wide reading.

Edward Muir, *Ritual in Early Modern Europe* (Cambridge: Cambridge University Press, 1997). A fascinating account of the transformations in concepts of time and the body in early modern Europe.

J. L. Price, *Dutch Society, 1588–1713* (New York: Longman, 2001). A general social history of the Dutch "Golden Age."

Barry Reay, *Popular Cultures in England, 1550–1750* (New York: Addison Wesley Longman, 1998). A sound and insightful thematic survey.

Private Life

Peter Burke, *Popular Culture in Early Modern Europe* (New York: Harper & Row, 1978). A lively survey of cultural activities among the European populace.

Roger Chartier, ed., *A History of Private Life, vol. 3, Passions of the Renaissance* (Cambridge, Mass.: Harvard University Press, 1989). A lavishly illustrated study of the habits, mores, and structures of private life from the fifteenth to the eighteenth centuries.

Stuart Clark, *Thinking with Demons: The Idea of Witchcraft in Early Modern Europe* (Oxford: Oxford University Press,

1997). A sensitive reading of the sources for the study of witchcraft.

Beatrice Gottlieb, *The Family in the Western World From the Black Death to the Industrial Age* (Oxford: Oxford University Press, 1994). An outstanding introduction to the transformations in the lives of families.

Ralph Houlbrooke, *The English Family, 1450–1700* (London: Longman, 1984). A thorough survey of family history for the society that has been most carefully studied.

Brian Levack, *The Witch-Hunt in Early Modern Europe* (London: Longman, 1987). A study of the causes and meaning of the persecution of European witches in the sixteenth and seventeenth centuries.

R. Muchembled, *Popular Culture and Elite Culture in France, 1400–1750* (Baton Rouge: Louisiana State University Press, 1985). A detailed treatment of the practices of two conflicting cultures.

Keith Thomas, *Religion and the Decline of Magic* (New York: Scribners, 1971). A gargantuan descriptive and anecdotal account of the forms of religious and magical practice in England.

Merry E. Wiesner, *Women and Gender in Early Modern Europe* (Cambridge: Cambridge University Press, 1993). The best introduction to European women's history.

THE ROYAL STATE IN THE SEVENTEENTH CENTURY

FIT FOR A KING

BEHOLD VERSAILLES, the greatest palace of the greatest king of the greatest state in seventeenth-century Europe. Everything about it was stupendous, a reflection of the grandeur of Louis XIV and of France. Sculptured gardens in dazzling geometric forms stretched for acres, scenting the air with exotic perfumes. Nearly as beautiful as the grounds were the 1,400 fountains, especially the circular basins of Apollo and Latona, the sun god and his mother. The hundreds of water jets that sprayed at Versailles defied nature as well as the senses, for the locale was not well-irrigated and water had to be pumped through elaborate mechanical works all the way from the Seine. Gardens and fountains provided the setting for the enormous palace with its hundreds of rooms for both use and show. Five thousand people, one tenth of whom served the king alone, inhabited the palace. Thousands of others flocked there daily. Most lived in the adjacent town,

which had grown from a few hundred people to over 40,000 in a single generation. The royal stables quartered 12,000 horses and hundreds of carriages. The cost of all of this magnificence was equally astounding, estimated to be over 100 million French pounds. Louis XIV ordered the official receipts burned.

Like the marble of the palace, nature itself was chiseled to the requirements of the king. Forests were pared to make leafy avenues or trimmed to conform to the geometric patterns of the gardens. In spring and summer, groves of orange trees grown in tubs were everywhere; in winter and fall they were housed indoors at great expense. Life-size statues and giant carved urns lined the carefully planned walkways that led to breathtaking views or sheltered grottoes. A cross-shaped artificial canal, more than a mile long, dominated the western end of the park.

Despite all the extravagance, the palace was so uncomfortable to live in that Louis had a separate chateau built on the grounds as a quiet retreat. His wife and his mistresses complained constantly of accommodations in which all interior comforts had been subordinated to the external facade of the building. Versailles was a seat of state as well as the home of the monarch, and it is revealing that the private was sacrificed to the public.

Soldiers, artisans, and the merely curious clogged the three great avenues that led from Paris to the palace. When the king dined in public, hordes of Parisians drove out for the spectacle, filing past the monarch as if he were an exhibit at a museum. The site itself was poorly drained, and the stench of sewage was particularly noxious in the heat and the rain. Even the gardens were too vast to be enjoyed. In the planted areas, the smell of flowers was overpowering while the acres of mown lawn proved unattractive to an aristocracy little given to physical exercise. In these contrasts of failure amid achievement, Versailles stands as an apt symbol of its age: a gaudy mask to hide the wrinkles of the royal state.

Versailles expressed the contradictions of its age. The seventeenth century was an era when the rich got richer and the poor got poorer. It was a time when the monarchical state expanded its power and prestige even as it faced grave challenges to its very existence. It was an epoch of unrelenting war amid a nearly universal desire for lasting peace.

LOOKING AHEAD

The great palaces of European absolute monarchs were designed to intimidate those who visited them. They were the representation of royal power at its apex. As we will learn in this chapter, not since Rome's emperors were at the height of their glory had power been more concentrated in the hands of rulers, and what they had consolidated over centuries they now had to protect against competing dynasties or rebellious subjects.

THE RISE OF THE ROYAL STATE

The wars that dominated the early part of the seventeenth century had a profound impact on the western European states. Not only did they cause terrible suffering and deprivation, but they also demanded efficient and better-centralized states to conduct them. War was both a product of the European state system and a cause of its continued development. As armies grew in size, their material needs grew in volume. As the battlefield spread from state to state, defense became government's most important function. More and more power was absorbed by the monarch and his chief advisers; more and more of the traditional privileges of aristocracy and of towns were eroded. At the center of these rising states, particularly in western Europe, were the king and his court. In the provinces were tax collectors and military recruiters.

Divine Kings

In the early sixteenth century, monarchs treated their states and their subjects as personal property. Correspondingly, rulers were praised in personal terms, for their virtue, their wisdom, or their strength. By the early seventeenth century, the monarchy had been transformed into an office of state. Now rulers embodied their nation, and, no matter what their personal characteristics, they were held in awe because they were monarchs.

Thus, as rulers lost direct personal control over their territory, they gained indirect symbolic control over their nation. This symbolic power was manifested everywhere. By the beginning of the seventeenth century, monarchs had permanent seats of government attended by vast courts of officials, place seekers, and servants. They no longer moved from place to place with their vast entourages. The idea of the capital city emerged, with Madrid, London, and Paris as the models. Here, the grandiose style of the ruler stood proxy for the wealth and glory of the nation. Great display bespoke great pride and strength.

Portraits of rulers conveyed the central message. Elizabeth I was depicted astride a map of England or clutching a rainbow and wearing a gown woven of eyes and ears to signify her power to see and hear her subjects. The Flemish artist Sir Anthony van Dyck (1599–1641) created powerful images of three generations of Stuart kings of England. Diego Velázquez (1599–1660) was court painter to Philip IV of Spain. His series of equestrian portraits of the Habsburgs—kings, queens, princes, and princesses—exude the spirit of the seventeenth-century monarchy, the grandeur and pomp, the power and self-assurance. Peter Paul Rubens (1577–1640) represented 21 separate episodes in the life of Marie de Médicis, queen regent of France.

Monarchy was also glorified in literature. National history, particularly of recent events, enjoyed wide popularity. Its avowed purpose was to draw the connection between the past and the present glories of the state. A popular French history of the period was entitled *On the Excellence of the Kings and the Kingdom of France*. Francis Bacon (1561–1626), who is remembered more as a philosopher and scientist, wrote a laudatory history of England's Henry VII, founder of the Tudor dynasty.

▼ Queen Elizabeth I of England. This portrait was commissioned by Sir Henry Lee to commemorate the queen's visit to his estate at Ditchley. Here the queen is the very image of Gloriana—ageless and indomitable.

In England, the seventeenth century was a period of renaissance. Poets, playwrights, historians, and philosophers gravitated to the English court. Ben Jonson (1572–1637), a commoner whose wit and talent brought him to court, made his mark by writing and staging masques, light entertainment that included music, dance, pantomime, and acting. Jonson's lavish productions, with sets designed by the great architect Inigo Jones (1573–1652), were frequently staged at Christmastime and starred members of the court as players. The masques took for their themes the grandeur of England and its rulers.

Shakespeare and Kingship. Many of the plays of William Shakespeare (1564–1616) also dealt with monarchy. Like Jonson, Shakespeare came from an ordinary family and began his career as an actor and producer of theater. He soon began to write as well as direct his plays, and his company, the King's Players, received royal patronage. He set many of his plays at the courts of princes, and even comedies such as *Measure for Measure* (1604) and *The Tempest* (1611) centered on the power of the ruler to dispense justice and to bring peace to his subjects. Shakespeare's history plays focused entirely on the character of kings. In *Richard II* (1597) and *Henry VI* (three parts, 1591–1594), Shakespeare exposed the harm that weak rulers inflicted on their states, while in *Henry IV* (two parts, 1598–1600) and *Henry V* (1599) he highlighted the benefits to be derived from strong rulers. In Shakespeare's tragedies a flaw in the ruler's personality brought harm to the world around him. In *Macbeth* (1606) this flaw was ambition; in *Hamlet* (1602) it was irresolution. Shakespeare's concentration on the affairs of rulers helped to reinforce their dominating importance in the lives of all of their subjects.

Monarchy and Law. The political theory of the divine right of kings further enhanced the importance of monarchs. This theory held that the institution of monarchy had been created by God and that the monarch functioned as God's representative on earth. One clear statement of divine right theory was actually written by a king, James VI of Scotland, who later became King James I of England (1603–1625). In *The True Law of Free Monarchies* (1598), James reasoned that God had placed kings on earth to rule and had charged them with the obligations "to minister justice; to establish good laws; and to procure peace." God would also judge them in heaven for their transgressions.

The idea of divine origin of monarchy was uncontroversial, and it was espoused not only by kings. The French Estates-General, for example, in 1614 agreed that "the king is sovereign in France and holds his crown from God only." This sentiment echoed the commonplace view of French political theorists. The greatest writer on the subject, Jean Bodin (1530–1596), called the king "God's image on earth."

In *The Six Books of the Commonwealth* (1576), Bodin defined the essence of the monarch's power: "The principal mark of sovereign majesty is essentially the right to impose laws on subjects generally without their consent."

Kings were nevertheless bound by the law of nature and the law of nations. They could not deprive their subjects of their lives, their liberties, or their property without due cause established by law. As one French theorist held, "While the kingdom belongs to the king, the king also belongs to the kingdom." Wherever they turned, kings were instructed in the duties of kingship.

The Court and the Courtiers

In reality, the day-to-day affairs of government had grown beyond the capacity of any monarch to handle them. The expansion in the powers of the western states absorbed more officials than ever. At the beginning of the sixteenth century, the French court of Francis I employed 622 officers; at the beginning of the seventeenth century, the court of Henry IV employed over 1,500. Yet the difference was not only in size. Members of the seventeenth-century court were becoming servants of the state as well as of the monarch.

Expanding the court was one of the ways in which monarchs co-opted potential rivals within the aristocracy. In return, those who were favored received royal grants of titles, lands, and income. As the court expanded, so did the political power of courtiers. Royal councils—a small group of leading officeholders who advised the monarch on state business—grew in significance. The council assumed management of the government and soon began to advocate policies for the monarch to adopt.

Yet the court still revolved around the monarch. The monarch appointed, promoted, and dismissed officeholders at will. As befitted this type of personal government, most monarchs chose a single individual to act as a funnel for private and public business. This was the "favorite," whose role combined varying proportions of best friend, right-hand man, and hired gun. Some favorites, like the French Cardinal Richelieu and the Spanish Count-Duke Olivares, were able to transform themselves into chief ministers. Others, like the English Duke of Buckingham, simply remained royal companions. Favorites lasted only as long as they retained their influence with the monarch. Richelieu claimed that it was "more difficult to dominate the four square feet of the king's study than the affairs of Europe." The parallel careers of Richelieu, Olivares, and Buckingham neatly illustrate the dangers and opportunities of the office.

Cardinal Richelieu (1585–1642), a younger son of a minor French noble family, trained for the law and then for a position that his family owned in the Church. He was made a cardinal in 1622. After skillful participation in the meeting of the Estates-General of 1614, Richelieu was

A GLIMPSE OF A KING

Louis de Rouvroy, duc de Saint-Simon, spent much of his career at the court of Louis XIV. His Memoires provide a fascinating study of life at Versailles, as well as poison pen portraits of the king and his courtiers. Here he describes some habits of the king.

FOCUS QUESTIONS

How does the king maintain his power over the nobles? Why does so much in this political system depend on personal skills and self-presentation?

HE ALWAYS TOOK GREAT PAINS to find out what was going on in public places, in society, in private houses, even family secrets, and maintained an immense number of spies and tale-bearers. These were of all sorts; some did not know that their reports were carried to him; others did know it; there were others, again, who used to write to him directly, through channels which he prescribed; others who were admitted by the backstairs and saw him in his private room. Many a man in all ranks of life was ruined by these methods, often very unjustly, without ever being able to discover the reason; and when the King had once take a prejudice against a man, he hardly ever got over it. . . .

No one understood better than Louis XIV the art of enhancing the value of a favour by his manner of bestowing it; he knew how to make the most of a word, a smile, even of a glance. If he addressed any one, were it but to ask a trifling question or make some commonplace remark, all eyes were turned on the person so honored; it was a mark of favour which always gave rise to comment. . . .

He loved splendour, magnificence, and profusion in all things, and encouraged similar tastes in his Court; to spend money freely on equipages and buildings, on feasting and at cards, was a sure way to gain his favour, perhaps to obtain the honour of a word from him. Motives of policy and something to do with this; by making expensive habits the fashion, and, for people in a certain position, a necessity, he compelled his courtiers to live beyond their income, and gradually reduced them to depend on his bounty for the means of subsistence.

From duc de Saint-Simon, *Memoires*.

---

given a court post through the patronage of Queen Marie de Médicis, mother of Louis XIII. The two men made a good match. Louis XIII hated the work of ruling, and Richelieu loved little else.

Though Richelieu received great favor from the king—he became a duke and amassed the largest private fortune in France—his position rested on his managerial abilities. Richelieu never enjoyed a close personal relationship with his monarch, and he never felt that his position was secure. In 1630, Marie de Médicis turned against him, and he was very nearly ousted from office. His last years were filled with suppressing plots to undermine his power or to take his life.

The Count-Duke Olivares (1587–1645) was a younger son of a lesser branch of a great Spanish noble family. By the time he was 20, he had become a courtier with a title, a large fortune, and, most unusually, a university education. Olivares became the favorite of King Philip IV (1621–1665). He was elevated to the highest rank of the nobility and used his closeness to the monarch to gain court appointments for his relatives and political supporters.

But he was more interested in establishing political policy than in building a court faction. His objective was to maintain the greatness of Spain, and he attempted to

further the process of centralizing Spanish royal power, which was not very advanced. Olivares's plans for a nationally recruited and financed army ended in disaster. His efforts at tax reform went unrewarded. He advocated the aggressive foreign policy that mired Spain in the Thirty Years' War and the eighty years of war in the Netherlands. As domestic and foreign crises mounted, Philip IV could not resist the pressure to dismiss his chief minister. In 1643, Olivares was removed from office; two years later, physically exhausted and mentally deranged, he died.

The Duke of Buckingham (1592–1628) was also a younger son but was not of the English nobility. He received the aimless education of a country gentleman, spending several years in France learning the graces of fashion and dancing. He was reputedly one of the handsomest men in Europe, and his looks and charm eventually brought him to the attention of Queen Anne, the wife of James I. She recommended Buckingham for a minor office that gave him frequent access to the king, and in less than seven years he rose from commoner to duke, the highest rank of the English nobility.

Along with his titles, Buckingham acquired political power. He assumed a large number of royal offices, among them Admiral of the Navy, and placed his relatives and dependents in many others. Buckingham took his obligations seriously. He began a reform of naval administration, for example, but his rise to power was so sudden that he found enemies at every turn. These increased dramatically when James I died in 1625, but Buckingham still managed to become the favorite and chief minister of the new king, Charles I (1625–1649). With Charles I firmly behind him, his accumulation of power and patronage proceeded unabated, as did the enmity he aroused. In 1628, Buckingham was assassinated by a discontented naval officer. While Charles I wept inconsolably at the news, ordinary Londoners drank to the health of Buckingham's killer.

The Drive to Centralize Government

Richelieu, Olivares, and Buckingham met very different ends, but they shared a common goal: to extend the authority of the monarch over his state and to centralize his control over the machinery of governance. One of the chief means by which kings and councilors attempted to expand the authority of the state was through the legal system.

Administering justice was one of the sacred duties of the monarchy. The complexities of ecclesiastical, civil, and customary law gave trained lawyers an essential role in government. As the need for legal services increased, royal law courts multiplied and expanded. In France, the Parlement of Paris, the main law court of the state, became a powerful institution that contested with courtiers for the right to advise the monarch.

In Spain the *letrados*—university-trained lawyers who were normally members of the nobility—were the backbone of royal government. Formal legal training was a requirement for many of the administrative posts in the state. In Castile, members of all social classes frequently used the royal courts to settle personal disputes. The expansion of a centralized system of justice thus joined the interests of subjects and the monarchy.

In England, central courts situated in the royal palace of Westminster grew, and the lawyers and judges who practiced in them became a powerful profession. They were especially active in the House of Commons of the English Parliament, which, along with the House of Lords, had extensive advisory and legislative powers. More important than the rise of the central courts, however, was the rise of the local ones. The English crown extended royal justice to the counties by granting legal authority to members of the local social elite. These justices of the peace, whose position can be traced to medieval times, became agents of the crown in their own localities. Justices were given power to hear and settle minor cases and to imprison people who had committed serious offenses until the assizes, the semiannual sessions of the county court.

Assizes combined the ceremony of rule with its process. Royal authority was displayed in a great procession to the courthouse that was led by the judge and the county justices, followed by the grand and petty juries of local citizens who would hear the cases and finally by the carts carrying the prisoners to trial. Along with the legal business that was performed, assizes were occasions for edifying sermons, typically on the theme of obedience. Their solemnity, marked by the black robes of the judge, the Latin of the legal proceedings, and the public executions, served to instill a sense of the power of the state in the throngs of ordinary people who witnessed them.

Efforts to integrate center and locality extended to more than the exercise of justice. The monarch also needed officials who could enforce royal policy in localities where the special privileges of groups and individuals remained strong. By the beginning of the seventeenth century, the French monarchy had begun to rely on new central officials known as intendants to perform many of the tasks of the provincial governors. Cardinal Richelieu expanded the use of the intendants, and by the middle of the century they had become a vital part of royal government.

The Lords Lieutenant were a parallel institution created in England. Unlike every other European state, England had no national army. Every English county was required to raise, equip, and train its own militia. Lords Lieutenant were in charge of these trained bands. The lieutenants were chosen from the greatest nobles of the realm, but they delegated their work to members of the local gentry, large landholders who took on their tasks as a matter of prestige rather than profit. Perhaps not surprisingly, the English military was among the weakest in Europe, and nearly all its foreign adventures ended in disaster.

Efforts to centralize the Spanish monarchy could not proceed so easily. The separate regions over which the king ruled maintained their own laws and privileges. Attempts to apply Castilian rules or implant Castilian officials always drew opposition from other regions. In 1625, Olivares proposed a plan to help unify Spain and solve the dual problems of military manpower and military finance. After 1621, Spain was fighting in the Netherlands and Germany. Olivares called for a Union of Arms to which all the separate regions of the empire, including Mexico, Peru, Italy, and the dominions in Iberia, would contribute. Olivares was able to establish at least the principle of unified cooperation, but not all of the Iberian provinces were persuaded to contribute. Catalonia stood on its ancient privileges and refused to grant either troops or funds.

The Taxing Demands of War

More than anything else, the consolidation of the state was propelled by war, which required increased governmental powers of taxation. Perhaps half of all revenue of the western states went to finance war. To maintain its military forces, the state had to squeeze every penny from its subjects. Old taxes had to be collected more efficiently, and new taxes had to be introduced and enforced. Such unprecedented demands for money on the part of the state were always resisted. The privileged challenged the legality of levying taxes; the unprivileged tried to avoid paying them.

The economic hardships caused by the ceaseless military activity touched everyone. Those in the direct path of battle had little left to feed themselves, let alone to provide to the state. The disruption of the delicate cycle of planting and harvesting devastated local communities. Armies plundered ripened grain and trampled seedlings as they moved through fields. The conscription of village men and boys removed vital skills and labor from the community. Peasants were squeezed by the armies for crops, by the lords for rents, and by the state for taxes.

In fact, the inability of the lower orders of European society to finance a century of warfare was clear from the beginning. In Spain and France, much wealth was beyond the reach of traditional royal taxation. The nobility and many of the most important towns had long enjoyed exemption from basic taxes on consumption and wealth. European taxation was regressive, falling most heavily on those who were least able to pay. Rulers and subjects alike recognized the inequities of the system, and regime after regime considered overhauling the national tax system but ultimately settled for new emergency levies. Nevertheless, the fiscal crisis that the European wars provoked did result in an expansion of state taxation.

Military spending also increased in England. War with Ireland in the 1590s and with Spain between 1588 and 1604 depleted the reserves that the crown had obtained when Henry VIII dissolved the monasteries. Disastrous wars against France and Spain in the 1620s provoked fiscal crisis for a monarchy that had few direct sources of revenue. While the great wealth of the kingdom was in land, the chief sources of revenue for the crown were in trade. In the early seventeenth century, customs duties became a lucrative source of income when the judges ruled that the king could determine which commodities could be taxed and at what rate.

Because so much of the crown's revenues derived from commerce and because foreign invasion could come only from the sea, the most pressing military need of the English monarchy was for naval defense. Even during the Armada crisis, the largest part of the English fleet had been made up of private merchant ships pressed into service through the emergency tax of Ship Money. This was a tax on each port town to hire a merchant ship and fit it out for war. In the 1630s, Charles I revived Ship Money and extended it to all English localities.

Still, no matter how much new revenue was provided for war finance, more was needed. New taxes and increased rates of traditional taxation created suffering and a sense of grievance throughout the western European states. Opposition to taxation was not based on greed. The state's right to tax was not yet an established principle.

Monarchs received certain forms of revenue in return for grants of immunities and privileges to powerful groups in their state. The state's efforts to go beyond these restricted grants was viewed as theft of private property. In the Ship Money case, challengers argued that the king had no right to such demands except in a case of national emergency. The king argued that such an emergency existed, since pirates were attacking English shipping. But if Charles I did not make a convincing claim for national emergency, the monarchs of France and Spain, the princes of Germany, and the rulers of the states of eastern Europe all did.

Throughout the seventeenth century, monarchy was consolidating its position as a form of government. The king's authority came from God, but his power came from his people. By administering justice, assembling armies, and extracting resources through taxation, the monarch ruled as well as governed. The richer and more powerful the king, the more potent was his state. His subjects began to identify themselves as citizens of a nation and to see themselves in distinction to other nations.

THE CRISES OF THE ROYAL STATE

The expansion of the functions, duties, and powers of the state in the early seventeenth century was not universally welcomed in European societies. The growth of central government came at the expense of local rights and privileges held by organized bodies such as the Church and the towns or by individuals such as provincial officials and aristocrats. The state proved to be a powerful competitor for the meager surplus produced on the land. As rents and prices stabilized in the early seventeenth century, after a long period of inflation, taxation increased, especially with the gathering momentum of the Thirty Years' War. State exactions burdened all segments of society. Peasants lost the small benefit that rising prices had conferred on producers. The surplus that parents had once passed on to children was now taken by the state. Local officials, never altogether popular, came to be seen as parasites and provided easy targets for peasant rebellions. Larger landholders, whose prosperity depended on rents and services from an increasingly impoverished peasantry, suffered along with their tenants. Even the great magnates were appalled by the state's insatiable appetite.

It was not only taxation that aroused opposition. Social and economic regulation meant more laws, more lawyers, and more agents of enforcement. State regulation was disruptive and expensive at a time when the fragile European economy was in decline. The early seventeenth century was a time of hunger in most of western Europe. Subtle changes in climate reduced the length of growing seasons and the size of crops. Bad harvests in the 1620s and 1640s left disease and starvation in their wake. And the wars ground on.

EUROPEAN POPULATION DATA (IN MILLIONS)							
Year	1550	1575	1600	1625	1650	1675	1700
England	3.0	—	4.0	4.5	—	5.8	5.8
France	—	20.0	—	—	—	—	19.3
Italy	11.0	13.0	13.0	13.0	12.0	11.5	12.5
Russia	9.0	—	11.0	8.0	9.5	13.0	16.0
Spain	6.3	—	7.6	—	5.2	—	7.0
All Europe	85.0	95.0	100.0	100.0	80.0	90.0	100.0

By the middle of the seventeenth century, a Europe-wide crisis was taking shape. Bread riots and tax revolts had become increasingly common in the early seventeenth century. As the focus of discontent moved from local institutions to the state, the forms of revolt and the participants also changed. Members of the political elite began to formulate their own grievances against the expansion of state power. A theory of resistance, first developed in the French wars of religion, came to be applied to political tyranny and posed a direct challenge to the idea of the divine right of kings. By the 1640s, all of these forces converged, and rebellion exploded across the Continent. In Spain, the ancient kingdoms of Catalonia and Portugal asserted their independence from Castilian rule; in France, members of the aristocracy rose against a child monarch and his regent. In Italy, revolts rocked Naples and Sicily. In England, a constitutional crisis gave way to civil war and then to the first political revolution in European history.

The Need to Resist

Europeans lived more precariously in the seventeenth century than in any period since the Black Death. One benchmark of crisis was population decline. In the Mediterranean, the Spanish population fell from 8.5 million to 7 million, and the Italian population from 13 million to 11 million. The ravages of the Thirty Years' War were most clearly felt in central Europe. Germany lost nearly one-third of its people; Bohemia lost nearly half. England, the Netherlands, and France were hardest hit in the first half of the century and only gradually recovered by 1700. Population decline had many causes, and direct casualties from warfare were only a very small component. The indirect effects of war—the disruption of agriculture and the spread of disease—were far more devastating. Spain alone lost half a million people at the turn of the century and another half million between 1647 and 1652. Severe outbreaks of plague hit England in 1625 and in 1665, and France endured three consecutive years of epidemics from 1629 to 1631.

All sectors of the European economy from agriculture to trade stagnated or declined in the early seventeenth century, but peasants were hardest hit. The surplus from good harvests did not remain in rural communities to act as a buffer for bad ones. Tens of thousands died during the two great subsistence crises in the late 1620s and the late 1640s.

Acute economic crisis led to rural revolt. As the French peasants reeled from visitations of plague, frost, and floods, the French state was raising the taille, the tax on basic commodities that fell most heavily on the lower orders. A series of French rural revolts in the late 1630s protested tax increases. The *Nu-Pieds* ("barefooted") rose against changes in the salt tax; other peasants rose against new levies on wine. These revolts typically began with the murder of a local tax official, the organization of a peasant militia, and the recruitment of local clergy and notables. The rebels forced temporary concessions from local authorities but never achieved lasting reforms. Each revolt ended with the reimposition of order by the state. In England, the largest rural protests, such as the Midland Revolt of 1607, centered on opposition to the enclosure of grain fields and their conversion to pasture.

The most spectacular popular uprisings occurred in Spanish-occupied Italy. In the spring of 1647, in the Sicilian city of Palermo, violence broke out in the wake of a disastrous harvest, rising food prices, and relentless taxation. As grain prices rose, the city government subsidized the price of bread, running up huge debts in the process. When the town governors could no longer afford the subsidies, they decided to reduce the size of the loaf rather than increase its price. The women of the city rioted when the first undersized loaves were placed on sale, and soon the entire city was in revolt. Commoners who were not part of the urban power structure led the revolt, and for a time they achieved the abolition of Spanish taxes on basic foodstuffs. Their success provided the model for a similar uprising in Naples, the largest city in Europe. The revolt began in 1647 after the Spanish placed a tax on fruit. A crowd gathered in protest, burned the customs house, and murdered several local officials. The rebels again achieved the temporary suspension of Spanish taxation. But neither of the Italian urban revolts could attract support from the local governors or the nobility. Both uprisings were eventually crushed.

The Right to Resist

Rural and urban revolts by members of the lower orders of European society were doomed to failure. Not only did the state control vast military resources, but it could count on the loyalty of the governing classes to suppress local disorder. Only when disgruntled local elites joined the angry peasants did the state face a genuine crisis. Traditionally, aristocratic rebellion was sparked by rival claimants to the throne. By the early seventeenth century, however, hereditary monarchy was too firmly entrenched to be threatened by aristocratic rebellions. When Elizabeth I of England died without an heir, the throne passed to her cousin, James I, without even a murmur of discontent. In France the assassination of Henry IV in 1610 left a child on the throne, yet it provoked little more than intrigue over which aristocratic faction would advise him. The principles of hereditary monarchy and the divine right of kings laid an unshakable foundation for royal legitimacy. But if the monarch's right to rule could no longer be challenged, was the method of rule equally unassailable? Were subjects bound to their sovereign in all cases whatsoever?

Resistance Theory.   Luther and Calvin had preached a doctrine of passive obedience. Magistrates ruled by divine will and must be obeyed in all things, they argued. Both left a tiny crack in the door of absolute submission, however, by recognizing the right of lesser magistrates to resist their superiors if divine law was violated. During the French civil wars, a broader theory of resistance began to develop. In attempting to defend themselves from accusations that they were rebels, a number of Huguenot writers responded with an argument that accepted the divine right of kings but maintained that kings were placed on earth by God to uphold piety and justice. When they failed to do so, lesser magistrates were obliged to resist them. Because God would not institute tyranny, oppressive monarchs could not be acting by divine right. Therefore, the king who violated divine law could be punished. In the most influential of these writings, *A Defense of Liberty Against Tyrants* (1579), Philippe Duplessis-Mornay (1549–1623) took the critical next step and argued that the king who violated the law of the land could also be resisted.

In the writings of both the French Huguenots and the Dutch Protestants there remained strict limits to this right to resist. These authors accepted divine right theory and restricted resistance to other divinely ordained magistrates.

Logic soon drove the argument further. If it was the duty of lesser magistrates to resist monarchical tyranny, why was it not the duty of all citizens to do so? This question was posed by the Jesuit professor Juan de Mariana (1536–1624) in *The King and the Education of the King* (1598). Since magistrates were first established by the people and then legitimated by God, magistrates were nothing other than the people's representatives. If it was the duty of magistrates to resist the tyranny of monarchs, Mariana reasoned, then it must also be the duty of every individual citizen. "If the sacred fatherland is falling into ruins, he who tries to kill the tyrant will be acting in no ways unjustly."

In his defense of the English Revolution, the great English poet John Milton (1608–1674) built on traditional resistance theory. Kings were instituted by the people to uphold piety and justice. Lesser magistrates had the right to resist monarchs. An unjust king forfeited his divine right and was to be punished like any ordinary citizen. In *The Tenure of Kings and Magistrates* (1649), Milton expanded on the conventional idea that society was formed by a covenant, or contract, between ruler and ruled. The king, in his coronation oath, promised to uphold the laws of the land and to rule for the benefit of his subjects. The subjects promised to obey. Failure to meet obligations—by either side—broke the contract.

Resistance and Rebellion.   By the middle of the seventeenth century, resistance theory provided the intellectual justification for a number of attacks on monarchical authority. In 1640, simultaneous rebellions in the ancient kingdoms of Portugal and Catalonia threatened the Spanish monarchy. The Portuguese successfully dissolved the rather artificial bonds that had been created by Philip II and resumed their separate national identity. Catalonia, the easternmost province of Spain, which Ferdinand of Aragon had brought to the union of crowns in the fifteenth century, presented a more serious challenge. Throughout the 1620s, Catalonia, with its rich Mediterranean city of Barcelona, had consistently rebuffed Olivares's attempts to consolidate the Spanish provinces. The Catalan Cortes—the representative institution of the towns—refused to make even small contributions to the Union of Arms or to successive appeals for emergency tax increases. Catalonian leaders feared that these demands were only an entering wedge. They did not want their province to go the way of Castile, where taxation was as much an epidemic as was plague.

Catalonia resisted demands for contributions to the Spanish military effort, but soon the province was embroiled in the French war, and Olivares was forced to bring troops into Catalonia. The presence of the soldiers and their conduct inflamed the local population. In the spring of 1640, an unconnected series of peasant uprisings took place. Soldiers and royal officials were slain, and the Spanish viceroy of the province was murdered. But the violence was not directed only against outsiders. Attacks on wealthy citizens raised the specter of social revolt.

It was at this point that a peasant uprising broadened into a provincial rebellion. The political leaders of Barcelona sanctioned the rebellion and decided to lead it. They declared that Philip IV had violated the fundamental laws of Catalonia and that in consequence their allegiance to the crown of Spain was dissolved. They turned to Louis XIII of France, offering him sovereignty if he would preserve their liberties. In fact, the Catalonians simply exchanged a devil they knew for one they did not. The French happily sent troops into Barcelona to repel a Spanish attempt to crush the rebellion. Now two armies occupied Catalonia. The Catalan rebellion lasted for 12 years. When the Spanish finally took Barcelona in 1652, both rebels and ruler were exhausted from the struggle.

The revolt of the Catalans posed a greater external threat to the Spanish monarchy than it did an internal one. In contrast, the French Fronde, an aristocratic rebellion that began in 1648, was more directly a challenge to the underlying authority of the state. It too began in response to fiscal crises brought on by war. Throughout the 1640s, the French state, tottering on the edge of bankruptcy, had used every means of creative financing that its ministers could devise. Still, it was necessary to raise traditional taxes and to institute new ones. The first tactic revived peasant revolts, especially in the early years of the decade; the second led to the Fronde.

The Fronde was a rebellion against the regency government of Louis XIV (1643–1715), who was only four years old when he inherited the French throne. His mother, Anne of Austria (1601–1666), ruled as regent with the help of her Italian adviser, Cardinal Mazarin (1602–1661). In the circumstances of war, agricultural crisis, and financial stringency, no regency government was going to be popular, but Anne and Mazarin made the worst of a bad situation. They initiated new taxes on officeholders, Parisian landowners, and the nobility. Soon all three groups united against them, led by the Parlement of Paris, the highest court in the land, in which new decrees of taxation had to be registered. When the Parlement refused to register a number of the new taxes proposed by the government and soon insisted on the right to control the crown's financial policy, Anne and Mazarin struck back by having a number of Parlement members arrested. But in 1648, barricades went up in Paris, and the court, along with the nine-year-old king, fled the capital. Quickly, the Fronde—which took its name from the slingshots that children used to hurl stones at carriages—became an aristocratic revolt aimed not at the king but at his advisers. Demands for Mazarin's resignation, the removal of the new taxes, and greater participation in government by nobles and Parlement were coupled with profuse statements of loyalty to the king.

The duc de Condé, leader of the Parisian insurgents, courted Spanish aid against Mazarin's forces, and the cardinal was forced to make concessions to prevent a Spanish invasion of France. The leaders of the Fronde agreed that the crown must overhaul its finances and recognize the rights of the administrative nobility to participate in formulating royal policy. But they had no concrete proposals to accomplish either aim. Nor could they control the deteriorating political situation in Paris and a number of provincial capitals, where urban and rural riots followed the upper-class attack on the state. The catastrophic winter of 1652, with its combination of harvest failure, intense cold, and epidemic disease, brought the crisis to a head. Louis XIV was declared old enough to rule, and his forces recaptured Paris, where he was welcomed as a savior. The Fronde accomplished little other than to demonstrate that the French aristocracy remained an independent force in politics. Like the Catalonian revolt, it revealed the fragility of the absolute state on the one hand, yet its underlying stability on the other.

The English Civil War

The most profound challenge to monarchical authority in the seventeenth century took place in England. In 1603, James I succeeded his cousin Elizabeth I without challenge. He was not a lovable monarch, but he was capable, astute, and generous. His principal difficulties were that he was Scottish and that he succeeded a legend. Elizabeth I had ruled England successfully for over forty years. As the economy soured and the state tilted toward bankruptcy in the 1590s, the queen remained above criticism. She sold off royal lands worth thousands of pounds and ran up huge debts at the turn of the century. Yet the gleaming myth of the glorious virgin queen was not the least bit tarnished, and when she died, the general population wept openly.

At first, James I endeared himself to the English gentry and aristocracy by showering them with the gift of social elevation. On his way to London from Scotland, the first of the Stuart kings knighted thousands of gentlemen. But he showered favor equally on his own countrymen, members of his royal Scottish court who accompanied him to England. A strong strain of ethnic prejudice combined with the disappointed hopes of English courtiers to generate immediate hostility to the new regime. Though he relied on Elizabeth's most trusted ministers to guide state business, James was soon plunged into financial and political difficulties. He never escaped from either.

Charles I. James's financial problems resulted directly from the fact that the tax base of the English monarchy was undervalued. For decades the monarchy had staved off a crisis by selling lands that had been confiscated from the Church in the mid-sixteenth century. But this solution reduced the crown's long-term revenues and made it dependent on extraordinary grants of taxation from Parliament. Royal demands for money were met by parliamentary demands for political reform. The most significant, in 1628, during the reign of Charles I, led to the formulation of the Petition of Right, which restated the traditional English freedoms from arbitrary arrest and imprisonment (habeas corpus), from nonparliamentary taxation, and from the confiscation of property by martial law.

Religious problems mounted on top of economic and political difficulties. Puritans were demanding thoroughgoing church reforms. One of the most contentious issues raised by some Puritans was the survival in the Anglican Church of the Catholic hierarchy of archbishops and bishops. These Puritans demanded the abolition of this episcopal form of government and its replacement with a presbyterial system similar to that in Scotland, in which congregations nominated their own

▼ Charles I by Daniel Myrtens. The antagonism between Charles and Parliament sparked a civil war in England.

representatives to a national assembly. Neither James I nor his son, Charles I, opposed religious reform, but to achieve their reforms, they strengthened episcopal power. In the 1620s, Archbishop William Laud (1573–1645) rose to power in the English church by espousing a Calvinism so moderate that many denied it was Calvinism at all. Laud preached the beauty of holiness and strove to reintroduce decoration in the church and a formal decorum in the service. One of Laud's first projects after he was appointed archbishop of Canterbury was to establish a consistent divine service in England and Scotland by creating new prayer books.

It fell to the unfortunate dean of St. Giles Cathedral in Edinburgh to introduce the new Scottish prayer book in 1637. The reaction was immediate: someone threw a stool at his head, and dozens of women screamed that "popery" was being brought to Scotland. Citizens rioted, and the clergy and the nobility resisted the use of the new prayer book. To Charles I the opposition was rebellion, and he began to raise forces to suppress it. But the Scots fought back, and by the end of 1640 an army of Charles's Scottish subjects had successfully invaded England.

Now the fiscal and political problems of the Stuart monarchs came into play. For 11 years, Charles I had managed to live from his own revenues. He had accomplished this by a combination of economy and the revival of ancient feudal rights that struck hard at the governing classes. He levied fines for unheard-of offenses, expanded traditional taxes, and added a brutal efficiency to the collection of revenue. While these expedients sufficed during peacetime, they could not support an army and war. Charles I was again dependent on grants from Parliament, which he reluctantly summoned in 1640.

The Long Parliament. The Long Parliament, which met in November 1640 and sat for thirteen years, saw little urgency in levying taxes to repel the Scots. After all, the Scots were resisting Laud's religious innovations, and many Englishmen agreed that they should be resisted. Parliament proposed a number of constitutional reforms that Charles I reluctantly accepted. The Long Parliament would not be dismissed without its own consent. In the future, Parliaments would be summoned once in every three years. Due process in common law would be observed, and the ancient taxes that the crown had revived would be abolished.

At first, Charles I could do nothing but bide his time and accept these assaults on his power and authority. Once he had crushed the Scots, he would be able to bargain from a position of strength. But as the months passed, it became clear that Parliament had no intention of providing him with money or forces. By the end of 1641, Charles's patience had worn thin. He bungled an attempt to arrest the leaders of the House of Commons, but he successfully spirited his wife and children out of London.

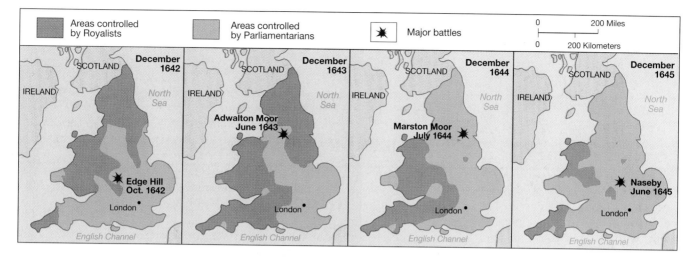

▲ The English Civil War. The maps show the gradual triumph of the parliamentarians whose control of London and the coastal areas gave them a profound logistical advantage during the wars.

Then he too left the capital and headed north, where, in the summer of 1642, he raised the royal standard and declared the leaders of Parliament rebels and traitors. England was plunged into civil war.

There were strong passions on both sides. Parliamentarians believed that they were fighting to defend their religion, their liberties, and the rule of law. Royalists believed that they were fighting to defend their monarch, their church, and social stability. After nearly three years of inconclusive fighting, Parliament won a decisive victory at Naseby in June 1645 and brought the war to an end the following summer. The king was in captivity, bishops had been abolished, a Presbyterian church had been established, and limitations were placed on royal power. All that was necessary to end three years of civil war was the king's agreement to abide by the judgment of battle.

But Charles I had no intention of surrendering either his religion or his authority. Despite the rebels' successes, they could not rule without him, and he would concede nothing as long as opportunities to maneuver remained. In 1647 there were opportunities galore. The war had proved ruinously expensive to Parliament. It owed enormous sums to the Scots, to its own soldiers, and to the governors of London. Each of these elements had its own objectives in a final settlement of the war, and they were not altogether compatible. London feared the parliamentary army, unpaid and camped dangerously close to the capital. The Scots and the English Presbyterians in Parliament feared that the religious settlement that had already been made would be sacrificed by those known as Independents, who desired a more decentralized church. The Independents feared that they would be persecuted just as harshly by the Presbyterians as they had been by the king. In fact, the war had settled nothing.

The English Revolutions

Charles I happily played both ends against the middle until the army decisively ended the game. In June 1647, parliamentary soldiers kidnapped the king and demanded that Parliament pay their arrears, protect them from legal retribution, and recognize their service to the nation. Those in Parliament who opposed the army's intervention were impeached, and when London Presbyterians rose up against the army's show of force, troops moved in to occupy the city. The civil war, which had come so close to resolution in 1647, had now become a military revolution. Religious and political radicals flocked to the army and encouraged the soldiers to support their programs and to resist disbandment. New fighting broke out in 1648, as Charles encouraged his supporters to resume the war. But forces under the command of Sir Thomas Fairfax (1612–1671) and Oliver Cromwell (1599–1658) easily crushed the royalist uprisings in England and Scotland. The army now demanded that Charles I be brought to justice for his treacherous conduct both before and during the war. When the majority in Parliament refused, still hoping to reach an accommodation with the king, the soldiers again acted decisively. In December 1648, army regiments were sent to London to purge the two houses of Parliament of those who opposed the army's demands. The remaining members, contemptuously called the Rump Parliament, voted to bring the king to trial for his crimes against the liberties of his subjects. On 30 January 1649, Charles I was executed, and England was declared to be a commonwealth. The monarchy and the House of Lords were abolished, and the nation was to be governed by what was left of the membership of the House of Commons.

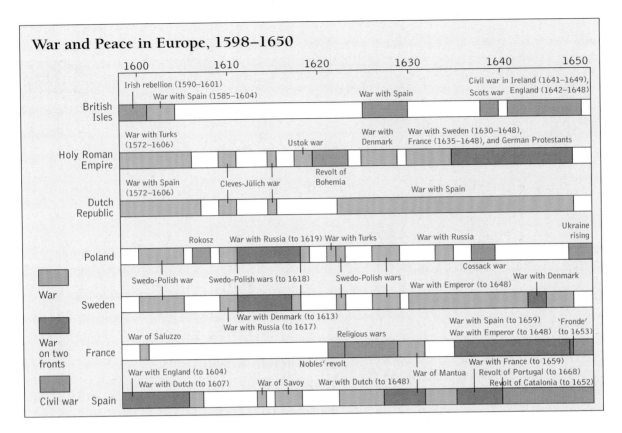

War and Peace in Europe, 1598–1650

Oliver Cromwell. For four years, the members of the Rump Parliament struggled with proposals for a new constitution, achieving little. In 1653, Oliver Cromwell, with the support of the army's senior officers, forcibly dissolved the Rump and became the leader of the revolutionary government. At first he ruled along with a Parliament that had been handpicked from among the supporters of the commonwealth. When Cromwell's Parliament proved no more capable of governing than had the Rump, a written constitution, The Instrument of Government (1653), established a new polity. Cromwell was given the title Lord Protector, and he was to rule along with a freely elected Parliament and an administrative body known as the council of state.

Cromwell was able to smooth over conflicts and hold the revolutionary cause together through the force of his own personality. He was a devout Puritan who had opposed the arbitrary policies of Charles I and who believed in a large measure of religious toleration for Christians. Though many urged him to accept the crown of England and begin a new monarchy, Cromwell steadfastly held out for a government in which fundamental authority resided in Parliament. Until his death he defended the achievements of the revolution.

But a sense that only a single person could effectively rule a state remained strong. When Cromwell died in 1658, his oldest son Richard was proposed as the new Lord Protector, but Richard had very little experience in either military or civil affairs. Nor did he have the sense of purpose that was

his father's greatest source of strength. Without an individual to hold the movement together, the revolution fell apart. In 1659, the army again intervened in civil affairs, dismissing the recently elected Parliament and calling for the restoration of the monarchy. After a period of negotiation in which the king agreed to a general amnesty with only a few exceptions, the Stuarts were restored when Charles II (1649–1685) took the throne in 1660.

Twenty years of civil war and revolution had their effect. Parliament became a permanent part of civil government. Royal power over taxation and religion was curtailed, though in fact Parliament proved more vigorous in suppressing religious dissent than the monarchy ever was. England was to be a reformed Protestant state, though there remained much dispute about what constituted reform. Absolute monarchy had become constitutional monarchy with the threat of revolution behind the power of Parliament and the threat of anarchy behind the power of the Crown.

The "Glorious Revolution." The threats of revolution and of anarchy proved potent in 1685 when James II (1685–1688) came to the throne. A declared Catholic, James attempted to use his power of appointment to foil the constraints that Parliament imposed on him. He elevated Catholics to leading posts in the military and in the central government and began a campaign to pack a new Parliament with his supporters. This proved to be too much for the governing classes, which entered into negotiations with William, Prince of Orange, who was the husband of Mary Stuart, James's eldest daughter. In 1688, William landed in England with a small force. Without support, James II fled to France, the English throne was declared vacant, and William and Mary were proclaimed king and queen of England. There was little bloodshed and little threat of social disorder, and the event soon came to be called the Glorious Revolution. Its achievements were set down in the Declaration of Rights (1689), which was presented to William and Mary before they took the throne. The Declaration reasserted the fundamental principles of constitutional monarchy as they had developed over the previous half-century. Security of property and the regularity of Parliaments were guaranteed. The Toleration Act (1689) granted religious freedom to nearly all groups of Protestants. The liberties of the subject and the rights of the sovereign were to be in balance.

The events of 1688 in England reversed a trend toward increasing power on the part of the Stuarts. This second episode of resistance resulted in the development of a unique form of government, which, a century later, spawned dozens of imitators. John Locke (1632–1704) was the theorist of the Revolution of 1688. He was heir to the century-old debate on resistance, and he carried the doctrine to a new plateau. In *Two Treatises on Government* (1689), Locke developed the contract theory of government. Political society was a compact that individuals entered into freely for their own well-being. It was designed to maintain each person's natural rights: life, liberty, and property. Natural rights were inherent in individuals; they could not be given away. The contract between rulers and subjects was an agreement for the protection of natural rights. When rulers acted arbitrarily, they were to be deposed by their subjects, preferably in the relatively peaceful manner in which James II had been replaced by William III.

The efforts of European monarchies to centralize their power came at the expense of the Church, the aristocracy, and the localities. It was a difficult struggle that took place over decades. In France, the Fronde was an aristocratic backlash; in Spain, the revolt of the Catalans pitted the Castilian crown against a proud ethnic province. In England, the excesses of monarchy were succeeded by the excesses of parliamentary rule. But the lesson that the English ruling elites learned was that for a nation to enjoy the benefits of a powerful central authority, it was necessary to restrain that authority. The Revolution of 1688 helped to create a constitutional balance between ruler and ruled.

THE ZENITH OF THE ROYAL STATE

The midcentury crises tested the mettle of the royal states. Over the long term, the seventeenth-century crises had two different consequences. First, they provided a check to

the exercise of royal power. Fear of recurring rebellions had a chilling effect on policy, especially taxation. Reforms of financial administration, long overdue, were one of the themes of the later seventeenth century. Even as royal government strengthened itself, it remained concerned about the impact of its policies. The memory of rebellion also served to control the ambitions of factious noblemen and town oligarchies.

If nothing else, these episodes of opposition to the rising royal states made clear the universal desire for stable government, which was seen as the responsibility of both subjects and rulers. By the second half of the seventeenth century, effective government was the byword of the royal state. The natural advantages of monarchy had to be merged with the interests of the citizens of the state and their desires for wealth, safety, and honor. After so much chaos and instability the monarchy had to be elevated above the fray of day-to-day politics to become a symbol of the nation's power and glory.

In England, Holland, and Sweden a form of constitutional monarchy developed in which rulers shared power, in varying degrees, with other institutions of state. In England it was Parliament, in Holland the town oligarchies, and in Sweden the nobility. But in most other states in Europe there developed a pure form of royal government known as absolutism. Absolute monarchy revived the divine right theories of kingship and added to them a cult of the personality of the ruler. Absolutism was practiced in states as dissimilar as Denmark, Brandenburg-Prussia, and Russia. It reached its zenith in France under Louis XIV, the most powerful of the seventeenth-century monarchs.

The Nature of Absolute Monarchy

Locke's theory of contract provided one solution to the central problem of seventeenth-century government: how to balance the monarch's right to command and the subjects' duty to obey. By establishing a constitutional monarchy, in which power was shared between the ruler and a representative assembly of subjects, England found one path out of this thicket. But it was not a path that many others could follow.

The English solution was most suited to a state that was largely immune from invasion and land war. Constitutional government required a higher level of political participation of citizens than did absolute monarchy. Greater participation meant greater freedom of expression, greater toleration of religious minorities, and greater openness in the institutions of government. All were dangerous. The price that England paid was a half-century of governmental instability.

The alternative to constitutional monarchy was absolute monarchy. It, too, found its leading theorist in England. Thomas Hobbes (1588–1679), in his greatest work, *Leviathan* (1651), argued that before civil society had been formed, humans had lived in a savage state of nature, "in a war of every man against every man." This was a ghastly condition without morality or law. People came together to form a government for the most basic of all purposes: self-preservation. Without government they were condemned to a life that was "solitary, poor, nasty, brutish, and short." To escape the state of nature, individuals pooled their power and granted it to a ruler. The terms of the Hobbesian contract were simple. Rulers agreed to rule; subjects agreed to obey. When the contract was intact, people ceased to live in a state of nature. When it was broken, they returned to it. With revolts, rebellions, and revolutions erupting in all parts of Europe, Hobbes's state of nature never seemed very far away.

For most states of Europe in the later seventeenth century, absolute monarchy became not only a necessity but an ideal. The consolidation of power in the hands of the divinely ordained monarch, who, nevertheless, ruled according to principles of law and justice, was seen as the perfect form of government.

The main features of absolute monarchy were all designed to extend royal control. As in the early seventeenth century, the person of the monarch was revered. Courts grew larger and more lavish in an effort to enhance the glory of the monarchy and thereby of the state. "L'état, c'est moi" ("I am the state"), Louis XIV was supposed to have said. As the king grew in stature, his competitors for power all shrank. Large numbers of nobles were herded together at court under the watchful eye of monarchs who now ruled rather than reigned. The king shed the cloak of his favorites and rolled up his own sleeves to manage state affairs. Representative institutions were weakened or cast aside. Monarchs needed standing armies trained in the increasingly sophisticated arts of war, so the military was expanded and made an integral part of the machinery of government. The military profession developed within nations, gradually replacing mercenary adventurers who fought for booty rather than for duty.

Yet the absolute state was never as powerful in practice as it was in theory. Nor did it ever exist in its ideal shape. Absolutism was always in the making, never quite made. Its success depended on a strong monarch who knew his own will and could enforce it. It depended on unity within the state, on the absence or ruthless suppression of religious or political minorities. The absolute ruler needed to control information and ideas to limit criticism of state policy. Ultimately, the absolute state rested on the will of its citizens to support it. The seventeenth-century state remained a loose confederation of regions, many acquired by conquest, whose loyalty was practical rather than instinctive. There was no state police to control behavior or attitudes, no newspapers or mass communication to spread propaganda. Censorship might restrict the flow of forbidden books, but it could do little to dam up the current of ideas.

Absolutism in the East

Frederick William, the Great Elector of Brandenburg-Prussia (1640–1688), made highly effective use of the techniques of absolutism. In 1640, he inherited a scattered and ungovernable collection of territories. The nobility, known as *die Junker*, enjoyed immunity from almost all forms of direct taxation, and the towns had no obligation to furnish either men or supplies for military operations beyond their walls.

When Frederick William attempted to introduce an excise—the commodity tax on consumption that had so successfully financed the Dutch Revolt and the English Revolution—he was initially rebuffed. But military emergency overcame legal precedents. By the 1650s, Frederick William had established the excise in the towns, though not in the countryside.

With the excise as a steady source of revenue, the Great Elector set about forming one of the most capable and best disciplined standing armies of the age. He organized one of the first departments of war to oversee all of the details of the creation of his army, from housing and supplies to the training of young officer candidates. This department was also responsible for the collection of taxes. By integrating military and civilian government, Frederick William established an efficient state bureaucracy that was particularly responsive in times of crisis. The creation of the Prussian army was the force that led to the creation of the Prussian state.

The same materials that forged the Prussian state led to the transformation of Russia. Soon after the young Tsar Peter I, known later as "the Great" (1682–1725), came to the throne, he realized that he could compete with the western states only by learning to play their game.

Like Frederick William, Peter concentrated on military reform. He understood that if Russia was to flourish in a world dominated by war and commerce, it would have to reestablish its hold on the Baltic ports. This meant dislodging the Swedes from the Russian mainland and creating a fleet to protect Russian trade. Neither goal seemed likely. The Swedes were one of the great powers of the age, constant innovators in battlefield tactics and military organization. Peter studied their every campaign. His first wars against the Swedes ended in humiliating defeats, but with each failure came a sharper sense of what was needed to succeed.

First Peter introduced a system of conscription and created a standing army. He unified the military command at the top and stratified it in the field. He established promotion based on merit and established military schools to train cadets for the next generation of officers.

Finally, in 1709, Peter realized his ambitions. At the battle of Poltava the Russian army routed the Swedes, wounding King Charles XII, annihilating his infantry, and capturing dozens of his leading officers. After the battle of

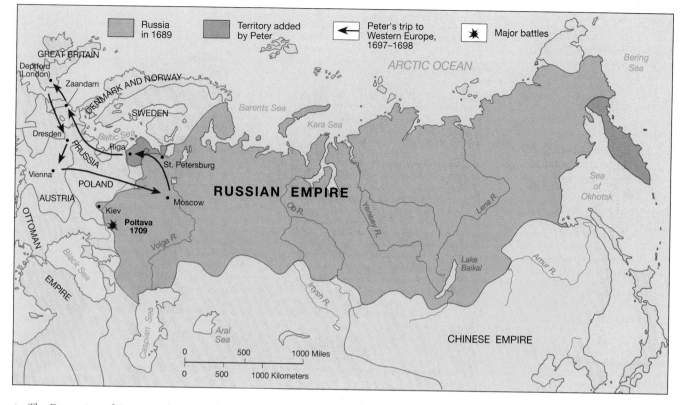

▲ The Expansion of Russia under Peter the Great. Peter added vital territory on the Baltic Sea to the vast Russian empire.

Poltava, Russia gradually replaced Sweden as the dominant power in the Baltic.

As an absolute ruler, Peter the Great's power was unlimited, but it was not uncontested. He secularized the Russian Orthodox church, subjecting it to state control and confiscating much of its wealth. He broke the old military service class, which attempted a coup d'état when he was abroad in the 1690s. By the end of his reign, the Russian monarchy was among the strongest in Europe.

The Origins of French Absolutism

Nowhere was absolutism as successfully implanted as in France. Louis XIII (1610–1643) was only eight years old when he came to the throne, and he grew slowly into his role under the tutelage of Cardinal Richelieu. It was Richelieu's vision that stabilized French government. As chief minister, Richelieu saw clearly that France's survival and prosperity depended on strengthening royal power. He preached a doctrine of *raison d'état* ("reason of state"), in which he placed the needs of the nation above the privileges of its most important groups. Richelieu saw three threats to stable royal government: the Huguenots, the nobles, and the most powerful provincial governors.

Richelieu took measures to control all three. The power of the nobles was the most difficult to attack. The nobles' long tradition of independence from the crown had been enhanced by the wars of religion. The ancient aristocracy, the nobility of the sword, felt themselves to be in a particularly vulnerable position. Their world was changing, and their traditional roles were becoming obsolete. Professional soldiers replaced them at war, professional administrators at government. Mercantile wealth threatened their economic superiority, and the growth of the nobility of the robe—lawyers and state officials—threatened their social standing. They were hardly likely to take orders from a royal minister such as Richelieu.

To limit the power of local officials, Richelieu used intendants to examine their conduct and to reform their administration. He made careful appointments of local governors and brought more regions under direct royal control. Against the Calvinists, who were called Huguenots in France, Richelieu's policy was more subtle. He was less interested in challenging their religion than their autonomy. In 1627, when the English sent a force to aid the Huguenots against the government, Richelieu and Louis XIII abolished the Huguenots' privileges altogether. They were allowed to maintain their religion but not

▶ Anne of Austria acted as a regent during her son's minority, though in practice she delegated most power to her adviser Cardinal Mazarin. This painting emphasizes the piety of the royal family, as Anne, Louis, and his younger brother Philippe kneel in prayer against a backdrop of God, Jesus, and their heavenly and worldly servants.

their special status. Finally, in 1685, Louis XIV revoked the Edict of Nantes, which had guaranteed civil and religious rights to the Huguenots. All forms of Protestant worship were outlawed, and the ministers who were not hunted down and killed were forced into exile. Despite a ban on Protestant emigration, over 200,000 Huguenots fled the country, many of them carrying irreplaceable skills with them to Holland and England in the west and to Brandenburg in the east.

Richelieu's program was a vital prelude to the development of absolute monarchy in France. The cardinal did not act without the full support of Louis XIII, but there can be no doubt that Richelieu was the power behind the throne. Louis XIII hated the business of government and even neglected his principal responsibility of providing the state with an heir. For years, he and his wife slept in separate palaces, and only a freak rainstorm in Paris forced him to spend a night with the queen, Anne of Austria, in 1637. It was the night of the conception of Louis XIV. Louis XIII and Richelieu died within six months of each other in 1642–1643, and the nation again endured the turmoil of a child king.

Louis le Grand

Not quite five years old when he came to the throne, Louis XIV was tutored by Cardinal Jules Mazarin (1602–1661),

Richelieu's successor as chief minister. Mazarin was more ruthless and less popular than his predecessor, but like Richelieu, he was an excellent administrator.

The King and His Ministers. In order to pacify the rebellious nobility of the Fronde, who opposed Mazarin's power, Louis XIV was declared to have reached his majority at the age of 13. But it was not until Mazarin died ten years later, in 1661, that the king began to rule.

Louis was blessed with able and energetic ministers. The two central props of his state—money and might—were in the hands of dynamic men, Jean-Baptiste Colbert (1619–1683) and the Marquis de Louvois (1639–1691). Colbert, to whom credit belongs for the building of the French navy, the reform of French legal codes, and the establishment of national academies of culture, was Louis's chief minister for finance. Colbert's fiscal reforms were so successful that in less than six years a debt of 22 million French pounds had become a surplus of 29 million. Colbert achieved this astonishing feat not by raising taxes but by increasing the efficiency of their collection. Until Louis embarked on his wars, the French state was solvent.

To Louvois, Louis's minister of war, fell the task of reforming the French army. During the Fronde, royal troops were barely capable of defeating the makeshift forces of the nobility. By the end of the reign, the army had grown to 400,000, and its organization had been thoroughly reformed.

Louis XIV furthered the practice of relying on professional administrators to supervise the main departments of state and to offer advice on matters of policy. He built on the institution of the intendant that Richelieu had developed with so much success. Intendants were now a permanent part of government, and their duties expanded from their early responsibilities as coordinators and mediators into areas of policing and tax collection. It was through the intendants that the wishes of central government were made known in the provinces.

The Court of Versailles. Though Louis XIV was well served, it was the king himself who set the tone for French absolutism. "If he was not the greatest king he was the best actor of majesty that ever filled the throne," wrote an English observer. The acting of majesty was central to Louis's rule. His residence at Versailles was the most glittering court of Europe. When the court and king moved there permanently in 1682, Versailles became the envy of the Continent. But behind the imposing facade of Versailles stood a well-thought-out plan for domestic and international rule.

Louis XIV attempted to tame the French nobles by requiring their attendance at his court. Louis established a system of court etiquette so complex that constant study was necessary to prevent humiliation. While the nobility studied decorum, they could not plot rebellion. Leading noblemen of France rose at dawn so that they could watch Louis be awakened and hear him speak his first words. Dozens followed him from hall to gallery and from gallery to chamber as he washed, dressed, prayed, and ate. There was no greater concern than the king's health, unless it was the king's mood, which was as changeable as the weather.

During Louis's reign, France replaced Spain as the greatest nation in Europe. Massive royal patronage of art, science, and thought brought French culture to new heights. The French language replaced Latin as the universal European tongue. France was the richest and most populous European state, and Louis's absolute rule finally harnessed these resources to a single purpose. France became a commercial power rivaling the Netherlands, a naval power rivaling England, and a military power without peer. It was not only for effect that Louis took the image of the sun as his own. In court, in the nation, and throughout Europe, everything revolved around him.

Louis XIV made his share of mistakes. His aggressive foreign policy ultimately bankrupted the crown. But without doubt, his greatest error was to persecute the Huguenots. As an absolute ruler, Louis regarded the Huguenots, with their separate communities and distinct forms of worship, as an affront to his authority. Supporters of the monarchy celebrated the revocation of the Edict of Nantes in 1685 as an act of piety. But the persecution of the Huguenots was a social and political disaster for France. The Huguenots who fled to other Protestant states spread stories of atrocities that stiffened European resolve against Louis. Those who remained became an embittered minority who pulled at the fabric of the state at every chance. Nor did the official abolition of Protestantism have much effect on its existence. Against these policies the Huguenots held firmly to their beliefs. There were well over one million French Protestants, undoubtedly the largest religious minority in any state. Huguenots simply went underground, practicing their religion secretly and gradually replacing their numbers. No absolutism, however powerful, could succeed in eradicating religious beliefs.

▼ This Hyacinthe Rigaud portrait of Louis XIV in his coronation robes shows the splendor of *Le Roi Soleil* (the Sun King), who believed himself to be the center of France as the sun is the center of the solar system.

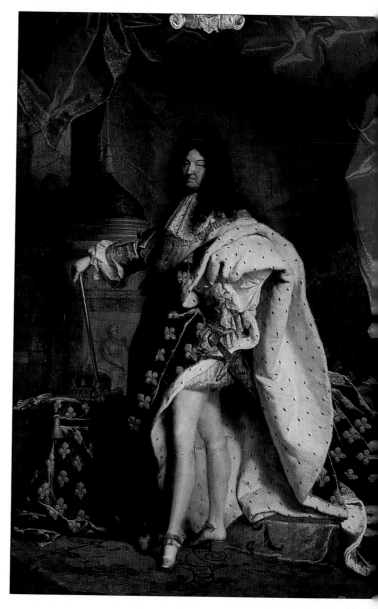

Conclusion

LOUIS XIV GAVE HIS NAME TO THE AGE THAT HE AND HIS NATION DOMINATED, but he was not its only towering figure. The Great Elector, Peter the Great, Louis the Great—so they were judged by posterity—all had forged nations for a new age. Their style of rule showed the royal state at its height, still revolving around the king but more and more dependent on permanent institutions of government that followed their own imperatives. The absolute state harnessed the economic and intellectual resources of the nation to the political will of the monarch, who ruled by incorporating vital elements of the state into the process of government. In England, the importance of the landholding classes was recognized in the constitutional powers of Parliament. The rights of the monarch were balanced against the liberties of the subject. In Prussia, the military power of the Junker was asserted through command in the army, the most important institution of the state. In France, Louis XIV co-opted many nobles at his court, while he made use of a talented pool of lawyers, clergymen, and administrators in his government. A delicate balance existed between the will of the king and the will of the state, a balance that would soon lead these Continental powers into economic competition and military confrontation.

QUESTIONS FOR REVIEW

1. How did war in the seventeenth century contribute to the creation of more powerful monarchical states?
2. What religious and political ideas were developed to justify resistance to monarchical authority?
3. What political and religious problems combined to bring England to civil war, and what results did the conflict produce in English government?
4. How did rulers such as Frederick William of Brandenburg, Peter the Great, or Louis XIV, and theorists such as Hobbes, justify absolute monarchical power?

DISCOVERING WESTERN CIVILIZATION ONLINE

You can obtain more information about the royal state in the seventeenth century at the websites listed below. See also the companion website that accompanies this text: www.ablongman.com/kishlansky, which contains an online study guide and additional resources.

The Crises of the Royal State

www.fordham.edu/halsall/mod/modsbook06.html
Links to sources relating to the reign of Charles I and the revolution against him.

www.baylor.edu/BIC/WCIII/Essays/charles.1.html
Excerpts from primary sources describing the execution of Charles I.

www.thegloriousrevolution.com
A site with links all relating to the Revolution of 1688 in England.

The Zenith of the Royal State

www.kipar.org/
A site on the Golden Age of France in the seventeenth century but with extensive links to English and Dutch materials on a variety of subjects.

www.bc.edu/bc_org/avp/cas/fnart/arch/versailles.html
Views of the gardens and rooms inside the palace with special emphasis on architecture.

www.loc.gov/exhibits/bnf/bnf0005.html
The Library of Congress's exhibition on the Age of Absolutism shows manuscripts, medals, and portraits of leading figures at the French court.

SUGGESTIONS FOR FURTHER READING

General Reading

Euan Cameron, ed., *Early Modern Europe: An Oxford History* (Oxford; New York: Oxford University Press, 1999). Up-to-date essays by leading historians with well-chosen topics and illustrations.

William Doyle, *The Old European Order* (Oxford: Oxford University Press, 1978). An important synthetic essay, bristling with ideas.

Thomas Munck, *Seventeenth Century Europe, 1598–1700* (New York: St. Martin's Press, 1990). The most up-to-date survey.

The Rise of the Royal State

Yves-Marie Bercé, *The Birth of Absolutism* (London: Macmillan, 1996). A history of France from the reign of Louis XIV to the eve of the Revolution by a leading historian of France.

J. H. Elliott, *Richelieu and Olivares* (Cambridge: Cambridge University Press, 1984). A brilliant dual portrait.

J. H. Elliott and Jonathan Brown, *A Palace for a King* (New Haven, Conn.: Yale University Press, 1980). An outstanding work on the building and decorating of a Spanish palace.

The Crises of the Royal State

Trevor Aston, ed., *Crisis in Europe, 1600–1660* (Garden City, N.Y.: Doubleday, 1967). Essays on the theme of a general crisis in Europe by distinguished historians.

Jonathan Israel, ed., *The Anglo-Dutch Moment* (Cambridge: Cambridge University Press, 1991). Essays by an international team of scholars on the European dimensions of the Revolution of 1688.

M. A. Kishlansky, *A Monarchy Transformed* (London: Penguin Books, 1996). The most recent survey of a remarkable era.

Quentin Skinner, *The Foundations of Modern Political Thought*, 2 vols. (Cambridge: Cambridge University Press, 1978). A seminal work on the history of ideas from Machiavelli to Calvin.

Lawrence Stone, *The Causes of the English Revolution* (New York: Harper & Row, 1972). A vigorously argued explanation of why England experienced a revolution in the mid-seventeenth century.

The Zenith of the Royal State

William Beik, *Louis XIV and Absolutism: A Brief Study with Documents* (Boston: Bedford/St. Martin's, 2000). A useful short history and selection of documents by a leading historian of French absolutism.

Joseph Bergin, *The Rise of Richelieu* (New Haven, Conn.: Yale University Press, 1991). A fascinating portrait of a consummate politician.

Claire Constans, *Versailles, Absolutism and Harmony* (New York: Vendome Press, 1998). A richly illustrated architectural history of the center and symbol of French absolutism.

Paul Dukes, *The Making of Russian Absolutism* (London: Longman, 1982). A thorough survey of Russian history in the seventeenth and eighteenth centuries.

H. W. Koch, *A History of Prussia* (London: Longman, 1978). A comprehensive study of Prussian history, with an excellent chapter on the Great Elector.

Geoffrey Parker, *The Military Revolution* (Cambridge: Cambridge University Press, 1988). A lucid discussion of how power was organized and deployed in the early modern state.

David Sturdy, *Louis XIV* (London: Macmillan, 1998). A concise survey of the reign organized topically.

CREDITS

DOCUMENT CREDITS

Chapter 1: "The Code of Hammurabi": From Pritchard, James B. *The Ancient Near East Anthology of Texts and Pictures.* Copyright © 1958 by Princeton University Press. **Chapter 2:** "Hector and Andromache": From *The Iliad of Homer,* translated by Richmond Lattimore. Copyright © 1951 by the University of Chicago. Reprinted by permission of the University of Chicago Press. **Chapter 3:** "The Two Faces of Athenian Democracy": Excerpts from Thucydides, *History of the Peloponnesian War,* translated by Rex Warner. **Chapter 4:** "Polybius Describes the Sack of New Carthage": From Polybius, *Rise of the Roman Empire,* translated by Ian Scot-Kilvert. **Chapter 5:** "The Reforms of Tiberius Gracchus": From *Roman Civilization,* Volume 1, by Naphtali Lewis and Meyer Reinhold. Copyright © 1951 Columbia University Press. Reprinted by permission of the publisher. **Chapter 6:** "Tacitus on the Germans": From Tacitus, *Germany.* **Chapter 7:** "The Justinian Code": Excerpts from *Justinian: The Digest of Roman Law,* translated by C. F. Kolbert (Penguin Classics, 1979). Copyright © C. F. Kolbert, 1979. Reproduced by permission of Penguin Books Ltd. **Chapter 8:** "From Slave To Queen": From *Sacred Women of the Dark Ages* by Jo Ann McNamara, John E. Halborg, and George Whatley. Copyright © 1992 Duke University Press. All rights reserved. Used by permission of the publisher. **Chapter 9:** "Pope Urban II Summons a Crusade": From *The First Crusade,* edited by Edward Peters. Copyright © 1971 University of Pennsylvania Press. **Chapter 10:** "Convivencia": Excerpt from *Las Siete Partidas,* translated by Samuel Parson Scott. Chicago: Published for the Comparative Law Bureau of the American Bar Association by Commerce Clearing House, Inc. © 1931. All rights reserved. Reprinted with permission. **Chapter 11:** "On The Family": From Leon Battista Alberti, "On the Family" in *The Family in Renaissance Florence* by Renee Watkins. Reprinted by permission of Renee Watkins. **Chapter 12:** "The Halls of Montezuma": From Bernal Diaz, *The True History of the Conquest of New Spain,* in *The Bernal Diaz Chronicles,* translated and edited by Albert Idell, pp. 169–171. **Chapter 13:** "The Eternal Decree": From John Calvin, *Institutes of the Christian Religion,* in *John Calvin, Selections from His Writings,* edited and with an introduction by John Dillenberger. **Chapter 14:** "War Is Hell": From Hans Jacob Christoph von Grimmelhausen, in *The Adventurous Simplicissimus,* translated by A. T. S. Goodrick, 1912. **Chapter 15:** "The Devil's Due": From "Medieval Witchcraft," from *Translations and Reprints from the Original Sources of European History, Volume III,* published for the Department of History of the University of Pennsylvania, Phildelphia. **Chapter 16:** "A Glimpse of a King": From *Memoirs of the Duke of Saint-Simon,* translated by Bayle St. John. (London: Swan Sonnonschein & Co., 1900).

PHOTO CREDITS

Unless otherwise acknowledged, all photographs are the property of Pearson Education, Inc. Page abbreviations are as follows: (T) top, (B) bottom, (L) left, (R) right.

Prints appearing on the following pages were hand-colored for Pearson Education, Inc., by Cheryl Kucharzak: 263, 265, 373, 467.

Introduction: 3 European Space Agency/Science Photo/Photo Researchers, Inc. **Chapter 1: 5** Augustin Ochsenreiter/South Tyrol Museum of Archaeology; **7** Kazuyoshi Nomachi/Pacific Press Service; **12** © British Museum; **17** The Metropolitan Museum of Art, Rogers Fund, 1931, (31.3.157) Photograph © 1983 The Metropolitan Museum of Art; **22** Erich Lessing/Art Resource, NY **Chapter 2: 27** William Francis Warden Fund. Courtesy, The Museum of Fine Arts, Boston (63.473); **30** Nimitallah/Art Resource, NY; **31** Hirmer Fotoarchiv, Munich; **35** Scala/Art Resource, NY; **38** Hirmer Fotoarchiv, Munich; **41** Lee Boltin Picture Library **Chapter 3: 47 (T)** Scala/Art Resource, NY; **(B)** Scala/Art Resource, NY; **51** Metropolitan Museum of Art, Fletcher Fund, 1931; **55** Alinari/Art Resource, NY; **59** Scala/Art Resource, NY; **64** Giraudon/Art Resource, NY **Chapter 4: 69** A. De Gregorio/Instituto Geographico De Agostini, Milan; **73** Hirmer Fotoarchiv, Munich; **81** Giraudon/Art Resource, NY; **83** Scala/Art Resource, NY **Chapter 5: 87 (B)** Nimatallah/Art Resource, NY; **(T)** Scala/Art Resource, NY; **88** Romische-Germanisches Zentralmuseum Mainz; **96** Erich Lessing/Art Resource, NY; **101** Catacomb of Priscilla/Benedettine di Priscilla/Pontificia Commissione de Archeologia Sacra **Chapter 6: 111** © British Museum; **113** Erich Lessing/Art Resource, NY; **118** Andre Held; **123** Réunion Des Musées Nationaux/Art Resource, NY **Chapter 7: 129** © SuperStock, Inc.; **130** Scala/Art Resource, NY; **136** Monastery of St. Catherine, Mt. Sinai, Egypt/Bridgeman Art Library; **143** Istanbul University Library **Chapter 8: 151** © Domkapitel Aachen, Foto: Ann Münchow; **152** Fototeca Unione, American Academy, Rome/Bridgeman Art Library; **160** Giraudon/Art Resource, NY; **166** Universitetets Oldskasamling, Oslo **Chapter 9: 173** Erich Lessing/Art Resource, NY; **177** By permission of the British Library (MS Harl. 4431. fol. 376); **183** By permission of the British Library (MS ROY 15 E III, fol. 269r); **184** © bpk, Berlin; **186** Scala/Art Resource, NY **Chapter 10: 195** Erich Lessing/Art Resource, NY; **201** Lambeth Palace Library (MS.6,f.43); **204** The Metropolitan Museum of Art, Cloisters Collection, 1969 (69.86) Photograph © 1991 The Metropolitan Museum of Art; **206** Stadtarchiv Soest (Bestand A Nr. 2771) **Chapter 11: 217; 224; 226; 232** Scala/Art Resource, NY **Chapter 12: 237** Michael Holford; **240** Giraudon/Art Resource, NY; **243** Reproduced by courtesy of the Trustees, © The National Gallery, London; **251** Thyssen Bornemisza Collection; **255** Musée du Louvre, Paris/Bridgeman Art Library, London/© SuperStock, Inc. **Chapter 13: 261** Library of Congress; **265** Kunstsammlungen Der Veste Coburg; **275** Erich Lessing/Art Resource, NY **Chapter 14: 281** Giraudon/Art Resource, NY; **282** Art Resource, NY; **283** François Dubois, Saint Bartholomew's Day, 1572–1584, oil on canvas, 94 cm x 154 cm, Musée Cantonal des Beaxu-Arts de Lausanne, Photo: J.-C. Ducret, Musée Cantonal des Beaxu-Arts de Lausanne; **287** Erich Lessing/Art Resource, NY; **293** Musée des Beaux-Arts de Strasbourg (2.86.12970) **Chapter 15: 299** Roudnice Lobkowicz Collec-tion/Bridgeman Art Library; **307** La Tour, Georges de (1593–1652) *The Fortune Teller.* Oil on canvas. J. 40 /8 in. W. 48 5/8 in. (101.9 x 123.5 cm.) Signed (upper right): G. de La Tour Fecit Luneuilla Lothar: Metropolitan Museum of Art, Rogers Fund, 1960 (60.30) Photograph © 1982 The Metropolitan Museum of Art **309** Rijksmuseum Foundation, Amsterdam; **311** Scala/Art Resource, NY **Chapter 16: 319** Réunion des Musées Nationaux/Art Resource, NY; **320** National Portrait Gallery, London; **328** The Granger Collection, New York; **334** Chateau de Versailles, France/Bridgeman Art Library; **335** Scala/Art Resource, NY

CONTEMPORARY EUROPE

Land Elevation

Feet		Meters
13,123		4,000
6,562		2,000
3,281		1,000
1,640		500
656		200
0		0
Below sea level		Below sea level

0   250   500 mi.

0   250   500 km

ICELAND

Norwegian Sea

Arctic Circle

30°W   20°W   10°W

N
W — E
S

KJØLEN MOUNTAINS

SCANDINAVIAN PENINS'

FAROE IS.

NORWAY   SWEDEN

SHETLAND IS.

L. Vänern

HEBRIDES IS.   *ORKNEY IS.*

L. Vättern

Scotland

JUTLAND PENINSULA

Northern Ireland

North Sea

DENMARK

Baltic

UNITED KINGDOM

BRITISH ISLES

IRELAND

Elbe R.

NORTH EU

50°N

Oder R.

Wales

England

NETHERLANDS

RUHR VALLEY

Celtic Sea

Thames R.

GERMANY

POL

ATLANTIC OCEAN

English Channel

BELGIUM

Rhine R.

CZECH REPUBLIC

BRITTANY PENINSULA

LUXEMBOURG

SLOV

Loire R.

Danube R.

Seine R.

LIECHTENSTEIN

Bay of Biscay

FRANCE

SWITZERLAND

AUSTRIA

HUN HU

Garonne R.

L. Geneva

A L P S

CENTRAL MASSIF

Rhône R.

SLOVENIA

Drava R.

Sava R.

Po R.

CROATIA

40°N

PYRENEES

ITALY

SAN MARINO

BOSNIA

IBERIAN PENINSULA

Ebro R.

ANDORRA

APENNINES

DINARIC

Duero R.

MONACO

CORSICA

Adriatic Sea

PORTUGAL

Tagus R.

SPAIN

Guadiana R.

Guadalquiver R.

BALEARIC ISLANDS

SARDINIA

Tyrrhenian Sea

SIERRA NEVADA

Strait of Gibraltar

Mediterranean Sea

Ion Se

A F R I C A

SICILY

MALTA